Rethinking Society for the 21st Century

Report of the International Panel on Social Progress

Volume 2: Political Regulation, Governance, and Societal Transformations

This is the second of three volumes containing a report from the International Panel on Social Progress (IPSP). The IPSP is an independent association of top research scholars with the goal of assessing methods for improving the main institutions of modern societies. Written in accessible language by scholars across the social sciences and humanities, these volumes assess the achievements of world societies in past centuries, the current trends, the dangers that we are now facing, and the possible futures in the twenty-first century. It covers the main socio-economic, political, and cultural dimensions of social progress, global as well as regional issues, and the diversity of challenges and their interplay around the world. This particular volume covers topics such as democracy and the rule of law, violence and wars, international organizations and global governance, and media and communications.

The International Panel on Social Progress brings together more than 300 scholars from all disciplines of social sciences and the humanities, and from all continents. Since 2014, the mission of the Panel has been to gather expertise and disseminate knowledge on the perspectives for social progress around the world in the coming decades. The Panel is an independent initiative supported by more than 30 scientific or academic institutions and international foundations. With Amartya Sen as President, and Nancy Fraser, Ravi Kanbur, and Helga Nowotny as co-chairs of the Scientific Council, the Panel has been co-directed by Olivier Bouin and Marc Fleurbaey.

Rethinking Society for the 21st Century

Report of the International Panel on Social Progress

Volume 2: Political Regulation, Governance, and Societal Transformations

CAMBRIDGE
UNIVERSITY PRESS

CAMBRIDGE
UNIVERSITY PRESS

University Printing House, Cambridge CB2 8BS, United Kingdom

One Liberty Plaza, 20th Floor, New York, NY 10006, USA

477 Williamstown Road, Port Melbourne, VIC 3207, Australia

314–321, 3rd Floor, Plot 3, Splendor Forum, Jasola District Centre, New Delhi – 110025, India

79 Anson Road, #06-04/06, Singapore 079906

Cambridge University Press is part of the University of Cambridge.

It furthers the University's mission by disseminating knowledge in the pursuit of
education, learning, and research at the highest international levels of excellence.

www.cambridge.org
Information on this title: www.cambridge.org/9781108423137
DOI: 10.1017/9781108399647

First published 2018

Printed in the United Kingdom by TJ International Ltd. Padstow Cornwall

A catalogue record for this publication is available from the British Library.

Library of Congress Cataloging-in-Publication Data
Names: International Panel on Social Progress, author.
Title: Rethinking society for the 21st century : report of the International Panel on Social Progress. Other titles: Socio-economic
transformations. | Political regulation, governance, and societal transformations. | Transformations in values, norms, cultures.
Description: Cambridge, United Kingdom; New York, NY: Cambridge University Press, 2018. | Includes index. |
Volume 1. Socio-economic transformations – Volume 2. Political regulation, governance, and
societal transformations – Volume 3. Transformations in values, norms, cultures.
Identifiers: LCCN 2018003514 | ISBN 9781108399593 (Set of 3 hardback volumes) | ISBN 9781108423120 (vol. 1 : hardback) |
ISBN 9781108423137 (vol. 2 : hardback) | ISBN 9781108423144 (vol. 3 : hardback) | ISBN 9781108399579 (Set of 3 paperback volumes) |
ISBN 9781108436328 (vol. 1 : paperback) | ISBN 9781108436335 (vol. 2 : paperback) | ISBN 9781108436342 (vol. 3 : paperback)
Subjects: LCSH: Social change. | Progress. | Political science. | Civilization – 21st century.
Classification: LCC HN18.3.I568 2018 | DDC 306–dc23
LC record available at https://lccn.loc.gov/2018003514

ISBN 978-1-108-39959-3 Set of 3 hardback volumes
ISBN 978-1-108-42312-0 Volume 1 Hardback
ISBN 978-1-108-42313-7 Volume 2 Hardback
ISBN 978-1-108-42314-4 Volume 3 Hardback
ISBN 978-1-108-39957-9 Set of 3 paperback volumes
ISBN 978-1-108-43632-8 Volume 1 Paperback
ISBN 978-1-108-43633-5 Volume 2 Paperback
ISBN 978-1-108-43634-2 Volume 3 Paperback

Contents

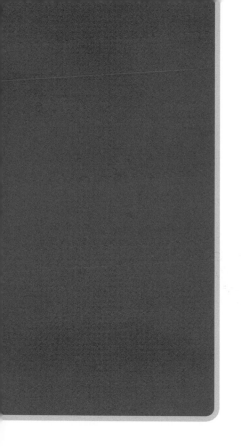

Introduction to Volume 2

Authors:[1]
Olivier Bouin, Marie-Laure Djelic, Marc Fleurbaey, Ravi Kanbur, Elisa Reis

---

[1] Affiliations: OB: RFIEA; MLD: Sciences-Po; MF: Princeton University; RK: Cornell University; ER: Federal University of Rio de Janeiro.

0.1 The IPSP Report: Aims and Method

This section briefly recalls elements that are expounded in more detail in the Introduction to Volume 1.

The International Panel on Social Progress (IPSP) is an academic, bottom-up initiative, aiming to assess the perspectives for social progress in the coming decades, in the world. Mobilizing large numbers of social scientists and humanities scholars, the IPSP project is complementary to many ongoing efforts by various groups and organizations with which it is collaborating, such as the United Nations and its Agenda 2030, the Organisation for Economic Co-operation and Development (OECD) and its multiple initiatives for a "better life" and "inclusive growth," the World Bank and its work against poverty and inequality, the ILO and its "decent work" agenda, the Social Progress Imperative and its measurement initiative supplementing economic indicators, and many others.

The IPSP distinguishes itself from other initiatives by examining not just policy issues for the medium term but also structural and systemic issues for the long term, by mobilizing a uniquely wide set of perspectives, from all relevant disciplines as well as from all continents, and by speaking to actors who are or will be the "change makers" of society. The Panel mobilizes the notion of "social progress" to emphasize that social change is not a neutral matter and that a compass is needed to parse the options that actors and decision makers face. The message of this Panel is a message of hope: We can improve our institutions, curb inequalities, expand democracy, and secure sustainability. Importantly, there is not a unique direction of progress but multiple possibilities and many ideas that can and should be experimented.

The Report presented has 22 chapters spread over 3 volumes. Every chapter is co-signed by a multidisciplinary team of authors and represents the views of this team. In total, more than 260 authors have been involved, with about 60 percent of contributions coming, in roughly equal proportions, from economics, sociology, and political science. Each chapter starts with a long summary of its contents, so as to help readers navigate the Report.

Every chapter is meant to be a critical assessment of the state of the art in the topic covered in the chapter, acknowledging ongoing debates and suggesting emerging points of consensus. Most chapters contain recommendations for action and reform, with an effort to make the underlying values explicit. This Report provides the reader with a unique overview of the state of society and possible futures, with a wealth of ideas and suggestions for possible reforms and actions. For scholars and students, it also offers an exceptional guide to the literature in the relevant academic disciplines of social sciences and the humanities. Readers are invited to take this Report as a resource, as a mine for ideas and arguments, as a tool for their own thought and action. They are also invited to engage with Panel members and share their views and experiences.

0.2 Outline of the Report and of Volume 2

The Report is divided into three parts, with two introductory and two concluding chapters. The introductory chapters lay out the main social trends that form the background of this Report (Chapter 1), and the main values and principles that form a "compass" for those who seek social progress (Chapter 2).

The first part of the Report deals with socioeconomic transformations, and focuses on economic inequalities (Chapter 3), growth and environmental issues (Chapter 4), urbanization (Chapter 5), capitalist institutions of markets, corporations and finance (Chapter 6), labor (Chapter 7), concluding with a reflection on how economic organization determines well-being and social justice (Chapter 8).

The second part of the Report scrutinizes political issues, analyzing the ongoing complex trends in democracy and the rule of law (Chapter 9), the forms and resolutions of situations of violence and conflicts (Chapter 10), the mixed efficacy of supranational institutions and organizations (Chapter 11), as well as the multiple forms of global governance (Chapter 12), and the important role for democracy of media and communications (Chapter 13). It concludes with a chapter on the challenges to democracy raised by inequalities, and the various ways in which democracy can be rejuvenated (Chapter 14).

The third part of the Report is devoted to transformations in cultures and values, with analyses of cultural trends linked to "modernization" and its pitfalls, as well as globalization (Chapter 15), a study of the complex relation between religions and social progress (Chapter 16), an examination of the promises and challenges in ongoing transformations in family structures and norms (Chapter 17), a focus on trends and policy issues regarding health and life-death issues (Chapter 18), a study of the ways in which education can contribute to social progress (Chapter 19), and finally, a chapter on the important values of solidarity and belonging (Chapter 20).

The two concluding chapters include a synthesis on the various innovative ways in which social progress can go forward (Chapter 21) and a reflection on how the various disciplines of social science can play a role in the evolution of society and the design of policy (Chapter 22).

The present volume (Volume 2) contains the second part of the report, with six chapters covering a wide range of issues from democracy and the rule of law to national and supranational institutions of governance, conflicts, and the media.

Chapter 9 considers the apparently contradictory trends that seem to both expand and shake democracy and the rule of law in different ways across the world. It emphasizes the link between those trends and deeper economic and social evolutions. Chapter 10 deals with violence and conflicts, drawing a contrasting picture of a world that is increasingly peaceful and secure while, still, persistent forms of latent and open conflicts and emerging forms of violence make it look no less frightening. It insists on the fact that inequalities in security are strongly correlated with other socioeconomic inequalities. Chapter 11 studies global governance and its coordination by international organizations and through supranational arrangements. It provides a thorough analysis of how these international bodies handle human rights, women's rights, refugees and migrations, health, conflicts, intellectual property, and climate change. Chapter 12 pursues the analysis of global governance by analyzing the trends by which national governments have been slowly deprived of many of their prerogatives, to the benefit of a more informal web of public and private transnational institutions and norms that embody the current form of globalization of finance and investment, trade, as well as the global management of labor and environmental issues. Chapter 13 puts the spotlight on media and communications, studying ongoing dramatic changes in the flow of information and the interconnection between people across the world and across communities of ideas. This chapter highlights the serious dangers in the current "business model" of the media (including the social media), and, relying on examples, advocates a public-good approach to the management of access to information and the governance of the media system. Chapter 14 concludes this part of the Report, and this Volume, by emphasizing the challenges to democracy that growing inequalities between social groups generate, and offers many thought-provoking examples of democratic innovation (especially from the Global South) as well as reflections on essential democratic issues such as the relation between state and religion or the role of the nation-state in a globalized world.

This part of the Report is central not just in its position between the two other volumes. Actually, there are two ways in which its importance must be recognized. First, while injustice is often depicted either in terms of inequalities in resources (see Volume 1, and especially Chapter 3 for a focus on this topic) or in terms of discriminations and exclusions for characteristics such as gender, race, religion, or sexual orientation (topics appearing in all parts of this report, but especially prominent in Volume 3), the distribution of power and the ability for individuals and groups to control their destiny is a dimension that is as important to stakeholders as the other dimensions. Even the mere possibility to live in peace and without immediate physical threat (the topic of Chapter 10) is one of the dimensions where, these days, one finds the starkest inequalities in the world.

The second way in which this part of the Report is central is that implementing societal change is ultimately a matter of collective action, which requires pulling levers and putting pressure on power centers. In a world that is now controlled by a very small global elite, social progress will not happen without a redistribution of power to bring more democracy not just in the classical sphere of politics but in all organizations where power determines the fate of members in important ways. This will also involve enhancing the role of supranational organizations (of states, NGOs, civil society actors) that have the unique capacity of coordinating action at the level needed to address global challenges. This perspective actually pervades the Report as a whole, and one can find important discussions of these issues in Volume 1 (e.g. in Chapter 6 for the corporation) and Volume 3 (e.g. in Chapter 17 for the family). The reflections offered in Volume 2 about democracy should be understood as going well beyond a narrow conception of power and politics. They can inform our understanding of power issues in all aspects of social life.

0.3 Contentious Words in a Report

Social sciences, unlike natural sciences, work with words that are also used in public debates and are sometimes used as weapons across the ideological battlefield. Social scientists themselves are of course not immune to value judgments influencing their choice of topics and their embrace of certain arguments or theses. While value judgments should be resisted when they can pollute positive analysis of facts, they should be recognized as necessary and made transparent when recommendations are proposed. This is why the IPSP has a full chapter on values and principles, and many recommendations about how to promote social progress understood in a certain way.

But the choice of words is especially sensitive for the analysis of social systems, when the same words are already weapons in the social and political battles of the day. In the preparation of the IPSP, this has raised debates about certain words. The case of "capitalism," for instance, is rather easy. Almost everyone in current debates accepts the characterization of the dominant economic system as "capitalist," and both critics and champions can use the word and understand approximately the same thing – though, interestingly, the special subordinate relation that labor has with capital under capitalism is not something that everyone spontaneously identifies as a defining feature of this economic and social system.

The case of "neoliberalism" has not been so easy and has not found a solution that would satisfy everyone in the Panel. What is special about this word is that it does not seem to be used by conservatives or libertarians anymore, and instead plays the role of a punching ball in the discourse of the critics (Springer, Birch, and MacLeavy 2016). Therefore, many see its being used as the signal of a particular position in the ideological spectrum, a signal of bias that undermines the credibility of the discourse.

However, there is a real phenomenon in search of a less fraught word. Liberal pro-market ideas have been revived, with remarkable dedication, by thinkers such as Hayek and Friedman, and when Keynesianism was shaken by the exhaustion of demand-side economic policies in the 1970s, an alternative was readily available and was very effectively pushed by the wealthy interests with which it was naturally congenial – although other ideas such as Ordoliberalism have also been influential at this juncture in Europe. Reagan and Thatcher could then launch the conservative revolution with an ideological base that was simple (indeed, some would say simplistic) and powerful. The Washington Consensus would soon unleash its injunctions for liberalization, structural adjustment, and shock therapy throughout the world, with all the damages that have ensued for the most vulnerable populations. This wave was, like most overambitious ideologies, even ready to fraternize with dictators in order to force its peculiar conception of "freedom" on reluctant peoples.

The last financial crisis may have momentarily shaken the arrogance of free market ideologues and politicians, but institutions have not changed much and liberal pro-market ideas remain dominant in most governmental spheres. However, scientific analysis cannot use the word "neoliberalism" without caution, given the multiplicity and diversity of phenomena and discourses under scrutiny. For instance, Chapter 9 notes that pro-market ideas, focused on competition, must be distinguished from pro-corporate ideas, which favor corporate interests even when this undermines market competition.

The Panel coordinators, facing this difficult equation, suggested, whenever that was possible, to use alternative words that could be more precise and more neutral in the final version of the Report, in view of the non-academic audience of the Report and its potential role in public debates. The Report that is offered here contains a mixture of conventions. Some chapters do not use the word at all, or very pointedly to refer to the conservative wave of the end of the twentieth century, while others use it extensively, following the usual academic conventions in certain disciplines and schools of thought. It is hoped that readers will understand that when the authors use it here, it is as a notion that is useful to describe a set of ideas and societal phenomena, not as a pejorative weapon meant to cast shame on ideological opponents. The general tendency of the Report is to approach the market as a useful mechanism for the creation and allocation of resources, provided its limitations are recognized and its function, "embedded" (in Polanyi's words) within suitable social institutions, is made compatible with general social objectives attuned to the common good.

Acknowledgments

The preparation of this Report has benefited from support by many individuals and organizations. Please refer to the Introduction to Volume 1 for details.

Reference

Springer, S., K. Birch, and J. MacLeavy (eds.). 2016. *Handbook of Neoliberalism*. London: Routledge.

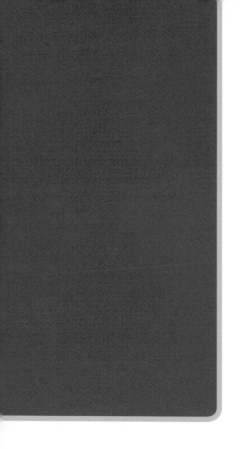

Political Regulation, Governance, and Societal Transformations

9

The Paradoxes of Democracy and the Rule of Law

Coordinating Lead Authors:[1]
Donatella della Porta, Michael Keating

Lead Authors:[2]
Gianpaolo Baiocchi, Colin Crouch, Sheila Jasanoff, Erika Kraemer-Mbula, Dina Kiwan,
Abby Peterson, Kenneth M. Roberts, Philippe C. Schmitter, Alberto Vannucci, Antoine Vauchez,
Asanga Welikala

[1] Affiliations: DDP: Scuola Normale Superiore, Italy; MK: University of Aberdeen, UK.
[2] Affiliations: GB: New York University, USA; CC: University of Warwick, UK; SJ: Harvard University, USA; EKM: University of Johannesburg, South Africa; DK: American University of Beirut; AP: University of Gothenburg; KMR: Cornell University; PCS: European University Institute; AV: University of Pisa; AV: University of Paris; AW: University of Edinburgh.

Summary

The promise of modernization after the Second World War was that economic growth, equality, the rule of law, and democracy would proceed together. In many ways, this has happened. Yet many of the promises of social progress developed after the Second World War have been undermined by internal tensions within the democratic project, as well as by social and economic trends. While stating the challenges that these trends have posed for democratic institutions and actors, we also look at the responses (both proposals and practices) that have emerged in order to address those challenges. In doing this, we note that the very conception of democracy as liberal democracy (based on delegation and majority voting) is under stress as the neoliberal wave has attacked those very intermediary institutions (parties, unions, voluntary associations) that had been at the basis of the development of the welfare state and democratic capitalism.

We start by noting the growth in inequality, which means that formal democracy is shaped by uneven power resources as concentration of wealth provides advantages in the capacity to influence public decision-making with mutual convertibility of economic and political resources. The spiral of inequality and corporate political power is reflected in a growing legitimacy crisis in old and new democracies. Liberalism, which promised the separation between the state and the market, has evolved into a neoliberalism based on the domination of the corporation, exacerbated by privatization and de-regulation. This has raised private profit criteria above considerations of the broader public good and in many cases encouraged corruption. The ensuing inefficiency and lack of transparency foster institutional mistrust, with perverse effects.

Challenges are also related to the fact that democracy has been mainly defined in a national mode, with the demos identified as the nation. Economic rescaling produced by global capitalism has, however, produced both de-territorialization and re-territorialization, which requires a (yet unachieved) rethinking of the basis for democracy but also of welfare and its foundation in both identities and institutions. In the North and (with different characteristics) in the South of the globe, movement of capital and of people pose challenges of national pluralism and its constitutional recognition, questioning key concepts such as the definition of political community and popular sovereignty and the relationship between human rights and citizenship. Citizenship is more appropriately considered as related not to fixed institutions but rather as "acts of citizenships" requiring subjectivity and agency and more inclusive conceptions.

The main actors in democratic development have been affected by these challenges. Political parties are an important element in democracy but they have become an interest in their own right. A crisis of representation has emerged from growing social detachment of political parties from social cleavages as well as of elected representatives from the citizens. This had most dramatic effects on the Left, when left-wing parties have supported liberalization reforms. Relying on expertise for the development of progressive policies is not a solution given the non-accountable power of science as well as the increasing challenges of privatization of knowledge-making, opacity of knowledge production, and persistence of fundamental class imbalances in access to knowledge. Participatory channels of access to institutions have been opened to "ordinary citizens" but they are often based on individualist conceptions and do not address fundamental issues of inequalities. While citizens often call for direct participation, existing experiments rarely empower the citizens.

While the judiciary has been seen as a surrogate for democratic participation for marginalized minority groups, its capacity for rights enforcement is limited by the expansion (in particular at the international level) of a *lex mercatoria* as well as the use of courts in order to protect economic freedom from democratic dynamics. The rule of law has also been subverted by unequal access to the law and by the influence of money while the judiciary also has its own particular interests, and corporate lawyers assume a brokerage function in globalized markets. On the other hand, in the control of political dissent, the state, rather than being weakened from globalization, increases its reach and power. The "war on terror" has been used to challenge the rule of law by states of emergency as well as authoritarian drifts with attempts at imposing a permanent "state of exception."

On the other hand, progressive social movements have addressed growing inequalities and democratic crises by developing alternative visions of democracy, stressing participation over delegation and deliberation over majoritarian decision-making. Participatory and deliberative conceptions have been prefigured as well as elaborated in recent waves of protests. The consolidation of oppositional actors, however, faces challenges in the fragmentation of the potential social bases, the need to build a new collective identity as well as to establish channels of access to power. This has resulted from, but also triggered, the reduction in citizens' entitlements and the weakening of the social contract upon which social progress depends.

9.1   Introduction

Our concern in this chapter is democracy and the rule of law as conditions for social progress. Democracy is at its most basic, rule by the people. This encompasses universal suffrage, free competitive elections, alternation in government, and the absence of obstacles to participation in public life. Conceptions of democracy, however, have been extended to other sites, including the workplace and the community, and even the international order. The idea of democracy has been expanded beyond representative democracy and passive participation through elections, towards new forms of participative democracy. Democracy requires an institutional framework for its own protection to secure civil equality, without which it would be meaningless in practice. It has to protect against arbitrary government and the tyranny of majorities; to protect minority rights; to sustain opposition; to provide predictability and security; and to safeguard against corruption. This is where the rule of law comes in. This requires an impartial legal system, free from political coercion, and the equality of all citizens before it. In the past some conceptions of the rule of law were quite conservative, focused on defending existing privileges and property rights against the spread of democracy and demands for equality. The political left in some countries (such as the UK) were wary of charters of rights and legal limitations on the scope of government, fearing the rule of lawyers and of private interests. This opposition has largely disappeared. Yet in our day, there remains the danger that the law will be captured by private power holders.

During the second half of the twentieth century, there was a widely held belief that democracy and equality before the law were a part of a broader process of modernization that carried the promise of global progress across a set of complementary spheres. Continuous economic growth under the impetus of technology would eradicate poverty and raise living standards. Social inequality would be reduced, bringing equality of opportunity and greater substantive equality. Rising living standards and greater equality were seen as conducive to the extension and deepening of democracy, allowing citizens to participate fully. Civil rights would extend to embrace the entire population on an equal basis. The nation-state provided both the demos and the institutional frame for democracy, and the model was adopted widely by peoples liberated from colonial domination. These elements would reinforce each other as prosperity would enhance democracy and secure political stability. Possible excesses of democracy, such as oppression of minorities and abuse of power were limited by its combination with liberalism in *liberal* democracy and by the rule of law itself. Political parties mobilized electors to participate, while providing programmatic policy alternatives. While different models of economic management competed during the first half of the twentieth century, a form of liberal regulated capitalism seemed finally to predominate, generating steady growth while curbing excesses of economic power. Remaining issues concerned the exact balance between the market and state, dividing pure market liberalism from social democracy. States possessed sufficient policy, regulatory and fiscal capacity to translate citizens' aspirations into substantive outcomes.

Our paradox arises from the circumstance that many of these promises have been met but they have been undermined by their own internal conflicts or by other social and economic trends. There were successive waves of democratization during the twentieth century, affecting most parts of the world. Legal orders have been strengthened and separated from politics in many states. Formally equal civil rights were extended without regard to class, ethnicity, or gender. National welfare bargains within states secured a strengthening of social benefits and the extension of education, health, and social benefits to larger sections of the population. Although these took place to very different extents depending on the country and region, there was hope for general progress.

In the early twenty-first century, we see less room for optimism. The formal apparatus of democracy and rule of law is intact across much of the world, but the conditions for their substantive exercise are weakening.

Formal political equality is undermined by the massive increases in social and economic inequality across much of the democratic world, which limits the ability of all to participate on equal terms. In the late twentieth century, there was a lot of talk about "globalization" seen as an ineluctable process curtailing the autonomy of the nation-state. It is now apparent that globalization is a stretched concept, which means many different things. Rather than an ineluctable force, it is often the work of nation-states themselves as they seek new scales of action to regain control of social and economic change. We define globalization as a new division of labor at the world level, eroding national markets and national systems of regulation. Its agents are states, corporations seeking new sites of production and markets, and international institutions. What is interesting for our purposes is not the broad concept but the form that globalization takes.

In its early twentieth-century form, it has opened up a new class division, in some cases obliterating older cleavages including those from the industrial revolution. In a familiar form, it may pitch multinational corporations against nation-states as the former engage in regulatory arbitrage and demand packages of taxes and services in exchange for investment. Its reach is often even deeper, as it often pitches individuals with high levels of education, mobile skills, and international connections, against those who lack these.

Within states, formal democracy is undermined by the ways in which economic power can be transformed into political power. This takes numerous forms, including the purchase of political machinery required in modern elections; the privileged power of large business in lobbying government, given their ability to relocate beyond the nation-state; and outright corruption.

Law similarly is formally open to all, but has become expensive, giving advantages to the rich and to corporations, which can claim some of the rights of persons. International trade deals can give corporations a privileged status against democratic governments, protected by a private form of arbitration outside the regular courts. Equal civil rights may be protected formally but social and economic rights may not. There is still corruption in many legal systems.

Political parties, which used to be a means for broadening political recruitment and transmitting voter preferences into government, have become detached from society while at the same time monopolizing

9

state power. The old parties have become self-perpetuating, sustaining a closed elite of professional politicians.

This has opened the way for the rise of new political movements offering simplistic solutions to the problems of rising inequality and global change, often appealing both to the beneficiaries and losers from change. Populism is a broad term, used differently in different historical and political contexts, but our concern here is with the rise of nationalist populism on the political right. We define national populism by a number of key features (Müller 2016): that the "people" has a single will and interest; that it is being frustrated by special interests and "elites"; that opposition is unpatriotic and therefore illegitimate; that the national will is to be interpreted by a supreme leader. This is the basis for Viktor Orbán's call for illiberal democracy. Other national populists include Trump, Duterte, Modi, and Le Pen. In the UK, a 52 percent vote in the Brexit referendum is taken as a wide-ranging mandate for a specific manner of withdrawing from the European Union, with as little parliamentary intervention as possible; judges ruling that parliament must be involved were lampooned by the tabloid press as "enemies of the people."

Minorities and migrants are made scapegoats for the consequences of social and economic inequality. Populist nationalism can serve to induce working-class electors to vote against their own economic interests, in the name of the national interest and against foreigners and elites. Not the least of ironies is that many of the politicians railing against the domination of "elites" are themselves insiders of the old ruling circles and moneyed classes.

All this is facilitated by the decline of the old print and broadcast media and the concentration of media ownership in the hands of wealthy individuals and organizations, often beholden to private or state-controlled economic or ideological interests. In many cases, truth itself has become a commodity, to be purchased or constructed at will. Social media are sometimes seen as emancipating, allowing citizens to communicate freely but they are also unencumbered by regulation of standards. The phrase "post-truth" politics has come into fashion, referring to the disappearance of shared empirical or epistemic knowledge upon which rival policy proposals can be debated. Donald Trump's spokeswoman can, without irony, talk of "alternative facts," while the blatant untruth that the UK pays £350 million a week to the EU, which could be diverted to the National Health Service after Brexit, was displayed on the side of a bus.

The nation-state, traditionally the main object of political competition, is less able to manage the process of social and economic change, so that democracy is detached from substantive policy capacity; hence governments of different political hues end up with similar policy outcomes. Faced with intractable social and economic challenges, states have sought various forms of automatic pilot that would guarantee success while relieving pressures on themselves. Hence, for example, the fashion for monetary policy as the master instrument of macro-economic stability, to be assured by giving central banks operational independence. Direct state intervention in many fields has been replaced by privatization, combined with regulatory agencies to ensure competition and public goals. Yet the regulatory state has itself become a massive reservoir of power, not always subject to democratic control and operating according to its own norms. This represents less of a retreat of the state than a reconfiguration in new forms.

At the same time as the state loses its capacity to produce social and economic change, its repressive capacity is enhanced in the face of real or constructed threats of disorder and terrorism. As the political agenda shifts from social progress to security, democracy itself produces a restriction of civil liberties.

The rule of law is also vulnerable to internal interests. Like political parties, the judiciary itself may become a class with its own vested interests, providing an obstacle to democratic change.

We also emphasize the role of ideas and shifting dominance ideologies. Over the last quarter of the twentieth century, monetarism displaced Keynesianism as the dominant economic paradigm. The failures of the new model in the financial crash of 2008 only briefly dented confidence in it. Democratic politicians failed to provide a convincing counter-narrative to underpin alternative strategies.

The idea of liberalism was also transformed and radicalized into "neoliberalism." Liberalism as a political doctrine emphasizes individual freedom and a secure public domain for the expression of ideas. Economic liberalism is based on free markets, competition and a limited role for the state in economic management, beyond ensuring the conditions for competition. The two have often been associated as part of the modernizing, emancipatory project. In practice, there has always been a tension between political and economic liberalism. The former has been prepared to use the state to ensure the equality of opportunity without which formally equal rights would be emptied of meaning. The latter has emphasized the primacy of markets. The outcome in the twentieth century was a form of regulated market order; and a system of social protection to compensate for market-generated inequalities.

This equilibrium has been upset by the rise of neoliberalism. The concept of neoliberalism has, like most social science concepts, been stretched and given a normative charge. Defined precisely, however, it provides a valuable insight into the malaise of modern democracies. We define neoliberalism as an ideology and political doctrine that asserts the superiority of free markets over most other forms of decision-making, especially over the actions of government. It differs from classic economic liberalism in two respects. First, market competition is extended to most domains of public action, notably the provision of public services. Second, the idea of the market has become confounded with the interests of corporations.

Starting in universities and think tanks, this form of neoliberalism gained hegemonic status in the face of states' inability to handle the challenge of economic change after the 1970s. This has entailed dismantling a citizenship regime of civic, political, and social rights. Privatization, deregulation, and liberalization have reduced public resources to mitigate social inequalities. The very notion of democratic capitalism, implying that democracy favors the development of capitalism, was challenged (Streeck 2015). Neoliberalism thus undermines

9

the historic principles of liberalism itself. Adam Smith, often invoked by neoliberals, was well aware of this. The paradoxes we are going to discuss in this chapter are embedded in the crisis and "strange non-death" of neo-liberalism (Crouch 2011).

Developments in the first part of the twenty-first century thus represent not a mere swing of the pendulum from left to right but a fundamental challenge to the liberal democratic order toward which the world seemed to be evolving during the latter part of the twentieth century. The very conception of democracy as liberal democracy (based on delegation and majority voting) is under stress as neoliberalism has attacked those very intermediary institutions (parties, unions, voluntary associations) that had been at the basis of the development of the welfare state and democratic capitalism.

Yet we do not want to be totally despondent. Neoliberalism, as we have shown, is not a coherent doctrine but an ideological cover for selective dismantling of public institutions. There have been notable reactions to neo-liberalism. Some may have represented what Karl Polanyi (1957) called "counter-movements" for social protection, conceived of as spontaneous and backward-looking. Other societal responses seek to promote alternative visions of democracy, stressing participation over delegation and deliberation over majoritarian decision-making.

While electoral accountability is jeopardized by a growing investment of economic resources in the political sphere, other visions and practices of "counter-democracy" develop. While elections are a central feature of democracy, stressing only elections can distract attention from the need for critical citizens who can render governments accountable. Representative democracy thus needs to be matched by participatory practices, continually linking policy to citizen concerns.

Another requirement is an informed public sphere, with some shared standards of truth. This is not to say that objective facts will produce political consensus but that arguments can at least be tested. This in turn can produce communication, deliberation, the exchange of reasons, the construction of shared definitions of the public good, as fundamental for the making and legitimation of public decisions. By relating with each other – recognizing the others and being recognized by them – citizens have the chance to understand the reasons of the others, assessing them against emerging standards of fairness. Communication not only allows for the development of better solutions, by allowing for carriers of different knowledge and expertise to interact, but it can also change the perception of one's own preferences, making participants less concerned with individual, material interests, and more with collective goods.

There is also a need to question the nation-state as the primary site of democracy and the rule of law. Talk of "globalization" and the end of the nation-state around the end of the Cold War was overblown and the nation-state remains a formidable center of power as well as object of political attachment. Yet the challenges of inequality and democracy arise at multiple levels, below, above, and across states as well as within them. The nation has been a force for progress and

solidarity but also for exclusion and aggression. Rather than illusory slogans about "taking back control" (as in the Brexit referendum) or appeals to common enemies (as in national populism), it is important to democratize the multiple scales at which policies are made. This requires new forms of institutional design.

There are inescapable dilemmas in all this. The rule of law cannot be the mere plaything of politics, as with a Silvio Berlusconi. Nor, however, can law be separate from the rest of the public domain. Governments should be subject to the rule of law but judges should not be made into legislators. The market has been a powerful generator of wealth but, left to its own devices, can undermine democracy itself. In the 1930s, democracy and the rule of law collapsed widely because of their enemies offering a radical alternative. In the twenty-first century they risk being undermined by forces purporting to act in their own name and by their own excesses and contradictions.

In the following sections, we observe specific challenges to the liberal model of democracy, but also opportunities for the development of different models of democracy, more participatory and deliberative.

We observe how neoliberalism allowed the owners of economic resources to influence political decisions, and the effect this had in spreading corruption and reducing citizens' rights. The very conception of the rule of law is challenged by unequal access to the judicial system. Public life is rescaling at multiple territorial levels, posing questions about equality and democracy but also opening up new forms of engagement. Democratic paradoxes are also visible in the development of some of the principal democratic actors, from parties to social movements, which see their organizational structures and modes of functions transformed. The very right of dissent is challenged, as neoliberalism spreads insecurity, but at the same time different paths of political participation emerge.

9.2   Capitalism, Inequality, and Democracy

In the days of the Cold War it was usually taken for granted that capitalism and democracy were natural partners. The situation has now changed. Some serious writers on contemporary politics have even begun to doubt whether democracy and capitalism are mutually compatible (Kocka 2014; Merkel 2014; Streeck 2015). A major source of disquiet is the implications for democracy of rising inequality. This disquiet comprises the following elements:

1. Unless significant regulatory measures are taken, there are no means within a capitalist economy to prevent the conversion of economic into political resources, and the dominant capitalist ideology, neoliberalism, is hostile to such regulation.
2. In an open political system, concentrations of wealth have particular advantages in exercising influence because they are spared the problems of collective action that limit the activities of other groups.
3. This influence is used to extract political favors in the interests of the wealthy, further increasing inequality and interfering with the

market order, producing a spiral of growing inequality and economic distortion.

We shall examine each of these contentions in turn.[3]

9.2.1   The Mutual Convertibility of Economic and Political Resources

In a perfectly competitive market economic resources should not be converted into power, and therefore can have no political implications; spending money on politics would be a business cost, and a firm engaging in such activity would have to raise prices and lose out to firms that did not so engage. All firms in a sector might avoid this problem by combining to lobby for their political interests, but coordination among a large number of firms runs into the collective action problem (see below), defection from the coordinated action bringing cost advantages to the defectors. However, the situation changes when many markets are only imperfectly competitive. Here economists divide into those who accept no other solution than trying to establish perfect competition and those (associated with the anti-antitrust movement, mainly in the United States) who argue that advantages flow from imperfect competition (Bork 1993; Posner 2001). These are not concerned with the political implications but claim that returns to scale are more or less infinite, and that therefore there are no reasons to seek to establish perfect markets. For them, unlike pure neoclassical theorists and *Ordoliberalen*, a competitive order exists where some firms win the competition and thereafter dominate, not one where competition is permanent.

We can here draw a distinction between two types of neoliberalism, which will be important to the general argument: market neoliberals, whose main concern is that markets function; and corporate neoliberals, who defend the role of large, oligopolistic corporations. The latter rarely confront the political implications of the build-up of large profits that their approach implies, but if they do they argue that if governments abstained from interference in the economy, there would be nothing to lobby about and firms would have no incentive to be politically active (Bork 1993). However, as was demonstrated in the financial crisis, certain sectors can be both dominated by a small number of firms and so strategically important for a national (or the global) economy, that the collapse of a small number could provoke a massive shock. This is the "too big to fail" argument. It is clearly the case for banking; it is probably also true for energy, defense, and for certain privatized public services. Firms in these sectors have a clear incentive to become politicized, as they have much to gain from government. The uneven distribution of political influence that this implies, even among businesses in different sectors, let alone in comparison with the rest of the population, embodies part of the asymmetry and inequality that make business lobbying questionable on both market-economic and democratic grounds.

The barrier that pro-corporate ideologues would erect between polity and economy is a semi-permeable membrane; restraints are imposed on the state's ability to intervene in the market, but not on

corporations' intervention in the polity. Indeed, in the United States such activity has been explicitly accepted by the Supreme Court. In 2010 it rejected a ruling by the Federal Election Commission that there were limits to the sums of money that organizations could spend on election campaigns, on the grounds that the US Constitution should be seen as having granted the same rights to organizations as to individuals, though it maintained the existing limits on such donations to individual candidates (US Supreme Court 2010). Four years later, however, it also removed the ban on the second kind of donation (US Supreme Court 2014). It is primarily large corporations that are able to make donations of this kind.

9.2.2   Wealth and the Problem of Collective Action

There are two aspects to liberal democracy: the formal processes of elections, where rules to ensure strict equality among all citizens are accepted as paramount; and the informal debating, lobbying, and other activities that link the world of government to society between elections. Here there are no guarantees of equality. The theory to support the latter was developed, largely by US political theorists, in the 1950s and 1960s under the general banner of pluralism or polyarchy (Dahl 1971). This dealt with the risk of an undemocratic inequality of influence in the informal arena by positing that the need for relative equality would be met if there were large numbers of groups trying to influence government, using a diversity of non-overlapping types of resource, and usually being effective only within specific, limited areas of policy. In that way, no one interest would dominate. As in the free market, provided that there are many participants in the market/polity, all are price-takers and none can exercise significant influence by acting alone.

There remained the risk of a hyperactive polity, with governments vulnerable to lobbying at every moment. Pluralist theorists dealt with this by pointing out that in general people were not politically active; Robert Dahl (1961: 305) remarked that "politics is a sideshow in the great circus of life." Such observations were placed on a stronger theoretical basis when Mancur Olson (1965) developed his theory of collective action. This demonstrated the difficulties of participation in collective action. First, if a movement were big enough to be likely to succeed, it would do so without the participation of any one individual, whose contribution would be infinitesimal to the movement though costly to that individual; therefore individuals had only a very low incentive to participate. Second, if the movement were aimed at a collective good rather than a membership good, individuals would benefit from its success even if they did not participate; again the incentive to take part was very low.

The pluralist account of Western democracy was being developed during the historical period when inequality was lower than at any time in the recorded past (OECD 2011; Piketty 2013). Now that inequality is increasing again, the account is becoming unrealistic. Olson envisaged a world in which people had no means of coordinating their actions except through voluntary individual action. This does not apply to persons and corporations possessing considerable wealth. They do not

---

[3]   An extended version of some of the arguments in this section will be found in Crouch (2016a), pp. 156–171.

need members; if they need human resources they employ people. The very wealthy are therefore an exception to the collective action problem, provided that they have enough incentive to bother to take action. They have this where governments might be in a position either to favor or frustrate their private interests. The assumption of pluralist theory that in a market economy firms are just some among many interests then falls – a circumstance that was indeed perceived and warned against by two of the leading US pluralist theorists right at the start of the current period of growing inequality – one of them being Robert Dahl himself (Dahl 1982; Lindblom 1977).

9.2.3 The Spiral of Inequality and Corporate Political Power

The ways in which growing inequality, corporate power, and politics interact take many forms. The OECD's (2011: 122ff.) analysis of growing inequality identified several causes, among them sectoral change; the growing finance and related business services sector being a particular source of growing inequality. It also identified "institutional" and "policy" factors. The latter can be seen particularly clearly in taxation, changes in which have been responsible for producing some of the growing inequality (OECD 2011). In the face of growing pre-tax income inequality a democratically responsive fiscal regime would be expected to improve the progressivity of taxation, while one caught up in mutually reinforcing inequalities of economic and political power would make regressive changes. The fiscal changes of the neoliberal period have been consistent with the latter hypothesis.

An institutional change that the OECD identified was the decline of coordinated collective wage bargaining. There is a close though not perfect relationship between the extent of coordinated collective bargaining and trade-union power. There is also a correlation between trade-union power and post-tax-and-transfer inequality: the greater the degree of union power, the greater the extent of redistribution produced by the fiscal system (Crouch 2016b). Interestingly, union strength correlates far more strongly with post-tax than with pre-tax inequality, suggesting a political rather than an economic effect of union challenge. Almost everywhere coordinated bargaining, union strength and fiscal redistribution have been in decline, reducing the role of what had been a major form of countervailing power against capital in more pluralist times.

9.2.3.1 Business Lobbying

The above discussion has concentrated on the challenge to the mutual compatibility of capitalism and democracy presented by growing inequality. But this is not the only reason why corporate interests are exercising a political influence that is seriously unbalancing a democratic pluralism. Since the collapse of Keynesian demand management, according to which governments undertook to sustain the level of employment, the dependence of the population on a high level of employment has become an important argument at the disposal of neoliberals. For market neoliberals this means the contention that wages and non-wage labor costs must be allowed to fall until all idle labor can find employment. This is, for example, a major part of the policy package imposed on Greece in the wake of the Euro crisis. For corporate neoliberals it means arguing that if governments want to reduce unemployment, they must listen to what corporations say they want. This can mean labor-market measures less harsh than the market neoliberal recipe, but it also involves granting privileged political access for the corporate leaders, who of course interpret a general interest in the light of their own private ones.

For market neoliberals, efficiency is achieved when markets clear. Aspects of life that, looked at more broadly than through the framework of economic theory, might be seen as important but that are not or by their nature cannot be represented within market exchanges are either insufficiently important to merit consideration, or are just unfortunate not to be able to be taken into account. Examples would be a perceived need to safeguard poor people's basic standard of living when they cannot find work that would provide such a standard, or most types of environmental damage. For this ideology, attempts to take such issues into consideration through regulation necessarily reduce efficiency because this is *per definitionem* measured only through the market.

9.2.4 Conclusion: Growing Tension Between Capitalism and Democracy

In the light of all the above, we are forced to ask whether capitalism and democracy are today as mutually dependent as they seemed to be during the Cold War. Is "republican democracy" still "capitalism's best possible shell," as Lenin claimed? Capitalists are believed to have a preference for democracy, because they tend not to like dictatorships, which use a lot of state power, can be arbitrary, and change rules without due process. Modern democracy more or less guarantees the rule of law, and clear procedures for changing law and lobbying around proposed changes. On the other hand, democracy can produce a mass of regulations to protect non-market, non-corporate interests. Capitalists' preferred regime is post-democracy, where all the forms of democracy continue, including importantly the rule of law, but where the electorate has become passive, responding to parties' carefully managed election campaigns, but not engaging in disturbing activism, and not generating a civil society vibrant enough to produce awkward counter-lobbies that try to rival the quiet work of business interests in the corridors of government (Crouch 2004).

The major phenomena that to date have disturbed this system are the xenophobic movements that played powerful roles in the votes of the British and US electorates respectively to leave the European Union and make Donald Trump president, and in becoming serious contenders for power in France, the Nordic countries, Austria, and the Netherlands. While these movements include "liberal elites" in their critique of contemporary society, they are ambiguous about whether they include business elites in that category; Donald Trump is himself at the heart of the US business elite. In any case they concentrate their serious attacks on ethnic minorities and immigrants, as well as fear of Islamic terrorism, and it seems to be for this reason that they attract most support.

It is unlikely that these movements constitute a serious democratic challenge to capitalist dominance over politics. If anything, their use of powerful emotional xenophobic rhetoric against formal political institutions raises doubts about their commitment to the procedural rules and open debate that underpin democratic institutions. This became clear in the UK following the EU referendum, when newspapers that had campaigned for the vote to leave the EU attacked the law courts for ruling that the national parliament should be involved in the Brexit process.

In any case, post-democratic capitalism does not require a formal renunciation of democracy any more than corporate neoliberalism requires a renunciation of the market; indeed, democracy and the market continue to be used as the primary legitimation of the evolving political system of dominant corporate power, because this latter lacks any legitimation of its own. Elements for such a legitimation are there, but they are used in a supplementary way (Crouch 2015). For example, anti-antitrust theory provided a justification for protecting market-dominating corporations from market-making competition law. New public management theory legitimates the abolition of boundaries between public officials and corporate personnel, seen so important to an earlier age of liberal economy. Corporate social responsibility both gives business leaders a social legitimation going beyond their role as profit-maximizers and suggests that public policy is not needed to tackle many market failures. In the absence of Keynesian demand management, the widespread desire for a high level of employment gives priority to the policy preferences of business interests.

We have not yet arrived at a situation where corporate dominance of our politics is complete, otherwise all consumer protection and labor laws would have already been abolished; governments would not be continuing to develop regulations to try to reduce smoking. But this is the direction of travel, strengthened by continuing growth in inequality and the mutual reinforcement of political and economic power. Democracy in some form probably continues to be the best possible shell for capitalism; but vice versa may no longer apply.

## 9.3	Corruption, Neoliberalism, and Democracy

In recent decades a chain of scandals has fueled a growing popular awareness of corruption as a factor that may negatively affect political and economic decision-making, distorting public policy through growing ineffectiveness and inequality, not only in less developed and authoritarian regimes, but also in advanced, capitalist, liberal democracies. The observable nexus between established democracy and transparency (Pellegata 2013) does not protect against reversals: Australia, Iceland, Spain, Argentina, Brazil, Cyprus, Hungary, for instance, have experienced since 2012 a sharp increase in the level of perceived corruption according to the Corruption Perception Index of the NGO Transparency International, the most widely used proxy that estimates its diffusion through subjective experts' assessments.

Citizens' beliefs in the same years follow a trend to harsher feelings about corruption, driven by at least two factors. First is the repeated uncovering of grand corruption networks in some democratic countries from the 1990s Italian "clean hands" investigation to the recent Petrobras and Lava Jato cases in Brazil. These often also involve the private sector, as in the stream of banking and financial scandals (from the United States to Germany). Second is the extensive use in the political debate of a "corruption issue" against traditional elites, often framed within populist appeals. The perception of rampant corruption in the political, economic, and financial arenas has been a leading factor in a growing dissatisfaction with elites, expressed in radical protest against the wealthiest people who exercise an opaque political influence, converting their disproportionate share of financial and material capital into hidden relationships with public actors. According to the 2013 Global Corruption Barometer (GCB) international survey, on average in the 54 democratic countries considered, 53 percent of respondents believed corruption had increased in the previous years; 33 percent thought it had stayed the same and 15 percent thought it had reduced. The 2016 Regional GCB provides a similar picture of distrust in EU countries, where 65 percent of citizens think that wealthy individuals often use their influence on government for their own interests and support stricter rules to prevent this. Liberal democracies where bribery is perceived as significant suffer a mounting de-legitimization of elected representatives and political institutions. Responses have included anti-establishment movements; an 'exit' strategy of abstention or disengagement from political activity; and the rise of populist political leaders waving the issue of corruption to challenge "old" and "crooked" political representatives, occasionally threatening the stability of democratic institutions. Large-scale corruption in the public sector is at the same time a signal of the failure of the institutional and societal mechanisms of control over the integrity and effectiveness in public agents' delegation of power, and a challenge to the basic principles of democratic government, such as equality, responsiveness, accountability, and transparency. Corruption *within* democracy is necessarily also corruption *of* a democracy.

### 9.3.1	Beyond the Neoliberal Paradigm of Corruption

In the economic literature, corruption is a rational response to contextual opportunities, generated by distortions of the relationship between a principal (the state, in case of the public sphere) and agents, often induced by the involvement of a third actor, the corruptor (Banfield 1975; della Porta and Vannucci 1999). This theoretical framework underlines how institutional variables such as monopoly power, opacity, and discretion in decision-making, create opportunities and incentives for individuals to enter into corrupt exchanges (Klitgaard 1988). Neoliberal doctrines have provided the basic theoretical toolkit underlying anticorruption measures and reforms sponsored in the last decades by inter-governmental and international organizations, particularly the OECD, World Bank, United Nations, and IMF. Bribery is seen as the predictable by-product of the undue intrusion of the state into the activity of competitive markets, both through public services (which should be replaced by a market for equivalent private commodities) and through regulation (whose burden is unnecessary given economic agents' self-restraining and free contractual agreements). Privatization, liberalization, cuts in public spending, and deregulation are the recommended policy for an effective and long-lasting reduction of corruption. The adoption of an anticorruption regulatory framework consistent with the limitation of state interference with markets has often been imposed as a prerequisite for the distribution of economic aids and investments.

In its practical application the neoliberal paradigm has shown severe drawbacks. The retreat of the state underlying neoliberal policies may itself be corruption-enhancing. This is exemplified by the bribery aimed at distorting or manipulating privatization processes of public enterprises and assets (Rose-Ackerman 1999), as well as by the strategic interest of large corporations, merchant banks, and other oligopolistic actors in obtaining a more favorable and looser regulatory environment of their high-profit activities, while discharging social, environmental, as well as financial costs onto the public. The externalization of public services or the recourse to contractual provisions allowing private corporations to play a crucial role even in the definition and satisfaction of public needs has increased managerial discretion and weakened public accountability. Coherently with the New Public Management approach, shifting between public and private roles has been encouraged, breaking down barriers that prevented revolving doors between government departments and firms. As a consequence, corrupting penetration of private businesses' interests into policy-making has been often observed, rather than the presumed adoption of efficiency-based organizational models in the public sector. In an extreme manifestation of this – Berlusconi in Italy and Trump in the United States – businessmen who were previously used to influence (and bribe) public decision makers enter into politics in order to get protection, invoking the rhetoric of entrepreneurial success as a rewarding strategy in their direct appeal to the "people." Moreover, any reduction of the state's role in the economy necessarily generates a large set of un-regulated, opaque, unaccountable interactions between public and private agents, lobbies, large corporations, and other organized economic interests.

The failure of anticorruption policies inspired by the application of the neoliberal paradigm has been widely observed and criticized (Ivanov 2007). Moreover, all international rankings, like Transparency International's *Corruption Perception Index*, or the World Bank's *Corruption Control Indicators*, consistently show the (apparently) paradoxical outcome: the world's maximum degree of integrity in the public sector can be observed in Scandinavian countries where public regulation and state intervention in the economy and the society are highest. This calls for additional explanations and alternative policy measures.

9.3.2 Corruption and the Blurred Boundaries Between Political and Economic Power

While the complementarity between capitalism and democracy was usually taken for granted, corruption is a symptom of subterranean frictions between the two. Liberal-democratic regimes establish, through institutional and informal constraints, a boundary between *internal* power, deriving from the occupation of roles of public authority, and economic power, deriving from the market process. In a wider perspective we can look at corruption as a practice – more or less "institutionalized" in itself – that *covertly* and therefore *unaccountably* converts economic into political resources and vice versa, blurring

the frontier separating the public and the private sphere. Corrupt activities are usually but not necessarily illegal, since this condition depends on the capability of the legal order to identify and sanction them. Additionally, the very definition and effective enforcement of corruption in legal terms may be influenced by corrupt politicians and judges, becoming the object of a symbolic contention on the acceptable boundaries between state, markets, and society; individual and collective interests and rights; the proper extent and limits of market, bureaucratic and patrimonial allocation of resources; and public and private roles (Johnston 1996).

Corruption implies the application of the price system to legal procedures and rights. Therefore it is not only contrary to democratic values, it also obstructs the efficient functioning of the market itself (Arrow 1972). The development of inclusive, as opposed to rent-seeking and extractive, economic and political institutions, provides more effective and credible commitments of rulers and economic actors to a limitation of excessive privatization and conversions of the public goods into privately appropriable rents (Acemoglu and Robinson 2012). When corruption happens in a liberal-democratic regime, a market for the exercise of public authority replaces official procedures that, under the rule of law, should provide impartial and universalistic criteria in the allocation of goods and services. Privatization can hardly be a remedy against bribery, since behind any form of corruption lies precisely a hidden and unaccountable privatization of resources in which secret networks of public and private agents exchange rents. This invisible "privatization" process implicit in bribery explains the strong relationship between economic inequality and corruption across both developed and developing countries (Gupta, Davoodi, and Alonso-Terme 1998). The *inequality trap* is the outcome of a positive-feedback mechanism fueled by the impact of perceptions of pervasive corruption on both mistrust in the quality of government's services and unequal allocation of resources, which in turn encourages both tax evasion and the search for selective inclusion in the cliques of privileged ones, through hidden influence and corruption, therefore further increasing unfairness (Uslaner 2013). Successful attempts of corrupt agents to minimize public scrutiny, visibility and risk, through the strategic use of their official roles, further undermines vertical and horizontal accountability. The potential for corruption generates economies of scale in a wider set of other illicit activities, since corrupt exchanges with regulators, public supervisors, and enforcers to avoid control and sanctions are intertwined with other ills including fiscal evasion, financial frauds, bankruptcies, and irregular industrial waste dumping (della Porta and Vannucci 2012).

9.3.3 Corruption as an Enduring Challenge to Democratic Principles and Practices

After the ephemeral triumph celebrated with the collapse of Communism in Eastern Europe, the democratic model has been shaken in the last decades by a series of tensions. Evidence and perceptions of widespread corruption are among the most acute symptoms of democracy's unresolved challenges, and a hidden factor that tends to exacerbate them. They contribute to the spiraling costs of political activity and the decline of political participation and traditional parties, linked to the impotence of political leadership, in the face of recurrent economic crisis and deterioration in public budgets, to resist the capturing influence of the strongest economic and financial interests. But they also facilitated the rise of populist or extremist parties and leaders, openly questioning liberal-democratic values and the sustainability of the welfare state.

Far beyond the inflated cost of public works and services, inefficient contractor selection, and the waste of resources due to rent-seeking, other long-term negative consequences of corruption affect the quality of democratic processes (Johnston 1986). Pervasive corruption alters the relative allocation of public spending, penalizing sectors where rents are more difficult to extract, such as education, social security, and welfare. A relatively higher portion of the public budget is allocated to huge infrastructural projects, defense and other sectors where monopolistic or oligopolistic corporations control the public markets (Mauro 1998). In the longer term, countries with a lower public investment in education will suffer a diminished level of accountability, due to a weakened capability of citizens to effectively control their decision makers, mobilize in collective actions, recognize and sanction malfeasance (Arnone and Borlini 2014).

Even the way out of rampant corruption offered by populist right-wing leaders is incoherent with the neoliberal perspective they criticize. The basic solution they envision against the multiplication of abuses of entrusted power is a drastic simplification. Bypassing the traditional multiple subjects of political delegation of power in representative democracy, they propose the strengthening of a unique, direct linkage between the masses and Trump-like charismatic leaders, whose reliability in anticorruption should be assessed by their capacity to "speak straight" and plain, by their success as entrepreneurs and non-involvement in "old" politics, and by their wealth – which is supposed to make them immune to temptation. But the "unconditional trust" they ask for from the people is the most vulnerable to arbitrary abuses of power and unaccountability, especially when – as the media tycoon and former Italian Prime Minister Berlusconi clearly shows – it is instrumentally invoked to justify a weakening of the rule of law, gaining impunity from judicial inquiries through special laws.

A basis for alternative, more effective anticorruption reforms lies instead in a simultaneous promotion of bottom-up initiatives, empowering societal actors, allowing them to influence those political entrepreneurs with the authority to change the formal "rules of the game." The mobilization from below of civil society and local communities' participation in anti-corruption policies may set in motion a positive interplay between actors' interests in integrity and optimistic expectations that an exit from systemic corruption can be found. In recent years, social movements denouncing kleptocratic practices have developed a radically different explanatory framework, where the fight against corruption is a basic constituent of a wider effort of citizens to oppose deterioration in the quality of democracy. Experiences that increase the citizens' opportunities to participate in public policies increase information available to the public, spreading a broad awareness and knowledge that in the "technocratic" conception of politics is kept hidden (della Porta, Font, and Sintomer 2014). The fight against corruption, re-framed as a public good, requires an effective defense of citizens' rights against the arbitrary power of the political

bosses to whom particularistic demands are addressed. Among the crucial factors that increase the possibility of success are better access for individual and collective actors to an independent judiciary, in order to denounce discrimination and privileges, especially when such practices strengthens social awareness (see Section 9.10).

In recent mobilizations from below, corruption is defined as a problem of social justice, rather than a mere obstacle to good government, and could be effectively curbed by widening the forms of political involvement through participative democracy (see Section 9.13). Decentralized knowledge and citizen awareness are often as insightful as experts' understanding. Public responsiveness spreads thanks to a wide stigmatization of political malfeasance. Spanish *indignados* ironically set the 'Estado de malestar' against the 'Estado de bienestar' (the state of malaise against the welfare state). In recent years, information about and censure of corruption circulated thanks to the support of NGOs, movements, groups, and activists, from Wikileaks to individual bloggers, to networks and e-platforms. This process encouraged the development of both vertical and horizontal accountability mechanisms, oriented not to punishment and enforcement, but also to raising public awareness. The fight against systemic corruption, a factor of degeneration and injustice affecting many representative democracies, cannot be a single-issue policy, nor delegated only to experts' advice to policy makers, but rather must be linked to a wider rethinking of politics and participation (della Porta 2013).

9.4   The Territorial Dimension

9.4.1   The Bounded Nation-State

For a long time, social and political theory presented modernization as a process of territorial integration and functional differentiation (Durkheim 1964). This stemmed from functional factors, including the expansion of markets, the division of labor and the diffusion of language and cultural norms (Deutsch 1972). States promoted cultural homogenization and uniform administration and services. State boundaries turned social and economic demands, and their political articulation, inwards (Rokkan 1999). Capitalism developed within a national framework in symbiosis with the state; labor organization followed. Economic and social systems were thus "caged" by the nation-state (Mann 1993).

There was a strong normative component to these theories as the nation-state was seen as the necessary framework for social progress. Democracy, from the nineteenth century, was usually defined in a national mode, the nation providing the demos. Civil and human rights were based on unitary and national citizenship.

Following the Second World War, Keynesian macro-economic policies were predicated on integrated national economies. Spatial development policies aimed at further integration by bringing lagging regions into national markets. Post-colonial states also pursued national economic integration sometimes through protectionism.

For the welfare state the unitary nation-state provided affective solidarity and the necessary scale for redistribution. Welfare settlements

9

rested on a positive-sum social compromise between capital and labor, both confined to national boundaries so unable to "exit" (Bartolini 2005).

The European state model became the precedent for state-building elsewhere in the world, where new states were aware of their own precariousness. Again there was a strong normative bias, with diversity, pluralism, and dispersed authority being associated with pre-modern political tradition, and unity and integration with modernization, democracy, equality, and welfare.

There was a central paradox at the heart of this deterritorialization and integration perspective. Territory was disappearing within states while becoming the supreme factor in differentiating states, economies, and social systems from each other. Solidarity, too, worked within states but not across them. The paradox became apparent with the rise of new forms of transnational economic, social, and political order.

9.4.2 Rescaling the State

In the aftermath of the Cold War, there was a brief moment of triumphalism as some scholars celebrated the end both of history and of territory with the victory of American liberal capitalism and "globalization." Progress had reached its logical conclusion as particularism gave way to a universal normative order.

In fact, what ended was not territory but the nation-state's monopoly over the definition and management of it. Rather than deterritorialization there is a re-territorialization. This is "spatial rescaling" by which functional systems, identities, and institutions are migrating to new territorial levels, above, below, and across the state system (Keating 2013). This process may be progressive or regressive.

Economic processes are reconstituting at the global and transnational levels, with free trade, mobility of capital, and the large corporation. At the same time, sub-state territories are sources of economic dynamism. The emerging global division of labor is by no means blind to territorial differentiation. Indeed, some of the industries that might appear to be prime candidates for deterritorialization, like financial services or software design, are the most concentrated spatially.

One perspective sees places as subordinated to a global division of labor as capital seeks out locations for production, jumping national boundaries. The city-region concept (Sassen 2000; Scott et al. 2001) presents urban locations tied together in global production chains, dislocated from their host states. Another perspective sees cities and regions as more than mere locations of productions but production systems, with their own internal logic (Crouch et al. 2001).

In a further move, these systems are portrayed as being in competition with each other as Ricardian comparative advantage gives way to absolute advantage (Scott 1998). This is a contentious point (Bristow 2010). Many economists insist that only firms compete and that talking of regional competition reifies spatial entities. The idea of inter-regional competition is an interpretation promoted by certain actors

for specific purposes. States and transnational agencies have taken it as a complement to models of endogenous development based on what regions can do for themselves, to supersede the old diversionary regional policies and permit a disengagement from spatial equity. All regions and cities are told to become more competitive although, logically, this is impossible; territories can become more productive, but that is another matter. For local and regional leaders, it provides the opportunity to expand their support base by postulating a common territorial interest.

This new regionalist thesis has been taken up by the political right, the left and the center. On the right, Ohmae (1995) argues that globalization means the end of the nation-state, to be replaced by regions, competing in a rigorous market order. Alesina and Spoloare (2003) derive the size of "nations" (by which they mean states) by reference to external trading conditions. In eras of protectionism, there is a tendency to large states, to secure extensive home markets. In times of free trade, global markets are open, home markets are less important, and small states are more viable. With a smaller population, they can achieve greater homogeneity of public policy preferences through ethnic homogeneity. The argument is neither theoretically coherent nor empirically sustainable (Keating 2013) but provides the intellectual underpinnings for the political right to deploy policies based upon a mixture of neo-liberalism, neo-mercantilism, and ethnic particularism.

The consequence might be a "race to the bottom." As localities compete for investment, they may cut taxes and social and environmental provision. Inter-regional solidarity will suffer as states reduce support for territorial cohesion.

Intra-regional solidarity can also suffer as social and economic actors may engage in "partial exit" from national social compromises (Bartolini 2005). Mobile actors and businesses can physically relocate or play regions off against each other. Such an outcome may be attractive to the political right but seen as a threat by the left.

The race to the bottom is neither inevitable nor free from contestation. Austerity, plant closures, and service retrenchment are often felt first at the local level, generating territorialized responses. State spatial development strategies and the intrusion of global economic forces generate local conflicts over land use and displacement. Oppositional social movements often mobilize at a local level. Urban struggles often focus on land use, pitting private profit against public utility in specific places, and on access to, spatially delivered public services. This has made the city and metropolitan area key sites for distributional conflicts and for a left-wing regionalism. Mobilization of indigenous peoples in the face of the intrusion of international capital and state development strategies will often take on a territorial form.

Contestation also comes from movements based on the revival of old, or creation of new, territorial identities and demands for political autonomy. In the 1970s there was a tendency to write this off as evidence of retarded modernity, a violation of the national integration teleology. A less prejudicial view is that political identities are continually in flux, with the nation-state providing one historically specific fix. Some new nationalisms are linked to exclusion, xenophobia, welfare chauvinism and opposition to immigration, and associated with the political far right. Others are socially liberal and politically social democratic. Many have fastened onto the new regionalism in economics to make an argument for the economic viability of smaller places in the context of global change, and support transnational integration as a way of constructing a broader external support system for small polities. In many cases, sub-state territories have emerged as spaces for resistance to welfare retrenchment. Where there is an existing affective solidarity based on a competing national identity, this may provide the basis for defense of welfare.

In the political center there is a vision of the region as a space of consensual governance, where that term refers to cooperation on agreed policy goals. Rescaling has been accompanied by depoliticization of key policy tasks. A new managerialism has focused on "delivery," without asking what is to be delivered. Depoliticization is matched with a change of scale, as with monetary policy in the Euro zone. At the regional level, development agencies have often been given a degree of operational independence and insulation from local distributive pressures. These forms are often legitimated (by states and international agencies) in the language of "governance," given a positive normative spin as politics-free problem solving.

So rescaling is, in itself, neither progressive nor conservative but, rather, a field of contestation. Territory is not a mere topological concept but a sociological concept whose substantive content is filled in through political and social struggle. Decentralization may not produce a race to the bottom but a race to the top if the territory concerned is more solidaristic than the state level.

9.4.3   Institutions

States have responded in various ways to rescaling as representation, accountability, and welfare as social and economic processes have escaped their purview. One strategy involves centralized or technocratic forms of territorial administration, matching the scale of policy systems. Another is decentralization to regional and local levels, while retaining strategic control at the center. The old idea that there is an optimal level for each governmental competence has been revived in arguments about structural reform, both in domestic politics and in recommendations of global agencies for structural reform. Yet, the optimal level for any function will depend on what the objective is and cannot be deduced from abstract principles.

State territorial management strategies are challenged by bottom-up forces seeking the democratization of territorial *governance* by seeking responsible *government*, based upon representation and democracy. They challenge technocratic and economistic conceptions of territory by pressing social, environmental, and distributional issues.

This has provoked a series of conflicts over institutions. The boundaries of territorial institutions can define the scope for distributive politics by including rich and poor, as well as the balance of political power. The internal constitution of territorial institutions may privilege central government, technocrats, or elected bodies. Decentralization may

expose vulnerable territories to the discipline of global competition or offload welfare responsibilities and expensive commitments. It may equally be a way to re-establish democratic input to, and control of, social and economic change.

Rescaling poses a challenge to a vision of the integrated nation-state as the inevitable outcome of modernization or as the normatively desirable ideal. It reminds us that, historically, there have been other forms of political order and there is no teleological necessity for a particular spatial order (Ferguson and Mansbach 1996; Sassen 2008). The response need not therefore entail the recreation of the twentieth-century state form, which had its bad sides, including exclusion, aggression, and domination. Inclusion and solidarity can no longer be entrusted to the centralized state alone, but must be built into systems of public policy-making at all levels.

9.5   The Constitutional Challenge of National Pluralism

As noted in the previous section, the central concept of political and constitutional modernity is the idea of the nation-state, which assumes the consolidation of modern states around the notion of a single cohering national identity. One of the most significant ways in which the pretensions of the nation-state to be the natural mode of modern political organization has been challenged is by the persistent autonomy claims made by sub-state or stateless nations within extant state polities. The condition of "national pluralism," which denotes the existence of more than one group claiming a *national* identity within the historical and territorial space of a state, and the accompanying rights claims asserted by these groups as *nations*, raise fundamental questions for established conceptual categories of law and politics in relation to nationality and statehood.

9.5.1   National Pluralism: A Global Policy Challenge?

Identifying what is and what is not a multinational polity can be analytically very difficult, not least because sub-state groups themselves are often unclear about the type of constitutional claims they wish to assert. Sometimes the "national" character of these claims is motivated primarily by strategic considerations in the face of unaccommodating host states. In others, such claims may be impossible to articulate due to the hostile and repressive political atmosphere created by the host state. In yet others, groups may make "nationalist" claims without necessarily demanding recognition as distinct nations. Most commonly and with only a handful of unusual exceptions across the world, however, nation-states do not recognize multiple nationality claims within their territorial boundaries at a constitutional level, even where some states may adopt sub-constitutional policies to address the challenges of national pluralism.

Even with these analytical difficulties, it is nevertheless possible to readily observe the empirical reality of national pluralism within a larger number of countries across the world than is often assumed, with one account even asserting that "90 percent or more" of existing states cannot be considered mono-nation-states (van den Berghe 2006). Based on the Minorities at Risk (MAR) data, Bertrand and Laliberté calculate that there are 126 ethnic groups in 23 countries in Asia, out of which 15 are classified as "sub-state national groups"; 362 ethnic groups in 43 countries in sub-Saharan Africa, out of which 4 are sub-state national groups; and 74 ethnic groups in 19 countries in North Africa and the Middle East, out of which 4 are sub-state national groups. This means that there are sub-state national groups in 39 percent of countries in Asia, 9 percent of countries in sub-Saharan Africa, and 21 percent of countries in North Africa and the Middle East (Bertrand and Laliberté 2010). In very few of these multinational states do sub-state nations receive the constitutional recognition they demand, and where they do, political practice often serves to negate any constitutional commitments as do exist. This suggests that the issue of national pluralism constitutes a constitutional and policy challenge that ought to engage social scientists at a more general level than the interests of area studies specialists who are often the only ones to study this phenomenon in any depth.

9.5.2 The Modern World of Nation-States

The international order as we know it today took shape with the dissolution of the Western European empires after the Second World War, which saw the creation of many new states in Asia and Africa. With the collapse of the Soviet empire, a number of new states were created. During these successive waves of state formation, the dominant model was what was described later as "classical modernist" nation-state building (Smith 1998). The classical modernist post-colonial nation-building model sees the sovereign nation-state as the essential condition of modernity (Smith 1983). Based on the general principles of this heuristic blueprint, proponents of the model seek to build territorial, civic nations corresponding to states through a wide array of techniques, including communications, mass education, political mobilization, and constitution-making, in much the same way as an architect designs a building or an engineer a machine. It takes the distilled experience of nation and state formation in the post-industrial West as the exemplary path to the universal modernity to which they strive. In other words, societies escape feudalism and religious and ethnic primordialism in Asia and Africa by making good copies of the predecessor civic nations and territorial states in the West (Smith 1998).

If those are the broad sociological and historical theses of post-colonial modernism, there are also a number of key normative propositions associated with it. These may be listed as follows. Nations are primarily territorial not ethnic entities. They are made up of political communities constituted by the principle of equal citizenship and civic participation. The nation defined in this way is the wellspring of sovereignty, which constitutes the sovereign state. The nation and the state cannot be separated; they only make sense as a conjoined concept ("nation-state"). Nation-states command the loyalty of their members to the unity of the community, and this is desirable in that it gives coherence and substance to the ideals of democratic participation, civic community, and popular sovereignty. Individual as well as communal disloyalty to the nation-state – for example, in the form of attempted secession – can be dealt with by force, and this is in

principle ethically defensible, for otherwise both internal and international order collapses. Finally, the intertwining of nation, state, and sovereignty generally favors centralization and unitary forms of constitutional organization (although it is not inconsistent with orthodox, mono-national federalism). In most if not all post-colonial states, this model continues to exert a powerful influence on the constitutional imagination of political elites.

By fusing the very notion of democratic modernity with a particular state form, this discourse invested the nation-state with a normative superiority that permitted sub-state nationalisms to be dismissed as backward and revanchist. At the same time, however, in the post-colonial context, state practice did not live up to the civic ideal of the nation-state in a number of ways. In many countries, post-colonial nation-building became not so much a process of modernization as a convenient vehicle for ethnic majorities to consolidate their hold on state power at the expense of minorities. Such states became 'ethnocracies' rather than nation-states reflecting the republican ideals of the French and American revolutions or the liberal principles of the European Enlightenment more broadly (Yiftachel 2006: ch. 2). Similarly, in many cases, the authoritarian apparatuses of the colonial state continued unreformed, providing the new elites with old instruments of oppressive power now legitimated by the discourse of modernism (Rae 2002).

In these ways, many sub-state nations found themselves trapped within nation-states (and a system of international order that presumed the legitimacy of state boundaries), which had little sympathy with their claims to recognition let alone accommodation. With few exceptions, this continues to be the overriding systemic context that sub-state nations in Asia and Africa have to contend with even today. Yet the widening and deepening of processes of democratization in many of these states reopens the sub-state national question, and demands constitutional responses consistent with the normative commitments of democratization.

9.5.3 Democratization and National Pluralism

Most states now subscribe to – or at least claim to uphold – the basic procedural requirements of democracy in the form of periodic elections, and the democratization challenge has moved on to deeper questions of substantive democracy (Whitehead 2002). It is in conceptualizing the substantive content of democracy, however, that current thinking in the social sciences has been unable to adequately respond to the multinational conundrum. Due to the dominance of the unitary nation-state, many democratization theorists and policy makers who are otherwise attentive to the demands of societal pluralism, assume that the demos within states is monistic, whereas the presence of multiple national groups within states demand approaches that recognize multiple *demoi* (cf. Stojanović 2010). From that analytical understanding a number of structural and normative implications for constitutional design follow if the democratic ideal is to be fully realized within multinational societies. Unless those questions are attended to, the nation-state's "crisis of the hyphen" (Anderson 1996: 8) would only perpetuate injustice, instability, and conflict.

9.5.4 National Pluralism's Analytical and Normative Challenges to Traditional Democratic Constitutionalism

The first challenge that the empirical reality of national pluralism poses for the dominant unitary conception of the nation-state is that "nation" and "state" have to be (re)understood as separate analytical categories (Keating 2001). It follows from the fact of multiple nations within the territory of the state that unless nation and state are disaggregated, the continued assumption that the nation is something that is exclusively associated with the state renders sub-state nations unable to realize their own claims to recognition (Tierney 2006).

Similarly, it is routinely assumed that the unitary nation-state is the sole repository of sovereignty within its territory. In the multinational context, such a monistic conception of sovereignty makes little sense, because the multiple nations that constitute the state's constitutional order would assert their own sources of constituent power. It follows from this that the concept of sovereignty has to be understood in both plural and relational terms. It may not be the case that the unique European Union-style multilevel normative order and pluralized sovereignties are replicable in other parts of the world (Welikala 2015), but the division and sharing of internal sovereignty is a common practice in federations and this needs to be amplified in multinational contexts to take explicit account of sub-state nationalities. The relational concept of sovereignty eschews the notion that sovereignty belongs exclusively to either the state or the people in favor of the view that sovereignty is a product of an ongoing relationship between the two (Loughlin 1992). This conception suits plurinational constitutionalism especially well, in determining the location and exercise of sovereignty as a constantly negotiated and dynamic political process between the sub-state nations and their host-states.

The nation, separated from the state, has both political and cultural dimensions. It is a form of collective identity defined by a group's shared culture, history, and social institutions; and it is a normative concept in that the assertion of nationhood involves claims to territory and self-government. In both senses but especially the latter, the nation is a space of collective deliberation, decision-making, and self-determination. Individual autonomy only makes real sense within the social context in which choices are made (Kymlicka 1995) and in multinational contexts, the sub-state national society rather than the state-national society is the primary space within which individuals make their cultural and political choices. Democratic constitutionalism's commitments to individual and collective self-determination therefore must extend to sub-state nations and the individuals who comprise them, and must not be limited to conceiving this relationship as being limited to individuals and the traditional nation-state.

However, there are two important provisos to traditional understandings of nationhood in the multinational context. The first is that individuals in the contemporary world can and do often entertain multiple "national" identities, and this needs to be treated as a reality rather than as a threat. Thus, plurinational constitutionalism must correspond to a reality in which individuals will have allegiances to both sub-state and state national identities, and in some cases to regional identities above the state. The second caveat is that the claims to constitutional accommodation of sub-state nations often do not and certainly need not take the form of separate states (Keating 2001: ix). States' fear of acknowledging sub-state national claims to even cultural autonomy stems from the assumption that any recognition of national status inevitably would lead to separatist claims to independent statehood. However, while many sub-state nationalists do make separatist claims for reasons of both strategy and conviction, separatism is not often the primary goal of many within sub-state nations. Instead, they seek accommodation of their national status within the constitutional arrangements of their host-states, in such ways as to give them recognition, representation, and autonomy (Tierney 2006: 18–19, 92–98). This no doubt presents a set of difficult challenges for constitutionalism, but as the experience of both the Western plurinational states as well as a number of recent examples of transitional constitution-making in conflict-affected states have shown, they are hardly insurmountable as technical problems (Ghai and Woodman 2013).

These observations lead to a range of implications for constitutionalism in dealing with the challenge of national pluralism, so as to accommodate sub-state claims to autonomy, recognition, and representation, balanced by adequate reciprocal requirements of state unity. Of these, the most fundamental are the disaggregation of nation from state, and the recognition of multiple national spaces within the state, which in turn demand the design of multilevel constitutional orders with highly decentralized forms of legal authority and political power. It also demands a methodology of constitutional practice that is pluralist, empiricist, pragmatic, flexible, and asymmetrical, or to put it conversely, a constitutional culture that is not hierarchical, rigid, and monistic as most modern liberal constitutional democracies tend to be.

9.6 Rights and Citizenship

9.6.1 Introduction

There is a substantive multidisciplinary literature – from anthropology, law, sociology, politics, philosophy and public policy – that engages with and critically reflects on the relationship between human rights and citizenship and the practical implications of different ways of understanding this relationship. Yet scholarship and public policy debates on human rights and citizenship have broadly been situated in liberal democratic societies, where the predominant concerns have been the integration of migrants and managing national minorities, with the presumption of a trajectory towards legal citizenship in the given nation-state. More recently, the changing conditions of global migration pose challenges for citizenship in liberal democratic societies. While some have argued that we are witnessing the demise of 'national' citizenship, and that instead rights are available to non-citizens through 'post-national' means, others have highlighted that international human rights laws and norms cannot operate outside of national politics. Going further, it has been argued that human rights discourses and legislation have actually led to greater inequalities through creating a number of sub-statuses (Nash 2009), and that it is only through citizenship that "we become human" and can claim rights (Douzinas 2000: 106). In some regions of the world, for example, in the Arab region, there are significant non-citizen populations, where typically there is no route to legal citizenship. While multiculturalism is evident as a discourse at the level of international organizations where respect for minority rights is a normative expectation also being applied to Arab states, it is conspicuous in its absence at the regional and national levels. Where there are forms of minority accommodation (as in Lebanon), this is decoupled from discourses on democratic inclusive citizenship.

This section re-examines the relationship between human rights and citizenship in a comparative frame, starting with a consideration of theoretical understandings of human rights and citizenship and the tensions or paradoxes arising between these conceptions. It then explores the tensions and paradoxes between democratic assumptions underpinning international human rights discourses of multiculturalism and trajectories of inclusive citizenship, with regionalized and localized political discourses of minority rights and the nation-state.

9.6.2   Between "Human Rights" and Citizenship

A significant debate in the field relates to justifications for human rights, and how these justifications are linked to claims of universality. Douzinas (2007: 9) has argued that the term "human rights" is problematic and paradoxical in that it "combines law and morality, description and prescription." The word "rights" indicates that it is a legal category, while the term, "human" refers to a moral framing of the individual in relation to the law. As human rights can be claims that may not actually be recognized in law, this entails operating in the domain of aspiration as opposed to legal reality – what Douzinas describes as the "confounding of the real and the ideal characteristic of human rights discourse" (2007: 10). There have also been attempts to define what is meant by "universality" of human rights. Connelly acknowledges that some accounts of the universality of human rights are problematic – "empirically, philosophically or politically" (2007: 281). As a way forward he attempts to delineate different forms of universality where he defends "functional" and "legal" accounts of universality, while conceding the probable indefensibility of "anthropological" and "ontological" universality. He also talks of an "overlapping consensus" universality and the notion of a "relative universality," distinguishing between universality at the level of the concept and at the level of practice (Connelly 2008). In contrast, Goodhart (2008) argues that human rights are a resource for people providing "aspiration" rather than "moral truth" and as such the legitimacy of human rights does not come from "proving" universality. He is troubled by Donnelly's concept of the "relative universality" of human rights, arguing instead that the legitimacy of human rights comes from their global appeal. Clearly, however, legitimacy does not stem from universality, rather than the reverse, as this reduces legitimacy to democratic popularity (Connelly 2008), confounding legal grounding with democratic grounding (Ferrara 2003), and also potentially raising the accusation of "imperial humanitarianism" (Gott 2002 cited in Connelly 2007: 298).

In contrast to justice approaches to human rights, "care" perspectives emphasize connection, concern for relationships and responsibilities, with an emphasis on obligation that does not arise from rights per se. Such perspectives potentially lend themselves to greater sociopolitical

and local contextualization, operationalizing human rights in the context of the political interests of the state and its negotiations. This raises a structural problem with respect to the operationalizing of human rights. While human rights claims can challenge existing inequalities, they must appeal to those very structures to make their claims (Benhabib 2005; Douzinas 2007; Soysal 1994). Human rights also act to depoliticize exclusion and conflict by framing these issues as individual claims with a corresponding legal remedy (Douzinas 2000).

Furthermore, while human rights discourses suggest that the cosmopolitanization of international law benefits non-citizens, it has been argued that it is only through being fully recognized as a member of the political community, that we become "human" and can claim our "human rights." While legal migrants in Western liberal democracies are often entitled to many civil and social rights, as well as being protected by legislation at the transnational level and sub-nationally, the same cannot be said for refugees, asylum seekers, and illegal (or "irregular") migrants. In this regard, it could be argued that Soysal's conclusion that "the logic of personhood supersedes the logic of national citizenship" (1994: 164) does not apply to refugees or those of irregular status. It is premature to claim that universal human rights have superseded national citizenship "by disrupting the territorial closure of nations" (1994: 164) when we witness, not only the tight control of state borders, but also the differential application of human rights with respect to those irregular migrants, refugees, and asylum seekers. Nash (2009) goes further, arguing that the cosmopolitanization of law does not lead to greater equality, and that rather than legally promoting universal human rights, legalization of international human rights law has led to inequality as evidenced through a proliferation of sub-statuses. Critiquing Benhabib, she argues that such political theorizing is at a level of abstraction that is not sociologically contextualized, and so does not engage with what happened in practice. Rather than simply a matter of legal entitlement, claiming rights depends on social structures through which power, material resources, and meanings are created and circulated. She conceives of refugees as "sub-citizens," arguing that this status is created through international law. In addition, Nash (2009) argues that we can witness forms of sub-citizenship even when people hold legal citizenship, but are nevertheless marginalized because of gender, ethnicity, "race," religion, sexuality, or socioeconomic class. Taking sociological account of these lived realities is critically important to recognize, and increasingly so with the rise of right-wing populist discourses and movements globally that challenge these "differences."

There is a substantial literature on group rights and one of the central debates or paradoxes relates to the very conception of group rights itself. Are rights inherently individual rights or can a group itself be deemed to hold rights, or is it as individuals or the group (Miller 2002)? In addition, are group rights defined as "human rights" or are they the rights of citizenship? In addition, there is the question of what counts as a "group," as opposed to people holding certain characteristics. Group rights typically refer to "external protection" rights – that is rights that an individual of the group can claim for against the state (Kymlicka 1995). However, there are concerns about individuals' rights within the group, especially more vulnerable members. Justifications for group rights can be framed as human rights principles or as principles of citizenship. Miller (2002) asserts that typically those arguing to defend group rights make the case that they are fundamental rights of citizenship appealing to equality; language rights for minority groups, or group rights for political representation would be examples. It could be deemed paradoxical that rights for certain groups are based on calls for equality. However, when looking at actual examples, it is evident that calls for group rights are often calls for achieving equality – for example, in rights to language, culture, education, and practice of religion.

Another paradox pertains to market citizenship, where citizens are presented with a discourse of having more choice and freedom, yet on the other hand, there is increasing social inequality, political apathy, and lack of agency (Root 2007). In addition, in relation to immigration and citizenship, the market is a central force shaping who is deemed worthy of residency and ultimately a route to citizenship. Shachar and Hirschl (2014) use "Olympic citizenship" to refer to nation-states' strategies of selecting those deemed highly desirable – including, for example, the very wealthy, scientists, and athletes. Skills-based programs attest to this trend, as is evident in the UK's highly skilled temporary migrant program, introduced in 2008, which allows highly skilled individuals to immigrate, initially for one year, without sponsorship from an employer. On securing employment, this stay can be extended with subsequent entitlement to apply for British citizenship after five years (Kiwan 2010). This invokes a moral conception of citizenship on economic grounds, and contrasts with securitization discourses surrounding the concerns of integrating migrants who are unskilled or semi-skilled.

Rather than focusing on the relationship between human rights and citizenship, Isin's (2008, 2009) approach is somewhat different in that he suggests that we need to think in a new way about citizenship. He proposes the idea of "acts of citizenship," where citizenship is not reduced to status or practice, but instead has its focus on subjectivity and agency. It has been proposed that refugees and other marginalized groups are participative actors constructing their own identities and acting to mediate their own fate (Nyers 2010) and that these actions constitute "acts of citizenship" (Isin 2008, 2009). This has been written about in Western liberal democratic contexts, for example, in Canada and the United States, where there have been political movements by groups of irregular migrants, refugees, and non-citizens making claims. It could also be argued that this conception of "acts of citizenship" has resonance in other parts of the world, for example, in the Arab region, where disempowered groups have publically made claims in the context of the Arab uprisings (Kiwan 2014), and also in Lebanon, where there are examples of political and moral agency in Syrian refugees' "acts of citizenship" in political, cultural and "moral" domains (Kiwan 2016a). The linking of "performativity" and "precarity" as theorized by Butler (2009: x) makes an argument that the different ways of "laying claim to public space and to citizenship require both translation and performative modes of expression." For Butler, precarity is a condition of being at increased risk of violence; furthermore, gender norms relate to this notion. So precarity can refer to a range of vulnerable populations, including refugees, and women refugees in particular. She thinks of performativity not only as "speech acts," but also in what she calls the "reproduction of norms," which is necessarily iterative in nature – so that through repeated discourses or acts, a norm is created.

She links performativity to precarity arguing that even "vulnerable" populations lacking the "right to have rights" can claim its voice and make its claims.

9.6.3 Multiculturalism, Minority Rights, and Inclusive Citizenship

While citizenship has been an exclusionary concept, academic theorizing and policy approaches illustrate an engagement with developing more inclusive conceptions of citizenship, with a particular interest in citizenship and ethnic and religious diversity. The literature illustrates a range of constructions of citizenship, which can broadly be categorized into "moral," "legal," "participatory" and "identity-based" conceptions (Kiwan 2008). While these are certainly not mutually exclusive traditions, they illustrate dominant ways of understanding citizenship in theory and practice. It should also be recognized that the intellectual history of citizenship is a highly gendered conception, where the public sphere is characterized as rational and masculine, in contrast to the private sphere as emotional and feminine (Shafir 1998). "Legal" conceptions of citizenship draw from the tradition of modern liberal developments in seventeenth-century Europe linked to the rise of the modern nation-state (Held 1993) and the idea of a "social contract" between "free and equal" human beings premised on human (male) rationality. Participative conceptions also have a long intellectual history dating back to Ancient Greece, evident in contemporary communitarian approaches to citizenship and civic republican notions emphasizing civic bonds and active participation in the community (Kiwan 2016a). With regards to identity-based conceptions, the twentieth century has been called the "ethnic" century, as many civil and international conflicts have been framed in these terms (Cornell and Hartmann 2007), and the twenty-first century looks to be continuing in this vein (Kiwan 2016b). One of the central debates in the citizenship literature relates to whether we are witnessing "renationalization," with negative consequences for immigrants and ethnic minorities (Kiwan 2013). In the context of securitization discourses, it can be argued that immigration and refugee policies, integration policies, and education policies in Western liberal democracies are illustrating a "restrictive turn" (Joppke 2010 Pacquet 2012; Wright 2008). In contrast, post-national accounts suggest the decline of national citizenship. Despite homogenizing state discourses, individuals and groups contest, construct, and negotiate their citizenship identities and practices in relation to official citizenship policies across a range of domains, including, immigration, refugee policy, and education policy.

9.7 Political Parties and the Challenge of Democratic Representation

Social progress on a wide range of issues requires that citizens and civil society groups achieve effective representation through democratic channels. Although many types of societal organizations can perform representative functions, political parties have long been seen as vital agents of representation that mediate between states and societies. Parties historically articulated and aggregated diverse societal interests, structured electoral competition, developed policy alternatives, and formed national governments. As such, parties were essential institutions for holding governments accountable to societal interests and preferences.

Nevertheless, the ability of parties to perform these roles has increasingly been questioned in many parts of the world, under both new and established democratic regimes. Although democratic institutions spread to some 60–70 new countries after the mid-1970s in Southern and Central Europe, Latin America, Africa, and Asia, there exists a widespread belief that a "crisis of representation" is undermining the quality and responsiveness of democratic rule (Mainwaring and Zoco 2007). Even in the long-standing democracies of Europe and North America, signs of representational decay are readily apparent in declining voter turnout, reductions in party membership and identification, rising electoral volatility, and the growth of populist or anti-establishment parties, leaders, and movements (della Porta 2015b; Mair 2013).

Although democratic governance involves a mix of representative and participatory practices, some sort of representation is integral to modern large-scale democracies. It is only through acting in concert with others that citizens can hope to influence democratic outcomes. Acting in concert can take a number of different forms, including social movements, civil associations, and political parties, all of which play a role in articulating competing interests and identities. Parties, however, have a central role as representative agents in formal democratic institutions, as they are the primary actors who compete in the electoral arena, craft public policies, and organize national governments. As E.E. Schattschneider (1942: 1) famously asserted, "political parties created democracy and modern democracy is unthinkable save in terms of the parties." As such, parties are a natural starting point for understanding contemporary challenges of representation.

Theories of representation derived from the West European experience have long assumed that parties are anchored in, and give political expression to, societal conflicts (or "cleavages") that structure policy preferences and electoral competition (Bartolini and Mair 1990; Lipset and Rokkan 1967). Parties, in short, are traditionally seen as organizational intermediaries between societal interests and state institutions; they are expected to simplify a plurality of societal interests by aggregating complementary preferences and "bundling" issues into a reasonably coherent set of rival policy platforms.

With the spread of electoral competition to new countries in the developing world, however, these classic representative functions are often in short supply. Parties are sometimes coercive instruments of previous autocratic rulers (Hicken and Kuhonta 2015; Riedl 2014), or clientelist machines that allow political elites to control popular constituencies by manipulating economic dependency (Kitschelt and Wilkonson 2007; Stokes et al. 2013). Parties founded during recent periods of democratic transition are less likely to be rooted in deep class cleavages and more likely to rely on the mass media or charismatic personalities to mobilize support, rather than strong grassroots branches and organized social blocs (Mainwaring and Zoco 2007). Party systems with such shallow social roots are prone to high levels of electoral volatility, and they are ineffective vehicles for translating societal preferences into public policy-making arenas. That is especially true for working- and lower-class groups, which are highly dependent on political organization to mobilize their strength in numbers as a counterweight to the more privileged forms of influence and access that elite groups enjoy.

These representational deficiencies are hardly unique to new democracies in developing regions, however. Even in Europe, the historical birthplace of socially grounded, programmatically defined mass party organizations, "parties are not what they once were," as Schmitter (2001) pithily noted. In part, this reflects changes in the social, economic, and cultural landscape on which parties compete. Social cleavages based on class and religion have loosened over time. A wide range of interest groups and activist organizations have emerged alongside and independent of parties to articulate societal preferences and identities. Mass broadcast and social media have partially displaced party organizations from their central roles as agents of political communication, socialization, and electoral mobilization. In this more heterogeneous and pluralistic sociocultural landscape, citizens have become increasingly detached from party organizations, giving rise to a phenomenon that Dalton and Wattenberg (2000) call "parties without partisans" (see also Mair 2013). This societal detachment is especially pronounced among the younger generation of voters whose life experiences are far removed from the sociopolitical cleavages and organizational forms of the industrial era.

Furthermore, as parties' social roots withered they became increasingly professionalized, embedded in state institutions, and dependent on state resources. Rather than representatives of societal interests, parties may come to be seen as collusive and self-interested political cartels that share in the spoils of public office (Katz and Mair 1995). Cartelization threatens to create an insular and professionalized political caste that is poorly attuned to societal needs and largely unaccountable to them. It also expands opportunities to exploit public office for purposes of corruption, self-enrichment, and influence peddling, practices that seriously distort the democratic process.

Such rent-seeking practices thrive when the rule of law is weak and institutional checks and balances are inoperative. They are also encouraged when the exorbitant costs of electoral campaigns induce politicians to cultivate ties to private donors, tilting the democratic playing field and undermining institutional responsiveness to popular constituencies (Gilens 2012; Winters 2011). Party competition can thus open channels for private wealth to skew the democratic process by converting economic power into political leverage (see Section 9.2). Taken together, varied forms of cartelization, corruption, and rent-seeking drive a wedge between citizens and the political class, and they exert a corrosive effect on citizens' trust and confidence in political institutions (see Section 9.3). Ultimately, they make democracy susceptible to anti-establishment forms of populist backlash.

The erosion of parties' societal linkages has been compounded by their diminished capacity to perform a key historical representative function – that of crafting alternative policy platforms in response to a broad range of societal interests. A gradual programmatic convergence of mainstream conservative and social democratic parties has long been noted in Europe. This process intensified when the

9

post-2008 financial crisis narrowed the programmatic options available to national governments and forced those with sovereign debt crises to adopt orthodox austerity measures dictated by transnational European institutions (Streeck 2013).

In Southern Europe, where the economic crisis was especially severe, political dislocations are strikingly reminiscent of those seen in Latin America following that region's debt crisis and market-based neoliberal reforms in the 1980s and 1990s. Party system upheaval in Latin America was especially pronounced where such neoliberal reforms were imposed by labor-based or left-leaning parties that were traditional proponents of state-led development and redistributive social policies (Lupu 2016; Morgan 2011; Roberts 2014). Such patterns of reform dealigned party systems programmatically, leaving them without a major party to channel societal opposition to neoliberal orthodoxy. Such opposition, therefore, tended to be channeled outside and against traditional party systems, leading to widespread social protest and the eventual rise of populist outsiders or new "movement parties" on the left flank of mainstream parties (Silva 2009; Yashar 2005). Similarly, the adoption of orthodox austerity measures by mainstream center-left parties in the early stages of the Southern European crisis triggered widespread social protest and the rise of new, anti-establishment populist or movement competitors. Paradoxically, as Mair (2013) suggested, a course of action that was 'responsible' in terms of securing international market integration made parties less responsive to – and representative of – their domestic constituencies.

Too often, citizens respond to failures of representation by withdrawing from active democratic participation, as evidenced by declining levels of partisan identification and voting turnout in many countries. In much of Europe, however, citizens have also lent support to far-right nationalist or populist parties that are hostile to globalization, transnational institutions, and ethnic or religious minority and immigrant communities. Parties that cater to such exclusionary forms of nationalism may advocate forms of "welfare chauvinism" that defend traditional social programs while narrowing their pool of eligible beneficiaries. A version of such right-wing populism recently triumphed in US presidential elections, where Donald Trump capitalized on economic insecurities, cultural resentments, fears of globalization and immigration, and widespread disillusionment with the two-party establishment.

As pointed out later in this chapter (see Section 9.13), however, other societal responses are possible. Social movements, for example, often emerge in the political void created by deficits in institutionalized political representation. By articulating issue positions or societal values that mainstream parties have neglected, social movements can transform the policy-making agenda, realign electoral competition, and give voice to new or marginalized social groups. Typically, they do so in extra-institutional arenas through diverse forms of social protest or "contentious politics" (McAdam, Tarrow, and Tilly 2001).

Social movements, however, need not remain on the margins of democratic institutions. Movement organizations and activists often work within established parties, or even found new "movement parties" that carry their agendas into electoral and parliamentary arenas (della Porta, Fenandez, et al. 2017). In the process, they may realign or reconfigure national party systems. Such was the case with the Green

parties spawned in the 1980s by European environmental, peace, and women's rights activists. Examples from Latin America include the Workers Party in Brazil, which was founded by labor and community activists, and the Movement Towards Socialism (MAS) in Bolivia, which gave partisan expression to a range of indigenous, peasant, and community-based movements (Madrid 2012). More recently, the *indignados* anti-austerity movement in Spain set the stage for a new movement party, *Podemos*, which challenged the programmatic convergence of mainstream parties. *Podemos* and other movement or leftist parties in a number of countries have repoliticized economic policy-making around issues of inequality, austerity, social citizenship, and workers' rights, expanding the range of policy debate in the aftermath of the post-2008 global financial crisis.

Similarly, a plethora of civil society actors are performing interest articulation and representation functions that parties once monopolized. Many civic groups work with parties and local governments to shape the policy-making agenda and respond to social needs. Reforms to decentralize government have sometimes facilitated these public–private partnerships, opening new channels for grassroots participation by community-based civic networks. In many cities community organizations are playing an important role in budgeting, program design, policy implementation, and the monitoring of public agencies (Baiocchi, Heller, and Silva 2011; Heller 2001). Such pluralistic forms of civic engagement provide opportunities for societal input that are a vital complement to the activities of party organizations.

Other types of institutional reforms can also enhance parties' responsiveness to societal concerns. Serious efforts at campaign finance reform and the regulation of media-based political advertising might reduce the incentives and opportunities for corruption, shielding the democratic process from the influence of private wealth. Likewise, independent judiciaries and electoral agencies are vital to safeguard against abuses of power and maintain the integrity of the electoral process. It should be recognized, however, that institutional reforms can have unintended consequences or potential trade-offs between conflicting goals. Primary elections, for example, may give citizens greater voice in the selection of party candidates for public office, but as seen in the United States they can also inflate the costs of elections and make party leaders dependent on wealthy private donors to finance internal campaigns. Moreover, primaries may encourage polarizing or populist tendencies in party systems, or even provide access to party leadership positions by populist outsiders, as seen in Donald Trump's stunning displacement (and eventual cooptation) of the Republican Party establishment in the United States.

Ultimately, modern democracy has seen a proliferation of new societal actors in the public sphere, but it has yet to discover a substitute for party organizations in a number of essential representative functions. For better or worse, parties continue to structure electoral alternatives, form governments, and shape policy initiatives. The ability of parties to craft meaningful programmatic alternatives at the national level would be well-served by coordinated international efforts to govern global markets. Indeed, vigorous advocacy of such coordinated efforts could offer a new opportunity for parties to craft progressive platforms that are clearly differentiated from the technocratic convergence of mainstream parties around market orthodoxy. In the meantime, both

9

traditional and emerging parties face the challenge of giving institutional expression to the broad range of societal actors and interests that are clearly dissatisfied with conventional forms of representation.

9.8 Expertise and Democracy

Since the beginning of the Scientific Revolution, science and expertise have acquired large roles as facilitators of democracy. The rise of experimental science, it is argued, gave citizens a new model for witnessing rulers' claims and holding them to higher standards of public justification (Ezrahi 1990). By the late nineteenth century, scientific knowledge, interpreted and communicated by experts, provided indispensable rationales for political action, ensuring that governments would not stray outside the limits of reasonableness and that publics, too, would agree on the need for new agenda items and policy decisions. Progressive politics at the turn of the twentieth century accepted and largely celebrated the growing delegation of policy responsibility to experts. Despite the shocks of two World Wars and subsequent pessimism about technology's power to reduce human autonomy and freedom (Habermas 1970), faith in government based on facts and evidence has only grown.

Many developments over the past 100 years bear out the belief that scientific knowledge increases civic participation, encourages interstate collaboration, and enhances the quality of public reason. Nineteenth-century divisions based on race and gender gave way to biological and sociological knowledge that established the equality of all human beings and laid the foundation for equal political treatment of all.[4] More recently, environmental and health knowledge spurred the formation of national, and to some extent global, "epistemic communities" (Haas 1990) on issues from biodiversity to pandemics and climate change.

Yet, faith in the democratizing influence of enlightened knowledge has long been troubled by countervailing doubts: in particular, the threat that superior expertise creates hierarchies of non-accountable power and excludes the demos from choosing its own purposes. Moreover, if public facts are made in ways that reinforce prior constellations of power, dominance, and injustice (Foucault 1980), then how can democracy realize its promises of accountability and self-governance?

Constructivist studies of science and technology have added new dimensions of concern, replacing a naturalistic account of scientific truth, in which science unproblematically mirrors nature, with perspectives that treat science as a mode of representation and interpretation (Felt et al. 2016). How such representations achieve and maintain authority becomes highly relevant to analyses of democracy and law. Work in the field of science and technology studies (STS) shows that knowledge about the world and norms for inhabiting the world are coproduced (Jasanoff 2004) – that is, our factual depictions of how the world is cannot be disentangled from our understandings of how we should live with the fruits of that knowledge. On this view,

scientific claims are neither neutral nor universal but rather reflect their conditions of production. Facts, put simply, are endpoints of social and political struggle (Latour 1987). And if facts are established through politics, then the hope that facts can create a level playing field for politics seems more mirage than reality.

9.8.1 Paradoxes of Progress

Does more knowledge lead to greater social progress? Is the Enlightenment promise that civic maturity will grow along with scientific understanding still valid, or is a more complex restatement warranted? What is the evidence on either side, and how should democracies take note not only of what science delivers but also of the limits of public knowledge? Further, if knowledge is a form of power, do means exist in contemporary democracies to ensure that this power will be accountably wielded?

It is widely accepted today that investments in science and technology are necessary if societies are to remain healthy and viable, whether by escaping from entrenched poverty and its assaults on human dignity or by promoting growth in jobs and economic opportunities. Those investments increasingly include not only research driven by scientists' curiosity about fundamental aspects of nature, but also science answering to governmental demands for useful knowledge. By the late twentieth century, the world's collective knowledge-producing capabilities included large amounts of what came to be called Mode 2 science (Gibbons et al. 1994): applied, transdisciplinary, multi-sited, and reflexive or conscious of its own value-ladenness.

Technological developments enabled economic growth and reduced poverty, as dramatically illustrated in the rise of the "Asian tigers" – Hong Kong, Singapore, South Korea, and Taiwan. Yet, the Tigers, along with neighboring countries such as Indonesia, Malaysia, Vietnam, and Thailand, embraced very different pathways to involving publics in governance. China's emergence as a global economic superpower only magnified the lack of congruence between the welfare benefits of scientific and technological activity and the spread of democracy.

In Western democracies, as well, fractures appeared in the alignment between knowledge and social harmony. First, contradicting the presumption that increasing knowledge resolves ambiguities and provides more reliable grounds for politics, more science opened up new frontiers of doubt and uncertainty. In this period of 'reflexive modernization' (Beck 1992), people used science to question the very facts that science produces in such abundance. The results range from what Ulrich Beck termed "organized irresponsibility" – the lack of accountable rulership – to "science for hire," with claims generated to serve parochial political interests. Increasing privatization of knowledge-making produced pockets of non-accountable expertise: models and algorithms that govern vast tracts of economic and social policy were shielded against critique by intellectual property laws and secretive corporate practices. Additionally, in most technologically advanced

---

[4]   Petitioners' briefs for two of the most progressive decisions by the Supreme Court of the United States – *Muller* v. *Oregon*, 208 U.S. 412 (1908) (legitimating limits on working hours to protect women's health) and *Brown* v. *Board of Education of Topeka*, 347 U.S. 483 (1954) (holding that educational systems separated by race could not be equal) – both argued in part on the basis of social science evidence.

societies, expert knowledge related to military strategy remained largely outside of democratic supervision.[5]

Second, in spite of the contingency of policy-relevant expert knowledge, science in the abstract provides a powerful deskilling discourse with which politicians deflect democratic criticism by accusing publics of scientific illiteracy. Canonical cases include protests against childhood vaccination; rejection of genetically modified crops and foods; skepticism toward the expert consensus around anthropogenic climate change; and, especially in the United States, rejection of evolutionary theory in favor of beliefs grounded in the Bible. Some commentators ascribed Britain's referendum vote to leave the European Union in June 2016 ("Brexit") to an ignorant rejection of economic expertise. Similarly, Donald Trump's surprise 2016 victory in the US presidential election was seen as a win for ignorant populism. Together, these examples support a "deficit model" of citizenship (Wynne 1994), which holds that a knowledge-deficient demos cannot be entrusted with the rights and obligations of self-rule.

Third, especially in the United States, where political disputes often spill over into litigation, the law's claims to impartial authority and commitment to reason have been compromised by accusations of scientific illiteracy. Judges, like other members of the lay public, are frequently charged with lack of scientific understanding. More insidiously, legal institutions are themselves complicit in ratifying a bright-line distinction between facts and values, and the corollary assumption that fact-finding must precede normative judgment. This is most apparent in the discourse of the "law lag," which declares that law is unable to keep up with the rapidity of scientific and technological advances and thus constantly arrives too late in its efforts to resolve situations of moral ambiguity or indeterminacy created by those developments.

These phenomena highlight the need to complicate the relationship between knowledge and social progress. A growing literature points to the varied and subtle ways in which tacit assumptions about the right ways to organize collective behavior impinge on and shape a society's approaches to producing shared knowledge, reasoning, and technological applications. Those underpinnings, because tacit, tend to be reproduced and reaffirmed by largely unreflective institutions. Therefore, although robust democracies continually give rise to new expert bodies, new technologies, and new knowledge-based policies, many deeper commitments to forms of politics rarely get exposed to critical scrutiny. These constitutional dimensions of political culture shape the conditions of possibility for modern politics, both democratic and authoritarian.

9.8.2 Cultures of Public Reason

Technological determinism is the commonplace notion that possibilities unlocked through material inventions drive human progress. There is, however, nothing deterministic about how societies respond to technological innovation. To be sure, technologies with enormous implications for society sometimes disperse quickly throughout the global marketplace – such as cars, cell phones, computers, and to some extent contraceptives. But on a great variety of technologies, from fossil fuels to agricultural biotechnology, neither lay nor official responses have converged transnationally, even when there is strong scientific consensus about the nature of the risks and benefits.

The public uptake of expert claims is a phenomenon to be understood in its own right in comprehensive accounts of democracy and the rule of law. "Civic epistemologies" (Jasanoff 2005), or public ways of knowing, refer to the institutionally stabilized ways in which citizens assess the public reasoning of powerful state organs. States differ in the practices by which they generate public knowledge, select and authorize experts, subject epistemic claims to public testing, and construct the very idea of objectivity in public discourse. These practices affect the credibility of expert claims. It matters, for instance, whether public knowledge is built as a "view from everywhere," with all interested parties gathered around the same table, or as a "view from nowhere," constructed through clashes among interest groups so as to produce claims that appear to stand above and outside of identifiable interests. The more inclusive practices of "view from everywhere" reasoning have led to markedly fewer public knowledge controversies than the "view from nowhere" approach. The latter, however, encourages a more skeptical style of citizenship, with lay publics more willing to generate their own expertise and question claims of higher epistemic authority.

No theory of political legitimacy questions (as yet) that sovereign states have a right to organize their public knowledge practices in accordance with their own cultural understandings of how to constitute relations between experts and citizens. If, however, divergent practices lead to different appraisals of the state of the world – whether the matter is climate change or plant genetic modification or threats to public health – then there could be democratic justification for epistemic subsidiarity, that is, an acknowledgment that different assessments of the same evidence may be allowed to coexist without needing to be standardized or brought into complete harmony. How and under what circumstances such subsidiarity may be tolerated remains an open question for political theory.

9.8.3 Epistemic Democracy: A New Constitutional Form?

The paradoxes and divergences identified above are likely to increase as technical expertise makes its way into new domains of decision-making and is disseminated through the ever more accessible digital medium. The proliferation of social media allows wider access to information, empowering popular sovereignty, but it also encourages the formation of bubbles or "echo chambers" among like-minded individuals, displacing deliberative exchange across varying belief systems.

Democratic societies are not insensitive to these challenges, and developments over a half century indicate growing awareness that the workings of government must include forms of public epistemic engagement. However, institutions for delivering on this insight, as

---

[5]   For example, the civilian death toll from US drone strikes has been contested, and independent organizations making such estimates have little faith in numbers generated by the government (Savage and Shane 2016).

well as the capacity to forge closure in situations of deep epistemic conflict, have not necessarily kept pace. Even in cultures committed to open access, pressures may form to exclude participation that rulers see as unreasonable. In turn, the moves by which such exclusions are made are themselves culturally conditioned.

To sum up, 350 years since the beginning of the Scientific Revolution, modern societies find themselves caught in novel binds about the role of knowledge in fostering democracy and the rule of law. The wide dissemination of knowledge and knowledge-making capabilities has not necessarily fostered well-deliberated, let alone wise or even rational, judgments. Fundamental challenges remain in the form of increased splintering and privatization of knowledge-making, the loss of trust in expert bodies, the opacity of transnational organizations, the persistence of power imbalances between rich and poor, and (not least) the unreflective uses of science to reinforce dominant problem framings that exclude genuinely challenging alternatives.

9.9 Participatory Democracy in the Neoliberal Era

In speaking of democratic deficits and paradoxes in our current era, it is impossible not to address the issue of citizen participation. Partially as a result of disappointments with democratic institutions, we are living today through a veritable "participation revolution." The idea that citizens ought to be at the center of governance has, since at least the late 1990s, become a central part of mainstream policy thinking. Although many – if not most – of the ideas about participation emerged with social movements and the political Left, enthusiasm for "citizen participation" today spans the political spectrum (as well as the globe) and is today widely endorsed and promoted by mainstream public policy experts, pro-market actors, as well as social movements. From deliberative polls to plebiscites, to e-governance, to participatory budgets and all manner of citizen forums, it is hard to find a democratic government today that does not invoke citizen participation in some form. Today we are witnessing a new political moment in which citizen participation is no longer the assumed domain of outsiders but has become widely encouraged, if not directly mandated, by governments and multilateral agencies. As Matt Leighninger (2006: 2) writes in his enthusiastically titled 2006 book, *How Expert Rule Is Giving Way to Shared Governance – And Why Politics Will Never Be the Same*, "In the 20th century, public life revolved around government; in the 21st century, it will center on citizens." Similarly many others discuss the dawning of an era in which citizens have come to participate in all sorts of matters previously reserved for government bureaucrats and politicians. To talk of citizen participation today is to address something being invoked by *Podemos* in Spain, by the Bolivarian Revolution in Venezuela, as well as by the World Bank and the European Union.

Yet, despite the enthusiasm, citizen participation is today deeply paradoxical, and in this small section we briefly explore what we see as its premises and limits. Participation, generally speaking, is today understood as a compelling way to gather governmental input, build trust in government, and create communities of engaged citizens. More sanguine promoters also hold the view that participation, properly

instituted, can help solve all kinds of modern-day problems of governance and politics. Yet, citizen participation today is fundamentally compatible with neoliberal tenets. It has emerged at the time of neoliberal reforms and government rollbacks and in some cases been deployed with the purpose of legitimating those reforms. It is, moreover, based on the idea of the individual, self-responsible citizen who solves problems without recourse to politics, movements, or sectoral representation. Mechanisms of citizen participation very seldom address the fundamental questions of power and inequality at the heart of the neoliberal project. This is not all, however. Participation does bring together communities of equals under a logic of inclusion, which causes tensions in neoliberalism. Participation can also bring to life ideas of collective, shared interests that cannot be dealt with at all within the neoliberal frame, for which politics is just about the sum of individual needs and demands. Participation can come to mean very different things in different places, depending on the power of movements, associations, and unions to shape the experience. These are the very actors that current understandings of participation do not recognize.

9.9.1 The History and Development of Participation: The "Perverse Confluence," Top-Down Influences, and Travel

Although numbers are difficult to come by, most experts agree that the number of experiences of citizen participation has exploded in the last two decades across the Global North and the Global South. As Archon Fung suggests, part of the difficulty in estimating the extent of participation is that "the forms of participatory innovation are often local, sometimes temporary, and highly varied" (Fung 2015: 514). But all indications suggest it is a very major trend. There is general agreement that we are living through what Caroline Lee, Michael McQuarrie, and Edward Walker (2015: 7) have called a "participatory revolution." Today, they note, "across the political spectrum, increasing citizen voice is viewed as a necessary counterweight to elite power and bureaucratic rationality." If contemporary ideas of participation emerged among social movements in the 1960s, these ideas were first appropriated by mainstream policy makers two decades later. Caroline Lee, who has studied what is today known as the "Public Engagement Industry," dates its appearance to the late 1980s but notes a tremendous growth in the 2000s. Demand for services by the International Association for Public Participation, for example, tripled between 2005 and 2008 (Lee 2015). In addition, participatory instruments now quickly travel the world as processes of 'fast policy transfer' (Peck and Theodore 2010).

Dagnino, Olvera, and Panficci (2006), in the context of Latin America, have described a "perverse confluence" between left democratizing projects and multilateral agencies around the desirability of participation. This resulted from the meeting of genuine "democratizing projects that were constituted during the period of resistance to authoritarian regimes" and "neoliberal projects" at the end of the 1980s. "In effect," they write, "they are based on the same references: the construction of citizenship, participation, and the very idea of civil society" (Dagnino et al. 2006: 16). All manner of New Left parties, movements and NGOs turned away from Leninist practices and took a "local" and a "social" turn, with a central focus on ideas of civil society and participation (Castañeda 1993: 200). This new thinking was eclectic, influenced by sources as wide as debates with European New Left, Liberation Theology, and Radical Pedagogy. Throughout Latin America in the 1990s, there were demands and claims from social movements and new progressive actors who sought to reform the state and deepen democracy through participation. This discourse ranged from the Zapatistas, to the Civil Society Assembly in Guatemala, to local administrations run by the Workers' Party in Brazil, to the Movement for Socialism in Bolivia, among many others. At the same time, agencies like the Inter-American Development Bank, USAID, the World Bank, and other bilateral and multilateral donors like DFID (UK), CIDA (Canada), UNDP, and major foundations like Ford, Kettering, Rockefeller, and MacArthur had all adopted the language of civil society and participation. For one indicator among many, at the global level, the World Bank has invested $85 billion in development assistance for participation in the last decade (Mansuri and Rao 2013, cited in Fung 2015: 514).

Citizen participation in the Global North follows a similar timeline and similarly wide cast of characters. There has been a sea-change in thinking about governance and the role of the citizenry since the late 1990s. The original interest in participation, of course, dates to social movements like Students for a Democratic Society, in the United States, and post-68 mobilizations in Europe. But it took disappointment with New Public Management and ideas of the minimal state for these ideas to move to the mainstream. In the early 2000s, in particular, there was growing concern about the quality of democracy and democratic participation in industrialized democracies. At the same time as "anti-globalization" activists expressed their desire for a more genuine global democracy, and innovated through the practices of NGOs and new movements – sometimes directly inspired by Global South movements like the Zapatistas or Brazil's Landless Movement – mainstream scholars and government officials worried as well. While the tenor was slightly different in Europe and in North America, the worry about declining citizen engagement, growing apathy, mistrust in government, and atomization was shared. As a result, there were a number of reforms and policy initiatives in several countries meant to encourage participation and bring citizens back into the work of government. Some have called this broad move a turn to "Public Governance," even if there is no consensus yet for the reforms and policies intended to increase citizen participation. But the trend is very clear. For North America a survey from 2009 found that almost all cities responded that they provided "opportunities for civic engagement in community problem solving and decision-making" and that nearly three-fourths of them had instruments in place for citizen decision-making in strategic planning that year.[6] In Western Europe the figures are similar, and several countries now mandate citizen participation as part of recent local government reforms.[7] Bingham, Nabatchi, and O'Leary (2005) catalogue and describe the tools of this new governance, which include deliberative democracy, e-democracy, public conversations, participatory budgeting, citizen juries, study circles, collaborative policy-making, and alternative dispute resolutions that permit citizens and stakeholders to actively participate in the work of government.

9.9.2 Compatibility with Neoliberalism: Marginal Experiments, Self-Responsible Citizens, Conflict-Free Deliberations, and Absence of Sectoral Representation

While they range in format, new forms of participation share some common features. They are open, and inclusive, and place "ordinary citizens" at the center. That is, they are not mediated by what are nowadays described as representatives of "the old ways," like unions, social movements, or political parties. Participation is not supposed to be conflictive, as it promises a win-win for all: governments get better input, citizens are heard, new solutions are dreamed up, and a more encompassing and inclusive sense of the common good emerges out of deliberation for all involved. By and large, participatory experiments have brought new participants to the demos. Though there is significant variation, there are significant successes in attracting non-traditional and vulnerable participants to forums that in some instances have surpassed the capacity of social movements in creating inclusive spaces. There is evidence of democratic learning, and some evidence of increased civic capacity that has been spurred by these.

Nonetheless, there is reason to worry, and critical scholars have begun to point to the ways that participation is part and parcel of neoliberal reforms (Hickey and Mohan 2004), with some, like Pablo Leal, referring to "the buzzword of the neoliberal era?" (Leal 2007: 539). It is more than the fact that participatory democracy has spread as governments have retrenched, or that local governments have, in some cases, introduced participation to improve the fiscal management of dwindling resources.

The first worry is that these experiments often take place at the margins of the state apparatus, without significant government reform, and without transforming the functioning of state institutions. They invoke the language of empowerment without devolving significant decision-making to participants. Many experiments are introduced "from above" and do not allow for participants to define the terms of participation itself. Many of these experiments – particularly consultative forums – do not wield decision-making power, or if they do, they do not wield decision-making power over significant decisions, such as economic policies. These experiments are fundamentally not able to challenge inequalities that are one of the principal threats to democracy. Second, there is the worry that participation paves the way to a depoliticization of the public sphere. Participation today emphasizes important characteristics of the neoliberal citizen: self-regulation, responsibility for individual problems, and a non-conflictive partnership with the state (Li 2005). In this formulation people are "conceived as individuals who are to be active in their own government, and shifting responsibilities for problems to individuals and communities" (Rose 1996: 330). As the state pulled out of the realm of social policy, these participatory

---

6   National League of Cities, Making local democracy work. Goodwin explores the data further to show "that a large majority (69 percent) had citizens serve on ad hoc task forces and a fairly high percentage of cities held neighborhood meetings (48 percent) and town meetings (39 percent)" (Godwin 2014: 253).

7   Recent research in Southern Europe highlights that most municipalities "have developed considerable participatory activity" (Font, della Porta, and Sintomer 2014: 42).

citizens are charged with shouldering the burden. And third, there is the move away from sectoral representation. It is not uncommon for promoters of participation today to frame their appeals as a way of going beyond unions, social movements, neighborhood associations, or interest groups, and placing emphasis on "regular citizens." There is no role for such organizations. This changes the structures of collective negotiation between the organizations and the public authorities with a direct system of decision-making. But this emphasis on direct voice can conflict with, and disempower, associations and movements formed around conflicts. Thus, the worry by Frances Cleaver and many others, that a central postulate of the thinking on participation today is that while there is a lot of emphasis on "getting the techniques right," "considerations of power and politics on the whole should be avoided as divisive and obstructive" (Cleaver 1999: 598).

9.9.3 Tensions with Neoliberalism, and Recapturing Democracy From Below: Associational Power, Camps, and other Demands

The idea of citizen participation in matters of common concern has very clear origins in social movements and progressive instincts. Yet, participation today is a different phenomenon. If participatory democracy's scope has expanded, its emancipatory dimension has all but disappeared. The question, rather than whether participation is neoliberal, is what its potential to mitigate the neoliberal project might be. More and more, democracy appears to spread while its meaning seems to be ever more modest. There are more ways than ever to participate democratically today, but the range of decisions within the reach of the demos seems narrower than ever. "We are all democrats now," writes Wendy Brown (2010: 45), but, as she also poignantly asks, "what is left of democracy?"

While today's very widespread institutions of citizen participation by themselves would not have much to offer to address the current challenges to democracy as detailed elsewhere in this chapter, they are not seamless parts of the neoliberal project either. There are some important ways that citizen participation can come to be in tension with neoliberal projects. First, is that while it is difficult to track with any precision because participation is so ubiquitous, we can say that some participatory experiments, like Participatory Budgeting, have brought new participants to the demos (Baiocchi and Ganuza 2016). Though there is significant variation, of course, and in some instances there are significant successes in attracting non-traditional and vulnerable participants to forums. The evidence is clear that this is not the case all of the time, but there are important examples of forums with otherwise disenfranchised participants, whether we are speaking of urban denizens in Brazil, lower-caste women in India, or formerly incarcerated or undocumented immigrants in New York.[8] This is not a trivial accomplishment, especially in that these are formally spaces of equals, where all, in principle, are allowed equal voice. And in some of these instances, forums have surpassed the capacity of social movements in creating inclusive spaces. There is also evidence of democratic learning, and some evidence of increased civic capacity

that has been spurred by these spaces (Talpin 2012). And of course, in a world of increasing inequality and segregation, these can be very significant spaces.

Finally, there is recurring finding by the scholarship that what participation comes to mean is ultimately contingent on local configurations of actors. Whether we are speaking of the Andes, of Brazil, of Southern Europe, or India, one recurring and robust finding has been that social movements, political parties, and unions can push citizen participation to be more transformative, more empowering, more responsive to local context, and more tied to fundamental decisions that matter.[9] A comparative study of cities that adopted participatory budgeting reforms in Brazil in the late 1990s, for example, showed that the outcome of the implementation of the same reform in otherwise similar contexts was conditioned by the presence of these collective actors. In particular the quality of democratization heavily depended on the autonomy of social movements to provide a counterweight to participatory forums. From that vantage point movements were able to push the limits of participation and force greater inclusion as well as more meaningful decision-making. Participation, in fact, continues to be a platform of social movements and other collective actors around the world who see in it the potential to deepen democratic institutions and foster social change (see Section 9.13). Yet, these are the very actors that are excluded in current modes of citizen participation.

9.10 The Judiciary as a Challenger

9.10.1 The Changing Role of the Courts

Since the 1960s, the social and political role of judges and courts has dramatically changed, prompting a shift in the balance of powers within democracies. Although the intensity and the timing of this transformation has differed from one country to another, the judicial branch has been endowed with new functionalities, including social progress, the fight against corruption, identity recognition, the "free market," and antitrust regulation. In a large variety of countries, from India to South Africa, Brazil to Italy or Germany, courts have become a central and relatively autonomous arena for the mediation of political, economic, and social interests. The ubiquitous rise of the judiciary in democracies has triggered optimistic scholarly and political discourses on the emancipatory and democratic potential of this new path. Many have viewed judicial empowerment as fulfilling the promises of liberal democracies on equality and rights, taking "law" out of the hands of bureaucrats and politicians and bringing it back to the 'people' and civil society. With the active support of international and regional organizations involved in promoting "democracy and the rule of law," a standard of the "independent judiciary" has consolidated based on equal access to courts, fair trial, and professional judges. It has become increasingly valued to settle the hard cases of democracies and to act as a substitute to the failures of representative politics and to the pitfalls of international *realpolitik*. Yet, the progressive potential of this rights- and courts-centered approach is ambivalent. While the rise of the judiciary has opened up new avenues for social

---

[8] There is a vast literature based on case studies. Some exemplars include Su (2017), Rao and Sanyal (2010), and Baiocchi (2005).

[9] This is a finding in Font et al. (2014), Baiocchi et al. (2011), Baiocchi and Ganuza (2016), Van Cott (2009), and in many other works.

progress, it has, in a "boomerang effect," contributed to the further weakening of the traditional channels of representative democracy. In addition, the instrumental role given to courts in the rise of neo-liberal modes of governance now threatens their capacity to live up to the new democratic and social promises that they have generated over the past decades.

9.10.2 An Alternative Use of Rights

For a long time, the "rule of law" and the judiciary were viewed by progressives as belonging to a broader block of socially and politically conservative elites that protected economic freedoms including property and freedom of contract, thereby impeding the unfolding of more progressive social and economic deals. In various Western countries, however, the 1970–1980s brought an important change as new claims for equality, often framed as minority rights, have been pursued through litigation strategies before courts. In the wake of politicization of the public debate in the late 1960s, new conceptions of law and of courts emerged within the legal professions in Western Europe, North America and in part in Latin America. New social movements have contested the monopoly of trade unions and left-wing parties over the realm of progressive politics, in part through the progressive discovery of the emancipatory potential of rights' claims. The world of human rights' activism that has emerged around transnational NGOs such as Amnesty international, Human Rights Watch, Oxfam or FIDH, philanthropic foundations, and professional lawyers has come to consider "courts and rights" as a key avenue to fulfill the political and social promises encapsulated in liberal democratic founding declarations. Following the successes of civil rights' movements in 1960s America, advocacy groups have embraced forms of "cause lawyering" in domains such as gender equality, the inclusion of indigenous people, or the non-discrimination of sexual minorities. To some extent, the judicial avenue has therefore become a surrogate for democratic participation for minority groups structurally marginalized in the political field.

In turn, rights and courts have been profoundly transformed. Historically framed in the liberal tradition as *political* and symbolic in nature, texts such as the European Convention of Human Rights, national constitutions or bills of rights, and principles such as rule of law and equality have turned into justiciable legal entitlements. A new blend of "constitutionalism" has been empowering constitutional courts with the task to protect "fundamental" individual rights. In the process, new rights have emerged, including privacy and data protection, non-discrimination, and human dignity, which are now justiciable before national and international courts. In addition, the weakening legitimacy of legislatures has prompted new delegations of powers to constitutional courts extending the scope of their judicial review into new domains, including political campaigning, same-sex marriage, and affirmative action policies. In parallel, the various "Clean Hands" operations against political corruption in Italy, Spain, or Brazil solidified a coalition of civil society movements, new sections of the media as well as moral entrepreneurs around the defense of judges and prosecutors as the best controllers of "political virtues" (Pizzorno 1998). In turn, these changes have triggered a transformation of the judicial branch itself. Under the lead of regional or international

organizations that have promoted higher "standards" of independence and forms of judicial cooperation across national borders, courts have made a drift away from the state-centric conceptions of their role. In parallel, thanks to the development of legal aid and the diffusion of class actions, they have become more accessible and responsive institutions, thereby opening more ways to use judicial arenas as a venue to settle political and social conflicts.

9.10.3 Judicialization and Its (Dis)Contents

Yet, this dramatic change in the role of courts has prompted a wider shift in the allocation of political authority within representative democracies. Against all naïve narratives of the judicialization as a process of democratic empowerment, the politics of counter-majoritarianism is itself deeply embedded in and driven by political and social elites. At times, they may even be an essential lever through which threatened political and social elites attempt to preserve their hegemony and lock in their policy preferences and worldviews, as Ran Hirschl (2004) has argued in the case of the rise of constitutional courts in countries such as South Africa or Israel. Emblematically, the recent anti-corruption inquiries in Brazil and the related impeachment procedure against the democratically elected president, Dilma Rousseff, have been led by conservative political elites. The role of legal elites is equally ambivalent. While the rise of courts has also increased the statute of the judicial and legal professions, the latter are not necessarily more diverse, socially and ideologically, than the elected representatives (Bellamy 2007); in the end, they may act more as "gate-keepers" than as "transmission belts," narrowing down social claims into a preexisting set of legal alternatives (and, thereby, sidelining potentially innovative arguments and causes).

Because of the very individualizing of features of rights' claiming, judicial petitioning has also brought its own contribution to processes of "depoliticization." The development of a "rights' talk" that has hampered public debate has often led to an "impoverishment of political discourse" mostly centered on individualism and liberty at the expense of more collective causes and solidarity campaigns. While it has helped concretize the claims for "equality before the law," the rise of courts has further undermined the political relevance of the traditional arenas of representative democracy. The gradual prevalence of a liberal-constitutionalist conception of the judiciary has in turn fueled the development of new forms of populism that have pointed at the judges' lack of social and political legitimacy. Revamping old criticisms of the "*gouvernement des juges*" and old concerns over the "counter-majoritarian difficulty," new waves of contestation of judicial review and constitutionalism have emerged as shown by campaigns in the UK led by UKIP and some sections of the Conservative Party against the European Court of Human Rights (ECHR) or by the recent "political backlash" led by a variety of a variety of African states against the jurisdiction of International Criminal Court. Last but not least, the capacity of this "new constitutionalism" to secure citizen's political and civil rights is nowadays profoundly challenged by the massive increase of States' repressive capacities to face post-September 11 terrorist threats – from the 2001 Patriot Act to the ongoing "state of emergency" in France and Turkey (see Section 9.11).

9.10.4   Courts in Neoliberal Politics

The promises raised by the rise of rights, however, face an ever bigger challenge given the instrumental role that courts have gained with the rise of neo-liberal economics. With the general retreat of state interventionism in the economic realm, courts have become the new pivot institution of the development of "competitive market," together with regulatory agencies, themselves shaped most often on a quasi-judicial model. Under the umbrella of the "regulatory state" championed by neo- and ordo-liberal doctrines of market regulation, courts have increasingly become instrumental. The liberalization of trade and the promotion of free markets have been fostered by the creation of specialized economic courts such as the Court of Justice of European Union or the World Trade Organization appellate body, thereby marginalizing alternative understandings of other diffuse interests such as social protection or human rights. Segments of the public administration, business elites and interest groups have used them to insulate economic freedoms from the dynamics of democratic politics, securing a constitutional statute for economic freedoms through judicial or quasi-judicial bodies such as regulatory or competition agencies. Courts have become powerful levers to reduce governments' restriction to competition and undermine cartelized industries and state monopolies. The European Court of Justice (ECJ), arguably the most effective international/regional court in the world, provides a clear example. While economic freedoms have gained a very powerful stance in Luxembourg, their dominance has prompted a selective protection of human rights, favoring the rights that were instrumental to the building of a Single Market such as non-discrimination, and sex equality while disregarding or dismantling others such as labor rights, which remain weakly protected at the EU level.

This connection between neoliberalism and courts has brought large companies and transnational interest groups in closer contact with courts. With the rise of multinational companies and the increasing international flows of trade, finance, and production, a growing market for legal services has emerged that transcended the traditional national boundaries of legal systems. Starting in the United States and the United Kingdom in the 1970s, a new organizational model began to spread internationally, that of global law firms with branches in Europe and, later, in the new BRICS markets, especially in Asia. These mega-law firms, such as Baker & McKenzie (with 77 branches in 47 countries) or Clifford Chance, now provide full and standardized services to their corporate clients ranging from transnational legal counseling to worldwide legislative and administrative lobbying. Positioned across the globe, they have the resources to pursue long-run interests in changing the state of the law through litigation and they are able to play across national and sector-specific legal domains, seizing fault lines, opportunities, and loopholes. The recent cases of the Panama papers or LuxLeaks have further exemplified the brokering role corporate lawyers may play in globalized markets. Together with their clients, they engage in judicial forum-shopping, circumventing state regulations in domains like taxes or social rights. This autonomization of the international field of *lex mercatoria* has led to an unprecedented development of commercial arbitration and similar forms of *private* justice shielded from public scrutiny and forms of accountability. Most trade liberalization treaties now include arbitral mechanisms – so-called Investment State Dispute Settlements (ISDS) – which circumvent states' judicial apparatus. On the whole, the increasing capture of this new judicial terrain of market regulation by big law firms and large interest groups has contributed to strengthening the political capacity of their clients and further undermined states' capacity to promote an agenda of "social progress."

Courts and rights have progressively been integrated into a larger neo-liberal compact, thereby tuning down the initial promises of equal civil and social rights. Ever since the mid-1990s, international organizations such as the International Monetary Fund (IMF) or the World Bank (WB), as well as law and economics scholars, have come to view the independence of the judiciary and the protection of economic rights such as property rights and freedom of contract, as a key lever in the transformation of emerging countries into competitive markets. Similarly, in Western democracies, courts have played an instrumental role in the rise of the neoliberal mode of governance that combines regulatory agencies, private actors' enforcement of legal norms, and a certain style of dispute resolution (so-called "adversarial legalism"). This judicialized mode of governance has proved to be a powerful challenger of the more cooperative and neo-corporatist style of government typical of Welfare State politics (Kelemen 2011). With its limited administrative capacity, weak redistributive policies, and salient non-majoritarian institutions including courts, regulatory agencies such as the Directorate General for Competition, and central banks, the European Union is the most emblematic case. Beyond the fact that this new governance scheme arguably obscures decision-making, it also contributes to circumventing the scope and the efficiency of representative politics, turning various intermediaries, be they consultants, lobbyists, advocacy coalitions, or lawyers, into de facto political actors.

In the end, the rise of rights and courts is highly ambivalent. Their progressive role in fulfilling the liberal and social promises written down in the grand declarations and bill of rights of liberal democracies is nowadays undermined by the instrumental role that courts and lawyers play in the rise of neoliberal policies and the demise of the Welfare State. In ways akin to what Luc Boltanski and Eve Chiapello have described as *The New Spirit of Capitalism* (2006), the progressive potential of rights' claim for recognition and autonomy has been in part incorporated and diverted into the neoliberal compact in ways compatible with its development. And yet, this tipping back of the judiciary is far from complete and still encounters a variety of professional and political counter-movements.

9.11   The Construction and Governance of Democratic Political Spaces in Times of Perceived Crises

A central paradox of democracy is between conflict and consensus. "Democracy implies *dissent and division*, but on a basis of consent and cohesion. It requires that the citizens assert themselves, but also that they accept the government's authority. It demands that the citizens care about politics – even if not too much" (Diamond 1990: 56). Consequently, a healthy democratic state invites its inhabitants into its decision-making and implementation processes, even dissident inhabitants. So in order to retain their legitimacy liberal democracies are constitutionally committed to allow dissent. The public spaces for assembly and freedom of speech are essential elements in democracies and these spaces of contention, according to liberal constitutions, must be protected. The conundrum lies in that while domestic dissent must be allowed, governments are determined to steer this dissent in ways that do not fundamentally threaten the political and economic order. The spaces for the maneuver of political challengers must be protected without jeopardizing the rule of law. Demonstration rights must be made secure but political violence on the part of challengers, such as terrorist attacks on refugee centers or mosques, must be rigorously policed. In other words, institutional actors meet the perceived threats of oppositional forces with actions designed to "steer the conduct of civil society" (Loader 2000: 344). Repression or policing contention is a dispersed mechanism *for* the governance of the dominant political and economic order. Dissent *is* governed, by sheer coercive force or by less strong-arm and subtle means, in order to maintain the status quo (Peterson and Wahlström 2015).

Policing contention is typically thought of as exercised at the national scale, and in many cases this is correct in so far as it concerns the steering, that is, law-making and coordination of repressive capacities. However, since September 11, 2001 the US-defined "war on terror" has dramatically extended the geopolitical scope of the governance of dissent to the global scale and with this extension clouded the traditional distinction between domestic threat and foreign threats. Post-September 11 has witnessed an unparalleled international cooperation and intelligence sharing between police authorities and security services and private corporate intelligence agencies in this new situation for the governance of dissent.

In response to terrorist actions or the threat of terrorist actions, numerous democracies across the globe enacted anti-terrorist legislation, such as the Patriot Act in the United States and the Prevention of Terrorism Act in India, which have radically expanded the repressive powers of the federal government thereby infringing on the civil rights of assembly and protest (Cole 2003). Abdolian and Takooshian (2002: 1446) point out that "historically, during times of crisis, it has been natural for democratic nations, including the United States, to temporarily abridge individual liberties in ways that would never be considered in more halcyon times." The rule of law, in Agamben's (2005) understanding, becomes lawless. For example, the US Patriot Act of October 2001 dramatically expanded the definition of terrorism to include what the Act defined as domestic terrorism, thus enlarging the number of activities to which the Patriot Act's extended law enforcement powers could be applied. For example, animal rights and ecological organizations could fall within its reach making it potentially a "felony to, among other things, 'deter' the business activities of industries engaged in the exploitation of animals and natural resources" (Eddy 2005: 262). These changes in the statutes have, according to Eddy, boosted the governance capacities in some states to protect economic interests and threaten to significantly raise the costs of involvement in non-violent environmental protest.

Furthermore, policing theorists have warned that democratic societies have progressively shifted towards becoming "surveillance societies" where "surveillance displaces crime control for the efficient production

of knowledge useful in the administration of suspect populations" (Ericson 1994: 139), thereby more and more and effectually extending in liberal democracies the legal scope of repression away from respect for the constitutionally protected rights of individuals to encompass collectives of individuals. For example, since September 11 and further accelerated in face of the threat posed by ISIL (Islamic State of Iraq and the Levant), security services are increasingly targeting Muslim communities as suspect populations. By casting a wide net in their counter-terrorism measures, security services have introduced a "religious profiling," such as Trump's anti-Muslim executive order, which in effect risks criminalizing Muslims per se (Peterson 2012). Counter-terrorism policing in many Western European countries now gives priority to what are called preventive strategies, which in effect extends the scope of repression from political dissidents to targeted communities and away from the constitutionally protected rights of individuals, which is a cornerstone in the rule of law in liberal democracies.

Political actors – both social movements and political parties – are found across the political spectrum; not all political actors are benign nor democratically progressive. We have in addition *the basic democratic paradox of majoritarian rule* in liberal democracies in which majorities can suppress minorities and, with the support of an electoral majority, the processes of democracy can be turned back or even overturned; for example, the current cases of Hungary, Poland, and Turkey.

In the wake of the fiscal crisis in 2008 and the waves of refugees seeking entry into Europe, far-right extremist movements and far-right parties are mobilizing the "losers" in ever increasing numbers across Europe, as well as the United States. Democracies, through an ordinary "free and fair" election, can take a turn away from the rule of law. In Hungary in 2010, Viktor Orbán's Fidesz Party won 53 percent of the vote and a seat bonus big enough to give it powers of constitutional amendment, moving toward what Orbán himself has called an "electoral revolution." The speed and the scale of the changes have indeed been revolutionary. The new 2011 Constitution and its enabling acts have turned what are supposed to be politically neutral bodies such as the Constitutional Court, the Central Bank, and the offices of the Ombudsman and the Public Prosecutor into arms of the ruling party. In short, according to Rupnik (2012: 133), "Orbán and his lieutenants have downgraded or done away with the checks and balances that are widely considered essential for the rule of law." If you add to this an act that creates a state agency meant to ensure "media objectivity," thereby undermining the public space for critical opposition, you have the main components of an authoritarian drift in the construction of political spaces and the governance of dissent.

The ruling Law and Justice Party (PIS) in Poland passed laws in 2015 that make it more difficult for the Constitutional Court, to overturn any of the government's decisions. The Court itself refused to follow the new laws, which it declared were unconstitutional – a textbook definition of a constitutional crisis (see Section 9.10) – and a full-blown domestic democratic crisis has erupted. KOD, a new pro-democracy movement established in 2015, put an estimated 250,000 people on the streets for a protest in May 2016. The Council of Europe's Venice Commission, which focuses on constitutional rights and the rule of law, issued a report condemning the moves. On the border of the EU in Turkey we find a similar authoritarian drift in the governance of dissent. President Erdogan has gradually been reversing two decades of democratic progress in Turkey and had in 2016 pushed through a tough anti-terrorism law – condemned by the EU – that was used to target even democratically minded opponents, when placing under arrest the pro-Kurdish HDP party leaders together with 10 MPs. In short, after the failed coup in July 2016 the ruling AKP party has launched draconian measures to silence dissent. Tens of thousands have been purged in the effort to rid the civil services and education system of alleged Gülenists reaching far beyond the proponents of the putsch to target other dissidents.

In the 2014 European elections in the UK the Eurosceptic far-right party UKIP achieved first place with 27.5 percent of the total vote marking the first time that a third party garnered the largest share of the votes. That election paved the way for the 2016 advisory referendum when, led by UKIP and some Conservative Party members, 52 percent of the votes were cast in favor of leaving the EU. Negotiations for a Brexit are underway.

While the developments in Hungary, Poland, Turkey, and the UK are perhaps the most dramatic, these movements and parties have found varying traction within civil societies and among electorates across Europe. The response by many citizens across Europe to the so-called refugee crisis has been to cast their votes for authoritarian, nationalist, xenophobic, and anti-EU parties. These far-right parties are flourishing, now further fueled by Trump's presidential election victory in the United States. During his campaign Trump had openly and repeatedly attacked basic democratic and constitutional norms; not least his support for physical violence as a response to political disagreement and his virile attacks against critical journalists. These political developments are unsubtle reminders that majoritarian rule must be tempered by robust constitutionalism that protects the civil rights of minorities and defends free speech.

Events, whether these are terrorist attacks or the perceived threat of terrorism, fiscal crises, or a refugee crisis, demonstrate the fragility of democratic processes in so-called new democracies as well as in consolidated democracies. Democratic processes can be rolled back. The still ongoing fiscal crisis is challenging democracy from both a technocratic and a populist direction. In Greece and Italy, democratically elected but insolvent governments have succumbed under pressure from the Eurozone and the European Central Bank and ceded (temporarily) vast policy-making powers to unelected experts. According to Donatella della Porta (2015a) a shared element of the recent anti-austerity protests she studied in Latin America, Eastern Europe, and South Africa was the discontent at what was perceived as a violation of acquired entitlements by a small and corrupt oligarchy of businessmen and politicians.

The authoritarian tendencies we are witnessing across the globe appear to marry well with the "liberal state." In the wake of the global fiscal crisis della Porta (2015b) identifies a concomitant "crisis of responsibility." Committed to protecting neo-liberal markets, for example with bail-outs of banks, which more or less undermines government finances, liberal governments are unable to protect their citizenry from the deleterious effects of global neoliberalism. Facing the real challenges from an aggrieved and concerned citizenry, dissent is increasingly governed in more repressive ways.

In conclusion, democracy is under siege and from a number of fronts, not least from the state itself. The responses of governments across the globe to real and perceived crises, even of governments that with some justification claim to be "liberal" and "democratic," provide substance to Giorgio Agamben's (2005) portentous warning that we have entered a "permanent state of exception"; "the state of exception has become a paradigm of government today" (Agamben and Raulff 2004: 609) and security has become *the* political vernacular. The existence of derogation-like clauses permits states to suspend the protection of certain basic human and civil rights thereby undermining meaningful political action. For example, after the failed coup in Turkey mid-July 2016 a state of emergency was decreed and has since been prolonged for an indefinite period. The decree has allowed the Erdogan government to shut down the Internet in 11 Kurdish cities and restrict access to social media services throughout the country; the top executive of Turkey's most influential opposition newspaper together with 9 other staff members have been likewise incarcerated.

Declaring war on terror the Bush administration invoked a *global state of emergency* to wage infinite war on an indefinite enemy. The war on terrorism is highly ambiguous, more or less infinite; the Pentagon originally named the "war against terrorism" "Operation Infinite Justice" (cited in Kellner 2007: 626). The present "permanent state of exception" should, Agamben indicates, be understood as "a fiction sustained through military metaphor to justify recourse to extensive government powers" (Agamben and Raulff 2004: 610), which can be introduced to cope with political dissent more generally – we see increasingly the conjunction of sovereign power and the police in the governance of dissent in contemporary democracies. As Ian Loader and Neil Walker (2007: 7) point out, the state itself must be civilized – "made safe by and for democracy." States can only do so by engaging with all inhabitants, even the poor and dispossessed, in constitutionally protected spaces for democratic dialogue and dissent regarding the exercise of its power. A vigilant and engaged citizenry offers the sole protection against the potential excesses of democratic states. It is upon their shoulders that the responsibility for "taming states" lays. Rule *by* the people must also be rule *for* (all) the people.

9.12 Internet and the Paradoxes of Democracy and the Rule of Law

The Internet has become a central feature of contemporary societies. According to the International Telecommunication Union (ITU), at the end of 2016 nearly half of the world's population had an internet connection while in 1995 it had been less than 1 percent. The bulk of internet users can be found in developing countries, with 2.5 billion users compared with one billion in developed countries in 2016. The rise of the Internet has led several commentators to describe the last two decades as the "cybersociety" (Jones 1998), "Internet society" (Bakardjieva 2005) or the "Internet age" (Castells 2015). These views give special attention to digital media as a major driving force shaping the structures of modern "networked" societies.

The Internet has facilitated new forms of structuring the ways humans relate to one another, and influence one another. The profound impact that the Internet has had and continues to have in modern societies has triggered a growing literature on the effects it has on democratic processes. This section discusses how communication technologies are shaping social movements, activism, and other forms of political participation.

In the context of deliberative democracy, true democracy requires citizen participation and engagement through active discussion with other citizens (Habermas 1996). The Internet brought the hope of an expanded and new public sphere, capable of embracing a broader set of ideas and a broader set of citizens.

The high rate of internet penetration, low cost of online communications, and global reach, have brought attention to the possibilities of the Internet as a source of citizen empowerment (Benkler 2006). In this respect, the Internet holds the potential to generate "communicative power" (Dutton and Peltu 2007), bringing participatory opportunities to traditionally "voiceless" agents to express their demands – a platform where individuals and communities are able to express their needs and desires. In addition, the combination of an increased access of citizens to government information and the possibilities of electronic voting, enables new types of internet-based engagement with democratic processes. Moreover, the dissemination power of the Internet brings a new dimension to citizen journalism and grassroots documentary-making, significantly altering relations of power in the media (Goode 2009). The importance and appeal of the empowering potential of the Internet in democratic processes is multifaceted and undeniable.

However, less is known about the negative impact that ICTs can have in democratic processes. Some arguments include the potential of further social polarization, with the Internet becoming a public sphere for the educated and affluent (Dahlberg 2001; Streck 1998); the dangers of information overload and misinformation (see the viral widespread of fake news reported during the 2016 US presidential elections and elsewhere);[10] and the way in which such rapid widespread of radical collective action can lead to violent conflict escalations.

The possibility to build stronger democracies in times of digital media and the Internet is still not well understood. It has already been argued that technology and democracy have had a "deeply ambivalent relationship" (Barber 1998).

Thanks to emerging online platforms, citizens find new ways to engage in the democratic discourse. The African continent, where the extensive use of cell phones has been coupled with a more recent and massive interest in social media, provides an example of the development of comprehensive an internet-based tool that allowed people to gather crisis-related data in Kenya (see the case of Ushahidi).[11] These online platforms, designed to be used by ordinary people, allowed users to report a violent incident through text message, email or web submission, and to portray the information on an online map.[12] These modes of citizen monitoring have reportedly performed better than mainstream media by gathering more cases of violence and covering wider geographic areas. The ability of citizens to write their own news and monitor events has deep implications on political voice (Hindman 2008). Such valuable examples also raise questions about the dangers of lowering the gates of free-flowing information and the risks of misinformation; with the absence of gatekeepers it becomes more difficult to establish the accuracy of shared information.

Along with ordinary citizens, political leaders are also increasingly reliant on ICTs, and the 2004, 2008, and more recently the 2016 US presidential elections are testimony to that. Newspaper and television-based electoral campaigns have been largely replaced by those conducted through social media. Twitter becomes a key tool used by political parties and candidates to inform the public about their stances and express their grievances. A recent study has shown that 62 percent of US citizens get their news via social media (Gottfried and Shearer 2016).

Activists and dissenters are also adapting the ways in which they communicate, collaborate, and protest to the possibilities brought by new online platforms (Kelly Garrett 2006). The speed at which ICTs are able to spread information about a particular event or concern, accelerates the reach of support communities across geographical areas, leading to rapid intensification of social movements. Activist mobilizations in Tunisia, Egypt, Spain, and elsewhere have been partly credited to the creative use of social media platforms such as Facebook and Twitter.

Making political statements through non-violent direct actions such as activism and civil disobedience constitute important acts of democratic participation.[13] These forms of democratic participation have taken new forms with the evolution of ICTs, especially through social media. As stated by Youmans and York: "Information technologies have become indispensable to reformers, revolutionaries, and contemporary democracy movements. They serve as venues for the shared expression of dissent, dissemination of information, and collective action" (Youmans and York 2012: 315). In this respect, there is a considerable amount of research that has pointed out the ability of ICTs and in particular the Internet to nurture the development of collective identities across dispersed populations, to the extent that can lead to collective action. Many studies have found evidence of protest groups that have formed and acted collectively on the basis of concerns shared through social media and internet-enabled blogs and websites (Castells 2015). The growing belief that "The Revolution Will Be Twittered" comes together with predictions of a "revolution 2.0" and a "Facebook revolution." Nevertheless, in response to such perceived power, others have questioned the ability of social media to bring about radical change. Such cautions are based on the observation that social media activism involves low risk and weak ties (Gladwell 2010) leading to "slacktivism" (Morozov 2010) and an

---

10 www.nytimes.com/2016/11/18/technology/fake-news-on-facebook-in-foreign-elections-thats-not-new.html?_r=0.

11 www.un.org/en/africarenewal/vol24no1/ushahidi.html.

12 Ushahidi's software has been adapted to other geographical areas, to help rescue earthquake victims in Haiti, and monitor violence in the DRC, South Africa, and Gaza.

13 Although civil disobedience remains controversial given that it violates and ignores existing laws.

illusion of meaningful participation with political matters with minimum effort such as joining a Facebook group or adding your name to an online campaign.

These are not, however, static relationships and interactions, and internet-enabled technologies, especially social media are surrounded by a changing ecosystem of actors and institutions. They are constantly evolving, and so their governance and use also evolve.

The Internet has facilitated the adoption of more decentralized, non-hierarchical organizational forms of democracy. However, at the same time there is reference to a "crisis in democracy" visible in the general disengagement of young people from traditional forms of political participation. Youth and their relationship with digital media deserve particular attention, as they have been key drivers of important contemporary online-enabled movements such as the Arab Spring, Anonymous, and Wikileaks.

Hacktivism has become one of the ways for civil society to communicate ideas and promote the principles of democracy and enhance individual freedoms using technology. The role of hacktivism has gained visibility in recent years and speaks directly to the issue of power, technology, and society. Hacktivism, or the actions of politically motivated hackers, emerge from the marriage of political activism and computer hacking. They differ from other types of hackers in their motivation, as they are driven by the pursuit of social change, rather than profit. Wikileaks and Anonymous have become some of the best known hacktivist networks.

Wikileaks started operating in 2006, offering a platform for whistle blowers to expose secret material anonymously. Its purpose is to achieve higher levels of government transparency by exposing sensitive files to the public, thereby subjecting them to societal scrutiny. Their existence and high levels of activity has ignited worldwide debate on the extent to which sensitive information should be publicly available.

Anonymous has been described as a collective of "hackers, technologists, activists, human rights advocates and geeks" who organize collective actions online and offline that "advance political causes" but are also organized "for sheer amusement" (Coleman 2012: 83). Anonymous advocates a culture of grassroots democracy based on "decentralized non-hierarchical modes of interaction" and a "commitment to consensus" (Coleman 2011 quoted in Fuchs 2014: 92).[14]

Electronic disobedience and hacktivism are new controversial forms of civic participation, and are likely to have a continued and growing impact on the Internet and the world. They represent a way for civil society to participate in global politics through the new public sphere, communicate their ideas, and promote the principles of democracy using the technology. Through their actions, hacktivists have raised important questions related to the issue of freedom of expression and the freedom of information. By running whistle-blower campaigns against government practices, hacktivism is challenging the existing

structures of power as well as the traditional channels of challenging power (such as independent press and traditional NGOs and CBOs).

Driven by a clear ethic and norms, some hacktivists disrupt the status quo of politics, holding politicians accountable by bringing their actions to the media spotlight. However, there is still a need to differentiate between different types of hacktivists – as they vary in their motives, ethical adherence, and willingness to engage in illegal or legally ambiguous activities – while some forms of hacktivism are clearly illegal other types remain in the grey area of transgression. In this respect, the delimitation over boundaries of what are socially acceptable protest activities, remains under scrutiny. What is becoming clear, is that the criminalization of political dissent can have long-term consequences in the understanding of political participation and the emergence of new configurations of social movements (Bosch 2017).

In summary, it is important to understand the intricacies of the complex, dynamic, and multifaceted relationship between online platforms and new forms of democratic participation in order to ensure that they assist the democratic process by encouraging open debates while engaging the public and delivering reliable information.

9.13 Progressive Social Movement and the Crisis of Responsibility in Late Neoliberalism

Social movements affected, affect, and can be expected to affect the development of states in democratic as well as non-democratic regimes (della Porta 2014). While not all movements have been oriented to expand citizens' rights, progressive social movements have struggled for civil, political, and social rights, also addressing the meta-issue of what politics and democracy are about. Social movements on the Left have in general challenged a definition of progress as optimization of economic conditions or economic growth, reflecting instead on issues of justice and democracy.

9.13.1 Social Movements and Citizens' Rights

Historical work on the evolution of citizens' rights has stressed the role of mobilization from below in achieving them. Civil, political, and social rights developed with the mobilization of the labor movement, bringing about institutional change. At the origins of democracy lies "the entrance of the masses into history" (Bendix 1964: 72). In the protest campaigns for the widening of citizenship rights, other models of democracy were also conceptualized and practiced, including direct, horizontal, and self-managed democracy. Social rights began then to be discussed as indispensable conditions for a true enjoyment of political rights (Marshall 1992: 28). As with the labor movement in the past, more recent movements became arenas for debating and experimenting with different conceptions of democracy. The protest movements of the late 1960s were interpreted as an indication of the widening gap between parties and citizens, and of the parties' inability

---

[14] It became better known in 2010 through their support of Wikileaks, by launching a series of Distributed denial of service (DDoS) attacks to shut down the websites of several companies that disabled donations to WikiLeaks.

to represent new lines of conflict (Offe 1985). The anti-authoritarian frame, central for these movements, was articulated in claims for "democracy from below." Democracies of councils and self-management were also discussed in the workers' movements of those years. In part, these conceptions penetrated the democratic state through reforms that widened participation, in schools, in factories, and in local areas but also through the political recognition of movement organizations and the "right to dissent."

9.13.2   Social Movements in the Neoliberal Juncture

As liberal democracy remained dominant, an understanding of contemporary challenges requires an assessment of the mechanisms whose functioning was needed in order for liberal democracy to be legitimate. Three such mechanisms were necessary. First, liberal democracies needed functioning political parties as actors that could implement the principles of electoral accountability. Second, majoritarian conceptions of democratic decision-making needed a nation-state as defining the border of the demos in whose name and interest decisions were made (see Section 9.4). Third, and more subtly, even though liberal democracy did not call for social equality, it still relied upon the assumption that political equality would reduce a social inequality that threatened the very principle of free access to political rights (see Section 9.2). The liberal form of democracy developed, that is, in contexts characterized by three elements: well-established welfare states, party democracies, and the full sovereignty of the nation-state. At the turn of the millennium, these conditions have been challenged as neoliberal globalization as well as other evolutions in contemporary democracies have produced a shift of power from parties (and representative institutions) to the executive; from the nation-state to international governmental organizations (IGOs); and from the state to the market, which also implies a shift from welfare state to warfare state. Even though these are neither complete nor natural or irreversible trends, they do challenge the legitimacy of the (neo)liberal vision of democracy, which is based upon an elitist conception of electoral participation for the mass of the citizens and free lobbying for stronger interests, along with low levels of state intervention (Crouch 2003: 5). While the weakening of political parties, nation-states, and welfare states challenges some definition of democracy, they might have produced some opportunities for other conceptions of democracies, less reliant upon electoral accountability (Rosanvallon 2006: 8).

Social movements have long been considered as children of affluent times, or at least of times of opening opportunities. The protests against first the austerity policies in the Global South and then the Great Recession in the European periphery defy these expectations, developing in moments of declining opportunities at both economic and political levels (della Porta 2015b, 2017b; Silva 2009). What is more, in many parts of the world, these movements have been able to radically change the party system, promoting the emergence of new actors, sometimes able to experiment with new policies (della Porta et al. 2017; Roberts 2015). If there is potential for change in a progressive direction, the challenges for a progressive politics from below remain high; in the mobilization capacity of a fragmented social basis, the development of a collective identity and solidarity, and the construction of a sustained organizational structure.

9.13.3   Class Structures and the Social Base for Protest: The Challenge of Fragmentation

Social movement studies have seen recent changes in the social structure as not particularly conducive to mobilization. Not only have processes such as deindustrialization and migration weakened the structural preconditions that had facilitated the emergence of a class cleavage, particularly in the working-class model of collective action, but recent developments have also jeopardized citizens' rights through poverty, unemployment, and job insecurity. Anti-austerity protests have challenged the new social movement paradigm. Sometimes called 'multitude' or 'precariat', those who protested against austerity represented coalitions of various classes and social groups that perceived themselves as losers of neoliberal development and its crisis.

Precariousness is certainly a social and cultural condition for many movement activists (Standing 2011). Overwhelmingly present in protests is a generation (that in Portugal defines itself as "without a future") characterized by high level of unemployment or employment in ill-paid and un-protected jobs. Young people took the lead in the Arab Spring, and those affected by the financial crises mobilized in different forms in Southern Europe. These young people are not those that have traditionally been described as losers. They are rather the well-educated and the mobile, which were once described as the "winners" of globalization but no longer perceived themselves as such.

Together with them, however, are other social groups that have lost most from the neoliberal attacks to social and civil rights, from public employees to retired individuals. Once considered as the most protected social groups, they have seen their rights continuously reduced, becoming precarious themselves in terms of their life conditions, losing fundamental rights such as those to health care, housing, and education (della Porta 2015b). Similarly, blue-collar workers of the small but also large factories, shut down or at least in danger of being shut down, have participated in the wave of protest. With high levels of participation by young people and well-educated citizens, the anti-austerity protests brought into the street a sort of (inverted) "2/3" society of those most hit by austerity policies. Traditional workers participated, but so did retired people, unemployed, and precarious workers (although these were more present in other types of protests). Therefore, the protests brought together coalitions of citizens with different sociobiographic backgrounds, but united by their feeling of having been unjustly treated.

The capacity of protest waves to mobilize this broad but heterogeneous basis has been varied, however, with very different opportunities for coalition building as well as international networking (della Porta 2017a).

9.13.4   The Construction of Collective Identities: The Challenge of Individualism

Recent progressive movements have to face a particular challenge in building collective identity. If neoliberalism strengthened a liquid culture, destroying old bases for personal, collective, and political identity through forced mobility and related insecurity (Baumann 2000), identification processes among anti-austerity protestors seemed to challenge the individualization of liquid society as well as its fear and exclusivism, calling instead for state intervention and inclusive citizenship, with the re-emergence of a social criticism of capitalism. Defining themselves broadly – as citizens, persons, or the 99 percent – activists of the anti-austerity activists developed a moral discourse that called for the reinstatement of welfare protections, but they also challenged the injustice of the system (della Porta 2015b). A call for solidarity and a return to the commons has been juxtaposed to an unjust and inefficient neoliberal ideology. Referring often to the nation, as the basis of reference of a community of solidarity, they, however, developed a cosmopolitan vision combining inclusive nationalism with recognition of the need to look for global solutions to global problems. Differing from the global justice movement, which had presented itself as an alliance of minorities in search of a broad constituency, the anti-austerity movements have constructed a broad definition of the self (della Porta 2015b). Backward looking, the anti-austerity protests called for the restoration of lost rights, vehemently denouncing the corruption of democracy. However, they also looked forward, combining concerns for social rights with those for cultural inclusivity. As precariousness and lost security about life development itself spread from young unemployed and under-employed to large social groups once protected, identification with the overwhelming majority in the society might provide some certainty.

What remains open is, however, the capacity of these movements to build new collective identities. The recognition of the great diversity within the movement does not seem sufficient to build long-term solidarities. The populist reasoning, as reconstruction of an idea of the people (Laclau 2005), is still at early stage.

9.13.5 Movements and Political Legitimacy: The Challenge of Power

Social movements active against austerity policies are embedded in a crisis of legitimacy that takes the particular form of a crisis of lack of responsibility towards citizens' demands (della Porta 2015b, 2017b). However, rather than developing anti-democratic attitudes, protesters claim that representative democracy has been corrupted by the collusion of economic and political power, calling for participatory democracy and a general return to public concern with common goods. Given the extremely low trust in existing representative institutions, these movements have addressed requests to the state, but also experimented with alternative models of participatory and deliberative democracy. *Acampadas* became places to prefigure new forms of democracy. In comparison with the global justice movement, the declining confidence in representative institutions is reflected in the weakening of the search for channels of access to public decision-making through lobbying or collaboration. Even if there is still a search for politics, its traditional forms are mistrusted and autonomous ones explored. In this sense, these movements are not anti-political but rather propose a different – deliberative and participatory – vision of democracy that they prefigure in their own organizational forms. Deliberation through high-quality discourse rather than charismatic power is called for as a way to find solutions to common problems. In the presence of an institutional system felt as more and more

distant, a direct commitment is asked for. Deliberative and participatory conceptions and practices of democracy are combined with an emphasis on the direct participation of the citizens rather than through networks of associations.

Very successful in addressing the public and at times capable of sudden and dramatic political effects, these protests have been based upon new strategies with, however, still uncertain capacity for organizational resilience and the stabilization of collective identities.

9.13.6 Progressive Versus Regressive Movements: Some Concluding Remarks

Donald Trump's victory in the 2016 US presidential election has been widely perceived as a sign of the triumph of regressive over progressive movements. Similarly, the Brexit referendum has been taken as an indicator of a wave of parochialism that threatens to wash away once-dominant cosmopolitan sentiment. It should come as no surprise that moments of crisis also engender political and social polarization. In fact, social movements have frequently emerged simultaneously on both the Left *and* the Right. In the crisis of neoliberalism, counter-forces (similar to what Polanyi had called counter-movements) emerged, developing in two directions: some were progressive, seeking to expand citizens' rights within an inclusive, cosmopolitan conception, and others were regressive, yearning for a bygone order in which only a restricted number of insiders were protected. However, it remains to be seen whether the Brexit or Trump campaigns can truly be conceived of as populist *movements*, rather than other forms of populist politics.

If we look indeed at the forms that this discontent takes on the Right, they appear to be very different from the ones we can observe on the Left: not only with respect to the sociopolitical content of their claims, but also with regard to organizational models. Research on right-wing populism has long identified a cultural demarcation – with cosmopolitanism on the one side and xenophobia on the other – that separates the political Left from the Right (Kriesi et al. 2012). This is all the more the case today. Additionally, politics on the Right is characterized by a specific organizational form that builds on strong, personalized leadership rather than citizen participation. This clearly differentiates it from progressive movements.

The question of under which political conditions a regressive countermovement can develop remains to be addressed. Research on progressive movements has clearly shown that the specific characteristics of discontent under neoliberalism and its crisis are influenced by the political responses to the great recession, particularly by the strategies of center-left (especially party) politics. Notably, research on anti-austerity protests in Latin America has shown that the most destabilizing waves of protests occurred where party politics failed to offer channels of anti-neoliberal dissent, as all major parties supported neoliberal policies (Robert 2015). A similar situation seems to be emerging in Europe, where the consequences of repositioning on the Right in terms of (exclusive) visions of social protection seem all the more dramatic when the Left is perceived as championing free markets and lacking a significant alternative.

9.14 Social Progress, Economic Factors, and Political Conditions

At the end of the 1980s and into the beginning of the twenty-first century, all of the political conditions for a qualitative leap forward in social progress seemed to be in place. The triumphal declaration of "the End of History" was regarded by many as credible. It implied that no longer did citizens (except for the diminishing proportion of them living in autocracies) have reason to expect any radical challenges to their established institutions. Liberal democracy, the rule of law and social equity had become solidly entrenched and mutually supportive. The Wall dividing East and West had fallen. The Soviet Union had collapsed and fragmented into new republics. The countries of East-Central Europe were well on the way to a successful transition to democracy, following the trajectory established earlier in Southern Europe, Latin America, and a few countries in Asia. Centrist political parties with convergent and moderate programs dominated most elections. Parties opposing capitalism and/or democracy barely existed and, if so, were confined to the fringes of political life. The European Union had completed its "Internal Market" and just made a "Great Leap Forward" with the creation of a common currency. Regional organizations were spouting up all over the globe, lowering barriers to trade and investment. All of this seemed to promise further economic growth, less inflation, full employment, more and better well-being – undisturbed by political threats.

The conjuncture of these events presaged a peaceful and prosperous evolution for the foreseeable future, especially in social progress. National states were expected to be much less pre-occupied with external or internal security. The bounty from the presumed decline in military and police expenditures was supposed to be diverted to new or improved welfare and educational policies. Poverty would be eliminated; public health would improve; education levels would rise; pensions would become more bountiful; inequalities in personal and regional income would diminish; access to and fairness within the judicial system would be assured. Thanks to this convergence of "all good things," the legitimacy of public institutions would be guaranteed and the grateful citizens would come to support and trust the politicians that would be associated with the production of such manifestly superior public goods.

It would not be an exaggeration to observe that virtually all of these expectations were frustrated. The "Dog of Social Progress" did not bark in the 1980s and has remained silent into the twenty-first century. This reversal of expectations has led to widespread disillusion and distrust with both the new and old liberal democracies and mistrust of the politicians that make them work. Traditional political parties lost members; voters no longer identified with them; fringe parties increased their presence in elections and in the public debate. The judicial process has achieved more attention than before, if only because of persistent stalemates in the political process, and issues involving access to courts and the fairness of their decisions increased. The institutions and performance of capitalism are under greater criticism than at any time since the 1930s. Instead of the expected progress in social conditions, citizens and denizens in countries across the globe have suffered from decreases in policy entitlements and in public spending on programs designed to combat poverty, ill health, poor

education, and income inequality – with the result that virtually all indicators of social distress have risen since the 1990s.

Why did this happen? What intervened during this period to so dramatically frustrate expectations? And why has it persisted into the following century?

No doubt economic factors played an important role. Growth rates declined and remained low in the developed countries; they increased but became more erratic in the developing ones. Where the aggregate demand of consumers declined, so did the incentives for investment and the margins of profitability. This, in turn, reduced public revenues and augmented resistance to redistributive policies – at the same time that the need for insuring against social risks and for compensating in response to market failures became more acute. One response of both private persons and state authorities was to borrow more funds in an effort to fill the widening gap – and that subsequently generated a massive crisis in currency markets, credit institutions, fiscal policies, and public confidence. If all that were not enough, the very core of capitalist accumulation shifted from industry to services and within the service sector, to financial services. Much of the reduced growth was gained through speculation by firms that employed few people and rewarded them generously – at the expense of the general public. Inequalities in income and wealth climbed to levels not experienced since the end of the nineteenth century – before the policy foundations for improved social progress were laid.

Changes in political conditions were quick to follow and even more disruptive of the trend toward social progress. Centrist and especially Leftist parties – historically the main supporters of increases in citizen entitlements – lost members and vote share. They have been increasingly replaced by populist fringe parties and candidacies that promise to address the decline in well-being, but have no concrete proposals for accomplishing this. At the same time, fewer and fewer citizens identify with any party and more and more of them do not bother to vote at all. Labor unions and employer associations became less representative of their respective class interests, and previously stable patterns of collective bargaining between them have dissolved into purely individual or plant-level agreements. Those segments of the working class that are unemployed or precariously employed and, hence, no longer covered by collective agreements or eligible for public entitlements have become increasingly alienated from the political process altogether and more likely to respond to populist and national appeals.

As significant as they may be, these economic factors and political conditions might have been insufficient to explain the reversal in trend were it not for an even more important change in the nature of the unit responsible for deciding on the public policies that affect social progress. That unit is (or, better, was) the sovereign national state. It was presumed that it alone had the capacity to impose regulations, redistribute benefits, subsidize production, promote education, and to do so by exercising its legitimate and exclusive authority over a distinct territory. Beginning in the 1980s, its capacity to do all of this in a sovereign manner has declined. A combination of transformations – conveniently summarized by the concept of globalization – has emerged that limit the extent to which any state takes these policies without reference to public and/or private actors outside its territory and beyond its jurisdiction. Whether these constraints are imposed by supra-national institutions at the global or regional level is less important than the extent to which they must be respected and the consequences that will follow if they are not. Putting the matter bluntly, social progress is no longer the exclusive product of national states.

In retrospect, it has become apparent that the increase in social progress that followed the Second World War was the product of an unusual coincidence of economic factors and political conditions. There was a shortage of labor for physical reconstruction, a manifest need for investment, and enormous opportunities to satisfy pent-up consumer demand (and to make assured profits). Moreover, governments had made extensive promises to disfavored groups during the war in order to ensure their loyalty and their willingness to make sacrifices. National states had won the war and exercised uncontested authority over their respective territories (with the exception of those who lost the war and were occupied by the victors). If this were not enough, there was also the persistent menace of the Soviet Union and national communist parties to justify making concessions to less favored groups. This constellation of factors and conditions was anchored in a relative balance between competing classes and converging ideologies that persisted for some 40 years or so. It has been labeled "the post-war settlement" and it contributed very substantially to the expansion of welfare and educational policies during this period. While it was particularly characteristic of post-war Europe and North America, it set precedents and produced policy innovations that affected public decision makers and private interest representatives in other parts of the world.

"Social progress depends upon social contract," that is the lesson to be gleaned from the post-war history of the North and West and from the post-colonial history of the South and East. Needless to say, the socioeconomic content of that contract and the political process that produces it has varied a great deal – as has its durability. Everywhere that it has existed, it has rested on two generic features: (1) the self-organization of the conflicting class interests at stake; and (2) the relative balance of power between them – as well as on the competing presence of other cleavages that cut across the functional conflict between capital and labor and serve to divide or weaken their respective capacities to act collectively, as well as to complicate the process of ideological justification. In pre-capitalist economies and traditional societies, both the interests at stake and the balance of power between them will be significantly different. A viable and effective social contract will depend more upon cultural norms of responsibility and reciprocity, rather than calculations of material advantage. But once capitalism has penetrated the society and undermined traditional groups and norms, social progress will depend primarily upon arriving at a compromise between capital and labor. This will, no doubt, be made more difficult by the persistence of tribal, religious, linguistic, generational, gender, and center-periphery conflicts in any specific case, but the core remains a mutually consensual agreement on how the economic surplus is to be distributed and the production of wealth is to be regulated – and by whom for the benefit of whom. Needless to say, such contracts are not always likely to be self-enforcing, hence, the need for the intervention of public authority to ensure that the contract will be observed. Without a state to monitor behavior, redistribute

benefits, regulate production, implement policies without discrimination, and sanction non-compliance, all social contracts would be vulnerable to "opportunistic" defections in response to momentary advantage. In other words, regardless of the type of regime (although democracies are far more reliable in this regard than autocracies), their viability and longevity depends, not just on the perceived fairness of their distributive impact, but also on the existence of an established and reliable legal system to adjudicate eventual conflicts and compensate victims. Without the rule of law in the background to enforce them, no social contract is likely to persist for long – and, hence, no social progress is likely to emerge or to be sustained.

In the advanced capitalist economies and established democratic polities of Western Europe and North America, considerable social progress was achieved during the 40 or so years after the end of the Second World War. This was accomplished, however, as the result of two quite different processes of social contracting. The first favorable scenario has been called pluralist; the second corporatist.

In the former, characteristic of polities dominated by Conservative or Liberal political parties, the contract was "unsigned." It emerged spontaneously from the exchanges, largely among individuals and firms, in product and labor markets. By combining supply and demand in a competitive manner, they would create a "fair" and "consensual" distribution of benefits – provided that these markets were neither monopolistic nor oligopolistic and provided that public authority was licensed to ensure that contracts were obeyed, that regulations were followed, and that weak and marginalized citizens were compensated. Social justice (or progress) depended primarily upon the efforts of individuals to realize their potential according to their competitive advantage in contributing to growth in the general economy. Failure to do so was a matter of personal responsibility, not a failure of the system as a whole. In accordance with liberal principles, shortcomings in this distributive process would (and should) be cared for by the voluntary actions of "charitable" organizations in civil society, not by governments. The fact that labor was then relatively scarce and had a momentarily greater capacity for collective action that could plausibly affect the profitability of firms provided a relative balance in class forces that encouraged moderation and compromise. The ideological hegemony of liberalism in these polities ensured that the "freedom" to compete for goods and services was regarded as preferable to the "tyranny" of state intervention – and the Soviet Union was there to demonstrate what that would mean.

In the latter, characteristic of polities dominated by Social Democratic or Christian Democratic parties, the contract was "signed." It emerged as the result of explicit bargaining between organizations representing conflicting class interests and capable of ensuring the compliance of their respective members. Supply and demand were monitored and controlled by both public and semi-public institutions, as was the distribution (and, in some case, re-distribution) of eventual benefits by ensuring that wages more or less tracked the evolution of productivity and that working conditions and skill levels would continuously improve. Critical for the success of such an allocation process was the high level of self-organization of the contracting parties. Not only were a large proportion of the respective social classes incorporated (whether voluntarily or involuntarily) into the institutions that represented their interests, but these organizations were comprehensive and hierarchically ordered with regard to the classes and sectors they represented, monopolistic in that they faced no competition from other organizations, and officially recognized by the state and granted assured access to decision-making and a role in implementing the policies eventually taken. The ideological justification for such arrangements was weaker than that provided by the "freedom" of liberalism. They were legitimated more by their success in increasing well-being than by their conformity to existing doctrine.

Signed or unsigned, the social contract no longer provides a reliable basis for social progress – and has not been doing so since, roughly, the early 1980s. The two elements that combined to produce it – the self-organization of conflicting class interests and the relative balance of power between them – have changed beyond recognition. Associations representing capital, labor, and the profession have lost members and the capacity to act collectively and credibly – as have the so-called "sister political parties" that supported them in the electoral and legislative process. Due to the globalization of capitalism and the shift of its center of accumulation to finance from industry, the reciprocal capacity of labor and capital to influence each other's behavior and, thereby, compel them to resort to compromises in the distribution of their joint product has literally disappeared in favor of the latter. In the absence of these two elements, it is difficult to imagine any significant increase in social progress for the foreseeable future, at least in those Northern and Western countries that had previously played a leading role in its advent. Hopefully, there may exist more favorable conditions for it in some of the countries of the South and East that are more protected from globalization and whose capitalism is still more industrial.

References

Abdolian, L.F., and H. Takooshian. 2002. "The USA Patriot Act: Civil Liberties, the Media, and Public Opinion." *Fordham Urban Law Journal* 30/4: 1429–1453.

Acemoglu, D., and J.A. Robinson. 2012. *Why Nations Fail: The Origins of Power, Prosperity and Poverty*. New York: Crown.

Agamben, G. 2005. *State of Exception*. Chicago, IL: University of Chicago Press.

Agamben, G., and U. Raulff. 2004. "Interview with Giorgio Agamben – Life, a Work of Art Without an Author: The State of Exception, the Administration of Disorder and Private Life." *German Law Journal*. www. germanlawjournal. com/article.php.

Alesina, A., and E. Spolaore. 2003. *The Size of Nations*. Cambridge, MA: MIT Press.

Anderson, B. 1996. *Imagined Communities: Reflections on the Origins and Spread of Nationalism*. Revised edition. London: Verso.

Arnone, M., and L.S. Borlini. 2014. *Corruption: Economic Analysis and International Law*. Cheltenham: Edward Elgar.

Arrow, K. 1972. "Gifts and Exchanges." *Philosophy and Public Affairs* I/4: 343–362.

Baiocchi, G. 2005. *Militants and Citizens: The Politics of Participatory Democracy in Porto Alegre*. Stanford, CA: Stanford University Press.

Baiocchi, G., and E. Ganuza. 2012. "No Parties, No Banners: The Spanish Experiment with Direct Democracy." *Boston Review*, January.

Baiocchi, G., and E. Ganuza. 2016. *Popular Democracy and the Paradoxes of Participation*. Stanford, CA: Stanford University Press.

Baiocchi, G., P. Heller, and M. Silva. 2011. *Bootstrapping Democracy: Transforming Local Governance and Civil Society in Brazil*. Stanford, CA: Stanford University Press.

Bakardjieva, M. 2005. *Internet Society: The Internet in Everyday Life*. London: Sage.

Banfield, E.C. 1975. "Corruption as a Feature of Governmental Organization." *Journal of Law and Economics* 18: 587–605.

Bartolini, S. 2005. *Restructuring Europe: Centre Formation, System Building, and Political Structuring Between the Nation State and the European Union*. Oxford: Oxford University Press.

Bartolini, S., and P. Mair. 1990. *Identity, Competition, and Electoral Availability: The Stabilization of European Electorates 1885–1985*. Cambridge: Cambridge University Press.

Baumann, S. 2000. *Liquid Modernity*. Cambridge: Polity.

Beck, U. 1992. *Risk Society: Towards a New Modernity*. London: Sage.

Bendix , R. 1964. *Nation Building and Citizenship*. New York: Wiley & Sons.

Benhabib, S. 2005. "Borders, Boundaries, and Citizenship." *PSOnline*, October, 673–677.

Bellamy, R. 2007. *Political Constitutionalism*. Cambridge: Cambridge University Press.

Benkler, Y. 2006. *The Wealth of Networks: How Social Production Transforms Markets and Freedom*. New Haven, CT: Yale University Press.

Bertrand, J., and A. Laliberté (eds.). 2010. *Multination States in Asia: Accommodation of Resistance?* Cambridge: Cambridge University Press.

Bingham, L.B., T. Nabatchi, and R. O'Leary. 2005. "The New Governance: Practices and Processes for Stakeholder and Citizen Participation in the Work of Government." *Public Administration Review* 65/5: 547–558.

Boltanski, L., and E. Chiapello. 2006. *The New Spirit of Capitalism* . London: Verso.

Bork, R.H. 1993 (1978). *The Antitrust Paradox: A Policy at War with Itself*. New York: Free Press.

Bosch, T. 2017. "Twitter Activism and Youth in South Africa: The Case of #RhodesMustFall." *Information, Communication & Society* 20/2: 221–232.

Bristow, G. 2010. *Critical Reflections on Regional Competitiveness*. Abingdon: Routledge.

Brown, W. 2010. "We Are All Democrats Now ..." *Theory & Event* 13/2: 44–57.

Brown, W. 2015. *Undoing The Demos: Neoliberalism's Stealth Revolution*. Cambridge, MA: MIT Press.

Butler, J. 2009. "Performativity, Precarity and Sexual Politics." *AIBR. Revista de Antropología Iberoamericana* 4/3: i–xiii.

Castañeda, J. 1993. *Utopia Unarmed: The Latin American Left After the Cold War*. New York: Knopf.

Castells, M. 2015. *Networks of Outrage and Hope: Social Movements in the Internet Age*. New York: John Wiley & Sons.

Cleaver, F. 1999. "Paradoxes of Participation: Questioning Participatory Approaches to Development." *Journal of International Development* 11/4: 597–612.

Cole, D. 2003. *Enemy Aliens: Double Standards and Constitutional Freedoms in the War on Terror*. New York: The New Press.

Coleman, E.G. 2011. *Anonymous: From the Lulz to Collective Action. In Politics in the Age of Secrecy and Transparency*. http://mediacommons.futureofthebook.org/ tne/pieces/anonymous-lulz-collective-action.

Coleman, G. 2012. "Our Weirdness Is Free." *Triple Canopy* 15: 13.

Connelly, J. 2007. "The Relative Universality of Human Rights." *Human Rights Quarterly* 29: 281–306.

Connelly, J. 2008. "Human Rights: Both Universal and Relative (A Reply to Michael Goodhart)." *Human Rights Quarterly* 30: 194–204.

Cornell, S., and D. Hartmann. 2007. *Ethnicity and Race: Making Identities in a Changing World*. Newbury Park, CA: Pine Forge Press.

Crouch, C. 2003. *Postdemocracy*. Cambridge: Polity Press.

Crouch, C. 2004. *Postdemocracy*. Cambridge: Polity Press.

Crouch, C. 2011. *The Strange Non-Death of Neoliberalism*. Cambridge: Polity Press.

Crouch, C. 2015. "Can There Be a Normative Theory of Corporate Political Power?" in V. Schneider and B. Eberlein (eds.), *Complex Democracy: Varieties, Crises, and Transformations*. Heidelberg: Springer.

Crouch, C. 2016a. "The Paradoxes of Privatisation and Public Service Outsourcing," in M. Jacobs and M. Mazzucato (eds.), *Rethinking Capitalism: Economics and Policy for Sustainable and Inclusive Growth*. Oxford: Wiley Blackwell.

Crouch, C. 2016b. *Society and Social Change in 21st Century Europe*. Basingstoke: Palgrave Macmillan.

Crouch, C., P. Le Galès, C. Trigilia, and H. Voelzkow. 2001. *Local Production Systems in Europe. Rise or Demise?* Oxford: Oxford University Press.

Dagnino, E., A. Olvera, and A. Panficci (eds.). 2006. *La disputa por la construcción democrática en América Latina*. Mexico City: Fondo de Cultura Económica.

Dahl, R.A. 1961. *Who Governs?: Democracy and Power in an American City*. New Haven, CT: Yale University Press.

Dahl, R.A. 1971. *Polyarchy, Participation and Opposition*. New Haven, CT: Yale University Press.

Dahl, R.A. 1982. *Dilemmas of Pluralist Democracy: Autonomy Versus Control.* New Haven, CT: Yale University Press.

Dahlberg, L. 2001. "The Internet and Democratic Discourse." *Information, Communication & Society* 4/4: 615–633.

Dalton, R.J., and M.P. Wattenberg (eds.). 2000. *Parties Without Partisans: Political Change in Advanced Industrial Democracies.* Oxford: Oxford University Press.

della Porta, D. 2013. *Can Democracy Be Saved?* Cambridge:Polity Press.

della Porta, D. 2014. *Mobilizing for Democracy.* Oxford: Oxford University Press.

della Porta, D. 2015a. *Late Neoliberalism and Its Discontents in the Economic Crisis.* Basingstoke: Macmillan.

della Porta, D. 2015b. *Social Movements in Times of Austerity.* Cambridge: Polity Press.

della Porta, D. 2017a. *Global Diffusion of Protest.* Amsterdam: Amsterdam University Press.

della Porta, D. (ed.). 2017b. *Riding the Wave.* Amsterdam: Amsterdam University Press.

della Porta, D. et al. 2017. *Late Neoliberalism and its Discontent.* Basingstoke: Palgrave.

della Porta, D., J. Fernandez, H. Kouki, and L. Mosca (eds.). 2017 in press. *Movement Parties in Times of (Anti)austerity.* Cambridge: Polity Press.

della Porta, D., J., Font, and Y. Sintomer. 2014. *Participatory Democracy in Southern Europe: Causes, Characteristics and Consequences.* New York: Rowman & Littlefield International.

della Porta, D., and A. Vannucci. 1999. *Corrupt Exchanges.* New York: Aldine de Gruyter.

della Porta , D., and A. Vannucci. 2012. *The Hidden Order of Corruption.* Farnham: Ashgate.

Deutsch, K.W. 1972. *Nationalism and Social Communication: An Inquiry into the Foundations of Nationality.* Cambridge, MA: MIT Press.

Diamond, L.J. 1990. "Three Paradoxes of Democracy." *Journal of Democracy* 1/3: 48–60.

Douzinas, C. 2000. *The End of Human Rights.* London:Hart.

Douzinas, C. 2007. *Human Rights and Empire: The Political Philosophy of Cosmopolitanism.* London:Routledge.

Durkheim, E. 1964. *The Division of Labour in Society,* New York: Free Press.

Dutton, W.H., and M. Peltu. 2007. *Reconfiguring Government–Public Engagements: Enhancing the Communicative Power of Citizens.* https://ssrn.com/abstract= 1295337

Eddy, E.C. 2005. "Privatizing the Patriot Act: The Criminalization of Environmental and Animal Protectionists as Terrorists." *Pace Environmental Law Review* 22/2: 261–327.

Ericson, R.V. 1994. "The Royal Commission on Criminal Justice System Surveillance," in M. McConville and L. Bridges (eds.), *Criminal Justice in Crisis.* Aldershot, UK: Edward Elgar.

Ezrahi, Y. 1990. *The Descent of Icarus: Science and the Transformation of Contemporary Democracy.* Cambridge, MA: Harvard University Press.

Felt, U., C. Miller, L. Smith-Doerr, and R. Fouché (eds.). 2016. *Handbook of Science and Technology Studies.* Cambridge, MA: MIT Press.

Ferguson, J. 1990. *The Anti-Politics Machine: Development, Depoliticization, and Bureaucratic Power in Lesotho.* Cambridge:Cambridge University Press.

Ferguson, Y.H., and R.W. Mansbach. 1996. *Polities: Authority, Identities, and Change.* Columbia, SC: University of South Carolina Press.

Ferrara, A. 2003. "Two Notions of Humanity and the Judgement Argument for Human Rights." *Political Theory* 31/3: 392–420.

Font, J., D. della Porta, and Y. Sintomer. 2014. *Participatory Democracy in Southern Europe: Causes, Characteristics and Consequences* London: Rowman & Littlefield.

Foucault, M. 1980. *Power/Knowledge: Selected Interviews and Other Writings, 1972–1977* (trans. Colin Gordon et al.). New York: Pantheon.

Fuchs, C. 2014. "Hacktivism and Contemporary Politics," in D. Trottier and C. Fuchs (eds.) *Social Media, Politics and the State: Protests, Revolutions, Riots, Crime and Policing in the Age of Facebook, Twitter and Youtube.* New York: Routledge.

Fung, A. 2015. "Putting the Public Back Into Governance: The Challenges Of Citizen Participation And Its Future." *Public Administration Review* 75/4: 513–522.

Ghai, Y., and S. Woodman (eds.). 2013. *Practicing Self-Government: A Comparative Study of Autonomous Regions.* Cambridge: Cambridge University Press.

Gibbons, M., C. Limoges, H. Nowotny, S. Schwartzman, P. Scott, and M. Trow. 1994. *The New Production of Knowledge.* London: Sage.

Gilens, M. 2012. *Affluence and Influence: Economic Inequality and Political Power in America.* Princeton, NJ: Princeton University Press.

Gladwell, M. 2010. "Small Change." *The New Yorker* 4: 42–49.

Godwin, M.L. 2014. "Civic Engagement and Fiscal Stress in American Cities : Insights From The Great Recession." *State and Local Government Review* 46/4: 249–259.

Goode, L. 2009. "Social News, Citizen Journalism and Democracy." *New Media & Society* 11/8: 1287–1305.

Goodhart, M. 2008. "Neither Relative nor Universal: A Response to Donnelly." *Human Rights Quarterly* 30/1: 183–193.

Gott, G. 2002. "Imperial Humanitarianism: History of an Arrested Dialectic," in B.E. Hernández-Truyol (ed.), *Moral Imperialism: A Critical Anthology.* New York: New York University Press.

Gottfried, J., and E. Shearer. 2016. *News Use Across Social Media Platforms 2016.* Washington, DC: Pew Research Center.

Gupta, S., H.R. Davoodi, and R. Alonso-Terme. 1998. "Does Corruption Affect Income Inequality and Poverty?" *IMF Working Paper* 76/98: 1–41.

Haas, P.M. 1990. *Saving the Mediterranean: The Politics of International Environmental Cooperation.* New York: Columbia University Press.

Habermas, J. 1970. *Toward a Rational Society: Student Protest, Science, and Politics.* Boston, MA: Beacon.

Habermas, J. 1996. *Between Facts and Norms: Contribution to a Discursive Theory of Law and Democracy.* Cambridge: MIT Press.

Held, D. 1993. *Political Theory and the Modern State.* Cambridge: Polity Press.

Heller, P. 2001. "Moving the State: The Politics of Democratic Decentralization in Kerala, South Africa, and Porto Alegre." *Politics and Society* 29/1: 131–163.

Hicken, A., and E.M. Kuhonta (eds.). 2015. *Party System Institutionalization in Asia: Democracies, Autocracies, and the Shadows of the Past.* Cambridge: Cambridge University Press.

Hickey, S., and G. Mohan (eds.). 2004. *Participation: From Tyranny to Transformation? Exploring New Approaches to Participation in Development.* London: Zed Books.

Hindman, M. 2008. *The Myth Of Digital Democracy.* Princeton University Press.

Hirschl, R. 2004. *Towards Juristocracy: The Origins and Consequences of the New Constitutionalism.* Cambridge, MA: Harvard University Press.

Isin, E.F. 2008. "Theorizing Acts of Citizenship," in E.F. Isin and G.M. Nielsen (eds.), *Acts of Citizenship,* London: Zed Books.

Isin, E.F. 2009. "Citizenship in Flux: The Figure of the Activist Citizen." *Subjectivity* 29: 367–388.

Ivanov, K.S. 2007. *The Limits of a Global Campaign against Corruption, in Corruption and Development The Anti-Corruption Campaigns* (S. Bracking, ed.). Basingstoke: Palgrave.

Jasanoff, S. (ed.). 2004. *States of Knowledge: The Co-Production of Science and Social Order.* Abingdon: Routledge.

Jasanoff, S. 2005. *Designs on Nature: Science and Democracy in Europe and the United States.* Princeton, NJ: Princeton University Press.

Johnston, M. 1986. "Corruption and Democracy in America," in J.B. McKimey and M. Johnston (eds.), *Trend, Waste and Abuse in Government.* Philadelphia, PA: ISHI Publications.

Johnston, M. 1996. "The Search for Definitions: The Vitality of Politics and the Issue of Corruption." *International Social Science Journal* 149: 321–336.

Jones, S. (ed.). 1998. *Cybersociety 2.0: Revisiting Computer-Mediated Community and Technology* (Vol. 2). London: Sage.

Joppke, C. 2010. "The Inevitable Lightening of Citizenship." *European Journal of Sociology* 51/1: 9–32.

Katz, R.S., and P. Mair. 1995. "Changing Models of Party Organization and Party Democracy: The Emergence of the Cartel Party." *Party Politics* 1/1: 5–31.

Keating, M. 2001. *Plurinational Democracy: Stateless Nations in a Post-Sovereignty Era.* Oxford: Oxford University Press.

Keating, M. 2013. *Rescaling the European State: The Making of Territory and the Rise of the Meso.* Oxford: Oxford University Press.

Kelemen, D. 2011. *The Rise of Eurolegalism: The Transformation of Law and Governance in Europe.* Cambridge, MA: Harvard University Press.

Kelly Garrett, R. 2006. "Protest in an Information Society: A Review of Literature on Social Movements and New ICTs." *Information, Communication & Society* 9/2: 202–224.

Kellner, D. 2007. "Bushspeak and the Politics of Lying: Presidential Rhetoric in the 'War On Terror'." *Presidential Studies Quarterly* 37/4: 622–645.

Kitschelt, H., and S.I. Wilkinson (eds.). 2007. *Patrons, Clients, and Policies: Patterns of Democratic Accountability and Political Competition.* Cambridge: Cambridge University Press.

Kiwan, D. 2008. *Education for Inclusive Citizenship*. London: Routledge.

Kiwan, D. 2010. "Highly Skilled Guest-Workers in the UK." *Policy and Society* 29/4: 333–343.

Kiwan, D. 2013. "Introduction," in D. Kiwan (ed.), *Naturalization Policies, Education and Citizenship: Multicultural and Multination Societies in International Perspective*. Basingstoke: Palgrave Macmillan.

Kiwan, D. 2014. "Emerging Forms of Citizenship in the Arab World," in E.F. Isin and P. Nyers (eds.), *Routledge Global Handbook of Citizenship Studies*. Abingdon: Routledge.

Kiwan, D. 2016a. "Syrian and Syrian Palestinian Women in Lebanon: 'Actors of Citizenship'?" in M. Shalaby and V. Moghadam (eds.), *Empowering Women After the Arab Spring*. Basingstoke: Palgrave Macmillan.

Kiwan, D. 2016b. "Race, Ethnicity and Citizenship in Education: Locating Intersectionality and Migration for Social Justice," in A. Peterson, R. Hattam, M. Zembylas, and J. Arthur (eds.), *The Palgrave International Handbook of Education for Citizenship and Social Justice*. Basingstoke: Palgrave Macmillan.

Klitgaard, R. 1988. *Controlling Corruption*. Berkeley, CA and Los Angeles, CA: University of California Press.

Kocka, J. 2014. *Geschichte des Kapitalismus*. Munich: C.H. Beck Verlag.

Kriesi, H. et al. (eds.). 2012. *Political Conflicts in Western Europe*. Cambridge: Cambridge University Press.

Kymlicka, W. 1995. *Multicultural Citizenship: A Liberal Theory of Minority Rights*. Oxford: Oxford University Press.

Laclau, E. 2005. *On Populist Reason*. London: Verso.

Latour, B. 1987. *Science in Action: How to Follow Scientists and Engineers Through Society*. Cambridge, MA: Harvard University Press.

Leal, P. 2007. "Participation: The Ascendancy of a Buzzword in the Neoliberal Era." *Development in Practice* 17/4–5: 539–548.

Lee, C.W. 2015. *Do-It-Yourself. Democracy: The Rise of the Public Engagement Industry*. Oxford: Oxford University Press.

Lee, C.W., M. Mcquarrie, and E.T. Walker. 2015. *Democratizing Inequalities: Dilemmas of the New Public Participation*. New York: New York University Press.

Leighninger, M. 2006. *The Next Form of Democracy: How Expert Rule Is Giving Way to Shared Governance – and Why Politics Will Never Be the Same*. Nashville, TN: Vanderbilt University Press.

Li, T.M. 2005. "Beyond 'the State' and Failed Schemes." *American Anthropologist* 107/3: 383–394.

Lindblom, C.E. 1977. *Politics and Markets*. New York: Basic Books.

Lipset, S.M., and S. Rokkan. 1967. "Cleavage Structures, Party Systems and Voter Alignments," in S.M. Lipset and S. Rokkan, *Party Systems and Voter Alignments*. New York: Free Press.

Loader, I. 2000. "Plural Policing and Democratic Governance." *Social and Legal Studies* 9/3: 323–345.

Loader, I., and N. Walker. 2007. *Civilizing Security*. Cambridge: Cambridge University Press.

Loughlin, M. 1992. *Public Law and Political Theory*. Oxford: Oxford University Press.

Lupu, N. 2016. *Party Brands in Crisis: Partisanship, Brand Dilution, and the Breakdown of Political Parties in Latin America*. Cambridge: Cambridge University Press.

McAdam, D., S. Tarrow, and C. Tilly. 2001. *Dynamics of Contention*. Cambridge: Cambridge University Press.

Madrid, R.L. 2012. *The Rise of Ethnic Politics in Latin America*. Cambridge: Cambridge University Press.

Mainwaring, S., and E. Zoco. 2007. "Political Sequences and the Stabilization of Interparty Competition: Electoral Volatility in Old and New Democracies." *Party Politics* 13/2: 155–178.

Mair, P. 2013. *Ruling the Void: The Hollowing of Western Democracy*. London: Verso.

Mann, M. 1993. *The Sources of Social Power, Volume II: The Rise of Classes and Nation-States, 1760–1914*. Cambridge: Cambridge University Press.

Mansuri, G., and R. Vijayendra. 2013. *Localizing Development: Does Participation Work?* Washington, DC: World Bank.

Marshall, T.H. 1992. *Citizenship and Social Class*. London: Pluto.

Mauro, P. 1998. "Corruption and the Composition of Government Expenditure." *Journal of Public Economics* 69: 263–279.

Merkel, W. 2014. "Is Capitalism Compatible with Democracy?" *Zeitschrift für Vergleichende Politikwissenschaft* 8/2: 109–128.

Miller, D. 2002. "Group Rights, Human Rights and Citizenship." *European Journal of Philosophy* 10/2: 178–195.

Morgan, J. 2011. *Bankrupt Representation and Party System Collapse*. Philadelphia, PA: University of Pennsylvania Press.

Morozov, E. 2009. *The Brave New World of Slacktivism*. http://neteffect.foreignpolicy.com/posts/2009/05/19/the_brave_new_world_of_slacktivism

Moyn, S. 2010. *The Last Utopia: Human Rights in History*. Cambridge, MA: Harvard University Press.

Müller J.-W. 2016. *What Is Populism?* Philadelphia, PA: University of Pennsylvania Press.

Nash, C. 2009. "Between Citizenship and Human Rights." *Sociology* 43/6: 1067–1083.

Nyers, P. 2010. "No-One Is Illegal: Between City and Nation." *Studies in Social Justice* 4/2: 127–143.

OECD. 2011. *Divided We Stand: Why Inequality Keeps Rising*. London: OECD.

Offe, C. 1985. "New Social Movements: Changing Boundaries of the Political." *Social Research* 52: 817–868.

Ohmae, K. 1995. *The End of the Nation State: The Rise of Regional Economies*. New York: The Free Press.

Olson, M. 1965. *The Theory of Collective Action*. New Haven, CT: Yale University Press.

Pacquet, M. 2012. "Beyond Appearance: Citizenship Tests in Canada and the UK." *International Migration and Integration* 13: 243–260.

Peck, J., and N. Theodore. 2010. "Mobilizing Policy: Models, Methods, and Mutations." *Geoforum* 41/2: 169–174.

Pellegata, A. 2013. "Constraining Political Corruption: An Empirical Analysis of the Impact of Democracy." *Democratization* 20/7: 1195–1218.

Peterson, A. 2012. "Legitimacy and the Swedish Security Service's Attempts to Mobilize Muslim Communities." *International Journal of Criminology and Sociology* 1/1: 1–12.

Peterson, A., and M. Wahlström. 2015. "Repression: The Governance of Domestic Dissent," in D. della Porta and M. Diani (eds.), *Oxford Handbook of Social Movements*. Oxford: Oxford University Press.

Piketty, T. 2013. *Le capital au 21e siècle*. Paris: Éditions du Seuil.

Pizzorno, A. 1998. *Il potere dei giudici. Stato democratico e controllo della virtu*. Bari: Laterza.

Polany, K. 1957. *The Great Transformation*. London: Beacon Press.

Posner, R.A. 2001. *Antitrust Law*. Chicago, IL: University of Chicago Press.

Rae, H. 2002. *State Identities and the Homogenization of Peoples*. Cambridge: Cambridge University Press.

Rao, V., and P. Sanyal. 2010. "Dignity Through Discourse: Poverty and the Culture of Deliberation in Indian Village Democracies." *Annals of the American Academy of Political and Social Science* 629/1: 146–172.

Riedl, R.B. 2014. *Authoritarian Origins of Democratic Party Systems in Africa*. Cambridge: Cambridge University Press.

Roberts, K.M. 2014. *Changing Course in Latin America: Party Systems in the Neoliberal Era*. Cambridge: Cambridge University Press.

Roberts, K. 2015. *Changing Course*. Cambridge: Cambridge University Press.

Rokkan, S. 1999. *State Formation, Nation-Building and Mass Politics in Europe. The Theory of Stein Rokkan*, edited by P. Flora, S. Kuhnle, and D. Urwin. Oxford: Oxford University Press.

Root, A. 2007. *Market Citizenship: Experiments in Democracy and Globalization*. London: Sage.

Rosanvallon, P. 2006. *La contre-démocratie: La politique a l'age de la defiance*. Paris: Seuil.

Rose, N. 1996. "The Death of the Social? Re-Figuring the Territory of Government." *International Journal of Human Resource Management* 25/3: 327–356.

Rose Ackerman, S. 1999. *Corruption and Government*. Cambridge: Cambridge University Press.

Rupnik, J. 2012. "How Things Went Wrong." *Journal of Democracy* 23/3: 132–137.

Sassen, S. 2000. *World Cities in a Global Economy*. 2nd ed. Thousand Oaks, CA: Sage.

Sassen, S. 2008. *Territory, Authority, Rights. From Medieval to Global Assemblages*, updated edition. Princeton, NJ: Princeton University Press.

Savage, C., and S. Shane. 2016. "U.S. Reveals Death Toll From Airstrikes Outside War Zones." *New York Times*, July 1.

Schattschneider, E.E. 1942. *Party Government*. New York: Rinehart.

Schmitter, P.C. 2001. "Parties Are Not What They Once Were," in L. Diamond and R. Gunther (eds.), *Political Parties and Democracy*. Baltimore, MD: Johns Hopkins University Press.

Scott, A. 1998. *Regions and the World Economy. The Coming Shape of Global Production, Competition, and Political Order*. Oxford: Oxford University Press.

Scott, A., J. Agnew, E. Soja, and M. Storper. 2001. "Global City-Regions," in A. Scott (ed.), *Global City-Regions. Trends, Theory, Policy*, Oxford: Oxford University Press.

Shachar, A., and R. Hirschl. 2014. "On Citizenship, States and Markets." *Journal of Political Philosophy* 22/2: 231–257.

Shafir, G. 1998. "Introduction," in G. Shafir (ed.), *The Citizenship Debates*. Minneapolis, MN: Minnesota University Press.

Silva, E. 2009. *Challenging Neoliberalism in Latin America*. Cambridge: Cambridge University Press.

Smith, A.D. 1983. *State and Nation in the Third World*. London: Wheatsheaf.

Smith, A.D. 1998. *Nationalism and Modernism: A Critical Survey of Recent Theories of Nations and Nationalism*. London: Routledge.

Soysal, Y. 1994. *Limits of Citizenship: Migrants and Postnational Membership in Europe*. Chicago, IL: University of Chicago Press.

Standing, G. 2011. *The Precariat: the New Dangerous Class*. London: Bloomsbury Academic.

Stojanović, N. 2010. "Mononational and Multinational States: A Valid Dichotomy?" Paper for Conference on Legal Reasoning and European Law: The Perspective of Neil MacCormick, European University Institute, May 21, 2010.

Stokes, S.C., T. Dunning, M. Nazareno, and V. Brusco. 2013. *Brokers, Voters, and Clientelism: The Puzzle of Distributive Politics*. Cambridge: Cambridge University Press.

Streck, J.M. 1998. "Pulling the Plug on Electronic Town Meetings: Participatory Democracy and the Reality of the Usenet," in C. Toulouse and T.W. Luke (eds.), *The Politics of Cyberspace*. London: Routledge.

Streeck, W. 2013. *Buying Time: The Delayed Crisis of Democratic Capitalism*. Verso.

Streeck, W. 2015. "Comment on Wolfgang Merkel, 'Is Capitalism Compatible with Democracy?'" *Zeitschrift für Vergleichende Politikwissenschaft* 9/1: 49–60.

Su, C. 2017. "Beyond Inclusion: Critical Race Theory and Participatory Budgeting." *New Political Science* 39/1: 126–142.

Talpin, J. 2012. *Schools of Democracy: How Ordinary Citizens (Sometimes) Become Competent in Participatory Budgeting Institutions*. Colchester: ECPR Press.

Tierney, S. 2006. *Constitutional Law and National Pluralism*. Oxford: Oxford University Press.

Uslaner, E.M. 2013. "Trust and Corruption Revisited: How and Why Trust and Corruption Shape Each Other." *Quality & Quantity: International Journal of Methodology* 47/6: 3603–3608.

US Supreme Court. 2010. *Citizens United* v. *Federal Election Commission*, 08–205. Washington, DC: US Supreme Court.

US Supreme Court. 2014. *McCutcheon* v. *Federal Election Commission*, 12–536. Washington, DC: US Supreme Court.

Van Cott, D.L. 2009. *Radical Democracy in the Andes*. Cambridge: Cambridge University Press.

van den Berghe, P. 2006. "Ethnies and Nations: Genealogy Indeed," in A. Ichijo and G. Uzelac (eds.), *When Is the Nation? Towards an Understanding of Theories of Nationalism*. London: Routledge.

Welikala, A. 2015. "Southphalia or Southfailure? National Pluralism and the State in South Asia," in S. Tierney (ed.), *Nationalism and Globalization*. Oxford: Hart.

Whitehead, L. 2002. *Democratization: Theory and Experience*. Oxford: Oxford University Press.

Winters, J. 2011. *Oligarchy*. Cambridge: Cambridge University Press.

Wright, S. (ed.). 2008. "Citizenship Tests in a Post-National Era." *International journal on Multicultural Societies* 10/1: 1–94.

Wynne, B. 1994. "Public Understanding of Science," in S. Jasanoff, G. Markle, J. Peterson, and T. Pinch (eds.), *Handbook of Science and Technology Studies*. Thousand Oaks, CA: Sage.

Yashar, D. 2005. *Contesting Citizenship in Latin America: The Rise of Indigenous Movements and the Postliberal Challenge*. Cambridge: Cambridge University Press.

Yiftachel, O. 2006. *Ethnocracy: Land and Identity Politics in Israel/Palestine*. Philadelphia, PA: University of Pennsylvania Press.

Youmans, W.L., and J.C. York. 2012. "Social Media and the Activist Toolkit: User Agreements, Corporate Interests, and the Information Infrastructure of Modern Social Movements." *Journal of Communication* 62/2: 315–329.

9

10

Violence, Wars, Peace, Security

Coordinating Lead Authors:[1]
Peter Wallensteen, Michel Wieviorka

Lead Authors:[2]
Itty Abraham, Karin Aggestam, Alexander Bellamy, Lars-Erik Cederman, Jerôme Ferret, Jean Baptiste Jeangène Vilmer, Wilhelm Heitmeyer, Angela Muvumba-Sellström, Laurie Nathan, Hideaki Shinoda, Ekaterina Stepanova

Contributing Author:[3]
Olga Odgers Ortiz

---

[1] Affiliations : PW: Uppsala University, Sweden and University of Notre Dame, USA; MW: FMSH and EHESS, France.
[2] Affiliations : IA: National University of Singapore, Singapore; KA: Lund University, Sweden; AB: Queensland University, Australia; LEC: ETH Zentrum, Switzerland; JF: EHESS-CNRS and University of Toulouse 1, France; JBJV: Collège d'études mondiales and Science Po, France; WH: University of Bielefed, Germany; AMS: Uppsala University, Sweden; LN: University of Pretoria, South Africa; HS: Tokyo University, Japan; ES: National Research Institute of World Economy and International Relations, Russia.
[3] Affiliation: El Colegio de la Frontera Norte, Mexico.

Summary

The issues of conflict, violence, and social progress and their interrelations have long been topics of philosophical discussion. Underling this chapter is the necessity to achieve social change and social progress through public action. Violence, especially in its more intense and extreme forms, often serves as a major impediment to social progress; it leads to or catalyzes a range of direct physical and humanitarian harms for the population (such as human losses and displacement), as well as socioeconomic, environmental, and other damage. However, social change may itself imply popular protest against repressive conditions such as repressive governments, foreign occupation, or colonial rule. This protest may be exercised through non-violent means, but sometimes through violence.

The chapter notes a long-term decline in number and intensity of wars, at least since the Korean and Vietnam wars. However, there are also data demonstrating a troubling rise in armed conflicts since the early 2000s, including historically high levels of terrorism. Significant geographical variations are suggestive for managing this phenomenon. Some regions have seen a steady decline in organized political violence (East Asia, South and Central America); some regions or countries experience far more terrorism than others (notably the Middle East, South Asia, some states in Europe). Homicide rates decline with increasing human development and social integration, while suicide rates do not follow the same pattern. Also the sexual and gender-based violence in conflict situations show variations, indicating that this phenomenon too can be averted among non-state actors (guerilla groups, liberation movements).

In respect to the means of violence, notably weapons development, nuclear weapons inventories have been reduced, but remain at very high levels. Global military expenditures have seen a marked rise, not least in the Middle East and for some major powers (China, Russia), while still not even close to the arsenals of the United States.

These powers are the top producers of small arms, the types of weapons mostly used in conflicts in Africa, for instance.

The continued prevalence of violence and weapons impede the possibilities of social progress and needs to be reversed. However, the international actions for controlling this lacks in commitment and enforcement. The UN system has been activated since the end of the Cold War, but has had difficulties in responding to the challenges of the past few years, most obviously revealed in the highly internationalized civil war in Syria. Similarly, disarmament measures have not moved forward. There seems to be little prospect for further nuclear weapons reductions, although the international agreement on Iran's nuclear technology is encouraging. A significant recent treaty is the Arms Trade Treaty, which now is being tested in monitoring illicit arms trade, and still lacks support of key major powers.

There is headway in the field of peacemaking and mediation, and where the negotiated endings to armed conflicts have become more frequent and of increasingly quality. Similarly, the notion of peacebuilding has emerged as a new and evolving response. As is the case with peacemaking there is a need for building international, regional, and new national institutions. State capacity is important as the state is expected to be the responder to increases in violence and to lead society toward social progress. "Weak" states need to be understood in terms of a lack of state capacity or legitimacy, or both. Of high importance is also the degree of ethnic and/or ethno-confessional diversity and representation. There is ample proof that the lack of participation in policy-making, as well as other forms of inequality and marginalization of large population groups increases the risk of conflict and violence. Gender inequality has a connection to the onset, in particular of civil wars. New social media play a role – not in the creation of conflict as such – but in the mobilization of a population.

Decreasing inequalities among ethnic groups and along gender lines suggest a more hopeful long-term trend, as does democratization. However, if a democratic system does not address the issues of ethnic, religious, and sociopolitical inclusion, territorial divisions, and power sharing, it may result in increased tension, conflict, and violence.

In addition, this chapter addresses the issues of global governance with respect to the management and prevention of conflicts and violence. It observes that there are geo-political variations, i.e. that the same issue may be substantially different from one region to another, thus making uniform measures inapplicable. It is also noteworthy that much global cooperation still rests on informal arrangements, which make UN Security Council action possible at certain instances, but may also impede implementation of decisions. There is a need for global, national, and local institutions that are stable, solid, and sustainable.

This chapter invites the readers to come with suggestions for conclusion building, for instance, on notions such as resilience, human security, and human rights.

10

10.1   Introduction

Chapter 10 deals with the human experience of physical violence from the individual to the global level. This relates to social progress in two different ways. First of all it is argued that *an overall reduction in violence in itself constitutes social progress*. It means meeting the ambitions "to save succeeding generations from the scourge of war" as expressed in the first sentence of the UN Charter from 1945. This could be done by reducing (or even eliminating) organized violence and war from human existence. This goal is, of course, colored by two world wars and an unprecedented genocide, the Holocaust, all taking place within half a century, a uniquely violent experience for human-kind. On the whole, the UN position is likely to be shared by most peoples and governments, as all UN member states have signed the UN Charter. Still, there is a contradiction, as most states build power on their monopoly on the legitimate use of violence. Furthermore, through a series of the international agreements on human rights states have agreed to restrain their use of physical powers. This should be regarded as an element of social progress in its ability to curtail state violence.[4]

This notwithstanding, one must be aware that a reduction of violence does not necessarily or automatically mean social progress. For instance, violence may disappear from a neighborhood with a history of riots as drug dealers impose local "peace" in order to pursue their business without the presence of police and media. And there are theoretical and philosophical arguments for the necessity of violence or its positive role in at least certain extreme cases. It has been said that in order to achieve social change, violence may be a means for social progress. Some would argue that without violence, colonial domin-ation, for example, would not have come to an end (or at least not as quickly). This can be debated. Also, the idea that some revolutionary processes have brought social progress can be discussed. Even if not as influential as in the past, there is a strong intellectual and political tradition that connects violence and emancipation of some groups, notably the working class, as pursued within Marxism and Leninism, but also in writings by committed intellectuals, notably Georges Sorel or Franz Fanon.[5] At the same time there are equally strong traditions of principled as well as pragmatic refusal to use violence for social progress, as witnessed in cleavages between reformists and revolu-tionaries in most liberation movements.

Empirically, it can be observed that social change may itself imply popular protest against repressive governments, foreign occupation or colonial rule. Such protest can often be exercised through non-violent means, as was the case in series of examples of decolonization, not-ably India, Ghana, or South Africa. The extent of repression may some-times direct legitimate protest into violent liberation. Great revolutions certainly achieved change of political leadership, notably in the United States, France, Russia, and China, but real social progress was in fact limited and often undone by the continued resort to violence to uphold the influence of the new holders of state power. Furthermore, it is quite clear that non-state actors' use of violence also legitimizes the state's use of violence.

Intellectually and morally this provides room for change through other means, notably active non-violence, national mass mobilization for social change as well as international sanctions and other forms of external pressure that may support internal transformations. Empirical evidence supports the idea that change through non-violence tends to bring more democracy and human rights than violent revolutions.

A second way to see the relations between violence and social pro-gress is to argue that *social progress means adding something to society that prevents continued recurrence of violent conflict*. For instance, if the resort to violence is rooted in discrimination, inequality and injustice (which often is the case, as this chapter demonstrates), then the attainment of human rights and human dignity as well as daily physical safety for all inhabitants for the foreseeable future *is* social progress.[6] Once the fear of physical attack on individuals, groups, or the society is no longer present human capacity is released for building a more reliant, sustainable society. This is a world society that approaches quality peace. Such a positive vision is enshrined in the second sentence of the UN Charter that reaffirms "faith in funda-mental human rights, the dignity and worth of the human person, in the equal rights of men and women and of nations large and small." This has more recently been included in the Sustainable Development Goals for 2030 set up by the UN General Assembly in September 2015, notably Goal 16 that aims to "promote just, peaceful and inclusive societies."

In this chapter, we depart from the assumption that the *reduction of violence is not the same as the rejection of conflict*.[7] On the contrary, social conflict is needed for progress. This is the essence of public debate, popular protest, and non-violent campaigns. However, we point to the importance of a line where conflicts no longer become constructive and that this line can be drawn at the threshold of system-atic violence. Once a number of people have been killed, a conflict no longer becomes constructive and loses its ability to continuously move a society towards social progress. This means that we must analytic-ally distinguish between conflict and violence. In many historical cases, violence is the contrary of a social movement. For instance, during a century and a half in some industrial countries, the working-class movement contributed by means of their joint struggle to build a wel-fare state through progressive relations with the owners of industrial production. Their conflict was generally the contrary of violence. But it may also happen that violence is part of a social conflict. It would be too simple to argue that there is always and necessarily a contrary rela-tionship, but nevertheless these are two different phenomena. Social

---

[4]   There are such agreements covering most regions of the world, for instance, the Universal Declaration of Human Rights (1948), the UN Covenants on Human Rights (1966), the Helsinki Final Act of 1975, the Charter of Paris (1990), the Istanbul Document 1999, the African Charter on Human and People's Rights (1998), and the Inter-American Commission on Human Rights within OAS (1978).

[5]   Today one would expect there to be parallel Islamic discussions on the use of violence to promote Islamic value. There is a violence-legitimizing position associated with certain militant Islamic groups, but evidence suggests that this is not likely to be shared by most Muslims. A within-Islam discussion on the limits of violence should be encouraged.

[6]   This is parallel to notions such as "quality peace." See Wallensteen (2015).

[7]   See Wieviorka (2009).

progress may always require conflict, but not always violence, while systematic violence normally impedes social progress. The Colombian case is a good illustration of this point: the peace agreement between the Government and the guerilla (FARC) includes ending of armed action, but also the inclusion of the FARC in the legal political system, where it will be a combative but non-violent actor.

We should also note that *"violence" comes in many different forms*, for instance, as "structural" and "cultural" violence (Galtung 1969). Structural violence refers to the life chances that a society denies some of its inhabitants, while privileging others. In the field of health care it is associated with some having lower life expectancies than others. Direct violence refers to the actual killing of human beings. It can be seen as a discussion between developed and underdeveloped continents facing different challenges (e.g. Global North vs. Global South; poor, developing states vs. industrialized ones), sub-regions (e.g. urban vs. rural areas), classes (e.g. rich vs. poor, land owners vs. tenants and landless), or identity groups (e.g. dominant ethnic minorities vs. dominated majorities, as exemplified in Apartheid South Africa). There could also be an additional understanding of this notion of violence, as the *structures of violence*. It leads to a focus on the social institutions that exert direct violence, e.g. the state as such and those that speak in its name and with its authorizations, notably the military forces, police institutions, intelligence operations, prison services, etc. To this we may add *cultural violence*, which includes the cultures that justify or legitimize structural or direct violence (Galtung 1990).

The issues of conflict, violence, peace, and security vary considerably across the globe due to historical conditions (e.g. colonialism, occupation, repression, and earlier wars) and present predicaments (e.g. underdevelopment, humanitarian challenges, drugs, and organized crime) and we are not able here to attend to all these as closely as they deserve. Still, this chapter aims to illustrate the intimate connection between social progress and the issues of violence, war, peace, and security. In this chapter we approach this, by first dealing with the origins and dynamics of violence and war (Section 10.2), followed by a treatment of matters relating to the building of peace and security (Section 10.3), after which we take up a set of overarching, general issues that affect both the previous sections (Section 10.4) followed by some remarks on implications for the future (Section 10.5). The time frame largely builds on the developments since the Second World War, and more specifically since the end of the Cold War.

10.1.1   Approach of this Chapter

In the classical social and political sciences, the analysis of war and political violence distinguishes between various forms of these phenomena. A treatise may concentrate on one or several levels, notably, individual, local, national, supranational, international, and world levels. This is a frequent framework that can be seen as a European legacy of the seventeenth century, often attributed to the Westphalian treaties following the Thirty Years War. It organized "the world" (in fact, only Europe) in states that related to each other through diplomacy

and war, what today is termed "international relations." This led to or contributed to the principle of "methodological nationalism" as observed by Ulrich Beck (2002). The main patterns of thinking and examining political violence and war focused either on relations *within* the nation-state, or *between* nations. This has the advantage of making it possible to pursue international comparisons, for instance, between countries. When connected to the idea of state sovereignty, however, it meant that internal affairs were no longer the legitimate concern of other states.[8]

It is useful to distinguish various levels, from the individual to the world. At the same time we know that it is no longer enough, or fully satisfactory, since these levels constantly interact with each other, particularly in the contemporary world. Frequently, a local expression of violence cannot be understood if one doesn't take into account distant elements, either concretely or symbolically: if a Jewish institution is destroyed by an explosion in Latin America, it is may be an expression of local anti-Semitism, but such hatred could certainly be nurtured by the Israeli-Palestinian conflict and by the Middle East situation, if not perpetuated by terrorists coming from the Middle East. The interaction may be a question of meaning, and it is then not concrete, but rather virtual, the fruit of the Internet and modern technologies of communication. This means, in line with Beck, that we should adopt a "cosmopolitan" perspective to understand important issues such as violence. He called this way of thinking "methodological cosmopolitanism:" a very local event should be analyzed taking into account non-local logics, such as world risks (Beck 2002).

But it is not only a question of more or less abstract meaning, the fruit of imagination of some actors, since many expressions of violence and war, today, develop simultaneously in a very concrete manner at different levels, and make impossible a simple use of "methodological nationalism." For instance, contemporary terrorism is frequently global, a mixture of both local and geopolitical dimensions. Radical Islamism often emerges in a society, with, for instance, post-colonial difficulties in integrating migrants, inequalities, racism, etc., on the one hand, and on the other hand, it may be organized far from this society, e.g. in the Middle East, by organizations such as al-Qaeda or IS, the Islamic State. In order to understand the terrorist attacks, for instance, in Paris (January and November 2015), Brussels (March 2016), Nice (July 2016), Stockholm, St. Petersburg, and London (April 2017), Manchester, UK (May 2017), Barcelona and Cambrils (August 2017), etc., one must take into account the individual trajectories of young people that were born in these countries, but also the existence of organizations based in Iraq, Syria, Libya, Caucasus, or other places where they may be planning local and international actions. These acts are both domestic and international. The patterns may be somewhat different from actions that we also have seen in the Middle East (including Turkey) and parts of Africa, where the recruitment pattern may differ, but still takes place within a context of cross-border actions. The classical, often legal, distinction between what is internal and what is external is not sufficient in order to understand this type of extreme violence. Of course, nation-states and their borders exist, and define a central level for analysis. But this is not the only level,

---

[8]   The Westphalian Treaty of 1648, however, included provisions attempted at protecting civilians that did not share religion with the ruler, a first admission of human rights extending beyond sovereignty. This is often not mentioned in writings on this particular treaty. See Osiander (2001).

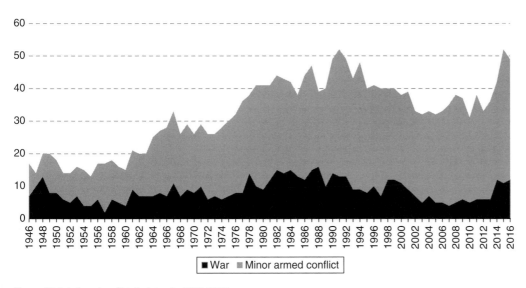

Figure 10.1 | Armed conflicts by intensity, 1946–2015.
Source: Uppsala Conflict Data Program, reproduced with permission.

Box 10.1 | Armed Conflict

An *armed conflict* is a contested incompatibility that concerns government and/or territory where the use of armed force between two parties, of which at least one is the government of a state, results in at least 25 battle-related deaths in one calendar year. An armed conflict with more than 1,000 battle-related deaths in a calendar year is a *war* (Uppsala Conflict Data Program www.ucdp.uu.se).

and in this chapter one must think globally, i.e. taking into account the various forms of articulation and interpenetration of levels that go from the more general and global to the more specific and individual or local.

10.2   Violence and War

10.2.1   Conflict Trends

There is considerable discussion on the trends in armed conflict. Steven Pinker's work *The Better Angels of our Nature: Why Violence Has Declined* received global attention when it appeared in 2011. Several other studies argued the same thing at about the same time (Gleditsch et al. 2013; Goldstein 2011; Norberg 2016; Väyrynen 2006).[9] Some evidence was based on data produced by the Uppsala Conflict Data Program (UCDP), but the arguments for this decline in violence differed. Pinker referred largely to a civilizational change, building on the increasing capacity of the state to control violence. Others referred to the effectiveness of international organizations (Goldstein 2011), the democratization of societies (Gleditsch et al. 2013) and the declining attractiveness of violence as a political instrument (Mueller 1989). The data that spurred the arguments observed the decline in armed conflicts and wars over time, as well as decreasing destructiveness of

the conflicts. In particular, the focus was on the periods since the end of the Second World War. The end of the Cold War has certainly also exerted an influence on armed conflicts.

The argumentation can be said to reflect an optimism that characterized a world of increasing globalization, universal economic growth, and strong improvements in health care. Five years later, the conclusions seemed premature, as armed conflicts again increased. This is what is demonstrated in the following two curves, drawn from UCDP using the definition in Box 10.1.

Figure 10.1 demonstrates that the trend, at the time of the debate and writings by Pinker, Goldstein, and Gleditsch had considerable face validity. They reflected a situation that seemingly could be observed and confirmed around the world. The wars appeared to be ending, either through comprehensive peace agreements (notably in Sudan and Indonesia, the Balkan wars were not restarting following the Dayton accords, etc.) or victories (Sri Lanka's armed forces decisively defeating the Tamil Tigers, in 2009). Barack Obama was elected president of the United States partly because of war fatigue in the United States. However, Figure 10.1 demonstrates the difficulty of making predictions: at about the same time as these observations were made new armed conflicts were brewing and soon changed the global outlook. In the years 2014–2015 Islamic jihadist groups made remarkable

---

9   John Mueller (1989) was actually first to argue along these lines.

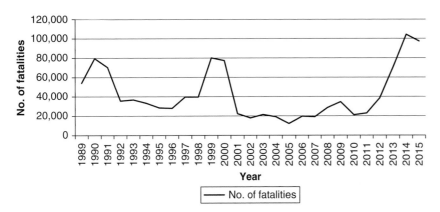

Figure 10.2 | Battle-related deaths in armed conflicts, 1989–2015.
Source: Uppsala Conflict Data Program, reproduced with permission.

territorial gains (IS in Iraq and Syria, Boko Haram in Nigeria, other affiliates in Libya, Mali, Yemen, al-Shabaab in Somalia). The contours of a transnational coordinated movement based on military capacity and terrorist activity suggested a real challenge to the existing world order. More predictable, perhaps, the United States, France, the United Kingdom, and Russia began to strike back, not the least after terrorist attacks in Western Europe. By 2017 many of these groups were weakened, but still able to inflict considerable harm and much fear.

In this more unpredictable global situation, the actions by Russia in unilaterally occupying and annexing Crimea coupled with the military de facto control over other parts of Ukraine through various separatist groups, also demonstrated that the custodians of world order, the permanent members of the UN Security Council, could act outside Charter obligations without effectively being rebuffed. Indeed, a precedent had already been set by the US and UK invasion of Iraq in 2003 and, even earlier, in Kosovo 1999. The world order as it was known, found itself in crisis. Furthermore, the control by the state of means of violence was no longer necessarily something that promoted civilizational values, as "legitimate" weapons were used for repression, civil wars, and external interventions by Western powers but also in Turkey, Thailand, the Philippines, and Myanmar. These were countries that only a few years earlier had been seen as examples of peaceful democratization. What they did drew international criticism, but international institutions had difficulties in garnering concerted reaction. These institutions were sidelined while democracy was retreating.[10]

As Figure 10.1 recounts the number of conflicts, also their destructiveness needs to be added to the picture. This is presented in Figure 10.2, which includes the battle-related deaths in the period since the end of the Cold War. Figure 10.2 confirms the picture that the world now faces challenges unprecedented since the end of the Cold War. Compared to the big wars of that period, e.g. the Korean War, the Vietnam War, the Iran-Iraq War, and the war in Afghanistan 1979–1989, these conflicts are still limited. However, the picture of a constant decline of wars has to be questioned. That picture may still be correct in a longer term, e.g. if one looks to decade-long changes. There is hope that the declining

trend may return. But the challenges for the immediate future, e.g. the next 5 to 10 years is likely to be a traditional one: how to manage the threats of organized violence in such a way that the amount of violence is not increasing even more?

The statistics of Figures 10.1 and 10.2 are global. However, we have emphasized the importance of studying the phenomenon of violence at different levels. Some regions of the world show patterns that deviate from the global one, in important ways. There are reasons to consider too, in particular: South America and East Asia. Both of them demonstrate a remarkable reduction in armed conflicts during the past three or four decades.

South America has passed through a transition away from military rule to democratization of most of state leadership. The conflicts have largely been ended through peace processes, notably in Central America and Colombia (as recent as in 2016), or through a few victories (notably the defeat of the Maoist Sendero Luminoso in Peru). There are other problems of violence in this region, something we will return to in this chapter.

Furthermore, East Asia has not seen a major war since 1980, but has instead been the region of exemplary economic growth. Although democratization is less common, the character of repression may have changed in some of the countries, notably China where human rights are still continuously violated but without the types of massacres that we saw in Tiananmen Square in Beijing in 1989 (Eck 2016). South Korea, Japan, the Philippines all seems solidly democratic. At the same time, however, the region includes a closed and unpredictable regime in North Korea. Also, the Communist Party of Vietnam has shown little interest in democratization. The uniting factor is, instead, an interest in economic growth and stability.[11]

This means that there are other regions that exhibit the largest extent of violence, particularly the Middle East. Thus, half of the deaths making up the 2015 number in Figure 10.2 refer to the internationalized civil war in Syria. Other countries with many war victims are Iraq, Libya,

---

[10] The 2017 Annual Report of the Varieties of Democracy Institute, Göteborg University, reported in May 2017 on the "global democratic backslide," pp. 8–9, https://issuu.com/ante/docs/v-dem_annualreport2017.

[11] See, for instance, Tønnesson (2015).

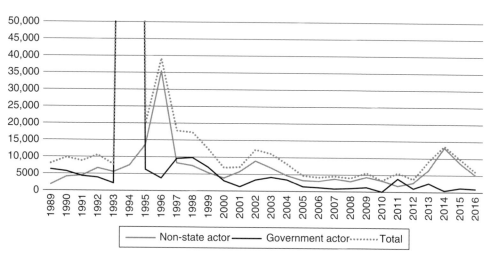

Figure 10.3 | Fatalities in one-sided violence, by type of actor, 1989–2016, with the outlier case of Rwanda indicated. Source: Uppsala Conflict Data Program, reproduced with permission.

and Yemen, all belonging to the Arab world, and countries close by, notably Somalia, Pakistan, Afghanistan, Mali, Nigeria, Turkey, and Ukraine. The present dynamics of these conflicts suggest that they are likely to continue throughout this decade and perhaps beyond, in the same form as today or involving even more actors. Even if these wars were to end in one way or the other, the rehabilitation of the societies is likely to be a long-drawn-out development. The experience from peace negotiations suggests that agreement is a reasonable way to end conflict, but also that they are likely to be very protracted. For instance, the recent agreement in Colombia has taken 4 years, and this came after many other attempts during the last 40 years; the process on Guatemala took 7 years; and negotiations between Israel and Palestinian representatives have continued, off and on, for more than 25 years.

Furthermore, as these involve regional connections, the complications in reaching an agreement (as well as a victory) are many and intertwined with other issues. The restoration of peace in the Middle East requires extraordinary commitments of regional as well as global actors. For the time being, there is no such dedication, apart from achieving victory for the preferred parties or preventing the victory of their enemies. And one may think that the deficit of solid states in this part of the world will make sustainable peace difficult to implement.

10.2.2   One-Sided Violence and Civilian Victimization

There is a legitimate and increasing concern about the fate of civilians in political conflicts. The UN has approved the protection of civilians as a most important international concern whether in armed conflict or in other situations, notably genocide, ethnic cleansing, and terrorism. Figure 10.3 gives recent data from the Uppsala Conflict Data Program on what is fruitfully termed one-sided violence for the post-Cold War period.

Figure 10.3 demonstrates the magnitude of the problem in terms of fatalities, as well as the variations over time. The case of Rwanda stands out at the most destructive event, in terms of human lives, since the end of the Cold War. It was largely government driven, and governments tend to be responsible for a considerable amount of such violence. However, the graphs also reveal that this is not the full story, and that various non-state actors are also capable to deliver considerable human destruction. Since 2012 that has been the dominant actor in one-sided violence. This leads this chapter to consider three types of violence: terrorism, genocide, and targeted killings.

10.2.2.1   The Issue of Terrorism

The field of organized violence does not only include the armed conflicts. There are also other categories. Some of them can be labeled one-sided, i.e. when a state or non-state actor deliberately targets civilians for explicit and political reasons. There are two forms that we need to consider. Here we deal with terrorism, and in the following section with genocide.

The notion of terrorism is of political, rather than academic, background. It dates back to the nineteenth century, as an elaboration of the term "terror" originally associated with the Jacobines of the French Revolution. The first interpreters and "students" of terrorist violence were revolutionary ideologues and their political opponents. Academic research on terrorism has only evolved since the 1970s. The analysis of terrorism in all its form is still not as advanced as one might expect, in view of its role in policy-making.[12]

The term is often used to label actions by others, and is only exceptionally part of the self-description of the actors. Many governments apply this term to classify their political and/or armed opponents, regardless of whether their actions fit with nationally or internationally acceptable

---

[12]   For a recent assessment, see Englund and Stohl (2017).

Box 10.2 | Definitions of Terrorism

(1) Terrorism involves deliberate use or threat of violence against "soft" (non-combatant) targets, or intentionally indiscriminate violence, in the name of political, religious, or ideological goals, employed by non-state actors to intimidate, destabilize, and exercise pressure on the society and the state (Working Definition, applied here).[13]

(2) Terrorism is "any action … that is intended to cause death or serious bodily harm to civilians or non-combatants, when the purpose of such act … is to intimidate a population, or compel a Government or an international organization to do or to abstain from doing any act" (High-Level Panel 2004: para. 164)

(3) Terrorism constitutes "Intentional acts of violence by non-state actors that satisfy at least two of the following three inclusion criteria:

   1. The violent act was aimed at attaining a political, economic, religious, or social goal;

   2. The violent act included evidence of an intention to coerce, intimidate, or convey some other message to a larger audience (or audiences) other than the immediate victims; and

   3. The violent act was outside the precepts of International Humanitarian Law (Global Terrorism Database)."

definitions. Thus, the term "terrorism" and "terrorists" largely belongs to the language of ordinary or political life, which easily results in confusion when used for scientific purposes (Wieviorka 1993).

From a conflict resolution point, labeling a party as "terrorist" leads to a strong normative statement, such as "you shall not negotiate with terrorists" – which actually may be a public posture while allowing for simultaneous, secret negotiations. The term is also used to call for unity behind one side. An example is the announcement by US President George W. Bush, Jr. on September 20, 2001: "Either you are with us, or you are with the terrorists." Indeed, the post-September 11, 2001 term "war on terrorism" spurred further confusion, especially when it comes to distinctions between "terrorism," "war," "rebellion," and "insurgency," as well as between non-state terrorism and "state terror." There is still no formally agreed international legal definition at the UN level. A 2011 overview lists 260 different definitions of terrorism (Schmid 2011).

This does not mean, however, the identifying terrorism is an impossible task. While most experts acknowledge the highly context-specific nature of multiple forms and manifestations of terrorism, mainstream terrorism research is at least in agreement on terrorism as a violent tactic to achieve political goals, broadly defined to include sociopolitical, ideological, or religious motivations. It is important to stress that terrorism itself is not a society-building philosophy or religion, comparable for instance, to liberalism, socialism, nationalism, Christianity, Islam, or Hinduism. To both perpetrators and observers it is a deliberate choice of a tactical option, where there in fact are alternatives. For the victims, however, terrorism is a human disaster, involving death and destruction for purposes not understood or shared by victims.

A common thread in most definitions is that terrorism involves actions that aim at civilians and other "soft targets" (non-combatants in conflict areas, civilian-dressed soldiers at vacation spots, people at civilian workplaces, public transportation, restaurants, hotels, schools, markets, sporting and entertainment events, religious services, etc.). It is the immediate target of violence – civilians (non-combatants) – that distinguishes terroristic actions from armed attacks against national or foreign government military and security forces or the capturing of geographical points for strategic or tactical reason. However, what is labeled terrorist action could also refer to military targets. Early examples are from Beirut in 1983, when two terrorist attacks killed soldiers at the American Embassy and in the French "Drakkar" building; it was also the case with 9/11 in Washington, DC where Pentagon was a target.

This is what insurgency or guerrilla warfare is about. It is the duty of governments to provide safety for the general public, and thus a typical terrorist ambition is to demonstrate that the government is not capable to deliver its part of the social contract. Attacks against "soft targets" are also meant to serve as staged, dramatic news-setting events for communicating the terrorists' message as widely as possible through real-time information flows, thus, creating a broader sense of insecurity and putting pressure on the state (or a group of states, international organization, or the world at large).

These three definitional criteria of terrorism – (1) a tactic choice to achieve a political goal, (b) through the use or threat of violence against civilians, (3) employed as an asymmetrical, "violent communication" tool – are summed up in the Working Definition used in this chapter and presented in Box 10.2. Box 10.2 includes three different definitions that seem to be in frequent use.

Two of the definitions in Box 10.2 are general, whereas the third one from the Global Terrorism Database (GTD) is operational with clear definitions, where it is enough if two of the three criteria are met. It

---

13   For more detail, see Stepanova (2008), pp. 5–13.

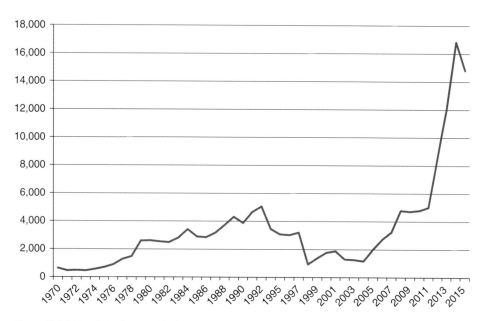

Figure 10.4 | Terrorist incidents worldwide, 1970–2015.
Source: Global Terrorism Database, National Consortium for the Study of Terrorism and Responses to Terrorism, University of Maryland. www.start.umd.edu/data/gtd.

may make for a longer list of cases. Also it risks including situations that are not entirely comparable. Still, the data from GTD constitutes basic information for this section and is used in the following figures and tables.

The most serious objection to all three definitions in Box 10.2 is that they do not cover political violence by states (Schmid 2011: 86–87). State terrorism, thus, is left as a phenomenon of its own. It is not difficult to document that a number of governments pursue actions targeting civilians for political purposes, which thus also could be seen as terroristic in methods and intentions.[14] Another complaint is that these definitions can be applied under occupation and, thus, possibly, define what is legally accepted resistance against occupation as terrorism. This objection is often heard from representatives of Palestine or other Arab countries.

This has led to the development of the notion of "one-sided violence" by the Uppsala Conflict Data Program, and that has been used in the heading above. When applied to situations of violence it becomes clear that states are highly responsible for a considerable share of such actions. Indeed, leaders of non-state actors targeting civilians often excuse this by referring to government actions. This is important, as there often is an interaction between the terror used by governments and by the armed opposition groups. Regimes based on terror often breed oppositional terror, which in turn may serve to reinforce the use

of terror by regimes. This may result in seemingly never-ending action–reaction cycles, where both sides see the defeat of the other as the only way out.

As mentioned the data presented here stems from the Global Terrorism Database at the University of Maryland (GTD). Figure 10.4 shows that the world in the mid-2010s finds itself at unprecedentedly high levels of terrorist actions. This is true for the period when statistics were available, i.e. since 1970. The year 2014 seems to have hit an all-time high. The number of terrorist incidents (16,840) and fatalities (32,765) exceeded those of the year 2000 by almost 10 times.[15] The year 2015 saw a minor decline in terrorist incidents and fatalities. Still, it was the second deadliest year on record.[16] The economic impact of these actions is not negligible.[17]

While no state is immune to violent extremism,[18] in the early twenty-first century much of global terrorist activity was concentrated to two regions – the Middle East and South Asia (Figure 10.5). In 2014, five countries were the scenes for 78 percent of all terrorism fatalities worldwide and for 57 percent of all terrorist attacks.[19] In 2000–2014, Western states saw 2.6 percent of all terrorist fatalities and 4.4 percent of terrorist attacks.[20] There was a decline in activity that might be attributed to the relative weakening of the Islamic State (ISIL) in Iraq and Boko Haram in Nigeria. We can note that many of these movements combine systematic use of terrorist means with active

---

[14] Early work on this was Stohl 1988.

[15] Ibid.

[16] With a global total of 14,806 terrorist incidents and 29,376 fatalities, 2015 was a 12 percent and 10 percent decline, respectively, from all-time peak numbers in 2014. See also the Global Terrorism Index (GTI 2016), p. 2 and Stohl (1988). Deterioration of the terrorism situation in several other countries resulted in the overall increase in Global Terrorism Index score for 2016 by 6 percent.

[17] In 2014, 16,818 terrorist attacks and 32,658 fatalities were registered, compared to 1,778 attacks and 3,329 fatalities in 2000. Economic damage reached USD 52.9 billion, compared to USD 4.93 billion in 2000 (GTI 2015: 2, 9, 63; GTI 2016).

[18] In 2014, terrorism affected 93 out of 162 countries as rated by the Global Terrorism Index.

[19] GTI 2015, p. 4.

[20] Ibid., p. 49.

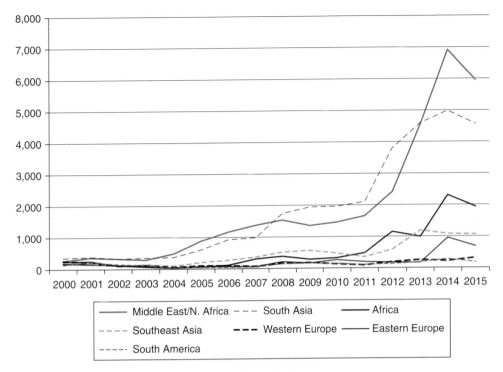

Figure 10.5 | Terrorist attacks by region (top seven regions), 2000–2015.
Source: Global Terrorism Database, National Consortium for the Study of Terrorism and Responses to Terrorism, University of Maryland. www.start.umd.edu/data/gtd.

combat, state-building ambitions, and social experiments in major armed conflicts, i.e. conflicts that have been mentioned in the previous section.

However, one of the main specifics of terrorism is that quantitative parameters do not fully reflect the political significance and impact of terrorist attacks. In the age of globalization and continuing rapid development of information and communication technologies, the capacity of violence to affect politics becomes more important than its actual scale and direct harm. For instance, destabilizing effect of terrorism on international politics and security largely depend on the comparative "centrality" of a specific context to global politics. Furthermore, in contrast to the trends in terrorism in its main regional centers, we can observe that after 2014, Europe in particular has seen the sharpest spike ever, with the largest increase in France and Turkey.[21] Attacks on centers of Western European centers gains global attention through international media and produce asymmetrical global resonances far exceeding the international effect from the more frequent and deadly attacks in, for instance, Baghdad, Kabul, Lahore, or Mogadishu.

There is today a large set of approaches to terrorism. It is not enough to say that it is a communication-oriented form of political violence, which is tailored to the information-intense post-industrial societies and their vulnerabilities, since its targets can be located in other societies. Some focus on select "root causes" considering that each form of terrorism is an outcome of certain combinations of factors – some of

which may be more fundamental than others (Bjorgo 2005; Crenshaw 2010). They may differentiate between *structural*, or *macro-level drivers* (demographic imbalances, globalization, "traumatic" modernization and relative deprivation, transitional societies, social alienation, and marginalization of segments of the population), *facilitating factors* (symbiotic relationship between terrorism and mass media, advances in weapons and information technology, weak state control of territory, interconnections with crime), and the more direct and context-specific *motivational causes* (discrimination and other grievances among a subgroup, elite dissatisfaction, lack of opportunity for political participation, or human rights abuse). Some look for and combine, where appropriate, explanations *at different levels of social structure* – at the individual psycho-sociological level, the social group, societal (national), and systemic (international) levels.

An important dimension of terrorism is its relationship with any kind of meaning. In many cases, terrorism is more violent and unlimited when the actors speak artificially in the name of a people, a class, a Nation, when they act far from any real social or cultural group. This was the case, for instance, in the 1970s and the 1980s with extreme-left terrorists were acting on behalf of the working class, while real workers didn't recognize their demands in their murders. Today, Islamic terrorist frequently want to die, and not only to kill, and there are important debates among scholars in order to know what actually comes first: religion, including martyrdom; or radicalization due to social and cultural factors.[22] Sometimes, too, the relationship

---

[21]   The OECD countries showed a 650 times increase in deaths from terrorism, from 77 in 2014 to 577 in 2015 (GTI 2016: 4).

[22]   See, for instance, the debate between the two main French specialists, Gilles Kepel and Olivier Roy. Kepel considers religion to be the core of Islamic terrorism, while Roy is much more interested in the social making of radicalized people. See de Bellaigue (2017).

to meaning is so strange that scholars introduce psychiatric or psycho-analytical explanations (Benslama 2016).

This implies an important point for those that deal with the importance of finding ways of ending violence: if terrorism is such a complex phenomenon, then, excessively mono-dimensional and simple approaches will necessarily fail. For instance, war with IS may be considered as necessary in order to end Islamic terrorism in many countries, but it will not solve the psycho-sociological problems or the domestic sociological crisis that make martyrdom and extreme violence attractive to many young people in these countries.

Trends in contemporary terrorism include bottom-up processes of expansion of a militant-terrorist actor from the more local to the regional, transnational, and geopolitical levels. Some of today's most deadly militant-terrorist actors went through this trajectory. A prime example is the Islamic State of Iraq and Levant (ISIL), which started as a Sunni-based reaction to Shia control in Iraq, later entered the Syria civil war and then began drawing attraction across the Middle East (e.g. Libya and Sinai in Egypt) as well as attracting individuals in Western Europe, North Africa, and North America joining them due to logics of action mainly rooted in their own countries. Boko Haram in Nigeria began as a local revolt in Northern Nigeria and later reached out to other parts of Western Africa. Many of these radical movements combine terror with actual territorial control. Many aim at changes in the government of their own states, rather than inviting a confrontation with the West (unlike IS and al-Qaeda). For a period these movements entered into a loose alliance. As can be seen in Figure 10.5 some of these movements are involved in a large share of all terrorist deeds.

Some analysts see terrorism in the Western world as an emergence of small, self-generating militant-terrorist cells, autonomous "lone wolves." The main "glue" for such networks are universalist radical anti-system ideologies (in the early twenty-first century, at the global level this role has been played by ideology of "global jihad"). Fragmented cells and networks emerge and operate in many countries, and may be found among homegrown, but religiously inspired jihadist followers in the West. One must be careful with the notion of "lone wolves:" in most cases, the so called "lone wolf" of the first moments after a terrorist attack appears in further police and justice investigations, not to be so "lone."

One must also note that radical Islam doesn't have a monopoly on contemporary terrorism. There can be other religions with similar phenomena – Hinduism, for instance. And some actions may have nothing to do with religion, and instead be connected to nationalist ideologies, or extreme-right motivations. The concern over "foreign fighters" has been great in Western Europe, building on cases of individuals that are radicalized, move to IS-controlled territory and then return, ready to carry out terrorist acts in major centers. The centers of gravity for this circulation of militants seem to correspond to areas of protracted armed conflicts.

Finally, it is worth keeping in mind that the dynamic interaction of asymmetrical and communication functions of terrorism may also take unexpected forms, depart from established patterns and generate new types and manifestations of threats that are hard to predict or forecast.

This means that the task of reducing terrorism cannot be confined to protection against expected terrorist threats only. It also requires identifying *structural weaknesses* of a sociopolitical system that is under terrorist threat(s) and increasing general political, ideological, social, and security resilience *of the system itself*, thus genuinely contributing to social progress.

To this can be added – as stated in the introduction of this chapter – another important point: if violence, particularly in its most extreme form such as terrorism, is more frequently the opposite to social movements, non-armed conflicts, i.e. to constructive change, then, the reduction of terrorism should be sought through re-inventing or re-launching of debates between actors able to talk and negotiate with each other. This could be true at all levels, including the transnational one, and this should combine different levels of action – something that is not easy to achieve.

10.2.2.2   One-Sided Violence: Mass Murder and Genocide

Coined in 1944 by Raphael Lemkin in order to analyze the crimes committed towards Armenians by the Turkish power, the massacres of Assyrians in Iraq in 1933 and the destruction of European Jews by the Nazis, the concept of genocide received international stature on December 9, 1948, when the Convention for the Prevention and Punishment of the Crime of Genocide was adopted by the United Nations General Assembly. The parties to the convention state that genocide is a crime under international law that they "undertake to prevent and to punish" (Article I). It provides that genocide is a set of acts with the "intent to destroy, whole or in part, a national, ethnical, racial or religious group" (Article II). Thus, it is a strong commitment and, by now, all the Permanent Members of the Security Council have ratified this convention.

The study of genocide was not developed academically until the 1980s, with work by Helen Fein (1979) on the one hand and Ted Gurr and the Minorities and Risk project on the other (1993). Certainly, the pursuit of the Nazi criminals continued, but most energetically only by Israel, as demonstrated by the spectacular capture of Adolf Eichmann and the subsequent trial, or by some individuals such as Serge and Beate Klarsfeld, campaigning for instance in 1986 against Kurt Waldheim, a former officer in the Wehrmacht before becoming the Austrian's president. Still, the Cold War period (from 1955 to 1990) saw 33 events that met the definition of genocide (and politicide) according to data published by Barbara Harff (2003). However, the descriptions of the time were not in these terms. Events listed by Harff include genocides during the wars in Sudan, Vietnam, and Tibet, as well as mass persecutions in Iraq, Indonesia, and Cambodia. The leading actors of the Cold War, in a remarkable way, were not giving the same attention to the sufferings of peoples in the many conflicts that together constituted this global conflagration between East and West. Their strategic significance in the struggle was all that mattered. The issue was not about the human consequences but whether a victory would be to the benefit of the Soviet Union or the West (or China). This overriding question neglected the sufferings that were an integral part, indeed the necessary element, in the conflict: people were killed, starved, turned into

10

refugees, and succumbed to famine and epidemics. Outside powers poured weapons, soldiers, expertise, intelligence, and funding to "their" respective sides. The long-term argument was that "when our side wins" the conditions would be so much better for all, and that would outweigh all the suffering.

Thus, only with the end of the Cold War could the issue of genocide again take its appropriate place in academia and international politics. The experiences of Bosnia (1992–1995) and Rwanda (1994) again convincingly demonstrated the relevance of the notion of genocide and the fact that contemporary situations were covered by the genocide definition: There was the intention to actually eliminate/exterminate national, ethnical, racial and religious groups in whole or in part.

Harff 2017 provides an operation definition. It may be argued that her work from 2003 is still the most important study. Data provided by UCDP demonstrates that genocides with considerable civilian fatalities are not a daily occurrence, as is the case with other forms of violence. The graph in Figure 10.3 demonstrates this very strongly: Rwanda constitutes a distinctive event. Certainly, the wars over Bosnia-Herzegovina 1992–1995 have also had a genocidal character, particularly associated with the term "ethnic cleansing." This resulted in mass population movements within and across borders and severe human victimhood. As both these examples demonstrate, however, genocide is often linked to other political developments, notably armed conflicts (Wallensteen, Melander, and Möller 2012). The Rwandan genocide took place in the midst of a civil war and the massacre of young Muslims in Srebrenica was an element in an ongoing war in the region. Thus, a predictor of genocide may very well be the existence of an armed conflict in the first place. The origins of genocide are also touched in Section 10.2.3.8.

10.2.2.3   One-Sided Violence: Targeted Eliminations – Efficiency, Legality, and Ethics

Consolidated democratic government can also resort to actions that are close to the definitions of terror, targeting and killing particular individuals without the resort to customary rules of law. Targeted killing is "the intentional, premeditated and deliberate use of lethal force, by States or their agents acting under color of law, or by an organized armed group in armed conflict, against a specific individual who is not in the physical custody of the perpetrator" (UN Human Rights Council 2010: 3). Illustrated today by the strikes conducted – mostly by drones, by the United States and Israel, for example – on suspected terrorists, such a practice has triggered a virulent academic and public debate on at least two questions.

First, its efficiency: On the one hand, its opponents pretend it is ineffective because the person killed would be immediately replaced, because terrorist organizations are adapting, flattening their organization, less hierarchical, and centralized, therefore less vulnerable to decapitation, and because of the cost of the operation (one targeted

killing at the right place and the right time necessitate a permanent deployment of intelligence, aircrafts, men, etc.). It would even be counterproductive, as it would trigger retaliation, create martyrs that strengthen cohesion of the adversary, make collateral damage that also reinforce its popular legitimacy and have a recruiting effect, and complicate peace negotiations.

On the other hand, its proponents respond that targeted persons are not that easily replaced, as leaders, recruiters, experts in explosives, etc., often have rare qualities and they are in limited numbers. Arresting or killing them disrupts the organization for a certain time. It is plausible to assume that the efficiency of the targeted killings therefore depend on their frequency: Frequent strikes allow no time for the organization to recruit and train, and are therefore more disrupting. Furthermore, retaliation is not systematic, does not always have the means to be very lethal, and is not always easy to distinguish from an attack that would have occurred anyway.

Second, its legality. In the context of an armed conflict, international humanitarian law (IHL) applies: Targeted killing may be legal if the target is a combatant or a civilian participating directly in hostilities, if it is necessary, proportional, and all precautions must be taken to minimize damage to civilians. In the absence of armed conflict, however, international human rights law applies and the state is allowed to kill only if necessary to protect life and if there is no other means, such as capture or neutralization, to prevent the threat. Targeted killing, in the sense of an intentional, premeditated and deliberate killing, is illegal because, unlike in wartime, in peacetime it is never allowed to have the sole purpose to kill.

Therefore, the crux of the matter is to know if the strikes – often drone strikes – are taking place in or outside the framework of an armed conflict. The problem of course, is that the definition of armed conflict is ambiguous, a declaration of war has never been a good indicator of a state of war, and the evolution of conflicts, particularly with the multiplication of transnational non-state armed groups such as ISIS and Boko Haram puts many situations into very grey areas, as has been discussed earlier in this chapter. If using the UCDP definition, as done here, many of these strikes may be found in the context of armed conflict, however.

Many states practice targeted killings but only two publicly acknowledge a targeted killings policy, Israel and the United States.[23] They have a similar normative framework, based on a rather extensive interpretation of self-defense, and criteria such as the primacy of capture, and respect for IHL. Their framework redefines imminence: someone who has already attacked, from which it can be assumed that he intends to attack again, and who has the ability to do so is considered an imminent threat. It is no longer necessary to have an even vague idea of the time, place, or nature of the attack: it is assumed that any alleged member of al-Qaeda is "continuously" planning an attack. A question is, however, how such a case can be brought to a court, where and with what consequences?

---

[23]   In media and other accounts, certain regimes notably those in North Korea (a recent example is the lethal attack on Kim Jong Un's half-brother in the airport of Kuala Lumpur, March 2017) and Russia/Soviet Union; have been accused of conducting such actions outside their own territories, against individuals they fear.

10.2.3 Violence in Societies

10.2.3.1 Framework

Violence can be seen as a demonstration of *power* (Imbusch 2003). It can manifest as the violation or destruction of the physical and psychological integrity of killed or injured persons or groups, or in threat to or destruction of a social order. Violence is always also characterized by *ambiguity* (Heitmeyer and Hagan 2003) when it comes to defining the diversity of its expressions, in the sense of what different cultures define as violence. There is no equivocation, however, in the case of killing of people, whether by an individual murderer, political groups, or actors under state authority.

Social progress depends on reducing threatened and actual criminal, political, and state killings of individuals and groups. There is, however, a specific *ambivalence* of violence, especially in connection with social progress: for example, where the removal of a murderous social order by individual or collective violence leads to dramatic escalation in society and potentially even civil war. Any member of society may become a victim, above all weak groups and minorities. In this section we single out the type of violence that is not directly seen as political or organized for political purposes, such as armed conflicts and one-sided violence that we have dealt with in Sections 10.2.1 and 10.2.2.

10.2.3.2 Human Development and Violence

Violent deaths can be disaggregated into three distinct forms: conflict-related, non-conflict-related, and suicides (UNODC 2013: 9). With non-conflict-related violence (Section 10.2.3.3) and suicide (Section 10.2.3.5) we focus on the most frequent instances. Conflict-related violence is the subject of other sections of this chapter. The approach in this section is to depart from the fact that countries can be categorized according to their level of human development (UNDP 2013). We combine such levels of development with different forms of violence to identify chances of social progress.

First, this means the *prevalence* of homicide in societies (Section 10.2.3.3) and cities (Section 10.2.3.4), suicide (Section 10.2.3.5), domestic violence (Section 10.2.3.6) school shootings (Section 10.2.3.7), violence against minorities (Section 10.2.3.8), organized crime and violence (Section 10.2.3.9), and right-wing violence (Section 10.2.3.10). The available datasets, maintained for example by the United Nations Office on Drugs and Crime (UNODC), the World Health Organization (WHO), and the World Bank, suffer various validity problems, especially in relation to the regions worst affected by crisis and violence.

Second, the extent of such violence is known to differ depending on the *social constellation*, in the sense of different *structural* levels of integration opportunities, living conditions, and danger to life. Several indices have been developed to enable international comparison of life chances. Economic development (GDP, GNI), human development (Human Development Index, HDI), and inequality (Gini coefficient) are prominent predictors of homicide rates (Nivette 2011: 117; Ouimet 2012: 239ff.; Pridemore 2011: 742ff.). The HDI was developed to counter a one-sided overemphasis on the economic, adding the categories of education and health to the economic dimension (GNI). It does not, however, address distribution within society (inequality).

That is achieved by the Inequality-Adjusted Human Development Index (IHDI), which supplies the best available measurement of social development taking account of inequality (Peterson 2013). This is therefore the index used in the following to compare development levels with homicide rates, seeking a macro-sociological background for the explanation of deadly violence (Messner 2003: 701f.).

In the question of a connection between HDI and homicide rates, research has produced diverging findings. Most studies, however, confirm that homicides decline as development increases (Altheimer 2008: 110; Cao and Zhang 2015; Lee and Pridmore 2014: 114f.; Messner, Raffalovich, and Shrock 2002; Nivette 2011: 118f.). The point of interest now is what happens to that relationship when application of the IHDI introduces the additional factor of inequality, which to our knowledge has never been examined.

Third, the various manifestations of violence occur in different *sociospatial contexts*, the places where people live (by choice or compulsion), with their respective integration opportunities and disintegration risks. Here, in the context of global urbanization, the focus is on urban areas, as this is where the greatest opportunities for social integration and hopes for a better life appear to exist. Whether such expectations can be fulfilled depends to a significant extent on the structural development of the country in which the urban area is located. For this reason, the IHDI is compared with the homicide rates of the most dangerous cities, in order to arrive at findings about level of development and living conditions.

Finally, the *limits* of such analyses must always be noted. These include a frequent lack of the long-term data required to identify social trends in structural development, rates of violence, and urban living conditions (Fearon 2011: 4). This also applies to change over time, for example when state violence increases or decreases after the political order changes, or a civil war breaks out or ends.

10.2.3.3 Human Development and Homicide Rates

The homicide rate is a reasonable indicator of the extent of violence in a society (Cao and Zhang 2015: 3; Marshall and Summers 2012: 39; Messner 2003: 701f.; Nivette 2011: 104 and 106; Ouimet 2012: 244; Smit, de Jong, and Bijleveld 2012: 5; UNODC 2013: 11). Among available datasets the WHO data enjoy great international recognition and are regarded as relatively valid (Cao and Zhang 2015: 8; Koeppel, Rhineberger-Dunn, and Mack 2015: 51; LaFree 1999: 133; Levchak 2016: 8; Messner et al. 2002: 383; Messner et al. 2011: 67), and will therefore serve as the principal basis for the following discussion.[24]

---

[24]   WHO Global Health Observatory Homicide Estimates 2012.

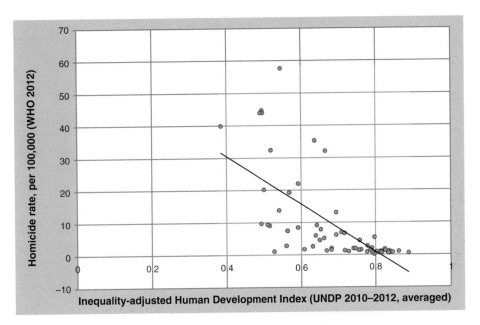

Figure 10.6 | Scatterplot of homicide rate and IHDI, correlation −.816** (n = 65).
Note: ** Correlations significant at 0.01 level (two-tailed).
Source: calculations by Kanis, Heitmeyer, and Blome; IKG/University of Bielefeld/Germany.

Table 10.1 | Homicide rate by development group (IHDI) (n = 132)

IHDI 2012		
Human development[a]	Number of countries	Mean homicide rate (WHO 2012) and standard deviation
Very high	19	1.2 (1.1)
High	17	2.8 (2.1)
Medium	29	8.5 (10.1)
Low	67	13.6 (15.8)
Total	132	9.3 (13.2)

[a] Based on HDI fixed cut-off values.

An initial exploration of the relationship between IHDI and homicide rate in a sample of 65 countries found a significant correlation of −.816 (Figure 10.6).[25] Noteworthy is the much higher variation in homicides within the group of countries with a low IHDI. Contrary this exhibits a considerable convergence in homicide rates as the inequality-adjusted human development increases.

When inequality is taken into consideration, it is found that the mean homicide rate decreases as level of development (IHDI) increases (see Table 10.1).[26] The value in the least developed group is 11 times that of the most developed.

Moving on, the IHDI allows us to investigate the loss of development attributable to inequality, finding almost all the countries with the greatest losses to be in sub-Saharan Africa. Of the 33 countries concerned, only 5 are outside that region.[27] The mean homicide rate in these countries is 12.1 (SD 8.3), more than six times the rate for countries with the smallest losses.

In this context, social progress – especially for the younger generation – occurs where there is an absence of temporary or permanent experiences of disintegration (manifested above all in social inequality, poverty, poor educational opportunities, and lack of health care). The dangers of social disintegration consist in interpersonal violence offering an option for changing personal and/or group-specific living conditions. Another relevant factor is the way new means of communication enable social comparisons to be made, in the sense of learning how young people are able to live in societies with higher levels of development. The other alternative is to direct violence against the self. These two forms of violence find their strongest expression in homicide, respectively suicide.

To put this into perspective, 79 percent of all homicide victims and 95 percent of all perpetrators are male (UNODC 2013: 13). The high proportion of male perpetrators is consistent across all countries. The proportion of female victims is correspondingly smaller at 21 percent, of which the 15–29 age group accounts for 8 percent (UNODC 2013: 14). Another mentionable difference between men and women is the context in which homicides occur. While men are mostly killed in public spaces and by unknown perpetrators almost half of all female homicide victims are murdered by intimate partners or family members (UNODC 2013: 14).

---

25   Spearman on grounds of lack of normal distribution of variables (Pearson with logarithmic homicide rate shows a similar result of −.770). Estimates based on homicides from vital registration and criminal justice data (WHO 2014a: 62ff.).

26   Note: The following statistics employ WHO homicide rates with adjusted and model-based estimates to cover more nations (WHO 2014a: 62ff.). While it is not advisable to use these types of estimates for inferential analysis it is feasible to use them for description. Nonetheless, model-based estimates should be interpreted with caution (Kanis et al. 2017).

27   Based on IHDI quartiles.

10

Table 10.2 | Homicide victims, rate by age group and sex

Homicide victims: rate per 100,000 population		
Age group	Male	Female
0–14	2.0	1.9
15–29	16.7	3.8
30–44	14.4	3.1
45–60	8.6	2.1
60+	5.6	2.4
Total	9.7	2.7

Source: UNODC 2013: 28ff.

The young are over-represented among homicide victims: Homicide rates are highest within the age group 15–29 (Table 10.2). Given the global population distribution, 43 percent of the victims are aged 15–29, while including victims aged under 15 increases the figure to 51 percent (UNODC 2013: 14). Thus in 2012 more than half of the 437,000 homicide victims were children, adolescents or young adults (UNODC 2013: 11). It must always be remembered that survivors experience temporary or permanent physical and/or psychological harm that negatively affects their prospects of social integration.

While victims can be distinguished by demography, differentiation is not possible for questions of involvement in crime or gangs, or status as victim of politically, ethnically, or religiously motivated violence. The data for perpetuators is even more deficient (UNODC 2014: 91).

As already noted, 43 percent of homicide victims are aged 15–29. In combination with the high homicide rates in Central and South America, this means that about 14 percent of all male homicide victims worldwide are persons aged 15–29 in that region (UNODC 2013: 13). The reasons for this are gang-related crime, narcotics trafficking and drug consumption (including alcohol), post-conflict situations, and the availability of arms, anchored in a societal culture of violence (Cao and Zhang 2015: 6; Cole and Gramajo 2009: 766; Del Felice 2008: 83f.; Neapolitan 1994: 5f.; Waldmann 2007: 62ff.). Networking between organized crime, politics, and elites exacerbates the situation, while capital generated by criminal violence flows into charitable causes, undermining state structures (Rodgers and Jones 2009: 7). Deadly violence becomes a "successful" business model. In some contexts, like in Mexico, this model has been more prevalent while the state appeared increasingly weaker and more corrupt. Violence, in some Latin American countries, was highly political in the 1960s, 1970s, and 1980s, it is now highly criminal. More generally, war and terror may include or open the way to more classical criminal violence, connected, for instance, to drug traffic.

10.2.3.4   Homicide Rates and Urbanization

While 43 percent of the global population lived in cities by the 1990s, the proportion rose to 54 percent by 2015 (UN-Habitat 2016: 6). The UN forecasts that by 2050, 66 percent of the world's population will be urban (UN 2015c: 1). This lends the urban living environment special importance for the question of social development. Cities form magnets – especially for young people willing to migrate – where social integration (or at least temporary integration into the labor market) secures the individual's economic reproduction and social recognition.

There does not appear to be any clear connection between urbanization and homicide rates. Most of the studies that have investigated this question find neither a positive nor a negative link (Levchak 2016: 5). There is discussion as to whether the growth process is a more relevant factor than the level of urbanization, in the sense of rural–urban migration driving the urbanization process generating competition for resources and greater anonymity – and with it increased willingness to pursue criminality (Cole and Gramajo 2009: 754). Such urban environments can thus become both attractive and dangerous when integration mechanisms fail to function. This creates a source of violence, especially by young men, in particular where culturally anchored norms of masculinity exclude failure.

The tension between the attraction of supposedly diverse opportunities in highly differentiated urban areas and frequently empty promises of a better life by legal means creates the breeding ground for aggression, where individual criminal violence and collective deadly violence represent significant options. The role of education, especially where migrants originate from rural areas, and ever-present comparisons with lives and possibilities in other parts of the world conveyed via the new media represent important background conditions.

Relating the major cities with the highest homicide rates (CCSPJP 2016: 3f.) to the findings using the IHDI concept, it is found that 13 of the 15 most dangerous cities in the 2015 ranking are geographically located in Central and South America (Figure 10.7). With the exception of the United States, all these cities are located in countries with a low level of development, according to the IHDI concept.

10.2.3.5   Suicide in Social Contexts

Suicide has to be seen in the societal and social context with a broad spectrum of risk factors. The WHO Report (2014b: 31) shows this including mental disorder as one factor. Even before homicide, suicide is one of the most frequent causes of death among adolescents and young adults (WHO 2014b: 3). The following descriptions are derived from WHO (2014b) suicide data for 130 nations.[28] Groups of countries can be categorized as follows: *very high* and *high* development 18 nations each, *medium* development 28, *low* development 66.[29] The total number of suicides in 2012 is estimated at 804,000 ((WHO 2014b: 7), with the number of attempts put 20 times higher ((WHO 2014b: 9). Globally, young men are more likely to kill themselves than women of the same age. Considering the values for both genders for the 15–29 age group, the suicide rate for males (14.5) is almost three times higher than for females (5.3). Within the same age group the values for males are relatively evenly distributed across development levels ranging from 13.5 to 16.0 and an average of 14.7. The female rate is less clear-cut with suicide rates ranging from 3.5 to 6.6 across development categories. It

---

[28]   The WHO report lists 172 countries. Due to deletion of cases no HDI/IHDI value is available for the count reduces to 130.

[29]   Based on HDI fixed cut-off values.

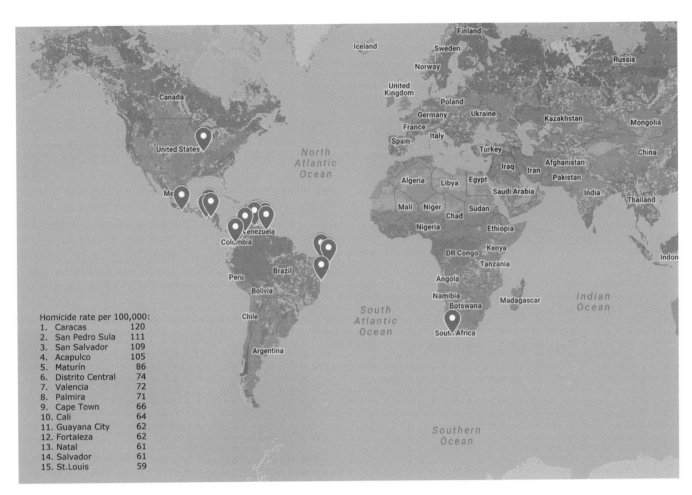

Homicide rate per 100,000:
1. Caracas   120
2. San Pedro Sula   111
3. San Salvador   109
4. Acapulco   105
5. Maturín   86
6. Distrito Central 74
7. Valencia   72
8. Palmira   71
9. Cape Town   66
10. Cali   64
11. Guayana City   62
12. Fortaleza   62
13. Natal   61
14. Salvador   61
15. St.Louis   59

Figure 10.7 | The 15 most dangerous cities, 2015.
Source: CCSPJP 2016.

is notable that the rate in less developed nations (6.6) is almost twice the rate for high developed countries (3.5). However, a general pattern is not identifiable, since the second highest rate is found in the very high developed nations. That is not so for the general suicide rate (10.0), which is noticeably higher in countries with high (15.9) or very high (12.8) development than in countries with medium (9.7) or low (7.7) development. In comparison with the homicide rate, it is of interest that this finding shows the opposite relationship to IHDI level.

Although the number of suicides is estimated to be almost twice that of homicides, it is less suited as an indicator of violence. As a rule, the recording of suicide is more complex. In certain countries suicide is illegal or taboo, leading to its prevalence being underestimated, especially in countries where registration is incomplete (WHO 2014b: 7). As complex as the recording are the explanations for suicide, with causes ranging from geographical to biological, psychological, and sociocultural factors. The figures for suicide rates clearly illustrate that high development and relatively low inequality are not the same as the absence of violence (Wilkinson and Pickett 2009).

10.2.3.6   Domestic Violence

Domestic violence is a complex phenomenon. It includes child maltreatment, violence in intimate relationships, homicide of intimates,

elder abuse, etc. It is known that violence in intimate relationships is extensive and not limited to one socioeconomic group, one society, one culture, or one time period. Researchers have found violence and abuse in every type of intimate relationship (Gelles 2003). The question of the extent of family violence has not been easy to answer and still leads to contentious debates over the scientific adequacy and rigor of incidence and prevalence estimates (Sommers 1994).

There are several social risk factors to take into account. One of the most consistent is the age of offenders. Violence is most likely to be perpetrated by those between 18 and 30 years of age. As is the case with non-intimate violence, the offenders in acts of intimate violence are generally male. Although most poor parents and partners do not use violence toward intimates, self-report surveys and official report data find that the rates of all forms of family violence, except sexual abuse, are higher for those whose family incomes are below the poverty line than for those above the poverty line (Gelles 2003: 850).

The situational and environmental factors related to violence include stress, unemployment, being a teenage mother, and sexual difficulties. Additional factors include social isolation and a lack of social support (Gelles and Straus 1988). A special problem is the intergenerational transmission of violence (Kaufman and Zigler 1987).

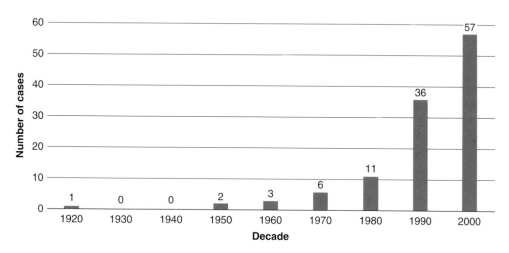

Figure 10.8 | Rampage school shootings worldwide by decade.
Source: Böckler et al. 2013: 10.

One of the most important risk factors for violence against women is gender inequality. Individual, aggregate, and cross-cultural data find that the greater the degree of gender inequality in a relationship, community, and society, the higher the rates of violence toward women (Browne and Williams 1993; Levinson 1989; Morley 1994).

10.2.3.7 School Shootings in the Spectrum of Multiple Homicides

Holmes and Holmes (1998) distinguished three basic categories of multiple homicide: serial killings, spree killings, and mass murders. Rampage killings are a subcategory of mass murder. School shootings are mostly committed by adolescent perpetrators and occur at school or in a school-related place. They wish to take revenge on the community, or to experience or demonstrate power (Sweatt et al. 2002; Newman et al. 2004).

The frequency of the phenomenon has clearly increased over the past decades (Figure 10.8).

In terms of geographical distribution, by the end of 2011 the US total had reached 76 (63 percent of all recorded cases) while there had been 44 cases in the rest of the world (37 percent). It is conspicuous that school shootings occur predominantly in highly developed industrial countries; the three with the highest totals, the United States, Germany, and Canada, are among the world's most economically prosperous nations.

That leads to the question of explanations. Several theories seek to explain the phenomenon: Social Disintegration Theory stresses the lack of recognition (Böckler et al. 2013; Heitmeyer and Anhut 2008), while others focus on the role of the media (Muschert and Ragnedda 2011; Muschert and Sumiala 2012), the Strain Theory (Levin and Madfis 2012), or the adolescent culture (Newman et al. 2004). Muschert (2007) notes that school shooting incidents need to be understood as resulting from a constellation of contributing causes.[30]

10.2.3.8 Group-Focused Enmity, Hate Speech, and Violence Against Minorities

Violence against minorities is a cause of great worldwide tragedies (Gurr 1993; Gurr and Pitsch 2003). It affects people without distinction of age and gender. The continuum of escalation begins with *Group-Focused Enmity* (Heitmeyer 2002; Zick, Küpper, and Heitmeyer 2009), under which people become targets for devaluation, discrimination, and violence purely on the basis of their chosen or externally attributed group membership, without heed to individual behavior. The legitimacy of this form of violence derives from the ideology of unequal worth (Heitmeyer 2002), which asserts a categorization into superior majority population and inferior minority population according to "racial," ethnic, gender-based, sexual, political, and/or social attributes. The associated hate crime is widespread (Hall et al. 2015) and the role of religion in conflicts has received increased attention since the late 1990s (Fox, James, and Yitan 2009). Concerning sexual and gender-based-violence, see Section 10.2.4.

Violence against minorities always involves power interests of the majority population and its intellectual and political elites. It is fostered by attitudes of Group-Focused Enmity, which serve to legitimize violent political, ethnic, and religious extremist groups, as well as state institutions such as the police and paramilitary units.

The global situation concerning violence against minorities is unclear and it is impossible to assemble a credible empirical overview. All that can be said comparatively is that violence is greatest in those countries where the group divisions are made visible (salient) by the media and by political and intellectual elites. This violence against minorities is further encouraged where those in power succeed in initiating "either/or" conflicts where there are no compromises or negotiated solutions, but only a dichotomous choice between victory and defeat (or destruction).

Minority Rights Group International (MRG) publishes regular reports on developments concerning hate crimes and mass killings. Reservations

---

[30] See also Paton (2015), constituting innovative research based on materials extracted from YouTube.

over the validity of data – estimates in particular, although official figures must also be viewed critically – apply here too (Kanis et al. 2017). These reservations notwithstanding, we note that in 2014 a very large number of minorities in 70 countries were threatened by hate crime, violence, and mass killing (Lattimer 2014). The worst-rated countries in 2014 included Somalia, Sudan, Syria, DR Congo, Afghanistan, Iraq, Pakistan, Myanmar, Ethiopia, and Yemen. At the same time, political developments cause shifts in the rankings; in 2015 the situation worsened in the Russian Federation, Libya, Egypt, Ukraine, and China (Lattimer and Verbakel 2015).

Particular dangers are faced by ethnic minorities that are not recognized as such by the state in which they live. For example, the heavily persecuted Rohingya minority in Myanmar is not on that country's official list of 135 ethnic groups, and lacks specific protection against the police and the army. A different quality of threat arises through authoritarian regimes that feel their power is threatened by minorities, such as China and the Muslim Uigurs or Russia against minorities in the Caucasus region. But these problems also exist in democratic systems where state institutions such as the police act violently against the black population, for instance in the United States.

Another threat constellation against minorities is characterized by violence exercised by non-state groups (under the eyes of state institutions), for example when nationalist Hindus in India take violent action against the Muslim minority. Minorities in many countries will face increasing violence. This also applies to the people involved in the global refugee movements, whose future extent we can only guess at. A huge problem is the reduced effectiveness of international law, which could continue to decline to dangerously low levels if further states, in particular African states with high levels of violence, choose to withdraw from the International Criminal Court in The Hague.

10.2.3.9   Organized Crime and Violence in the Context of Migration and Development

Global migration has increased drastically. The United Nations (2016, 1) reported that the total number of migrants grew from 200 million in 2000 to 244 million in 2015. Migration flows exist in several regions of the world, have different causes, and generate diverse variations of individual and especially organized crime and violence.

In the Middle East (e.g. Syria, Iraq, Libya) a migration flow has emerged as a result of civil wars and armed conflicts forcing refugees and asylum seekers to migrate to neighboring countries and Europe. In Africa, in countries like Somalia, Nigeria, Congo, and Chad (Grawert 2008), civil wars and failed or weak states combine with low levels of development (Whitaker 2003). The main destination for migration is the North. Migrations in the Americas are often based on the consequences of civil wars (e.g. El Salvador, Honduras, Guatemala) or drug wars, e.g. Mexico or Columbia (Cantor 2014; Durand and Massey 2010; Ramírez-de-Garay 2016).

All the constellations generate different forms of crime and organized violence in the several settings: youth gangs like the Maras in El Salvador; organized drug violence, for example, in Mexico or Columbia; violent criminal networks of human traffickers who organize the migration flows from the Middle East and North Africa (and Afghanistan or Pakistan) to Europe. There are also organized, violent xenophobic and racist groups in the arrival countries, e.g. the United States, Germany, and Hungary.

While there is well-developed research on the migration-development nexus (e.g. De Haas 2012; Faist 2008; Faist, Fauser, and Kivisto, 2011), there still seems to be a deficit concerning the integration of violence research in this setting. Future research needs to incorporate the IHDI measure (see Section 10.2.3.3) as well as the homicide-urbanization link (see Section 10.2.3.4). Additionally, there is an alarming research gap concerning women and children as victims of violence in the global migration flows.

10.2.3.10   Violence by Right-Wing Extremist Groups

Right-wing extremism (political parties and movements and right-wing extremist violence) not only represents a growing threat of ideological targeting of groups (Group-Focused Enmity), it also is threatening democracies, liberal values, and the chances of social progress.

A broad spectrum of organized groups exists in Europe (see Figure 10.9) in Sweden, the United Kingdom, and Germany, in the eastern parts of Europe, and in Russia, as well as violent militias in the United States. The events of Charlottesville, Virginia, in August 2017 seem to have surprised the American public at large and led to a feeble response from the US President.

A violent form of right-wing extremism is more likely to develop where there is no political representation through political parties (Koopmans 1996). The greater the level of violence perpetrated by right-wing extremist groups, the lower the political weight attributed to legitimate power-sharing – one should nevertheless note that some extreme-right parties try to avoid any kind of violence that could affect their respectability. The French Front National, for instance, neither uses nor supports violence.

There are different theoretical approaches to explain this phenomenon. Social-psychological approaches emphasize the Authoritarian Personality (Adorno 1950) or Social Identity Theory (Tajfel 1981) to establish the ingroup–outgroup relationship. Movement Theory concepts try to explain why a collective action comes about (McAdam, Tarrow, and Tilly 1996). Deprivation Theory emphasizes the degree of disadvantage in society (Gurr 1972) as a result of social inequality. Political Culture Theory targets the attraction or failure of the democratic system, corresponding opportunities for participation, and state benefits (Sprinzak 1995). Modernization Theory approaches take as their starting point the dynamics of integration and disintegration (Anhut and Heitmeyer 2000; Wieviorka 1999).

Concerning the further development of right-wing extremist violence there is an obvious need to observe what happens with the movement of refugees to Europe.

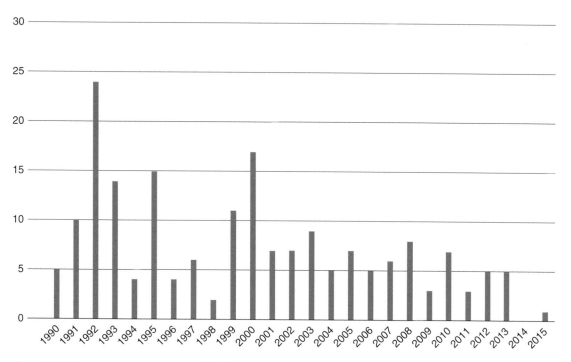

Figure 10.9 | Right-wing terrorism and violence (RTV) killing incidents across Western Europe, 1990–2015 (n = 190). Source: Ravndal (2016: 9).

10.2.3.11 Conclusion: Social Progress and the Chance of the Future Generations

Identifying favorable conditions for social progress and thus reductions in deadly violence against individuals and groups – in order to enable social and political intervention – now depends on the theoretical framing.

One starting point is the *dynamics of integration and disintegration processes* in societies with different levels of integration concerning social inequality, education, health, etc. With respect to social progress, especially for the younger generation, *Social Disintegration Theory* (SDT) (Heitmeyer and Anhut 2008) emphasizes opportunities for *reproduction* (access to employment and housing), *socialization* (individual and group access to public and political life), and *communitization* in the sense of developing personal and group identity. Where these opportunities are lacking, the probability of disintegration rises, and with it deficits in recognition that can in turn lead to violence. The dynamics of integration and disintegration processes are always also permeated by cultural and religious tradition and ethnic composition, and embedded in constellations of power and authority.

In terms of social progress and the associated decrease in violence, the societal challenges faced by political decision makers and civil society actors are extraordinarily diverse. These include preventing or minimizing an accumulation of increasing inequality and poverty, which also represent indications of social disintegration. To the extent that the data showing global poverty are declining statistically (UN 2015b: 4)

are correct (for criticisms see Klasen 2013; Reddy and Lahoti 2016), average figures for social progress and social integration are not very helpful; the IHDI concept identifies numerous societies where a low level of development is associated with high levels of violence.

This raises the question of which type of political regime impedes social progress, notably to the disadvantage of the young generation, while at the same time promoting the attraction of violence.

This applies especially in relation to *demographic developments* in societies of the Global South, where often rapidly growing young populations – for example, in Arab societies – find few legal chances for social integration and thus recognition, or none at all. Frequently the only means left for them to secure an existence is crime and violence or internal mass migration to the big cities (where their perspectives are also often uncertain), or increasing international migration from South to North – as currently occurring not only from civil war regions to Europe – in order to be able to live a decent life. This generates new conflicts, in some cases adopting violent forms. It is also an open question whether the European cities will continue to function as "integration machines."

10.2.4 Sexual and Gender-Based Violence

Sexual and gender-based violence during conflict (or "conflict-related sexual violence"),[31] has become a new focus of social science research across a range of traditions, as well as international action by the

---

[31] "Gender-based" violence is not always conflict-related sexual violence, though the terms are often conflated. Gender-based violence is defined by the Committee for the Elimination of Discrimination Against Women (CEDAW) in its General Recommendation 19 to the Convention for the Elimination of Women. It is considered a fundamental violation of women's human rights, *because* they are women (CEDAW 2006). It includes physical, emotional, economic, political, and psychological harms. It can occur in the form of a direct act, as well as by omission. The term is used in both peace and conflict settings (see CEDAW 2006 paras. 1–4). However, in this chapter, the concurrent use of

United Nations (UN) and regional organizations and human rights and women's non-governmental organizations (NGOs). While addressing the problem of impunity through international law[32] and UN Security Council Resolutions 1325 (2000), 1820 (2008), 1888 (2009) and 1960 (2010) has made visible this once "invisible" feature of war, global attention in terms of peace and security has also led to new insights. First, conceptual challenges have arisen. It is no longer enough to say that gender inequality or patriarchal norms are the primary explanation for variation in the perpetrators, motives, frequency, scale, or type of abuses during conflict. Perpetrator groups do not only select victims because of their gender. And, men are also victims. Second, this violence is not always a "weapon of war." Sometimes it is not organized or strategic (Cohen 2013; Cohen and Nordås 2014; Eriksson Baaz and Stern 2009, 2013; Henry 2016; Hoover Green 2016; Marks 2013; Muvumba Sellström 2015a, 2015b; Wood 2006, 2009, 2010, 2014). There are important variations in the commission and therefore causes of these assaults, with a few actors carrying out the majority of atrocities (Cohen 2013; Cohen and Nordås 2014; Muvumba Sellström 2015a). New research shows how some actors prevent their fighters from committing conflict-related sexual violence (Hoover Green 2016; Lieby 2009; Muvumba Sellström 2015a, 2015b).

Describing these harms has grown increasingly complex. Sexual violence includes rape, sexual slavery, enforced prostitution, forced pregnancy, enforced sterilization, or any other similar act of comparable gravity, as defined by the 1998 Rome Statute of the International Criminal Court (ICC) (UNGA 1998). Abuses and assaults of a sexual nature can cover a wide range of phenomena (Wood 2006, 2009, 2010, 2014) in many different combinations, in the midst of war, as well as in militarized post-conflict settings (Muvumba Sellström 2015a). The relationship between gender-based violence, such as intimate partner abuse, and conflict-related violence is mainly anecdotal. The patterns can differ dramatically between war and peace (Wood 2014). It has therefore become helpful to focus on wartime acts and delineate the conflict-basis for these deeds from peacetime. For instance (and not without controversy), the UN's use of the term "conflict-related sexual violence" maintains an explicit basis in terrorism; organized, political armed violence; or war where assaults are "directly or indirectly linked (temporally, geographically or causally) to a conflict" (UN SG 2016: 1).

Gender is not always the main criteria for selection for conflict-related sexual violence. Victims are chosen because of other categories, such as political affiliation, ethnicity, religion, or geographic origins. In Rwanda, between 250,000 and 500,000 ethnic Tutsis and Hutu moderate women were raped (Binaifer 1996; UN Commission on Human Rights 1996). Certainly, their gender was the ground for targeting, but it was not a sufficient reason for their ill-treatment. Victims had to be "constructed" as representing the rival interests of, or as a threat to the identity of Hutu extremist perpetrators. The Islamic State in Iraq and the Levant (ISIL) in Iraq and Syria has committed systematic

abduction and sexual slavery. Ethnic or religious minority women and girls have been kidnapped to serve as sexual slaves for ISIL fighters (UN Secretary-General 2016). While these abuses are gendered – the Islamic extremist group used women's bodies as a form of currency to pay its fighters – ISIL's agenda was genocidal and it "intended to destroy the Yazidis of Sinjar, composing the majority of the world's Yazidi population, in whole or in part" (UN Human Rights Council 2016: 1). Such systematization lends conflict-related sexual violence to formulation as a gendered "weapon of war" (Quinn Thomas and Ralph 1994).

Of late, feminist scholarship has motivated for the use of gender as an analytical tool for disaggregating patterns in sexual violence. Davies and True (2015) contend that it is not only a matter of gender as a unitary, single [or binary] variable, but a question of relations, motivations, and processes that are predicated on how power is accrued, shared, and contested. As such, wartime sexual violence should be analyzed within a gender paradigm, if only to better assess its tactical use for political gains (see Cockburn 2010; Davies and True 2015). For instance, it is not yet clear how perpetrator attitudes about who can be victimized and what sorts of acts are permissible, shape their actions. Nor have social scientists settled questions about to what extent different degrees of discrimination and their social practice in peacetime correspond to particular patterns of violence during conflict. Indeed, the heterogeneous nature of beliefs and practices, which may also be contingent on interests and notions of class, ethnicity, and religion, will always challenge social science orthodoxies that seek to explain sexual and gender-based violence. These other factors create fluidity and at least at the individual level, deepen the complexity of the causal dynamics at play.

For now, there is no scientific consensus that gender inequality generates sexual violence in all conditions (Cohen 2013; Gottschall 2004; Wood 2014). Even when they have been exposed to similar gendered practices, with the same social construction of masculinity, marriage and sex, practices of sexual violence vary (Eriksson Baaz and Stern 2009, 2013; Muvumba Sellström 2015a, 2015b; Wood 2014). This problematizes the weapon-of-war framework (see, for example, Buss 2009; Eriksson Baaz and Stern 2009, 2013; Kirby 2013). Wood demonstrated that wartime sexual violence is puzzlingly varied (2006, 2009, 2010, 2014). Research by Lieby (2009) on the Guatemalan and Peruvian civil wars and Hoover Green's (2011) study of El Salvador has also drawn out additional evidence. Although this approach fails to capture the way that different power relations influence the political nature of this violence, and thus its gendered hue, it nonetheless offers a useful entry point into understanding the variation of sexual violence in conflict.

The *pre-conflict* phase may include a range of acts that include gender-based psychological and physical abuses. However, systematic scholarly investigation of temporal variation in sexual violence remains limited.

---

the terms "gender-based" and "sexual" is limited or used explicitly. In general, the emphasis of this section is on sexual crimes committed in conflict settings, which may also be directed at males and are direct acts.

[32] The International Criminal Tribunal for Rwanda (ICTR) issued a historic conviction for rape and sexual violence as a serious crime of genocide (*Prosecutor* v. *Akayesu* 1998). Article 7 of the Rome Statue of the International Criminal Court (ICC) names widespread or systematic sexual violence as a crime against humanity (UNGA 1998: para. 1g). The International Criminal Tribunal for the former Yugoslavia (ICTY) further expanded the scope for conviction for sexual violence from rape to include sexual torture, enslavement and various forms of penetration (*Prosecutor* v. *Dragoljub Kunarac, Kovac and Vukovic* 2001).

In general, pre-conflict sexual violence may be obscured. Observers may call it intimate partner abuse, or civilian rape. Violence that takes place behind closed doors may not be accounted for as conflict-related. Theoretically, intimate partner abuse may arise because of increased militarization and recruitment. Perpetrators might target victims along ethnic or political fault lines.

Violence against men may require special attention and monitoring of prisons, particularly before more open armed hostilities. Sexual violence acts against men and boys are an empirical reality in all phases of conflict (Ferrales, Brehm, and Mcelrath 2016; Jakobsen 2014). Sexual violence against males has occurred in ancient wars, in every region of the world, and in many of the conflicts of the past and present centuries (Sivakumaran 2007). However, attacks of males are too often equated with torture, which can feature in pre-conflict repression by the state. Though they may be under-reported as "tortured" (Lieby 2012), male victims are anally raped, forcibly sterilized, beaten on their genitals, forced to masturbate before their abusers or other victims, and forced to remain naked. Any combination of these acts can also occur (Sivakumaran 2007).

Evidently, not all armed political actors commit widespread sexual violence *during conflict* (Wood 2006, 2009, 2010, 2014). Cohen and Nordås collected reports of sexual violence prevalence, covering 129 active conflicts, involving 625 armed actors for the period 1989–2009, in the Sexual Violence in Armed Conflict (SVAC) dataset. They found that 43 percent of individual conflicts had no reports of this violence (Cohen and Nordås 2014). Even in wars that could feature systematic conflict-related sexual violence, some actors may diverge from the weapon-of-war narrative.

To exemplify, in 2004, the Party for the Liberation of the Hutu People-Forces for National Liberation (FNL) was rarely associated with wartime rape or similar abuses (Muvumba Sellström 2015a) during or after the civil war in Burundi. The lack of sexual violence is particularly striking if we consider that the coinciding and bordering genocide in Rwanda, between similar "ethnic" groups and root causes of conflict, included widespread sexual violence against Tutsis committed by the Hutu militia group known as *Interahamwe*. Palipehutu-FNL and *Interahamwe* each aimed to defeat their respective Tutsi minorities. Both attacked Tutsi civilians. Yet, FNL did not permit or order sexual violence.

Post-conflict sexual violence is also varied, though research on this particular phase is also limited. As during conflict, few actors commit the majority of acts. Muvumba Sellström's (2015a) events-based dataset between 1989 and 2011, of 23 armed actors who concluded their conflicts with a negotiated settlement in sub-Saharan Africa, shows that only a minority of actors (eight) was responsible for the majority (68 percent) of abuse. However, the type of assaults was also complex. Many of the 137 events involved more than one type of sexual violence. Approximately 30 combinations of violence were identified, ranging from single incidents of rape, gang rape, mass rape, sexual slavery, torture, harm to children, or combinations of these. About 44 percent of post-settlement sexual violence events had an unknown number of victims. However, there did appear to be a downward trend, with the armed actors in the study reducing their levels of sexual violence within the three years after settlement of their conflict.

Research has further sought to explain the willingness of armed actors to control the behavior of their combatants. Such studies entail cross-national and case study examination of the institutional (or organizational, see Wood 2014) conditions that contribute to sexual brutality by soldiers (Butler, Gluch, and Mitchell 2007; Cohen 2013; Lieby 2009; Nordås 2012). Wood's (2006, 2009) study of the Liberation Tigers of Tamil Eelam (LTTE) of Sri Lanka underscored Butler et al.'s (2007) contribution, which introduced the control of sexual violence as a principal-agent-problem. Wood highlighted the role of strong hierarchal structures and disciplinary practices through the chain of command. Hoover Green's (2011) examination of the *Frente Farabundo Martí para la Liberación Nacional* (FMLN) in El Salvador interprets the principal-agent problem (Butler et al. 2007) as the "commander's dilemma," whereby leaders have to control their fighters while simultaneously inculcating their fighters with a will to kill for the cause (Hoover Green 2016: 621–622). One solution is standard operating procedures (more often found among state actors), and de-legitimization of problematic values. This echoes Butler et al.'s (2007) conclusion that breakdowns in institutional bureaucratic oversight among state agents will increase abuses.

A robust code clarifies Palipehutu-FNL's behavior. It instituted a prohibition on sexual violence and leveled the death penalty, applicable throughout the chain of command. Leaders indoctrinated followers during group prayers and trainings, ritualized good conduct through naming and shaming, and fostered peer pressure (Muvumba Sellström 2015a). Sexual violence was depicted as amoral and an act of weakness. This is in contrast to its rival rebel group, the National Council for the Defence of Democracy–Forces for the Defence of Democracy (CNDD-FDD), which never instituted clear and constant codes of conduct against sexual violence. While FNL had a lower rate of sexual violence, CNDD-FDD, even as the ruling, governing party in the post-conflict period, was responsible for intense levels of sexual and gender-based violence (Muvumba Sellström 2015a).

However, as with gender inequality, the lack of institutional prohibitions may not be a sufficient explanation (see also Henry 2016). Wood proposes that ideology is an understudied and important basis for an armed group's likelihood to prevent abuse (Gutiérrez and Wood 2014; Wood 2015). Hoover Green (2011) suggests that actors espousing a Communist vision for society are amenable to discipline. Peace and conflict research indicates that economic endowments (Humphreys and Weinstein 2006; Weinstein 2006) might explain the permissiveness of indiscriminate sexual abuse. Cohen (2013) provides a picture of sexual violence as a tool for building cohesion when a non-state armed group forcibly recruits fighters. Ex-Palipehutu-FNL members point to their dependence on civilians as a reason for putting in place the edict against sexual violence in the first place. Muvumba Sellström (2015a) posits that this is what motivates rebel group conduct.

Other important distinctions require further study. Tentative evidence shows that state actors (government security agents, police, military) are more likely to commit sexual violence during and immediately after conflict (Muvumba Sellström 2015a, 2015b; Nordås 2011, 2012). These findings are drawn from reports from international human rights groups such as Human Rights Watch (HRW) and Amnesty International (AI), news reports, and US State Department Human Rights reports. It is possible

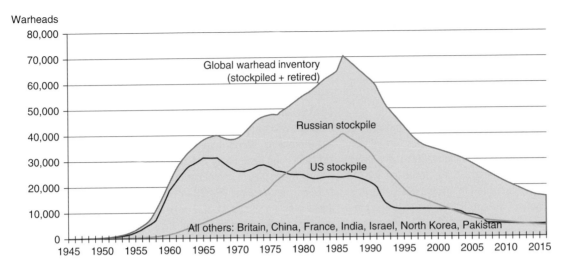

Figure 10.10 | Nuclear weapons inventories, 1945–2016.
Source: Federation of American Scientists (FAS). https://fas.org/wp-content/uploads/2014/05/warheadhistory.jpg

that these sources focus on the state. At least, state abuses may be more observable to the press and to NGOs.

To conclude, the deeper appreciation for variation offers an opportunity. If some armed actors control their fighters, despite gender inequality, then conflict-related sexual violence is preventable. Finding out why and how, will be an important contribution to our collective social progress.

10.2.5   Nuclear Weapons and Military Expenditures

10.2.5.1   Developments in Global Nuclear Weapons Arsenals

The previous sections have dealt with ongoing uses of violence for political purposes. One of the bases for military action is the military capability that the parties command. Thus, it is important to observe the trends both in nuclear weapons and in the conventional arsenals. Figures 10.10 and 10.11 have pertinent information with respect to nuclear weapons issues.

While nuclear weapons reduction has slowly continued – due primarily to the United States and Russia, which collectively have over 93 percent of the world's nuclear weapons – the leading nuclear weapons-possessing countries continue to invest in expensive, comprehensive nuclear modernization programs. This takes place despite these two countries recently renewing their commitment to nuclear arms reduction with the successor to START, the 2011 bilateral Treaty on Measures for the Further Reduction and Limitation of Strategic Offensive Arms. The states with smaller such arsenals have begun following suit, and many are expanding their nuclear arsenals, namely, China, India, and Pakistan (SIPRI 2016a).

As the head of the SIPRI Nuclear Weapons Project, Shannon Kile, recently pronounced, "Despite the ongoing reduction in the number of weapons, the prospects for genuine progress towards nuclear disarmament remain gloomy" (SIPRI 2016b).

Figure 10.11 demonstrates the differences in nuclear capacity. North Korea's capacity is not included but it is likely to be smaller than what

is often project to be the Israeli inventory (which is not acknowledged by the Israeli government). However, it may be more strategically significant for the North Korean regime.[33] Increasingly unified international pressure on North Korea has not been able to stop the country's move towards a more advanced capacity in weapons as well as in delivery system. There are no negotiations going on to deal with this problem. Instead, the developments add to the gloom expressed by SIPRI research Kile.

At the same time, the agreement with Iran on its nuclear program is likely to effectively halt the possibility of this country becoming the tenth nuclear weapons state. The likelihood of any other country initiating a nuclear weapons program today seems remote. In that sense, the Nuclear Non-Proliferation Treaty has slowed down the spread of such weapons around the world. This points to the ability of negotiations to actually achieve results in this field, and thus suggests the urgency of increasing the international efforts in this regard.

10.2.5.2   Developments in Military Expenditures

Military expenditures are a further indication of the ability and willingness of states to undertake military and violent action for their own defense and, possibly, global security. Figure 10.12 shows the trends in global military spending. Table 10.3 then provides the total expenditure for key countries as well as trends in spending for these countries during the past 10 years. Both these graphs are drawn from SIPRI, which is seen to be a reliable source for such estimates.

After declining precipitously with the fall of the Soviet Union and the end of the Cold War, world military expenditures began sharply rising in the first decade of the twenty-first century. With the global economic crisis, military spending in much of the world halted or declined. World military expenditures rose in 2015 for the first time since 2011, partially reflecting the recovery of North American and European countries from

---

[33]   See Baker (2016).

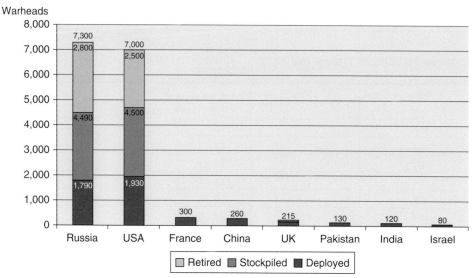

Note: North Korea has produced fissile material for 10–12 warheads and detonated 4 nuclear test assemblies, but we're not aware of public information that shows it has yet stockpiled weaponized warheads.

Figure 10.11 | Estimated nuclear weapons inventories, 2016.
Source: Kristensen and Norris 2016

the economic crisis. Likewise, this recent rise has been propelled by the continued military spending growth in China, Russia, Saudi Arabia, and other countries in Asia, Central and Eastern Europe, and the Middle East, which have offset the expenditure declines experienced in other parts of the globe.

According to Table 10.3 world military expenditure in 2015 totaled 1,676 billion dollars, the 15 top spenders were responsible for more than 80 percent of this. It is notable that the five permanent members of the UN Security Council (USA, UK, France, Russia, and China) alone spent close to 60 percent of the world expenditures. Thus, the accumulated military power, if these states acted in concert, would be overwhelming. For many countries, these statistics also suggest that military expenditures is done at a considerable price for the national economy, constituting more than 5 percent of GDP, for instance, for Saudi Arabia, United Arab Emirates, Israel, and also Russia. For the first three it may be a response to the turmoil facing the region, as can be seen in the fact that Saudi Arabia's military expenditures have risen by almost 100 percent in the past 10 years. Only the United Arab Emirates and China have growth rates exceeding this, in the first case certainly also an effect of the regional turmoil, while for the latter it has increased concerns in East Asia about China's long-term ambition.

Thus, the military data reinforces the picture that emerges from the analysis of armed conflicts and terrorism. There are some regions that find themselves in particularly challenging circumstance. When facing immediate security challenges from conditions in the neighborhood, there are strong incentives to invest in defense, and, as a corollary, be attempted to intervene in one form or another.

The type of weapons and the military expenditures reported in Figure 10.12 and Table 10.3 largely related to major arms. It also highlights the importance of major manufacturers of arms and their interest in export of weapons as a factor.[34] Many of the wars in, say, Africa, do not use such heavy equipment. It is notable that there are no African countries among the 15 top spenders. The estimate made by SIPRI military expenditures for all of Africa is set at US€ 37 billion, which is about 2 percent of the world total.[35] It would put the entire continent (of more than 50 countries) at number 10 in Table 10.3. Still it is a continent that has large share of all armed conflicts, regularly around a third (Pettersson and Wallensteen 2015). This means that these wars are fought with smaller weapons, which thus are capable of creating considerable havoc in poor countries and dilute their resources even more. A recent report of the Small Arms Survey points out that just two countries (China and Russia) hold almost 25 percent of the total global inventory of such weapons. It also states that newly manufactured weapons outstrip the destruction of surplus firearms.[36] This means that the world's holding of such weapons increases. It is likely that they are not only used for politically motivated wars, but also find their ways to organized crime and to individuals, making possible school shootings and other events with less overt political motivations. In other words, there is a considerable undocumented trade in small arms.

---

[34]   There is a major discussion as to the role of the military industry in security affairs. Clearly, industry is highly important in issues of procurement, planning and development of weapons. It is more difficult to document its role in decisions to go to a particular war, military intervention, or other forms uses of weapons. The debate of the 1980s on military-industrial complexes needs to be revisited.

[35]   Table 10.5, SIPRI.

[36]   www.smallarmssurvey.org/about-us/highlights/highlight-rn34.html

Table 10.3 | Military spending: 15 top spenders, 2006–2015

Rank 2015	2014[a]	Country	Spending, 2015 ($ b.)	Change, 2006–2015 (%)	World share 2015 (%)	Spending as a share of GDP (%)[b] 2015	2006
1	1	USA	596	3.9	36	3.3	3.8
2	2	China	[215]	132	[13]	[1.91]	[2.01]
3	4	Saudi Arabia	87.2	9	5.2	13.7	7.8
4	3	Russia	66.4	91	4.0	5.4	3.5
5	6	UK	55.5	−7.2	3.3	2.0	2.2
6	7	India	51.3	43	3.1	2.3	2.5
7	5	France	50.9	−5.9	3.0	2.1	2.3
8	9	Japan	40.9	0.5	2.4	1.0	1.0
9	8	Germany	39.4	2.8	2.4	1.2	1.3
10	10	South Korea	36.4	37	2.2	2.6	2.5
11	11	Brazil	24.6	38	1.5	1.4	1.5
12	12	Italy	23.8	30	1.4	1.3	1.7
13	13	Australia	23.6	32	1.4	1.9	1.8
14	14	UAE[c]	[22.8]	136	[1.4]	[5.]	[3.2]
15	15	Israel	16.1	2.6	1.0	5.4	7.5
Total top 15			1,350		81		
World total			1,676	19	100	2.3	2.3

[a] Rankings for 2014 are based on updated military expenditure figures for 2014 in the current edition of the SIPRI Military Expenditure Database. They may therefore differ from the rankings for 2014 given in the SIPRI Yearbook 2015 and in other SIPRI publications in 2015.

[b] The figures for military expenditure as a share of gross domestic product (GDP) are based on estimates of 2015 GDP from the International Monetary Fund (IMF) World Economic Outlook Database, October 2015.

[c] The figures for UAE are for 2014, as no data is available for 2015. The percentage change is from 2006 to 2014.

Source: SIPRI (2015).

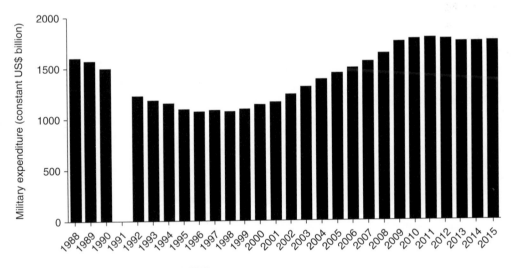

Figure 10.12 | Military expenditures, 1988–2015.
Note: No data for USSR 1991, thus no total.
Source: SIPRI. www.sipri.org/media/press-release/2016/world-military-spending-resumes-upward-course-says-sipri.

10.2.6   Conclusion

In this section, we have scrutinized some of the trends and insights into the most devastating forms of violence: armed conflicts, war, terrorist acts, homicide, and suicide. The trends that can be observed do not necessarily all point in the same direction. The long-term trends have been one of declining violence of all forms. However, lately armed conflicts, wars, and terrorism have again been on the rise. As studies of homicide show, there is a close connection between armed conflict and homicide. One may thus fear an upsurge also in such violence, even if some of the presently ongoing wars are terminated. This means that the world faces intense challenges to deal with the threats of violence. Thus, we turn to the possibilities of dealing with such challenges.

10

10.3 Peace and Security

10.3.1 International Peace and Security

The challenges we have indicated in the previous sections directly relate to the security of the inhabitants of this planet. The challenges may be more acute to some regions than to others and some individuals than others, but it is all part of the same global threat. The insecurity of some can quickly be the insecurity of all, particularly in this globalized age. The task for the world is thus both conceptual and practical. How shall the present situations be analyzed and how can it be approached? The methodologies and conclusions are likely to vary, but the importance of concerted action may be less disputed. As the assignment is global in nature, it should be the domain of international institutions in general and the UN in particular. The purpose of the UN according to Article 1 is exactly to "maintain international peace and security, and to that end take effective collective measures for the prevention and removal of threats to the peace." Thus, in this section we will study some of the means available for such responses.

Figure 10.13 presents the activity of the UN Security Council as the main organ for deciding on the collective measures for the worlds as a whole. The increased work of the Council can be seen in the number of decisions in general (resolutions) and in particular the resolutions taken under Chapter VII (which are binding for the entire membership). This includes decisions on sending out mediators and peacekeepers, or imposing sanctions, supporting disarmament measures, or initiating peacebuilding work. The third line in the Figure shows the number of draft resolutions that have been vetoed by one or more permanent members of the Council. The Figure demonstrated an impressive activation of the Council since the end of the Cold War.

When comparing this curve to the one of Figure 10.1 it can be observed that the increased activity of the Council in the 1990s actually corresponds to a reduction in armed conflict. However, the increase of armed conflict observed since 2011 does not see an accompanying increasing of Council activity, at least not in terms of making more decisions. A study of the actual texts of the resolutions would, however, most likely demonstrate the increased complexity and the difficulty in handling some of the conflicts. Some of the most urgent wars, however, have not seen concerted action by this UN body, notably those over Syria and Ukraine. It may point to an important deficiency in the international set up. However, before looking for remedies, let us pursue some of the means commonly used by the international, regional, and national bodies involved in dealing with global issues of violence and war.

10.3.2 Disarmament Issues

The availability of weapons, munitions, and spare parts as well as training of soldiers, refining equipment, and finding bases for action are important for the initiation and continuation of wars,

armed conflicts and terrorist deeds. The trends were observed in Section 10.2.3. A radical way of dealing with this is to find effective forms of disarmament. Table 10.4 lists all major international disarmament treaties that have been agreed among states since 1963, i.e. 27 treaties in 53 years. It is not an impressive rate, as it suggests only one treaty every second year. Given the size of nuclear arsenals, the extent of military expenditures, the increase in armed conflicts, and the challenge of terrorism, this is not an inspiring record. On the contrary, it demonstrates an inability of the international community to face the challenge of political organized violence in a joint manner. As several of the treaties have been quite effective, it is possible for states to agree in ways that are sufficiently detailed to stand the tests of implementation. We have mentioned the Non-Proliferation Treaty earlier. In the case of the ban on chemical weapons the world was able to act jointly against Syria's use of such weapons in 2013 and have them abolished within a year. Thus, the world can conclude agreements of high quality and make sure they are implemented, if this is given shared priority. The latest agreement, the Arms Trade Treaty of 2013 is now in place and has begun its work to control illicit transfers of arms. It remains to be seen and there are many suggestions for its improvement, for instance, as expressed by the Small Arms Survey: the need for a standardized international reporting system.[37] It is, however, the only treaty that would actually have an impact on all the three types of violence we have scrutinized here: wars, terrorism and homicide.[38]

As can be seen in Table 10.4 most of the treaties have concerned weapons of mass destruction (i.e. nuclear, chemical, and biological weapons), delivery systems (missiles in particular) and some very specific conventional weapons (land mines, in particular). Some of the measures are regional, rather than global, and some treaties have replaced or deepened earlier agreements. As could be seen in Figure 10.10, the agreements on nuclear weapons have resulted in substantial reductions in the inventories, but by no means led to the type of removal of entire systems as was discussed in the 1980s, and resulted in the complete elimination of intermediate-range nuclear weapons in 1988. As indicated by the increase in global military expenditures, the world seems close to facing a new upsurge in weapons development, not the least as some of the leading nuclear weapon states are engaged in new weapons projects. Thus, the achievements of international disarmament remain disconcerting and the international actions to deal with them are not convincing.

10.3.3 Peacemaking and Mediation

10.3.3.1 Introduction

Since the end of the Second World War and particularly since the demise of the Cold War, the settlement of conflicts through mediation has become increasingly common. In the 1990s there were more mediation attempts than during the preceding four decades combined (Grieg and Diehl 2012), and the proportion of conflicts ending in peace agreements exceeded those ending in military victory (Kreutz 2010). Other prominent trends over the past two decades include a shift in

---

[37] www.smallarmssurvey.org/about-us/highlights/highlight-rn34.html
[38] UNODC (2013: 69) gives considerable attention to this treaty.

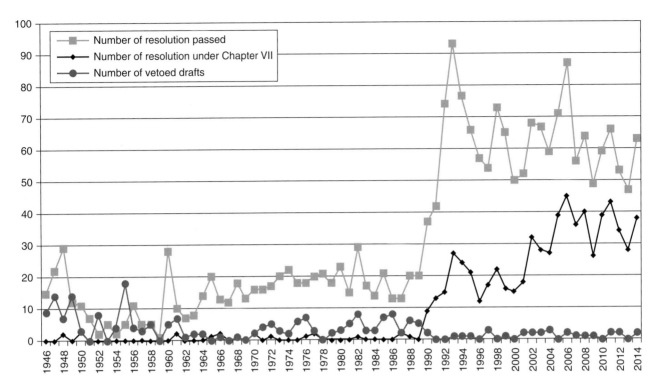

Figure 10.13 | UN Security Council Resolutions 1946–2014.
Source: Wallensteen and Johansson 2015.

mediation from inter- to intrastate conflict (DeRouen and Bercovitch 2012); a growing involvement or regional organizations in peacemaking (Gartner 2011) and the institutionalization and professionalization of international mediation (Convergne 2016).[39]

This section identifies factors relating to the success or failure of mediation and highlights the importance of mediation but also warns against exaggerating the role and influence of the mediator; it covers the institutionalization of the field as well as the major deficiencies and challenges; it identifies ways of reducing the risk that peace agreements break down; and it suggests that more attention should be paid to post-conflict constitutions as the definitive peace agreements. The discussion focuses on the resolution of intrastate conflict, which are more common than interstate conflict.

10.3.3.1.1 The Relative Importance of Mediation

The importance of international mediation in deadly conflict is unquestionable. It is frequently the only bridge from hostilities to peace and it can forge among mortal enemies a consensual platform for long-term reconciliation, reconstruction and state building. Where it fails, as in Darfur from 2004 to the present, Syria from 2012 to date and Rwanda prior to the 1994 genocide, the fatalities and destruction can reach catastrophic proportions. By contrast, in 1996 UN mediation ended the civil war in Guatemala, in 2005 the Inter-Governmental Authority on Development mediated an end to the decades-long war in Sudan and

in 2008 the African Union mediation in the Kenyan electoral conflict prevented a descent into protracted violence.

Increasingly, mediation research is concerned with the durability of peace agreements. A key question in this regard is whether mediated settlements are more or less likely than military victories to lead to a recurrence of violence. According to Kreutz, 9.5 percent of military victories in the 1990s restarted and this rose to 40 percent of victories in the early 2000s; by contrast, 46.1 percent of negotiated settlements led to resumed hostilities in the 1990s and this fell to 21 percent in the early 2000s (cited in Wallensteen and Svensson 2014: 323). Others paint a more pessimistic picture: coinciding with the shift in war termination from military victory to negotiated settlement, the relapse rate has progressively increased since the 1960s, with 60 percent of conflicts in the early 2000s relapsing within five years (von Einsiedel 2017).

The scholarly literature on international mediation is primarily concerned with the question of what accounts for success and failure. The dependent variable is mediation outcomes and the main independent variables can be divided into two categories, i.e. those concerning structural condition and those having to do with the process (Kleiboer 1996).[40] Among the first are matters relating to the conflict (its duration, its intensity, the issues, and whether it is ripe for resolution through negotiations [Zartman 2001]). Then, there are variables relating to the disputant parties (their cohesiveness, political orientation, motivation to mediate, and previous and ongoing

---

39   For a review of the scholarly literature on international mediation, see Wallensteen and Svensson (2014).
40   For recent reviews of the literature, see Wallensteen and Svensson (2014) and Wall and Dunne (2012).

Table 10.4 | International arms control treaties

International disarmament treaties and agreements	
Arms Trade Treaty	June 25, 2013
New Strategic Arms Reduction Treaty	May 10, 2010
Mine Ban Treaty	March 21, 2010
Convention on Cluster Munitions	May 30, 2008
International Code of Conduct against Ballistic Missile Proliferation (ICOC)	November 25, 2002
Strategic Offensive Reductions Treaty (SORT)	May 24, 2002
Open Skies Treaty	January 1, 2002
Strategic Arms Reduction Treaty II (START II)	September 26, 1997
Chemical Weapons Convention (CWC)	April 1, 1997
Comprehensive Test-Ban Treaty (CTBT)	September 17, 1996
African Nuclear-Weapons-Free Zone Treaty	April 11, 1996
Treaty of Pelindaba	October 26, 1994
Missile Technology Control Regime (MTCR)	January 7, 1993
Strategic Arms Reduction Treaty I (START I)	October 1, 1992
Latin America Nuclear Weapons Free Zone Treaty (Treaty of Tlatelolco)	January 1, 1989
Intermediate-Range Nuclear Forces Treaty	December 27, 1988
South Pacific Nuclear Weapons Free Zone Treaty (Treaty of Rarotonga)	August 6, 1985
Strategic Arms Limitation Talks II (SALT II)	June 18, 1979
Peaceful Nuclear Explosions Treaty (PNET)	April 4, 1976
Biological Weapons Convention (BWC)	March 26, 1975
Threshold Test Ban Treaty (TTBT)	July 1, 1974
Strategic Arms Limitation Talks (SALT I)	May 26, 1972
Anti-Ballistic Missile (ABM) Treaty	May 26, 1972
Seabed Arms Control Treaty	May 18, 1972
Outer Space Treaty	October 10, 1970
Nuclear Non-proliferation Treaty (NPT)	March 5, 1970
Limited Test Ban Treaty (LTBT)	October 10, 1963

Source: Arms Control Association. www.armscontrol.org/treaties?page=2

relationships). Furthermore there are factors relating to the mediator variables, (impartiality, status, identity, and power) and finally international context (superpower involvement in the conflict, regional dynamics, and related conflicts).

The process variables have to do with the mediator's style and strategies. A useful typology is that of Touval and Zartman, distinguishing between the mediator as a "communicator," "formulator," and "manipulator" (Touval and Zartman 1985). The mediator as communicator is a "passive conduit and repository," serving as a channel of communication and conveyer of messages and proposals between the parties. The mediator as formulator plays a more active role, assisting the parties to redefine issues or devise solutions to their conflict. At the most assertive end of the spectrum, the mediator as manipulator uses leverage to push and pull the parties towards an agreement. While examples of each of these roles can readily be found, it is often the case that the mediator and mediating organization play all three roles in a conflict, sometimes sequentially and sometimes concurrently, and almost always in parallel with interventions by other external actors.

There is no consensus in the literature on which style and strategy of mediation is most effective (Wallensteen and Svensson 2014: 319).

Notwithstanding the importance of mediation, however, the mediator's role and influence should not be overstated. By definition, mediation requires the consent of the conflict parties, who must be willing to transcend their mutual hatred and suspicion and embark on a cooperative process of negotiation and problem-solving. Without this willingness, there may be little that a mediator can do. The mediator's assets are soft and intangible, encompassing stature, credibility, and a distinct set of personal attributes and skills. Even if the mediator is backed by powerful actors that offer attractive inducements and put concerted pressure on the parties, mediation will not make progress unless the adversaries believe that their interests are likely to be served through a negotiated settlement. In short, the burden of peacemaking lies more with the parties (and their allies and patrons) than with the mediator.

Nevertheless, the fallacy of the mediator as a demi-god is widespread. It is evident in policy perspectives that they expect mediators to craft agreements in perfect compliance with liberal norms, regardless of the wishes of the conflict parties; in academic work that places too much weight on the mediator's characteristics and strategies as determinants of the outcome of negotiations; in the hubris of mediating organizations that imagine they can rapidly bring the parties to their senses through a combination of persuasion, carrots, and sticks; and in the pressure that donors put on mediators to broker a peace agreement quickly. Put differently, the fallacy here is to treat negotiations as sub-species of mediation when in fact it is the other way round.

10.3.3.2   Mediation Professionalism and Deficiencies

The UN has played a pioneering role in the professionalization and institutionalization of international mediation. It has established a mediation support unit in the Department of Political Affairs; a standby team of mediation advisers, available for rapid deployment to support peace processes throughout the world; an academic advisory council on mediation; and several specialist training programs (Convergne 2016). Similarly, the European Union, the Organization for Security and Cooperation in Europe, the African Union, and other regional bodies have set up mediation structures and made efforts to enhance the quality of their peacemaking endeavors.

The impact of this professionalization and institutionalization is unclear. There is certainly much greater knowledge, expertise, and capacity than in previous decades but the field remains wracked by serious deficiencies. Lakhdar Brahimi and Salman Ahmed refer to these deficiencies as the "seven deadly sins of mediation" (Brahimi and Ahmed 2008). The "original sin of mediation" is a mediator's ignorance regarding the conflict dynamics, parties, and history. This is compounded by the sin of arrogance, where mediators are untroubled by their ignorance, assuming that the conflict before them is pretty much like the previous ones. The other deadly sins, according to Brahimi and Ahmed, are partiality, impotence, haste, inflexibility, and false promises.

Quite often, moreover, mediators intervene in complex conflicts without a comprehensive plan, believing that the need for flexibility in volatile situations is antithetical to sound planning. But in the absence of a strategic plan, mediations lack cohesion and direction, they tend to be reactive rather than proactive and they do not inspire confidence among the conflict parties. Another general malaise lies in the sphere of evaluation, learning, and adaptation. There is an endless stream of "lessons learnt" workshops, and manuals on mediation but the findings do not lead to the requisite reform of practice and systems. Consequently, there is insufficient institutionalized learning over time and the same mistakes are repeated from one mediation to the next.

10.3.3.3 Mediation Challenges

Over the past 20 years regional organizations in some parts of the world have become more assertive in addressing conflicts in their neighborhood (Gartner 2011; Wallensteen and Bjurner 2015). This has often been accompanied by synergistic cooperation between these organizations, the UN and other external players.[41] The downside is that the multiplicity of mediation actors has also led to coordination problems, nasty competition over the leadership of a mediation, and "forum shopping" by the conflict parties.[42] In Africa there have been many divisive clashes between mediating bodies, including the cases of Burkina Faso (2015), the Central African Republic (2003, 2013, and 2015), Côte d'Ivoire (2011), Darfur (2011), Guinea (2009), Guinea-Bissau (2012), Libya (2011), Madagascar (2009), Mali (2012), Sudan (2008), and Zimbabwe (2008) (Nathan 2017; Wallensteen and Bjurner 2015). Although the UN Secretary-General has called for 'coherence, coordination and complementarity' among external actors involved in peace efforts (UN 2012: 18–19), the UN has not established reliable mechanisms to achieve this (Nathan 2017).

Other mediation challenges that have attracted attention over the past few years are the need for greater involvement of women in negotiation and mediation teams; broadening peace processes beyond the negotiating table and engaging women's groups and other civil society formations; the incorporation of gender provisions in peace agreements; the role of mediators during the implementation of agreements; the pressure on mediators to promote the UN's ever expanding normative agenda; the UN ban on amnesties for war crimes, which sometimes puts mediators at loggerheads with the conflict parties; the difficulty of mediating with parties that are fragmented; the many conundrums related to negotiations with extremists; and the development of national capacities for mediation and dialogue.

10.3.3.4 Implementation of Peace Agreements

Peace agreements are not self-implementing. Many of them break down, resulting in renewed hostilities.[43] One possible reason is that the parties, under pressure from external actors, sign an agreement without any intention of honoring it. Alternatively, they might initially be committed to implementing the agreement but then change their minds because of opposition from within a party or a change in the balance of power between the parties. A third possibility is that implementation disputes escalate because of the abiding enmity and suspicion among the parties. Fourth, there may be inadequate external support for implementation, especially in relation to security arrangements. Fifth, parties that did not participate in the negotiations might seek to wreck the settlement through violence.

A review of practice and the literature has identified a number of mediation approaches and strategies that might reduce the risk of breakdown (Stedman 2001). Some of these naturally relate to the content of the agreement. A sustainable agreement is likely to be one that, to the greatest extent possible, meets the primary needs, concerns, and aspirations of all parties and communities; avoids marginalizing any party or community; addresses the root causes of the conflict; and lays the basis for representative and inclusive governance. The agreement should also include an implementation plan that covers responsibilities, a time schedule and monitoring, and verification and dispute resolution mechanisms.

Mediators and donors are mistaken, though, if they believe that the "magic" lies in the text of the peace agreement. Rather, the key to success lies in changing the relationship between the parties. Violent intrastate conflict emerges not only from substantive disputes and grievances but also from a chronic deterioration in political and social relationships. The violence itself does massive damage to relationships. The mediator must therefore prioritize the challenge of political reconciliation, assisting the parties to shift their disposition from implacable enmity to non-violent political competition and cooperation. In deadly conflicts this cannot be done quickly and it is imprudent for donors and other international actors to urge mediators to move with undue haste.

A related imperative is that the agreement must be owned by the protagonists and not forced on them by mediators. In intrastate conflicts it is also desirable that the negotiations and resultant peace agreement are anchored in civil society and enjoy public support. This helps to minimize popular fears and suspicion about the talks, contributes to the legitimacy of the process and the agreements, cultivates national ownership and not merely elite ownership, and for all these reasons contributes to the sustainability of the agreement (UN 2012).

The period immediately after the signing of a peace agreement is one of great danger and uncertainty, which is heightened if there is a delay between the disbandment of the mediation team and the formation of the implementation support team and mechanisms. The implementation team should be set up, and implementation planning should begin, prior to the conclusion of negotiations. Conversely, it is unwise for a mediation team to disband as soon as the agreement is signed.

---

[41] See, for instance, United Nations (2015a).

[42] See, for instance, Crocker, Hampson, and Aall (1999).

[43] The estimates vary and may depend on definitions. See von Einsiedel (2017), Wallensteen and Svensson (2012) and the Centre for Humanitarian Dialogue (2007), p. 13. On implementation difficulties see Stedman, Rothchild, and Cousens (2002). The Peace Accords Matrix at the Kroc Institute, University of Notre Dame, maps the degree of implementation in comprehensive peace agreements, see https://peaceaccords.nd.edu.

The team ought to be retained, with some continuity in its membership, to support dispute resolution during the implementation phase.

10.3.3.5   The Post-Conflict Constitution as the Peace Agreement

The outcomes of peace agreements are not limited to the absence or recurrence of hostilities. Rather, they vary along a spectrum that covers renewed fighting, low-level instability, stability without social justice, and a durable peace characterized by justice, equitable development, and good governance. These outcomes are not determined solely by the content of the peace agreement. They emerge from a wide range of domestic and external factors and institutions that traverse the political, economic, and social realms.

A critical institution that has been neglected in studies on the durability and impact of peace agreements is the post-conflict constitution.[44] Many such constitutions incorporate key provisions of the peace agreement and some of them emerge directly from the peace agreement's stipulations on constitutional reform.[45] Examples include the constitutions of Bosnia and Herzegovina (1995), Bougainville (2004), Cambodia (1993), Kenya (2010), Mozambique (1992), South Africa (1993), and Sudan (2005). These constitutions may amount to legal versions of the peace agreements. In the long term they constitute the definitive peace agreements because, unlike the accords signed by the conflict parties, they enjoy the status of supreme law, they have enduring authority, they are justiciable and enforceable, they are binding on the state and all groups and citizens, and they can be amended if they become outdated. In addition, the content and the process of drafting a post-conflict constitution has sometimes played a conciliatory and unifying role, seeking to overcome historical divisions and forge a national vision and identity (Widner 2005). And in a broader sense, peace is maintained through a constitution's classic functions of regulating political competition, constraining the exercise of power, protecting individuals and groups, and establishing procedures and mechanisms for non-violent management and resolution of conflict.

In reality, of course, a post-conflict constitution might not live up to these ideals and it may well enshrine elite pacts and compromises on land, justice, and other matters, derived from the negotiated settlement, that lay the seeds for subsequent tension and instability. The constitution can be a much revered or much abused instrument, a site of political contestation, or a vehicle that serves to contain and resolve political disputes. In any event, the crucial point is that the salience of a peace agreement fades with the passing of time, whereas the constitution's strengths and limitations as a peacemaking institution may have abiding significance.

10.3.4   Prevention of War and One-Sided Violence

The responses to the threats of new wars and to one-sided violence, such as terrorism, mass murder and genocide largely seem to fall into two categories, which could be labeled *direct and structural approaches*. The first set of approaches are oriented towards detecting and preventing more or less imminent action, e.g. through measures of early warning, surveillance, and rapid reaction forces, as well as identifying potential perpetrators, their environment, resources, and movements (including international travel).

The latter approach points to broader changes in society that minimize the likelihood of violent action at large, e.g. through inclusion, respect for diversity and policy participation. This includes education, training, and providing jobs consonant with qualifications, where the purpose is to reduce social frustration in society.

It is not possible at this juncture the make an assessment of any of these strategies. An example can be given from studies of genocide prevention and one from the study of terrorism.

10.3.4.1   Preventing Genocide: Possible Approaches

Direct prevention requires detailed information on early warning signals and a capacity to act early. There are ideas about how to do this, notably in the form of a genocide watch. One approach has been the attempt to identify the steps that lead to genocide and, at the same time, demonstrating the urgency of action and what do to when the threats are at different stages. This approach is associated particularly with the work of Gregory Stanton. Initially he suggested 7 steps, later they were 8 steps, most recently 10 (Stanton 2016). The points are logical and make intuitive sense, and include matters such as classification, dehumanization, organization, polarization, identification, and extermination, later adding others, for instance, discrimination, persecution, and denial. However, these stages are difficult to research as they are hard to separate from each other. Genocides do not necessarily follow a logically ordered sequence. Thus, researchers have converted some of the stages into factors that can play a role, not the least adding historical experiences, as no society "starts" toward genocide from a "normal" condition.

In particular, it is difficult to separate genocide from other ongoing developments in a society. There is a very close connection to war or other violent upheavals. War can provide an opportunity for genocide, but genocide, as Lemkin noted, may also lead to war as it enhances government control over a society. Obviously, conditions of war may make government and populations more susceptible to ideas of genocide against imagined enemies. This is also one of the first observations Harff makes in her statistical study on genocides since 1955. She notes that almost all genocides "occurred in the immediate aftermath of internal wars, revolutions, and regime collapse" (Harff 2003: 57). Thus, preventing war may at the same time prevent genocide. There are, however, events included in Harff's list that are separate from civil or international wars. An example is Indonesia in 1965, where the authorities targeted Communists (who often were Chinese in origin). It followed on an attempted coup. Although the coup did not

---

44   For an exception that considers the constitution-making process in the context of peacebuilding, see Samuels (2005).

45   Peace agreement stipulations regarding constitutional reform are recorded in the Peace Accords Matrix of the Kroc Institute for International Peace Studies, University of Notre Dame (https://peaceaccords.nd.edu/).

lead to regime collapse, it still resulted in a change of power followed by a deliberate use of the state apparatus to target a large and well-organized group. About half a million persons were killed. As this, furthermore, took place during the Cold War, the anti-communism of the West and the strategic significance of Indonesia muted Western reactions. Notably, the case is not closed as, in June 2016, an international tribunal found the Indonesian government responsible for the events of 1965, describing them as a crime against humanity, while also criticizing Western governments.[46]

Direct prevention raises the question of whether it is enough to prevent the onset of civil war to also prevent genocides. One strain of thought suggests that focus should be on state failure and "weak states." If states are more stable and better integrated, the likelihood of genocides may be reduced. Of course, the Holocaust resulted from a highly organized and effective state, suggesting that too strong a state may not be desirable either. Harff's list includes a number of states that were well organized, resource rich and capable of acting, at the time of the atrocities, e.g. China in Tibet in 1959 and during the Cultural Revolution after 1966, Chile following the coup in 1973, Syria in 1982, and the Serbian state in Bosnia and Kosovo in the 1990s. Thus, it is not the weakness as such that is important. Instead, Harff concludes that it is the "political upheaval" that determines the events that follow. This description fits all but one of the cases listed (Harff 2003: 62). However, there are many upheavals that do not result in genocides. That leads to an additional conclusion: Exclusionary ideologies constitute an important part of the picture. There is often an ideological component to the persecution that takes place, and governments may in fact maintain power through the help of such ideological components. Thus, it is not likely that they will be willing to participate in preventive measures. The international community has to act. The UN Special Advisers on prevention of genocide and responsibility has now been merged into one office. It could be a sign of increasing international commitment to this issue.

What would a structural approach entail? As there is a close connection between war and genocide, the explanations for civil wars yield some suggestions. The concept of quality peace can help this discussion (Wallensteen 2015). It leads to three observations.

First, the issue of discrimination is often central. In the work of Harff it plays a role, as part of the "exclusionary" ideologies. There is a lot to say that diversity in a society may make the society complex to govern, but it does not in itself generate civil war or genocide. On the contrary, diversity is likely to be a stimulant to economic growth, culture, and political life.

However, when coupled with discrimination, matters become difficult and serious (Cederman, Gleditsch, and Buhaug 2013; Cederman, Weidmann, and Gleditsch 2011). If one group has more resources than another, and actively works to maintain its power, then violence, armed conflict, and genocide may follow. It can take many forms. A small elite that is in power and is identified along any of these markers (national, ethnical, racial, and religious) may fear the majority and turn into a repressive regime (e.g. Assad and the Alawites in Syria 2016). Or a

sizeable group may be marginalized, although it previously has been dominant or well resourced, thus becoming a basis for recruitment for rebels (e.g. Tamils in Sri Lanka, where some turned to LTTE, Sunnis in Iraq where some turned to IS). Thus, a society with quality peace is one that can respect the dignity of all human beings, whatever their identity may be. A very valid indicator is gender equality (Melander 2005).

Second, insecurity created by governments and/or rebels will make most inhabitants concerned, thus supporting measures that are expected to lead to their protection. Allegiance will go to the one that is the most effective. The easy availability of weapons, in other words, plays a role in the onset of civil wars. In terms of genocides, we may also see threats, notably semi-controlled militia groups or self-proclaimed defense forces that inject fear in other groups. Thus, providing safety for daily life is important for a society to maintain a peace with quality. In the immediate post-genocide conditions, international protection may be one of the most effective ways of setting a society on the path toward a peace with quality.

Third, the expectations for the future are most important. If the expectation is that peace will last, and that there will be no (re)occurrence of civil war or genocide, the inhabitants will invest (e.g. in education or production) and thus contribute to sustaining the peace. However, if there is fear that the conditions are likely to (again) result in war and/or genocide, defensive measures may add to a spiral of increasing antagonism and violence. Genocide studies demonstrate that there is a history of exclusion, previous persecution, and genocide. Thus, to break such historical cycles is a necessary ingredient in the construction of quality peace after a civil war as well as after genocide.

10.3.4.2　Preventing Terrorism: Possible Approaches

While the exact combination of strategies to counter-terrorism depends heavily on the specifics of the system in question and the respective sociopolitical and cultural contexts, some principles can be formulated:

A critical problem in strategies such as the global "war on terrorism" and national counter-terrorism is a lack of understanding counter-terrorism as a security activity distinct from military or policing operations. Thus, the primary goals of countering terrorism are not coercion, enforcement or retaliation, but prevention and preemptive disruption of terrorist activity.

The focus on countering terrorism financing, logistics, and access to weapons and other materials is important. At the same time considerable attention needs to be paid to pro-actively reducing terrorists' ability to exploit new information and communication technologies both for ideological propaganda and mobilization purposes, and, increasingly, as an organizing tool for network-building and operational purposes.

In short, it would mean that antiterrorism strategy is more effective if it systematically tries to undermine two key comparative advantages of militant-terrorist actors – their extremist ideologies and organizational

---

[46]　www.cnn.com/2016/07/21/asia/indonesia-genocide-panel/.

systems. Only a balance between functionality and legality, legitimacy and respect for human rights can ensure that antiterrorism does not produce more terrorism than it seeks to reduce.

To this can be added – as stated in the introduction of this chapter – if violence, particularly in its most extreme form such as terrorism, is more frequently the opposite to social movements, non-armed conflicts, i.e. to constructive change, then, the reduction of terrorism should be sought through re-inventing or re-launching of debates between actors able to talk and negotiate together. This could be true at all levels, including the transnational one, and this should combine different levels of action – something that is never easy to achieve.

Thus, preventing terrorism is a highly complex issue. It means dealing with various levels of action, various territories, and various temporalities, and articulating all this more or less at the same time.

The levels of actions extend from the very individual, for instance when the personality of some persons could lead to violence, to the more global or collective, for instance when international agreements are at stake. The issue of territories goes from the very local, for instance when one understands that a small town has been the place for the creation of a terrorist group or even a network, as was the case in France with Lunel (in the Gard department) or in Spain with Ripoll (Catalonia), to whole regions, today mainly the Middle East, but also parts of sub-Saharan Africa in order to understand Boko Haram. Preventing terrorism means in this regard not only taking into account these different types of territories, but also their articulation, for instance between what is at stake at the national level within a country such as France, or Spain, or Tunisia, and what is at stake in the whole Middle East, including Iraq or Syria, but also Israel, Jordan, Turkey, and Iran.

In addition, one has to take into account the temporal perspective going from the very short term to the "longue durée." Prevention in the very short term means first of all the use of intelligence, police, diplomacy, and it comes with an important concern: short-term policies may include measures that could threaten democracy, as clearly stated by those that criticize the Patriot Act in the United States. Prevention in the "longue durée" means public policies, in education, employment, etc., but also some diplomacy. Too often, when a country faces terrorism, prevention refers only to short-term measures, and when there appears to be no more attacks, governments and public opinion show very little interest in dealing with the issue in the "longue durée," which, after all, is the only effective preventive action for sustaining a society.

10.3.5   Peacebuilding

Peacebuilding is central to social progress as it seeks to address justice and the structural root-causes to conflict (Aggestam and Björkdahl 2013; Mani 2002; Philpott 2012). Peacebuilding is therefore closely connected to positive peace (Galtung 1969), social, economic, and political progress by its ambition to build peace beyond the cessation of direct and organized violence (negative peace). This brief section on peacebuilding provides an overview of recent trends in the field of practice as well as in theory. It concludes with a reflective note on the

current debates and how the contemporary peacebuilding is standing at the crossroads. This discussion recurs in the concluding chapter with a note on resilient peacebuilding.

The peacebuilding field is relatively new and evolved as a response to the growing number of intrastate conflicts in the early 1990s. It was triggered after the end of the Cold War by the initial optimism about new prospects for collective actions within the United Nations (UN). At the same time, it was a response to the increasing number of intrastate conflicts with their devastating consequences of ethnic cleansing and genocide that had taken place in areas such as the Western Balkans and Rwanda. A noticeable mobilization on the international arena to act was observed, which included humanitarian military interventions and long-term international engagement to build peace (Hoffman and Weiss 2006; Philpott and Powers 2010). Taking the lead, former UN General Secretary Boutros Boutros-Ghali launched a new peacebuilding agenda in the document *Agenda for Peace* (1995) where peacebuilding is "defined as action to identify and support structures which will tend to strengthen and solidify peace in order to avoid a relapse into conflict." The document contained an ambitious agenda that underlined the responsibility of the international community not only to manage but also to prevent conflict. Hence, peacebuilding was launched in an attempt to resolve problems associated with fragile, failing, and dysfunctional states in order to transform them into robust liberal democracies. The prospect of building peace and security was also to be bolstered and embedded by economic development, interdependence, and regional cooperation. Consequently, comprehensive peace support operations began to expand dramatically from the early 1990s onwards not only in numbers but also in their multifunctional tasks and mandates (Heldt and Wallensteen 2006). In sum, the practice of peacebuilding largely evolved into state building (Call and Wyeth 2008; Chandler 2010).

10.3.5.1   Institutionalization of Peacebuilding

Peacebuilding is often described as the institutionalization of peace, which aims to balance the twin objectives of consolidating peace and averting a relapse into conflict (Mani 2002). There are numerous definitions and concepts associated with peacebuilding, which reflects the broad range of activities associated with the term (Call and Wyeth 2008; Cousens and Kumar 2001; Jeong 2005). Furthermore, the concept of peacebuilding serves as an umbrella notion, which overlaps with many other spheres of peacemaking, peacekeeping, development, reconciliation, institution building, and democracy promotion.

Ramsbotham and others (2012) suggests a useful analytical overview of peacebuilding, which is summarized in four dimensions. The first regards the *military/security*, focusing on establishing order and security in the post-conflict phase. For instance, peacekeeping troops can rapidly be deployed as a way to bolster a ceasefire, peace agreement, and to restore the monopoly of violence after the violence has ceased. Thus, the quest to integrate various military branches in to one and to transform rebel groups to political parties is of critical importance for the security and order (Edmunds 2008; Ekengren and Simons 2013; Lyons 2005; Sriram and Herman 2009). This ambition is reflected in the number of programs that the international community

10

has launched in recent years on Demilitarization, Demobilization, and Reintegration (DDR) and with Security Sector Reforms (SSR). The second dimension of peacebuilding is *political/constitutional*, which focuses on supporting the political and democratic transition from war to peace by assisting in restoring law and order, for instance by drafting and making constitutional reforms and amendments, holding elections, and strengthening civil society. In addition, one central aim is to introduce and build good governance and to establish a strong justice sector, which can monitor the adherence of human rights and democratic norms (Call 2007; Jarstad and Sisk 2008; Sriram, Martin-Ortega, and Herman 2010).

The third dimension relates to *economic/social* peacebuilding practices, such as assisting with development and long-term sustainable macro-economic planning aimed to stabilize the economy of the state. Such efforts may include issues related to distributive justice and inequal-ities between groups, but may also include land ownership, prop-erty rights, employment, and welfare programs (Berdal 2009; Carey 2012; Donais 2005). The last dimension concerns the *psycho/social* of building peace in conflict-ridden and traumatized post-war societies. Thus, peacebuilding is here strongly associated with justice (Biggar 2003; Lambourne 2009; Lederach 1997; Murithi 2009).

In many ways, the transitional justice has moved to the forefront of the peacebuilding agenda (Bell 2009; Teitel 2000) as several contem-porary conflicts have suffered from ethnic cleansing, war crimes, and genocide. It is also a core priority of the international community to hold perpetrators accountable for crimes and violence committed during war. Accordingly, it marks an end to the culture of impunity that existed during the Cold War. Moreover, to address past atroci-ties is viewed as critical for any durable peace settlements. One overarching assumption is therefore that processes of democratiza-tion, peacebuilding, and transitional justice are mutually reinforcing (Fukuyama 2004; Ignatieff 2003).

There are numerous empirical cases where principles of retributive justice are ingrained within the peacebuilding paradigm and practice, such as the International Criminal Tribunal for the former Yugoslavia and the United Nations International Criminal Tribunal for Rwanda (Kerr and Mobekk 2007; Rotberg and Thompson 2000). Also restora-tive justice principles are promoted within peacebuilding, focusing on social and political processes to rebuild fractured relationships. The Truth and Reconciliation Commission in South Africa is an often-referred example of where peace is seen as being achieved through the empowerment of victims and offenders (Clark 2008; Menkel-Meadow 2007; Zehr 2002).

The strong emphasis on justice in peacebuilding, however, has also caused heated debates among practitioners and scholars (Albin 2009; Herman et al. 2013). One line of argument is that justice is an essen-tial good to be pursued, which may contribute to the consolidation of a sustainable peace. It claims that the urgency of reaching an end to violent conflict may fail to address underlying causes of conflict and violations of international humanitarian law and therefore cause peace accords to collapse. A contrasting argument considers the pur-suit of justice to undermine pragmatic and more realistic peacemaking efforts, causing counterproductive results and triggering new conflicts.

Yet, as Hughes, Schabas, and Thakur (2007) point out, while justice does not necessarily generate or equate to peace, it is necessary and appropriate to integrate justice in peace processes in order to produce conditions for a durable peace.

10.3.5.2   In Theory: Contesting Ideal Types of Peacebuilding

In the last two decades, the peacebuilding field has quickly been professionalized due to the increasing needs and demands of peace expertise, particularly from Western policy makers. To reduce and manage the complexities posed by contemporary conflicts, the international community has continuously strived towards a standardized, professionalized, and at times technocratic method-ology of peacebuilding (Aggestam 2015; Mac Ginty 2012). Yet, des-pite successful outcomes in some peace processes, the peacebuilding field is still struggling with a whole range of problems and challenges, such as those posed by collapsed peace processes (Mac Ginty 2006), the non-implementation of negotiated peace agreements (Stedman, Rothchild, and Cousens 2002), the resurgence of violence in post-conflict societies by so-called peace spoilers (Darby 2001; Newman and Richmond 2006), exclusion of women and other marginalized groups (Paffenholz et al. 2016), and widespread peace fatigue in long-drawn out peace processes where conflicts tend to be frozen (Aggestam and Björkdahl 2012; Perry 2009). Hence, a number of assessment studies and evaluation programs have been conducted on peacebuilding practices that aim to distil lessons learned and identify best practices (see, for example, Reychler and Schirch 2013).

The scholarly field on peacebuilding has therefore sought to generate policy relevant contributions, which, for example, is reflected in the large number of handbooks on peacebuilding produced, including tool-boxes and recommendations of suitable strategies (see, for example, UN 2010 and Ho Wong 2002). Several academic studies have examined the correlation between peacebuilding and sustain-able peace from a diversity of theoretical perspectives (Newman, Paris, and Richmond 2009) and methodological approaches ranging from large-sample studies (Wallensteen 2015) to ethnographic studies (Paffenholz 2001; Richmond 2011). Yet, despite its generic drive one shared conclusion from these studies is that there is no universal blue-print of peacebuilding. Hence, greater attention is now paid to local ownership, institutions, and capacity peacebuilding.

At the same time, these evaluations and assessments have triggered major debates among scholars who hold distinct ideas of what should be viewed as efficient and sustainable peacebuilding. Newman et al. (2009) have identified three ideal types of peacebuilding: transforma-tive, realist, and liberal. *Transformative peacebuilding* focuses on resolving the underlying causes to conflict and strive to promote a dur-able peace that rests on a positive interpretation of peace and social justice, which includes a desire to engage with local actors, bottom-up approaches, and the promotion of human security needs (Mac Ginty 2012). Accordingly, this is not a universalizing vision of peace but one that recognizes the importance of diverse contexts. In contrast *realist peacebuilding* puts less emphasis on resolving conflict and more on managing and containing conflict escalation. An overriding stra-tegic concern is the establishment of international stability and order

10

by establishing strong states. Societal change, on the other hand, is delinked from international peacebuilding (Barnett, Songying, and Christoph 2014). Finally, *liberal peacebuilding* may be the one that most clearly articulates its vision of peace by its democracy promotion, market economy, and state-building efforts. Thus, it has guided most peacebuilding interventions in recent years. This is also why the debates mostly have centered on liberal peacebuilding where critics highlight its limitations in practice (Campbell, Chandler, and Sabaratnam 2011).

Contemporary peacebuilding practices have been criticized for its top-down and hegemonic interventions, which tend to create more of virtual rather than real state institutions and hybrid forms of peace as a result of the international-local interplay (Mac Ginty 2010). Also the ambition to rapidly promote democracy and market based economic reforms in post-conflict societies risk causing instability and even exacerbate conflict. In addition, ill-timed and poorly organized political elections may backfire and trigger ethnic tensions, which we have seen in Bosnia-Herzegovina and Iraq. Scholarly work has highlighted the risk and vulnerabilities of conflict escalation particularly in partial democracies and transitional states. This is why Roland Paris (2004), for example, argues that institutionalization should precede liberalization.

10.3.5.3 Peacebuilding at the Crossroads

As these debates reflect, peacebuilding in practice has in many instances failed to live up to the high hopes and ambitious normative agenda articulated in the 1990s. Consequently, we are today witnessing an increasing pragmatism in peacebuilding (Barnett et al. 2014; Paris 2014), which is coupled with new major security and political challenges in global politics, such as the Russian aggression against Ukraine and annexation of Crimea, global jihadist terrorist attacks, and the expansion of the Islamic State's (IS) spheres of influence in the Middle East and elsewhere. These are taking place in parallel with the increasing failures of regional and international institutions to cope and manage these security threats with cohesive, comprehensive, and multilateral strategies, which the ongoing war in Syria tragically illustrates. The concept of resilience in peacebuilding has therefore taken hold and centers on capacity building and the strengthening of local communities themselves to prevent and manage conflict and violence (Chandler 2015). We will return to discuss resilience in further details in the concluding section of this chapter.

10.4 Particular Issues

10.4.1 State Capacity

This section discusses the link between state capacity and political violence, focusing on the outbreak of civil war and cases of state failure.[47] Indeed, some of the most influential explanations of internal conflict in recent years have singled out the lack of state capacity as a major cause of war. This perspective on "state weakness," derives directly from Hobbes' classical account of political order according to which only the Leviathan, that is the sovereign state, can guarantee peace

and political stability. Thus, weak territorial control opens up a window of opportunity to rebellion challenging the state's monopoly of violence. The modern understanding of sovereignty shows how this institution developed gradually in early modern Europe through a process of institutional centralization and elimination of competing power centers (Tilly 1990). This process saw a gradual shift from pre-modern "indirect rule," that relied on feudal intermediaries and warlords, to systematic imposition of "direct rule," which enabled the state to consolidate its control over its territory, by building up an effective state bureaucracy, disarming its internal rivals, and securing enough resources through tax revenues and other types of resource extraction.

Having inspired generations of realist scholars in international relations, the Hobbesian perspective on the state and political order pervades modern theories of civil war. According to Huntington (1968: 1), "the most important political distinction among countries concerns not their form of government but their degree of government." On this view, too little rather than too much state is the main problem. As an account of political violence, then, the Hobbesian approach expects civil war to erupt in areas of weak statehood, because it is precisely there that rebels fighting irregular war are able to overcome numerically superior state forces.

This logic is visible in Fearon and Laitin's (2003) highly influential account of civil war. Because of the asymmetric conditions facing rural rebels, state capacity is not primarily about raw military power so much as about the state's control of its population. Fearon and Laitin argue that administratively incompetent states, especially those that extract their resources through the shortcut of oil extraction, are less likely to do their policing effectively, with large-scale violence as a consequence. Similarly, Posen (1993) offers an explanation of ethnic civil war as "emergent anarchy" whereby competing ethnic groups launch offensive attacks on each other after the collapse of multi-ethnic states, such as the former Yugoslavia. Even more drastically, Mueller (2004) reduces civil war to opportunistic predation waged by hooligans and bandits in the absence of efficient statehood. State failure constitutes the most drastic type of state weakness. In such cases of state collapse, whatever remains of the government faces multiple typically ethnic rebellions that produce a state of ungovernability and pervasive political violence (Rothberg 2004). Under such conditions, warfare will tend to become especially chaotic bringing forth widespread criminality and human rights abuse.

While situations characterized by weak statehood have indeed produced considerable violence, especially in sub-Saharan Africa since the end of the Cold War, it would be premature to generalize from such cases to civil war in general (Kalyvas 2001). There can be no doubt about the importance of state capacity as a prerequisite for peace and long-term political stability, but the Hobbesian perspective suffers from a host of problems that makes it too limiting to be relied on as a general guide to peace and progress.

One obvious difficulty concerns the challenge of operationalizing and measuring state capacity. While Fearon and Laitin (2003) relied on GDP per capita and rough terrain as proxies, subsequent studies have stressed the multidimensional nature of the concept (e.g. Hendrix

---

[47] There is a long-standing literature on configurations of state capability as explanations of interstate conflicts (e.g. Maoz 1983).

2010). However, most of these alternative indicators also rely on averages over the entire territory of countries. Yet, there is no reason to believe that statehood is evenly distributed over the territory of states, especially in underdeveloped ones (Herbst 2000). Thus, it is essential to develop measures of local state capacity, which is becoming possible thanks to methodological advances involving geographic information systems (Tollefsen and Buhaug 2015). Road networks represent one particularly promising measure of local state capacity (Herbst 2000; Hunziker 2015).

Another problem afflicting explanations turning on state weakness is that they operate with a narrow, materialist notion of state capacity that focuses on the military might, territorial control of the population and the delivery of public goods. Yet, this somewhat "colorblind" rendering of sovereignty, fails to realize that the modern state also engages in identity formation that has the potential of generating loyalty that drastically reduces the likelihood of rebellion (Goodwin 1997). In fact, ethnically distinctive groups that differ from the center in terms of language, religion, or other markers, may react with protest and separatism if the state fails in its nation-building project (Flora 1999). Such reactions are especially likely to trigger separatist nationalism where a shift from indirect to direct rule deprives the local populations of previous autonomy (Hechter 2000) and exposes ethnically distinctive minorities to resource extraction and immigration (Weiner 1978) and "internal colonialism" (Hechter 1975). Even in Western Europe, in one of the paradigmatic cases of state strength, it took a long time to turn "peasants into Frenchmen" (Weber 1976).

Thus, the Hobbesian rendering of state capacity needs to be complemented with an understanding of how the state may serve as an instrument of established ethnic and class-based elites. Leaders of such states are prone to refer to rebels as criminals and terrorists who should be suppressed with repressive policies. Rather than producing peace, strengthening state capacity in such cases may offer repressive governments even more opportunities to marginalize and ultimately crush their domestic opponents. Whereas some scholars think that giving war a chance is the best way to bring order to war-torn countries (Luttwak 1999), it is very doubtful that lasting peace will be achieved without addressing underling injustices and inequalities (Cederman, Gleditsch and Buhaug 2013). Unless combined with inequality reduction and inclusion, the strengthening of state capacity will perpetuate violence in the long run.

10.4.2   Social Movements, Social Media, and Violence

The question posed here is about the actuality of dynamics between new "movements," conflict, and violence, and the importance of social digital media in these new dynamics. This means we are also discussing the future of social conflict theory and new conflictual intrastate dynamics.

By integrating long-time analysis on movements such as Occupy Wall Street, Indignados, and more recently Nuit Debout in France, we think that the definition of problems related to the economic crisis and cultural concerns in these new dynamics is now not weighted down by classical cultural references of "old" social movements ("nation,"

"revolution," "religion," for example) as it has been interpreted by including violence as a possibility in traditional social movements. New social and cultural issues seem to be expressed in *new conflicting forms pacified in their modes of action* (Ferret 2014; Wieviorka 2005, 2012).

Taken in this light, the open criticism of violence and social control in the core of these "movements" can be considered as a sign of a *real specific identity work* made by individuals or *sujets* (Touraine 1992) who plan to shape a critical opposition to global cultural values such as the verticality of social relations, the communicative power and dominant ideologies through several fields (politics, gender relations, relations between generations, etc.).

This *identity work* is based on the development of *hybrid organizations* (but it doesn't mean the end of organizations and the classic *loi d'airain d'oligarchie* of Michels) and animation against critical physical and virtual spaces dedicated to regulate and regulate the violence contained in the system of values we fight.

This *denied violence* may then be defined as the sign of a particular mediation maintained between a movement in construction and apprehended critical action, in the words of Touraine (1973, 1993), at the lowest level, that is to say, as protests manifested not by a priori guidelines framed but *positive resistances*. This construction of a *collective subject* released ideological macro-narratives should not be understood in a triumphant and heroic dimension (Touraine 1992) but as a painful work, anxious, people wary of democratic disciplines and mimetics without trying for long to break with the "system." In these new dynamics, Internet, Social Media, and powerful connectivity can be considered as *new confrontational spaces*.

On one hand, digital media can be used in the non-confrontational phase, when the opponents are at a distance. In fact, such opponents rarely communicate with each other. Each communicates with its own side, and with the unmobilized people in their network who they would like to bring in as allies. This could be analyzed with the C-Escalation/D-Escalation model of time-dynamics (Collins 2012; Collins and Sanderson 2015; Ferret 2015, 2016). In the early phase of these movements (Indignados, Nuit Debout, for example), we observed that Digital media are good for spreading narratives and images, especially since these corporate official media tend to simplify as much as possible the reality and show only the violence. These movements offer new medializations and they feed the polarization process because these digital media are prime bases for spreading rumors and reputation (the medialization of violence of the police units in the street with CopWatch). Even photo images can act as rumors, since they can be sent without attending to the surrounding context, and without giving accurate information about the identities of the persons represented. Thus, we can expect that digital media mobilize social networks to engage in more conflict and control the violence of the State.

But, on the other hand, these media have such diverse connections that they cannot generate a single, common focus of attention. They are prone to multiple definitions of reality, and tend to disperse attention to many different directions. So, we can make this into a researchable question: when do digital media generate a stronger collective focus of attention (more people circulating the same messages), and when are they more scattered?

The answer, from situations like mobilization in Madrid and Barcelona during Indignados' mobilizations in 2011 appears to be that physical action on the ground is what generates more common attention. The social media can mobilize little groups of friends and acquaintances to go out to a place to demonstrate or fight, and the events there create focus of attention. There is some evidence that many people stayed home to watch, so that the media inhibited participation, when there was publicity about the opponents' repressive violence. So far it appears that digital media operate above all in the mobilizing phase and not in the conflict itself.

There has been a certain amount of enthusiastic propaganda about the digital age and how it is transforming society. In reality, it has been adding on to existing structures of society but not supplanting them, or even changing them very much. A powerful social conflict is when social groups organize to generate one big Durkheimian collective consciousness, full of resounding emotions; and this is best done where there is a big central place where people gather and the conflict with the enemy takes place in the historic central places of a city. The media can help publicize this but it does not eliminate *the need to physically gather for the confrontation.*

10.4.3   Inequality

Few topics are more controversial in conflict research than the link between inequality and political violence. Yet, it is important to note that both concepts are multidimensional. Here we will narrow down the latter concept to revolutions and civil wars, but it is likely that inequality is related to other types of conflict as well, including interstate war.[48]

Inequality can also be divided into subcategories. While most social science research focuses on individual-level comparisons, there is a growing realization that inequality also needs to be conceptualized and measured at the level of groups. Whereas the former can be referred to as individual or "vertical" inequality, the latter has been labeled "horizontal" inequality between culturally defined groups (Stewart 2008), or even more generally "categorical" inequality, which also includes gender (Tilly 1999).

Regardless of the level, inequality can emerge along various key dimensions. With respect to conflict, political and economic differences are arguably the most important, but other social and cultural aspects are also relevant. Since individual-level political equality is to a large extent synonymous with democracy, we will discuss those issues in the section on democracy below.

The classical literature covering the link between vertical inequality and conflict focused on peasant revolutions (Paige 1975; Scott 1976). Stressing protest against exploitative social orders and unmet expectations, these studies postulate that widely held frustrations will

trigger violence (Gurr 1970). However, others questioned the extent to which grievances and inequality could be seen as causes (e.g. Tilly 1978). This classical literature failed to generate clear results (e.g. Lichbach 1989), partly because it focused almost entirely on socio-economic inequality among individuals rather than between identity groups.

This finally led many influential researchers to question the link between inequality and internal conflict altogether (e.g. Collier and Hoeffler 2004; Fearon and Laitin 2003). However, other researchers have made efforts to measure such distinctions systematically (e.g. Cederman, Gleditsch, and Buhaug 2013; Gurr 1993; Petersen 2002).

In summary, the literature tells us that individual-level inequality can generate conflict, especially in stark cases of socioeconomic exploitation (see e.g. Wood 2003), but there is no strong evidence that there is such a regularity at the global level (though see Boix 2008). The empirical record is much more robust when it comes to the link between both political and economic inequality among ethnic groups and civil war. Contrary to claims that greed trumps grievances, recent studies have shown that political marginalization of ethnic groups increases the risk of conflict (Cederman, Wimmer and Min 2010; Cederman, Gleditsch, and Buhaug 2013).

The same goes for horizontal inequality along economic lines, as shown by Cederman, Weidmann, and Gleditsch (2011). Yet, the jury is still out as regards the distinction between religious and non-religious conflict. While a number of scholars argue that religious conflict is on the rise (Toft 2007), others argue that there is no strong evidence that ethno-linguistic conflicts have become eclipsed by religious strife (Bormann et al. 2017). In contrast, there is growing evidence as regards gender inequality and the onset of internal conflict (see e.g. Melander 2005) and sexual violence during such conflicts (e.g. Wood 2009).

In many cases, horizontal inequality has major repercussions on political violence beyond the borders of the state. Most importantly, in cases where ethnic groups straddle state borders, governmental elites in homeland states may take a keen interest in the well-being of their ethnic kin in neighboring states. Where such groups are both politically and economically discriminated against, the risk of interventions orchestrated by the homeland increases. The worst-case scenario features a spiral of violence that causes civil war between the ethnic minority and the government in the host state, further spilling over into irredentist warfare between the two states (Weiner 1971). While some experts believe this pattern has become much less frequent in today's world (Saideman and Ayres 2008), the eruption of violence in the Eastern Ukraine and Nagorno-Karabakh illustrate that irredentism cannot be written off as a thing of the past.

There is also plenty of historical evidence for a link between horizontal inequality along ethnic lines and civilian victimization. Mann (2005) shows that ideological repression of indigenous populations by colonist settlers and ethnic minorities by ethnonationalists has generated waves of ethnic cleansing and genocide during the past two centuries. However, because the leading datasets have so far not been coded with respect to the ethnicity of the victim groups, there is less systematic comparative evidence on the link between political and economic

---

[48]   We will discuss some of these links in the section on democracy below.

dimensions of ethnic inequality and one-sided violence, but thanks to new data collection efforts, this situation is fortunately about to change.

What do all these findings imply for the prevention and reduction of political violence? If inequality causes violence, it can reasonably be expected that decreasing inequality will lead to pacification. Obviously, this presupposes that inequality can be changed in the first place, which is more likely in the case of political as opposed to economic asymmetries. But it is important to see how even political inclusion may be extremely difficult to achieve, especially in a climate of mistrust and resentment following a larger conflict. Exactly how to bring members of marginalized groups into politics is a matter of dispute. Whereas most scholars support various schemes of power sharing at the group level (e.g. Gurr 2000; Lijphart 1977; Mattes and Savun 2009), others are much more skeptical (e.g. Roeder 2005). The fear is that power sharing will cement societal, and especially ethnic divides, making it impossible to transcend them.[49] This, in itself, could lead to rigid and brittle arrangements that lock the country into a conflict spiral that will see violent conflict recur sooner or later. In addition, territorial power sharing, such as federalism and autonomy, may also provide potential secessionists with resources to stage future rebellions, thus creating a state in the state that is ready to secede at any time, as illustrated by the breakup of the former Yugoslavia and the USSR (e.g. Snyder 2000).

Such pessimism, however, is most likely exaggerated, at least as a general analysis, because the comparisons fail to take into account that power-sharing arrangements are typically invoked in particularly difficult conflict cases, which means that their pacifying tends to be underestimated (Wucherpfennig, Hunziker, and Cederman 2016). Furthermore, the power-sharing skeptics assume that the alternatives, such as US-style individualist centralized solutions, are even less likely to trigger violence, which is a dubious assumption in case of ethnically divided post-conflict settings (McGarry and O'Leary 2009).

If equalizing policies are likely to deliver peace, a decrease of inequality would be especially welcome. In fact, there is good news in this respect. Whereas economic inequality among households within the same countries has been increasing in most parts of the world (Bourguignon 2015; Milanovic 2016), the overall global trend in domestic horizontal inequality seems to be the opposite. Especially in Asia, marginalized ethnic groups have been able to partially catch up with their countries' average income. Yet, the main exception to this trend is sub-Saharan Africa, where marginalized groups are lagging further behind (Bormann et al. 2016). However, this unfortunate effect may be compensated by reduced political inequality. Particularly in sub-Saharan Africa, ethnic inclusion through power sharing and group rights has been increasing since the end of the Cold War. This pattern appears to be part of a more general "regime of accommodation" that has contributed to the decrease of violence during this period (Gurr 2000).

10.4.4 Regime Type and Peace

Following up the general discussion of inequality and conflict above, this section conceptualizes democracy as an issue of political equality at the individual level. Nevertheless, group-level equality remains pertinent as a background factor, since democratic governance presupposes a "demos" (Dahl 1989), that is a unit constituting the voting population, which is often defined in ethnic terms (Mann 2005).[50] Given a reasonably inclusive demos, democracy boils down to contestation open to participation (Dahl 1971), which in turn calls for effective participation, voting equality, enlightened understanding by the citizens, and control of the agenda (Dahl 1989).

What do we know about democracy and conflict? The democratic peace literature is a natural place to start. Building on Kant's (1795) famous political philosophy, contemporary scholarship tells us that there is virtually no warfare between democratic states.[51] Despite some dissenting voices, most researchers agree that there is a very robust link between the presence of democracy and no or little interstate conflict due to both institutional and normative mechanisms (e.g. Russett 1993; Russett and Oneal 2001; for a review, see Hegre 2014). The former mechanism tells us that democracies are better than authoritarian regimes at aggregating the (presumably) pacific preferences of the wider population that has to carry most of the costs of war. The latter mechanisms stresses that democracy is a system of peaceful conflict resolution that tends to externalize such peaceful norms to relations with other democracies.

The "domestic democratic peace" follows similar lines. Compared to authoritarian rule, democracy can be expected to exhibit less group-level exclusion, while offering peaceful means of contestation and constraints on the use of violence by governments (Hegre 2014). In this sense, democratic governance serves as a tool to overcome commitment problems between wealthy elites and poor masses (Acemoglu and Robinson 2005). Yet, as already indicated, all this presupposes that the demos problem has been resolved. Failure to do so can spawn ethnic separatist war and even repression along ethnic lines, as illustrated by long-standing conflicts in Turkey and Israel. Furthermore, incompletely institutionalized semi-democracies may be more prone to violence than established full democracies because they offer more opportunities to mass participation without institutional safeguards against populist extremism and manipulation of key institutions, including the courts, the media, and elections. Accordingly, Hegre et al. (2001) suggest that conflict risk follows an inverted U-curve, which means that it is really the semi-democracies that are the least stable, although the evidence remains somewhat mixed as regards this regularity (Hegre 2014). In contrast, there is no support for the simple linear proposition that more democracy means less civil war.

With respect to one-sided violence and repression, regime type also appears to play an important role. Davenport (2004) proposes that the domestic democratic peace does exist with respect to state repression.

---

49   Also, power sharing after conflict may marginalize moderate voices within each group, while giving the radicals a seat at the table (Jarstad 2008).

50   The crux is that this unit cannot be determined through voting for logical reasons, so in this sense democracy presupposes a high degree of agreement as to the membership criteria within the demos and cannot coexist with high degrees of horizontal inequality.

51   It should be noted, however, that the extent to which democracies are more peaceful in their relations with non-democratic states is much more controversial (see Hegre 2014).

In an influential study, Harff (2003) claims that democracy contributes to preventing genocide. At the same time, however, democracies may be more prone to be targeted by terrorists because the openness of such systems make them more vulnerable to extortion by violent groups (for a review, see Valentino 2014).

In contrast to the optimism expressed by Bill Clinton and George W. Bush's attempts to spread democracy as a foreign policy goal, the realization that democratization, as opposed to stable democracy, may be disproportionally vulnerable to both interstate and intrastate conflict needs to be taken seriously. Following similar lines as the arguments about semi-democracy and conflict mentioned above, these scholars stress how authoritarian elites may attempt to stay in power through ethnic outbidding by extremists who try to overtrump each other with increasingly extremist views (Horowitz 1985). Likewise, incomplete democracies appear to be more likely to experience diversionary war, implying that elites try to stay in power and deflect from their own weaknesses by launching foreign military adventures (Mansfield and Snyder 2005). Especially where the demos is contested, there is no guarantee that the opening of a previously authoritarian system will not produce a surge in exclusive ethno-nationalism.

While this literature has managed to convince many researchers that there are such adverse effects, serious measurement difficulties continue to haunt research on democratization and war, especially because the former concept is difficult to operationalize based on highly aggregated democracy indices. For this reason, a number of studies have tried to unpack the notion of democratic governance by focusing on aspects of democracy, such as for example elections (e.g. Wilkinson 2004). The evidence that civil wars may be more likely both before and after elections is growing (e.g. Brancati and Snyder 2013; Cederman, Gleditsch, and Hug 2013). Other aspects of regime type that call for increased scrutiny are the rule of law, the role of media, and the interaction with ethnic inclusion through territorial and governmental power sharing, or the extension of group rights.

Given these open empirical questions, it does not come as a surprise that there is a lively debate about how to approach democratization in the context of development of peacemaking (Crocker and Hampson 2007). Although there is general agreement that fully institutionalized democracy is peaceful and stable, the main issue concerns how to get there from a starting point characterized by both a lack of democracy and deep divisions, possibly including past or ongoing civil war. The ill-fated US intervention in Iraq in 2003 has been particularly sobering for the democratization enthusiasts and has arguably vindicated those who warn against the conflict-fueling effect of democratization. Yet Western support for authoritarian regimes in the Middle East along pragmatic geopolitical lines stressing "security first" does not seem to be a recipe for stability and peace either. It makes little sense to recommend a unified pace of democratization that would fit all societies, but the goal of establishing political equality, the rule of law, and popular legitimacy clearly cannot be postponed for ever. For sure, it would be futile to try to impose majoritarian democracy on deeply divided, conflict-torn states. As argued above, democracy needs to be combined with some type of governmental and possibly territorial power sharing, even though such systems deviate from basic democratic principles such as one-person-one-vote.

10.4.5   Geopolitics and Power Re-Configurations

The complexities of the present international order that we have illustrated in this chapter with respect to war, terrorism, violence, and (inadequate) global security measures has also prompted a discussion on geopolitics.[52] Today, the concept of geopolitics is often used as a synonym for "power politics" and presented as an alternative to international institutionalism represented by the idea of the "liberal" international order (Ikenberry 2001). Users of "geopolitics" imply that universal approaches are less valid today and that distinct geographically areas exhibit different political circumstances. It suggests that the Western-led type of international order envisaged after the end of the Cold War is now being challenged in regionally different ways. Thus, we need to consider these arguments and assess their validity.

Many argue that the decline of the power of the United States has a significant impact on international order. Unlike typical "power politics" among a limited number of powers in traditional European international society in the nineteenth century or the global confrontation between the two ideological camps during the Cold War period, the current world entails geographically distinctive power configurations. The rise of China may threaten US influence in East Asia. The withdrawal of the United States left the Middle East as a power vacuum, then experiencing serious confrontations among regional powers and sectarianism. Europe now finds itself in a "Great Game" style of confrontation between NATO and Russia. The impact of the war on terror-strategy on the spread of Islamic radicalism is associated with deteriorating security conditions in the Middle East, South Asia, and Africa.

Also security measures and peace operations vary in accordance with geopolitical configurations. We have observed regional variations in previous sections of this chapter, but additional examples can illustrate this. The United Nations is primarily active for peace and security in Africa, having operational partnerships with regional and sub-regional organizations, such as AU, ECOWAS, and IGAD. In Europe, regional organizations, notably EU, NATO, and OSCE, undertake their own operations without involving outside actors. In the Middle East regional organizations (Arab League, GCC, OIC) and regional powers (Saudi Arabia, Iran, Turkey) compete for greater influence in the region. As there are only modest regional organizations in South, South East, and East Asia, direct links to the United States are instead seen to be more important for peacemaking efforts. Regardless of one's views of geopolitics in the contemporary world, it seems true that the efforts on conflict and peace vary due to differing circumstances among the world's regions.

At this point, it may be instructive to recall traditional theorists of geopolitics, Halford J. Mackinder and Nicholas J. Spykman, to evaluate their significance in the context of the twenty-first century. The founder of "geopolitics," Mackinder, is known for concepts such as "pivot," "heartland," "crescent," "bridge head" in addition to "land power" and "sea power." Using this terminology, the United States is a special "sea power" maintaining worldwide alliance with other major "sea powers" such as Britain, Japan, and Australia. The traditional US stronghold in the Western Hemisphere is a large "outer crescent"

---

[52]   See, for instance, Mead (2014) and Ikenberry (2014).

area. To this is added traditional US "bridge heads" in the "inner crescent," today referring to NATO allies, Egypt, India, and Korea. On the other hand, the challenges against the American "sea power" exist in the "pivot" "heartland" area and some volatile parts of the Eurasian continent that constitute the "world island." The most famous dictum of Mackinder, referring to the two World Wars is "Who rules East Europe commands the Heartland; Who rules the Heartland commands the World Island; Who rules the World Island commands the World." Translating this to contemporary conditions it would suggest that the most significant geopolitical phenomenon at this moment is the possibility of NATO's eastward expansion and the counter-reactions by Russia over areas such as Ukraine and the Caucasus (Mackinder 1919).

Spykman asserted that Mackinder was misleading in his excessive emphasis on Eastern Europe by pointing to the importance of the "Rimland" with or against sea powers and land powers. According to Spykman, rephrasing Mackinder, those who dominate the Rimland will dominate the world. The United States as a hegemon failed over Rimland like the Korean Peninsula, Vietnam, Afghanistan, Iran, and Iraq during and after the Cold War by losing ground in its search for dominance of the world. One important observation is that the other superpower, China, in the Rimland, is in an "amphibious" zone and needs to cooperate or confront with both sea powers and land powers (Spykman 1944).

During the interwar period with the surge of founding fathers of theories of geopolitics, the type of international order based upon regional discrepancies was intensively discussed by researchers as well as practitioners. The Axis countries' ideas about a German Monroe Doctrine for Europe and the Japanese version for Asia reflected elements in the strategic debates before the Second World War. The United States as well as the European imperial powers sought to identify a way to accommodate regionalism in order to establish a worldwide system of international order (Rosenboim 2014). The advent of the Second World War and the creation of the post-1945 international order emerged in the wake of the collapse of regionalist views of power politics.

In the twenty-first century our quest for social progress would not allow us to simply reproduce the power configurations during the interwar period. But if geopolitical perspectives may entail critical insights into the reality of international politics, we may have to identify the appropriate manner we apply theories of geopolitics in our contemporary world. To consider geographically different circumstances is necessary for smooth and peaceful progress of international society, but does not necessarily require the vocabulary of geopolitics or its deterministic perspective.

10.4.6 Global Governance and International Institutions

Hedley Bull, a leading personality in the so-called English School in the discipline of international relations, defined "international society"

as a society of states, which, "conscious of certain common interests and common values, form a society in the sense that they conceive themselves to be bound by a common set of rules in their relations with one another, and share in the working of common institutions" (Bull 1977: 13). Following Bull's conception, we can still distinguish between formal and informal institutions of international society. Bull himself was interested in informal ones, for instance, the balance of power, war, and Great Powers, while he fully recognized the importance of treaty-based formal international organizations such as the United Nations as channels for international law and diplomacy.

In the contemporary world, there are a large number of international institutions including those created for the purpose of peace and security.[53] Ranging from the UN as a global body where the Security Council has far-reaching authority under Chapter VII to more mediation/arbitration style conflict resolution mechanisms by regional organizations such as EU, AU, and international courts, notably ICJ. Global governance of formal international institutions has developed considerably since the middle of the twentieth century compared to any other time in human history. The possibility of creating world government was discussed in conjunction with the creation of the League of Nations as well as its successor the United Nations. Instead of relying on one comprehensive international governmental body, international society in our age is constituted by numerous formal international institutions demarcated according to functions, geography, and politics. Perhaps the warning by Bull against the "domestic analogy" was heralded, but it is more correct to say that the state structures were stronger and have remained so. For instance, the state's welfare functions have made it important to the inhabitants in other ways than the traditional physical protection of the population. International order has to be maintained in a manner that is very different from any domestic order. Global governance by international institutions is advancing in a highly complex way, without any deliberate attempts to create any form of central world government. In fact, the 2010s has witnessed a backlash against, for instance, regional international organizations having too much influence.[54]

One may argue that informal institutions are quite important in international "anarchical society." As Bull pointed out, there are roles of major powers that also include the possibility of enforcement action. The recent discussion can be exemplified by concepts such as "PoC (protection of civilians)" and "R2P (responsibility to protect)," which all have a position in the UN documentation and have been referred to in Security Council decisions, although they have no formal standing in the UN Charter. The same is true for armed peacekeeping operations, which were first introduced in 1956 and now have evolved into multidimensional mission and with considerable flexibility in cooperation with regional and other international organizations, notably for support of intelligence, logistics, military technologies, professional civilian expertise, etc. Advanced activities to contribute to peace and security include the highly expanded spheres of development aid,

---

[53]   According to Wallensteen and Bjurner (2015: Appendix B) there are 31 regional or transregional interstate organizations dealing with peace and security. The total number of international organizations is estimated to be about 68,000 according to the Yearbook of International Organizations (www.uia.org/faq/intorgs1) of which some 5,000 are inter-governmental. Those dealing with security is thus but a fraction of the total.

[54]   The British referendum of June 2016 resulted in a rejection of the country's membership in the European Union, stimulating similar thoughts elsewhere. However, there has not been a debate about leaving the United Nations, not even under the UN-critical Bush Jr. administration in the United States.

humanitarian aid, rule of law reforms, human rights promotion, democratization assistance, etc.

What is striking is the ability to informally reorganize formal institutions. The concept of "partnership peacekeeping" is a key word in the current trend of international responses to crises of conflicts.[55] The United Nations is no longer a single or even a main implementer of international peace operations. When UN deploys large missions in Africa, for instance, UN seeks to collaborate with regional and sub-regional organizations such as AU and ECOWAS. Thus, in 2016, 9 of 16 UN peacekeeping missions were in Africa.[56] An additional five operations were based in the Middle East and the Balkans. It is a pattern that is likely to continue. A challenge will be to deploy a peacekeeping mission in Syria, once the war is over. One may think that there is a regional division of labor, where organizations such as EU, NATO, and OSCE act in Europe and in the Mediterranean area, where there are other arrangements for other regions. The special position of the United States in global governance is also an issue to be explored for the purpose of developing international institutions. These informal settings and considerations decisively affect the way peace operations are conducted by formal international institutions. The phenomenon of informal combinations of formal international institutions is a reflection of the complex reality of our contemporary world.

For instance, enforcement actions based upon Chapter VII authority is an institutional framework of the original design of the UN Charter. However, the use of Chapter VII has been developed through informal arrangements and consultations, not specified in the Charter. The now established pattern of granting Chapter VII authority to almost all the UN peacekeeping missions for specific mandates of PoC (protection of civilians) is an example of this. At the end of the Cold War the Security Council actually discussed other possible threats to international peace and security, such as those arising from economic, social, humanitarian, and environmental crises.[57] As we say in Section 10.3 of this chapter, for instance in Figure 10.13, the resort to action under Chapter VII is a crucial element in present global governance.

However, one may argue that the special power of the Security Council is also a serious problem due to its disproportionate representation. The permanent members of the Security Council have considerable power over decisions due to their legal right to use a veto, but also to the permanency of their position. While other states come and go as members, not staying longer than two years, the major powers have been in the Council since its inception, more than 70 years ago. Given that any reform of the composition of the Security Council is difficult to achieve in the foreseeable future, the legitimacy of the Security Council will continue to remain a crucial topic and thus require careful attention by the stakeholders in and outside of UN.

The special power of the permanent members of the Security Council is highly related to the ideological framework of contemporary international society. Some leading members of the Security Council regard their ideological foundation, which could be characterized as

"liberal values" of the West, as the natural framework for informal international institutionalism. Non-Western states are suspicious in this regard and worry that the United States and its allies are trying to impose their own standards on other states that may not share the same values at all or to the same extent. There is a danger that informal international institutionalism could lead to mistrust among various international actors. Fundamental consideration should be given to the importance of constant search for an appropriate balance between formal and informal international institutions of stable, solid, and sustainable global governance.

10.4.7 The Weakness of Global Society

The issue of violence and war requires the member states of the international society to find way to protect themselves. A typical way is to arm oneself against external threats, as well as against internal challenges. The logic of international threats would suggest that common activity against shared threats would be more logical. This is the reason for the existence of international and regional organizations within the field of peace and security. However, for most states the reliance on own national defense and national police remains the preferred option. Only Costa Rica and Iceland have opted for not having armed forces. Even the resort to shared peacekeeping operations is limited, although it would constitute a reasonable compromise between reliance on national vs. global resources. Table 10.5 demonstrates this very strongly. It lists the 10 countries that contribute the most to UN peacekeeping, as of 2016. The ordering of the countries follows the size of their assessed contributions (the third column) and the numbers can be compared to the military expenditures for the countries as a whole. By comparing to the GDP of the country the investment in national efforts can easily be compared to those going to international efforts for peace and security. For most of these countries the peacekeeping contributions are less than two hundredths of a percent of GDP compared to the 2 percent on average going to the national military expenditure. It is an illustration of the weakness of the resources going to the international efforts. The nationally controlled policies strongly outpace the global efforts. The logical solution of dealing with global challenges in common efforts still is far from the reality within the field of peace and security. The trends, furthermore, are not encouraging for international efforts, judging by pronouncement of the Trump administration in the United States.

10.5 Conclusion

International peace and security is at the crossroads with regards to agenda, practice, and theory. It has led to a search for alternative models of thought, sometimes explicitly aimed at replacing the 'liberal peacebuilding paradigm'. For instance, the notion of resilience has resurfaced and become attractive to academics and practitioners. Another concept is "sustaining peace," which has been incorporated in a number of UN resolutions, both by the Security Council and the General

---

[55] "Partnering for Peace: Moving Towards Partnership Peacekeeping: Report of the Secretary-General," UN Document, S/2015/229, April 1, 2015.

[56] Information provided by the UN Department of Peacekeeping Operations, website www.un.org/en/peacekeeping/operations/current.shtml.

[57] Statement by the President of the Security Council, UN Document, S/23500, January 31, 1992.

Table 10.5 | The top 10 providers of assessed contributions to UN peacekeeping operations 2016. Military expenditures versus UN peacekeeping contributions

Country	Military expenditure (100 millions USD)	Military expenditure as % of country's GDP	Peacekeeping contributions(100 millions USD)*	Peacekeeping contributions as % of country's GDP
United States	6189	3.3	2.2496	0.012
China	2184	1.9	0.8102	0.007
Japan	467	1.0	0.7622	0.016
Germany	416	1.2	0.5031	0.014
France	564	2.3	0.4968	0.020
UK	489	1.9	0.4566	0.017
Russia	701	5.3	0.3157	0.025
Italy	282	1.5	0.2952	0.016
Canada	157	1.0	0.2299	0.015
Spain	151	1.2	0.1921	0.015

* Peacekeeping contributions calculated from each country's percentage contribution relative to total UN Peacekeeping Operations for June 2016–July 2017 budget.
Data sources:
SIPRI World Military Expenditures Database
GDP by Country, World Bank Group
UN Department of Peacekeeping Operations
Source: UN Department of Peacekeeping Operations. Data Compiled by Global Policy Forum.

Assembly (e.g. in 2016) or the academically grounded "quality peace." These conceptions all acknowledge the complexity and multi-layered nature in the construction of peace. Also, they share the approach of not imposing a specific model or agenda for peace, but rather to facilitate, strengthen, and create space for existing national and local capabilities to cope with violent change and sustain peace within a global setting.

Some sections of this chapter indicate that the world has – for the past 25 years – seen a shift of authority from national states to more global cooperation, where coordination of interests has been the central concern, often captured by the term "globalization." There is much historical evidence to suggest that such forms of cooperation, particularly among major powers, ensure predictability and a reduction in the risks of wars among states. At the same time, the rise of civil wars, unilateral military interventions (notably in Iraq, Georgia, Ukraine, Syria) with novel techniques (drone warfare, targeted assassinations, cyberattacks, unidentified troops) and increasing emphasis on national interests (whether Chinese, Russian, British, or American) reduce the incentives for cooperation. Under such conditions mutual concerns are no longer seen as legitimate, unless they fit with particularistic interests. There are, thus, reasons to consider that the world in the middle of the 2010s finds itself at a crucial moment breaking away from some patterns of the past quarter-century. The expression used by Secretary-General Kofi Annan to the General Assembly in September 2003 when facing the situation when two permanent members of the Security Council had invaded a sovereign country without a UN mandate may be even more pertinent: "Excellences, we have come to a fork in the road. This may be a moment no less decisive than 1945 itself, when the United Nations was founded."[58]

The UN may have weathered the situation in 2003, the role of global institutions regained some standing. By 2015 the world had agreed both on new development goals (Agenda 2030, which includes Goal

16 for the development of peaceful societies) and actions for climate change (Paris Agreement 2015). Nevertheless, an undercurrent emphasizing exceptionality and nationalism surfaced strongly just a year later, 2016, exemplified by the referendum in the UK to leave the European Union, the negative Colombian popular vote on a peace agreement to end 50 years of civil war (but the process is finally going on reasonably) the election of Donald Trump as President of the United States, the authoritarian turn of Tayyip Erdogan in Turkey, and a global decline in the rate of democracy. More obviously than in a long time, there is a choice between a world with global governance based on concerns for universal human security (as advocated by Kofi Annan, above) and one based on forms of exclusive national sovereignty of ethnically and/or confessionally defined rights. And between these two levels, the global and the national, one should consider the role of regional cooperation, such as the European Union and the African Union.

The social progress documented in this chapter has largely required international cooperation and globally shared frameworks. Without that, much social progress is directly challenged. Thus, developing action to further cooperative solutions, with international, transnational, regional, or global forms appears more urgent than ever. This, of course, without promoting one particular societal form, but still building on globally shared values and empirically grounded policies.

In particular, the dangers arising from social inequalities within and between societies constitute a recurrent factor in analyses of cause of conflicts, wars, one-side violence, and terrorism. This refers to matters such as unequal access to power, protection, resources, education, and other basic goods for different segments of the population (whether considering gender, ethnic, religious, regional, or other social categories). Thus, a global agenda for lessening inequalities and increasing societal integration would have the benefit of reducing violence over the long term as well as constituting social progress in itself, by incorporating universal respect for human dignity.

[58] Kofi Annan to the UN General Assembly, September 23, 2003, www.un.org/webcast/ga/58/statements/sg2eng030923.htm

Furthermore, matters of physical security for social groups and vulnerable communities would need to be part of such an agenda. What happens after a war is important for the prevention of a recurrence of war. Respecting the rights to fair processes, democratic opportunities, and individual security for men and women alike is essential for long-term social progress, after termination of violent conflict and for the prevention of possible future violent conflicts. The problem in fact is not disputes and conflicts, but violence. In many respects, the transition of societies from violent to institutionalized, and continuous management and resolution of conflict is an important aspect of social progress.

Without a global agenda for dealing with violence and war through concerted action, the actors might instead find remedies, based on parochial efforts for social progress, for instance resorting to the local use of non-violent action, without an expectation of international support. This, furthermore, may be met with violent repression, particularly if there is a vacuum in international enforcement of human rights and humanitarian law. Such a decoupling between international, national and local norms and interests can result in greater harms being perpetrated against civilians, journalists and political dissidents. Finding ways to constructively connect the levels of global society may be necessary for making globally shared social progress, fairness, and human dignity attainable in the foreseeable future.

References

Acemoglu, D., and J.A. Robinson. 2005. *Economic Origins of Dictatorship and Democracy.* Cambridge: Cambridge University Press.

Adorno, T.W., E. Frenkel-Brunswik, D.J. Levinson, and N.R. Stanford. 1950. *The Authoritarian Personality.* New York: Harper & Brothers.

Aggestam, K. 2015. "Desecuritisation of Water and the Technocratic Turn in Peacebuilding." *Journal of International Environmental Agreement. Politics, Law and Economics* 15/3: 327–340.

Aggestam, K., and A. Björkdahl. 2012. "Just Peace Postponed: Unending Peace Processes and Frozen Conflicts," in K. Höglund and H. Fjelde (eds.), *Building Peace, Creating Conflict? Conflictual Dimensions of Local and International Peacebuilding.* Nordic Academic Press.

Aggestam, K., and A. Björkdahl (eds.). 2013. *Rethinking Peacebuilding: The Quest for Just Peace in the Middle East and the Western Balkans.* London and New York: Routledge.

Albin, C. 2009. "Peace vs. Justice – and Beyond," in V.K. Jacob Bercovitch and I. William Zartman (eds.), *The Sage Handbook of Conflict Resolution.* London: Sage.

Altheimer, I. 2008. "Social Support, Ethnic Heterogeneity, and Homicide: A Cross-National Approach." *Journal of Criminal Justice* 36/2: 103–114.

Anhut, R., and W. Heitmeyer. 2000. "Desintegration, Konflikt und Ethnisierung. Eine Problemanalyse und theoretische Rahmenkonzeption," in W. Heitmeyer and R. Anhut (eds.), *Bedrohte Stadtgesellschaft,* Konflikt- un Gewaltforschung. Weinheim, München: Juventa, 17–75.

Arms Control Association. www.armscontrol.org/treaties?page=2.

Baker, R. 2016. "Facing North Korea's Nuclear Reality." July 26. www.stratfor.com/weekly/facing-north-koreas-nuclear-reality

Barnett, M., F., Songying, and Z. Christoph. 2014. "Compromised Peacebuilding." *International Studies Quarterly* 58/3: 608–620.

Beck, U. 2002. *Macht und Gegenmacht im globalen Zeitalter: Neue welpolitische Ökonomie.* Frankfurt/Main: Suhrkamp.

Bell, C. 2009. "Transitional Justice, Interdisciplinarity and the State of the 'Field' or 'Non-Field.'" *International Journal of Transitional Justice* 3/1: 5–27.

Benslama, F. 2016. *Un furieux désir de sacrifice. Le surmusulman.* Paris: Le Seuil.

Berdal, M. 2009. *Building Peace After War.* London: Routledge.

Biggar, N. (ed.). 2003. *Burying the Past: Making Peace and Doing Justice after Civil Conflict.* Washington, DC: Georgetown University.

Binaifer, N. 1996. *Shattered Lives: Sexual Violence during the Rwandan Genocide and the Aftermath.* New York, Washington, London, and Brussels: Human Rights Watch/Women's WatchProject.

Bjorgo T. (ed.). 2005. *Root Causes of Terrorism: Myths, Reality and Ways Forward.* Abingdon: Routledge.

Böckler, N., T. Seeger, P. Sitzer, and W. Heitmeyer. 2013. "School Shootings: Conceptual Framework and International Empirical Trends," in *School Shootings.* New York: Springer.

Boix, C. 2008. "Economic Roots of Civil Wars and Revolutions in the Contemporary World." *World Politics* 60/3: 390–437.

Bormann, N., L. Cederman, Y. Pengl, and N.B. Weidmann. 2016. "Globalization, Exclusion and Ethnic Inequality." Unpublished paper.

Bormann, N., L. Cederman, and M. Vogt. 2017. "Language, Religion, and Ethnic Civil War." *Journal of Conflict Resolution* 61/4: 744–771.

Bourguignon, F. 2015. *The Globalization of Inequality.* Princeton, NJ: Princeton University Press.

Boutros-Ghali, B. 1995. *An Agenda for Peace.* New York: United Nations.

Brahimi, L., and S. Ahmed. 2008. *In Pursuit of Sustainable Peace: The Seven Deadly Sins of Mediation.* New York University: Center on International Cooperation.

Brancati, D., and J.L. Snyder. 2013. "Time to Kill the Impact of Election Timing on Postconflict Stability." *Journal of Conflict Resolution* 57/5: 822–853.

Browne, A., and K.R. Williams. 1993. "Gender, Intimacy, and Lethal Violence: Trends from 1976 through 1987." *Gender & Society* 7/1: 78–98.

Bull, H. 1977. *The Anarchical Society: A Study of Order in World Politics.* London: Macmillan.

Buss, D.E. 2009. "Rethinking 'Rape as a Weapon of War'" *Feminist Legal Studies* 17/2.08: 145–163.

Butler, C.K., T. Gluch, and N.J. Mitchell. 2007. "Security Forces and Sexual Violence: A Cross National Analysis of a Principal-Agent Argument." *Journal of Peace Research* 44/6: 669–687.

Call, C. (ed.). 2007. *Constructing Justice and Security after War.* Washington, DC: United States Institute for Peace.

Call, C.T., and V. Wyeth (eds.). 2008. *Building States to Build Peace.* Boulder, CO and London: Lynne Rienner.

Campbell, S., D. Chandler, and M. Sabaratnam (eds.). 2011. *A Liberal Peace? The Problems and Practices of Peacebuilding,* London: Zed Books.

Cantor, D.J. 2014. "The New Wave: Forced Displacement Caused by Organized Crime in Central America and Mexico." *Refugee Survey Quarterly* 33/3: 34–68.

Cao, L., and Y. Zhang. 2015. "Governance and Regional Variation of Homicide Rates: Evidence From Cross-National Data." *International Journal of Offender Therapy and Comparative Criminology* 61/1: 25–45.

Carey, H.F. 2012. *Privatizing the Democratic Peace: Policy Dilemmas of NGO Peacebuilding.* Basingstoke: Palgrave Macmillan.

CCSPJP 2016. "The 50 Most Violent Cities in the World 2014." Citizens' Council for Public Security and Criminal Justice. www.seguridadjusticiaypaz.org.mx/biblioteca/prensa/send/6-prensa/199-the-50-most-violent-cities-in-the-world-2014, 05.30.2016.

Cederman, L., K.S. Gleditsch, and H. Buhaug. 2013. *Inequality, Grievances and Civil War.* New York: Cambridge University Press.

Cederman, L., K.S. Gleditsch, and S. Hug. 2013. "Elections and Ethnic Civil War." *Comparative Political Studies* 46/3: 387–417.

Cederman, L., N.B. Weidmann, and K.S. Gleditsch. 2011. "Horizontal Inequalities and Ethno Nationalist Civil War: A Global Comparison." *American Political Science Review* 105/3: 478–495.

Cederman, L., A. Wimmer, and B. Min. 2010. "Why Do Ethnic Groups Rebel? New Data and Analysis." *World Politics* 62/1: 87–119.

Centre for Humanitarian Dialogue. 2007. *Charting the Roads to Peace: Facts, Figures and Trends in Conflict Resolution.* Centre for Humanitarian Dialogue: Geneva.

Chandler, D. 2010. *International Statebuilding: The Rise of Post-Liberal Governance.* Abingdon: Routledge.

Chandler, D. 2015. "Resilience and the 'Everyday': Beyond the Paradox of 'Liberal Peace.'" *Review of International Studies* 41/1: 27–48.

Clark, J.N. 2008. "The Three Rs: Retributive Justice, Restorative Justice, and Reconciliation." *Contemporary Justice Review* 11/4: 331–350.

Cockburn, C. 2010. "Gender Relations as Causal in Militarization and War: A Feminist Standpoint." *International Feminist Journal of Politics* 12/2: 139–157.

Cohen, D.K. 2013. "Explaining Rape during Civil War: Cross-National Evidence (1980–2009)." *American Political Science Review* 107/3: 461–477.

Cohen, D.K., and R. Nordås. 2014. "Sexual Violence in Armed Conflict: Introducing the SVAC Dataset, 1989–2009." *Journal of Peace Research* 51/3: 418–428.

Cole, J.H., and A.M. Gramajo. 2009. "Homicide Rates in a Cross-Section of Countries: Evidence and Interpretations." *Population and Development Review* 35/4: 749–776.

Collier, P., and A. Hoeffler. 2004. "Greed and Grievance in Civil Wars." *Oxford Economic Papers* 56: 563–595.

Collins, R. 2012. "C-escalation and D-Escalation: A Theory of the Time-Dynamics of Conflict." *American Sociological Review* 77/1: 1–20.

Collins, R., and S.K. Sanderson. 2015. *Conflict Sociology: A Sociological Classic Updated*. New York: Routledge.

Committee on the Elimination of Discrimination against Women (CEDAW). 2006. General Recommendation No. 19: Violence Against Women and Addendum, Draft General Recommendation No. 19 (1992): Accelerating Elimination of Gender-Based Violence Against Women. CEDAW/C/GC/19/Add.1.

Convergne, E. 2016. "The Mediation Support Unit and the Production of Expert Knowledge about Mediation at the UN." *Journal of Intervention and Statebuilding* 10/2: 181–199.

Cousens, E., and C. Kumar (eds.). 2001. *Peacebuilding as Politics*. Boulder, CO: Lynne Rienner.

Crenshaw M. 2010. *Explaining Terrorism: Causes, Processes and Consequences*. New York: Routledge.

Crocker, C.A., and F.O. Hampson (eds.). 2007. *Leashing the Dogs of War: Conflict Management in a Divided World*. New York: US Institute of Peace Press.

Crocker, C., F. Hampson, and P. Aall (eds.). 1999. *Herding Cats: Multiparty Mediation in a Complex World*. Washington, DC: United States Institute for Peace.

Dahl, R.A. 1971. *Polyarchy: Participation and Opposition*. New Haven, CT: Yale University Press.

Dahl, R.A. 1989. *Democracy and Its Critics*. New Haven, CT: Yale University Press.

Darby, J. 2001. *The Effects of Violence on Peace Processes*. Washington, DC: United States Institute of Peace Press.

Davenport, C. 2004. "The Promise of Democratic Pacification: An Empirical Assessment." *International Studies Quarterly* 48: 539–560.

Davies, S.E., and J. True. 2015. "Reframing Conflict-Related Sexual and Gender-Based Violence: Bringing Gender Analysis Back In." *Security Dialogue* 46/6: 495–512.

De Bellaigue, C. 2017. "Jihad and Death by Olivier Roy Review – The Global Appeal of Islamic State." *Guardian*, April 21.

De Haas, H., 2012. "The Migration and Development Pendulum: A Critical View on Research and Policy." *International Migration* 50/3: 8–25.

Del Felice, C. 2008. "Youth Criminality and Urban Social Conflict in the City of Rosario, Argentina." *International Journal of Conflict and Violence* 2/1: 72–97.

DeRouen, K., and Bercovitch, J. 2012, "Trends in Civil War Mediation," in J. Hewitt, J. Wilkenfeld, and T.R. Gurr (eds.), *Peace and Conflict*. Boulder CO: Paradigm.

Donais, T. 2005. *The Political Economy of Peacebuilding in Post-Dayton Bosnia*. Abingdon: Routledge.

Durand, J., and Massey, D.S. 2010. "New World Orders: Continuities and Changes in Latin American Migration," *The Annals of the American Academy of Political and Social Science* 630/1: 20–52.

Eck, K. 2016. "The Repressive Peace," in E. Bjarnegård and J. Kreutz (eds.), *Debating the East Asian Peace*. Copenhagen: Nordic Institute of Asian Studies Press.

Edmunds, T. 2008. *Security Sector Reform in Transforming Societies*. Manchester: Manchester University Press.

Ekengren, M., and G. Simons. 2013. *The Politics of Security Sector Reform*. Farnham, UK: Ashgate.

Englund, S., and M. Stohl. 2017. "Terrorism: Situations, Structure, and Dispositions as an Analytical Framework for Studying Terrorism," in M. Stohl, M.I. Lichbach, and P.N. Grabosky (eds.), *States and Peoples in Conflict. Transformations of Conflict Studies*. New York: Routledge.

Eriksson Baaz, M., and M. Stern. 2009. "Why Do Soldiers Rape? Masculinity, Violence, and Sexuality in the Armed Forces in the Congo (DRC)." *International Studies Quarterly* 53/2: 495–518.

Eriksson Baaz, M., and M. Stern 2013. *Sexual Violence as a Weapon of War?: Perceptions, Prescriptions, Problems in the Congo and Beyond*. London and New York: Zed Books.

Faist, T. 2008. "Migrants as Transnational Development Agents: An Inquiry into the Newest Round of the Migration–Development Nexus." *Population, Space and Place* 14/1: 21–42

Faist, T., M. Fauser, and P. Kivisto. 2011. *The Migration-Development Nexus: A Transnational Perspective*. London: Palgrave Macmillan.

Fearon, J.D. 2011. *Homicide Data: Third Revision Background Paper Prepared for the WDR 2011 Team*. Stanford, CA: Stanford University, Department of Political Science.

Fearon, J.D., and D.D. Laitin. 2003. "Ethnicity, Insurgency, and Civil War." *American Political Science Review* 97/1: 75–90.

Federation of American Scientists (FAS). https://fas.org/wp-content/uploads/2014/05/warheadhistory.jpg

Fein, H. 1979. *Accounting for Genocide: National Responses and Jewish Victimization during the Holocaust*. New York: Free Press.

Ferrales, G., H.N. Brehm, and S. Mcelrath. 2016. "Gender-Based Violence Against Men and Boys in Darfur: The Gender-Genocide Nexus." *Gender and Society* 4: 565–589.

Ferret, J. 2014. "La violence refusée des indignados espagnols." *Socio. La nouvelle revue des sciences sociales* 3: 375–391.

Ferret, J. 2015. *Violence politique totale. Un défi pour les sciences sociales*. Paris: Lemieux Editeur.

Ferret, J. 2016. *Crisis social, movimientos y sociedad en España hoy*. Zaragoza: Sibirana Ediciones.

Flora, Peter (ed.). 1999. *State Formation, Nation-Building, and Mass Politics in Europe: The Theory of Stein Rokkan*. Oxford University Press.

Fox, J., P. James, and L. Yitan. 2009. "State Religion and Discrimination Against Ethnic Minorities," in *Nationalism and Ethnic Politics*. London: Routledge.

Fukuyama, F. 2004. "The Imperative of State-Building." *Journal of Democracy* 15/2: 17–31.

Galtung, J. 1969. "Violence, Peace and Peace Research." *Journal of Peace Research* 6/3: 167–191.

Galtung, J. 1990. "Cultural Violence." *Journal of Peace Research* 27/3: 291–305.

Gartner, S.S. 2011. "Signs of Trouble: Regional Organization Mediation and Civil War Agreement Durability." *The Journal of Politics* 73/2: 380–390.

Gelles, R.J. 2003. "Violence in the Family," in J.L. Hagan and W. Heitmeyer (eds.), *International Handbook of Violence Research*. Netherlands: Springer.

Gelles, R.J., and Straus, M.A. 1988. *Intimate Violence*. New York: Simon & Schuster.

Gleditsch, N.P., S. Pinker, B.A. Thayer, J.S. Levy, and W.R. Thompson. 2013. "The Forum: The Decline of War." *International Studies Review* 15/3: 396–419.

Global Terrorism Database. National Consortium for the Study of Terrorism and Responses to Terrorism, University of Maryland. www.start.umd.edu/data/gtd.

Global Terrorism Index (GTI). 2015. *Global Terrorism Index 2015: Measuring and Understanding the Impact of Terrorism*. Sydney: Institute for Economics and Peace.

Global Terrorism Index (GTI). 2016. *Global Terrorism Index 2016: Measuring and Understanding the Impact of Terrorism*. Sydney: Institute for Economics and Peace.

Goldstein, J.S. 2011. *Winning the War on War: The Decline of Armed Conflict Worldwide*. New York: Penguin.

Goodwin, J. 1997. "State-Centered Approaches to Social Revolutions: Strengths and Limitations of a Theoretical Tradition," in J. Foran (ed.), *Theorizing Revolutions*. London: Routledge.

Gottschall, J. 2004. "Explaining Wartime Rape." *Journal of Sex Research* 41: 129–36.

Grawert, E., 2008. "Cross-Border Dynamics of Violent Conflict: The Case of Sudan and Chad." *Journal of Asian and African Studies* 43/6: 595–614.

Grieg, M., and P. Diehl. 2012. *International Mediation*. Cambridge: Polity.

Gurr, T.R. 1970. *Why Men Rebel*. Princeton, NJ: Princeton University Press.

Gurr, T.R. 1972. "The Calculus of Civil Conflict." *Journal of Social Issues* 28/1: 27–47.

Gurr, T.R. 1993. *Minorities at Risk: A Global View of Ethnopolitical Conflicts*. Washington, DC: United States Institute of Peace Press.

Gurr, T.R. 2000. "Ethnic Warfare on the Wane." *Foreign Affairs* 79: 52–64.

Gurr, T.R., and A. Pitsch. 2003. "Ethnopolitical Conflict and Separatist Violence," in W. Heitmeyer and J. Hagan (eds.), *International Handbook of Violence Research*. Dordrecht: Kluwer Academic.

Gutiérrez Sanín, F., and E.J. Wood. 2014. "Ideology in Civil War: Instrumental Adoption and Beyond." *Journal of Peace Research* 51: 213.

Hall, N., A. Corb, P. Giannasi, and J. Grieve (eds.) 2015. *The Routledge International Handbook on Hate Crime*. Abingdon and New York: Routledge.

Harff, B. 2003. "No Lessons Learned from the Holocaust? Assessing Risks of Genocide and Political Mass Murders since 1955." *American Political Science Review* 97/1: 57–73.

10

Harff, B. 2017. "Genocide and Political Mass Murder: Definitions, Theories, Analyses," in M. Stohl, M.I. Lichbach, and P.N. Grabosky (eds.), *States and Peoples in Conflict. Transformations of Conflict Studies*. New York: Routledge.

Hechter, M. 1975. *Internal Colonialism: The Celtic Fringe in British National Development, 1536–1966*. London: Routledge and Kegan Paul.

Hechter, M. 2000. *Containing Nationalism*. Oxford: Oxford University Press.

Hegre, H. 2014. "Democracy and Armed Conflict." *Journal of Peace Research* 51/2: 159–172.

Hegre, H., T. Ellingsen, S. Gates, and N.P. Gleditsch. 2001. "Toward a Democratic Civil Peace? Democracy, Political Change, and Civil War, 1816–1992." *American Political Science Review* 95(March): 33–48.

Heitmeyer, W. 2002. "Gruppenbezogene Menschenfeindlichkeit. Die theoretische Konzeption und erste empirische Ergebnisse" ["Group-Focused Enmity. The Theoretical Conception and First Empirical Results"], in W. Heitmeyer (ed.), *Deutsche Zustände, Folge 1* [*German States, Issue 1*]. Frankfurt/Main: Suhrkamp.

Heitmeyer, W., and R. Anhut. 2008. "Disintegration, Recognition, and Violence: A Theoretical Perspective." *New Directions for Student Leadership* 119: 25–37.

Heitmeyer, W., and J. Hagan 2003. "Violence: The Difficulties of a Systematic International Review," in W. Heitmeyer and J. Hagan (eds.), *International Handbook of Violence Research*. Dordrecht: Kluwer Academic.

Heldt, B., and P. Wallensteen. 2006. "Peacekeeping Operations: Global Patterns of Intervention and Success, 1948–2004," in B. Heldt (ed.), *Research Report*. Stockholm: Folke Bernadotte Academy.

Hendrix, C.S. 2010. "Measuring State Capacity: Theoretical and Empirical Implications for the Study of Civil Conflict." *Journal of Peace Research* 47/3: 273–285.

Henry, N. 2016. "Theorizing Wartime Rape: Deconstructing Gender, Sexuality, and Violence." *Gender and Society* 30/1: 44–56.

Herbst, J. 2000. *States and Power in Africa: Comparative Lessons in Authority and Control*. Princeton, NJ: Princeton University Press.

Herman, J., O Martin-Ortega, and C.L. Sriram. 2013. *Beyond Justice Versus Peace: Transitional Justice and Peacebuilding Strategies*. https://ecpr.eu/Filestore/PaperProposal/6e3e3742-d3fb-405e-aa53-56d810f1b4b2.pdf.

High-Level Panel (HLP) 2004. *Report of the Secretary-General's High-Level Panel on Threats, Challenges and Changes: A More Secure World: Our Shared Responsibility*. New York: United Nations.

Ho Wong, Jeong. 2002. *Approaches to Peacebuilding*. Basingstoke: Palgrave Macmillan.

Hoffman, P., and T. Weiss. 2006. *Sword and Salve: Confronting New Wars and Humanitarian Crisis*, Oxford: Rowman & Littlefield.

Holmes, R.M., and S.T. Holmes (eds.) 1998. *Contemporary Perspectives on Serial Murder*. London: Sage.

Hoover Green, A. 2011. "Rape Reporting During War: Why the Numbers Don't Mean What You Think They Do" (with Amber Peterman, Tia Palermo and Dara Kay Cohen), *Foreign Affairs*, 1 August.

Hoover Green, A. 2016. "The Commander's Dilemma: Creating and Controlling Armed Group Violence." *Journal of Peace Research* 53/5: 619–632.

Horowitz, D.L. 1985. *Ethnic Groups in Conflict*. Berkeley, CA: University of California Press.

Hughes, E., W.A. Schabas, and R. Thakur. 2007. *Atrocities and International Accountability: Beyond Transitional Justice*. New York: United Nations University.

Human Rights Watch (HRW). 2004. Burundi: The Gatumba massacre, war crimes and political agendas. New York, London, Brussels, Nairobi: HRW.

Humphreys, M., and J.M. Weinstein. 2006. "Handling and Manhandling Civilians in Civil War." *The American Political Science Review* 100/3: 429–447.

Huntington, S.P. 1968. *Political Order in Changing Society*. New Haven, CT: Yale University Press.

Hunziker, P. 2015. "Civil Conflict in Petroleum Producing Regions." Dissertation ETH Zürich.

Ignatieff, M. 2003. *Empire Lite: Nation-Building in Bosnia, Kosovo and Afghanistan*. New York: Vintage.

Ikenberry, G.J. 2001. *After Victory: Institutions, Strategic Restraint, and the Rebuilding of Order after Major Wars*. Princeton, NJ: Princeton University Press.

Ikenberry, G.J. 2014. "The Illusion of Geopolitics: The Enduring Power of the Liberal Order." *Foreign Affairs* 93: 80.

Imbusch, P. 2003. "The Concept of Violence," in W. Heitmeyer and J. Hagan (eds.), *International Handbook of Violence Research*. Dordrecht: Kluwer Academic.

Jakobsen, H. 2014. "What Is Gendered About Gender-Based Violence? An Empirically Grounded Theoretical Exploration in Tanzania." *Gender and Society* 28: 537–561.

Jarstad, A.K. 2008. "Dilemmas of "War-to-Democracy Transitions: Theories and Concepts," in A.K. Jarstad and T. Sisk (eds.), *From War to Democracy: Dilemmas of Peacebuilding*. Cambridge: Cambridge University Press.

Jarstad, A.K., and T.D. Sisk. (eds.) 2008. *From War to Democracy. Dilemmas of Peacebuilding*. Cambridge: Cambridge University Press.

Jeong H.W. 2005. "Peacebuilding in Postconflict Societies," in M. Keating, A. Le More, and R. Lowe (eds.), *Aid, Diplomacy and Facts on the Ground*. Bristol: Chatham House.

Kalyvas, S.N. 2001. " 'New' and 'Old' Civil Wars – a Valid Distinction?" *World Politics* 54/1: 99–118.

Kanis, S., S.F. Messner, M. Eisner, and W. Heitmeyer. 2017. "A Cautionary Tale About the Use of Estimated Homicide Data for Cross-National Research," mimeo.

Kant, I. 1795/1948. "On Eternal Peace," in C.J. Freidrich (ed.), *Inevitable Peace*. Cambridge, MA: Harvard University Press.

Kaufman, J., and E. Zigler. 1987. "Do Abused Children Become Abusive Parents?" *American Journal of Orthopsychiatry* 57/2: 186.

Kerr, R., and E. Mobekk. 2007. *Peace and Justice: Seeking Accountability After War*. Cambridge: Polity.

Kirby, P., 2013. "Refusing to be a Man? Men's Responsibility for War Rape and the Problem of Social Structures in Feminist and Gender Theory." *Men and Masculinities* 16/1: 93–114.

Klasen, S. 2013. "Is It Time for a New International Poverty Measure?" in *OECD: Development Cooperation Report 2013: Ending Poverty*. Paris: OECD.

Kleiboer, M. 1996. "Understanding Success and Failure of International Mediation." *Journal of Conflict Resolution* 40/2: 360–389.

Koeppel, M.D.H., G.M. Rhineberger-Dunn, and K.Y. Mack 2015. "Cross-National Homicide: A Review of the Current Literature." *International Journal of Comparative and Applied Criminal Justice* 39/1: 47–85.

Koopmans, R., 1996. "Explaining the Rise of Racist and Extreme Right Violence in Western Europe: Grievances or opportunities?" *European Journal of Political Research* 30/2: 185–216.

Kreutz, J. 2010. "How and When Armed Conflicts End: Introducing the UCDP Conflict Termination Dataset." *Journal of Peace Research* 42/2: 246.

Kristensen, H.M., and S. Norris. 2016. "Chinese Nuclear Forces." *Bulletin of Atomic Scientists* 72/4: 205–211.

LaFree, G. 1999. "A Summary and Review of Cross-National Comparative Studies of Homicide," in M.D. Smith and M.A. Zahn (eds.), *Homicide: A Sourcebook of Social Research*. Thousand Oaks, CA: Sage.

Lambourne, W. 2009. "Transitional Justice and Peacebuilding after Mass Violence." *International Journal of Transitional Justice* 3/1: 28–48.

Lattimer, M. 2014. "Peoples Under Threat 2014: Hate Crimes and Mass Killing," in Minority Rights Group International (MRG), *State of World's Minorities and Indigenous People 2014*. London: MRG.

Lattimer, M., and D. Verbakel. 2015. "People Under Threat," in Minority Rights Group International (MRG), *State of World's Minorities and Indigenous People 2015*. London: MRG.

Lederach, J.P. 1997. *Building Peace: Sustainable Reconciliation in Divided Societies*. Washington, DC: United States Institute of Peace Press.

Lee, A., and S. Pridmore. 2014. "Emerging Correlations Between Measures of Population Well-Being, Suicide and Homicide: A Look at Global and Australian Data." *Australian Psychiatry* 22/2: 112–117.

Levchak, P. 2016. "The Relationship between Urbanisation and Cross-National Homicide Rates: Robustness Across Multiple Estimation Methods.," in *International Journal of Comparative and Applied Criminal Justice* 40/3: 225–243.

Levin, J., and Madfis, E., 2012. "Conclusion: Cultivating Bias in the Media," in D.L. Bissler and J.L. Conners (eds.), *The Harms of Crime Media: Essays on the Perpetuation of Racism, Sexism and Class Stereotypes*. Jefferson: McFarland, pp. 239–246.

Levinson, D., 1989. *Family Violence in Cross-Cultural Perspective*. New York: Sage.

Lichbach, M.I. 1989. "An Evaluation of 'Does Economic Inequality Breed Political Conflict?' " *World Politics* 41/4: 431–470.

Lieby, M. 2009. "Wartime Sexual Violence in Guatemala and Peru." *International Studies Quarterly* 53: 445–468.

10

Lieby, M. 2012. "The Promise and Peril of Primary Documents: Documenting Wartime Sexual Violence in El Salvador and Peru," in M. Bergsmo, A. Butenschøn Skre, and E.J. Wood (eds.), *Understanding and Proving International Sex Crimes*. Beijing: Torkel Opsahl Academic.

Lijphart, A. 1977. *Democracy in Plural Societies: A Comparative Exploration*. New Haven, CT: Yale University Press.

Luttwak, E.N. 1999. "Give War a Chance." *Foreign Affairs* 784: 36–44.

Lyons, T. 2005. *Demilitarizing Politics*. New York: Lynne Rienner.

McAdam, D., S. Tarrow, and C. Tilly. 1996. "To Map Contentious Politics." *Mobilization: An International Quarterly* 1/1: 17–34.

McGarry, J., and B. O'Leary. 2009. "Must Pluri-National Federations Fail?" *Ethnopolitics* 8: 5–25.

Mac Ginty, R. 2006. *No War, No Peace. The Rejuvenation of Stalled Peace Processes and Peace Accords*. Basingstoke and New York: Palgrave.

Mac Ginty, R. 2010. "Hybrid Peace: The Interaction Between Top-Down and Bottom-Up Peace." *Security Dialogue* 41/4: 391–412.

Mac Ginty, R. 2012. "Routine Peace: Technocracy and Peacebuilding." *Cooperation and Conflict* 47/3: 287–308.

Mackinder, H.J. 1919. *Democratic Ideals and Reality: A Study in the Politics of Reconstruction*. London: Constable & Co.

Mani, R. 2002. *Beyond Retribution: Seeking Justice in the Shadows of War*. Cambridge: Polity Press.

Mann, M. 2005. *The Dark Side of Democracy: Explaining Ethnic Cleansing*. Cambridge: Cambridge University Press.

Mansfield, E.D., and J. Snyder. 2005. *Electing to Fight: Why Emerging Democracies Go to War*. Cambridge, MA: MIT Press.

Maoz, Z. 1983. "Resolve, Capabilities, and the Outcomes of Interstate Disputes." *Journal of Conflict Resolution* 27: 195–229.

Marks, Z. 2013. "Sexual Violence in Sierra Leone's Civil War: 'Virgination', Rape, and Marriage." *African Affairs* 113/450: 67–87.

Marshall, I.H., and D.L. Summers. 2012. "Contemporary Differences in Rates and Trends of Homicide Among European Nations," in M.C.A. Liem and W.A. Pridemore (eds.), *Handbook of European Homicide Research: Patterns, Explanations, and Country Studies*. New York: Springer.

Mattes, M.B.S. 2009. "Fostering Peace after Civil War: Commitment Problems and Agreement Design." *International Studies Quarterly* 53: 737–59.

Mead, W.R. 2014. "The Return of Geopolitics: The Revenge of the Revisionist Powers." *Foreign Affairs* 93: 69.

Melander, E. 2005. "Gender Equality and Intrastate Armed Conflict." *International Studies Quarterly* 49/4: 695–714.

Menkel-Meadow, C. 2007. Restorative Justice: What Is It and Does It Work? *Annual Review of Law and Social Science* 3: 161–187.

Messner, S. 2003. "Understanding Cross-National Variation in Crime Violence," in W. Heitmeyer and J. Hagan (eds.), *International Handbook of Violence*. Dordrecht: Kluwer Academic.

Messner, S.F., B. Pearson-Nelson, L.E. Raffalovich, and Z. Miner. 2011. "Cross-National Homicide Trends in the Latter Decades of the Twentieth Century: Losses and Gains in Institutional Control?," in W. Heitmeyer, H.G. Haupt, A. Kirschner, and S. Malthaner (eds.), *Control of Violence: Historical and International Perspectives on Violence in Modern Societies*. New York: Springer.

Messner, S.F., L.E. Raffalovich, and P. Shrock. 2002. "Reassessing the Cross-National Relationship between Income Inequality and Homicide Rates: Implications of Data Quality Control in the Measurement of Income Distribution." *Journal of Quantitative Criminology* 18/4: 377–395.

Milanovic, B. 2016. *Global Inequality: A New Approach for the Age of Globalization*. Cambridge, MA: Harvard University Press.

Minority Rights Group International (MRG). 2015. *State of World's Minorities and Indigenous People 2015*. London: MRG.

Morley, R., 1994. "Wife Beating and Modernization: The Case of Papua New Guinea." *Journal of Comparative Family Studies* 25–52.

Mueller, J.A. 1989. *Retreat from Doomsday: The Obsolescence of Major War*. New York: Basic Books.

Mueller, J.E. 2004. *The Remnants of War*. Ithaca, NY: Cornell University Press.

Murithi, T. 2009. *The Ethics of Peacebuilding*. Edinburgh: Edinburgh University Press.

Muschert, G.W. 2007. "Research in School Shootings." *Sociology Compass* 1/1: 60–80.

Muschert, G.W., and M. Ragnedda. 2011. "Media and Control of Violence: Communication in School Shootings," in W. Heitmeyer, H.G. Haupt, S. Malthaner, and A. Kirschner (eds.), *Control of Violence*. New York: Springer.

Muschert, G.W., and J. Sumiala (eds.). 2012. *School Shootings: Mediatized Violence in a Global Age* (Vol. 7). Emerald Group.

Muvumba Sellström, A. 2015a. *Stronger than Justice: Armed Group Impunity for Sexual Violence*. Doctoral Dissertation. Uppsala: University of Uppsala's Department of Peace and Conflict Research.

Muvumba Sellström, A. 2015b. "Impunity for Conflict Related Sexual Violence: Insights from Burundi's Former Fighters," in S.I. Cheldelin and M. Mutisi (eds.), *Deconstructing Women, Peace and Security: A Critical Review of Approaches to Gender and Empowerment*. Cape Town: Human Sciences Research Council (HSRC).

Nathan, L. 2017. "How to Manage Inter-Organizational Disputes Over Mediation in Africa." *Global Governance* 23/(2): 151–162.

Neapolitan, J.L. 1994. "Cross-National Variation in Homicides: The Case of Latin America." *International Criminal Justice Review* 4: 4–22.

Newman, E, R. Paris, and O. Richmond. (eds.) 2009. *New Perspectives on Liberal Peacebuilding*. Tokyo: United Nations University Press.

Newman, E., and O. Richmond. (eds.) 2006. *Challenges to Peacebuilding: Managing Spoilers During Conflict Resolution*. Tokyo: United Nations University Press.

Newman, K., C. Fox, D.J. Harding, J. Mehta, and W. Roth. 2004. *Rampage: The Social Roots of School Shootings*. New York: Perseus.

Nivette, A.E. 2011. "Cross-National Predictors of Crime: A Meta-Analysis." *Homicide Studies* 15/2: 103–131.

Norberg, J. 2016. *Progress: Ten Reasons to Look Forward to the Future*. London: Oneworld.

Nordås, R. 2011. *Sexual Violence in African Conflicts*. Centre for the Study of Civil Wars, Oslo: Peace Research Institute of Oslo (PRIO), Policy Brief 01.

Nordås, R. 2012. *Sexual Violence on the Decline? Recent Debates and Evidence Suggest 'Unlikely'*. Centre for the Study of Civil Wars, Oslo: PRIO, Policy Brief 03.

Osiander, A. 2001. "Sovereignty, International Relations and the Westphalian Myth." *International Organization* 55/2: 251–287. doi:10.1162/00208180151 140577.

Ouimet, M. 2012. "A World of Homicides: The Effect of Economic Development, Income Inequality, and Excess Infant Mortality on the Homicide Rate for 165 Countries in 2010." *Homicide Studies* 16/3: 238–258.

Paffenholz, T. 2001. *Peacebuilding: A Field Guide*. Boulder, CO: Lynne Rienner.

Paffenholz, T., N. Ross, S. Dixon, A.L. Schluchter, and J. True. 2016. *Making Women Count – Not Just Counting Women: Assessing Women's Inclusion and Influence on Peace Negotiations*. Report ITI, UN Women. www.inclusivepeace.org

Paige, J.M. 1975. *Agrarian Revolution: Social Movements and Export Agriculture in the Underdeveloped World*. New York: Free Press.

Paris, R. 2004. *At War's End: Building Peace after Civil Conflict*. New York: Cambridge University Press.

Paris, R. 2014. "The Geopolitics of Peace Operations: A Research Agenda." *International Peacekeeping* 21/4: 501–508.

Paton, N. 2015. *School Shooting, La violence à l'ère de Youtube*. Paris: Maison des Sciences de l'homme.

Peace Accords Matrix. Notre Dame, IN: Kroc Institute, University of Notre Dame. https://peaceaccords.nd.edu

Perry, V. 2009. "At Cross Purposes? Democratization and Peace Implementation Strategies in Bosnia and Herzegovina's Frozen Conflict." *Human Rights Review* 10: 35–54.

Petersen, R.D. 2002. *Understanding Ethnic Violence: Fear, Hatred, and Resentment in Twentieth-Century Eastern Europe*. Cambridge: Cambridge University Press.

Peterson, L. 2013. "The Measurement of Non-Economic Inequality in Well-Being Indices." *Social Indicators Research* 119/2: 581–598.

Pettersson, T., and P. Wallensteen. 2015. Armed Conflicts, 1946–2014. *Journal of Peace Research* 52/4: 536–550.

Philpott, D. 2012. *Just and Unjust Peace: An Ethic of Political Reconciliation*. Oxford: Oxford University Press.

Philpott, D., and G. Powers. (eds.) 2010. *Strategies of Peace: Transforming Conflict in a Violent World*. Oxford: Oxford University Press.

10

Pinker, S. 2011. *The Better Angels of Our Nature: Why Violence has Declined.* New York: Viking.

Posen, B.R. 1993. "The Security Dilemma and Ethnic Conflict," in M.E. Brown (ed.), *Ethnic Conflict and International Security.* Princeton, NJ: Princeton University Press.

Pridemore, W.A. 2011. "Poverty Matters: A Reassessment of the Inequality-Homicide Relationship in Cross-National Studies." *British Journal of Criminology* 51/5: 739–772.

Prosecutor v. Akayesu. 1998. International Criminal Tribunal for Rwanda (ICTR), Arusha, ICTR-96-4-T, September 2.

Prosecutor v. Dragoljub Kunarac, Radomir Kovac and Zoran Vukovic. 2001. International Criminal Tribunal for the former Yugoslavia (ICTY), The Hague, IT-96-23-T & IT-96-23/1-T, February 22.

Quinn Thomas, D., and R.E. Ralph. 1994. "Rape in War: Challenging the Tradition of Impunity." *SAIS Review* 14/1: 81–99.

Ramírez-de-Garay, D. 2016. "Las barbas del vecino. Los patrones de difusión del crimen violento en México (1990–2010)." *Foro internacional* 56/4: 977–1018.

Ramsbotham, O., T. Woodhouse, and H. Miall. 2012. *Contemporary Conflict Resolution.* Oxford: Blackwell.

Ravndal, J.A. 2016. "Right-Wing Terrorism and Violence in Western Europe: The RTV Dataset." *Perspectives on Terrorism* 10/3.

Reddy, S., and R. Lahoti. 2016. "$1.90 A Day: What Does It Say? The New International Poverty Line." *New Left Review* 97: 106–127.

Reychler, L., and L. Schirch. 2013. *Conflict Assessment and Peacebuilding Planning: Toward a Participatory Approach to Human Security.* Boulder, CO: Lynne Rienner.

Richmond, O. 2011. *A Post-Liberal Peace.* London and New York: Routledge.

Rodgers, D., and G.A. Jones. 2009. "Youth Violence in Latin America: Gangs and Juvenile Justice in Perspective," in G.A. Jones and D. Rodgers (eds.), *Youth Violence in Latin America: Gangs and Juvenile Justice in Perspective.* New York: Palgrave Macmillan, 1–24.

Roeder, P.G. 2005. "Power Dividing as an Alternative to Ethnic Power Sharing," in P. Roeder and D. Rothchild, *Sustainable Peace: Power and Democracy after Civil Wars.* Cornell University Press.

Rosenboim, O. 2014. "Geopolitics and Empire: Visions of Regional World Order in the 1940s." *Modern Intellectual History* 12/2.

Rothberg, R.I. (ed.). 2004. *When States Fail: Causes and Consequences.* Princeton, NJ: Princeton University Press.

Rotberg, R.I., and D. Thompson (eds.). 2000. *Truth v. Justice: The Morality of Truth Commissions.* Princeton, NJ: Princeton University Press.

Russett, B. 1993. *Grasping the Democratic Peace: Principles for a Post-Cold War World.* Princeton, NJ: Princeton University Press.

Russett, B.M., and J.R. Oneal. 2001. *Triangulating Peace: Democracy, Interdependence, and International Organizations.* New York: W.W. Norton.

Saideman, S.M., and R.W. Ayres. 2008. *For Kin or Country: Xenophobia, Nationalism, and War.* New York: Columbia University Press.

Samuels, K. 2005. "Post-Conflict Peace-Building and Constitution-Making." *Chicago Journal of International Law* 6/2: 663–682.

Schmid, A.P. (ed.). 2011. *The Routledge Handbook of Terrorism Research.* London: Routledge.

Scott, James. 1976. *The Moral Economy of the Peasant: Rebellion and Subsistence in Southeast Asia.* New Haven: Yale University Press.

SIPRI. 2015. *Military Expenditure Fact Sheet.* http://books.sipri.org/files/FS/SIPRIFS1604.pdf

SIPRI. 2016a. *Newsletter,* June 13. www.sipri.org/media/press-release/2016/global-nuclear-weapons-downsizing-modernizing

SIPRI. 2016b. *Nuclear Fact Sheet.* www.sipri.org/sites/default/files/FS%201606%20WNF_Embargo_Final%20A.pdf

Sivakumaran, S. 2007, "Sexual Violence Against Men in Armed Conflict." *The European Journal of International Law* 18/2: 253–276.

Smit, P.R., R.R. de Jong, and C.C.J.H. Bijleveld. 2012. "Homicide Data in Europe: Definitions, Sources, and Statistics," in M.C.A. Liem and W.A. Pridemore (eds.), *Handbook of European Homicide Research: Patterns, Explanations, and Country Studies.* New York: Springer.

Snyder, J. 2000. *From Voting to Violence: Democratization and Nationalist Conflict.* New York: W.W. Norton.

Sommers, C.H. 1994. *Who Stole Feminism? How Women Have Betrayed Women.* New York: Simon & Schuster.

Sprinzak, E. 1995. *Political Violence in Israel.* Jerusalem: The Jerusalem Institute for the Research of Israel.

Spykman, J.N. 1944. *The Geography of the Peace* (ed. H.R. Nicholl). New York: Harcourt, Brace & Co.

Sriram, C.L., and J. Herman. 2009. "DDR and Transitional Justice." *Conflict, Security & Development* 9/4:10–11.

Sriram, C.L., O. Martin-Ortega, and J. Herman (eds.). 2010. *Peacebuilding and Rule of Law in Africa: Just Peace?* Abingdon: Routledge.

Stanton, G.H. 2016. "The Ten Stages of Genocide." http://genocidewatch.net/genocide-2/8-stages-of-genocide/

Stedman, S.J. 2001. *Implementing Peace Agreements in Civil Wars: Lessons and Recommendations for Policymakers.* New York: International Peace Academy.

Stedman, S.R., D.S. Rothchild, and E.M. Cousens (eds.). 2002. *Ending Civil Wars: The Implementation of Peace Agreements.* Boulder, CO: Lynne Rienner.

Stepanova E. 2008. *Terrorism in Asymmetrical Conflict.* New York: Oxford University Press.

Stewart, F. (ed.). 2008. *Horizontal Inequalities and Conflict: Understanding Group Violence in Multiethnic Societies.* Basingstoke: Palgrave Macmillan.

Stohl, M. (ed.). 1988. *The Politics of Terrorism.* 3rd ed. New York: Marcel Dekker.

Sweatt, L., C.G. Harding, L. Knight-Lynn, S. Rasheed, and P. Carter. 2002. "Talking About the Silent Fear: Adolescents' Experiences of Violence in an Urban High-Rise Community." *Adolescence* 37/145: 109–120.

Tajfel, H. 1981. *Human Groups and Social Categories: Studies in Social Psychology.* Cambridge: Cambridge University Press Archive.

Teitel, R.G. 2000. *Transitional Justice.* New York: Oxford University Press.

Tilly, C. 1978. *From Mobilization to Revolution.* New York: McGraw-Hill.

Tilly, C. 1990. *Coercion, Capital, and European States, Ad 990–1990.* Oxford: Basil Blackwell.

Tilly, C. 1999. *Durable Inequality.* Berkeley, CA and Los Angeles, CA: University of California Press.

Toft, Monica. 2007. "Getting Religion? The Puzzling Case of Islam and Civil War." *International Security* 31/4.

Tollefsen, A.F., and H. Buhaug. 2015. "Insurgency and Inaccessibility." *International Studies Quarterly* 17: 6–25.

Tønnesson S. 2015. "The East Asian Peace: How Did It Happen? How Deep Is It?" *Global Asia* 10/4: 8–15.

Touraine, A. 1973. *Les mouvements sociaux.* París: Editions du Seuil.

Touraine, A. 1992. *Critique de la modernité.* Fayard.

Touraine, A. 1993. "Découvrir les mouvements sociaux." *Action collective et mouvements sociaux,* 17–36.

Touval, S., and W. Zartman. 1985, "Introduction: Mediation in theory," in S. Touval and I.W. Zartman (eds.), *International Mediation in Theory and Practice.* Boulder, CO: Westview.

UN. 2010. *Monitoring Peace Consolidation. United Nations Practitioners' Guide to Benchmarking.* New York: United Nations.

UN. 2012. *Guidance for Effective Mediation.* New York: United Nations.

UN 2015a. *Cooperation Between the United Nations and Regional and Subregional Organizations on Mediation. Report of the Secretary-General.* UN Doc. A/70/328. New York: United Nations.

UN 2015b. *The Millennium Development Goals Report 2015.* New York: United Nations.

UN 2015c. *World Urbanization Prospect. The 2014 Revision.* New York: United Nations.

UN Commission on Human Rights. 1996. Report on the Situation of Human Rights in Rwanda submitted by Mr. René Degni-Ségui, Special Rapporteur of the Commission on Human Rights, Under Paragraph 20 of Resolution S-3/1 of May 25, 1994, Fifty-Second Session, Item 10 of the Provisional Agenda, para. 16, Economic and Social Council, E/CN.4/1996/68.

UN, Department of Economics and Social Affairs, Population Division. 2016. "International Migration Report 2015: Highlights," ST/ESA/SER.A/375.

UN Department of Political Affairs 2012. *United Nations Guidance for Effective Mediation.* New York: United Nations.

UN Development Program. 2013. *The Human Development Report 2013.* http://hdr.undp.org/sites/default/files/reports/14/hdr2013_en_complete.pdf

UN General Assembly (UNGA). 1998. Rome Statute of the International Criminal Court (last amended 2010), United Nations Diplomatic Conference of Plenipotentiaries on the Establishment of an International Criminal Court, July 17.

10

UN-Habitat 2016. *Urbanization and Development. Emerging Futures.* World Cities Report. United Nations Humans Settlements Programme. New York: United Nations.

UN Human Rights Council. 2010. *Report of the Special Rapporteur on Extrajudicial, Summary or Arbitrary Executions.* Philip Alston. Addendum, Study on targeted killings, May 28. Geneva: UNRC.

UN Human Rights Council. 2016. *They Came to Destroy: ISIS Crimes Against the Yazidis.* Independent International Commission of Inquiry on the Syrian Arab Republic. Geneva: UNRC (A/HRC/32/CRP.2).

UNODC 2013. *Global Study on Homicide 2013.* New York: United Nations.

UN Secretary-General. 2016. *Report of the Secretary-General on Conflict-Related Sexual Violence.* New York: UN Security Council (S/2016/361).

UN Security Council (UNSC). 2000. Resolution. New York: UN Security Council (S/Res/1325).

UN Security Council (UNSC). 2004. *Joint Report of MONUC, ONUB and OHCHR into the Gatumba Massacre.* New York: UN Security Council.

UN Security Council (UNSC). 2008. *Resolution.* New York: UN Security Council (S/Res/1820).

UN Security Council (UNSC). 2009. *Resolution.* New York: UN Security Council (S/Res/1888).

UN Security Council (UNSC). 2010. *Resolution.* New York: UN Security Council (S/Res/1960).*Uppsala Conflict Data Program.* Department of Peace and Conflict Research, Uppsala University. www.ucdp.uu.se

Valentino, B.A. 2014. "Why We Kill: The Political Science of Political Violence against Civilians." *Annual Review of Political Science* 17: 89–103.

Väyrynen, R. (ed.). 2006. *The Waning of Major War: Theories and Debates.*, London and New York: Routledge.

von Einsiedel, S. 2017. "Civil War Trends and the Changing Nature of Armed Conflict." *Occasional Paper 10.* Tokyo: United Nations University Centre for Policy Research.

Waldmann, P. 2007. "Is There a Culture of Violence in Colombia?" *International Journal of Conflict and Violence* 1/1: 61–75.

Wall, J., and T. Dunne. 2012. "Mediation Research: A Current Review." *Negotiation Journal* 28/2: 217–244.

Wallensteen, P. 2015. *Quality Peace: Peacebuilding, Victory and World Order.* New York: Oxford University Press.

Wallensteen, P., and A. Bjurner (eds.). 2015. *Regional Organizations in Peacemaking. Challengers to the UN?* Abingdon: Routledge.

Wallensteen, P., and P. Johansson. 2015. "The UN Security Council: Decisions and Actions," in S. von Einsiedel, D.M. Malone, and B.S. Ugarte (eds.), *The UN Security Council in the 21st Century.* Boulder, CO: Lynne Rienner.

Wallensteen, P., E. Melander, and F. Möller. 2012. "The International Community Response," in I.W. Zartman, M. Anstey, and P. Meertz (eds.), *The Slippery Slope to Genocide: Reducing Identity Conflicts and Preventing Mass Murder.* Oxford, New York: Oxford University Press.

Wallensteen, P., and I. Svensson. 2014. "Talking Peace: International Mediationin Armed Conflicts." *Journal of Peace Research* 51/2: 315–327.

Weiner, M. 1971. "The Macedonian Syndrome: An Historical Model of International Relations and Political Development." *World Politics* 23/(4): 665–683.

Weiner, M. 1978. *Sons of the Soil: Migration and Ethnic Conflict in India.* Princeton, NJ: Princeton University Press.

Weinstein, J. 2006. *Inside Rebellion: The Politics of Insurgent Violence.* New York: Cambridge University Press.

Whitaker, B.E. 2003. "Refugees and the Spread of Conflict: Contrasting Cases in Central Africa." *Journal of Asian and African Studies* 38/2–3: 211–231.

WHO 2014a. *Global Status Report on Violence Prevention 2014.* WHO Library.

WHO 2014b. *Preventing Suicide: A Global Imperative.* WHO Library.

Widner, J. 2005, "Constitution Writing and Conflict Resolution." *Research Paper* 2005/51, UNU-WIDER, United Nations University.

Wieviorka, M. 1993. *The Making of Terrorism.* Chicago, IL: University of Chicago Press.

Wieviorka, M. 1999. "Le multiculturalisme: solution, ou formulation d'un problème?" in P. Dewitte (ed.), *Immigration et Intégration.* Paris: La Découvert.

Wieviorka, M. 2005. *La différence : Identités culturelles : enjeux, débats et politiques.* La Tour-d'Aigues: L'Aube.

Wieviorka, M. 2009. *Violence: A New Approach.* London: Sage.

Wieviorka, M. 2012. *Evil.* Cambridge: Polity Press.

Wilkinson, R., and K. Pickett. 2009. *The Spirit Level: Why More Equal Societies Almost Always Do Better.* London: Penguin Books.

Wilkinson, S.I. 2004. *Votes and Violence: Electoral Competition and Ethnic Riots in India.* Cambridge: Cambridge University Press.

Wood, E.J. 2003. *Insurgent Collective Action and Civil War in El Salvador.* Cambridge: Cambridge University Press.

Wood, E.J. 2006. "Variation in Sexual Violence During War." *Politics and Society* 34/3: 307–342.

Wood, E.J. 2009. "Armed Groups and Sexual Violence: When Is Wartime Rape Rare?" *Politics and Society* 37/1: 131–161.

Wood, E.J. 2010. "Sexual Violence During War: Variation and Accountability," in A. Smeulers (ed.), *Collective Crimes and International Criminal Justice: An Interdisciplinary Approach.* Antwerp: Intersentia.

Wood, E.J. 2014. "Sexual Violence in Armed Conflict." *International Review of the Red Cross* 96/894: 457–478.

Wood, E.J. 2015. "Social Mobilization and Violence in Civil War and their Social Legacies," in D. Della Porta and M. Diana (eds.), *The Oxford Handbook of Social Movements.* Oxford: Oxford University Press.

Wucherpfennig, J., P. Hunziker, and L.E. Cederman. 2016. "Who Inherits the State? Colonial Rule and Post-Colonial Conflict." *American Journal of Political Science* 60/4: 882–898.

Zartman, I.W. 2001, "The Timing of Peace Initiatives: Hurting Stalemates and Ripe Moments." *Global Review of Ethnopolitics* 1/1: 8–18.

Zehr, H. 2002. *The Little Book of Restorative Justice.* Intercourse, PA: Good Books.

Zick, A., B. Küpper, and W. Heitmeyer. 2009. "Prejudices and Group-Focused Enmity. A Sociofunctional Perspective," in A. Pelinka et al. (eds.), *Handbook of Prejudice.* Amherst, NY: Cambria Press.

10

11

International Organizations and the Technologies of Governance

Coordinating Lead Authors:[1]
Hilary Charlesworth, Sally Engle Merry

Lead Authors:[2]
B.S. Chimni, Javier Couso, Terence Halliday, Outi Korhonen, Vivian Lin, Eden Medina, Leslye Obiora, César Rodríguez-Garavito, Gregory Shaffer, Rene Urueña

Contributing Author:[3]
Ruth Okediji

---

[1] Affiliations: HC: University of Melbourne and the Australian National University, Australia; SM: New York University, USA.
[2] Affiliations: BC: Jawaharlal Nehru University, India; JC: Universidad Diego Portales, Chile; TH: American Bar Foundation, USA; OK: University of Turku, Finland; VL: La Trobe University, Australia; EM: Indiana University, USA; LO: University of Arizona, USA; CRG: Universidad de los Andes, Colombia; GS: University of California, Irvine, USA; RU: Universidad de los Andes, Colombia.
[3] Affiliation: University of Minnesota Law School, USA.

Summary

By "international organizations," we refer to organizations beyond a single state that engage in transnational or global governance. This chapter addresses five types of international organizations: intergovernmental organizations whose members are states; international non-state organizations that directly address transnational or global policy; international civil society organizations; international commercial organizations; and hybrid public–private international organizations. The chapter's case studies focus particularly on intergovernmental organizations, but in interaction with other organizations as they address issues of human rights; refugees and migration; women's rights; health; intellectual property; conflict, security, and terrorism; and climate change. In assessing international organizations, the chapter begins by examining the relationship of these organizations to global order and disorder. While robust empirical research is limited on norm-making and monitoring, it is clear that a handful of countries in the Global North[4] dominate intergovernmental organizations.

This chapter describes how international and global governance operates through varieties of governance technologies. These technologies vary in how fully they engage transnational, national, and local actors, state and non-state, in their design and implementation. Technologies of governance have been criticized because they have few mechanisms for tapping into creativity and tacit knowledge at local levels and they implicitly vest expertise and normative authority in the Global North and centers of geopolitics or finance. In so doing, they mute the voices of many domestic actors.

Our case studies demonstrate both the promise and problems of international organizations in enhancing human flourishing. They reveal the complexities of the engagement between the Global North and Global South and local and global processes. For transnational governance to produce social progress it will need to resolve difficulties of coordination, funding, accountability, and adaptability of governance technologies.

11

---

4   In this chapter, we use the term "Global North" interchangeably with the term "developed countries," and "Global South" with "developing countries."

11.1 Introduction: International Organizations and Technologies of Governance

Social problems are increasingly transnational in scope (Halliday and Shaffer 2015). In response, varieties of international organizations have proliferated to address areas of social life and promote social progress.[5] These international organizations have invented and expanded ways to govern aspects of topics ranging from security, economics, health, and the environment to human rights, labor, trade, investment, and consumer safety.

11.1.1 Scope of International Organizations

By "international organizations," we refer to organizations beyond a single state that engage in transnational or global governance. This chapter addresses five types of international organizations: intergovernmental organizations whose members are states; non-state international organizations that directly address transnational or global policy; international civil society organizations; international commercial organizations; and hybrid public-private international organizations. The chapter focuses particularly on intergovernmental organizations as they interact with other international organizations in addressing issues of human rights, intellectual property, climate change, public health, conflict, and security and migration.

(1) State-created intergovernmental organizations confront social issues through several generic forms, including regional, transnational, and global legislatures (such as the European Parliament, UN General Assembly, and World Health Assembly), international courts (such as the International Criminal Court, European Court of Justice, Andean Courts, and World Trade Organization Appellate Body), international regulatory bodies (such as the International Monetary Fund in its role in financial monitoring and surveillance, and the International Civil Aviation Organization) and international and regional development banks such as the World Bank and the African, Asian, and Inter-American Development Banks. State-based organizations can also be largely virtual through networks of state regulatory officials organized and hosted by states (such as the International Competition Network).

In principle, therefore, intergovernmental organizations offer a site for deliberative equality as national delegations engage in law-making with equal formal power. In practice, that equality in deliberation is not achieved, which creates challenges for invention of innovative practices to ensure the participation, influence, and reception of pragmatic local knowledge from states in the Global South. Global regulation of the financial sector, for example through the Financial Stability Board or G20, suffers from asymmetries of input and power in both global rule-making and international surveillance of national economies and transnational flows of capital.

While robust empirical research is limited on norm-making and monitoring, research indicates that a handful of countries in the Global North dominate intergovernmental organizations.

(2) A second class consists of international organizations that are not state-based but operate as international organizations: Two examples are the Internet Corporation for Assigned Names and Numbers (ICANN), which governs the Internet, and the International Committee of the Red Cross, which develops and monitors compliance with the laws of war. They, too, must be subject to scrutiny over equality and mutuality in global governance.

(3) A third class of international organizations is homologous with civil society organizations within states: international non-governmental organizations, including interest groups, religious bodies, political party alliances; international informal but stable networks of organizations or individuals; philanthropies; universities and educational institutions.

International civil society organizations cover every cluster or type of human right promulgated under UN auspices. Amnesty International (AI) and Human Rights Watch (HRW), for instance, articulate global norms, usually based on UN declarations, conventions, and findings in UN watchdog bodies, such as the Human Rights Council. AI and HRW hold countries accountable to those standards and rely heavily on public shaming as a sanction.

World religions, too, can exert great influence on vulnerable populations in poor countries and shape public policy in rich and powerful countries. These influences can both promote social progress and constrain it. The Roman Catholic Church and many Protestant denominations have worldwide infrastructures for medical services, education, and literacy. Islamic associations deliver essential welfare services to vulnerable populations across the Islamic world. Notable leaders of religious international organizations, such as the Dalai Lama and Pope Francis, exert powerful moral influence on the shaping of international public discourse through extensive media coverage of the poor, refugees, and victims of government repression or natural disasters. Yet religious organizations can also abuse human rights and resist their promotion.

Insofar as they are organized to bring about the realization of rights in practice, international non-governmental organizations can be considered emancipatory. Yet they often escape criticism and scrutiny because their ideals appear noble, or they privilege rights more salient to certain parts of the world than others. They are usually financed and led by actors in the Global North. For social progress, it is critical to ask how well their goals, leadership, practices, and effects reflect or suppress the views of actors in the Global South.

(4) Market international organizations include industry and professional associations; multinational business firms; informal and formal financial and investment institutions; labor organizations; and management and investor networks.

---

[5] Compare the count of 136 intergovernmental organizations and 980 international non-governmental organizations in 1956 with at least 7,757 intergovernmental organizations and 60,272 international non-governmental organizations in 2016 (UIA Yearbook of International Organizations 1956–1957, 2015–2016).

The globalization of professional services projects can be observed in huge law, accounting, engineering, and other professional firms that project a global footprint with the intent of serving clients throughout the world. It is an open question whether these firms project or indirectly underwrite progressive values or whether they subvert such values in search of profits. Professional and industry associations combine and recombine professionals and technical experts both in the creation of transnational norms and in their local application. Such professional and industry associations, which are often involved in global law or rule-making, require close scrutiny on a case by case basis to judge whether their actions have intended or unintended consequences adverse to social progress, most especially in weak states and on vulnerable actors in markets and civil society.

(5) In practice, these classes of international organizations interpenetrate and overlap in public–private partnerships and other ways that incorporate state and non-state actors in decision-making and implementation, including through networks that integrate state and non-state actors in common causes, often engaging international epistemic communities of service professionals, scientists, and academics, among others. For instance, in health, the World Health Organization has been struggling to develop partnerships with massively endowed private organizations, such as the Gates Foundation, in order to improve health outcomes. These efforts can promote progress, but they also can introduce contradictions and shift priorities in ways that can be harmful to it.

These five forms of international organizations exist in dense ecologies of organizations (Block-Lieb and Halliday 2017; Rodríguez-Garavito 2015). Competition, conflict, and confusion over goals and resources pose formidable challenges in the pursuit of significant opportunities for cooperation and social progress. Those of the Global North are typically more powerful and better funded than those of the Global South.

11.1.2   Technologies of Governance

Transnational and global governance operates through varieties of social technologies. The term technology refers to regular techniques and strategies of doing things that includes laws and legal practices, documents and forms, rules about how offices and bureaucracies should behave, habitual practices, and people trained to carry out governance activities.

(1) Global governance of markets through law occurs through the production in international organizations of legal technologies such as multilateral conventions, model laws, legislative guides, guides to practice, model contracts, standards and codes, and best practices (Block-Lieb and Halliday 2017). Research indicates that formal representation and procedural fairness do not commonly translate into actual and tangible participation. Voices, views, alternatives, and perspectives from outside the global center are rarely articulated, and, if expressed, have little effect on outcomes in global governance. These technologies generally rely on persuasion and moral pressure, but may also be conveyed through military coercion, economic coercion, along with systems of reward, modeling, and capacity-building (Braithwaite and Drahos 2000).

The critical difference among the technologies in their contribution to social progress turns on their degree of respect for sovereignty and participatory governance by states and non-state actors. More participatory and inclusive technologies typically support social progress more effectively. Yet technologies of governance contain few mechanisms for tapping into local creativity and tacit knowledge. They implicitly vest expertise and normative authority in the Global North and centers of geopolitics or finance, thereby denying dignity and agency to domestic actors.

(2) Governance technologies incorporate various accountability processes. These include: (a) formal processes, involving courts and administrative-like bodies (including networks of national officials and private associations); and (b) decentralized certification processes, including informal reporting and peer review assessment in light of hard and soft law norms.

Formal processes are significant. Transnational governance increasingly involves authoritative rulings by international courts. More than two dozen international courts have issued over 37,000 binding rulings (Alter 2014: 4) on trade, human rights, intellectual property rights, and international criminal law prosecutions. Decisions can be strongly conducive to social progress or can impede it, not only through direct effects, but also through the shadow of a potential judicial proceeding that can have effects without any formal claim being filed. For example, research shows that although the International Criminal Court (ICC) has had few actual prosecutions, the ICC prosecutor's office can place pressure on domestic proceedings, as evidenced in the Colombia peace dialogues in 2012–2016. By contrast, the threat of investment arbitration can exercise a chilling effect on progressive regulation. For example, big tobacco companies have pressured countries not to regulate cigarette packaging in ways that interfere with their brand names, even if done in line with the World Health Organization's (WHO) Framework Convention on Tobacco Control 2003.

Transnational networks of administrative officials meet regularly in multilateral and bilateral forums, including over the Internet, to address common regulatory challenges. For example, the 2015 Paris Agreement under the UN Framework Convention on Climate Change of 1992 provides for voluntary "soft law" targets to which countries commit. Competition officials regularly meet and share information to crack down on cartels that operate and have effects in multiple countries (Shaffer, Nesbitt, and Waller 2016).

An underappreciated technology in regulatory governance is peer review reporting mechanisms. The World Trade Organization (WTO), for example, has over a dozen committees that meet, in total, thousands of times per year. The Organization for Economic Cooperation and Development (OECD) is particularly known for diffusing norms through regular interaction of policy makers and government officials through peer review assessments. The OECD has no formal dispute settlement system, yet signatories act "as if" certain obligations are binding. Peer pressure is more readily applied in organizations with a strong institutional structure that provides for sustained interaction to clarify definitions and obligations, and to ensure monitoring, facilitate learning, and determine remedies. The human rights regime relies significantly on pressure through oversight committees, particularly at the multilateral level (Charlesworth and Larking 2014). For example, Japan changed its policies regarding the Ainu indigenous community after it was challenged before the international human rights monitoring system.

(3) A rapidly developing technology of governance relies on indicators (Merry 2016; Merry, Davis, and Kingsbury 2015). These vary from rigorous criteria deployed by international financial institutions to indicators developed by non-profit organizations to rate countries and corporations on human rights, rule of law, freedom, justice, and other social concerns.

Indicators purport to capture the presence or absence of an underlying phenomenon by the uniform application of a set of measures to all countries in the world. Countries are rated and those ratings are published as scales of conformity with the supposed norm. For example, both the World Bank and the private World Justice Project have developed rule of law indicators, each seeking to capture variation on differing conceptualizations of the rule of law. Freedom House rates countries on freedom of the press. International development banks rate countries on everything from poverty to education to welfare services to governance.

The use of monitoring indicators as a technology of governance came into prominence with the adoption of the Millennium Development Goals (MDGs) of 2000–2015. With eight goals that covered a range of issues related to human development, including poverty and hunger, primary education, gender equality, child mortality, maternal health, major communicable diseases, and environmental sustainability. A regular program of monitoring and reporting was instigated, and considerable funding from bilateral and multilateral agencies as well as private philanthropies was dedicated to the achievement of MDGs for developing countries.

In 2015, the MDGs were replaced by the Sustainable Development Goals (SDGs), following an extensive consultative process that was driven by member states, rather than by UN agencies. The SDGs cover economic, environmental, and social development, with a focus on equity and human rights. These 17 aspirational goals include: no poverty, zero hunger, good health and well-being, quality education, gender equality, clean water and sanitation, affordable and clean energy, decent work and economic growth, industry innovation and infrastructure, reduced inequalities, sustainable cities and communities, responsible consumption and production, climate action, life below water, life on land, peace and justice, and partnerships for the goals. The SDGs apply to all countries and are presented as integrated and indivisible. In the SDGs, each goal is supported by a series of targets. There are now 169 targets, with over 200 indicators. The monitoring and reporting on the SDGs is also accompanied by a voluntary national self-review process.

Indicators can be valuable as a stimulus to change. They can add measurement to show the frequency and distribution of social problems highlighted by stories. When valid and reliable they can serve as pressure points to stem decline in adherence to progressive values. But indicators can also undermine social progress. If their underlying conceptualization of a social problem is trivial or fails to reflect framings

salient to those being rated, or reflects an ideology inimical to the priority of social progress, scores can be misleading and even counter productive.

For indicators to be used constructively for social progress they will require (1) identifying who creates the indicators; (2) ensuring that participation in indicator development includes those frequently marginalized from standard-setting; (3) agreeing on underlying dimensions that properly capture the social phenomenon in question; (4) scrutinizing methodologies of operationalization to ensure they validly reflect the views and practices of those measured; and (5) interpreting findings with skepticism about the scope and limits of inferences that can be drawn from them.

These issues and concerns appear in a series of substantive case studies in the rest of this chapter. Each examines the operation of international organizations and governance technologies in a particular area, focusing on their ecosystems, contexts, inter-connections, complexities, and contradictions. The case studies show that, despite some areas of significant social progress, the technologies of global governance tend to reproduce existing global inequalities.

11.2   Case Studies

11.2.1   Human Rights

Human rights are central to the way international governance can promote social progress. They have become one of the main frames for articulating social progress and they are one of the most developed institutional technologies of global governance. Myriad hard-law and soft law human rights standards interact at global, regional, and national scales, forming a plural governance field that creates both opportunities and challenges for social justice.

11.2.1.1   The Challenge for Social Progress

These are paradoxical times for human rights in general, and for human rights international organizations in particular. On the one hand, human rights have achieved an unparalleled status as a global discourse on social progress and have been institutionalized through a wide range of organizations at the global, regional, and domestic levels. On the other hand, they are the focus of growing criticism regarding their limited effectiveness, Northern-centrism, and outdated institutional architecture and strategies at a time of increasing geopolitical multi-polarity, regulatory fragmentation, and technological change. This section outlines the key principles and practices shaping and transforming the structures, cultures and processes of human rights. We highlight the current challenges of the field and courses of action aimed at reinvigorating the contribution of human rights to social progress.

11.2.1.2   The Human Rights Field: Context

In keeping with the United Nations Charter, signed in 1945, the UN General Assembly adopted the Universal Declaration of Human Rights

(UDHR) in 1948, creating the intellectual foundation of the contemporary human rights system. Two treaties that articulated the basic principles of the UDHR into legally binding obligations entered into force in 1976. These treaties are the International Covenant for Civil and Political Rights (ICCPR) and the International Covenant for Economic, Social, and Cultural Rights (ICESCR). Other human rights treaties cover an array of issues, including racial and gender discrimination, torture and enforced disappearances, the rights of children, migrant workers, and people with disabilities. Each of the treaties is monitored by a committee, such as the Committee on the Elimination of Racial Discrimination and the Committee on the Rights of People with Disabilities. The treaties form the core of the human rights system of law. The human rights field also includes a wide range of international, regional, national, and civil society organizations that create, support, and monitor compliance with human rights. Many of these entities serve the critically important role of making violations known and bringing them to global attention. In addition, they develop new issues, share information among each other, and serve as watchdogs for compliance with the terms of human rights treaties.

International organizations are fundamental actors in this field. They include the core agencies of the United Nations universal system, such as the UN Human Rights Council, and numerous specialized UN agencies. There are also regional judicial and quasi-judicial bodies, such as the Inter-American Commission on Human Rights and the African, European, and the Inter-American courts of human rights. In addition to policy-making and enforcement-oversight bodies, there are information-gathering and monitoring organizations such as global and regional rapporteurs and working groups on specific rights; for example the UN Special Rapporteur on the Right to Food and the UN Working Group on the Issue of Human Rights and Transnational Corporations and Other Business Enterprises. These entities provide expertise to the system and have, along with transnational non-government organizations (NGOs) and networks, been decisive in setting and implementing human rights standards. International organizations also include numerous public, private, and public–private entities, such as the World Bank, the WTO, the European Central Bank, and transnational corporations which, while not explicitly concerned with human rights, have profound effects on the realization or frustration of human rights on the ground.

11.2.1.3   Human Rights in Transition: Drivers of Change

Four transformations are pulling the human rights field in different directions (Rodríguez-Garavito 2014). First, the rise of emerging powers to counter the dominance of Europe and the United States points to a broader and more fragmented multi-polar world order (de Búrca, Keohane, and Sabel 2013). In this context, states and NGOs in the Global North have less control over the creation and implementation of human rights standards, as new actors from transnational social movements to Global South states and NGOs are becoming more influential.

Second, the range of actors and strategies is changing. Time-honored techniques such as naming and shaming recalcitrant states into compliance with human rights standards are complemented by

new strategies that involve different actors, targets of activism and mechanisms, including social media and virtual networks. At the same time, both autocratic and elected governments are pushing back against transnational advocacy by promoting restrictive laws and policies that constitute what has been called a "global war against NGOs" (Bechenmacher and Carothers 2015; Editorial Board 2015).

Third, the growth of the knowledge economy fostered by advancements in information and communication technologies (ICTs) presents new challenges and opportunities for human rights. As shown by mobilizations exemplified by the Occupy Movement around the world, resources such as social networks, video documentaries, digital reporting, online learning, and long-distance education have considerable potential to accelerate sociopolitical change, reduce the informational disadvantages that buttress the marginalization of disenfranchised communities, and bring together national, regional, and global groups capable of having a direct impact on the protection of rights (Zuckerman 2013).

Fourth, extreme environmental degradation – climate change, water scarcity, rapid extinction of species and forests, uncontrolled pollution, etc. – has become one of the most serious threats to human rights. Insofar as human rights mean very little if what is at risk is life on earth itself, ecological questions are central to constructive dialogues about human rights (Santos 2014).

The combination of these four conditions has compounded intense debates in the field. Left with more questions than answers, human rights activists face a complicated situation in a field that tries to provide clear-cut legal solutions to complex moral and political dilemmas. Nonetheless, the seeming turbulence also presents opportunities. Transitions between strategic models, intellectual paradigms, governance structures, technologies and the like represent openings for creativity and innovation.

11.2.1.4   Problems and Prospects

A confluence of factors exacerbated by Cold War tensions protracted the promulgation of the ethical standards and political commitments enshrined in the 1948 UDHR into legally binding obligations. Geopolitical interests fostered the separation of the interdependent and indivisible rights espoused by the UDHR into two separate treaties, namely the ICCPR and the ICESCR. It was not until 1966 that these instruments opened up for signature. It took another decade, until 1976, to secure enough support for the covenants to enter into force. Countries that adopted the agreements typically ratified them with reservations, understandings, and declarations that watered down their potential effect. The implementation of socioeconomic and cultural rights was further curtailed by a provision in the ICESCR that qualified a state's commitment to uphold them "to the maximum of [a state's] available resources, with a view to achieving progressively the full realization [of these rights]" (Article 2).

Since the human rights system was formed during the colonial era, many nations were not able to contribute to the foundations for its formation. As these nations gained independence from colonial subjugation, some contested both the universalization of human rights that bore the imprint of the West and the primacy of civil and political rights in the system. Building on the centrality of the right of self-determination in the two core conventions, the ICCPR and the ICESCR, many countries from the Global South sponsored the Declaration on the Right to Development in the UN General Assembly in 1986. Although its champions failed to galvanize adequate support to translate the Declaration into a legally enforceable treaty, the concept of a right to development has influenced subsequent agreements, including the MDGs (2000), and the agenda for the SDGs (2015).

Human rights are frequently embodied in legal rules. However, their social impact does not depend only on their formal legal incorporation, but also on their moral status, which is based upon a vision of what is good and just in the world. In fact, the core claim of human rights that all persons have an intrinsic value that entitles them to certain freedoms does not depend on express legal recognition nor can it be eliminated by positive legal norms. In spite of the enduring overlap between legal entitlements and moral claims, human rights remain subject to interpretations that question perceived legitimacy, coherence, and cultural deficits (Sen 1999).

The cultural critique of human rights reflects the need for sensitivity to difference and mirrors debates between relativism and universalism. While relativists protest the globalization of human rights norms on the basis of their origin in the Global North, universalists denounce deference to cultural specificity, particularly in the domain of religion and the family. The legitimacy challenge derives from positivistic arguments akin to Jeremy Bentham's unequivocal dismissal of natural or moral rights devoid of legal recognition as anarchical fallacies or "nonsense upon stilts." The coherence debate implicates disagreements between proponents of positive rights who prioritize distributive justice and opponents who favor so-called negative rights that limit states' obligation to non-interference with individual liberties and laissez-faire institutional possibilities.

Those who question the coherence of human rights claims echo Wesley Hohfeld's classification of legal concepts that correlates rights with duties; these critics thus refute the validity of fundamental normative rights that purport to exist in the absence of corresponding duties. The African Charter on Human and Peoples' Rights (1992), which imposes both rights and duties on the individual, has not entirely resolved coherence concerns. Critics caution against the tendency of political elites to manipulate articulations of reciprocal benefits and burdens, to abdicate cardinal social obligations, diminish individual entitlements, shunt responsibility to individuals, and shirk legal claim to rights to life, liberty, and property.

Attempts to bolster the legitimacy, coherence, and cross-cultural purchase of human rights have engendered spirited discourses about the fundamentals for unforced consensus. Dignity, which defines a basic value across societies, has enjoyed ample affirmation in these discourses. However, historical appeal and cross-cultural ubiquity has not freed the notion of dignity from ambiguity. The constraints on enforcing fundamental liberties and immunities to protect human dignity speak volumes about the challenges of human rights guarantees, even when they are embedded in a constitution. Despite this, the cross-cultural resonance of the human rights regime as a bellwether for social progress continues to intensify.

Human rights accountability requires both adequate resources and support for financial stewardship practices. For example, development partners traditionally invoke governance deficits caused by corruption to criticize host governments for shortfalls in aid performance. However development agencies often do little better in managing effective aid delivery than host governments.

In some places, weak state institutions co-exist with resilient societies in which local organizations align indigenous struggles with universal norms and actively translate international human rights norms into local cultural terms, a process of vernacularizing human rights (Merry 2006). Promoting grassroots agency in communities caught in the tedious vacillations of dysfunctional state sovereigns allows us to reimagine state–society relations. It reinforces Eleanor Roosevelt's observation that, without concerted citizen action to uphold human rights close to home, "we shall look in vain for progress in the larger world."

11.2.1.5   Towards a Human Rights Ecosystem

A key trait of the contemporary human rights movement is its diversity. The twenty-first century has witnessed a proliferation of actors who use the language and values of human rights in social movements and local activism. This diversity far surpasses the traditional boundaries of human rights. Although this expansion has met with some resistance, we argue that human rights theory and practice must open spaces for new actors, themes, and strategies that have emerged in the last decades instead of guarding its traditional boundaries.

To capture and maximize this diversity, some have suggested that the field should be understood as an ecosystem, rather than as a unified movement or institutional architecture (Rodríguez-Garavito 2014). In this vein, the emphasis should be on symbiotic relationships and connections between discrete contributions of members of the ecosystem. The nature of the transnational human rights ecosystem is informed by a diversity of *actors*. A body of scholarly work on human rights examines its forms of social organization, its effects, and its success, revealing this multiplicity of actors. Current campaigns involve not only professional NGOs and specialized international agencies, but also many others. While lawyers play an important role, many actors are grassroots leaders, social movement activists, or local participants in NGOs.

There is also an expanding range of *topics* taken up by the human rights movement, for instance, in the realm of socioeconomic rights. Although initially raising doubts among scholars (Sunstein 1996) and advocates (Roth 2004) in the North, efforts by NGOs, social movements, and scholars in the South have successfully incorporated these rights into the legal and political human rights repertoire. As a result, socioeconomic rights are recognized in international law and in some national constitutions, and have become the focal point of some sectors of the human rights community, giving rise to new theories of justice and human rights (Sen 2009). Activists, academics, and courts in countries like India and South Africa have been on the frontline of developing sophisticated legal doctrines and theories that have improved

11

compliance with socioeconomic rights. International human rights actors such as the UN Special Rapporteurs, the African Commission, and the Inter-American Court of Human Rights are busy creating content and improving effectiveness for these rights (Rodríguez-Garavito and Rodríguez 2015). These outcomes buttress the idea of human rights as a vehicle for social justice without weakening civil and political rights. Indeed, effective judicial interventions demonstrate the interdependence of civil-political and socioeconomic human rights.

A pluralistic approach is also required with respect to *strategies* in the human rights field. "Boomerang effect" strategies (Keck and Sikkink 1998) whereby NGOs like Amnesty and Human Rights Watch have pressured Northern states to use their influence on Southern states to get the latter to comply with human rights continue to be important. But multi-polarity makes it difficult for strategies centered on Europe and the United States to be effective, as the crises in Syria and Ukraine bear witness. Thus, human rights organizations are trying new approaches. Through a "multiple boomerang" strategy, Global South NGOs are forming coalitions of national organizations, simultaneously lobbying their national governments and the emerging powers of the region to add their influence to protect human rights (Rodríguez-Garavito 2015).

As in any ecosystem, the strength of the human rights field will depend on symbiosis, that is, the interaction among its different actors, to the advantage of the latter and the broader cause they share. Collaboration and complementarity will thus become even more important to the survival and thriving of the field as a whole. Nurturing collaborations is easier said than done. For dominant global human rights NGOs, this implies a difficult challenge: transitioning from the vertical and highly autonomous modus operandi that has allowed them to make key contributions, to a more horizontal model that would allow them to work with networks of diverse actors. For the time being, NGOs' efforts to globalize their operations by opening offices in new centers of power in the Global South have failed to translate into new forms of engagement. They have not succeeded in the effort to interact with local, national, and regional organizations on an equal footing in terms of initiative, decision-making, and authorship. For domestic organizations, adjusting to the new ecosystem entails pursuing strategies that allow them to link up with each other. It requires using new leverage points created by increased multi-polarity and opening themselves up to non-legal professionals, social movements, and online activists.

In sum, in order for the human rights field to continue to contribute to social progress and to address the challenges it faces in the twenty-first century, it should operate as an ecosystem, rather than as a hierarchy. Competition for resources and for leadership can thus become competitive cooperation (Block-Lieb and Halliday 2017). In a complex and interdependent world, human rights actors should spend less time on gatekeeping and more time on symbiosis.

11.2.1.6   Conclusion

This overview of human rights as a technology of governance for achieving social progress emphasizes that the human rights field is a changing and developing complex of norms, structures, organizations,

people, and processes. The field is going through a paradigm shift, with basic questions about its actors, strategies, and organizational architecture open to novel solutions and approaches. The language and the values of human rights have become omnipresent, not just through traditional advocacy campaigns to pressure states and private actors to comply, but also to address a range of issues, many of them newly developed by innovative civil society organizations. These efforts have broken down the boundaries of the human rights field to foster novel strategies and accommodate creative solutions. The increased multi-polarity can allow the system to embrace diverse professionals, social movements, and activists. As the human rights regime becomes a multi-faceted ecosystem, it can accommodate more marginal organizations that link up with each other. Such an interactive, collaborative system could temper the stringent authoritative forces within states. This form of organization prioritizes learning, self-reporting, and peer review to advance the production and use of knowledge about the capacity of human rights to promote social progress.

In order for this collaborative approach to flourish, asymmetries between the Global North and South in the human rights field need to be taken seriously. Northern states continue to have a disproportionate voice and decision-making power in intergovernmental organizations that determine the fate of human rights, from the UN Security Council to the World Bank. NGOs in the North receive over 70 percent of the funds from philanthropic human rights foundations (Foundation Center 2013) and continue to have disproportionate power when it comes to setting the international agenda (Carpenter 2014). And too often they define this agenda based on internal deliberations, rather than through collaborative processes with NGOs of the Global South, social movements, activist networks, and other relevant actors.

Nurturing collaborations is easier said than done. For dominant human rights organizations, this poses a difficult challenge: transitioning from the vertical and highly autonomous modus operandi that has allowed them to make significant contributions, to a more horizontal model that would allow them to work with networks of diverse actors. For domestic organizations, adjusting to the new ecosystem entails pursuing strategies to link up with each other and using the new leverage points created by increased multi-polarity, as well as creating links with non-legal professionals, social movements, and online activists.

11.2.2   Refugees and Migration

11.2.2.1   The Problem of Social Progress

There are more than 50 million displaced persons in the world today of which about 20 million are refugees. Of the latter nearly 85 percent are hosted by states in the Global South (Gammeltoft-Hansen and Hathaway 2015: 242).

Refugees encounter two sets of problems. First, there is the *non-entrée* regime instituted in the Global North consisting of a number of "traditional" and "new generation" measures. The traditional *non-entrée* measures include visa controls, carrier sanctions, and interdiction on the high seas. The new generation measures involve "cooperation based *non-entrée*" measures that seek to make countries of origin and countries of transit control migration on behalf of the developed world (Gammeltoft-Hansen and Hathaway 2015: 242). Gammeltoft-Hansen and Hathaway have devised a seven-part typology of new generation *non-entrée* practices with the objective "to insulate wealthier countries from liability by engaging the sovereignty of another country" (2015: 243). These are: "reliance on diplomatic relations; the offering of financial incentives; the provision of equipment, machinery, or training; deployment of officials of the sponsoring state; joint or shared enforcement; assumption of a direct migration control role; and the establishment or assignment of international agencies to effect interception" (Gammeltoft-Hansen and Hathaway 2015: 243).

Second, there are the inadequate rights and welfare regimes in countries both of the Global North and the Global South. In the Global South refugees "face serious violations of their rights and extreme levels of poverty" (Harrell-Bond 2008: 13). A large number of them "are confined in camps and settlements where they are denied freedom of movement … Most spend decades 'warehoused' in camps, where life is characterized by sub-nutritional diets, neglect of separated children, sexual and gender-based violence, threats, detention, beatings, torture, and even extrajudicial killings" (Harrell-Bond 2008: 13). The situation in the Global North is as troubling because of regressive measures that include mandatory detention, the lack of right to work, deferred family reunification, and dismal living conditions in camps.

11.2.2.2 Forced Migration: Refugees – Technologies of Governance

In the Cold War period there was a relatively liberal approach in the West towards refugees, as they were seen as propaganda weapons against the former Soviet bloc countries. This era saw the adoption of the 1951 UN Convention on the Status of Refugees. The convention defines a refugee and catalogues a range of rights that are to be made available to them. The Convention, and/or its 1965 Protocol, which removed certain chronological and geographical limits, have been ratified by 148 states as of June 1, 2017. At the regional level there are conventions and declarations such as the 1969 OAU Convention on Status of Refugees and the Cartagena Declaration 1984. These instruments are playing a significant role in providing protection to refugees. There are also legal instruments applicable to asylum seekers at sea including the 1960 International Convention on the Safety of Life at Sea and the UN Convention on Law of the Sea of 1982. Finally, there is international human rights law, which complements international refugee law in providing protection to asylum seekers and refugees (Harvey 2015: 43).

In so far as international organizations are concerned, the Office of the UN High Commissioner for Refugees (UNHCR), created in 1950 as a subsidiary organ of the UN General Assembly, has the mandate to provide protection and assistance to refugees, which has to be renewed every five years. Over the decades the UNHCR has performed the tasks assigned to it reasonably well (Betts, Loescher, and Milner, 2012; Loescher 2001). First, it has taken important normative initiatives that comprise "conclusions" adopted by its Executive Committee (Milner 2014: 1). Second, the UNHCR has actively provided protection on the ground while facilitating the availability of material assistance. Third, it has helped find solutions to particular refugee flows. Fourth, the

UNHCR has played a broad supervisory role assigned to it under the 1951 convention.

There are other non-state actors that play a role in the working of the global refugee regime. These include regional organizations like the AU, the International Association of Refugee Law Judges (IARLJ), Southern Refugee Legal Aid Network (SRLAN), International Council for Voluntary Agencies (ICVA), and academic institutions like the Refugee Studies Centre (RSC) Oxford.

11.2.2.3 Forced Migration: Refugees – Failures

The global refugee regime suffers from many weaknesses. Two major deficiencies are: first, major refugee hosting countries have not ratified the 1951 UN Convention on the Status of Refugees. These include Jordan, Syria, Lebanon, Indonesia, Malaysia, Nepal, Pakistan, and Thailand. Only five countries in Asia have become parties to the Convention: Cambodia, China, South Korea, and Japan. It is worth noting that Asia does not possess a regional human rights regime.

The other weakness is that the role of UNHCR is constrained by several factors. First, UNHCR's mandate has been extended in some situations to include internally displaced persons (IDPs). This affects their protection function (Harrell-Bond 2008: 19). It can also lead to situations where the organization provides assistance to those responsible for persecution of refugees (Loescher, Betts, and Milner 2008: 122). Second, there is the problem of voluntary funding, which results in the lack of adequate and assured funding for performing its protection and assistance functions. The UNHCR is also far too dependent on funds from the Global North to effectively perform its supervisory role, which is also hampered by the lack of clear procedures.

11.2.2.4 Forced Migration: Refugees – Ecology

The international refugee regime is principally shaped by powerful states of the Global North, which argue that the *non-entrée* regime is consistent with their legal obligations either under the 1951 Convention or under international human rights law. The field of refugee studies is also dominated by scholars and academic institutions located in the Global North and proposed solutions to the global refugee problem tend to exclude the concerns of the Global South (Chimni 2009). At the same time there are a number of progressive researchers who have made out a case for a more liberal asylum regime embedded in international human rights law.

11.2.2.5 Forced Migration: Refugees – Recommendations

In order to address the global refugee problem a range of short- and medium-term recommendations can be gleaned from the literature. First, there must be increase in legal channels of migration through eliminating *non-entrée* measures (Clayton 2015). Second, the principle of *non-refoulement* must be strictly respected. In the instance of mass influx of refugees States must ensure that refugees "are welcomed into a safe and caring environment" (Clayton 2015). Third, there must

11

be institutionalized dialogue between countries of the Global North and the Global South to give effect to the principle of burden sharing addressing both financial and physical burden sharing (Chimni 2001). Fourth, a Refugee Rights Committee must be established consisting of independent legal experts to oversee the implementation of the 1951 Convention. Fifth, an adequate response to the problem of climate refugees must be shaped. There are several possibilities that may be explored including expanding the definition of refugee in the 1951 Convention on Refugees or adopting a protocol on climate refugees to the Geneva Convention. Sixth, there must be initiatives at the regional level. For example, in the case of EU, "a supranational institutional arrangement that guarantees the equitable sharing of responsibilities within the EU" must be established (Turk 2016: 58). It should create an EU Asylum Authority that would act throughout the territory of the EU. This would include the establishment of an independent EU Asylum Appeals Court, as well as one EU Asylum Code that would cover issues related to substantive and procedural rights and standards of treatment (Turk 2016: 58). Seventh, the root causes of refugee flows should be given due attention (Clayton 2015). In this regard much more needs to be done to prevent conflicts, interventions and wars that are among the root causes of refugee flows (Clayton 2015). Eighth, countries not parties to the 1951 Convention should be exhorted to join it. Ninth, international human rights law with its wider scope should be made the primary basis for refugee protection (Chetail 2014: 70–72).

11.2.2.6   Voluntary Migration: Problems of Social Progress

There were an estimated 232 million international migrants in 2013 (UN 2013: 1). Of these, about 59 percent lived in the developed world and 41 percent were hosted by developing countries (UN 2013: 1). The numbers include forced migrants as the definition of "migrants" used includes all foreign born or aliens (UN 2013: 1).

11.2.2.7   Voluntary Migration: Technologies of Governance

The international migration regime comprises migration policies and programs of individual countries, international norms and practices, interstate discussions and agreements, multilateral forums and consultative processes, and the activities of international organizations.

On the international plane a range of legal conventions deal with the rights of migrants in addition to the general human rights treaties. These include the 1949 ILO Convention concerning Migration for Employment (Revised 1949) (No. 97); 1975 ILO Convention concerning Migrations in Abusive Conditions and the Promotion of Equality of Opportunity and Treatment of Migrant Workers (Supplementary Provisions) (No. 143); 1990 International Convention on the Protection of the Rights of All Migrant Workers and Members of Their Families; 2011 ILO Convention concerning Decent Work for Domestic Workers (No. 189); 2000 Protocol to Prevent, Suppress and Punish Trafficking in Persons, Especially Women and Children; and 2000 Protocol against the Smuggling of Migrants by Land, Sea and Air. Besides, there are non-binding UN General Assembly Resolutions that usually call upon states to "promote and protect effectively the human rights and fundamental freedoms of all migrants, regardless of their migration status,

especially those of women and children" (UN Department of Economic and Social Affairs 2013).

There are a number of international organizations working in the field of migration. First, there is the International Organization for Migration (IOM), whose principal aim is to assist in "meeting the growing operational challenges of migration management; advance understanding of migration issues; encourage social and economic development through migration; and uphold the human dignity and well-being of migrants" (IOM 2014). Second, a number of forums for the discussion of migration issues have been created that include the International Centre for Migration Policy Development (ICMPD) created in 1993 and the Global Migration Group (GMG) established in 2006, which promote cooperation between states and relevant agencies (Geiger and Pecoud 2014: 866). In 2003 a Global Commission for International Migration was also established with the mandate to "provide the framework of a coherent, comprehensive and global response to the issue of international migration" (Martin 2015: 72). Third, there is WTO whose General Agreement of Trade in Services (GATS) regulates movement of natural persons as one mode of delivery of services. Fourth, there are regional and sub-regional consultative processes such as the Regional Migration Conference (RCM), otherwise known as the Puebla Process, which includes Canada, the United States, Mexico, the Central American countries, and the Dominican Republic (Martin 2015: 71). Finally, the UN human rights treaty bodies have clarified the rights of migrants through their General Comments and Recommendations.

11.2.2.8   Voluntary Migration: Failures

The weaknesses of the international migration regime are widely known. First, key conventions like the 1990 Convention on the Rights of Migrant Workers have been ratified by few migrant-receiving states. Second, international cooperation in the area of migration "is relatively limited in comparison to many other trans-boundary issue-areas" (Geiger and Pecoud 2014: 866). It is also "lightly institutionalized within the United Nations system" (Doyle 2004: 4). The IOM, since 2016 a "related organization" of the UN, remains essentially a "service provider to states" (Geiger and Pecoud 2014: 866). These problems give rise to challenges arising from the absence of strong coordinating action or evolving preventive strategies, and finding constructive solutions (Doyle 2004: 4). As a result, a central problem remains the absence of legal channels for migration and the lack of respect for migrant rights.

11.2.2.9   Voluntary Migration: Ecology

There is no policy area in which states more zealously safeguard their sovereignty than in the area of migration. Mainstream migration scholarship also favors restrictive policies. A number of reasons are advanced in support of this standpoint. First, it is argued that a population with common identity is essential to sustain democratic societies. Second, it is contended that accountability in a world of sovereign states is owed only to citizens and not to non-nationals. Third, it is pointed out that unilateral responses have always been the norm in the framing of policies towards aliens in distress. Finally, it is stressed that control over migration is required in order to ensure homeland security.

On the other hand, progressive scholars argue the case for relatively more open borders. In their view, first, a liberal migration regime has advantages in the era of accelerated globalization in which capital, goods, and services have become increasingly mobile. Second, it is argued that the recognition of the rights of non-nationals is fundamental to the claim of a society being considered a democratic society (Frost 2003: 109). Indeed, it is imperative that democratic societies "incorporate a vision of just membership" (Benhabib 2004: 3). Third, progressive scholars underscore the contribution of migrants to the economic, social, and cultural development of host economies.

Where international organizations are concerned, a case for establishing an International Migration Organization has been made (Bhagwati 2004: 218). However, others observe that creating a new organization in a contentious area is no easy task (Martin 2015). This is because of the preference of states for national level policies, the absence of legal protection mandate for migrants, the lack of a regular budget, and the reluctance to closely link it with UN (Martin 2015: 79). The impact of the IOM's new relationship with the UN remains to be seen.

11.2.2.10   Voluntary Migration: Recommendations

The following recommendations can be made to protect the rights of migrants. First, the sovereignty-based approach to migration must be replaced by a human rights-based approach. Second, migrant-receiving states should be called upon to ratify the 1990 Convention on the Rights of Migrant Workers. Third, as against managing migration for member states, the IOM should devote more attention to the rights of migrants. Fourth, the ILO should be called upon to play a greater role and think of new ways to protect the rights of migrant workers through enhancing its own resources for that purpose. Fifth, the ongoing dialogue in different forums must be sustained to arrive at viable solutions. Sixth, host states must undertake certain urgent measures including domestic legislation to ensure that the rights of migrant workers are protected, offering in particular legal guarantees against discrimination. Seventh, the concerns of migrant women, as identified by treaty bodies like the Committee on the Elimination of Discrimination against Women in its General Comment No. 26, must be effectively addressed. Eighth, states should be required to actively cooperate to stop smugglers and traffickers from exploiting the vulnerabilities of migrants. Finally, a World Migration Organization should be established with a comprehensive mandate on migration, leaving the UNHCR to deal with asylum seekers and refugees.

11.2.3   Women's Rights

11.2.3.1   The Challenge for Social Progress

Across the world, women face discrimination and oppression. While there is evidence of progress for women over the past two decades, for example in their increased representation in elected state institutions and the paid labor market, and in the growing enrolment of girls in primary and secondary education, there remain marked asymmetries between men and women's access to authority, income, and power. Apparent progress is often undermined by deep-seated structures of inequality. Thus, while more women are in paid work in most countries, terms and conditions of work have sharply deteriorated. For example, 83 percent of domestic workers globally are women, but only one half of them are entitled to the minimum wage (UN Women 2015). Beliefs and practices based on gender, prioritizing masculine approaches and values, contribute to this inequality. One response to this situation has been the growth of social movements for women's rights, framing women's inequality as a question of human rights.

11.2.3.2   How Are Existing Organizations Working?

Campaigners for women's rights have often resorted to the international arena. International institutions appear to offer hospitable and progressive sites to protect women's rights in the face of often hostile national environments. To a large extent, international organizations have been pressured by national and international women's movements to incorporate women's issues into their mandates. The proliferation of NGOs working on women's rights has been essential to bringing this issue into the international domain. However, incorporating women's rights into the overall human rights system has been difficult. While there have been a number of important developments in international protection of women's rights, international organizations have also been ambivalent on this topic. There are also sophisticated networks of civil society actors who are hostile to claims of women's rights, particularly those relating to reproduction and sexuality.

The engagement of international organizations with women's rights starts with the League of Nations, although women had begun to organize internationally before that. The Hague Women's Conference in 1915 is a good example of international mobilization, focused on preventing war (Baetens 2010). The League of Nations, established in 1919, paid attention to particular women's issues, such as nationality. Its contemporary, the ILO, adopted conventions dealing with women's labor rights, typically designed to protect women's role as mothers. The League's successor, the United Nations, had an explicit mandate to consider women's equality with men: the preamble to the UN Charter (1945) reaffirms faith in "the equal rights of men and women." The purposes of the UN included promotion of human rights "without distinction as to race, sex, language or religion." The UN established the Commission on the Status of Women in 1946 as a political body to elaborate this agenda. The UN created a new administrative and policy agency, UN Women, in 2010 to bring together the organization's work on women. Although the vocabulary of women's rights is evident within the UN, it does not appear to have made much general impact on the practices of the institution or on the lives of women and girls. There has been selective appropriation of feminist ideas and a formulaic approach to their implementation. A feature of the last two decades is the rise in influence of non-governmental groups as well as private sector actors.

11.2.3.3   Technologies of Governance

In this area, we see examples of the three types of technologies of governance noted above: hard and soft law documents, accountability processes through courts and administrative systems, and indicators of women's progress.

11

International organizations have developed a complex normative system to protect women's rights primarily through the adoption of international agreements and declarations. The Universal Declaration of Human Rights (1948) and the two major international human rights instruments, the International Covenant on Economic, Social and Cultural Rights (ICESCR) and the International Covenant on Civil and Political Rights (ICCPR), both adopted in 1966, provide that the rights they recognize should be respected "without distinction of any kind" including sex. The most detailed international statement on women's rights is the 1979 Convention on the Elimination of All Forms of Discrimination against Women (CEDAW). The adoption of an Optional Protocol to CEDAW in 2000 allowed individuals to bring international claims of breaches of the Convention. There are also a range of regional treaties dealing with women's rights. An important treaty adopted by the Council of Europe is the Istanbul Convention on Violence against Women and Domestic Violence (2011).

During the 1970s and 1980s, a series of national movements for women's rights coalesced into an international campaign for peace and for women's economic empowerment and equal participation in education, politics, and development. Between 1975 and 1995, a series of world conferences brought together government and civil society representatives in transformative events that produced important outcome documents. The first meeting, held in Mexico City in 1975, focused on equality, development, and peace. Subsequent conferences in Copenhagen in 1980 and Nairobi in 1985 reiterated these concerns, but attention gradually shifted from peace to human rights, with a growing focus on violence against women. The Nairobi Forward-Looking Strategies developed in 1985 identified reducing violence against women as a basic strategy for addressing the issue of peace (UN Secretary-General 1995: 125).

In 1990, the UN's Economic and Social Council adopted a resolution developed by the Commission on the Status of Women stating that violence against women in the family and society derives from their unequal status in society and recommended that governments take immediate measures to establish appropriate penalties for violence against women as well as developing policies to prevent and control violence against women in the family, workplace, and society (UN Secretary-General 1995: 131–132). This recommendation suggests developing correctional, educational, and social services approaches including shelters and training programs for law enforcement officers, judiciary, health, and social service personnel. CEDAW does not mention violence against women explicitly, but the committee monitoring the Convention developed an initial recommendation against violence in 1989 and formulated a broader recommendation that defined gender-based violence as a form of discrimination in 1992.

By the 1990s, with the increasing focus on human rights characteristic of this period, the global women's movement sought to define women's rights as human rights. At the 1993 UN Conference on Human Rights in Vienna, a worldwide campaign gathered over 300,000 signatures from 123 countries asserting that women's rights were human rights. The concluding document, the Vienna Declaration and Programme of Action, formally recognized the human rights of women as "an inalienable, integral and indivisible part of human rights" (Connors 1996: 27). It advocated "the elimination of gender bias in the administration of

justice and the eradication of any conflicts which may arise between the rights of women and the harmful effects of certain traditional or customary practices" (sec. II, B, para. 38, UN Doc. A/Conf. 157/24.) The Vienna Declaration specifically called for the appointment of a special rapporteur on violence against women and the drafting of a declaration eliminating violence against women, both of which occurred soon after.

In 1995, the Fourth World Conference on Women, held in Beijing, drew representatives from 189 countries and 30,000 civil society activists. They met for two weeks and developed a major policy document for women's rights, the Platform for Action. Many regard this document as a high-water mark for women's rights, and there is some reluctance to hold further meetings because of a fear that this document will be weakened. The Platform for Action noted the failure to achieve the goals of the Nairobi conference and identified 12 "critical areas of concern":

- The persistent and increasing burden of poverty on women.
- Inequalities and inadequacies in and unequal access to education and training.
- Inequalities and inadequacies in and unequal access to health care and related services
- Violence against women.
- The effects of armed or other kinds of conflict on women, including those living under foreign occupation.
- Inequality in economic structures and policies, in all forms of productive activities and in access to resources.
- Inequality between men and women in the sharing of power and decision-making at all levels.
- Insufficient mechanisms at all levels to promote the advancement of women.
- Lack of respect for and inadequate promotion and protection of the human rights of women.
- Stereotyping of women and inequality in women's access to and participation in all communication systems, especially in the media.
- Gender inequalities in the management of natural resources and in the safeguarding of the environment.
- Persistent discrimination against and violation of the rights of the girl child (UN 1995: Chapter III, par. 44, p. 31).

The Platform identified violence against women as a violation of human rights and fundamental freedoms, defining it broadly as "any act of gender-based violence that results in, or is likely to result in, physical, sexual or psychological harm or suffering to women, including threats of such acts, coercion or arbitrary deprivation of liberty, whether occurring in public or private life" (UN 1995: Sec. D. para. 113). It includes gender-based violence in the family, the community, or perpetrated by the state, including acts of violence and sexual abuse during armed conflict, forced sterilization and abortion, and female infanticide. By declaring protection from violence for women and girl children as a universal human right, the conference placed women's rights in transnational space, the domain of the international human rights system: "Violence against women both violates and impairs or nullifies the enjoyment by women of their human rights and fundamental freedoms. The long-standing failure to protect and promote those rights and freedoms in the case of violence against women is a matter of concern to all States and should be addressed" (UN 1995: sec. D, 112).

Thus, by the mid-1990s women's rights were recognized as human rights. A rapidly growing number of civil society organizations pressured governments and international organizations to recognize these rights. The shift from a national to a global platform for women's rights enhanced their visibility. In response, there was a growing resistance to women's human rights, regularly framed in terms of the protection of culture and tradition.

The MDGs, in effect from 2000 to 2015, identified the promotion of gender equality and women's empowerment as one of their eight goals. Progress toward this goal is measured by the proportion of women in parliament, the ratio of women to men in paid non-agricultural work, and the ratio of girls to boys in primary, secondary, and tertiary education. The SDGs, which replaced the MDGs, operative from 2015 to 2030, also specify gender equality and women and girl's empowerment among their goals. The targets under this goal are broader, including reproductive rights, economic rights, elimination of "harmful practices" and gender-based violence, access to technology, and recognition and valuation of unpaid care and domestic work.

Global initiatives have been important in bringing international attention to women's inequality in work, education, and political power. However, in practice the focus on women's rights has remained relatively narrow, zeroing in on violence to women's bodies such as domestic violence or sex trafficking, while neglecting wider inequalities such as reproductive rights, disproportionate poverty, and the burdens of unpaid care work. The prominence of violence against women as a central concern is compatible with older protectionist approaches to women's rights.

We can identify two major themes in the development of women's human rights. The first is the idea that women require special treatment, specifically protection. This theme characterizes early international instruments that aimed to prevent some types of exploitation of women, for example, ILO conventions prohibiting women working at night, or in mines. These instruments were not cast in the language of rights, and their aim was primarily to protect ideals about womanhood, such as women's physical weakness and vulnerability outside their families. The protective strand with respect to women has not disappeared, emerging, for example, in a suite of Security Council resolutions on women, peace, and security adopted since 2000, beginning with Resolution 1325. These resolutions depict women in conflict zones as particularly susceptible to sexual violence, requiring protection, rather than as potential agents in shaping their own futures. Similarly, the centrality of the issues of violence against women and sex trafficking indicate a persistent focus on state protection of women.

The second theme in the area of women's human rights is women's equality with men: the right to equal treatment and non-discrimination on the basis of sex. This principle is signaled in the UN Charter and the human rights treaties cited above. However, in general, efforts to achieve equality for women in education, work, and political participation and to prevent discrimination on the basis of sex have lagged in comparison to those focusing on the protection of women from physical and sexual violation.

Although during the early years of the women's rights movement there was little focus on sexuality and gender identity, more recently

organizations concerned with women's rights and lesbian, gay, bisexual, transgender, and queer rights, called in international parlance sexual orientation and gender identity (SOGI) rights, have worked in collaboration. Many civil society organizations now seek to pressure international organizations to include SOGI rights in their work, focusing in particular on the prevention of discrimination on the basis of sexual orientation and gender identity.

11.2.3.4   Achievements and Limits of Current Structure

Women's human rights have made precarious progress in the international arena. Although there is now elaborate scaffolding for these rights in terms of treaty provisions and jurisprudence, they are constantly at risk of erosion. One example is the raft of reservations entered to CEDAW by states that have ratified it.

As noted above, one of the areas of success has been highlighting the problem of violence against women. Through social movement activism, the UN has been encouraged to develop laws and programs to increase women's protection from violence. The UN Committee on the Elimination of Discrimination against Women and the UN Secretary-General have both taken a leading role in identifying the problem and urging states to take action.

Despite this progress, many other dimensions of women's equality have not been addressed adequately. Issues such as reproductive rights and the equality of work and education have languished. Violations of women's rights are often justified on the grounds that they are an aspect of particular religious or cultural practices, and rights to religious freedom or cultural integrity are often invoked to "trump" women's rights. While concerns of cultural diversity arise with respect to human rights generally, it is striking that the concept of "culture" is much more frequently invoked in the context of women's rights than in any other area. This issue has arisen in many conflict environments, such as Afghanistan and Iraq. Resistance to women's rights comes from local male political elites and religious leaders. For their part, international actors attach little priority to engaging women in peace processes and protecting women's rights. Indeed women's rights are often traded in political settlements to achieve an apparent stability.

The sense that the area of women's human rights is under constant siege has meant that much energy goes into preservation of a limited status quo and that there is a reluctance to develop new standards. Thus, 20 years after the Beijing Conference, UN Women decided not to hold another conference on women in 2015 because of the anxiety that even the modest gains contained in the Beijing Declaration and Program for Action might be wound back by coalitions of religious influences.

On the other hand, civil society mobilization on women's human rights is extensive, with strong participation by NGOs in international conferences and meetings of the Commission on the Status of Women. The international human rights system has proved valuable for many national and local organizations as the basis for making claims about women's rights that are legitimated by their acceptance by global institutions. Women's human rights are typically generated by concerns and issues at the local level, such as dowry murders or honor killing, which circulate to global arenas where they are packaged into broad statements of universal obligation, such as protection from violence. Such statements, conventions, and policy documents then serve as the basis for vernacularizing these rights: translating them into terms that are culturally appropriate and appealing to local communities (Merry 2006). For example, women's demands for protection from domestic violence may result in the creation of local women's courts, modeled after a male-dominated village court, as has occurred in parts of India.

The dynamism of civil society activism on women's issues and the process of vernacularizing global norms mean that, despite the resistance of some states and international organizations to women's rights, this is a growing and developing field. The international conventions, conferences, resolutions, and policy documents provide a rich set of resources for local activists to use, offering models for action and legitimation for claims that women's rights are global.

Nevertheless, there is an ongoing struggle to broaden the issues recognized by the international order beyond narrow individual ones to more systemic ones. For example, rather than seeing violence against women as a product of males who use violence inappropriately, civil society groups advocate a broad approach that critiques the social acceptance of violence against women, the inadequacy of state institutions and laws to protect women, systems of marriage and kinship that prevent women from leaving violent families, and structures of educational, economic, and political inequality that force women to be dependent on men even if they are violent. Successive Special Rapporteurs on Violence against Women appointed by the UN Human Rights Council have adopted an approach of this kind.

11.2.3.5   Possible Futures

International organizations are often reluctant to take up issues that cause controversy, such as women's reproductive rights. The challenge for local organizations seeking to appropriate concepts of women's human rights to improve the status of women is to mine the range of possibilities offered by international organizations in a way that is appropriate to local circumstances while resisting the pattern of trading women's rights off against other issues, such as the maintenance of tradition or political stability. Alliances with feminists working within international bureaucracies can be valuable (Eyben and Turquet 2013). Overall, this is a dynamic and contested social field, with coalitions and struggles among international organizations, civil society, and states. These contests continually redefine what women's rights mean and what these ideas and institutions can do to improve the status of women worldwide.

11.2.4   Health

11.2.4.1   Challenges for Social Progress

The World Health Organization (WHO) has become a "world government for health," the formal structure and mechanism by which nations come together to determine policies for global health. Its predecessor organizations, the Pan American Sanitary Organization (PAHO) (1902)

and the Office International d'Hygiène Publique (1907), arose from the need to balance interests of trade against those of health (Fidler 1999; Lee 2009; WHO 2016b). The issue of alignment of national standards of quarantine for infectious diseases remains a core concern today, but the globalized world now sees both increased population mobility and a wide array of products that pose risks to health. The tension between commercial and national health security interests remains central to global health (WTO and WHO 2002).

The governance challenge has also been made more complicated in the latter part of the twentieth century by the proliferation of international organizations involved in global health. The emergence of official development assistance through bilateral and multilateral agencies, the entry of large new philanthropies, the establishment of public–private partnerships, and the expansion of international NGOs have highlighted the issue of governance for global health. Underlying the debate about how best to progress global health is the friction between different approaches to achieving good health outcomes, that is, targeted strategies for disease eradication as opposed to sustainable health system development (Dieleman et al. 2016).

11.2.4.2   Ecology of International Organizations in Health

The origin of international organizations for health was the First Sanitary Conference in 1851. Convened by the French government, and attended by 12 countries each represented by a physician and a diplomat, concern was focused on whether to standardize international quarantine regulations against the spread of cholera, plague, and yellow fever. The impetus was a report by the French Minister for Commerce, released in 1834, that showed differing quarantine requirements for exotic diseases across these countries.

Until the founding of the WHO in 1946, most of the cross-national health actors were non-governmental. There were philanthropies such as the Rockefeller and Ford Foundations, established in 1913 and 1936 respectively, as well as church missions, which introduced Western medicine around the world. Their aim was not to govern global health, but to save lives. Nonetheless, the series of Sanitary Conferences led to the establishment of several intergovernmental bodies. PAHO was the first regional intergovernmental body set up to share information about health conditions in the Americas, and to formulate sanitary agreements and regulations so that quarantine requirements would be reduced to a minimum in respect of cholera, yellow fever, bubonic plaque, and smallpox. The Office International d'Hygiène Publique was established in Paris to distribute health information from national health departments. The League of Nations set up a health committee in 1920 that promoted technical assistance to countries to control epidemics.

The post-Second World War environment marks the beginning of contemporary history of global health. The WHO was established as a UN technical agency, its Constitution signed by 61 member states. Since then, health actors have proliferated in bilateral and multilateral organizations, such as the UK Department for International Development (DFID), the US Agency for International Development (USAID), the World Bank, and regional banks. Although these entities

11

focused largely on development assistance projects and loans for post-war or post-independence reconstruction, from the 1960s they moved increasingly into the health field. The influence of the donors on national health policies and systems grew through project funding as well as policy dialogues. Bilateral donors often served as a soft power instrument for promoting national foreign policy interests.

The 1990s saw another wave of organizations working in global health. This increasingly complex global health architecture now includes: public–private partnerships (PPPs), for example the Global Fund for AIDS, Tuberculosis, and Malaria, and the Global Alliance for Vaccines and Immunizations (GAVI); new philanthropies such as the Bill and Melinda Gates Foundation and Bloomberg Philanthropies; as well as strong influences from large international non-government organizations (INGOs), for example Médecins Sans Frontières, Oxfam, and Save the Children. The adoption of the MDGs by the UN General Assembly in 2000 saw substantial growth in funding for targeted health programs, aiming to reduce maternal and infant mortality, HIV/ AIDS, tuberculosis, and malaria. Funds from a wide variety of sources were channeled not only through governments but increasingly also through NGOs (Dieleman et al. 2016).

This case study examines the post-Second World War developments, particularly from the 1990s onwards. In reviewing the debates between ideologies and organizational and financing developments, the case study assesses the achievements and problems in this complex landscape for global health governance and social progress.

11.2.4.3   Technologies of Governance and Global Health Architecture

The WHO allows each member state one vote at the annual World Health Assembly. Its Constitution provides a mandate to set standards, convene policies, provide technical support to countries, monitor situations and trends, and undertake research (WHO 2016b). The work is carried out through 6 regional offices and 137 country offices. There is strict regulation of work with private sector and civil society organizations. As the secretariat to the World Health Assembly, the WHO is funded through assessed contribution from member states, as well as their voluntary contributions and the support of major philanthropies. The financial contribution is dominated by the major bilateral donors and the high-income economies of the world.

Two legal instruments are in place – the Framework Convention on Tobacco Control (FCTC) adopted in 2001 and the International Health Regulations (IHR) last updated in 2005. The FCTC has been the basis for successful introduction of tobacco control efforts across many countries, and serves as the basis for solidarity in the battle against the tobacco industry interests (Framework Convention Alliance 2016). The most recent revision of the IHR was hastened by the outbreak of SARS in China and elsewhere, but has again come under scrutiny following the Ebola crisis in West Africa, given that reporting by countries about their IHR core capacities is not externally validated.

The WHO's influence over global health is otherwise exercised through its normative work and supporting countries in program delivery.

WHO promulgates technical standards, ranging from how various health indicators should be defined and measured, to allowable exposure limits to various hazards, to evidence-based guidelines for public health interventions. Its regular World Health Report presents the "state of the world" on selected issues, be it health financing, non-communicable diseases, or human resources for health (WHO 2013, 2016m). The influence of the WHO extends beyond its member governments to civil society. Most notably, the Declaration of Alma-Ata in 1978 captured the world's imagination through its call for "health for all by the year 2000," and enunciating primary health care principles that relate not only to health equity and service delivery but also to community participation in the planning and implementation of health care (WHO 2016c).

The governance of global health has, however, become increasingly fragmented and uncoordinated. Bilateral and multilateral donors, working in countries since the 1960s through grant or loan-financed projects, offer substantial funding contributions and with it, sustained technical inputs. The global health landscape became even more complex when the World Bank turned its attention to normative standards in its 1993 World Development Report (World Bank 1993). In contrast to the universalist orientation of the Declaration of Alma-Ata, the World Bank advocated prioritized funding of benefit packages based on cost-effective analysis. This new approach framed large loan projects across developing country funding programs to provide immunization, combat micronutrient deficiencies, and control and treat infectious diseases.

The dissonance between a targeted ("vertical") approach with a systemic ("horizontal") approach was heightened initially in the global economic downturn shortly after the Declaration of Alma-Ata, when UNICEF promoted "selective primary health care" (through a package called GOBIFFF – growth monitoring, oral re-hydration, breast-feeding, immunization, food supplements, family spacing, and female education) as a way to achieve specific health outcomes in a resource-scarce environment. This was supported further through the 1993 World Development Report, and then reinforced by the emergence of institutions in the late 1990s focused on funding or supporting prevention and control efforts directed at particular diseases. UNAIDS was established outside the WHO. The Global Fund for AIDS, Tuberculosis, and Malaria was a public–private partnership as was the Global Alliance for Vaccine Initiative (GAVI). The US did not join the global effort on HIV/ AIDS and set up its own program, the President's Emergency Plan for AIDS Relief (PEPFAR). The 2000 MDGs, with their emphasis on health goals, promoted targeted programs coupled with performance management through reporting. In a sense, this was a criticism of slow governmental processes to reach agreement on normative standards through the WHO, and of the idealism embodied in the Declaration of Alma-Ata. It was also a response to reduced UN funding, caused by the US reluctance to pay its UN dues from 1985 onwards.

Relevant also is the fact that the new philanthropies of the 1990s, such as the Bill and Melinda Gates Foundation and Bloomberg Philanthropies, had a presence far exceeding established funding agencies such as Ford and Rockefeller. They seeded major initiatives, with funding that greatly outstripped the WHO's capacities. As private entities, they had minimal obligations to account for their actions.

The increased funding for global health was welcomed by the recipients and the advocates for particular causes, but there was no mechanism for coordination of global health initiatives, let alone a system of multi-stakeholder governance. Instruments such as the Paris Declaration and International Health Partnerships (IHP+) attempted to improve coordination at a national level with bilateral and multilateral donors and other public-private partnerships (International Health Partnerships 2016). A mechanism for policy coherence at the global level remained elusive.

There have been proposals variously for the constitution of an advisory committee of stakeholders for the WHO, such as "Committee C" (Kickbusch, Hein, and Silberschmidt 2010) and also for a Framework Convention on Global Health (FCGH) (Gostin and Friedman 2013) to coordinate financing of global health. The proposed Committee C would create an additional third committee of the World Health Assembly to deal with coherence, partnership, and coordination of global health actors, non-health actors, and the development of legal instruments, all within the existing infrastructure of the World Health Assembly. The FCGH proposes the development of a legally binding treaty for global health, from a human rights perspective and driven by civil involvement, based within the WHO, or the UN, or outside these existing forums.

Many observers have noted that the post-Second World War institutional arrangements for global health governance are inadequate for the challenges of the twenty-first century. A World Health Forum has been proposed, encompassing a broader range of participants than the World Health Assembly, including representatives from all major global organizations as well as the private sector. This would enable major actors to work more effectively together – globally as well as at country level – to address issues with coherence, accountability, fragmentation, and duplication of effort (WHO 2011). There have also been calls for WHO reforms along the lines of having regional directors appointed rather than elected, in the interest of "one WHO" (Gostin and Friedman 2015). The WHO has adopted a framework of engagement with non-state actors, in order to strengthen connections with NGOs, private sector entities, philanthropic foundations, and academic institutions, while providing protection from potential risks to reputation, conflicts of interest and undue influence from external actors (WHO 2016n). In the post-Ebola period, there have been calls for a separate UN agency to manage emergencies and disease outbreaks (Kickbusch 2016; United Nations 2016a). The WHO has now established the Health Emergencies Program in order to optimize intra-agency coordination, operations, and information flow (WHO 2016j).

11.2.4.4   Achievements

Health is the result of interaction between the person's biological make up and his/her environment, including family upbringing, social networks, educational experiences, living and working conditions, geographical location, political systems, and cultural expectations (Australian Institute of Health and Welfare 2014; Institute Medicine (US) 2006; WHO 1946). Health care services are part of the solution, alongside other public policy interventions.

Taking a long view, from the mid-twentieth century onward, the health of nations has generally improved. During this period life expectancy increased significantly for most countries and for the largest and poorest nations, China and India, life expectancy increased from less than 45 years to above 60 years (Gapminder 2015). However health inequalities between and within nations remain. Within China, for example, health status and life expectancy vary according to GDP, access to health care and geographical region, ranging from 71 to 82 years (Lin and Carter 2014; Liu et al. 2010). The largest variations occur within India, where life expectancy varies between states from 56 years to 74 years (Balarajan, Selvaraj, and Subramanian 2011). In all OECD countries life expectancy is over 70 years, whereas across G77 countries life expectancy varies from less than 50 to more than 80 years (Gapminder 2015).

Improved health is attributable to a wide range of factors beyond health care, including improved environment, housing, water, and sanitation, urban infrastructure, education, income, and food supply. In this respect, international organizations have made contributions, be they health specific, such as the WHO or development banks and bilateral donors, or philanthropies and civil society organizations. For example, over the last half century the World Bank's International Development Association has worked in the world's 77 poorest countries, advising governments on economic development and coordinating donor assistance for access to drinking water, schooling, employment, electricity, and roads (World Bank 2016). More recently Bloomberg Philanthropies have played a significant role in enabling improvements in education, energy supply, food supply, road safety, anti-tobacco efforts, and prevention of obesity (Bloomberg Philanthropies 2015). Oxfam International, since its beginnings as a small community-run organization in the 1940s in the UK, has become a global confederation of independent non-government organizations, raising awareness and funds to address global poverty and provide access to food, water, and education (Oxfam International 2016).

Globally, through the WHO and in partnership with other actors, some particular progress in health status and health governance can be seen:

- The Framework Convention on Tobacco Control encourages strict policy, regulatory, and financing strategies that are addressing one of the most deadly risk factors for health.
- The International Code of Practice on Marketing Infant Formula has highlighted the unethical practices that hinder opportunities for babies to receive the nutrition they need (WHO 1981).
- The International Health Regulations are requiring governments to share information about disease outbreaks and to strengthen domestic capacity to manage them (WHO 2016g).
- The eradication of smallpox (WHO 2016f); the near eradication of polio through the Polio Global Eradication Initiative, the largest public–private partnership for health involving multiple donors globally, the largest private donor being the Bill and Melinda Gates Foundation (Polio Eradication Initiative 2016; WHO 2015a); as well as advances in eradication of measles in partnership with American Red Cross, US Centers for Disease Control and Prevention (CDC), United Nations Foundation, and UNICEF (WHO 2016h); and advances in eradication of malaria through the Global Malaria Programme in partnership with endemic

country governments and authorities, UN agencies, National Malaria Control Programmes, and multiple intergovernmental organizations, private–public partnerships, and campaign groups (WHO 2016a).

Beyond these specific efforts, the normative frameworks of the WHO have also been important in providing a vision for social progress, such as the Declaration of Alma-Ata to promote primary health care and equity, and the Ottawa Charter for Health Promotion in 1986 (WHO 1986) pointing to how a multi-sectoral approach can support communities taking control over the factors that affect their health.

International organizations, through the UN system in particular, have instigated both health-specific norms and regulations as well as provided broader social frameworks and conventions. The most important instruments for the health of vulnerable populations include the Universal Declaration of Human Rights (1948), the Convention on the Elimination of All Forms of Discrimination Against Women (1979), the Convention on the Rights of the Child (1989), the Declaration on the Rights of Indigenous Peoples (2007), and the Codex Alimentarius International Food Standards (Food and Agriculture Organization of the United Nations 2016). These have allowed civil society and health sector actors to work in coalition, advocating to and holding governments to account for addressing problems of health inequity. Following the refugee crisis in Europe in 2015–2016, the International Organization for Migration has been officially incorporated into the UN system.

In the years since the new millennium, the UN General Assembly has also adopted a range of resolutions specifically for health, for example, the Declaration of Commitment on HIV/AIDs and the Report on Unhealthy foods, non-communicable diseases and the right to health (United Nations 2014). The MDGs had a strong health focus – on HIV, TB, Malaria, infant mortality, and maternal mortality – which allowed donors to coalesce their resources around these specific issues. The SDGs, adopted in 2015, provide a stronger global platform in being inclusive of all countries, and not just developing countries, and also embody a "social determinants of health" framework, that requires a multi-sectoral governance approach. Furthermore, they recognize that universal health coverage is fundamental to the achievement of equitable and sustainable health outcomes and this will require all countries to work on how to ensure all people and communities have access to needed quality services, ranging from prevention to treatment, without undue financial hardship. Universal Health Coverage (UHC) is one of the key targets under Goal 3 (on health and well-being) of the SDGs and is the platform for various health outcomes. UHC builds from earlier normative work of the WHO, including the World Health Reports of 2000 (Health Systems), 2008 (Renewal of Primary Health Care), and 2010 (Health Systems Financing), and indeed the 1978 Declaration of Alma-Ata (in particular sections VIII–X in relation to national systems, access to primary health care, and social and economic development).

11.2.4.5   Problems and Limitations

Health inequality is a major global challenge, as are the complex processes of global health governance. Underlying the problem of global governance are questions about both who funds global health and the knowledge base for global health.

Reducing health inequalities requires redistributional social and economic policies. Policy for health care systems is, however, also an important part of addressing health inequalities. The responsibility for improving health and well-being fundamentally rests at the local (and national) level. The extent to which international organizations are able to influence national policies is one limitation. Agreement to global rhetoric is easy while implementation is constrained by complex political and economic forces at work. At the national and local levels, there are powerful commercial interests in all countries and forceful religious influences in many countries. Trade interests may drive governments towards free trade agreements, and potentially sacrificing access to generic medicines (Lopert and Gleeson 2013; WHO 2016l).

Global normative frameworks can be important rally points for social movements, at local, national, and global levels. The People's Health Movement is an example of a global citizen's network, a monitoring report called Global Health Watch is published every few years, from the perspective of health as a human right requiring cross-sectoral and international policy. The ability of international organizations to communicate effectively, if not partner, with civil society to support holding governments to account is one reason behind the limited influence of international organizations on national policies. At the same time, some member states are wary about engagement with non-state actors (Lin and Carter 2014; Philanthropy News Digest 2016), for fear of losing the centrality of government and the place of the public sector in global health policy and governance, or for fear of corruption by commercial interests (Gulland 2016; WHO 2015b).

The roles played by public and private funders, including bilateral, multilateral, and philanthropic donors, can also create distortions in a country's health system, along with distortions in global health priorities (Lane and Glassman 2007). Funders are driven by their own imperatives and accountabilities – to the domestic politics of a country, to the passions of wealthy individuals, and to the institutional goals of a funding body. The short-term need to produce results may lead to improved overall health outcomes but may produce unequal distribution of health within a country. Underlying factors that produce ill-health, particularly health inequalities, may require longer investment periods than funders wish to do. The focus on vertical programs by high-income country donors also distorts the financing for WHO and in recipient countries by creating programmatic silos, often at the cost of focus on creating sustainable and resilient health systems. For example, highly targeted programs, such as the US PEPFAR, the Global Fund for AIDS, TB, and Malaria, and the GAVI, absorb large volumes of funding, as well as human resources, at national and even global levels, which may not reflect the burden of disease in different parts of the world (Fidler 2010).

The dominance of high-income countries in the financing of global health and of the WHO also drives the values and knowledge bases that inform the work of global health actors. Recent managerial tools such as "pay-for-performance" and "result-based financing," along with continuing emphasis on monitoring and evaluation indicators

11

(WHO 2016e), are all consistent with the neo-liberal "new public management" frameworks that have dominated the English-speaking developed world (Manning 2001; United Nations Research Institute for Social Development 1999). The emphasis by the World Bank on results-based financing and rigorous impact evaluation (Lin, Carter, and Yan 2016) advantages countries and regions where these approaches are in place or are familiar (World Bank 2010). The push for "evidence-based health policy" (CDC 2016) (or "evidence-based medicine," "public health," or "health care practice") privileges northern production of knowledge, given the funding and publication of knowledge over-whelmingly occurs in high-income countries (McMichael, Waters, and Volmink 2005). The use of English as the common language of govern-ance further perpetuates the hegemony of high-income Anglophone countries. These cultural barriers are difficult to overcome.

Lack of policy coherence at the global level will also influence the extent of policy coherence at the national level. Global health agreements reached through the WHO may be inconsistent with trade agreements that governments have signed (WTO and WHO 2002). Access to gen-eric medicines may be central for universal health coverage, but patent protection for the pharmaceutical industry may be a stronger driver for some countries (Lopert and Gleeson 2013; WHO 2001, 2016d). Standards for intake of sugar and fat may have sound scientific basis and be adopted globally, but the trade interests of food and beverage industry may be more influential in trade regimes (Friel et al. 2013; Legge et al. 2013).

The early history of global health saw difficulties in agreeing on standards for quarantine due to trade interests (Bashford 2014; Tognotti 2013; WHO 2007). While there has been important progress in communicable disease standards over the twentieth century, there is now tension between trade interests and the prevention of non-communicable diseases that exhibit a clear socioeconomic gradient in most countries (McQueen 2013; WHO 2008, 2016). If the rise of emerging diseases, such as Ebola and Zika, are shown to be related to disrupted ecosystems, then the future of global health is closely tied to global action on climate change (Epstein 2001; Redding et al. 2016; University College London 2016; WHO 2003, 2016e).

11.2.4.6   Possible Futures

The WHO and the UN system have been significant contributors to social progress in global health, using a variety of governance tools. The results are nevertheless a culmination of the efforts of many – including member states that champion issues on governance boards, advocates who push their governments to lead on global health issues, public and private financiers who make implementation pos-sible, researchers and teachers who provide the evidence and produce a capable public health workforce.

Health, at any level, is a collective effort. It is co-produced by indi-viduals, families, and communities with those who intervene, be it at the clinical or policy level, and at local or global levels. The twentieth-century global health landscape has been shaped by a relatively top-down, paternalistic set of institutions. This landscape has become complicated in the early twenty-first century. The three

major trends over the past two decades have been towards more discretionary funding (and away from longer-term funding), towards multi-stakeholder governance (and away from government-centered representation), and towards narrower mandates (or vertically focused initiatives rather than broader systemic goals) (Clinton and Sridhar 2017: 1). If the current scenario continues, is further progress possible?

A "business as usual" scenario is possible – perhaps likely – because of the deeply entrenched interests of elites, as major financial donors, sitting on the governance bodies as well as those within the institutions. Insufficient vigilance about the changing global health challenges may well lead to further breakdown of trust and social order, and perpetuate health inequalities within and across countries. A twenty-first-century fit-for-purpose international organization for health must pay greater attention to social inclusion and equity. Concerted action addressing political and commercial determinants of health will be necessary. This will require both active civil society engagement and consideration of new forms of global health governance.

11.2.5   Intellectual Property

11.2.5.1   The Challenge for Social Progress

Intellectual property rights are a bundle of time-limited exclusive rights granted to authors and creators in the intangible products of their cre-ative labor. From a utilitarian perspective, incentives to encourage pri-vate investment in creative endeavor can enhance social welfare by increasing the production of cultural goods such as useful inventions (protected by patents) and expressions of ideas (protected by copy-right). The grant of such monopoly rights, however, also creates social costs in the form of greater barriers to entry for competitors, higher prices for consumers, and may impede down-stream innovation. This requires a coordinated approach to intellectual property regulation in light of other legal frameworks such as human rights, public health, competition, and innovation.

With economic globalization, international protection of intellec-tual property rights became an important issue to rights holders in Europe and in the United States who persuaded their governments to pursue harmonization of intellectual property rules through inter-national organizations and technologies of governance under them, in particular through the international trade system. Substantive har-monization of intellectual property norms as a matter of trade policy through an international organization, however, raises a challenge of normative balance in light of the diverse situations of countries and peoples around the world. Moreover, tradeoffs involved at the multi-lateral bargaining table require knowledge of the technical subjects being negotiated and strong national interests that cannot easily be forfeited without serious political or constitutional challenge domes-tically. In the context of the Uruguay Round negotiations that led to the creation of the WTO in 1995, neither technical expertise nor domestic constituencies existed in developing and least-developed countries to counteract the powerful interest groups demanding stronger intellec-tual property rules through the WTO. Such strong intellectual property rules, without corresponding limits, constrain national policy space critical for countries to create conditions consistent with the cultural

11

and economic contexts in which innovation and cultural development can best flourish. In this way, international organizations and their technologies of governance may impede social progress.

The Agreement on Trade-Related Aspects of Intellectual Property Rights (TRIPS Agreement) is one of the WTO agreements that came into effect in 1995. It required new minimum substantive commitments to intellectual property rules backed by dispute settlement with the threat of trade sanctions to secure enforcement. These requirements since have been made more stringent through a web of bilateral, regional, and plurilateral trade agreements negotiated by the United States and the European Union (EU) with developed and developing countries. Importantly, while only governments may bring disputes under the WTO dispute settlement process, many of these bilateral and plurilateral agreements provide rights to private parties to bring claims under investor-state dispute settlement provisions, often overseen by the International Centre on the Settlement of Investment Disputes (ICSID) operating within the World Bank.

As countries sought to implement TRIPS standards in national law, new national institutions were created or powers of existing institutions enhanced, leading to the spread and development of professionals specialized in intellectual property law, affecting local legal practice. Because TRIPS requirements have penetrated state institutions and local legal practice, the result can be viewed as an example of a transnational legal order that has transformed law and practice within countries (Halliday and Shaffer 2015). However, in analyzing and implementing TRIPS obligations, some developing countries have successfully asserted local values or defended national interests by engaging other legal frameworks involving other international organizations, or appealing to constitutional principles that reflect values in the international human rights regimes and limit the domestic reach or effect of TRIPS rules (Okediji 2007, 2015a).

This case study assesses developments regarding pharmaceutical patent protection, copyright, and protection of traditional knowledge in relation to international organizations and technologies of governance. Overall, the case study exhibits the potential pathologies of international organizations when they reflect the interests of powerful states and interest groups within them, whether from the perspective of countries in the Global South or more broadly. Yet international law and international organizations also have been used to check some US and European initiatives through the discourses of development, human rights, health, and indigenous rights law, including as advanced through treaties and soft law.

11.2.5.2 Pharmaceutical Patents and Access to Medicines

The issue of access to medicines involved a high degree of contestation. Until the creation of the TRIPS Agreement, no international treaty or international organization required national protection of pharmaceutical patent rights. However, from the mid-1990s until around 2000, in light of the incorporation of mandatory patent protection in the TRIPS Agreement and the negotiation of new bilateral and plurilateral agreements containing TRIPS-plus provisions, countries around the world were required to adopt new patent laws providing for the patenting of pharmaceutical products. As a result, countries were considerably more constrained in exercising policy space to ensure optimal production and distribution of drugs at affordable prices (Shaffer and Sell 2014).

Although the TRIPS Agreement imposes significant obligations on states to protect the holders of patent rights, commentators now commonly refer to the flexibilities in its provisions to counter US and European demands for ever-greater protection. The TRIPS Agreement provides for some interpretive options, such as what constitutes novelty and inventive steps for the purposes of granting a patent that many developing countries have explored (Dreyfuss and Rodríguez-Garavito 2014; Kapczynski 2008). Among the most important of the limitations and exceptions for patents for developing countries are the rights of parallel importation, of granting compulsory licenses, and of so-called "Bolar" exemptions[6] for generic drug companies to prepare a drug under patent for marketing authorization once the patent expires (Correa 2000; Dreyfuss and Rodríguez-Garavito 2014). International non-governmental organizations, such as Médecins Sans Frontières and Knowledge Ecology International, have actively promoted the use of such flexibilities. In response to these pressures, in 2001, WTO members negotiated the Doha Declaration on Public Health and they adopted a waiver in August 2003 that enables any member country to import pharmaceuticals made under a compulsory license (although the conditions of the waiver are still contested for being too stringent).

In subsequent developments, the flexibilities incorporated in the TRIPS Agreement have prominently featured in US and EU bilateral and multilateral agreements. These agreements have eliminated or curtailed significantly many of the policy options provided in the TRIPS Agreement. For example, many of them prohibit parallel importation and restrict the use of compulsory licenses. As a result, these bilateral, regional, and multilateral agreements may reduce policy levers available to governments to provide access to lower cost health technologies.

Implementing the relatively high standards of the TRIPS Agreement nonetheless has been more of a challenge than the United States and Europe initially contemplated. This is, in large part, because a countervailing process of transnational legal ordering has emerged with a different normative frame, one with a human rights focus. Developing countries, civil society actors, and UN-based organizations have advanced this frame at the international and national levels both to counter the push for ever stronger pharmaceutical patent protection, and to spur recognition and application of a right to health in public policy more generally.

At the international level, developing countries have found support from the World Health Assembly, the UN Committee on Economic, Social, and Cultural Rights, the Office of the UN High Commissioner on Human Rights (OHCHR), the UN Special Rapporteur on the Right to Health, and the Joint UN Programme on HIV/AIDS. The WHO Constitution establishes that "the enjoyment of the highest attainable standard of health is one of the fundamental rights of every human

---

6   Named for a US law designed to overturn the case of *Roche Products Inc.* v. *Bolar Pharmaceutical Co. Inc.* 733 F 2d 858 (1954).

being" (WHO 1946). The right to health is also incorporated in multiple human rights instruments, including the 1948 Universal Declaration of Human Rights and the ICESCR. The OHCHR identified access to essential medicines as "a vital component of fulfilling the right to health" (OHCHR 2008). The MDGs included access to essential medicines; the MDG Gap Task Force Report 2012 advised that "developing countries should carefully assess possible adverse impacts on access to medicines when adopting TRIPS-Plus provisions" (UN 2012). Such rights advocacy helped to build an alternative normative framing, to establish new offices and initiatives in international organizations (such as in the WHO), as well as entirely new international institutions (such as UNAIDS), and generated pressure for the amendment and interpretation of the TRIPS Agreement in light of social welfare concerns.

11.2.5.3　Copyright

The international copyright system emerged from a dense network of bilateral agreements between European countries that shared similar social, cultural, and economic conditions. These countries eventually negotiated and agreed to the 1886 Berne Convention for the Protection of Literary and Artistic Works, which established minimum standards for cross-border protection of literary and artistic works. Those standards were extended to many colonial territories, many of which continued to govern and regulate cultural goods under Berne rules even after independence.

In the post-colonial era of the late 1960s and 1970s, the Berne standards were viewed as incompatible with the level of economic development in most former European colonies. Yet, international organizations regarded copyright protection as a major element of social and cultural advancement. As a result, these organizations promoted the protection of copyright as an important legal regime for economic growth and development but favored less stringent copyright standards such as those promulgated under the 1952 Universal Copyright Convention. Once the United States ratified the Berne Convention in 1989, however, it set the stage for the strengthened international copyright norms eventually codified in the TRIPS Agreement. The incorporation of Berne minimum standards into the TRIPS Agreement augmented the monopoly power of copyright owners and consolidated global market dominance in the creation and distribution of knowledge goods. Yet, as with patents, important limitations were also incorporated into the copyright provisions in TRIPS. For example, the idea-expression limitation (excluding ideas from copyright protection, and only protecting their expression) was codified for the first time in international copyright law through the TRIPS Agreement. Additionally, the Berne Appendix, a compulsory licensing protocol negotiated to accommodate the bulk access needs of developing countries particularly for educational purposes, was also preserved in TRIPS.

Nonetheless, one of the significant changes occasioned by TRIPS was a limitation on national policy to enact additional limitations and exceptions at the national level. Known as the three-step-test (TST), this provision in the TRIPS Agreement ostensibly constrains the extent to which countries can design copyright law to adapt to specific cultural and economic needs. Countries must "confine limitations and exceptions to exclusive rights to certain special cases which do not

conflict with a normal exploitation of the work and do not unreasonably prejudice the legitimate interests of the rights holder" (WTO 1995: TRIPS Art. 13). In this contested policy space, international copyright law constrains the pro-development and pro-competitive aspects central to national policy-making. Limitations and exceptions to copyright are precisely where national cultural, political, and social values are best exercised and defended, and where innovation and competition flourish. Accordingly, the defense and preservation of limitations and exceptions has become a central focus of international copyright norm-setting activities in the World Intellectual Property Organization (WIPO), emphasizing the role of copyright law in human and social development.

In seeking to constrain the scope of acceptable limitations and exceptions at the national level, international organizations that administer the various copyright treaties ultimately deny less-powerful countries the explicit right to shape national interests in the production and dissemination of cultural goods. Under TRIPS, the simultaneous expansion of copyright and reduction of policy space marked a significant change in international copyright law because it also signaled the growing power of private market actors in shaping regulatory policies in areas where fundamental rights are implicated. This is the case with privacy interests and copyright's role as an engine of free speech. As copyright industries in the United States and Europe sought to consolidate gains from TRIPS by advocating new treaties to gain stronger protection in the digital context, civil society groups, public agencies, and developing countries mobilized firm resistance to these expansionist efforts of the copyright industries by advocating for limitations and exceptions in the treaties. As concluded, the 1996 WIPO Copyright Treaty (WCT) and the WIPO Performers and Phonograms Treaty (WPPT) include provisions that preserve some important national flexibilities in ways that arguably are in tension with the TST. Negotiated on the heels of the TRIPS Agreement, the normative balance established in these WIPO treaties was made possible in part by the strong resistance to TRIPS that had galvanized an Access to Knowledge movement (A2K) directed at preserving the public welfare focus of national copyright laws (Kapczynski 2008).

The strong reaction to the welfare implications of more robust copyright rights imposed by TRIPS caused the A2K movement to seek international balance in copyright treaties, rather than just national policy space. National copyright regimes typically are predicated on utilitarian justifications. Put simply, copyright is a means to incentivize the production of cultural goods. This utilitarian emphasis was incorporated in TRIPS (Art. 7), which states that its objective is to "contribute to the promotion of technological innovation and to the transfer and dissemination of technology." However, national copyright laws can and should reflect several other justifications including the protection of an author's personality, advancement of cultural and technological interchange, and the expansion of the public domain. As stated in TRIPS Article 7, the terms of global copyright protection should insure "to the mutual advantage of producers and users of technological knowledge and in a manner conducive to social and economic welfare, and to a balance of rights and obligations."

The A2K movement, working through a network of private and public organizations, leveraged these TRIPS provisions to demand change within international institutions. The demands yielded developments such as the WIPO Development Agenda, which requires that development considerations inform WIPO's norm-setting and technical assistance programs. In addition to challenging the dominant ideology of international organizations involved in copyright norm-setting, the A2K movement sought to establish its own vision of copyright regulation, informed by human rights norms. Since 2008, developing countries and NGOs have pressed for mandatory limitations and exceptions for libraries and archives, for educational institutions, and for the blind. In 2013, the Marrakesh Treaty to Facilitate Access to Published Works (MAT) was concluded. It established a mandatory exception to copyright law – the first of its kind. Countries that ratify the MAT are obligated to establish an exception in their national copyright laws to allow visually impaired persons to have accessible format copies.

The MAT is the first treaty to use the international copyright regime to accomplish specific human rights ends. Although Article 27 (1) of the UDHR states that "everyone has the right freely to participate in the cultural life of the community, to enjoy the arts and to share in scientific advancement of its benefits" (UNGA 1948), the practical implications of this right have been difficult to work out given competing approaches to copyright. However, reconciling human rights goals with copyright is feasible and has instrumental benefits (Okediji 2007). To maintain and strengthen those benefits, however, will require ongoing collaboration between civil society groups, international NGOs, and developing countries. It will also require convergence between norms created in different international regimes and across different legal frameworks.

11.2.5.4   Intellectual Property and Traditional Knowledge

Indigenous peoples have been economically, politically, and socially marginalized by the modern state, and their knowledge has been subject to assimilation, appropriation, and disregard. International organizations such as the UN have played a key role in articulating the importance of protecting forms of traditional knowledge and connecting it to the cultural survival of indigenous peoples. Traditional knowledge is an umbrella term that includes recognition for a number of forms of indigenous cultural production, including traditional cultural expressions such as folklore, music, dance, and oral history; plant-based and ethnobotanical knowledge; environmental knowledge; and, in some cases, genetic resources. We adopt the term traditional knowledge as it is the legal term of art, but recognize that the term can be viewed as misleading, or even pejorative. Our use of the term, therefore, acknowledges that traditional knowledge should not be viewed as ancient, static, and natural, but as dynamic and inventive (Gana 1995; Sunder 2007).

UN organizations, such as the United Nations Educational Scientific and Cultural Organization (UNESCO) and International Labor Organization (ILO), have generated diverse legal instruments that address the need to protect forms of traditional knowledge and the rights of indigenous communities to control these forms of cultural production. These legal instruments have created narratives that legitimate indigenous claims to intangible property and assist in securing resources for the protection of these rights. However, most of these legal instruments lack enforcement mechanisms that provide recourse to indigenous peoples. Moreover, the UN structure does not always give voting rights to non-state actors, marginalizing the participation of indigenous peoples in intellectual property negotiations. UN organizations have also played a far smaller role than national governments in shaping the articulation and exercise of cultural property rights. Domestic law has played a more important role in determining how states articulate, protect, and limit the property rights of indigenous peoples to their cultural heritage and traditional knowledge.

Human rights law has provided many of the core principles for protecting forms of cultural heritage. From its inception in 1945, UNESCO recognized that the preservation of culture was an essential part of protecting such human rights as dignity, equality, and mutual respect. In the 1990s, the UN began to adopt an understanding of cultural preservation that included intangible forms of cultural heritage. This can be seen in the 1993 Convention on Biological Diversity that linked indigenous innovation, the preservation of biological resources, and support for sustainable development. It also appears in the 1993 UN report *Protection of the Cultural and Intellectual Property of Indigenous Peoples* (1993), which highlighted the lasting effects of colonialization, challenged the distinction between cultural and intellectual property from an indigenous perspective, and argued for changing intellectual property laws to ensure the survival of indigenous peoples. More recent UN efforts include the 2003 Intangible Heritage Convention, which expanded the definition of cultural heritage to include intangible forms of cultural production, such as ritual, behavior, oral history, knowledge, and practice. The 2005 Convention on the Protection and Promotion of Diversity in Cultural Expressions positioned such cultural rights as trade rights. The 2007 UN Declaration on the Rights of Indigenous Peoples similarly called for nations to enact domestic legislation to protect the intellectual and cultural property of indigenous peoples.

Such concerns about the protection of cultural heritage and traditional knowledge emerged in a context of shifting trade laws that expanded the reach of international intellectual property protection and strengthened them in ways that aligned with the interests of some large multinational corporations (Drahos and Braithwaite 2003). Developments such as the TRIPS Agreement drew increased attention from scholars, indigenous groups, and the Global South to the ways international intellectual property laws benefited the Global North, in particular the United States. For example, patent laws recognize an inventor's transformation of raw materials into something new and inventive. However, this definition may not easily encompass forms of knowledge that have been collectively produced, which communities have preserved for generations, and that have resulted from incremental change.

While multinational corporations ensured that their concerns about economic losses to "piracy" were codified in legal instruments such as the TRIPS Agreement, indigenous peoples saw their own forms of cultural production likened to the public domain and left open to appropriation. International intellectual property laws made it easier for corporations to extract resources from indigenous peoples and developing nations while enriching the economies of more industrialized nations, a relationship that critics likened to a new form

11

of colonialism (Boyle 1996; Shiva 1997). Such developments articulated a need for the rights of indigenous peoples to be protected from intellectual property laws, meaning they needed defensive protection from laws that permitted third parties to make forms of traditional knowledge part of their protected property claims (Helfer and Austin 2011). Human rights principles provided the underpinning for many of these defensive claims and served to counterbalance the market logic of international intellectual property law.

Indigenous communities have also used intellectual property rights as a form of positive protection for innovations based on traditional knowledge. For example, trademark protection has been used to safeguard traditional signs and symbols and trade secret law has been used to protect forms of secret and sacred traditional knowledge. However, framing traditional knowledge as an intellectual property right requires viewing the world in terms of authorship and ownership, a premise rejected by some indigenous groups and activists, who have looked for alternative framings. Attempts to define who counts as a member of an indigenous group or community for the purposes of exercising cultural heritage rights may prove challenging at a practical level. There are rifts within communities and some groups lack formal standing. Some communities may even come into being via their relationship to cultural property laws and the rights they provide (Coombe 2011). Moreover, forms of knowledge cannot always be matched clearly and easily with particular people and places. For example, aspects of indigenous medicinal knowledge may also be part of the folk medicinal knowledge of the poor (Hayden 2003).

Nation-states, especially those in the Global South, may also claim ownership of indigenous cultural heritage and view such forms of cultural production as part of their national heritage. State efforts to protect forms of indigenous cultural heritage through the use of geographical indications – labels for products with a specific geographic origin that have features tied to that origin – have increased the presence of traditional handicrafts and agricultural products in international markets. In some cases, they have increased the economic revenue of communities and state programs and prevented the appropriation of cultural heritage. However, such efforts can also increase distrust and conflict within communities, exacerbate unequal distributions of wealth, benefit distributors and purchasers of these goods more than the small-scale producers, and open indigenous communities to increased state involvement and regulation (Blakeney and Coulet 2011; Chan 2014; Drahos 2014). Future research and policy-making in this area should consider not only how intellectual property laws can prevent the appropriation of indigenous knowledge but also how expanding understandings of culture as property affects the lives of indigenous communities in multiple, and sometimes contradictory, ways.

11.2.5.5   Possible Futures

Aspects of intellectual property law disproportionately favor wealthy nations and multinational corporations, but the development of transnational human rights law, environmental law, and competition law provides ways to counterbalance this tendency. With the assistance of international organizations, countries could shape and tailor intellectual property legal norms and practices to specific cultural, economic,

and social priorities in ways that would benefit the less powerful. Several strategies could be useful.

(1) *Developing alternative or competing normative frames for the interpretation of international IP norms.* Braithwaite and Drahos (2000) contend that less-powerful stakeholders in global debates fare better if they invest resources in developing principle-based normative frames. These frames can then be combined with technical expertise to apply them. Otherwise, such expertise will tend to work only within normative frames created by powerful actors, such as the United States, EU, and business associations within them, and diffused through technical assistance programs, whether WIPO, WTO, bilateral, or private sector programs. Alternative frames can help catalyze social movements to challenge and call for the modification and reinterpretation of international intellectual property laws (Kapczynski 2008). These alternative frames can be developed and diffused with the assistance of international organizations in such fields as human rights, public health, and culture.

(2) *Developing local expertise and local institutional competence.* Developing countries and civil society groups need to develop not only new normative frames; they also need technical expertise embedded in local institutions. In this way, they become entrepreneurs of international norms and not simply passive recipients and adapters of norms that are institutionalized in the development-related initiatives of international organizations, which in practice may serve the interests of developed countries. This local institutional expertise will need to be broad-based, embedded within government institutions, and include civil society and relevant producer interests, such as representatives of generic producers of pharmaceuticals. Building local expertise in this way could serve to counter the ease with which international organizations, working through technical assistance programs, weaken the authority and credibility of domestic institutions that seek culturally appropriate approaches to intellectual property norms (Okediji 2015a). Understanding technical assistance programs as technologies of governance suggests that international organizations could play an important role in cultivating domestic institutional expertise (Okediji 2014) and should be required to design technical assistance to do so. They also can raise the visibility and reaffirm the legitimacy of successful legal innovations at the national, regional, and community level that promote the protection of national policy space for domestic institutions to adopt norms that are appropriate for national economic and cultural development.

(3) *Pooling resources.* One way that expertise can be built and diffused is by pooling resources through transnational alliances among governments and non-governmental groups specializing in intellectual property issues, linking where appropriate with international organizations. Centers can be developed in universities and think tanks to provide forums for sharing experiences and the identification of more effective practices. Broad-based initiatives that include health activists and generic pharmaceutical producers, for example, are central, as are initiatives that recognize the importance and complexities of protecting traditional knowledge and indigenous cultural heritage rights within existing international intellectual property rules (Shaffer 2004).

(4) *Coordinating with allies in industrialized countries.* Developing countries, civil society organizations, and indigenous groups can coordinate with groups in the United States and Europe to undercut industry pressure in the formation of US and EU negotiating positions and strategies, and counter them within international organizations. International negotiations involve a two-level game in which national constituencies compete in the formation of national positions and those national positions are then advanced in international negotiations. Developing countries, indigenous groups, and other constituencies can work with political allies in the United States and Europe to alter the US and European domestic political calculus as occurred with respect to the Marrakesh Treaty.

(5) *Seeking to better understand the effects of applying the IP frame to a diverse world.* Intellectual property law imposes particular categories, classifications, and Northern "market" values upon the world. Categories, such as "traditional knowledge," "property," "author," and "invention," are not natural but are brought into being as people interact with legal frameworks that tie these categories to the exercise of liberties and making rights claims. The application of these categories by international organizations can alter social structures, practices, and ways of seeing the world (Bowker and Star 1999; Okediji 2014, 2015b). For example, understanding culture as property emphasizes its market value and de-emphasizes other reasons for its production and protection. Viewing the right to health as a right to access patented pharmaceuticals may give priority to pharmaceutical-based policy solutions and foreclose more holistic interventions that take into account economic and social rights and combine them with forms of public medical assistance and education (Biehl 2014). Understanding copyright as an engine of free expression and as a tool for education, as some of the earliest national copyright statutes did, can catalyze important national limits to the property rights of content owners while also facilitating important social welfare policies such as access to education. International organizations involved in the area of intellectual property should bear in mind that the intellectual property frame not only involves the technical application of terms and categories to different cases but also remakes the world so that it conforms to its categories. While human rights law offers alternative frames for the interpretation of the law in this area, intellectual property can also conceptually alter our understandings of human rights.

11.2.6 Conflict, Security, and Terrorism

11.2.6.1 The Challenge for Social Progress

Since the first international organizations were created, scaling up authority to an international body has been used as a strategy to prevent violence, either as the result of cooperation between nation-states that may otherwise go to war, or as an intervention by an international body in domestic or regional settings that could end up in conflict. However, this strategy has also perpetuated colonial relations, the creation of "enemies" and "existential threats" to justify arbitrary policies, and the implementation of counterproductive political and development plans by international organizations.

The eradication of conflict, insecurity, and terrorism are major goals of international organizations; both those that work specifically in these fields, e.g. the North Atlantic Treaty Organization (NATO), and those of general jurisdiction. Conflict, insecurity, and terrorism/radicalization are often seen as connected through cycles of conflict driven by injustice, inequality, poverty, famine, environmental degradation, water shortage, poor health, unemployment, social exclusion, and other human rights problems (Korhonen, Gras, and Creutz 2006). The concept of complex emergency describes the cycles, linkages, and domino effects among these drivers and root causes (World Food Program 2005).

Traditionally, the policies and actions of international organizations have shifted between, and combined, two approaches: (1) repressive pacification (e.g. collective defense, peace enforcement, disarmament, criminalization of aggression) and (2) developmentalism and humanitarian relief (e.g. capacity-building, human rights instruments, development assistance). Financial, legal, and policy measures have been adopted. Major international organizations, e.g. the UN, the African Union (AU), the EU, and NATO, have mechanisms to employ troops from their member states. Also individual and ad hoc coalitions of states have acted with or without a mandate from the UN in cases of aggression against them and terrorism.

11.2.6.2 The Institutional Ecology of Global Security Governance

The number of organizations dealing with security and conflict keeps growing in a world in which governance has been fragmenting and specializing. In this context, coordination of problems among the various international organizations has been identified as one of the greatest challenges of conflict, security, and anti-terrorism governance. Indeed, the UN Millennium Declaration of 2000 called for "greater policy coherence and better co-operation between the UN, its agencies, the Bretton Woods institutions and the WTO" to prevent crises and to alleviate them. International organizations have responded through a "cluster approach" and "joint needs assessments" (UNGA 2000). The UN Office of the Co-Ordination of Humanitarian Assistance (OCHA) and the Department of Humanitarian Assistance (DHA) coordinate internally with over 20 bodies and externally with at least 30 main NGOs. Similarly, the leading organization in the field, the International Committee of the Red Cross (ICRC), engages in wide coordination with civil and military actors generally and in the field. Nevertheless, as international organizations, including NGOs, active in conflict and crisis areas are numerous, coordination, overlap, and both intra- and inter-institutional competition for funding, visibility, and policy leadership are an issue.

Inter-institutional interaction is, in this sense, a central dimension of the management of conflict, security, and terrorism by international organizations. Ultimately, global security governance is interactional. The law that constitutes the authority of international organizations often takes into account the interaction between institutions involved. Moreover, the institutions in charge of international security governance can develop through interaction, as did the AU/UN Hybrid Mission in Darfur (UNAMID) in 2007. Similarly, substantive policies and programs adopted by international organizations involved in international security governance can also be the result of interaction. It is now common for the UN Security Council to refer to international financial institutions in some of its resolutions. The World Bank, in turn, is actively engaged in the control of landmines, particularly through its Emergency Landmine Clearance Project. Finally, interaction becomes crucial when multiple institutions are active in a specific area or state. While international organizations have focused their efforts on coordination, the reality is that interaction between institutions may involve competition, mimicry, co-optation, and specialization.

Private actors are also important elements in this institutional ecosystem and the increase in the privatization of security and military services has sharpened questions of coordination and accountability. Corporations providing security and military services do not fall under the command structure or public control mechanisms of the states that employ them; their contracts are secret and their actions take place outside national jurisdictions of their home states (Francioni and Ronzitti 2011).

The quantity and heterogeneity of public, private, governmental, and non-governmental organizations involved in security, conflict, and counter-terrorism, and the ensuing coordination problems, have historical antecedents. In the era before the UN, powerful states or coalitions of interested states often took over areas that were both strategically and/or economically important to them. Some were exploited through colonialism or as mandates during the League of Nations period. Colonial powers frequently resorted to mercenaries for military campaigns. This legacy of public and private coalitions and intertwined interests still dominates the behavior of powerful states within and outside international organizations in situations of conflict, insecurity, or terrorism (Korhonen et al. 2006).

11.2.6.3 Technologies of Governance

Policies dealing with conflict oscillate between repression of violence and developmentalism, with corresponding changes in technologies and tools of governance. Historically, coalitions of states and colonial rulers used civilian administration of territories, taking over trade and economic governance combined with military repression. In 1863, the International Committee of the Red Cross (ICRC) was founded to protect the victims of war. Its efforts spread from relief work to preventative measures such as the coordination of policies, initiatives, and treaties promoting more humane rules of war and arms restrictions. The UN Charter contains the basic rules and principles of friendly relations between states. From 1945, the concept of collective security and peaceful settlement of international disputes became the normative foundation of international security; i.e. an attack against a sovereign state would be considered an attack against all and collectively defended. Mechanisms of dispute settlement ranging from negotiations, peace talks, mediation, conciliation, and good offices to court procedures were set up after the founding of the UN. Over the last 70 years, there has been a flowering of international specialist tribunals.

In the aftermath of the World Wars, the Bretton Woods institutions, the World Bank group, and the International Monetary Fund (IMF) were established. The World Bank supports vulnerable states susceptible to complex emergencies, and to post-conflict rebuilding by offering funds and coordination of pledges and assistance programs. The IMF offers advice and aid in stabilizing public finances that are either a driver or, at least, greatly compromised by conflict and insecurity, and the proper conduct of which can decrease terrorist financing.

The UN, the EU, and the AU provide a wide range of capacity-building, good governance, human rights, development assistance, dispute settlement, and, also, peacekeeping instruments; the Organization of American States (OAS) does most of these as well. UN peacekeeping is the oldest model and regional organizations such as the AU and EU can act through it, in concert with it, with its mandate or independently, similar to NATO. The AU also acts in concert with the Arab League. During the Cold War, the so-called first generation of UN peacekeeping was strictly limited to situations where the target state consented and consisted mainly of a military presence and monitoring of ceasefire lines (Ratner 1995). If fighting broke out, the Blue Helmets were only permitted to protect themselves. In the 1980s and early 1990s the second generation of "extended" peacekeeping emerged with multifunctional mandates including holding of elections and civil governance added to the missions, e.g. in Namibia and Cambodia. After the Brahimi report in 2000 and UN Secretary-General Kofi Annan's reform efforts, the third generation of peacekeeping developed to permit more robust force and peacebuilding powers. In 2005, the responsibility to protect (R2P) concept was endorsed by the UN. It marked a turn away from the debate on the right to intervene or to undertake a humanitarian intervention, towards the duty of states and international organizations to protect people. R2P was first invoked by NATO in its Libya operation (2011), which took place alongside a UN mission. The status of the R2P principle has, however, been roundly challenged by some states, notably by the BRICS group,[7] on the basis that it could be used to justify military intervention before all peaceful means for dispute resolution were exhausted.

In addition to peacekeeping and development, the UN is also the leading international organization in establishing tribunals (e.g. the International Court of Justice and ad hoc criminal tribunals), in promoting disarmament, arms control, and nuclear non-proliferation, in developing human rights instruments, mechanisms, bodies, and oversight, and in counter-terrorism. The counter-terrorism mechanisms include 14 treaties, and several subsidiary bodies that coordinate with other agencies internally and externally. The UN Global Counter-Terrorism Strategy was adopted in 2005 to prevent and combat terrorism; to take measures to build state capacity; to ensure the respect of human rights while countering terrorism, and to strengthen the role of the UN. Despite the aspiration of many states to enhance the international/UN response to terrorism, other states still insist on the primary role of national states. The lack of a general comprehensive counter-terrorism convention reflects these controversies, for example, as to the definition of a terrorist and to the sharing of intelligence. Similar tensions exist within NATO, the EU, and AU on this subject.

Complex emergencies put pressure on the kind of governance techniques required for effective international security governance,

---

7   Brazil, Russia, India, China, and South Africa.

beyond the traditional toolkit of legally binding norms and soft law instruments. These new technologies of governance pose questions of legitimacy for the involvement of international organizations in security governance, particularly because they imply a technocratic intervention in domestic issues that are, by definition, intensely political.

The policy applicable to internally displaced populations (IDP), and the reliance on indicators as a technology of governance, provide good examples of a technical intervention. Indicators in the context of global IDPs are useful to justify involvement of international organizations in a situation that is, in principle, recognized as merely domestic. Moreover, indicators are a useful mechanism to influence a political outcome. In this latter sense, they seem to work in a way similar to soft law instruments. They are not backed by armed enforcement, but rather change the terms of engagement. Just as soft law norms have been proven effective in the IDP context, so also indicators are able to influence the way domestic governments behave with regard to its IDPs. Yet, there are many questions as to whose ideas of progress seemingly "neutral" indicators represent and the risk of reducing complex social issues into quantifiable units.

11.2.6.4   Achievements and Limits

The achievements in the field of conflict prevention or alleviation, insecurity, and counter-terrorism are many, including the development of the norm against aggressive force and the availability of many international fora for negotiations and peace talks. Another key element is the realization that conflict cycles can be stopped only through eradication of the complex emergencies that drive them. Yet, the achievements contain inbuilt dilemmas. First, while war is outlawed, war-making has taken more covert modes. Hybrid war tactics, cyberattacks, use of proxies, unmarked uniforms, mercenaries, economic repression, and extortion to destabilize states and governments is on the increase. International organizations cannot keep up in launching policies, let alone actions. Addressing insecurity caused by conflict cycles through eradicating conflict drivers is comprehensive, long-term and, therefore, most often seems too costly. Although many fora for negotiations exist, the access to these fora is not easy and structural biases exist; many voices remain unheard.

Yet, there has been improvement in the peacekeeping mandates, legitimacy, accountability, and coordination. Periodic reviews have been made, ombudspersons appointed, the UN Peacebuilding Commission established (2005) and a dialogue for improvement, although slow, has taken place in all international organizations. Multinational negotiations are conducted on some of the most controversial and persistent crises.

Peacekeeping missions undertaken by intergovernmental organizations seem to have been most successful when managing the aftermath of conflicts already resolved or tentatively resolved by some sort of local or international political agreement. Success, then, is defined as stabilization, not necessarily improvement of social justice. In those cases, peacekeeping typically involves electoral missions, or even taking over foreign affairs, finance, and communications of a state (e.g. the UN Transitional Authority in Cambodia (UNTAC) in 1992). Another factor

contributing to the stabilization success by intergovernmental peacekeeping missions is the commitment of resources by states, particularly powerful states. Finally, a third factor that contributes to the effectiveness of peacekeeping operations is the acceptance of peacekeepers by conflicting parties along with the support of regional international organizations. The AU/UN Hybrid operation in Darfur referred to above is an example of this approach, which, with almost 20,000 uniformed peacekeepers at its peak in 2007, was among the largest peacekeeping missions. There are, however, operations where the amount of staff and troops has been much larger, such as those by the NATO and state coalitions in Iraq and Afghanistan.

Many challenges remain. These include the rapid development of technologies and tactics of war and violence, far more quickly than international organizations can respond. The rise of the Internet and novel communications technologies, for example, has taken international terrorism and other activity to a new level. More traditional problems include the selectivity of international organizations, constrained by their membership, in responding to particular crises, as illustrated by the failure of international organizations in Rwanda, Darfur, and Syria.

Balancing available resources and the needs of target areas is also very difficult; the intervention in Iraq in 2003 and the consequent change in governance has solved some issues, but also caused massive problems. Conflict, insecurity, and terrorist situations are always politically charged and international organizations tend to respond in ad hoc ways. As the UN counter-terrorism debate shows, powerful states want to maintain room to maneuver against, or in the absence of, multilateral consensus. The downside of "adhocism" is the diminished capacity to learn from the past and to increase effectiveness through critical self-assessment (Korhonen et al. 2006). On the other hand, delicate situations require tailored responses; an optimal balance between ad hoc techniques and improvement through systematic/critical review is not easily achieved.

11.2.6.5   Possible Futures

The shift in emphasis from traditional, hard, or repressive modes of responding to conflict, insecurity, and counter-terrorism towards preventative diagnosis and action is fruitful. International organizations move slowly in comparison to tactics and technologies of aggression, their interventions are politically constrained, targets highly selective, and military operations extremely costly and unpopular. Prevention, even if comprehensive and long-term, is simply more economical, not to mention humane. For instance, according to estimates, one day of the NATO bombing in 1999 cost as much as one year of the UN rebuilding mission in Kosovo (UNMIK) (Watt and Norton-Taylor 1999). Thus, if assistance funds had been put to use beforehand, much of the suffering and injustices could have been prevented without the destruction.

International security governance offers important lessons for social progress. Governance of complex conflicts and transitions demands economic and environmental choices from international organizations. "Security" and "economics" cannot be read as separate areas of global governance. Balancing them is a matter of political and ideological choices, which should be made explicit. Even though liberal peace theory with its emphasis on core civil and political rights, electoral democracy, constitutionalization, liberal economics, and free trade have provided the value basis for international security operations since the mid-twentieth century, it is questionable whether this peacebuilding package fits any particular target region. The contemporary neo-liberal agenda is not the only alternative, nor is it universally accepted.

Moreover, international security governance is the result of constant interaction between numerous organizations. In their interaction, some of these organizations adopt survival strategies – sometimes cooperating, sometimes competing with other actors. The shortcomings of accountability within international organizations involved with international security governance, particularly the UN, needs to be improved. International norms of immunity of international organizations, international civil servants, and contained in status of force agreements need to be revised and limited.

Governance of complex conflicts has triggered the use of new technologies of governance, different from formally legally binding instruments. These new technologies, though, risk sheltering crucial choices from political scrutiny and have the potential of redistributing power among different groups in conflict settings. International security governance needs thus to acknowledge that these new technologies of governance are not neutral, and consider the unintended consequences of their use.

In general, the way forward in anti-conflict, security, and counterterrorism for international organizations is to move from ad hoc or piecemeal efforts toward a willingness to develop early warning analysis, to learn from mistakes, and to engage in impact analysis of entry and exit strategies for missions before and after they occur. Checks on secrecy, espionage, destabilization, and unilateralism need to be developed given the importance of information and communication technologies for both progressive and regressive social outcomes.

11.2.7   Climate Change

11.2.7.1   The Challenge for Social Progress

One of the most serious global challenges of our time is human-induced climate change. It poses risks to human and natural life, but until recently, little was done to address the problem. Richardson et al. (2009: 6) summarize the gravity of this issue:

> Past societies have reacted when they understood that their own activities were causing deleterious environmental change by controlling or modifying the offending activities. The scientific evidence has now become overwhelming that human activities, especially combustion of fossil fuels, are influencing the climate in ways that threaten the well-being and continued development of human society. If humanity is to learn from history and to limit these threats, the time has come for stronger control of the human activities that are changing the fundamental conditions for life on Earth.

Given its global scope, the fight against human-induced climate change would benefit greatly from the use of innovative transnational technologies of governance. It requires a long-term perspective and a preparedness to take strong measures now to address a problem whose scope is still uncertain. Effective policies against human-induced climate change will require adjustments in the economic arrangements of both developed and developing nations.

11.2.7.2   Current Efforts

At the time of the inaugural conference of the International Panel on Social Progress in August 2015, attempts to address climate change in a meaningful way had largely failed. Indeed, in spite of the growing awareness of both the existence of human-induced global warming and the catastrophic impact that it could have on future generations, UN action over the last two decades had made slow progress. A major issue has been acknowledging the different responsibilities of the Global North and South for causing climate change. The UN Framework Convention on Climate Change (1992) (UNFCCC) and its Kyoto Protocol (1997) had established intricate systems to differentiate between the obligations of developed and developing states with respect to reductions in greenhouse gas emissions. This seemed out of step with the rising emissions and economic strength of some developing countries, as well as the relocation of some energy-intensive industries or production systems away from developed countries.

The 21st Conference of the Parties (COP) to the UNFCCC, which took place in Paris in 2015, adopted a different approach to the regulation of climate change, enshrined in a binding agreement. The Paris Agreement entered into force in November 2016 and, as at June 1, 2017, has been ratified by 146 countries.

The Paris Agreement is a complex and flexible international treaty. The main features relevant to international governance are:

a)   a formal commitment to hold the increase in the global average temperature to well below 2°C above pre-industrial levels, with an even greater ambition to limit increases to 1.5°C above pre-industrial levels (Article 2);

b)   its global scope in the sense that it contemplates that both developed and developing states will reduce their greenhouse gas emissions; all states have the same core obligations;

c)   obligations to ensure that finance flows are "consistent with a pathway towards low greenhouse gas emissions and climate-resilient development" Article 2 (1) (c); and (in the COP decision to which the Paris Agreement in annexed) a goal for developed countries to provide US $100 billion per year by 2020 for climate-change mitigation and adaptation efforts in developing countries;

d)   its mechanism for reducing greenhouse gas emissions through "nationally determined contributions," where parties undertake and communicate ambitious efforts to achieve the purpose of the Agreement (Article 3);

e)   a review system that commits countries to take stock of their level of emissions every five years, and to provide successive nationally determined contributions that represent a progression from the previous one (Article 4).

The goals set by the Paris Agreement are ambitious given that global temperatures are already 1°C above pre-industrial levels, and achieving "net zero" greenhouse gas emissions under current economic and technological conditions is impossible. Nevertheless, the goals are consistent with the "precautionary principle"[8] and, more specifically, with avoiding the risk of reaching a "point of no return" in terms of global warming.

The Paris Agreement represents a significant advance on the Kyoto Protocol in that it makes the fight against human-induced climate change a global task, through addressing the actions of both economically developed and developing nations. This suggests that the perceived threat of climate change is such that even developing nations have to adjust their national standards of living to be compatible with achieving the emissions reductions required by the Agreement. The Agreement nevertheless takes into account differences in states' circumstances and capacities, and preserves the UNFCCC and Kyoto Protocol's recognition of the principle of "common but differentiated responsibilities and respective capabilities, in light of different national circumstances" (Article 2).

11.2.7.3 Technologies of Governance

The Paris Agreement was designed to encourage broad participation. It achieves this through creating minimal substantive obligations, giving priority to national environmental policies. In this sense it is a "bottom-up" system, reflecting rather than regulating domestic positions. It depends on extensive peer and public pressure for its efficacy.

The implementation structure is to create a "pledge and review" system by which states commit to reductions in emissions, and then national pledges are reviewed in the light of a global stocktaking in five-year cycles. This represents a change from earlier international regulation, which depended on one-off pledges, by creating a long-term architecture to encourage continuous improvement: the Paris Agreement establishes an expectation that progressively stronger action will be taken over time.

The Agreement also endorses market-based approaches to climate change, to "incentivize and facilitate participation in the mitigation of greenhouse gas emissions by public and private entities" (Article 6.4.b). Without using the language of "markets" because of objections by some states, Article 6 encourages emission trading schemes and emission reduction offsets. These will be monitored by an international supervisory body, still to be established.

11.2.7.4 Achievements and Limitations

The global reach of the Paris Agreement is significant as is its setting of core legal obligations applicable to all countries. It is not yet clear whether it has been able to achieve a real consensus on tackling climate change, or whether the Agreement simply masks deep

divisions (Bodansky 2016). There is certainly a challenge in enforcing the commitments because the language of the Paris Agreement is often vague. Phrases such as "countries will aim to undertake rapid reductions" or that they will ensure that future pledges are "a progression beyond existing efforts" (Article 4) leave much room for divergent interpretations. This will in turn complicate access to reliable information regarding both the baseline of each country's greenhouse gas emissions and the periodical reductions they can achieve. The brevity of the Agreement means that many of its elements are still to be negotiated, including the specifics of the five-year cycle of national pledges and review.

Another problem that often complicates the life of international organizations such as the Conference of the Parties is a so-called "democratic deficit." The Paris Agreement was negotiated by states with different political regimes and public spheres, in terms of media coverage of the issue, participatory deliberations prior to the global negotiations, and public engagement with the issue. The often significant differences in the national settings of the parties makes enforcement of the international obligations imposed by the Paris Agreement complicated. They will also affect the legitimacy of an agreement that curtails national sovereignty over areas such as energy policy and economic policy-making.

The effectiveness of the Paris Agreement is critically dependent on transparency at national levels. The specifics of the transparency framework are yet to be determined. The experience of the EU with Greece's lack of openness about its financial situation in 2008 illustrates the risks for transparency when there are major economic, sociopolitical, cultural, and institutional differences between states within a particular treaty regime.

11.3 Conclusions

11.3.1 Interaction Between Local and Global Processes

International organizations are constantly interacting with a wide variety of other international, national, and local organizations, shaping their ability to promote social progress. As this chapter shows, both fragmentation and opportunity are characteristic of the modes of governance these international institutions provide. At the international level, there are myriad hard and soft law rules promulgated and overseen by international organizations that meet more or less regularly to address transnational and global problems. While some international law scholars despair about the fragmentation inherent in these processes, others describe the situation in terms of global legal pluralism and celebrate the openness and opportunity that such diversity and competing rules and institutions provide.

This chapter also emphasizes, however, the importance of interactions between international organizations and national and local ones. To some extent, this is an instance of the intersection of state and civil society organizations. Despite the common assumption that

---

[8] Kriebel et al. (2001: 871–872) identify four features of the precautionary principle "taking preventive action in the face of uncertainty; shifting the burden of proof to the proponents of an activity; exploring a wide range of alternatives to possibly harmful actions; and increasing public participation in decision making."

such organizations are quite discrete and distinguishable, in practice they often blur, with civil society groups sometimes receiving state funding and being assigned state regulatory functions, while state organizations incorporate the ideas, practices, and personnel of civil society groups. There is a growing tendency for states to turn their regulatory responsibilities over to private actors as budgets shrink and states seek to minimize their responsibilities. For relatively poor states, international foundations and donor agencies take on increasingly important roles in local service provision in fields such as health and security, leading to yet more imbrication of state and private action.

One of the most striking dimensions of the role of international organizations in governance is the way they interact with local communities. Through the work of international humanitarian agencies, human rights groups, and other social service providers, local communities often come under the direct supervision and influence of international actors. Poorer states may find their health care, police, and even environmental protection systems administered by international foundations or other international organizations. While this may imply a loss of sovereignty, local organizations can actively appropriate the resources, ideologies, and governance approaches of international organizations for their own purposes.

Such purposes may be compatible with those of the international organization, such as compliance with human rights, but they may also contradict them. Local actors may use the framework of human rights to promote goals quite at odds with the philosophy of human rights, for example. International organizations, unless they are donors, have little control over this process. As these case studies show, the relationship between the local and the global can range from consensus and eager appropriation to deep resistance. Between these extremes there are opportunities, too often unexplored and undeveloped, for creative collaboration.

Calls to protect tradition, to preserve religious values, and to return to nationalism and nativism are indications of resistance to international orders, ideas, and pressures. As globalization proceeds, such forms of resistance have become more conspicuous, although located more in rural than urban areas. Indeed, new international organizations have emerged opposed to the secular, rights-based ones, some based on religious ideas or the creation of a new kind of global order. It is too simple to see social progress as the global dissemination of international ideas and institutions, since while some celebrate this change, others see it as a loss of local distinctiveness, economic and political autonomy, culture, and power. The global/local interaction offers possibilities for social progress in some ways, such as the inculcation of more egalitarian ideologies, but also of social regress as local distinctiveness is swallowed up by homogenizing global institutions.

A fundamental challenge remains to transcend global–local tensions and asymmetries of respect and power. The effectiveness of governance technologies to produce human flourishing depends upon the willingness and creativity of all actors, non-state and state, transnational and local, to find cooperative ways of formulating mutually acceptable goals and the ways and means to achieve social progress.

11.3.2   Financial Issues and Role of Funding

Limited funding poses a major constraint to the effectiveness of international organizations. Growing consensus about the importance of leveraging other forms of capital to augment financial resources may mitigate this challenge. Recognizing and integrating non-financial assets ranging from sociocultural and political to intellectual capital helps foster local buy-ins for transnational technologies of governance and empower situated communities to engage as stakeholders. In the human rights arena, for example, the contingency of rights on the availability of resources has enhanced international cooperation via bilateral and multilateral funding arrangements to support implementation and enforcement. The historic commitments that spurred the MDGs and culminated in the SDGs are based both on revenue-generation and non-financial resources that accrue from institutional experience, knowledge, and capacity for example.

Many organizations have accumulated a wealth of knowledge, experience, and convening power that could generate income. In contexts marked by fragile and failing state sovereigns, civil society organizations can forge partnerships to test interventions that buttress evidence-based policy and operational models. For example, NGOs such as BRAC, a Bangladesh-based development organization, are gradually becoming self-sustaining by evolving profitable social enterprises, as part of broader social ecosystems, which underwrite expenditures and equip program participants to become agents for social change. Equally noteworthy is increasing business sector involvement exemplified by private–public partnerships, corporate social responsibility, and the rise of philanthropic vehicles. The growing significance of diaspora engagements and indigenous resource mobilization mechanisms suggest the effectiveness of transnational technologies of governance. These trends dovetail with growing interest in the devolution of relevant powers, authorities, and processes for state–society collaborations that can galvanize the agency of individuals. In this way, state–society relations can democratize the push for reform, invigorate popular sovereignty, enhance the power of ordinary citizens, and empower polities.

11.3.3   Cognitive Frameworks for Global Modes of Thinking

Technologies of governance, such as indicators, compilations of best practices, model laws, and court rulings, generate and impose particular ways of seeing the world. These cognitive categories may seem to be objective and universally applicable in the context of global governance, but they have been developed by epistemic communities of economists, lawyers, development experts, aid workers, and statisticians to make the world visible, knowable, and governable. We come to know and understand such phenomena as human rights, climate change, innovation and cultural production, immigration, health, and national security in terms of the economic, legal, or technical frame that international organizations have applied. This may facilitate the creation of policies and programs, enable communication across agencies and institutions, and make it easier for methods and findings to travel from one context to another. However, it also limits our vision and privileges particular kinds of expertise.

International organizations derive influence from the epistemic clout of their technical expertise. By framing an issue as technical, organizations are able to exert power over international and domestic political processes and, in the process, may shield political decisions from democratic scrutiny. Indicators, such as those that measure corruption or human rights abuses, reflect decisions about which variables organizations have decided to include, which they have left out, and how such variables should be measured. As numbers, indicators give the appearance of objectively measuring preexisting phenomena. Yet they reflect a particular normative view of the world, one that obscures the choices made when constructing the indicator.

Shared cognitive frameworks also function to hold international organizations together and allow them to function cohesively in a diverse institutional ecology. Highly specialized organizations may appear to be acting independently, but they in fact inhabit a densely populated space in which they interact constantly with one another. Commonalities in the language and practices of expertise facilitate communication among the staffs of different organizations, as well as their processes of data collection and the standardization of practices. As such, these frameworks provide stability and coherence in international work. However, this shared cognitive frame may make other ways of knowing invisible and contribute to a culture of elitism that gives greater recognition to the knowledges and practices of more powerful nations in the Global North. It may also further marginalize members of groups that do not have access to technical experts who can participate in these specialized conversations and represent and communicate the groups' interests.

International organizations should raise awareness of, and propagate, local knowledges from all parts of the world. They must identify successful innovations in nations, regions, and communities. They must discern in what contexts innovations work and adapt innovations to these contexts. International organizations must be especially sensitive to unreflective frameworks that simplify, homogenize, and force the world into categories that deny its complexity. The role of cognitive frameworks in knowledge production is therefore fundamental to the constructive role of international organizations in promoting social change.

11.3.4 Accountability for International Organizations

There are many calls for more accountability within international organizations. The distance from popular democracy, the isolation from domestic accountability mechanisms, the lack of transparency in financing, and the structural and gendered biases embedded in these organizations are common complaints. The scope of their activities, the vastness of the global arena, the multicultural and pluralist staffs, locales and goal-settings make management and oversight difficult. Accountability is, however, neither a simple issue nor a panacea. Internal accountability mechanisms of international organizations include financial control and audits that focus on economy, efficiency, and effectiveness. Large international organizations may have an audit court, as the EU does, or an administrative court, as the UN does, or other oversight bodies. For instance, the UN General Assembly receives some 70 reports from internal bodies annually. Organizations may also have a permanent ombudsperson or mission-specific one, as does the

UN Mission in Kosovo. Human rights courts and bodies also offer legal accountability in cases of grave violations of human rights.

The limits of the formal accountability mechanisms often derive from high transaction costs and difficulty of access to them because of insufficient knowledge or resources. Most accountability institutions are overwhelmed with cases. The most effective accountability mechanism may, therefore, be a healthy organizational culture and managerial commitment rather than any formal tool. Member states and the media also scrutinize international organizations although the interest tends to be much weaker than in the case of domestic organs.

One widely discussed example of the accountability *problématique* in the case of international organizations is related to the sexual exploitation of local women and girls by UN peace personnel. The issue prompted the UN Secretary-General to issue a "Zero-Tolerance" Bulletin (UN Secretary-General 2003). The Bulletin, while heralded by some, was criticized for individualizing responsibility and prohibiting sex in all circumstances while failing to recognize the complex and difficult political economies of peace operations in conflict areas. The claim was that the Bulletin diverted attention from the general failures of peace support, such as the failure to create economic opportunities for locals, specifically, for women and girls, for reinforcing conservative attitudes and local religious elites, and for ignoring the problems that derive from the hegemonic masculinities of UN humanitarianism, and the structural biases of the operations, the UN and international institutional life generally (e.g. Otto 2007).

Accountability mechanisms are important but they typically focus on individual responsibility rather than prompting structural reforms in complex political economies. Different types of mechanisms need to be supported by a responsive organizational and managerial culture in order to avoid the pitfalls of superficial accountability.

11.3.5 Summary

As social problems are increasingly transnational and global in scope, international organizations have proliferated, using many different technologies of governance. These organizations develop and advance different visions of social progress across areas of social life. This chapter has highlighted seven broad areas in which international organizations have operated, assessing their achievements and limits, their promise and their pathologies. International organizations remain crucial for advancing social progress in an interconnected world. Yet, given their remoteness from local contexts and stakeholders, they can be readily captured by well-organized constituencies from the Global North. To advance social progress, international organizations must be both bold in their ambitions and modest in their pretensions, working with local stakeholders to address local contexts.

References

Alter, K.J. 2014. *The New Terrain of International Law: Courts, Politics, Rights.* Princeton, NJ: Princeton University Press.

Australian Institute of Health and Welfare. 2014. "Australia's Health." www.aihw. gov.au/australias-health/2014/understanding-health-illness/.

Baetens, F. 2010. "The Forgotten Peace Conference: The 1915 International Congress of Women," in R. Wolfrum (ed.), *Max Planck Encyclopedia of Public International Law*. Oxford: Oxford University Press.

Balarajan, Y., S. Selvaraj, and S.V. Subramanian. 2011. "Health Care and Equity in India." *Lancet* 377/9764 (October 1): 505–515. doi:10.1016/S0140-6736(10)61894-6.

Bashford, A. 2014. *Imperial Hygiene: A Critical History of Colonialism, Nationalism and Public Health*. Basingstoke: Palgrave Macmillan.

Brechenmacher, S., and T. Carothers. 2015. "In for a Bumpy Ride: International Aid and the Closing Space for Domestic NGOs." *openGlobalRights*, April 9. www.opendemocracy.net/openglobalrights/saskia-brechenmacher-thomas-carothers/in-for-bumpy-ride-international-aid-and-closi.

Benhabib, S. 2004. *The Rights of Others: Aliens, Residents, and Citizens*. The John Robert Seeley Lectures. Cambridge and New York: Cambridge University Press.

Betts, A., G. Loescher, and J. Milner. 2012. *UNHCR: The Politics and Practice of Refugee Protection into the 21st Century*. 2nd ed. Global Institutions Series. Abingdon and New York: Routledge.

Bhagwati, J.N. 2004. *In Defense of Globalization*. Oxford and New York: Oxford University Press.

Biehl, J. 2014. "The Juridical Hospital: Patient-Citizen-Consumers Claiming the Right to Health in Brazilian Courts," in E. Medina, I. da Costa Marques, and C. Holmes (eds.), *Beyond Imported Magic: Essays on Science, Technology, and Society in Latin America*. Inside Technology. Cambridge: The MIT Press.

Blakeney, M.L., and T. Coulet. 2011. "Mid-Term Progress Report for the African, Caribbean, and Pacific Group of States." *The Protection of Geographical Indications (GI): Generating Empirical Evidence at Country and Product Level to Support African ACP Country Engagement in the Doha Round Negotiations*. African, Caribbean, and Pacific Group of States.

Block-Lieb, S., and T.C. Halliday. 2017. *Global Lawmakers: How International Organizations Make Commercial Law for the World*. New York: Cambridge University Press.

Bloomberg Philanthropies. 2015. *2015 Annual Report*. http://annualreport.bloomberg.org.

Boyle, J. 1996. *Shamans, Software, and Spleens: Law and the Construction of the Information Society*. Cambridge: Harvard University Press.

Bodansky, D. 2016. "The Paris Climate Change Agreement: A New Hope?" *American Journal of International Law* 110: 288–319.

Bowker, G.C., and S.L. Star. 1999. *Sorting Things Out: Classification and its Consequences*. Cambridge, MA: MIT Press.

Braithwaite, J., and P. Drahos. 2000. *Global Business Regulation*. Cambridge and New York: Cambridge University Press.

Brechenmacher, S., and T. Carothers. 2015. "In for a Bumpy Ride: International Aid and the Closing Space for Domestic NGOs." openGlobalRights, April 9. www.opendemocracy.net/openglobalrights/saskia-brechenmacher-thomas-carothers/in-for-bumpy-ride-international-aid-and-closi.

Carpenter, R.C. 2014. *"Lost" Causes: Agenda Vetting in Global Issue Networks and the Shaping of Human Security*. Ithaca, NY and London: Cornell University Press.

Centers for Disease Control and Prevention (CDC). 2016. "Health Policy Analysis and Evidence." www.cdc.gov/policy/analysis/index.html.

Chan, A. 2014. *Networking Peripheries: Technological Futures and the Myth of Digital Universalism*. Cambridge, MA: MIT Press.

Charlesworth, H., and E. Larking (eds.). 2014. *Human Rights and the Universal Periodic Review: Rituals and Ritualism*. Cambridge: Cambridge University Press.

Chetail, V. 2014. "Are Refugee Rights Human Rights? An Unorthodox Questioning of the Relations between Refugee Law and Human Rights Law," in R. Rubio-Marín (ed.), *Human Rights and Immigration*. Collected Courses of the Academy of European Law 21. Oxford: Oxford University Press.

Chimni, B.S. 2001. "The Reform of the International Refugee Regime: A Dialogic Approach." *Journal of Refugee Studies* 14/2: 151–161.

Chimni, B.S. 2009. "The Birth of a 'Discipline': From Refugee to Forced Migration Studies." *Journal of Refugee Studies* 22/1 (March 1): 11–29. doi:10.1093/jrs/fen051.

Clayton, J. 2015. "UNHCR Chief Issues Key Guidelines for Dealing with Europe's Refugee Crisis." UNHCR. September 4. www.unhcr.org/en-us/news/latest/2015/9/55e9793b6/unhcr-chief-issues-key-guidelines-dealing-europes-refugee-crisis.html.

Clinton, C., and D. Sridhar. 2017 "Who Pays for Cooperation in Global Health? A Comparative Analysis of WHO, the World Bank, the Global Fund to Fight HIV/AIDS, Tuberculosis and Malaria, and Gavi, the Vaccine Alliance." *Lancet*. published online January 27. http://dx.doi.org/10.1016/S0140-6737(16)32402–3.

Connors, J. 1996. "General Human Rights Instruments and Their Relevance to Women," in A. Byrnes, J. Connors, and L. Bik (eds.), *Advancing the Human Rights of Women: Using International Human Rights Standards in Domestic Litigation*. London: The Commonwealth Secretariat.

Coombe, R. 2011. "Cultural Agencies: The Legal Construction of Community Subjects and Their Properties," in M. Biagioli, P. Jaszi, and M. Woodmansee (eds.), *Making and Unmaking Intellectual Property: Creative Production in Legal and Cultural Perspective*. Chicago, IL: University of Chicago Press.

Correa, C. 2000. *Integrating Public Health Concerns into Patent Legislations in Developing Countries*. Geneva: The South Center.

De Búrca, G., R.O. Keohane, and C. Sabel. 2013. "New Modes of Pluralist Global Governance." *New York University Journal of International Law and Politics* 45/3: 723–786.

Dieleman, J.L., M.T. Schneider, A. Haakenstad, L. Singh, N. Sadat, M. Birger, A. Reynolds, et al. 2016. "Development Assistance for Health: Past Trends, Associations, and the Future of International Financial Flows for Health." *Lancet* 387/10037: 2536–2544. doi:10.1016/S0140-6736(16)30168-4.

Doyle, M.W. 2004. "The Challenge of Worldwide Migration." *Journal of International Affairs* 57/2: 1–5.

Drahos, P. 2014. *Intellectual Property, Indigenous People and Their Knowledge*. Cambridge: Cambridge University Press.

Drahos, P., and J. Braithwaite. 2003. *Information Feudalism: Who Owns the Knowledge Economy?* New York: New Press.

Dreyfuss, R.C., and C. Rodríguez-Garavito. 2014. *Balancing Wealth and Health: Global Administrative Law and the Battle Over Intellectual Property and Access to Medicines in Latin America*. New York: Oxford University Press.

Editorial Board. 2015. "The Global War Against NGOs." *Washington Post*, December 10. www.washingtonpost.com/opinions/the-war-against-ngos/2015/12/10/2ce59002-992b-11e5-b499-76cbec161973_story.html?utm_term=.bcab5b788d20.

Epstein, P.R. 2001. "Climate Change and Emerging Infectious Diseases." *Microbes and Infection* 3/9: 747–754. doi:10.1016/S1286-4579(01)01429-0.

Eyben, R., and L. Turquet (eds.). 2013. *Feminists in Development Organizations: Change from the Margins*. Rugby: Practical Action.

Fidler, D. 1999. *International Law and Infectious Diseases*. Oxford: Clarendon Press.

Fidler, D. 2010. "The Challenges of Global Health Governance." *International Institutions and Global Governance Program*. Council on Foreign Relations. http://ec.europa.eu/health/eu_world/docs/ev_20111111_rd01_en.pdf.

Food and Agriculture Organization of the United Nations. 2016. "Codex Alimentarius International Food Standards." www.fao.org/fao-who-codexalimentarius/codex-home/en/.

Foundation Center. 2013. *Advancing Human Rights: The State of Global Foundation Grantmaking*. New York: Foundation Center.

Framework Convention Alliance. 2016. "Tobacco Control Successes." www.fctc.org/fca-news/global-tobacco-control-success-stories.

Francioni, F., and N. Ronzitti (eds.). 2011. *War by Contract: Human Rights, Humanitarian Law, and Private Contractors*. Oxford and New York: Oxford University Press.

Friel, S., L. Hattersley, W. Snowdon, A.M. Thow, T. Lobstein, D. Sanders, S. Barquera, et al. 2013. "Monitoring the Impacts of Trade Agreements on Food Environments." *Obesity Reviews* 14: 120–134. doi:10.1111/obr.12081.

Frost, M. 2003. "Thinking Ethically about Refugees: A Case for the Transformation of Global Governance," in E. Newman and J. van Selm (eds.), *Refugees and Forced Displacement: International Security, Human Vulnerability, and the State*. Tokyo and New York: United Nations University Press.

Gammeltoft-Hansen, T., and J.C. Hathaway. 2015. "Non-Refoulement in a World of Cooperative Deterrence." *Columbia Journal of Transnational Law* 53/2 (January): 235–284.

Gana, R.L. 1995. "Has Creativity Died in the Third World? Some Implications of the Internationalization of Intellectual Property." *Denver Journal of International Law and Policy* 24/1 (September 22): 109.

Gapminder. 2015. "Is Child Mortality Falling? 200 Years That Changed the World." gapminder.org.

Geiger, M., and A. Pécoud. 2014. "International Organisations and the Politics of Migration." *Journal of Ethnic and Migration Studies* 40/6 (June 3): 865–887. doi:10.1080/1369183X.2013.855071.

Gostin, L.O., and E.A. Friedman. 2013. "Towards a Framework Convention on Global Health: A Transformative Agenda for Global Health Justice." *Yale Journal of Health Policy, Law, and Ethics* 13/1: 1–75.

Gostin, L.O., and E.A. Friedman. 2015. "A Retrospective and Prospective Analysis of the West African Ebola Virus Disease Epidemic: Robust National Health Systems at the Foundation and an Empowered WHO at the Apex." *Lancet* 385/9980: 1902–1909. doi:10.1016/S0140-6736(15)60644-4.

Gulland, A. 2016. "WHO Open To 'Lobbying' by Business." *British Medical Journal* 353. doi:10.1136/bmj.i3134.

Halliday, T.C., and G.C. Shaffer (eds.). 2015. *Transnational Legal Orders*. Cambridge Studies in Law and Society. New York: Cambridge University Press.

Harrell-Bond, B. 2008. "Building the Infrastructure for the Observance of Refugee Rights in the Global South." *Refuge* 25/2 (October 1): 12.

Harvey, C. 2015. "Time for Reform? Refugees, Asylum-Seekers, and Protection Under International Human Rights Law." *Refugee Survey Quarterly* 34/1 (March 1): 43–60. doi:10.1093/rsq/hdu018.

Hayden, C. 2003. "From Market to Market: Bioprospecting's Idioms of Inclusion." *American Ethnologist* 30/3: 359–371.

Helfer, L.R., and G. Austin. 2011. *Human Rights and Intellectual Property: Mapping the Global Interface*. Cambridge and New York: Cambridge University Press.

Institute Medicine (US). 2006. "The Impact of the Social and Cultural Environment on Health," in L.M. Hernandez and D.G. Blazer (eds.), *Genes, Behavior, and the Social Environment: Moving Beyond the Nature/Nurture Debate*. Washington, DC: National Academies Press (US). www.ncbi.nlm.nih.gov/books/NBK19924/.

International Health Partnerships. 2016. "Development Cooperation and Health." www.internationalhealthpartnership.net/en/about-ihp/.

IOM. 2014. "About IOM." International Organization for Migration, July 1. www.iom.int/about-iom.

Kapczynski, A. 2008. "The Access to Knowledge Mobilization and the New Politics of Intellectual Property." *Yale Law Journal* 117/5: 804–885. doi:10.2307/20455812.

Keck, M.E., and K. Sikkink. 1998. *Activists Beyond Borders: Advocacy Networks in International Politics*. Ithaca, NY: Cornell University Press.

Kickbusch, I. 2016. "Seize the Moment to Reform Global Health Governance." www.g7g20.com/articles/ilona-kickbusch-seize-the-moment-to-reform-global-health-governance.

Kickbusch, I., W. Hein, and G. Silberschmidt. 2010. "Addressing Global Health Governance Challenges through a New Mechanism: The Proposal for a Committee C of the World Health Assembly." *Journal of Law, Medicine & Ethics* 38/3: 550. doi:10.1111/j.1748-720X.2010.00511.x.

Korhonen, O., J. Gras, and K. Creutz. 2006. *International Post-Conflict Situations*. Helsinki: Erik Castrén Institute.

Kriebel, D., J. Tickner, P. Epstein, J. Lemons, R. Levins, E.L. Loechler, M. Quinn, R. Rudel, T. Schettler, and M. Stoto. 2001. "The Precautionary Principle in Environmental Science." *Environmental Health Perspectives* 109/9 (September): 871–876.

Lane, C., and A. Glassman. 2007. "Bigger and Better? Scaling Up and Innovation in Health Aid." *Health Affairs* 26/4 (July 1): 935–948. doi:10.1377/hlthaff.26.4.935.

Lee, K. 2009. *The World Health Organization (WHO)*. London and New York: Routledge, Chapman & Hall.

Legge, D., D. Gleeson, W. Snowdon, and A.M. Thow. 2013. "Trade Agreements and Non-Communicable Diseases in the Pacific Islands." www.who.int/nmh/events/2013/trade_agreement.pdf.

Lin, V., and B. Carter. 2014. "Changing Health Problems and Health Systems: Challenges for Philanthropy in China," in J. Ryan, L.C. Chen, and A. Saich (eds.), *Philanthropy for Health in China*. Bloomington, IN: Indiana University Press.

Lin, V., B. Carter, and G. Yan. 2016. "Policy, Research, and Behavioral Medicine," in E.B. Fisher, L.D. Cameron, A.J. Christensen Ehlert, Y. Guo, B.F. Oldenburg, and F.J. Snoek (eds.), *Principles and Concepts of Behavioral Medicine: A Global Handbook*. New York: Springer.

Liu, J., G. Chen, I. Chi, J. Wu, L. Pei, X. Song, L. Zhang, L. Pang, Y. Han, and X. Zheng. 2010. "Regional Variations in and Correlates of Disability-Free Life Expectancy among Older Adults in China." *BMC Public Health* 10: 446.

Loescher, G. 2001. *The UNHCR and World Politics: A Perilous Path*. New York: Oxford University Press.

Loescher, G., A. Betts, and J. Milner. 2008. *The United Nations High Commissioner for Refugees (UNHCR): The Politics and Practice of Refugee Protection into the Twenty-First Century*. Global Institutions Series. London and New York: Routledge.

Lopert, R., and D. Gleeson. 2013. "The High Price of 'Free' Trade: U.S. Trade Agreements and Access to Medicines." *Journal of Law, Medicine & Ethics* 41/1: 199.

McMichael, C., E. Waters, and J. Volmink. 2005. "Evidence-Based Public Health: What Does It Offer Developing Countries?" *Journal of Public Health* 27/2 (June): 215–221. doi:10.1093/pubmed/fdi024.

McQueen, D.V. (ed.). 2013. *Global Handbook on Noncommunicable Diseases and Health Promotion*. Dordrecht and New York: Springer.

Manning, N. 2001. "The Legacy of the New Public Management in Developing Countries." *International Review of Administrative Sciences* 67/2 (June 1): 297–312. doi:10.1177/0020852301672009.

Martin, S.F. 2015. "International Migration and Global Governance." *Global Summitry* 1/1 (May 28): 64–83.

Merry, S.E. 2006. *Human Rights and Gender Violence: Translating International Law into Local Justice*. Chicago Series in Law and Society. Chicago, IL: University of Chicago Press.

Merry, S.E. 2016. *The Seductions of Quantification: Measuring Human Rights, Gender Violence, and Sex Trafficking*. Chicago Series in Law and Society. Chicago, IL: University of Chicago Press.

Merry, S.E., K.E. Davis, and B. Kingsbury (eds.). 2015. *The Quiet Power of Indicators: Measuring Governance, Corruption, and the Rule of Law*. Cambridge Studies in Law and Society. New York: Cambridge University Press.

Milner, J. 2014. "Introduction: Understanding Global Refugee Policy." *Journal of Refugee Studies* 27/4 (December 1): 477–494. doi:10.1093/jrs/feu032.

Okediji, R. 2007. "Securing Intellectual Property Objectives: New Approaches to Human Rights Considerations," in M.E. Salomon, A. Tostensen, and W. Vandenhole (eds.), *Casting the Net Wider: Human Rights, Development and New Duty-Bearers*. Antwerp and Oxford: Intersentia.

Okediji, R. 2014. "The Role of WIPO in Access to Medicines," in R. Cooper Dreyfuss and C. Rodríguez-Garavito (eds.), *Balancing Wealth and Health: The Battle over Intellectual Property and Access to Medicines in Latin America*. Law and Global Governance Series. Oxford: Oxford University Press.

Okediji, R. 2015a. "Legal Innovation in International Intellectual Property Relations: Revisiting Twenty-One Years of the Trips Agreement." *University of Pennsylvania Journal of International Law* 36/1: 191–268.

Okediji, R. 2015b. "Law and Technology in a Neo-Liberal Age," in J.D. Wright (ed.), *International Encyclopedia of the Social and Behavioral Sciences*. Amsterdam: Elsevier.

Otto, D. 2007. "Making Sense of Zero Tolerance Policies in Peacekeeping Sexual Economies," in V. Munro and C.F. Stychin (eds.), *Sexuality and the Law: Feminist Engagements*. Abingdon: Routledge-Cavendish.

Oxfam International. 2016. "History of Oxfam International." www.oxfam.org/en/countries/history-oxfam-international.

Philanthropy News Digest. 2016. "China's New Charity Law to Loosen Rules But May Face Resistance." http://philanthropynewsdigest.org/news/china-s-new-charity-law-to-loosen-rules-but-may-face-resistance.

Polio Eradication Initiative. 2016. "Polio as of This Week 17 August 2016." www.polioeradication.org/Dataandmonitoring/Poliothisweek.aspx.

Ratner, S.R. 1995. *The New UN Peacekeeping: Building Peace in Lands of Conflict after the Cold War*. New York: St. Martin's Press.

Redding, D.W., L.M. Moses, A.A. Cunningham, J. Wood, and K.E. Jones. 2016. "Environmental-Mechanistic Modelling of the Impact of Global Change on Human Zoonotic Disease Emergence: A Case Study of Lassa Fever." *Methods in Ecology and Evolution* 7/6: 646–655. doi:10.1111/2041-210X.12549.

Richardson, K., et al. 2009. *Synthesis Report from Climate Change: Global Risks, Challenges & Decisions*. Copenhagen: University of Copenhagen, March. www.pik-potsdam.de/news/press-releases/files/synthesis-report-web.pdf.

Rodríguez-Garavito, C. 2014. "The Future of Human Rights: From Gatekeeping to Symbiosis." *Sur International Journal on Human Rights* 11/20 (December): 498–509.

Rodríguez-Garavito, C. 2015. "Multiple Boomerangs: New Models of Global Human Rights Advocacy." openGlobalRights, January 21. www.opendemocracy.net/openglobalrights/c%C3%A9sar-rodr%C3%ADguezgaravito/multiple-boomerangs-new-models-of-global-human-rights-advoc.

11

Rodríguez-Garavito, C., and D. Rodríguez. 2015. *Radical Deprivation on Trial: The Impact of Judicial Activism on Socioeconomic Rights in the Global South.* New York: Cambridge University Press.

Roth, K. 2004. "Defending Economic, Social and Cultural Rights: Practical Issues Faced by an International Human Rights Organization." *Human Rights Quarterly* 26/1: 63–73. doi:10.1353/hrq.2004.0010.

Santos, B. de Sousa 2014. *Derechos humanos, democracia y desarrollo.* 1st ed. Colección Dejusticia. Bogotá: Dejusticia.

Sen, A.K. 1999. *Development as Freedom.* 1st ed. New York: Knopf.

Sen, A.K. 2009. *The Idea of Justice.* Cambridge: Harvard University Press.

Shaffer, G. 2004. "Recognizing Public Goods in WTO Dispute Settlement: Who Decides Who Decides?: The Case of TRIPS and Pharmaceutical Patent Protection." *Journal of International Economic Law* 7/2: 459–482.

Shaffer, G., N.H. Nesbitt, and S.W. Waller. 2016. "Criminalizing Cartels: A Global Trend?" in J. Duns, A. Duke, and B. Sweeney (eds.), *Comparative Competition Law.* Northampton, MA: Edward Elgar.

Shaffer, G., and S. Sell. 2014. "Transnational Legal Ordering and Access to Medicines," in R.L. Okediji and M.A. Bagley (eds.), *Patent Law in Global Perspective.* New York: Oxford University Press.

Shiva, V. 1997. *Biopiracy: The Plunder of Nature and Knowledge.* Boston, MA: South End Press.

Sunder, M. 2007. "The Invention of Traditional Knowledge." *Law and Contemporary Problems* 70/2: 97–124.

Sunstein, C. 1996. "Against Positive Rights," in A. Sajó (ed.), *Western Rights? Post-Communist Application.* The Hague and Boston, MA: Kluwer Law International.

Tognotti, E. 2013. "Lessons from the History of Quarantine, from Plague to Influenza A." *Emerging Infectious Diseases* 19/2: 254–259. doi:10.3201/eid1902.120312.

Turk, V. 2016. "Envisioning a Common European Asylum System." *Forced Migration Review* 51 (January): 57–60.

UN Department of Economic and Social Affairs, Population Division. 2013. *International Migration Report.* United Nations.

Union of International Associations (UIA). 1956–1957, 2015–2016. *Yearbook of International Organizations.* https://uia.org/yearbook.

United Nations. 1945. *Charter of the United Nations.* 24 October. 1 UNTS XVI.

United Nations. 1948. "The Universal Declaration of Human Rights." Paris, December 10. www.un.org/en/universal-declaration-human-rights/.

United Nations. 1993. *Study on the Protection of the Cultural and Intellectual Property Rights of Indigenous Peoples/by Erica-Irene Daes, Special Rapporteur of the Sub-Commission on Prevention of Discrimination and Protection of Minorities and Chairperson of the Working Group on Indigenous Populations.* E/CN.4/Sub. 2/1993/28.

United Nations. 1995. "Beijing Declaration and Platform of Action." Beijing, September 15. www.un.org/womenwatch/daw/beijing/pdf/BDPfA%20E.pdf.

United Nations. 2012. *MDG Gap Task Force Report.* www.un.org/development/desa/dpad/wp-content/uploads/sites/45/mdg8report2012_engw.pdf.

United Nations. 2013. *UN High Level Dialogue on Migration and Development.* New York: United Nations. www.ilo.org/wcmsp5/groups/public/---ed_protect/---protrav/---migrant/documents/meetingdocument/wcms_226556.pdf.

United Nations. 2014. *Unhealthy Foods, Non-Communicable Diseases and the Right to Health.* New York: United Nations, www.ohchr.org/EN/HRBodies/HRC/RegularSessions/Session26/Documents/A-HRC-26-31_en.doc.

United Nations. 2016a. *Protecting Humanity from Future Health Crises. Report of the High-Level Panel on the Global Response to Health Crises.* January 25. www.un.org/News/dh/infocus/HLP/2016-02-05_Final_Report_Global_Response_to_Health_Crises.pdf.

United Nations. 2016b. *Report of the Conference of the Parties on Its Twenty-First Session, Held in Paris from 30 November to 13 December 2015.* Paris: United Nations Framework Convention on Climate Change, January 29. http://unfccc.int/resource/docs/2015/cop21/eng/10.pdf.

United Nations. 2016c. "Sustainable Development Goals." www.un.org/sustainabledevelopment/.

United Nations. 2016d. "UN Climate Change Paris Agreement." http://newsroom.unfccc.int/paris-agreement/.

United Nations General Assembly. 1950. "Statute of the Office of the United Nations High Commissioner for Refugees." UNGA. Vol. 428(V). www.unhcr.org/en-us/protection/basic/3b66c39e1/statute-office-united-nations-high-commissioner-refugees.html.

United Nations General Assembly. 2000. "Millennium Declaration." www.un.org/millennium/declaration/ares552e.htm.

UN Office of the High Commissioner for Human Rights. 2008. "The Rights to Health: Fact Sheet No 31." www.ohchr.org/Documents/Publications/Factsheet31.pdf.

United Nations Research Institute for Social Development. 1999. "The New Public Management Approach and Crisis States." www.unrisd.org/80256B3C005BCCF9/(httpPublications)/5F280B19C6125F4380256B6600448FDB.

United Nations Secretary-General. 1995. "From Nairobi to Beijing: Second Review and Appraisal of the Implementation of the Nairobi Forward-Looking Strategies for the Advancement of Women," in *Report of the UN Secretary-General.* New York: United Nations.

United Nations Secretary-General. 2003. *Special Measures for Protection from Sexual Exploitation and Sexual Abuse.* UN Doc. ST/SGB/2003/13.

UN Women. 2015. *Progress of the World's Women: Transforming Economies, Realizing Rights.* New York: United Nations. http://progress.unwomen.org/en/2015/.

University College London. 2016. "Predicting Disease Outbreaks Using Environmental Changes." www.ucl.ac.uk/news/news-articles/0616/130616-predicting-virus-outbreaks.

Watt, N., and R.D. Norton-Taylor. 1999. "Nato Counts £ 4.8bn Price of Campaign." *Guardian,* June 11. www.theguardian.com/world/1999/jun/11/balkans7

World Bank. 1993. *World Development Report 1993.* http://elibrary.worldbank.org/doi/abs/10.1596/0-1952-0890-0.

World Bank. 2010. *Challenges in Monitoring and Evaluation.* http://siteresources.worldbank.org/INTLACREGTOPPOVANA/Resources/840442-1255045653465/Challenges_in_M&E_Book.pdf.

World Bank. 2016. "IDA at Work in the Poorest Countries." https://ida.worldbank.org/content/infographic-ida-work-poorest-countries.

World Food Programme. 2005. *Policy Issues: Definition of Emergencies.* Rome: World Food Programme. www.wfp.org/sites/default/files/Definition%20of%20Emergencies%20-%20(2005).pdf.

World Health Organization. 1946. "Preamble to the Constitution of the World Health Organization as Adopted by the International Health Conference, New York, June 19–22; Signed on July 22, 1946 by the Representatives of 61 States (Official Records of the World Health Organization, No. 2, P. 100) and Entered into Force on April 7, 1948." www.who.int/about/definition/en/print.html.

World Health Organization. 1981. "International Code of Marketing of Breast-Milk Substitutes." www.who.int/nutrition/publications/code_english.pdf.

World Health Organization. 1986. "The Ottawa Charter for Health Promotion. First International Conference on Health Promotion, Ottawa." www.who.int/healthpromotion/conferences/previous/ottawa/en/index.html.

World Health Organization. 2001. "Globalization, TRIPS and Access to Pharmaceuticals – WHO Policy Perspectives on Medicines." Essential Medicines and Health Products Information Portal, March. http://apps.who.int/medicinedocs/pdf/s2240e/s2240e.pdf.

World Health Organization. 2003. "Climate Change and Infectious Diseases." www.who.int/globalchange/climate/summary/en/index5.html.

World Health Organization. 2007. "Chapter 1 Evolution of Public Health Security." *World Health Report 2007 – A Safer Future: Global Public Health Security in the 21st Century.* www.who.int/whr/2007/07_chap1_en.pdf.

World Health Organization. 2008. *Commission on Social Determinants of Health: Final Report. Closing the Gap in a Generation: Health Equity Through Action on the Social Determinants of Health.* Geneva: World Health Organization. www.who.int/social_determinants/thecommission/finalreport/en/index.html.

World Health Organization. 2011. "World Health Forum Concept Paper." www.who.int/dg/reform/en_who_reform_world_health_forum.pdf.

World Health Organization. 2013. "Research for Universal Health Coverage." www.who.int/whr/2013/report/en/.

World Health Organization. 2015a. "10 Facts on Polio Eradication." www.who.int/features/factfiles/polio/en/.

World Health Organization. 2015b. "Global Funding for Local Health Issues." *Bulletin of the World Health Organization* 93: 367–368. doi:10.2471/BLT.15.030615.

World Health Organization. 2016a. "About the WHO Global Malaria Programme." www.who.int/malaria/about_us/en/.

World Health Organization. 2016b. "Constitution of WHO: Principles." www.who.int/about/mission/en/.

11

World Health Organization. 2016c. "Declaration of Alma-Ata 1978." www.euro .who.int/__data/assets/pdf_file/0009/113877/E93944.pdf?ua=1.

World Health Organization. 2016d. "Essential Medicines and Generic Products Information Portal." http://apps.who.int/medicinedocs/en/d/Js21846en/.

World Health Organization. 2016e. "First World Health Assembly." www.who.int/ global_health_histories/first_world_health_assembly/en/.

World Health Organization. 2016f. "Frequently Asked Questions and Answers on Smallpox." www.who.int/csr/disease/smallpox/faq/en/.

World Health Organization. 2016g. "International Health Regulations." www.who .int/topics/international_health_regulations/en/.

World Health Organization. 2016h. "Measles Key Facts." www.who.int/mediacentre/ factsheets/fs286/en/.

World Health Organization. 2016i. "Monitoring and Evaluation (M&E)." www.who. int/hiv/strategic/me/en/.

World Health Organization. 2016j. "Reform of WHO's Work in Health Emergency Management WHO Health Emergencies Programme." www.who.int/ about/who_reform/emergency-capacities/RC_Reform-who-work-health-emergency-management-en.pdf?ua=1.

World Health Organization. 2016k. "Social Determinants of Health." www.who.int/ social_determinants/thecommission/finalreport/key_concepts/en/.

World Health Organization. 2016l. "The Doha Declaration on the TRIPS Agreement and Public Health." www.who.int/medicines/areas/policy/doha_declaration/ en/.

World Health Organization. 2016m. "What Is the World Health Report?" www.who .int/whr/en/.

World Health Organization. 2016n. "WHO's Engagement with Non-State Actors." www.who.int/about/collaborations/non-state-actors/en/.

World Trade Organization. 1995. "Agreement on Trade-Related Aspects of Intellectual Property Rights." www.wto.org/english/docs_e/legal_e/27-trips_ 01_e.htm

World Trade Organization and World Health Organization. 2002. "WTO Agreements and Public Health: A Joint Study by the WTO and the WHO Secretariat." www .wto.org/english/res_e/booksp_e/who_wto_e.pdf.

Zuckerman, E. 2013. *Rewire: Digital Cosmopolitans in the Age of Connection.* New York: W.W. Norton & Company.

11

12

Governing Capital, Labor, and Nature in a Changing World*

Coordinating Lead Authors:[1]
G. Balachandran, Grégoire Mallard

Lead Authors:[2]
Olufunmilayo Arewa, Lucio Baccaro, Tim Büthe, Andrea Nightingale,Pierre Pénet,
Dominique Pestre, Anthea Roberts

* The authors acknowledge the support of the Fonds National Suisse de la Recherche Scientifique (grant #166977) and the Graduate Institute for a preparatory conference in Geneva (May 13–14, 2016).
[1] Affiliations: GB and GM: Graduate Institute of International and Development Studies, Switzerland.
[2] Affiliations: OA: University of California Irvine School of Law, USA; LB: University of Geneva, Switzerland; TB: Hochschule für Politik/Bavarian School of Public Policy at the Technical University of Munich (TUM), Germany and Duke University, USA; AN: Swedish University of Agricultural Sciences, Sweden; PP: University of Geneva, Switzerland; DP: École des hautes études en sciences sociales, France; AR: School of Regulation and Global Governance (RegNet) at the Australian National University, Australia.

Summary

This chapter attempts a broad analytical compass for surveying the main actors, institutions, and instruments governing our world. Despite its seeming ubiquity, governance is a relatively new expression in this context, suggestive both of new modes of exercising power and an enhanced focus on ordering a world undergoing rapid change. Speaking generally, governance may be understood as the exercise of power organized around multiple dispersed sites operating through transnational networks of actors, public as well as private, and national and regional as well as local.

The turn to governance is often held to be coeval if not conjoined to profound changes in the meaning and nature of government associated with the ascendancy of neoliberal ideas and precepts. This has had significant implications for how governance tends to be understood. Critics associate it directly with the changing role of states in the economic and social sphere. Transnational governance, in particular, is criticized for foregrounding the priorities of corporate investors often to the detriment of social or environmental goals, subordinating principles of "comparative" or "cooperative" advantage to "competitive" advantage, and promoting micro-regulatory forms of regulation over strategic or structurally focused interventions (such as industrial policy). Associated shifts trace states' powers, otherwise a touchstone of sovereignty, being increasingly negotiated with transnational private actors and international financial institutions (IFIs), and placed under external jurisdictions. The turn to governance tends also to be framed directly or indirectly, justifiably or otherwise, as occurring alongside cuts in the public provisioning of health, education, housing, and social expenditures wherever they may have taken place, a parallel proliferation of managerial controls, and governments contracting out public services to private and quasi-private agencies, or relinquishing them to the voluntary sector. At the risk of oversimplifying its critics' views, if modern governments describe rule by/over citizens, governance describes rule over subjects.

This chapter maps a rather more fluid and differentiated landscape of governance across the five areas it surveys, i.e. finance, investment, trade, labor, and environment. In finance, while regulation may appear to have become more transnational and to an extent even voluntary, deregulatory outcomes have reconfigured the nature of risk and the cognitive and policy frameworks for dealing with it. At the same time a growing risk of states having to foot the ultimate bill may still become a point of departure for more differentiated regulatory approaches. On the other hand, not only are environmental agreements continuing to be implemented and enforced at national and sub-national scales, the ascendancy of market interventions and transnational institutions here has taken place in parallel with – and sometimes through mutual cooptations of – other kinds of interventions including those for promoting decentralization and community control over resources. Trends in labor regulation may also reflect individual state choices more than direct transnational pressures, or run contrary to the preferences of specialized international organizations in the domain. Even in the controversial sphere of investment treaties, there is considerable ongoing fluidity with regard to norms, jurisdiction, and actors within and between national and international arenas. Thus, upon closer inspection and with the benefit of a more domain-specific approach, we may not necessarily observe a sweeping or uniform shift, but more a mosaic of regulatory frameworks, quite disparate trends with regard to their negotiation, implementation, and impact, and a future rife with possibilities.

12.1   Introduction

This chapter attempts a broad analytical compass for surveying the main actors, institutions, and instruments governing our world. "Governance" is an increasingly ubiquitous expression used in this context. For centuries, governance was synonymous with government and conveyed little else of significance. From the 1980s it entered into more common and increasingly prescriptive usage in the context of "corporate governance," particularly in the United States (Cadbury 1992; Ocasio and Joseph 2005). During the 1990s, governance began to figure with greater frequency in World Bank reports (Moretti and Pestre 2015), accompanied by attempts to identify, measure, and compare its dimensions through worldwide indicators. The IMF also began using indicators of "good governance" in its conditional lending programs (Best 2014; IMF 1997). Indeed, even the currently common English language meaning of governance, as the "action or fact of governing a nation, a person, an activity, or one's desires" (*OED* 1989, 2015) is of relatively recent origin. This chapter endeavors to unpack the meanings and practices of governance broadly in relation to actors and instruments (who governs and how), subjects and objects (who and what is governed), and effects (with what consequences).

Speaking generally, governance may be understood as the exercise of power organized around multiple dispersed sites operating through transnational networks of actors, public as well as private, and national, regional as well as local (Djelic and Sahlin-Andersson 2006). It departs from the classical, albeit stylized, understanding of unbounded state sovereignty over one territory and population (Mallard and Sgard 2016): even realists no longer deny the transformation of global governance in economic matters, or their effects on decision-making processes and substantive outcomes (Kahler and Lake 2009: 253; Waltz 1999). While holding a low opinion of government, advocates of governance rarely distinguish between them explicitly or in an analytical way. Governance, according to them, signifies greater public accountability and participation at the expense of vertical and centralized authority (Slaughter 2004). Transnational governance and governance institutions, together with free, competitive markets lightly regulated by independent, rule-bound regulators, are also viewed in a positive light by comparison with governments that, even when not unrepresentative, corrupt, or beholden to special interests, are often alleged to be mired in red tape. As a form of government purportedly by experts, governance is viewed as being more conducive to coordinated solutions for trans-border problems, including through the circulation of institutional and regulatory "best practices" (Büthe and Mattli 2011; Mattli 2003; Sabel, O'Rourke, and Fung 2000). The latter have a bearing also on regulation at the domestic level: whether one speaks of "competition states" (Cerny 1990) or "regulatory states" (Jayasuriya 2002, 2004), states have increasingly resorted to management techniques (Lascoumes and Le Gales 2007; Maurer 1999; Supiot 2015) that shun strong legal provisions in favor of incentives and, on paper at least, penalties to orient business decisions (Foucault 1977: 177). The resulting shifts from post-Second World War methods of "command and control" regulation are regarded in this view as pragmatic adaptations to the more complex, interconnected world of the 1980s (Krisch 2005). Governance here represents a response to past failures and an attempt to fashion more efficient instruments of control through a recursive cycle of regulatory changes (Halliday and

Shaffer 2014). Enmeshed in "webs of rewards and coercion" or "dialogic webs" (Braithwaite and Drahos 2000: 551–552), the switch to governance may also signal a government's responsiveness to international economic actors' preference for national "regulatory systems and social practices … consistent with their general values, goals and desires" (Braithwaite and Drahos 2000: 15–19).

Governance evokes strong reactions from its critics. For many, it is a controversial political project coeval if not conjoined with neoliberalism and globalization, and inconsistent with meaningful economic advance and social progress (Blyth 2002; Dezalay and Garth 2002; Krippner 2005). It represents part of an ongoing "great transformation" driven by powerful actors seeking to aggrandize themselves at the expense of the state (Blyth 2002). Naturalizing particular forms of authority and power while foreclosing alternative possibilities, it promotes widening socioeconomic inequalities and a "race to the bottom" in labor, social, and environmental protections (Bourdieu 1987; Rist 2002; Sassen 1996). In lockstep with neoliberal precepts that place them, and societies more generally, at the mercy of international financial markets, "governance" diminishes rather than enhances the democratic accountability of governments. Critics of governance in the South, especially, view it as part of a "post-Washington consensus" project to develop a "political-institutional framework to embed structural adjustment policies": as such it "complements rather than replaces" the policies of the so-called Washington consensus (Jayasuriya 2002: 24). For such critics, governance describes or prescribes shifts in the distribution of power to the detriment of states and citizens, and in favor of markets, large corporations, and international financial institutions (IFIs) like the International Monetary Fund (IMF) and the World Bank (WB) (Ferguson and Gupta 2002; Rose 1999; Scholte 1997).

Since the 1980s, forceful calls for the retreat of "government" have indeed paralleled the growing power of business corporations and other private market actors to push states to abandon past forms of government regulation, adopt lighter forms of "governance," and create conditions conducive to individualized, self-representational forms of agency associated with market actors. Such pressures may doubtless be associated with the rise of "governance" without, however, being its full explanation. In this chapter, we map the trajectories of governance in five areas (i.e. finance, investment, trade, labor, and environment), in an effort to clarify the nature of the institutional shift to governance; the regulatory instruments and processes embodying it; and their implications. Central to grand narratives of "globalization," the prominence of these areas is mirrored equally in critiques of neoliberalism (Dezalay and Garth 2002; Ferguson 2005; Jayasuriya 2006; Krippner 2005; Lordon 2010; Piketty 2014), with complex interplays in both accounts between developments in each of these areas, and even when not so explicitly acknowledged, the rise of governance and the decline of representative governments and democratic institutions, and finally their implications for social and collective goods. At the same time they enable us to clarify, and wherever possible, nuance the shift to governance.

These are each broad areas, hence the focus of this chapter is unavoidably narrow and differentiated. Our main endeavor here is to present an account of the complex nature of the rise of governance, its most visible instruments in each area, and outline the main implications of the turn to "governance."

We find, mainly, that while developments in one area impinged on the others, there are nevertheless significant asymmetries of trajectory, impact, and learning in each area, and differences across them. For instance, finance may have witnessed a relative regulatory shift towards voluntary and transnational realms. Yet the resulting competitive pressures blindsided states to the risks and costs of regulatory failures not least to their own finances and credit, both private and public. In contrast, projects and experiences of environmental governance show that the ascendency of market interventions and transnational institutions have emerged in parallel with – and sometimes coopt – other kinds of interventions, including the promotion of decentralization and community control over resources. Furthermore, there appears to be more scope for differential scales and layers in environmental governance, with environmental agreements being negotiated and implemented at regional, national, and sub-national scales, with the latter also often crisscrossing national boundaries. Trends in labor regulation may reflect individual state choices more than direct transnational pressures, and run contrary to the preferences of specialized international organizations in the domain. Even in the controversial sphere of investment treaties, one may detect considerable ongoing fluidity with regard to norms, jurisdictions, and actors within and between national and international arenas, and an ongoing process of review and reform, both formal and informal.

12.2   The Rise of Global Governance

The nature, scope, and methods of economic regulation have changed greatly since the 1980s. The role of states, in particular, has been transformed, with welfare and distributional objectives yielding to the demands of competitive economic openness. Policies for "competitive advantage" place greater emphasis on promoting an investor-friendly environment, sidelining strategic economic or industrial objectives for more relational ones, and substituting market-focused, micro-economic regulation compatible with incentivizing private entrepreneurship for macro- or more structural interventions such as industrial policy (Cerny 1990: 260). Regulatory changes have also tended increasingly to be negotiated with transnational private actors and international financial institutions (IFIs), and placed under external jurisdictions (Carruthers 2016; Halliday and Carruthers 2009). The premise underlying many of these changes, that regulated private investment is more efficient than public provisioning, has encouraged the restructuring of vast spheres such as health, education, housing, and transport where many services formerly undertaken by governments have been contracted out or displaced to private entities, including in some places to private equity firms, or relinquished to the voluntary sector (Cooley and Spruyt 2010; Scahill 2011). If finance and modes of governance are interwoven, a key question relates to the ways in which the former reconfigured the balance of power and responsibilities not merely among, but importantly, between firms and states, between capital and labor, and between socioeconomic groups.

We commence here by mapping the main governing actors, institutions, and forums in the five areas surveyed in this chapter. This section focuses on two broad features characteristic of modern governance: a relative fragmentation of power and authority especially in the last three decades, and its dense concentration at particular sites (Hansen and Stepputat 2001; Jessop 2007; Rose 1999) that are also often nodes of accumulation of capital and wealth. On the surface these features may seem complementary: as large business, associations, lobbies, and interest groups become more powerful, they may fragment the authority of nation-states and redistribute power in ways that mirror and reinforce inequalities of income and wealth (Cafaggi and Pistor 2015; Piketty 2014). Fragmentation can also obscure or naturalize vertical power hierarchies, and even when not promoting complicit associations between regulatory bodies and their targets, enhance the power of larger, better-resourced and networked private actors to determine what constitutes knowledge, "optimal policies," "best practices," and so on (Lascoumes and Le Gales 2007). However, whatever its origins, governance is not reducible simply to the transmission and implementation of preformed "neoliberal" templates and prescriptions. The regulatory fields in these five areas too, suggest important tensions and differences.

12.2.1   Finance

The Bretton Woods system (1945–1971) severely curtailed international capital markets. Wary, in particular, of the destabilizing impact of short-term capital flows, the original IMF Articles of Agreement prioritized currency stability over capital mobility. At first fixed exchange rates and capital controls restricted the range and riskiness of financial transactions (Eichengreen 1996; Helleiner 1993). However, accumulating current account imbalances and the growth of offshore banking placed great strain on fixed exchange rates and the capital controls that had held them in place. They also intensified destabilizing speculation against coordinated attempts to realign exchange rates or limit their movement, hence prefiguring both the onset of generalized floating and the parallel expansion of international capital flows (Adams, Mathieson, and Schinasi 1999; Giry-Deloison and Masson 1988). These processes accelerated as a result of the 1970s oil shocks. Intensified cross-border capital flows weakened the independence of national monetary policies, while the slower but unmistakable internationalization of debt markets narrowed the scope for fiscal policy. National regulation of financial markets was also challenged by the growth in cross-border risk relationships, which outpaced the regulatory capacities of states or of any alternative mechanisms, and heightened possibilities for transnational evasion (Cerny 1994: 328).

These changes in the financial and regulatory landscape were not entirely systemic, spontaneous, or "market"-driven. "Loopholes" in UK banking regulations enabled London to emerge as a major off-shore banking center in the 1960s and facilitated the accumulation of overseas banking balances. Competing 1970s changes to US regulations allowed US-owned banks to expand abroad. In retrospect these were the thin edges of a deregulatory wedge that unfolded into more overtly ideological and political initiatives under the Thatcher and Reagan administrations to lift capital controls and free up banks and financial markets (Best 2005; Blyth 2002; Boyer 1996; Dezalay and Garth 2002; Helleiner 1996; Loriaux 1997; Mishra 1996). Financial deregulation continued largely without major interruptions in the 1990s and

2000s despite a change in government in both countries, with a bi-partisan House majority passing the Gramm-Leach-Bliley Act during the Clinton Administration to formally repeal the 1933 Glass-Steagall proscription on institutions "engaged principally" in banking under-writing or dealing in securities. A monumental piece of deregulation, GLBA represented the culmination of decades of lobbying efforts by the financial industry (Sherman 2009). But the ground for it was laid in the late-1980s when the Federal Reserve under successive Republican administrations allowed bank affiliates to underwrite an expanding variety of securities, including mortgage-backed securities and con-sumer finance assets.

Historically, normative priorities and legal norms in the international arena have been set by powerful countries. Financial regulations are no exception. Pressures from international financial institutions, for instance, reinforced the deregulatory push in the South and led unsur-prisingly to enhancing their authority vis-à-vis Southern states. At the same time, some norms and practices, at least, of Anglo-American finan-cial market governance may have diffused around the world through mimetic cross-country processes rather than through direct trans-national governance pressures (DiMaggio and Powell 1983). Textbook theories of rational expectations and new orthodoxies such as the effi-cient market hypothesis, and deregulatory policy prescriptions based on them, traveled from Chicago to Brussels to inform European economic policy (Blyth 2002; Majone 1994). The liberalization of domestic cap-ital markets in the United States, and to a lesser extent in the UK, was associated with realizing the supposed promises of "shareholder cap-italism." It is impossible to do justice here to the resulting regulatory shifts, or their effects. But we may note that one of their pronounced effects has been an emphasis on "shareholder value," which has had the further effect of transforming notions of value and meanings of per-formance, or even profitability (Fligstein and Shin 2007). Illustratively, fears of leveraged buyouts of firms judged by stock markets to be "underperforming" and "undervalued" lead to a reconfiguration of risks, incentives, and objectives including of large industrial firms, and to a transformation of their structures, organizational and employment practices, and relationships with local communities (Ho 2009).

In explaining the turn towards deregulation particularly beyond the Anglo-American world, therefore, it may be important to attend to the ways in which ideologies and external shocks and pressures were mediated to particular ends, and consequently their wider contexts and processes. The resistance of major European governments to what they perceived to be hegemonic US attempts to restrict the scope for inde-pendent national financial regulation, and its gradual bending in the 1990s, highlights the intimate connections between changes in gov-ernance, regulation, financial, industrial and employment structures, and business interests. Already in the 1980s the European Commission had begun to look at US norms and standards to free up and integrate European financial markets, becoming in the process an epistemic agent of neoliberal orthodoxy and affirming its own position as an important new actor in the governance of markets (Abdelal 2010). The Commission's 1989 resolution to form a monetary union and the 1991 adoption of the Maastricht Treaty soon came to emblematize this con-version while also adding a seemingly unstoppable momentum to the liberalization and integration of capital markets (Aglietta and Brand 2013: 42). One upshot was the enhanced traction for transnational

indicators such as, for example, the Basel capital adequacy norms for banks. Conventionally associated with banking stability, in Germany, Basel II norms were feared to undermine the ability of its banks to lend freely at their discretion to the small and medium enterprises that formed the backbone of "Rhine capitalism" and the associated social model of the "Mittelstand," and for whom bank loans had long been an indispensable source of investment finance (Kruck 2011: 11). The same was not true in France, with its more consolidated industrial structure and bank lending. Hence the French government, large French banks, and even the governing socialists had fewer qualms about overcoming their habitual skepticism for external norms to throw their weight behind the efforts of the Jacques Delors-led European Commission to promote financialization (Langohr and Langohr 2008: 195). This offers an apt illustration of how practices of financial market governance identified with Anglo-American capitalism could subdue overt resist-ance to make headway in Europe, expanding into spaces vacated by governments in Washington, London, Paris, and Brussels, and more broadly entrenching transnational governance norms, mechanisms, and regulations that spread subsequently around the world through processes of state-to-state diffusion.

In Southern states financial leverage in the form of multilateral lending and structural adjustment programs have played a major role, including by promoting retrenchment or privatization in spheres such as health, education, social and welfare services, transport and communications, and other infrastructure. International financial institutions, notably the IMF and the World Bank, played a crucial role in spreading neo-liberal agendas outside the West (Dezalay and Garth 2002). Indeed, until recently their main impact was felt in the developing world where, in varying degrees, the opening up of trade, abolition of price controls, privatization, and the rolling back of the state took the form of a "shock therapy" imposed from outside by the IMF and World Bank at the behest or with the active support of powerful Western states. By the mid-1970s the United States was, as noted above, relaxing capital controls, soon it began turning its attention to freeing up capital flows in other parts of the world (Best 2014: 61). Pinochet's Chile remains a textbook example of extensive deregulation promoted as an antidote to left-wing development agendas, but by the 1980s it had become merely the first candidate for the "shock therapy" inflicted by the IMF and the World Bank on other developing countries, including many in South America burdened by debts contracted in the 1970s that had become unsustainable in the wake of a sharp rise in US interest rates (Dezalay and Garth 2002; Johnson 1995; Nelson 2014; Silva 1997). In the 1980s stabilization and structural adjustment programs also became pervasive in Africa (Noorbakhsh and Paloni 1999, 2001) where unfavorable growth comparisons with Asia and Latin America helped advance programs seeking to foster growth through eliminating eco-nomic or structural "bottlenecks" (Konadu-Agyemang 2000).

Several explanations may be ventured for why the Bretton-Woods institutions became such redoubtable champions of neoliberal policies and supranational governance of financial markets. An important "insti-tutional effect" is of particular relevance here, i.e. their expanding sur-veillance responsibilities under conditions of free capital mobility and destabilizing speculation. Far from feeling inhibited about undertaking responsibilities it was ill-equipped for, the IMF, in particular, became an unabashed champion of capital account liberalization in the 1990s

(Shaffer and Waibel 2016: 307–311), and thus of its own enhanced influence. Its efforts may well have achieved greater success (Reserve Bank of India, 1997) had the 1997 East Asian crisis not intervened to demonstrate the perils of financial openness and lead to a brief period of reversal, and overall to a more measured approach towards financial liberalization notably in Asia, but also in other parts of the South.

12.2.2   Investment Treaties

The post-Uruguay Round liberalization of trade and the rapid growth of foreign direct investment (FDI) in the last three decades has deepened the stakes in international investment protection. The latter is mainly governed by two actors: states, which are parties to investment treaties, and arbitrators who resolve disputes about the interpretation and application of those treaties. Investors are granted protection under these treaties, which permit them to bring arbitral claims directly against the states in which they invest. But the system itself is largely governed by states and tribunals, even if the system is often designed for the benefit of investors and driven by them.

Though the late twentieth-century expansion of cross-border capital flows intensified demands for legal protection of overseas investments, the latter has a longer history rooted in European overseas empires and extra-territoriality treaties or clauses in bilateral agreements. Overseas investment protections were subsequently fleshed out bilaterally in decolonization agreements. Parallel attempts in the 1950s to formulate a multilateral investment treaty, however, failed because capital exporting and capital importing states were unable to agree on common standards. Consequently for over four decades from the 1950s, bilateral investment treaties remained the norm though their numbers remained quite small by the standards of the growth witnessed in the 1990s, when they mushroomed five-fold from around 385 in 1989 to nearly 1900 by the end of 1999 (UNCTAD 2000). In 1998 attempts to negotiate a Multilateral Investment Agreement under the auspices of the OECD failed, hence attention reverted to bilateral investment treaties whose numbers continued to rise (Van Harten 2016). In 2016 there were an estimated 3,200 international investment agreements worldwide.

In principle states have two broad motivations for entering into investment treaties. The explicit rationale for a predominantly capital exporting state is to secure protections for its nationals with investments abroad. The stated motivation for a capital importing state is to attract foreign investment on competitive terms. From the investors' perspective, investment treaties offer protection against expropriation without compensation, and the tendency of host states, however hospitably disposed they may have been at first, to engage afterwards in unfriendly behavior. Since relocating investments can be costly or impossible, investment treaties bind countries to treat foreign investors fairly after the investment is made (Guzman 1998). The evidence on whether investment treaties actually promote foreign investment is, however, mixed. Some studies find a positive effect on investment flows, others find no such effects. Tracking bilateral investment flows and attributing differences to investment treaties can also be fraught with methodological difficulties (see, e.g. Salacuse and Sullivan 2005; Webb Yackee 2010). In the absence of clear-cut evidence, some commentators argue that investment treaties serve no

purpose, or impose obligations on states without any clear benefits. Another growing concern relates to expansive notions of investors' rights in treaties and the jurisprudence, especially given that the sorts of violations the former were originally designed to protect against – such as direct expropriation of mineral rights or mining investments without compensation – are no longer common.

Investment obligations are also increasingly embedded in pluri-lateral and mega-regional free trade agreements, an early example of which was the North American Free Trade Agreement (NAFTA) between the United States, Canada, and Mexico. Other agreements, whether completed, under negotiation, or in a state of suspense, including the Trans-Pacific Partnership Agreement (TPP), the Regional Comprehensive Economic Partnership (RCEP) involving the ASEAN and six states in the Asia Pacific including China, and the Transatlantic Trade and Investment Partnership (TTIP), similarly incorporate investment provisions. While none of these count as worldwide multilateral treaties, the United States, Europe, and China have at different times attempted through such mega-regional agreements to compete in setting the standards that they hope will be adopted by the rest of the world.

The rise of investment treaties has led to a boom in the demand for private arbitration and may be said to signal a turn from government to governance. Investment treaties usually have two main features. First, on a substantive level, the treaty parties accept certain obligations with respect to the treatment of investing nationals from the other treaty party. These obligations typically include treating them fairly and equitably, not expropriating their investments without due process and adequate compensation, and not discriminating against nationals belonging to the treaty partner in favor of the state's own nationals (national treatment) or other foreign nationals (most favored nation treatment). Second, on a procedural level, investment treaties usually provide two forms of dispute resolution. The states may undertake state-to-state arbitration to resolve any disputes about the interpretation or application of the treaty. Investors may also bring investor-state arbitral claims if they believe that they have suffered damage as a result of the host state's violation of its treatment obligations (Roberts 2014). The most unusual feature of investment treaties is that they permit investors, who are non-state actors, to bring arbitral claims directly against states before ad hoc arbitral tribunals. But unlike human rights treaties like the European Convention on Human Rights (Douglas 2003; Paparinskis 2013; Roberts 2010, 2013) to which they are sometimes compared, investors can usually bring claims without first exhausting local remedies. Besides they have a role in selecting arbitrators to resolve the dispute. The main justification for this procedure is that it permits investment disputes to be depoliticized (Paparinskis 2010; Shihata 1986): previously, a foreign investor claiming mistreatment by the host state had to bring the dispute before its domestic courts or rely on its own home state for "diplomatic protection" (e.g. by bringing a claim on behalf of the investor on a state-to-state level). Investment-treaty arbitration was intended to enable foreign investors to take their claims directly to an ostensibly independent and unbiased international tribunal without being subject to the political decision-making processes of the home or host state. However, while granting them procedural rights to enforce substantive treaty protections (Douglas 2003; Roberts 2015), investment treaties usually do not impose reciprocal obligations on foreign investors, whether in regard to their treatment of the host state, or of the environment, its employees and workers, and so on. Host states cannot generally bring arbitral claims against foreign investors, though they can sometimes raise limited counterclaims. Workers, individuals and NGOs cannot use investment treaties to bring claims against foreign investors whether in domestic courts (which, however, they may do under domestic laws) or in arbitration tribunals.

This system results in governance through arbitration (Van Harten 2016), whereby states agree to bypass domestic courts in favor of private networks of international arbitration firms and judges. This form of "contracting out" a key element of sovereign authority – i.e. judicial power – is all the more notable since the older-style investment treaties tended to be short and vague (in contrast to newer ones that are often longer and more detailed), leaving many issues unaddressed, or their terms open to being interpreted in many ways. As a result a large measure of interpretive authority, particularly with regard to the older treaties, has passed to arbitral tribunals tasked with resolving particular disputes (Roberts 2010). Besides, even if in theory there is no system of precedent between investment treaty tribunals and arbitral awards, in practice, a de facto body of precedent has emerged because tribunals in one case often refer extensively to awards from other cases (Kaufmann-Kohler 2007) and because of the tight grouping of the "arbitration community," sometimes referred to as the "arbitration mafia" (Dezalay and Garth 1996). This has meant the emergence of a body of investment treaty jurisprudence, and of investment treaty tribunals as important governance actors in this regime. Thus, as in the case of finance, where IFIs have used the turn to de-regulation to claim more authority over governance in general, and national-level macro-economic policies in particular, the multiplication of investment treaties and arbitral awards has reinforced the judicial authority of transnational private networks of arbitration professionals, and the opacity, and in some degree the clubby backroom character, of governance (Dezalay and Garth 1996).

12.2.3   Trade

Global trade governance may be defined as encompassing attempts to manage, resolve, or supersede conflicts of interest in international trade. Some of the "behind-the-border" issues having a bearing on trade, such as the treatment of foreign investment, labor rights, and environment, are discussed elsewhere in this chapter and others, such as human rights, elsewhere in this volume. This section focuses on trade-related regulatory governance of products and services, as well as the governance of competition law and policy as a trade-related issue. It shows that the developments in global trade governance over the course of the last three decades have involved "the reallocation of authority upward, downward, and sideways" (Hooghe and Marks 2003: 233), thus illustrating the full spectrum of changes entailed in contemporary understandings of governance.

To examine the causes and consequence of these developments, it is useful to distinguish between the traditional "at the border" trade barriers (most centrally tariffs and import quotas) and the new behind-the-border issues that have increasingly been governed at

the international level conjointly with, or even entirely through, trade institutions. These "trade-plus" issues cover a wide swathe. They include standards and regulations (Büthe and Mattli 2011; Grieco 1990; Mattli 2003; Yarbrough and Yarbrough 1992), government procurement (Arrowsmith and Anderson 2011; Rickard 2015), competition policy (Bradford and Büthe 2015; Büthe 2014), services (Hoekman and Primo Braga 1997; Shingal 2015), exchange rates (Copelovitch and Pevehouse 2014), investments (Büthe and Milner 2008), labor rights (Mosley 2011), and even more broadly human rights (Aaronson 2014) and the environment (Barkin 2014; Esty and Geradin 1997; Schreurs and Economy 1997; Zeng and Eastin 2007).

Traditional core trade issues at first glance may seem like an example of an issue area where governments have successfully resisted demands to move from government to governance, and the associated shifts in authority. The agreement to replace quantitative restrictions such as import quotas with tariffs, for instance, was achieved through inter-governmental bargaining, in the case of many countries already during the era of GATT (the General Agreement on Tariffs and Trade) (Deardorff and Stern 1985; Goldin and van der Mensbrugghe 1997). Negotiating maximally permissible tariff levels in bilateral, mini-lateral, or multilateral trade agreements has similarly remained a governmental prerogative, and once such agreements have been struck, compliance with any such changes in trade governance is ultimately still up to each national government.

Closer inspection, however, reveals subtle, yet significant deviations from the ideal-typical notion of state sovereignty even with regard to the traditional core trade issues. Under GATT and WTO, the principal-supplier prerogative in tariff negotiations might be said to have amounted to a case of product-specific horizontal ("sideways") delegation from the smaller and less trade-intensive to the larger and more trade-intensive economies (Steinberg 2002). Under this procedural rule, the major importers and the major exporters of a given product conduct the primary negotiations, and the tariff reductions agreed by them (for the said product) then get multilateralized to all GATT/WTO member states. Preferential trade agreements (PTA), which are usually negotiated among a small group of countries (often just two countries bilaterally) entail less delegation. Many PTAs contain most-favored-nation (MFN) clauses committing the signatories to grant to each other the most favorable terms granted to any other trading partner, including in other PTAs. MFN, however, only applies to favorable terms granted by a signatory state to *its* other PTA partners in exercise of its sovereign authority. In that sense, the shift in further trade liberalization from the multilateral WTO-based trade regime to PTAs covering a smaller number of countries but often going much deeper, may be said to constitute something of a reversion of trade (negotiation) governance "back" to individual national governments beyond the extent of their commitment to their existing WTO obligations.

At the same time, the shift from the GATT to the WTO in 1994 involved a substantial strengthening of the dispute settlement mechanism for the multilateral trade regime. This was part of a broader trend toward the "legalization" of international relations (Goldstein et al. 2001) and often mirrored by the establishment of third-party dispute settlement mechanism provisions in PTAs (Allee and Elsig 2015). This element of the legalization of international trade governance empowers designated panels of trade law experts to issue *binding* decisions in disputes that arise under a trade agreement where the parties cannot resolve the disputes among themselves. It constitutes an upward shift of authority while increasing the binding-ness of negotiated commitments.

Changes in trade-related global governance, however, extend considerably beyond the traditional core issues of tariffs and quotas. They represent the particular focus of this section. As Steven Vogel (1996) famously pointed out, "freer markets" seem to require "more rules." Concretely, a market economy requires a legal and regulatory framework to help market participants reduce information asymmetries (Akerlof 1970), overcome time inconsistency (Kydland and Prescott 1977), and to inhibit forms of behavior, such as cheating and fraud, which, if unchecked, can adversely affect investment and accumulation (Hough and Grier 2015). These rules may also allow socioeconomic actors to turn paralyzing uncertainty into calculable risk, though the ability to do so might be illusionary (Blyth 2010).

Governments too, when they engage in economic liberalization – i.e. reduce the role of the state in the economy and no longer direct economic activity – may decide to put a stronger legal and regulatory framework in place for markets to work well (Vogel 1996). They may also not see the creation of market regulations as a purely domestic issue that each country should or can address independently. As research on the political consequences of economic interdependence has shown since the 1970s, market integration increases a country's stake in the laws and policies of its neighbors, creating both the potential for increased conflict and greater incentives for cooperation (Keohane and Nye 1972; Ruggie 1983). Consequently, there is an incentive now for governments – often but by no means always at the urging of domestic or transnational commercial or societal actors – to address a large and growing number of "trade-related" issues via the international trade regime. Specifically, the GATT/WTO and especially PTAs now contain numerous commitments to undertake certain steps and refrain from others. The international trade regime thus shapes domestic policy-making and constrains governments' ability to regulate markets as each separately at any particular moment sees fit.

Effective regulation of international trade has hence also come to mean the international regulation of product markets. Technical standards offer an apt illustration. They can be critical to having a market in the first place, for example because they define comparable and compatible products (Balleisen 2014; Spruyt 2001; Yarbrough and Yarbrough 1992: 92f.), and often help achieve important public policy objectives such as consumer protection (Vogel 1995) or workplace safety (Cheit 1990), at times even without the need for government regulations that make them binding (Morrison and Webb 2004). Here, the Technical Barriers to Trade (TBT) Agreement of the WTO – which is an integral part of the treaty that created the WTO and thus binding on all WTO member states (Marceau and Trachtman 2002) – and similar provisions in many PTAs oblige national and sub-national public authorities to use compatible international standards, where available, as the technical basis for non-trade distortionary public policies. However, neither the TBT Agreement nor corresponding provisions in PTAs contain or create standard-setting procedures for the vast array

of often complex traded products where the absence of standards might increase the costs and riskiness of market exchange, or make, say, the management of negative externalities, such as inadvertently putting users at risk, more challenging. Rather, the TBT Agreement recognizes two transnational, *non-governmental* organizations, the International Organization for Standardization (ISO) and the International Electrotechnical Commission (IEC) as sources of "international standards," and leaves it open whether other standards bodies might also be considered sources of international standards for WTO purposes. The TBT Agreement thus radically changed the status of ISO and IEC, greatly empowering the mostly private-sector experts in the two long-standing organizations whose "technical committees" may develop and revise the actual ISO and IEC standards (Büthe and Mattli 2011). Given their status under international trade law, many of these standards now determine market access and have given the non-governmental ISO/IEC and the private-sector technical experts they assembled, an influential role in the governance of international trade.

Similarly, for the sensitive issue of food safety (Ansell and Vogel 2006; Gaughan 2004; Liu 2010), the WTO's Sanitary and Phyto-Sanitary Measures (SPS) Agreement obliges governments to defer to the international food safety standards of the Codex Alimentarius Commission (Büthe 2008; Marceau and Trachtman 2002). The Codex Commission is formally a joint organ of two international organizations (the World Health Organization and the Food and Agriculture Organization). It may, however, be more accurately described as a hybrid public–private body, since the majority of the experts who wield power over global trade by developing its standards come from the private sector, often from the very food industry whose products are to be regulated, even if they happen nominally to represent Codex member governments (Avery, Drake, and Lang 1993; Büthe 2009; Veggeland and Borgen 2005).

The changes sketched above are important and carry the force of international trade law. But arguably even bigger changes have occurred in spheres where the rise of transnational private regulation and the increasing prevalence of non-governmental technical experts in shaping the rules for global markets are not limited to regulatory bodies empowered by governments. For objectives as diverse as organic agriculture, environmentally sustainable timber logging and industrial practices, "fair trade" (which is concerned with the distribution of gains from trade, particularly the share received by local producers, workers, and artisans in developing countries), and the prevention of child labor, "entrepreneurial" (Green 2014) private actors have sought and often gained regulatory authority through the creation of standards and accompanying certification schemes (e.g. Auld 2014; Djelic and Sahlin-Andersson 2006; Peters et al. 2009; Reed, Utting, and Mukherjee-Reed 2012). To the extent that these private rules and certificates govern market access, they constitute an important part of trade governance.

Another distinctive illustration of transnational governance relating to trade comes from the diffusion of competition law. There have historically been close links between trade policy and national competition laws, notably in late nineteenth-century Canada and the United States. The Havana Charter for the ill-fated International Trade Organization in the aftermath of the Second World War included a competition policy chapter, and the founding treaties of the European Community included competition rules in its framework for the governance of the eventual common market (Büthe 2014). However, the idea of a multilateral competition regime proved controversial in the context of GATT; proposals in the late 1990s and early 2000s to add a competition chapter to the WTO treaty (or drawing up an add-on agreement akin to TBT and SPS) also made little headway. Still, these setbacks have not deterred closer connections between trade and competition regimes, including a growing "backdoor" integration of competition policies in the international trade regime. The striking growth in the number of countries with a domestic competition law from about 30 in 1990 to more than 130 today may be traced to the conduit effect of institutionalized trade openness (Büthe and Minhas 2015). Besides, more than two-thirds of the PTAs since 1990 contain competition provisions, including for regulatory cooperation between national competition authorities. The latter is also a key objective of some 200 recent bilateral agreements relating to competition law and policy.

Many changes in the global trade regime have shifted rule- and decision-making up, down, and sideways from domestic politics and traditional inter-governmental institutions. National governments as unitary actors in the international sphere have yielded gradually to more complex webs of "governance" institutions, ranging in diversity across "trans-governmental" networks of specialized government officials working directly with their counterparts abroad largely outside the channels of traditional international diplomacy (Eberlein and Newman 2008; Keohane and Nye 2001; Slaughter 2004), hybrid public–private bodies such as the Codex Alimentarius Commission where government delegations mostly comprise corporate sector employees of the regulated firms or industries (Büthe and Harris 2011), non-governmental transnational bodies such as the International Electrotechnical Commission (Büthe 2010a) or the International Organization for Standardization (Büthe and Mattli 2011; Murphy and Yates 2008), and civil society or private sector-driven transnational bodies clamoring for regulatory influence in global markets (Auld 2014).

12.2.4   Labor

Labor regulation has traditionally been the province of national governments, which have, however, rarely operated in isolation. In addition to national governments, other relevant actors in the sphere of labor are domestic trade unions, employers, including multinational corporations, employer associations, and NGOs. National trade unions have historically pushed for protective measures for workers (e.g. limitation on working hours, minimum wages, employment protection legislation, unemployment benefits, etc.), which were adopted either through negotiating collectively with firms and employer associations, or through campaigns resulting in government legislation that might also sometimes take the form of "bargained laws" ratifying and giving general applicability to outcomes produced by collective bargaining between unions and employers. Alternatively labor laws have provided a procedural framework for collective bargaining procedures to give regulatory effect to legislated goals such as, for instance, those relating to health and safety at the workplace (Blainpain 2007; Hepple and Veneziani 2009).

In brief, private bodes such as trade unions and employer associations have always played an important role in the field of labor regulation. "Corporatist" policy-making may nevertheless still represent a distinctive Continental European and Scandinavian style by comparison with Anglo-American countries. In corporatist systems national governments have often been willing to share their policy-making prerogatives with their "social partners" (trade unions and employer associations) in the labor and social domains, i.e. they have involved private actors representing labor and capital in the conception and execution of public policy (Baccaro 2014; Berger 1981; Lehmbruch and Schmitter 1982). Empirical research suggests that corporatist societies tend to be less unequal than non-corporatist ones, while their macroeconomic performance in terms of growth and employment seems comparable (Hicks 1988; Kenworthy 2002; Wallerstein 1999).

At the international level, labor regulation was strongly influenced by a somewhat diluted version of the corporatist model illustrated by the governance structure of the most important institution at the global level, i.e. the International Labour Organization (ILO). Established in 1919 as part of the Versailles Peace Treaty, the ILO was the West's response to the "red scare" (Cox 1973: 102). After the Bolshevik revolution, the Western powers represented corporatism as an institutional alternative to communism in Europe. The ILO survived the collapse of the League of Nations and became a specialized agency of the United Nations after the Second World War. Today it is the only international organization to incorporate private actors in its structure, with its governing body being composed of governments, trade unions, and employer associations.

The ILO (1972 [1919]) discharges a vast mandate: reflecting the conditions under which it was founded, the preamble to its constitution describes the organization's goal as contributing to "universal and lasting peace" by bringing about "social justice" specifically, by removing "injustice, hardship, and privation" in conditions of work that can "produce unrest so great that the peace and harmony of the world are imperiled." The preamble also states that "the failure of any nation to adopt human conditions of labour is an obstacle in the way of other nations which desire to improve the conditions in their own countries." International labor regulation under the aegis of the ILO has thus aimed to protect states with generous worker benefits and protections from competition from others seeking to gain trade advantage through lower wages and protective standards. A notable sign of this commitment in the early years of the ILO was its efforts to legislate an eight-hour working day. The 1944 Philadelphia Declaration which gave the ILO a new foundation and *élan* added that its "fundamental objective" was to ensure that "all human beings, irrespective of race, creed or sex, have the right to pursue both their material well-being and their spiritual development in conditions of freedom and dignity, of economic security and equal opportunity" (ILO 1972 [1919]). The ILO was hence assigned "a responsibility … to examine and consider all international economic and financial policies and measures in the light of this fundamental objective."

Since the 1980s, principles and practices relating to labor regulation have been profoundly transformed by upbeat assessments of the benefits of free capital and labor markets in which the ILO itself had little direct say. First, new research in both macroeconomics and

12

labor economics tended to view policies for employment protection, unemployment insurance, national or industry-level collective bargaining, etc., as contributing to raising the non-accelerating inflation rate of unemployment (NAIRU), and advocated deregulation as a way to sustain employment in Western labor markets (Layard, Nickell, and Jackman 2005, Nickell, Nunziata, and Ochel 2005). Second, labor regulation has been blamed from a micro-level perspective for reduced efficiency and increased inequality in the labor market, notably between privileged "insiders" (generally male and older workers) with access to stable "legacy" employment offering good wages and good working conditions protected by legislation and collective bargaining rights, and "outsiders" (predominantly young and/or female) condemned to precarious working conditions (Boeri 2011; Lindbeck and Snower 1988; Saint-Paul 2002). Similar arguments are made for developing countries where labor regulation is said to lead to a rationing of formal jobs and the expansion of an unregulated informal economy. A less regulated labor market would, in this view, equalize conditions between organized and unorganized workers, and the formal and the informal sectors of the economy (Frölich et al. 2014; Heckman and Pagés 2000).

Such analyses have been very influential including within international organizations (IMF 2003; OECD 1994). Within the ILO, the 2000s saw the launch of a Decent Work agenda (ILO 1999). "Decent Work" was never precisely defined, but its emphasis on dignity, equality, fair income, and safe working conditions evokes a flexible and negotiable combination of rights and protections. Referring to "work" rather than "labor" was also an important rhetorical innovation with "work" capable of embracing a range of employment relationships without necessarily privileging stable employment. The ILO's decent "work" agenda implicitly acknowledged its earlier focus on formal employment and neglect of workers in the unorganized sector, a majority of them in the poorer countries (Baccaro and Mele 2012). This critical reassessment of labor institutions and regulation was accompanied by a rethinking of the effectiveness of state action in regard to labor. For advocates of this new approach, regulatory problems were far too complex, interrelated, and diverse to be effectively dealt with by the imposition of rigid standards. It was preferable instead to adopt "experimentalist" modes of governance in which regulators set the broad goals and parameters of public policy while leaving their execution to partnerships between firms and civil society actors sharing organizational learning anchored in quantifiable indicators of performance and information about best practices (Sabel et al. 2000). As a result, if traditional labor regulation was directed at restricting employer discretion and sought to strengthen the bargaining position of workers, the new prescriptions are premised on decent working conditions offering positive pay-offs to employers, including in the form of stronger worker motivation, commitment, and productivity (Elliott and Freeman 2003; Ruggie 2008; Vogel 2005).

With financial de-regulation and the opening of capital markets, economies have experienced a historic shift in the distribution of power and resources, reflected in a declining share of labor incomes and an accompanying surge in wealth inequalities within many countries (Piketty 2015). Labor has also been a direct target of deregulation affecting rights and concerns ranging from unionization and collective bargaining to employment conditions and health and safety at the workplace. Critics of worsening labor conditions, including the marginalization of young adults, women, older workers, and so on have traced these trends to the financialization of the economy (Krippner 2005). "Structural reforms" promoted by the IMF and the World Bank in the developing world, and by national governments and the EU Commission in Europe, undermined public investment, led to transfer of wealth from the working class and middle class to wealthier groups, increased inequalities, and reduced rates of social mobility (Piketty 2015). As a rule, the most vulnerable and those who relied on welfare benefits were among those who were hurt the most.

Their different contexts of transition (post-socialism vs. post-colonialism) are crucial to understanding differences in the actors, instruments, and results of "shock therapies" between Eastern Europe and, say, Africa, and their effects on labor regulations. In Africa from the start, structural adjustment programs affected individual and social well-being including through their effects on the rights of labor and conditions of employment (Logie and Woodroffe 1993). In Ghana, for example, structural adjustment programs led to significant cuts in the public sector workforce and in state expenditures on public services, with the imposition of user fees for health and education leading to reduced access to health and educational services. At the same time, besides inflation and declining real wages, steep currency devaluations led to a four-fold increase in Ghana's total debt between 1980 and 1995, and increased external debt from approximately 32 percent to 95 percent of GDP during the same period (Konadu-Agyemang 2000).

Labor in the richer countries has also been affected by the loss of many forms of industrial employment, the decline of unions, and the loss of bargaining power, both in greater or lesser degree a result of changes in labor laws and regulations, the widespread growth of contractual employment, and the emergence of a "precariat" (Standing 2008). These trends are by no means new. Prolonged periods of sluggish growth, rising inequalities, and decline in public services may also be traced back at least three decades. Yet recent years have seen a startling intensification of these trends, with reinforcing policy changes, and sharper distributive effects. While their direction was unmistakable, the rather more incremental implementation of deregulatory policies over a nearly two decades-long period and a still functional, though rapidly fraying, social safety net enabled the more affluent parts of the West to absorb the consequences of deregulation and liberalization. Public borrowing also compensated to some extent for declining revenues (Streeck 2014), while looser monetary policies and debt-financed increases in consumption helped offset the effects of falling public and private investment and lower incomes (Rajan 2010). Welfare systems too, helped cushion the effects of layoffs necessitated by the reduction in trade barriers (Esping-Andersen 1996). However, even in the West, the distributive consequences of policy choices made in the 1980s and 1990s have become increasingly clear and inescapable since the onset of the financial crisis in 2008. Their impact has been particularly harsh in the countries of southern Europe where successive cutbacks in public investments and roll backs of the state since 2010 have not only provoked acute social crises, they have in the absence of compensating increases in private investment led to an acute employment crisis, particularly among young adults.

12.2.5 Environment

The environmental domain differs from the other domains to the extent that nation-states have retained more control over environmental governance despite calls for international and supra national environmental governance mechanisms and bodies (Bulkeley 2005). To some extent it reflects the fact that there is not one "environment" but many: environmental questions range across different scales and across levels, from local concerns about air or water quality, protecting flora, fauna, or biodiversity, to regional (including trans-boundary) environmental management, say of rivers or curbing acid rain, to global level concerns like climate change, with each implying different types of actors, epistemic and ethical values, and solutions. Hence, as a domain, environment illustrates the impossibility of envisaging a single model or locus of regulation or governance (Bulkeley 2005; Dingwerth 2008; Jordan and O'Riordan 2004; Shove and Walker 2010; Steffen et al. 2015; Vaccaro 2007). Furthermore, regardless of scale, environmental governance is usually conceptualized as profoundly place-specific (Pestre 2008), more closely connected to local public spaces and politics (Swyngedouw 2005), and concerned also to govern non-humans, for example containing the spread of chemicals, managing global effects such as climate change, or regulating animal population levels. To a considerable extent environmental governance also reflects aspirations to manage the impact of markets on the use and exploitation of planetary resources.

Environmental governance's focus on the *environment*, rather than humans, has institutional and instrumental implications; it may also help explain why nation-states have remained powerful actors in this sphere of government. While environmental governance has not been immune to the turn towards market-based solutions and/or transnational governance, the combination of place-based environmental resources and "services" and the need to govern "global environmental goods" (like climate), means that even to their most ardent advocates markets may not always offer the best solutions. In the North, as explained below, government regulations, voluntary compliance, and limited market-based mechanisms have prevailed. In the South, in addition to these mechanisms, there has been greater emphasis on decentralization of resources such as forests and water, leading to the development of both state and donor supported community level users groups to govern resources (Lemos and Agrawal 2006), and ecosystem schemes that link local users to financial arrangements designed to promote environmental quality and sharing of scarce resources, especially water (Corbera, Kosoy, and Martínez Tuna 2007). Market-based solutions such as "cap and trade" for pollutants have been slow to develop or not been particularly stable or successful, especially at the international level. Thus, in general, nation-states remain central to environmental decision-making (Pestre 2008, 2016).

Interstate organizations have continued to play an important role in defining and managing environmental challenges, often in coordination with technical experts and scientists (Newell 2012; Bulkeley 2015; Sending and Neumann 2006). Engaged scientists within these IOs, often aligned with citizen groups, emerged as important voices on the environment, playing an influential role in setting environmental agendas and bringing expert knowledge to bear on them (Bäckstrand 2003; Hulme 2011). An important consequence was the growth of the "environment," as an object of regulation and of the

associated expertise in the natural sciences. The environment often refers to or implies forms of commons that are not always easy to study or interpret (Bakker 2007). Therefore, identifying environmental issues and evaluating them using appropriate tools, are intrinsic to the government of nature (Hulme 2010). The nature of environmental knowledge was one reason why the management and protection of the environment could not be left to the market. This applies to climate change – panel 1 of the International Panel on Climate Change (IPCC) for example – or to the state of the biosphere among many other environmental questions such as air and water pollution. The United Nations Environmental Programme (UNEP), the UNESCO, and international scientific organizations like the International Union for Nature Conservation (IUCN) and the Scientific Committee on Problems of the Environment (SCOPE), were central in setting up many of these environmental governance institutions particularly in the 1970s.

A distinct feature of environmental governance is also the extent to which it has been driven at various levels by horizontal and vertical mobilization crisscrossing states and embracing an enlarged political sphere occupied by new social movements and increasingly politicized civil society groups. Such mobilizations are often explicitly critical of neoliberal governance agendas (Rajagopal 2003; Valdivia 2008). For instance, environmental mobilizations have mutually fostered and brought together international groups of scientists like the IPCC (Beck 2012; Beck et al. 2014), transnational activist-advocacy groups like Green Peace and Friends of the Earth, national coalitions of Native American groups protesting environmental justice issues, and grassroots movements protesting large dam projects such as the Narmada in India (Swain 1997), and local, smaller-scale protests, for instance against garbage incinerators in Los Angeles (di Chiro 1996). One consequence of these mobilizations has been to force industry, including notably multinational corporations, and national governments to become more invested in the environment, leading to a range of outcomes from voluntary standards to negotiating regional and other cross-border agreements (Cashore 2002).

The impact of such movements is particularly evident in the contrast between the 1970s and the early 1980s, when the knee-jerk attitude of international businesses was to resist any action in favor of environmental protection, and the subsequent decades. In the 1970s, while the environment had begun to move up national and international governance agendas, international businesses continued to trivialize the issue and its consequences, in many instances even joining hands with authoritarian governments to victimize environmentalists and attack early environmental movements as disruptive extremist movements. This tendency is far from dead, not only in many poorer countries that are rich in minerals or resources like timber (Peluso 1993; Peluso and Vandergeest 2011; Neumann 2004; Swain 1997), but in some wealthy countries such as the United States where, as recently as 2017, attempts by a Native American band to block an oil pipeline on their territory (over which they have treaty rights) were met with police and government violence (Sammon 2016).

If Western governments have been frequently complicit when not actively engaged in protecting their nationals' concessions and investments both at home and abroad, from the late 1980s, major groupings of business such as the International Chamber of Commerce

(ICC) began in parallel to nuance their stance, overtly acknowledging the environment as a legitimate public and business concern and attempting to co-opt campaigning groups and NGOs in their efforts to beat back public regulation in favor of voluntary firm- or industry-level goals and targets, at best with some "independent" monitoring (Forsyth 2005). Such strategies, which, arguably from the perspective of the management were more "efficient" and "cost-effective" (Bennett and James 1998), multiplied through ICC initiatives and dedicated entities such as the Geneva-based World Business Council for Sustainable Development (WBCSD). As the environment became a growing and incontestable public concern, and in many cases a source of public scandal with reputational consequences, a potential drag on stock performance, and a source even of civil or criminal liability, businesses began to embrace environmental concerns, to the extent possible on their own terms (Pestre 2008, 2016).

However, the sovereignty of scientific knowledge and environmental concerns of local actors has not escaped challenge including from those who recognize the necessity of environmental governance. Particularly in official settings (e.g. government bureaucracies and international organizations), the link between the environment and the political sphere has tended to be mediated by economic experts playing an increasingly institutionalized role. The reasons for this may be said to be political, managerial, institutional, as well as epistemic. Right from the start protecting the environment was recognized to involve economic trade-offs, including in the South with efforts to reduce poverty, and soon such concerns began to feature prominently in World Bank lending agendas, particularly for large environmental projects such as dams. Whether, to what extent, or how this resulted in international financial institutions extending their clout to the sphere of the environment must remain a matter of speculation. More generally, as environment began to be framed as an "externality," debates about the environment and implementation of environmental norms and programs tended also to be expressed in terms of incentives and penalties (e.g. "polluter pays"), and more generally in cost-benefit terms. The notion of "ecosystem services" has also been generative of schemes to pay people for protection of valuable resources like upstream water, or most recently, for carbon sequestration. The "economization" of environmental discourses was also reflected at the institutional level in international financial institutions and intergovernmental organizations. A notable example is the OECD where the environment unit was detached from the scientific division that had created it, and placed under the charge of economists. The OECD soon became instrumental in proposing new rules, guidelines, voluntary agreements, for example relating to investment policies of multinational enterprises in the South, which were conceived as tools to organize global forms of regulation bypassing state-based measures. The World Bank likewise played a key role in standardizing environmental impact assessment exercises for Northern investments projects in the South, in doing so privileging "scientific" assessments over the perspectives of local people (Moretti and Pestre 2015). This trend towards "economism" may equally be seen in the functioning of the IPCC, which prioritizes economic and technical evaluations (Dahan Dalmedico and Guillemot 2008), and in international organizations such as the WTO and its arbitration tribunal whose decisions often hold implications for national environmental laws. (Charnovitz 2007; DeSombre and

Barkin 2002; Shaffer 2010). Demands to reconcile the environment with the purported demands of employment and growth have also given rise to concepts such as "sustainable development" and categories such as "green technologies," which, in turn, have arguably facilitated the constitution of a scaled-up "global" as the proper space or scale for environmental action (Bulkeley 2005; Hulme 2010; Mahony 2014).

12.3   Authority and Regulation

This section explores the forms of authority, instruments of governance, and calculative devices mobilized to regulate private and public actors in the five areas under study here. The turn from government to transnational governance is often identified with the expanding deployment of instruments of market self-regulation and thus associated with the spread of neoliberal ideologies and practices (Ferguson and Gupta 2002; Lascoumes and Le Gales 2007). There is indeed some confirmation that the turn to transnational governance has meant greater reliance on market discipline in some areas (for instance, labor and environment). At the same time, in finance and investment it correlates with innovations in monitoring, surveillance, techniques of risk calculation, arbitration, and so on more conducive to "governance by experts" whose panoply of regulatory instruments may work in tandem with the market but is not limited to it. Thus, transnational governance may not only enhance the sphere of private self-regulation, it has also the potential to change how public regulation operates.

12.3.1   Finance

Since the 1980s, changing forms of domestic financial regulation and the redistribution of regulatory roles between the public and private sectors were led by a series of innovations signifying a shift from statutory legal codes to more flexible, expert-based "risk-sensitive" rules, accompanied by the introduction of new techniques of risk calculation (Riles 2011). Statutory regulations in finance conventionally involved static provisions applicable to the whole sector, for example, in the case of banks separating banking and investment, restricting scale or overseas operations, licensing entry, etc. In Europe and the developing world after the Second World War, many central banks and governments adopted varying degrees of directed lending policies affecting the distribution of institutional credit between the public and private sectors as well as within them. Directed lending policies could be motivated by several objectives, and any impact they might have on asset quality and financial market stability were more easily manageable in closed economies (Balachandran 1998). Financial regulation in open economies is naturally more complex, not least since financial markets also tend to be more complex. Here, particularly for advocates of flexibility, instead of defining the scope of permissible and impermissible transactions, modulating regulation across sectors and contexts of exchange could make it more effective and reduce incentives for evasion.

The new modes of regulation have coalesced to a considerable degree around the use of indicators. This is particularly notable for regulation sensitive to risk (Davis et al. 2012). The expansion of private risk expertise is emblematic of a broader expansion in the knowledge infrastructure for regulation where private firms have been joined by international organizations (such as the IMF) and other entities as suppliers of knowledge. Such knowledge has implications for investors' decisions, functioning of markets, and directly as well as indirectly for macroeconomic policies and outcomes. The diverse sources of supply for this knowledge, in turn, raise important questions about the nature of modern financial markets and financial market signals.

Ratings offer a good example of "governance by indicators" with respect to financial and investment decisions, and more broadly of macroeconomic policies (Davis et al. 2012; Pénet and Mallard 2014). The dispersal of regulatory authority and knowledge following the deregulation of institutional lending and investment since the 1970s was accompanied by an increased reliance on ratings as private risk-based technologies of public regulation. Historically credit rating agencies emerged to provide, for a fee, financial market information to investors who, unlike say the big banks, lacked the means to produce their own information. Already in the 1930s, US regulators were enjoining the use of public ratings by banks and investment firms that did not devise or were unwilling to share their own internal ratings (Carruthers 2016). After the war, with stringent capital controls and the consequential reduction of systemic risk, regulatory demand for ratings remained sluggish. But from the mid-1970s ratings began to make their way back into regulatory provisions. In 1975, the US Securities and Exchange Commission (SEC) began using them to regulate capital-adequacy norms for broker dealers.

Since the 1980s ratings began to be incorporated into a broader variety of contexts in the United States, and subsequently in the European Union. Sometimes this could be opportunistic or symbolic: for instance, deployed as a test of national banks' qualifications to establish financial subsidiaries following the 1999 repeal of the Glass-Steagall Act, ratings became a rationale for dismantling a centerpiece of the New Deal regulatory framework. But regulators also used ratings for risk-sensitive restrictions on the types of securities which institutions such as pension funds and insurance companies may carry in their portfolios. Regulators use rating-based formulas when computing differential disclosure requirements. For instance, the SEC mandates higher disclosure requirements for financial institutions with riskier asset portfolios as measured by credit ratings (Crockett et al. 2003: 7). Ratings are used to determine the eligibility of securities for central bank accommodation. They are also embedded in private options contracts outside the regulatory framework of public exchanges, while platforms such as the International Swaps and Derivatives Association (ISDA) use rating triggers to reassess collateral (Riles 2011). Rather than appearing as an instrument of deregulation, ratings here serve as a means for voluntary compliance and oversight in what might otherwise be an unregulated industry.

The use of ratings, not to mention ad hoc and often opaquely based assessments put out from time to time by public and private bodies, is not without problems. For many critics credit ratings possess little intrinsic informational value (Partnoy 1999). Not only have they failed to forecast defaults, they may even aggravate instability when credit rating agencies appear to be following rather than leading markets (Ferri, Liu, and Stiglitz 1999; Pénet 2015; Rona-Tas and Hiss 2011). Though such critiques might be thought by some to beg the endogeneity of prices, the latter have been argued to be superior to ratings for regulatory purposes (Partnoy 2002). Recently, banks and investment funds have been distancing themselves from credit rating agencies by bolstering their internal expertise. However, ratings remain in use to compute capital reserve requirements, and banks remain reliant on them to risk-weight their exposures. Ratings continue to determine eligible securities for central banks' open market operations as in the case of the European Central Bank (Pénet and Mallard 2014). In other words, despite their limited informational value, demand for ratings appears to be institutionally well-entrenched. Yet with so much riding on them it is also open to question whether the real value of ratings, at least in the short term, may lie not in their informational value as much as in their utility as a tool of governance both whose supply and channels of impact conveniently fudge the boundaries of public/private, government/markets, and so on.

The management of sovereign debt and sovereign debt crises in recent decades also illustrates the complex relations and shifting boundaries between public and market regulation in the sphere of finance. From the 1950s until nearly the late 1970s, developing country governments' external borrowing requirements were largely met by IFIs, Western governments, and their consortia. A high, though declining proportion of securities issued by Western governments were also held by home lenders. In the 1970s many developing countries' governments turned to Western banks to escape IFI conditionalities. Latin American countries were among the first developing countries to do so, and thus among the first to return to international capital markets after the Second World War. At first, i.e. from the 1950s to the 1970s by comparison to the later decades, IFIs and Western banks kept a distance from each other. Yet within less than a decade of their turn to private borrowing, a combination of loan-pushing and over-borrowing, surging imports and declining export revenues, and a steep hike in US interest rates plunged the Latin American countries into a debt crisis. Western banks turned to their own governments at the first hints of trouble. In an early display of the tendency (in accord with realist theories of power) for multilateral lending institutions to act in collusion with sovereign creditors' interests (Cox, Jacobson, and Curzon 1973; Haas 1964; Stone 2002, 2004), soon governments and IFIs were back in play to negotiate structural adjustment programs for the debt-affected countries in return for rescheduling debts and new loans, the bulk of which went into paying off Western banks. This landscape has largely remained unchanged for over four decades during which, as discussed above, developments in the sphere of regulation, regulatory institutions, expertise, and behavior have further helped diffuse the lines between public/private, governments/markets, and so on.

Conditionalities are an essential feature of multilateral lending. Their modern origins may be traced to efforts by nineteenth-century private consortia such as the London-based Corporation of Foreign Bondholders to effectively collateralize public policy in lieu of tangible collateral assets or revenues in countries not subject to formal or informal colonial rule (Flandreau 2013; Flores-Zendejas 2016). From the perspective of lenders, colonial loans or guarantees entailing enforceable conditionalities accompanied by close monitoring represented the ideal model of lending to foreign governments.

Modern-day conditionalities can be assessed with respect to substantive demands, i.e. the actual conditions, or the instruments used to support them (Babb and Carruthers 2008). Loans may be made against the promise of meeting conditions; or fulfilling them may be a precondition for disbursing the loan. In both cases periodic monitoring and assessments would be the norm. Ex-ante conditionality can be coercive to the extent lending can cease if countries do not deliver on their promises. Ex-post conditionality may be more coercive and may partake in the nature of "hard law" (Abbot and Snidal 2000). It does not also preclude continuous monitoring of set performance targets, but in practice, it has been associated with the IMF's expanded surveillance role, which includes producing assessments of debt-servicing capacity and vulnerability indices. For the poorest countries such assessments play a role not unlike credit ratings in sovereign bond markets, and with a similar bearing on private investment decisions. For borrowers with access to sovereign bond markets they complement private assessments of credit risk by rating agencies (Best 2014; Nelson 2016). In the wake of the 1997 East Asian crisis, conditionality programs even expanded to include institutional policies in the judicial sphere (Best 2014; Halliday and Carruthers 2009).

The 1980s were a "lost decade" not only in Latin America but also in sub-Saharan Africa where World Bank and IMF programs led to a decline in incomes, investment, and even trade, as well as increased levels of poverty. While these failures did little to cause the IFIs to pause, with the late-1990s Asian crisis, "the question of what kind of failure this represented itself became a subject of contestation" within the IMF and World Bank (Best 2014: 75). However, no amount of failure seemed to make a difference to conditionality-based lending, indeed by the late 2000s, it was no longer confined to developing countries. Since the 2010s conditional lending has come to form an accepted feature of debt restructuring and austerity packages within the Eurozone, notably in Greece, Portugal, and Ireland. At the same time, conditionality procedures, terms, and practices have grown more diverse and complex.

Overall, conditionality is a powerful, yet blunt and flawed mechanism of "expert" governance over sovereign debt issues. Its persistence may perhaps be attributed to IFIs and powerful governments, and perhaps even borrowing governments privileging technical or "calculative" surveillance instruments as a means to exert, or for the latter negotiate, both political and market pressures. Although sovereign defaults and debt restructuring have been on the rise since the 1980s, the international law on sovereign debt remains notoriously underdeveloped, and attempts to frame a comprehensive multilateral framework for resolving sovereign debt disputes through interstate negotiation remain controversial and have made little headway (Helleiner 2008; Krueger 2002).

12.3.2 Investment

Governance of cross-border investment continues mainly to operate through interstate negotiation (treaties) and litigation (mostly in the form of arbitration). As already noted, the two most important instruments used to regulate public actors in this sphere are the investment treaties themselves, which impose obligations on host states,

and investment treaty awards, which are made by investment treaty arbitral tribunals in the context of resolving a specific dispute about the interpretation or application of an investment treaty. This institutional development is particularly worthy of note in the context of governance, for the triangulation of its interstate framework with the needs and interests of private investors in the lending countries.

In terms of treaties, in addition to various mega-regional free trade agreements with investment obligations (like NAFTA, TPP, and the RCEP), the 3,200 international investment agreements that have been signed up to now represent a complex spaghetti bowl of bilateral, pluri-lateral and regional agreements, which may be said to make up a "global" system despite the absence of a single, overarching multilateral treaty. Indeed, even though the vast majority of these treaties are bilateral, this dense web of investment treaties is regarded as a global system for several reasons (Schill 2009). First, many treaties contain similar substantive terms, as previous treaties are used as legal "boilerplates" (Gulati and Scott 2013) for future negotiations. So despite their bilateral form, they often partake of a shared multilateral substance. Second, investment treaties usually contain most-favored-nation (MFN) provisions enabling investors under one treaty to gain the benefit of favorable provisions in a state's other treaties. Third, governance through arbitration is a key shared attribute of the investment treaty system. Investment treaties are subject to interpretation by arbitral tribunals, which often interpret provisions in one treaty by reference to decisions under other treaties.

However, the investment treaty system does not have a supreme court or an appellate body and an arbitral tribunal might not follow the decisions of another tribunal through a formal doctrine of precedent. This has meant that different arbitral tribunals have interpreted the same provisions in different ways. In some controversial cases, different tribunals have even ruled on the same scenario in different ways, leading to concerns about inconsistent or conflicting decisions (Franck 2005; Van Harten 2016). For instance, in two cases against the Czech Republic arising out of the same facts, one tribunal found no liability and the other found liability and awarded the investor USD$350 million. In practice, a de facto body of precedent has nevertheless emerged because tribunals in one case often refer extensively to awards from other cases (Kaufmann-Kohler 2007). This does not always create consistency, however, as on some key issues such as whether MFN provisions apply to dispute resolution, investment treaty tribunals have split between two or more approaches.

Under international law, subsequent agreements and practice of the treaty parties can be taken into consideration when interpreting a treaty (Gordon and Pohl 2015; Roberts 2010; Vienna Convention on the Law of Treaties, article 31(3)), though it is not clear that a subsequent interpretation of the treaty parties would be binding on investment treaty tribunals. Still, the power of states to negotiate and enter into treaties, and arbitral tribunals to interpret and apply these treaties, should be understood as an iterative dialogue (Roberts 2010; UNCTAD 2011). After tribunals interpret treaties, treaty parties have the power to confirm, reject, or qualify these interpretations by leaving the treaty terms the same or changing them in their next rounds of treaty negotiations. This can be seen most clearly in the evolution of

US investment treaties, which include specific changes that confirm or reject the reasoning given in particular investment treaty awards. Following a series of early cases, NAFTA states grew concerned enough over the broad interpretations of the treaty language by some investment arbitral tribunals for the Free Trade Commission (FTC), which is made up of cabinet-level representatives of the signatory states and has the power to issue binding interpretations of NAFTA provisions, to clarify their intent by issuing its interpretations of the investment provisions. Despite some initial controversy about the effect of these interpretations on ongoing cases, arbitral tribunals generally now interpret NAFTA in light of these FTC interpretations. Given this, many newer-style investment treaties contain a clause giving treaty parties the power to adopt interpretations that bind arbitral tribunals under the treaty. To some extent, therefore, investment treaty law is being developed through interactions between states and tribunals. But not all states have the resources to engage in this iterative process (Gordon and Pohl 2015).

The regulatory sphere with regard to foreign private investment extends beyond the realm of hard law (i.e. investment treaties and arbitration awards). We may count, among tools of "soft" regulation, the recommendations and advisory opinions of private consulting firms and large, multinational law firms, influential think tanks, and international organizations like the OECD, which advise countries on their investment policies as well as the "soundness" of their investments abroad. In recent years, multilateral coordination against money laundering through forums such as the G20 has investors, states, and other institutions coalescing around the "rule of law" and "transparency" frameworks developed as part of the World Bank and IMF's anti-corruption initiatives in the 1990s (Halliday, Levi, and Reuter 2013). As part of their anti-money laundering agendas, entities like the Financial Action Task Force (FATF) and the IMF have promoted "financial transparency" measures and banking reforms that extend the reach of reporting requirements like those promoted by the OECD. With the rise of counter-terrorism financing (CTF) campaigns after 2001, "financial transparency" regulations have gained teeth to a point it is doubtful whether they form only a "soft law" even with respect to the transnational legal order regulating foreign investment (Biersteker 2009). This is a notable difference from the 1980s, though it is perhaps too early yet to speculate about the jurisdictional and knowledge asymmetries arising from the rapid creation of a global system for monitoring cross-border investment transactions (Mallard 2018; Zarate 2013).

12.3.3   Trade

Recent trends in international trade governance have impacted the regulation of private actors (how they are governed and by whom) and reshaped the role of governments and other public actors who have also themselves become to some extent subjects of governance. Two developments may be particularly worthy of note here, not least because rather than being simply opposed tendencies as often supposed, they appear to possess interesting complementarities: first, traditional instruments of interstate negotiation and interstate litigation continue to be central to trade governance; at the same time, governance by "expertise" has burgeoned, and states have delegated

regulatory authority in some areas to expert bodies including those composed of "experts" with close ties to the regulated entities. To add to the apparent paradoxes, these developments have taken place against the backdrop of increased state control over territory, at least "at the border" (Thomson and Krasner 1989).

A key difference between the GATT and WTO, which were both founded on a set of common, mutual, and more or less binding interstate commitments, lies the latter's judicialization of the multilateral trade regime (Shell 1995; Zangl 2008). By rendering violations of trade agreements more easily punishable, the WTO system aimed to render the international integration of markets beneficial to competitive producers and consumers independent of the political power of their countries (Bagwell and Staiger 2010). By assisting the weaker states vis-à-vis the powerful, judicialization might also act as something of a corrective to long-standing power imbalances, and enhance the stability and legitimacy of the trade regime.

Such optimism about the "rule of law" is, however, tempered by the recognition that formal-legal international institutions that seem to empower the weak might operate in the shadow of a possible resort to "informal governance" that favors the powerful (Héritier and Eckert 2008; Stone 2011). "Realist" observers of the politics of international economic relations have long held that international law was made by powerful states, and as such for their benefit (Drezner 2007; Krasner 1991). Early studies of the WTO dispute settlement mechanism, which found that it disproportionately benefitted rich and powerful countries (Bown 2004; Esserman and Howse 2003), indeed seemed to bear out this interpretation and suggest that the rules governing international commerce are no exception. One of the insights from the World Justice Project's multi-dimensional comparative analysis of the rule of law is that the broader institutional context of law and courts generates new and complex forms of inequality in the "access to justice" among otherwise very similar countries (Haggard and Tiede 2011). Even legal forms of redress at the international level require political will, money, and specialized expertise, so perhaps unsurprisingly, few developing countries were found to have used the dispute settlement mechanism during the WTO's first decade (Busch and Reinhardt 2003; Kim 2008; Shaffer 2003).

More recent research on the WTO dispute settlement mechanism suggests, however, that over time and with a modest amount of experience, many developing countries appear to be quite able to "learn" how to use the system to their advantage (Davis and Bermeo 2009). Though there is insufficient data at present to draw firm conclusions, a similar trend may be in evidence in regard to developing country experiences with bilateral and minilateral agreements on competition law and policy that have mushroomed in recent years (Waverman, Comanor, and Goto 1997; Petrie 2015). In particular, stronger dispute settlement provisions in many preferential trade agreements (PTAs) appear to have acted as a restraint on anti-competitive behavior or lessened indirect protectionist measures, brought more broadly symmetrical benefits to competitive producers and consumers in the partner countries, and thus institutionalized trade openness on more sustainable foundations (Abbott and Snidal 2009; Koremenos 2007). In short, despite the limited evidence, a shift of regulatory authority in the sphere of

12

trade to the transnational level through an international govern-ance mechanism offering an assured path to legal redress may yet hold out prospects for developing countries.

The trajectory of scholarship seems broadly similar with respect to the relationship between public and private actors where the latter play an enhanced role in trade governance: initial optimism about the progressive nature of transnational regulatory governance giving way to concerns about potentially severe downsides, followed by a more differentiated view that recognizes considerable variation in outcomes and a better understanding of conditional effects. Consider, for example, the practically and normatively important realm of tech-nical standard-setting where the key actors tend mostly to be private sector firms rather than governments. Even here, access to conducive "complementary" institutions (Büthe and Mattli 2011) seems to allow firms from small, poor, or less powerful countries to exercise substan-tial influence if they feel persuaded by the stakes to make suitable investments in learning-through-participation.

The rise of transnational private regulation is regarded at least in part as an attempt to overcome limitations of traditional national regu-latory regimes, especially when traditional international (Dashwood 1983; Raustiala 1997) and even newer trans-governmental forms of regulatory cooperation (Slaughter 2004: 36–64) were unavailable or ineffective. Transnational private regulation seemed under these conditions to be a means to overcome the incapacity of public (i.e. governmental) regulation to address negative externalities – and pos-sibly achieve broader regulatory policy objectives – in global markets. It promised to lead to less costly (but at least equally effective) regulations, give regulated firms a stake both in the content of the standards and regulations and their implementation, and reduce enforcement costs (Haufler 2001). It also seemed to offer opportun-ities for participation by non-commercial stakeholders who are often marginalized in domestic regulatory decision-making and generally excluded from direct participation in intergovernmental regulatory cooperation (Cashore, Auld, and Newsom 2004).

More recent research calls this optimistic view into question. Creating and maintaining truly self-regulatory (or genuinely democratic) and effective regulatory institutions at the transnational level is difficult. Even though private actors face a range of market and non-market incentives to comply with nominally voluntary standards (Büthe 2010c), careful analyses of their practices reveal barely nominal compliance with transnational private regulatory regimes, and little effective enforcement (Locke 2013). Often – some might argue inevit-ably – transnational private regulatory bodies appear to be dominated by commercial stakeholders, with few effective safeguards for the interests of other stakeholders, so that even under complete compli-ance private standards skew outcomes in favor of commercial actors (Mayer and Gereffi 2010). The rise of transnational economic regu-lation thus tends, in this view, to have long-lasting *political* distribu-tional implications, further empowering the private sector, especially the larger corporate actors, vis-à-vis other interests (Cafaggi and Pistor 2015).

For those who adopt a zero-sum view of power, this trend toward empowering private commercial actors has also, by necessity, meant

a loss of power for states or governments in the governance of trade and trade-related issues. Indeed, a prominent concern about the rise of transnational regulation is its undermining of the state as the only legitimate collective institution of a political community (Teubner 1996). The proliferation of transnational bodies where private actors make and enforce rules in trade-related governance moreover raises concerns about the disenfranchisement of citizens and consumers for whom participation in governance is now costlier and more diffi-cult, and brings few corresponding benefits. Beyond issues where civil society stakeholders are already well organized and/or have strong ex-ante preferences (e.g. human rights or environmental concerns), and unless private regulation is subject to strong public oversight, trans-national private regulation can lead commercial actors, particularly the larger ones, to gain a disproportionately strong voice in setting market standards.

Yet a zero-sum view may be too one-sided. As noted above, for many countries these ongoing changes in global trade governance have taken place in the context of longer-term processes of state forma-tion and technological change that have generally enhanced their governments' territorial control, both at and behind the border. Besides, the notion of "orchestration" (Abbott et al. 2015) may, if suitably adapted to the realm of transnational regulation, see states fostering transnational fora of governance (while retaining a certain level of control) as a potentially congenial way to supplement their own ability to regulate in areas where they can no longer afford or possess the necessary capability.

Domestic producers and states can be resourceful and successful in protecting their interests in yet another way. A possible recourse is to non-tariff barriers (NTBs) that are not (yet) prohibited by existing trade agreements. And indeed as tariffs have fallen, NTBs have proliferated (Baldwin 2000). Political-economic analyses of international trade pro-vide increasing support for Bhagwati's (1988) concern that there may be something like a "law of constant protection," according to which international agreements to open markets to more foreign competition result only in temporary increases in openness, followed by reversion to a comparable level of protection by other, often novel means. Research on the politics of trade shows that the use of new NTBs is particularly common in trading states, including democracies more likely to sign away their freedom to use recognized trade barriers and developing countries whose consumer-voters may embrace trade openness, where political institutions ensure a high level of responsiveness to the pri-vate sector (Ehrlich 2007; Kono 2006; Milner and Kubota 2005). Of course, calling on governments to protect them from increased for-eign competition is not the only possible response of domestic firms. As long as producers in a newly integrated international market are similarly competitive, openness creates both incentives and opportun-ities for private transnational protection (Büthe and Minhas 2015). The formation of price-fixing or market-sharing cartels or other collusive anti-competitive practices become, under these conditions, a "rational business strategy" (Connor and Lande 2012). The available evidence of the scale and geographic scope of international cartels suggests that firms are well aware of such opportunities, though given the ongoing global diffusion of competition law, transnational enforcement cooper-ation, and the spread of whistleblower protection, it is difficult to ascertain whether the detection of international cartels reveals an increase in anticompetitive behavior, or is the result of more effective enforcement (Connor 2015).

12.3.4   Labor

As noted above, the ILO partakes of a corporatist tripartite structure comprising representatives of governments, employers, and unions. It has no hard law instrument at its disposal, and has to rely on its power to persuade (Maupain 2013). Lacking hard law instruments, the ILO disposes of essentially two regulatory instruments, Conventions and Recommendations. Conventions are meant to be legislated into national laws by the states ratifying them. Recommendations, by contrast, are not obligatory. But they need no ratification and are intended to guide national and international policy, as well as adjudication processes at the national level.

Member states have to be persuaded to ratify Conventions. Once they do, the ILO, possessing no implementation capacities of its own, has perforce to rely on national capacities. The ILO, however, has a highly developed reporting system for national-level application of Conventions. Countries that have ratified a particular Convention are required to submit periodic reports on the measures they have taken to give effect to its provisions (Art. 22 of the ILO Constitution). Each country produces as many reports as it has ratified Conventions on the basis of which a Committee of Experts evaluates national laws with respect to the relevant Conventions and proceeds where necessary to nudge ratifying states to modify their domestic laws and practices. Even member states that have not ratified a particular Convention are under obligation to report on the matters it deals with, "showing the extent to which effect has been given, or is proposed to be given, to any of the provisions of the Convention … and stating the difficulties which prevent or delay" the ratification of the Convention (Art. 19.5(e)). This constitutional provision has provided the basis for a new reporting mechanism built around the Declaration of Fundamental Principles and Rights at Work adopted in 1998, on which more is said below. In addition, a semi-judicial body, the Committee on Freedom of Association, examines complaints about violations of freedom of association whether or not the country in question has ratified the relevant Conventions (i.e. Convention 87 of 1948 on Freedom of Association and Protection of the Right to Organize, and Convention 98 of 1949 on the Right to Organize and Collective Bargaining). Complaints can be lodged by each of the tripartite constituents, including from foreign countries, and by international associations of unions and employers. The committee's awards have been used to chastise anti-union policies followed by many countries, including Britain under Margaret Thatcher, the United States under Ronald Reagan, or in more recent years, countries such as Colombia.

A serious attempt to strengthen the ILO's regulatory "teeth" was made in the course of the 1990s debate on "social clauses" in trade agreements (Leary 1996). The effort here was to make core ILO Conventions a condition for market access, with violations offering just cause for retaliatory trade measures. Not surprisingly, to the Southern governments who vigorously opposed and managed to block the proposal, it smacked of an ill-disguised Western attempt at protectionism. In 1996 the WTO's Ministerial Conference in Singapore determined

that the WTO lacked the competence to deal with labor standards and reiterated the ILO's exclusive mandate in this domain (Singapore Declaration). This was not motivated by a resolve to strengthen the ILO, more by developing countries' desire to head off a stronger, even possibly a punitive regime governing international labor standards.

ILO Conventions cover very specific issues concerning conditions of work in various industries, such as health and safety, provisions for vocational training, wage-setting provisions, social security, and so on. Many are arguably obsolete. The standards prescribed in the Conventions are not rigid, nor are they spelt out with great precision. Some simply require national authorities to introduce a national policy on a particular issue, for example on child labor, others offer regulators different options to choose from. Conventions can also make room for consultations or negotiations with "social partners" (unions and employers) at the national level. The overall record of ratification of ILO Conventions nevertheless remains dismal. Between the early 1960s and the late 1980s the ILO passed on average two Conventions per year, but fewer than 13 countries had on average ratified them within five years. Ratifications as a rule came from countries whose laws are already in line with a Convention. Where that is not the case, the ILO has little choice than to rely on the political will and implementation capacity of member states.

In 1998 the ILO adopted a Declaration of Fundamental Principles and Rights at Work, whereby all member countries confirmed their commitment to freedom of association and collective bargaining, non-discrimination, and the abolition of child labor and forced labor. The Declaration also introduced an important distinction between "rights" and "principles." Principles are meant to be upheld by all states by virtue of their membership of the organization regardless of whether they have ratified the relevant Conventions. Principles indicate a goal and a direction, but leave member states free to implement them as they see fit. Rights, on the other hand, flow from the relevant Conventions and associated jurisprudence, and give rise to precise legal obligations.

Its defenders see the 1998 Declaration as a positive development that marks the transition from understanding standards as constraining the actor's self-interest to re-conceptualizing them as legal devices that help actors achieve a more enlightened notion of their own self-interest (Langille 2005). To its critics, the shift from rights to principles represents a debasement of ILO norms since member states are no longer required to abide by the obligations that the Conventions embodied (Alston 2004). Principles can also be fuzzy enough to allow countries like the United States, which has not ratified most ILO core Conventions and that has several problems of its own particularly with regard to freedom of association and collective bargaining, to claim the moral high ground vis-à-vis developing countries who may have a better record of ratifying and legislating ILO Conventions.

The ILO's reliance on state-based, territorially discrete actors and capacities hinders its ability to adapt to the restructuring of production through global supply chains. Even when developing country governments have the capacity to implement minimum labor standards, they might refrain from doing so for fear of damaging their competitiveness and losing export markets, investments, and employment.

The ILO's own approach towards transnational production chains has been hampered by conflicting priorities, with some officials continuing to emphasize the importance of labor treaties (i.e. Conventions and Recommendations), others more concerned with employment creation and sensitive to possible trade-offs between labor standards and jobs. Conflicts of this nature highlight the main challenge under which the ILO has always labored, but that has only grown deeper in recent decades, i.e. that its constituents hold divergent views as to what represents feasible and just outcomes. While the ILO continues to pride itself on its tripartite structure, employers tend to see the ILO in a largely symbolic role that leaves local actors free to adopt their own solutions. However they may express it, Southern governments are to be found more often than not siding with employers. Unions are more likely to argue for universal standards based on appeals to human rights while also being chary of Western paternalism (and protectionism). Governments remain for the most part less engaged in ILO proceedings than union and employer representatives. That said, Western governments tend to be more aggressive champions of labor standards in Southern countries than the latter's own governments (Baccaro and Mele 2012), or within their own countries.

In this backdrop, the regulation of labor standards has come to rely increasingly on private initiatives by multinational firms or industry consortia. Such interventions have often been reactive to fears of reputational damage following public scandals that broke out with increasing frequency from the early 1990s when NGOs began targeting global brands such as Nike for the abysmal conditions under which their products were made. Such targeted campaigns and broader attempts to sensitize consumers to conditions of employment in the poor countries where their labels are produced have forced global brands to introduce private monitoring systems in global supply chains. Corporate codes of conduct sometimes drew on the ILO's 1998 Declaration, firms also began employing monitors to undertake site visits to check their suppliers' compliance with national labor laws and their own codes. But the credibility of such monitoring remains an acknowledged problem. Several consortia have been created to ensure independent monitoring, with mixed results: for instance, Locke (2013) has analyzed internal monitoring by three large brands in footwear, apparel, and electronics to conclude that private monitoring is of limited effectiveness, with little improvement in outcomes over time. In particular, freedom of association (i.e. the right of workers to join unions of their own choosing) is rarely respected. The threat of sanctions against violators has been of limited deterrent value. In addition, private monitoring does not address the root causes of labor violations, especially abuse of overtime regulations or of the rights of contract workers. These violations are ultimately the result of the practices of the brands themselves, which typically impose tight deadlines and squeeze suppliers' margins as much as possible.

To a great extent, therefore, global labor regulation has come to rely on private monitoring systems where the relevant actors include global brands and buyers, local suppliers, industry consortia, and NGOs (Gereffi, Humphrey, and Sturgeon 2005; Locke 2013; Seidman 2007). The ILO's own limited monitoring of supply chains is an exception that confirms the rule. The first program in this area was the Better Factories Cambodia project (Ang et al. 2012; Oka 2015; Polaski 2006), which was launched in the early 2000s after the ILO was tasked by the US government to inspect and certify working conditions in Cambodia's apparel industry. Cambodia's access to the US market was made contingent on the results of these inspections. The Cambodia project acquired international renown and was continued even after the Multi-Fiber Agreement came to an end in 2005. For its part the Cambodian government decided to issue export licenses only to companies that passed ILO inspections. Although Better Factories was replicated in other countries such as Jordan, Lesotho, and Vietnam in collaboration with the International Finance Corporation (or IFC – the financial arm of the World Bank – these programs are known as ILO/IFC "Better Work" programs), it remains limited.

Private monitoring represents a different approach to regulation from that advocated by the ILO, with rather different notions of effectiveness, accountability, and justice. It also suffers from severe limitations. First, accountability in private codes is largely limited to commercial accountability: suppliers are required to abide by their principal's code of conduct and as part of their commercial and contractual liability. The notion of democratic accountability to workers, for example by promoting the formation of free trade unions, rarely if ever forms part of private governance systems. Second, effectiveness is operationalized as reduction in workplace violations. However, the use of standardized scorecards for plant evaluation has generated various attempts to "game" the system by suppliers and better scores do not necessarily translate into better performance (Locke 2013). Justice is also ultimately subordinated to the bottom-line: companies may genuinely be committed to being socially responsible; certainly they are willing to spend millions of dollars setting up and running internal inspection systems. However, profits and returns to shareholders remain the ultimate goal and may explain why, rather than drop suppliers, brands might opt to ride out any short-term impact of supplier controversies on their share prices.

12.3.5 Environment

Environment presents a diverse picture in regard both to its nature and scale. This impression is enhanced when one considers the varied instruments for regulating it, devised by a diverse cast of actors. Nation-states control territory and resources, particularly forests, waterways, and mineral resources and, whatever their motivation, are unavoidably in the position of making laws and regulations relating to their exploitation and use. Since the 1970s several international treaties, mainly devised through the UN system (notably the UN Environment Program, UNEP), set goals and standards for environmental protection that are ultimately expected to be enforced by nation-states. A list of illustrative if not landmark treaties here might include the 1973 Convention on International Trade in Endangered Species (CITES), the 1987 Montreal Protocol on chlorofluorocarbons (CFCs), the 1997 Kyoto Protocol and the 2015 Paris Agreement on climate change. Thanks to such treaties and conventions, the role and responsibilities of governments and public actors in environmental governance have greatly expanded in recent decades. Private actors are often here the main targets of regulation.

Rules and mechanisms for ensuring effectiveness, accountability, and efficiency differ profoundly from one treaty to the next. They vary between texts with unenforced or unenforceable promises (e.g. the Kyoto Protocol), to controlled arrangements like the Montreal Protocol (whose success has been attributed to the chemical industry's ability to develop alternatives to CFCs). Some Conventions are routinely violated (e.g. CITES or the Convention on International Trade in Wild Flora and Fauna), while other initiatives (e.g. the REDD+ initiative for Reducing Emissions from Deforestation and Degradation) may be diverted from their main objective – in this case carbon mitigation – to address goals such as economic and social development, which are ancillary to the initiative.

This expanding interstate dispensation for environmental protection has been accompanied by a growing reliance on scientific expertise on the environment. At the international level, environmental treaties are framed by interpretations and definitions of the "environment" produced within biophysical sciences, and based on abstract models that reduce, decompose, reconstitute, and measure the world in ways that make it amenable to governance (Hulme 2010, 2011).

Historically, scientists and states have often worked in collaboration to understand and govern nature (Drayton 2000; Dresner 2008; Dryzek 2013). In our own times, the International Panel on Climate Change (IPCC) marks an important intervention in its domain. Reflecting an enhanced level of cooperation between states and scientists, the IPCC has been able to put large resources behind building conceptual and computer models to capture complex interactions between diverse elements with a view to generating a better understanding of climate and climate change. Global Circulation Models (GCMs) were developed first in the 1980s to understand how emissions in one place might have an impact at other places, but the models were limited by data as well as in their capacity to address the challenge of scale. Technical and data constraints both meant that models could not aspire to fine-grained scales. Data for large parts of the South was either poor or simply unavailable. This was paradoxically a crucial reason why climate change became a "global" problem, i.e. it was not possible to model atmospheric circulation on smaller scales (Eriksen, Nightingale, and Eakin 2015; Mahony 2014). In turn, the inability of models to capture local dynamics mostly confined our understanding of climate change to a global level, with countries in the South being left to highlight major blind spots in GCM-based perspectives on climate change, demand regional downscaling, and insist on regionally focused interventions and adaptation measures (Beck et al. 2014; Mahony 2014).

A quite different set of instruments binding public actors has been designed at the regional level, through regional treaties or arrangements adopted more especially since the 1990s (Pestre 2008). These are particularly numerous in Europe, and have led in most cases to notable environmental improvements – acid rain, Baltic and North Sea agreements, agreements relating to the Rhine and the Danube come to mind here. Such "control and command" agreements are particularly effective when problems are not difficult to identify, large segments of the population are affected, and local action can provide solutions. Some of these questions – e.g. pollution, water quality, and so on – lie also at the boundary between health and environmental concerns. Fewer such instances may be cited in the South where attempts at regional cooperation have met with limited

success. The Transboundary Haze Agreement in Southeast Asia, for example, has been severely hampered by governments that are often suspected to be in collusion with large agri-businesses or logging interests, lacking clear or legitimate authority over diverse, dispersed, and often poor and oppressed small holders whose combined actions (e.g. burning small forest plots for cultivation) can produce sizeable environmental impacts (Tsing 2005). Where environmental problems originate in poverty, and states lack legitimacy, accountability, or effective authority, the immediate absence of options for people on the ground can present insurmountable difficulties even in the presence of shared norms and desire for environmental protection (Peet and Watts 2004).

Green audits and management rules are the key instruments for holding businesses accountable for the environment. Initiated in the 1980s, their use exploded in the 1990s. As already noted, large Western companies began taking environmental challenges in their stride to champion voluntary approaches, sometimes using the vocabulary of "contract," "internalizing" the environment as a firm-level management problem, and advancing their environmental credentials, including through developing niche markets and premium products via enhanced public interfaces (Bailis and Baka 2011; Perkins 2009). By the 2000s the portfolio of environmental instruments extended to green finance and the sustainable management of assets. Such initiatives for self-regulation were shadowed by a growing view, notably within the OECD and UNEP, that it would be more efficient to internalize environmental protection in the process of production, rather than at the end of the pipe. A major consideration here was the needs of trade, in particular a concern to avoid disrupting markets and businesses, with business associations (notably the ICC and WBCSD) emerging as fervent advocates of a business-friendly approach to environmental challenges on the eve of the 1992 Rio Summit.

An upshot of private, firm-level self-regulation was that concrete rules remain concentrated in the hands of managers and auditors – *le secret des affaires* – leaving relatively limited room for public disclosure and monitoring. Environmental considerations were incorporated into management processes for energy savings and recycling on the principle of "pollution prevention pays." In the aftermath of the introduction of ISO 14000 series in the 1990s many industrial agreements defining technical standards of products and processes were devised in cooperation between firms, states, and international organizations (notably the EU), with the World Bank and other multilateral organizations later accepting and rendering them "international" (Moretti and Pestre 2015). However, such voluntary industry-level engagements tend to be based on loose guidelines and monitoring processes restricted to audits by competing firms in contexts that may be rife with conflicts of interest. For example, in the chemical industry, where production tends to change rapidly on account of high rates of innovation and where diffusion of pollutants can be extensive, dispersed, or not easy to contain, regulation has remained weak and extremely sensitive to industrial lobbying. One may observe the same phenomenon in other fields like energy production, transport, paper pulp, or mechanical industries where the most common instruments are Best Available Technologies (BAT) based on available processes considered less harmful to the environment. Conflictual elements tend to be glossed by scientific and business experts defining and

12

standardizing vocabulary, meanings, assessment techniques, process comparisons, ranking methods, and so on.

BAT benchmarks have also made their way into Environmental Impact Assessments mandated as conditions for project loans from the World Bank and other multilateral institutions. BATs and environmental impact assessments based on them may be contestable, but they lie beyond the authority and technical expertise of social movements, local communities, or even national governments in poor countries to challenge. Voluntary engagements are also not real contracts – for instance they typically do not involve independent, even if business-led, regulation or arbitration. Hence there are few effective mechanisms to enforce agreed upon standards and targets.

Despite the limitations inherent to voluntary environmental governance mechanisms, many public bodies in association with business consortia have placed growing reliance on industry-administered labels, certification schemes, and public campaigns (e.g. industry environmental awards) to promote and publicize adherence to voluntary environment norms. Initiatives such as self-regulation by market actors and standard-setting practices that, as noted above, began to proliferate from the 1990s anticipate post-2000 innovations by major global companies in partnership with international NGOs such as the World Wildlife Fund (WWF), major Southern states, and in a few instances other locally based entities, to set environmental quality standards for many agricultural products. The "Round Tables" for palm oil and soya are among the better-known examples here (Bailis and Baka 2011; Fairhead, Leach, and Scoones 2012; Fortin 2013; Ponte 2013). Such quality standards may be considered a form of "soft law," but they are voluntary and the initiative for their design and enforcement rests with corporations rather than the states or local communities to whom such "Round Tables" may sometimes be a pre-emptive response.

Mechanisms of this nature share some kinship with environmental labeling. Though its origins lie in the labeling of bio or organic produce in the 1970s, environment labels really turned "green" in the 1990s alongside businesses embracing voluntary engagements, with the Forest Stewardship Council label for a sustainable management of forests (Klooster 2005) and the Marine Stewardship Council label leading the way among a host of others (Boström and Hallström 2010). Since then labeling has expanded into many sectors (including mining), with certifications varying in quality and amounting in some cases to a form of "greenwashing." As with many tools and instruments of this nature, it is impossible to talk about a "general form of accountability." Because rules of accountability are privately defined and quite varied, and because audits are closed black boxes and rarely open to counter-expertise, it is impossible to judge them against universal criteria or standards notwithstanding attempts, such as the so-called "gold standards," to rank them (Spencer 2010). Compliance with such codes may also be selective and opportunistic – for instance in many countries of the South, enterprises might comply with restrictive EU standards in order to gain access to EU markets but cut corners in producing for domestic markets. The ability of such mechanisms to target the supply end of environmental degradation is therefore open to doubt.

Another important trend in the regulation of corporate environmental conduct is the valuation of environments based on the services they provide (Carpenter et al. 2009) and the adverse results of corporate actions on non-corporate actors. The former has led to the growth of consultancy firms and rating bodies employing biologists and economists to "value" the "services" rendered by ecosystems for purposes of compensation schemes arising from large projects such as dams and airports. Methods of valuation can be opaque or even circular, with valuations and estimates of compensation sometimes based on assets, whether actually, prospectively, or even notionally, created by "rehabilitation projects" in unspecified locations or locations far from the developments in question, and that are available to be bought or benchmarked as compensation for destruction elsewhere. Ecosystem system valuations are also used in many Southern schemes to promote conservation goals, for example preserving upland forest ecosystems in order to protect water sources "downstream" (Dempsey and Robertson 2012).

As already observed, such methods and schemes raise significant epistemic and ethical questions. Social and environmental cost-benefit analysis, environmental cost estimates, their throughput into prices of goods and services such as power are all in greater or lesser degree premised on the assumption that the health or environmental consequences of particular products or manufacturing processes can be assessed in economic terms and rendered commensurable with other production costs. However one regards the inherent economic logic, three issues are worth flagging. First, the idea that health and environmental impacts can be reduced to economic costs is contentious. Second, economic valuation can often serve as one of several possible mechanisms through which victims of environmental impacts are inadequately "compensated." Third, as several behavioral studies show, financial penalties can be a weaker instrument for compliance than binding legal prohibitions and may hence offer less effective protections against delinquent behavior.

In addition to such concerns, the actual governance of environmental issues can also be far removed from the idealized world of social or environmental cost-benefit analysis. Not least, public authorities rarely have an adequate grasp of production processes and environmental systems, hence norms and policies end up being conceived jointly with the firms that are the targets of these policies (Bailis and Baka 2011). Moreover, strong lobbying by corporate interests has largely helped normalize the approach managers and management consultants have taken since the last three decades, i.e. promoting a large menu of options offering relatively open-ended choices, time frames, and modalities for disputes and deferrals. The success of the tobacco industry is worth recalling in this light, so too the pattern it set for effective climate change denial in the United States (Oreskes and Conway 2010). However, despite the absence of any evidence in their favor, there has been no letup in the determination of businesses and conservative ideologues who profess to take the environment seriously, to persist with voluntarist mechanisms in preference to binding legal frameworks for environmental regulation.

12.4 Implications and Assessments

What are the broader implications for social progress of recent trends in international economic, labor, and environmental governance?

As the preceding sections document, the shift from government to governance has been rather uneven across the five areas. Yet there seems sufficient ground to suggest that inter-governmental, trans-governmental, transnational, and non-governmental ordering and rule-making processes have combined to create the impression of a world of "governance without government" (Rosenau and Czempiel 1992). However, the actual experience of such processes, say in the form of relative empowerment and dis-empowerment, as well as the popular and "populist" responses to them, lie outside the scope of this chapter. Though some appear widespread, for example the recourse to "expertise"and the use of indicators and ratings (Davis et al. 2012; Pénet and Mallard 2014), the apparent shift from government to governance has been accomplished by distinct instruments in each area. This shift has paralleled the decline in the power of states, yet some of it has been an outcome of interstate treaties or inter-governmental agreements. Such paradoxes cannot also be resolved here. In this section, we draw on the survey of regulatory landscapes attempted above to assess, or enable the reader to assess, unfolding governance scenarios in the five areas, and their broader social and political implications.

12.4.1 Finance

The impact of financial openness and more broadly the financialization of contemporary capitalism on the key indicators of social progress are addressed in other chapters in this volume; so too, the meanings and goals of social progress and a "good life." What may be safely ventured from the perspective of governance is that for nearly four decades there has been a growing and unmistakable global shift of power in favor of finance and the services directly and indirectly associated with it. The shift may be more pronounced in some countries than others, in some it may not even be easily distinguishable or may only become visible when the gaze is shifted to overseas and off-shore entities. However, what seems indisputable is that financialization and its associated transformations have imposed severe constraints on the horizon of possibilities at least with respect to the strategies and instruments for achieving social progress. This is true for both the advanced nations as well as those of the South. While such constraints may bite most deeply for the populations and governments of nations with high levels of external debt or in various stages of a debt crisis, their effects are by no means limited to the latter.

By the free-wheeling standards of the 2000s, "casino capitalism" in the 1980s (when Susan Strange [1986] coined the expression), described a world of slot machines. However, the dice had already become heavily loaded against developing countries that looked to inflows of private capital to finance domestic investment. Besides, while the incentives and rewards for risk were high, private, and largely external, the systemic consequences of risk were costly, public, and domestic. Unable to ride out these risks or withstand their political consequences, the state in many developing countries had dissolved into chronic crisis by the 1990s (Fukuyama 2004). A sobering revelation during the recent financial crisis has been the limited capacity or willingness of states even in the advanced countries to pursue independent policies to rekindle growth and reduce unemployment (Aglietta and Brand 2013). Whether or not this represents a loss of sovereignty – here again

we would be well advised to take a differentiated view – it certainly represents a marked change from the time when states had considerably greater freedom to set and pursue their own welfare goals and objectives (Amadae 2003). The wider and longer-term social and political consequences of states' weakened capacities in this respect could yet emerge as a source of concern from the point of view of social progress.

Against this broader backdrop, power shifts in favor of large Western institutional creditors seem particularly worthy of note. The Greek crisis offers a good illustration, though, of course, the point is far more general. Aglietta and Brand (2013: 76) have remarked on the kinship between the early 1990s speculative attacks on the British pound, the Italian lira and the French franc, and the more recent relentless shorting of Greek and Italian debt. But one may observe a relatively new element, at least for the West, in the management of the recent (or current) financial crisis in southern Europe, i.e. that policy makers have felt under great pressure to coordinate their response with private actors including in order to lend credibility to their own actions, such as even, say, the austerity packages demanded by lenders and debt markets (Aglietta and Brand 2013: 79). Yet it is not all carrots: attempts at coordination are more likely to be effective in the presence of close central bank cooperation and expansion of central banks' "lender of last resort" responsibilities (a potential stick) to ward off speculative attacks and staunch a potentially perverse cycle of deleveraging, depreciation, liquidity crises, and seizure of inter-bank credit. The mix of carrots and sticks may thus bear watching to trace the course of financial (de)regulation and the social and political responses to it.

There is a case to be made that deregulation is not necessarily about reducing the role of the state even in the sphere of finance, but instead about redirecting it to particular purposes. This may be exemplified by trends in the governance of risk. In the wake of financial deregulation, larger actors embraced risk to power financial innovation and boost returns. It is far more likely, however, that for smaller, more vulnerable actors, whether workers or small entrepreneurs, risk was involuntary and came for the most part with the possibility of little sustained reward. Besides, while neoliberal governance models offloaded risk on to insurance or financial markets, states continued to provide the backstop when the latter failed, or in the event of a crisis. Consequently risk became a systemic feature whose distributional consequences were liable to be managed in ways that aggravated inequalities, including in respect of government support. Hence, while the financial crisis and its aftermath may suggest the return of governments, it has not yet, for all that, meant the end of neoliberal governance and its implications for social outcomes (Mirowski 2013).

12.4.2 Investment

The investment treaty system has also been a source of considerable concern in recent years and an object of ongoing reform. Concerns about the asymmetric nature of investment treaties have already been discussed. Among concerns relating to the functioning of existing treaties, an important one is the nature of their juridical process. For instance, when a foreign investor initiates an investor-state claim under an investment treaty, the dispute is typically heard by an ad hoc

12

arbitral tribunal instead of a national or international court (Van Harten 2016). Some commentators argue that arbitrators suffer from an actual or apparent bias in favor of foreign investors, particularly on jurisdictional questions, as only foreign investors can bring arbitral claims and thus create "repeat business" (Van Harten 2016). Investment treaty tribunals differ from international courts in important ways, as the arbitrators are selected ad hoc for a single case and the tribunal disbands after pronouncing on the respective claim. Lawyers working for major international firms have played an important role in helping to create and expand this investment treaty system that not coincidentally shifts power from state judicial institutions to private law firms (to the particular benefit of multinational law firms specializing in arbitration disputes), and that some argue reinforces a pro-investor bias in the system (Corporate Europe Observatory and the Transnational Institute 2012; Dezalay and Garth 1996). An associated concern is that many lawyers wear two hats, as counsel for one of the parties in some cases and arbitrators resolving claims in others. The investment treaty system is hence criticized for being rife with conflicts of interest where individuals' roles as arbitrators in one case may not be independent of their interest as counsel for one of the parties in other cases (Corporate Europe Observatory and the Transnational Institute 2012). Some recent investment treaty proposals, such as, for instance the TPP, EU proposals in TTIP negotiations (EU Proposal 2015), and more recently the EU and Canada's proposal to work toward a multilateral investment court, sought to resolve this conflict by requiring investment arbitrators not to take on work as counsel in other cases. However, for the most part, investment treaties do not have this provision. Consequently "double hatting" remains a common practice.

A larger concern relates to the use of private dispute resolution mechanisms to resolve issues of significant public concern (Van Harten 2016). International commercial arbitration usually involves private law disputes about contracts between two private parties or between a private party and a state acting in a private capacity. By contrast, investment treaty arbitrations involve claims by foreign investors against states often for acts undertaken in their public capacity. For example, Philip Morris challenged Uruguay's and Australia's decision to introduce regulations on the packaging of tobacco and Vattenfall challenged Germany's decision to phase out nuclear power. But it is important to distinguish between investors bringing claims and doing so successfully: it is worth noting that both Australia, and perhaps more significantly Uruguay, successfully defended themselves against Philip Morris' claims. But states can still be required to spend considerable amounts defending their regulatory measures. Australia is reported to have spent around $40 million in its defense against Philip Morris, and the award on costs remains pending. The average amount spent on legal fees in investor-state disputes is estimated to be $8 million (Corporate Europe Observatory and the Transnational Institute 2012). A successful state is likely to receive some of this money back in a costs award. But Uruguay still had to bear 30 percent of its legal fees; besides the lengthy period of uncertainty created by the case was arguably of benefit to Philip Morris and may have persuaded other states to defer or abandon similar regulations.

Investment treaties seem, however, to be in transition from being mainly protective of foreign investors to also protecting important state prerogatives. As to procedure, new proposals are on the table to address some of the present inadequacies, though no one proposal has yet gained significant momentum. Older-style investment treaties with strong investor protection and few express protections for state sovereignty (Alvarez 2010; Vandevelde 2009) were typically based on models developed by capital exporting states with little fear of being sued by foreign investors in their own countries. The North American Free Trade Agreement (NAFTA) was unusual because it included investment protections in a treaty between three states of which two were developed states. One result was that both Canada and the United States found themselves being sued by investors belonging to the other country. They hence decided to revise their model investment treaties to strike a better balance between investment protection and state sovereignty (Canadian Model BIT 2004; US Model BIT 2012). This marked a beginning for developed states to realize that they had interests as both capital exporters and capital importers, and an opening to incorporate clauses that sought to distinguish non-discriminatory regulatory actions to advance legitimate public welfare objectives such as public health, safety, and the environment, from acts of indirect expropriation.

In recent years more developed states have been named as respondents in investor-state claims. Many developing countries are also beginning to recognize their growing interests as capital exporters. Their nationals may sometimes elect to invest in politically unstable regions. The resulting convergence of interests between developed states and developing states is visible in a new generation of investment treaties that appear to be more balanced in their protection of investors' and states' interests (Alvarez 2010; Vandevelde 2009). More cognizant of the prerogatives of domestic law-making bodies such as legislatures, newer investment treaties seek to go beyond merely protecting foreign investors and foreign investment, and indeed beyond a narrow focus on economic goals, to reconcile them with broader social and environmental objectives (van Aaken 2014; van Aaken and Lehmann 2013; Bonnitcha 2014; Roberts 2015). Such treaties may prove to be of longer-term benefit to investors and states particularly if they can help to create a level playing field without a regulatory race to the bottom (van Aaken 2014; van Aaken and Lehmann 2013; Bonnitcha 2014; Roberts and Braddock 2016).

Newer investment treaties also attempt to address the concern that pleadings, hearings, and sometimes even awards are confidential in the private dispute resolution mechanism of most existing treaties. In response to NGO and civil society objection to this lack of transparency, some newer treaties allow interested third parties to intervene as amicus. More investment treaty awards are now being made public. However, the cases and documents are, with some exceptions such as NAFTA, still typically less public than in domestic courts or international tribunals. One potential reform that is gaining ground is the European Union's proposal to establish a permanent investment treaty court and an appellate body. This proposal would have the advantage of arbitrators being selected by the treaty parties, given security of tenure, and encouraged to act more independently than if they were reliant on ad hoc reappointment by the disputing parties. The prohibition on double hatting can be a further protection against conflicts of interest. An appellate mechanism may also permit greater consistency in interpreting claim resolutions. The EU has already agreed to Free Trade Agreements containing this procedural innovation with

Canada and Vietnam, but it remains to be seen whether this proposal gains broader traction, and how awkward legacies such as multiple investment courts and appellate bodies under different treaties could be resolved. There may hence be room for proposals such as the one currently being considered by UNCITRAL, to have a new convention establishing a multilateral court and/or appellate body that states could sign onto, and that would then apply to their existing investment treaties (Kaufmann-Kohler and Michele Potestà 2016).

12.4.3   Trade

The transformation of trade governance has occurred in the context of the differential capacity or willingness of national governments to regulate markets beyond the borders of their jurisdiction (Cutler, Haufler, and Porter 1999; Hall and Biersteker 2002), resulting in various forms of trans-governmental and transnational forms of governance of economic activity or production/value chains (Gereffi et al. 2005; Gourevitch 1999; Kahler and Lake 2003). Some changes have been largely driven by governments, for instance the delegation of regulatory authority to private bodies such as the ISO and IEC in the TBT-Agreement (Büthe and Mattli 2011) and to hybrid public–private bodies such as the Codex Alimentarius Commission for food safety standards (Büthe 2009). Other changes have been driven by civil society activists, even broad social movements, or initiated by firms or business associations to head off the development of more onerous standards and certification schemes by civil society groups, or to forestall other sources of regulatory uncertainty (Bartley 2003; Cafaggi 2011; Green 2014). Furthermore, the legitimacy of transnational and global governance has been challenged on both procedural and consequential grounds and from a variety of perspectives (Bernstein and Cashore 2007; Joerges 2004; Keohane 2003; Zürn 2004).

To some extent such concerns might be alleviated by recognizing that trans-governmental and transnational governance may strengthen rather than undermine the ability of states to govern trade-related issues, even if somewhat indirectly. To the extent that new forms of governance help governments overcome limitations in nation-state-based regulatory capabilities in global markets, we may conclude – at least as long as the activities and the impact of trans-governmental networks and transnational private actors continue to be conditioned by public institutions at the domestic level (Risse-Kappen 1995) – that the new forms of governance may complement and augment, rather than simply undermine, traditional public authority (Abbott et al. 2015; Büthe 2010b). Concerns about the marginalization of various societal interests (Kaiser 1969) may also be open to redress through administrative law procedures at the inter- and transnational level (Kingsbury, Krisch, and Stewart 2005) even if the substantive effectiveness of such safeguards would still depend on the ability of marginalized interests to make use of them (Mattli and Büthe 2005).

The shift in the regulatory authority traditionally associated with the modern state "upward, downward, and sideways" (Hooghe and Marks 2003: 233) and the consequent reduction in the state's centrality as the site of political contestation over priorities, trade-offs, and the

distribution of costs and benefits, poses a stiffer challenge. It is hardly possible to overestimate the significance of such contestations for the formation of political communities and representative institutions at the national level (e.g. Boix 2015; Caporaso 1996; Skocpol 1992). Since many countries in the South remain far from consolidated as political communities and even a number of Western countries face centrifugal political demands (Jolly 2015), the declining importance and influence of states, let alone their failure, may have profound political and social consequences.

What this means for social progress is not at all obvious except in perhaps superficial ways, for example for those living in a country with a repressive or kleptocratic ruler (Levi 1988). By contrast for those who live in liberal-democratic societies, "social progress" may be best assured by international regimes that retain a central position for their governments – or assure the full range of stakeholders' voice and influence in regulatory governance at the inter- or transnational level. In such cases the balance between power and public welfare would remain subject to active negotiation by stakeholders holding fluid structural positions in the traditional sense, yet subscribing to common principles and procedures for rule-making and account-ability norms, and sensitive to the marginalization of some potential stakeholders, the differential ability of others to take advantage of them, and the dynamic consequences of regulation in any form (Büthe 2010c).

12.4.4   Labor

It is difficult to assess the impact of regulation in the field of labor as far as "social progress" is concerned. Hard measures such as trends in real wages, share of wages to GDP, or wage and income inequalities do not suggest that attempts at regulating employment and working conditions have met with much success. In the last two to three decades real wage growth has lagged productivity growth in most countries, leading to income distribution being skewed in favor of profits at the expense of wages, particularly for unskilled labor (ILO 2009; OECD 2008). The causes of this phenomenon may be debated. Some point to the relative decline in the price of capital goods (Karabarbounis and Neiman 2014), others to the decline in unionization and the diminished bargaining power of workers and unions, and a generalized widening in income inequalities (Avdagic and Baccaro 2014; ILO 2008, 2015; Stockhammer 2013). Debates over causality are complex enough without invoking shortcomings in global labor governance. Few would disagree, however, that labor regulation has been unable to counter these trends. This is consistent with the findings of empirical studies of private monitoring that it has little impact on improving even firm-level outcomes (Locke 2013).

The ILO's declining ability to secure ratification and application of its Conventions by member states (Baccaro and Mele 2012; Maupain 2013; Standing 2008) does not also augur well for global labor regulation. The ILO aims to prevent a race to the bottom by promoting the adoption of minimum labor standards by both developed and developing countries, but lacking the necessary wherewithal, whether carrots or sticks, can only rely on its own powers of persuasion. Some countries, notably

China and India, suspect developed country protectionism behind ILO efforts to promote international labor standards. Second, the employer constituency within the ILO has felt more emboldened to block the organization's attempts to increase regulatory effectiveness (Baccaro 2015). The ILO has, however, scored some symbolic successes, notably the widespread acknowledgment, including in major international policy documents, of its goal of "decent work."

The last three decades have seen the failure of the model of private governance of labor, centering on the initiatives of multinational companies. As already noted, major global supply chains responded to NGO and consumer mobilizations in the West by establishing supplier norms and private monitoring mechanisms. Yet such efforts may be deceptive when the main causes of non-compliance stem from the commercial practices of the brands themselves, i.e. tight deadlines, meager margins, and in many instances a preference for captive suppliers whose margins and deadlines can be squeezed more than would be possible with suppliers having a diversified clientele. In addition, freedom of association and collective bargaining plays a very limited role in corporate codes of conduct, which can seem inspired by a "unitarist" view of the employment relationship wherein labor and capital face no conflict of interest (Kaufman 2004) and problems calling for regulatory solutions are best left to the benevolence of firms and managers. In contrast, recent empirical research suggests that international labor standards may work best when private initiatives are accompanied by a strengthening of state capacities (Locke 2013).

While the path remains rocky for attempts to regulate labor standards globally, the future is not without opportunity. At the political and policy level much could depend on how the growing evidence of a link between inequalities, over-saving, and slowing growth is translated into actionable policies for improving labor standards (Baccaro and Pontusson 2016; Summers 2014) as a means to reversing the slowdown and restoring growth. Second, international coordination is essential to this process, which has also the potential to make improvements in labor standards a positive sum game. Embedding globalization in an architecture of protective institutions, including to assure a minimum set of labor standards, may therefore well be seen to necessitate inventing an institution such as the ILO were one not already in existence.

12.4.5 Environment

Recent changes in environmental governance have significant implications for social progress, even if the overall results present a mixed picture. First, there has been a marked push towards certification, labeling, and auditing as mechanisms of regulation, opening up environmental governance to a wider array of actors and decentralized mechanisms of accountability. These new actors and mechanisms both bring regulation "closer to the ground" and serve to dispense information about, and authority to govern, environments. Second, there has been a move from national-level sectoral environmental policies that were common until the 1990s in areas such as forestry, water, grazing, and agriculture, towards sub-national level regulation of ecosystems viewed as "watersheds," "corridors," and similar frames intended to better capture the interconnected nature of environmental processes (Purdon 2003). Though it has led to conflicts between different forms

of expertise and priorities for governance, ecosystem management has been important in reshaping the inter-connected and multi-level logic of regulation by forcing foresters, water experts, wildlife biologists, and so on to cooperate to devise integrated management plans for designated territories. Third, the impact of popular mobilization has brought environmental concerns into the mainstream. Now most nation-states and many private actors seek at least to cast a veneer of "environmental friendliness" over their policies and practices.

These three general trends have resulted in both a tendency to carry on "business as usual" with some industries and governments continuing to treat evidence of their adverse environmental impact with skepticism, as well as attempts at instituting environmental safeguards before major problems are revealed. Their effects also appear to be uneven, notably in industries such as chemicals or mining with a marked bias against environmental regulation and a tendency to evade them whenever possible. Lessons have no doubt been learnt from past mistakes – some major oil companies, for example, now prefer registering their tankers in countries like Denmark with strong industrial and environmental regulations to risking costly and damaging oil spills by vessels registered in countries with more lenient norms (Dryzek 2013). It is sobering at the same time that many practices still elude radical change (carbon emissions being a notable example).

Taken as a whole, environmental policies also illuminate the debate over the relative merits of statutory versus disciplinary regulation. The costs of cleaning up polluted environments, for example through the US Environmental Protection Agency's Super Fund sites, has helped push a variety of state and non-state actors to take environmental impact into account at the beginning of projects rather after the fact. However, culpable evidence of environmental damage can be hard to come by at the best of times. Particularly for some kinds of environmental damages such as loss of biodiversity or atmospheric contamination, it can be difficult if not impossible to link individual firms or industries to observed impacts. This can have an eventual bearing on the effectiveness of environmental laws (Ellerman 2003; Goulder and Parry 2008).

Last but not least, the extension of transboundary cooperation in environmental governance can come at the expense of effectiveness or binding enforcement (Bulkeley 2005). Today the impetus for integrated management has grown, not least because of the specter of climate change (McLaughlin 2011). But as noted above, the modeling approach to such integration can expose epistemological tensions between interdisciplinary data, as well as other limitations. In climate domains, modeling continues to be hampered by the underlying Global Circulation Model platform: as noted above, regional models have proven nearly impossible to "downscale" and if modelers start over and build regional models, they cannot be easily integrated with existing GCMs. These epistemic issues translate into governance contestations on the ground as transboundary challenges encompass governmental and private actor cooperation, but also into national and disciplinary differences in environmental knowledge and sensibilities. Such challenges can supersede ecological goals (Mahony 2014): for instance, scientists invested in research framed in terms of "planetary boundaries" (Steffen et al. 2015) may be more likely to advocate supra-national governance bodies based on abstract anthropocentric conceptions that disregard the social and political dimensions of the environment.

12.5   Conclusion

Scale is a notable feature of projects for governing the world today, and "global" their seemingly natural aspiration. "Global" can claim a long genealogy for projects to make sense of the world if not necessarily to order it (Subrahmanyam 2005). But "global" and "governance" reflect scalar and other shifts in meaning with implications especially for how lives and societies are organized and governed. The world of empires obviously has different implications for how we are governed from that of nation-states, likewise a world where nation-states may be ceding authority to other institutions. What is governed and how that object is specified are affected by, and affect, visions of scale as well as the spaces and nature of authority. Who governs and how has a mutual bearing on knowledge, norms, and subjectivities, and both together for the loci and relationships of power. None of this is new or original, yet it is useful in conclusion to remind ourselves that the expanded usage of "governance" as a generalized description of all forms of rule coincides with a period of rapid shifts in the nature and distribution of sovereign authority and power. "Global" and "governance" may therefore describe, as well as constitute and naturalize, such shifts.

This chapter has surveyed governance in five areas, in an effort to add more shades to our understanding of contemporary government and governance. It is diagnostic rather than overtly prescriptive even in the individual areas, where the turn from government to governance reveals important similarities and differences. These relate both to the nature of the turn and the main actors (Section 12.2) as well as the modes of authority and regulation (Section 12.3). The resulting diversities underline that governance cannot avoid being work that, after a fashion, may be said to be in progress: what is governed, how it is framed, who governs and how – these are subjects of ongoing political contestation with a range of possible outcomes. Equally, while shifts in the actors, instruments, and mechanisms of governance have only partially transformed the role of nation-states, the resulting social impact depends on the accountability of governments as well as their ability to regulate and hold institutions of governance to account.

The contested and fluid nature of governance rules out easy operational "fixes." Government, governance, and any combinations thereof involve and reflect trade-offs between *accountability*, *equity/ justice*, and *efficiency*, among other considerations. Such choices are fundamentally political rather than technical.

Expert knowledge is indispensable for government/governance; however, as is commonplace, the former is fragmentary and limited, and the interventions it fosters in one context can undo or set back progress in others. The state's "ways of seeing" have been justly criticized (Scott 1998). Governance can also seem a "utopian project" and governance mechanisms have been argued too often to suffer from a "democratic deficit" (Follesdal and Hix 2006). To what extent they do depends partly on counterfactual assumptions. Yet some governance institutions – e.g. central banks – are designed to be independent of governments if not unaccountable to representative institutions. Not coincidentally independence emerged as the "Ark of the Covenant of central banking" alongside the post-First World War expansion of popular franchise. Monetary policy consequently became the first domain for which "experts" claimed monopoly, as well as immunity from democratic politics (Balachandran

2013). Likewise the revival of central bank independence in the 1990s coincided with burgeoning faith in the regulation of financial markets and services by "experts" often belonging to the industry or inhabiting its intellectual silos and echo chambers (Balachandran 1998).

The implications of knowledge – i.e. its sources, nature, etc. – for governance and its relationship with government are visible across the five areas surveyed here. Governance seems more natural, and more amenable or vulnerable to being scaled up where the regulatory expertise is backed or entrenched by powerful interests (e.g. finance, trade, investment). Here the role of governments seems to be mainly to facilitate governance, help societies adapt, and should an opportunity arise, strive to reform governance mechanisms. Governance would seem more elusive or scale-bound where countervailing knowledges prevail, or hegemonic claims to knowledge and expertise may be unable to subdue local diversity. Where entrenched knowledge has been displaced and the intellectual and political capital for revising or restoring it seems wanting (for example in labor as a domain), the resulting impasse may lead to a domain's relegation or reconfiguration (Lordon 2010). The nature of authorized knowledge seems also to have a bearing on the scale of governance/government – the more credible or effective its claim to universal relevance and application, the more it might be available to be mobilized for enlarging the space of governance or escalating its level.

Governments function more often than not in the same knowledge echo chambers as experts and may be as susceptible to "silo thinking." Yet their greater public accountability offers a better possibility of self-correction. Democratic and responsive political leaderships are also, generally speaking, better able to dispose of knowledge in more integrative ways or act with greater sensitivity towards the interactive effects of their interventions on social progress.

Sustaining shared conceptions of the social good and expanding programmatic possibilities for social progress both demand broadening deliberative processes (De Tocqueville 1835). The latter are too often limited to "stakeholders" – a gatekeeping term that can privilege some participants (e.g. organized private actors such as businesses and their representative organization), exclude others, or configure them into institutions such as NGOs more able to sidestep concerns of representativeness and accountability (Elyachar 2005). While there is surely a place for such consultations, the latter cannot substitute for social progress agendas and their diagnoses and prognoses being subjected to public debate and scrutiny, and their legitimacy established through democratic mandate. In the long run, democratic politics sensitive to scale and supported by the broadest possible deliberative processes can alone ensure that modes of government/governance reflect concerns for accountability, equity/justice, and symmetrical trade-offs with efficiency, and that they possess sufficient legitimacy to unite diverse actors around a shared platform for social progress.

References

Aaronson, S.A. 2014. "A Match Made in Heaven? The Wedding of Trade and Human Rights," in L.L. Martin, *Oxford Handbook of the Politics of International Trade*, New York: Oxford University Press.

Abbott, K.W., and D. Snidal. 2000. "Hard and Soft Law in International Governance." *International Organization* 54/3: 421–456.

Abbott, K.W., and D. Snidal. 2009. "The Governance Triangle: Regulatory Standards Institutions and the Shadow of the State," in W. Mattli and N. Woods (eds.), *The Politics of Global Regulation*. Princeton, NJ: Princeton University Press.

Abbott, K.W., P. Genshel, and D. Snidal (eds.). 2015. *International Organizations as Orchestrators*. Cambridge: Cambridge University Press.

Abdelal, R. 2010. *Capital Rules: The Construction of Global Finance*. Cambridge, MA: Harvard University Press.

Adams, C., D.J. Mathieson, and G. Schinasi. 1999. *International Capital Markets: Development, Prospects and Key Policy Issues*. Washington, DC: International Monetary Fund.

Aglietta, M., and Th. Brand. 2013. *Un New Deal pour l'Europe*. Paris: Odile Jacob.

Akerlof, G.A. 1970. "The Market for Lemons: Quality Uncertainty and the Market Mechanism." *Quarterly Journal of Economics* 84/3: 488–500.

Allee, T., and M. Elsig. 2015. "Dispute Settlement Provisions in PTAs: New Data and New Concepts," in A. Dür and M. Elsig (eds.), *Trade Cooperation: The Purpose, Design and Effects of Preferential Trade Agreements*. Cambridge: Cambridge University Press.

Alston, Ph. 2004. "'Core Labour Standards' and the Transformation of the International Labour Rights Regime." *European Journal of International Law* 15/3: 457–521. doi: 10.1093/ejil/15.3.457.

Alvarez, J.E. 2010. "The Once and Future Foreign Investment Regime," in M. Arsanjani, J.K. Cogan, R.D. Sloane, and S. Wiessner (eds.), *Looking to the Future: Essays on International Law in Honor of Michael Reisman*. Amsterdam: Brill/Niijohff.

Amadae, S.M. 2003. *Rationalizing Capitalist Democracy: The Cold War Origins of Rational Choice Liberalism*. Chicago, IL: University of Chicago Press.

Ang, D., D. Brown, R. Dehejia, and R. Robertson. 2012. "Public Disclosure, Reputation Sensitivity, and Labor Law Compliance: Evidence from Better Factories Cambodia." *Review of Development Economics* 16/4: 594–607. doi: 10.1111/rode.12006.

Ansell, C., and D. Vogel (eds.). 2006. *What's the Beef? The Contested Governance of European Food Safety*. Cambridge, MA: MIT Press.

Arrowsmith, S., and R.D. Anderson (eds.). 2011. *The WTO Regime on Government Procurement: Challenge and Reform*. Cambridge: Cambridge University Press.

Auld, G. 2014. *Constructing Private Governance: The Rise and Evolution of Forest, Coffee, and Fisheries Certification*. New Haven, CT: Yale University Press.

Avdagic, S., and L. Baccaro. 2014. "The Future of Employment Relations in Advanced Capitalism: Inexorable Decline?" in A. Wilkinson, G. Wood, and R. Deeg (eds.), *The Oxford Handbook of Employment Relations: Comparative Employment*. Oxford: Oxford University Press.

Avery, N., M. Drake, and T. Lang. 1993. *Cracking the Codex: An Analysis of Who Sets World Food Standards*. London: National Food Alliance.

Babb, S.L., and B.G. Carruthers. 2008. "Conditionality: Forms, Function, and History." *Annual Review of Law and Social Science* 4:13–29.

Baccaro, L. 2014. "Similar Structures, Different Outcomes: Corporatism's Surprising Resilience and Transformation." *Review of Keynesian Economics* 2/2: 207–233.

Baccaro, L. 2015. "Orchestration for the 'Social Partners' Only: Internal Constraints on the Ilo," in K.W. Abbott, P. Genschel, D. Snidal, and B. Zangl (eds.), *International Organizations as Orchestrators*. New York: Cambridge University Press.

Baccaro, L., and V. Mele. 2012. "Pathology of Path-Dependency? The Ilo and the Challenge of 'New Governance.'" *Industrial & Labor Relations Review* 65/2: 195–224.

Baccaro, L., and J. Pontusson. 2016. "Rethinking Comparative Political Economy: The Growth Model Perspective." *Politics & Society* 44/2: 175–207. doi: 10.1177/0032329216638053.

Bäckstrand, K. 2003. "Civic Science for Sustainability: Reframing the Role of Experts, Policy-Makers and Citizens in Environmental Governance." *Global Environmental Politics* 3/4: 24–41.

Bagwell, K., and R.W. Staiger. 2010. "The World Trade Organization: Theory and Practice." *Annual Review of Economics* 2: 223–256.

Bailis, R., and J. Baka. 2011. "Constructing Sustainable Biofuels: Governance of the Emerging Biofuel Economy." *Annals of the Association of American Geographers* 101/4: 827–838. doi:10.1080/00045608.2011.568867

Bakker, K. 2007. "The 'Commons' Versus the 'Commodity': Alter-globalization, Anti-Privatization and the Human Right to Water in the Global South." *Antipode* 39/3: 430–455. doi:10.1111/j.1467-8330.2007.00534.

Balachandran, G. 1998. *The Reserve Bank of India, 1951–67*. Delhi and Oxford: Oxford University Press.

Balachandran, G. 2013. *John Bullion's Empire: Britain's Gold Problems and India between the Wars*. London: Routledge.

Baldwin, R.E. 2000. "Regulatory Protectionism, Developing Nations, and a Two-Tier World Trade System." *Brookings Trade Forum* 3: 237–280.

Balleisen, E.J. 2014. "Right of Way, Red Flags, and Safety Valves: Business Self-Regulation and State-Building in the United States, 1850–1940," in P. Collin et al. (eds.), *Regulierte Selbstregulierung in der westlichen Welt des späten 19. und frühen 20. Jahrhunderts*. Frankfurt am Main: Vittorio Klostermann.

Barkin, J.S. 2014. "Trade and Environment," in L.L. Martin (ed.), *Oxford Handbook of the Politics of International Trade*. New York: Oxford University Press.

Bartley, T. 2003. "Certifying Forests and Factories: States, Social Movements, and the Rise of Private Regulation in the Apparel and Forest Products Field." *Politics & Society* 31/3: 433–464.

Beck, S. 2012. "Between Tribalism and Trust: The IPCC Under the 'Public Microscope.'" *Nature and Culture* 7/2: 151–173.

Beck, S., M. Borie, J. Chilvers, A. Esguerra, K. Heubach, M. Hulme, R. Lidskog, E. Lövbrand, E. Marquard, and C. Miller. 2014. "Towards a Reflexive Turn in the Governance of Global Environmental Expertise: The Cases of the IPCC and the IPBES." *GAIA-Ecological Perspectives for Science and Society* 23/2: 80–87.

Bennet, M., and P. James (eds.). 1998. *The Green Bottom Line: Environmental Accounting for Management. Current Practice and Trends*. London: Routledge.

Berger, S. (ed.). 1981. *Organizing Interests in Western Europe*. New York: Cambridge University Press.

Bernstein, S., and B. Cashore. 2007. "Can Non-State Global Governance Be Legitimate? An Analytical Framework." *Regulation and Governance* 1/4: 341–371.

Best, J. 2005. *The Limits of Transparency: Ambiguity and the History of International Finance*. Ithaca, NY: Cornell University Press.

Best, J. 2014. *Governing Failure: Provisional Expertise and the Transformation of Global Development Finance*. Cambridge: Cambridge University Press.

Bhagwati, J. 1988. *Protectionism*. Cambridge, MA: MIT Press.

Biersteker, T. 2009. "Targeted Sanctions and Individual Human Rights." *International Journal* 65/1: 99–117.

Blainpain, R. 2007. *Comparative Labour Law and Industrial Relations in Industrialized Market Economies*. Alphen aan den Rijn: Kluwer.

Blyth, M. 2002. *Great Transformations: Economic Ideas and Institutional Change in the Twentieth Century*. Cambridge: Cambridge University Press.

Blyth, M. 2010. "Coping with the Black Swan: The Unsettling World of Nassim Taleb." *Critical Review: A Journal of Politics and Society* 21/4: 447–465.

Boeri, T. 2011. "Institutional Reforms and Dualism in European Labor Markets," in D. Card and O. Ashenfelter (eds.), *Handbook of Labor Economics*, Volume 4, Part B. Amsterdam: Elsevier.

Boix, C. 2015. *Political Order and Inequality: Their Foundations and Their Consequences for Human Welfare*. Cambridge/New York: Cambridge University Press.

Bonnitcha, J. 2014. *Substantive Protection under Investment Treaties: A Legal and Economic Analysis*. Cambridge: Cambridge University Press.

Boström, M., and K.T. Hallström. 2010. "NGO Power in Global Social and Environmental Standard-Setting." *Global Environmental Politics* 10/4: 36–59.

Bourdieu, P. 1987. "The Force of Law: Toward a Sociology of the Juridical Field." *Hastings Law Journal* 38: 9–14.

Bown, C.P. 2004. "Developing Countries as Plaintiffs and Defendants in GATT/WTO Trade Disputes." *The World Economy* 27/1: 59–80.

Boyer, R. 1996. "State and Market: A New Engagement for the Twenty-First Century?" in R. Boyer and D. Drache (eds.), *States Against Markets: The Limits of Globalization*. Abingdon: Routledge.

Bradford, A., and T. Büthe. 2015. "Competition Policy and Free Trade: Antitrust Provisions in PTAs," in A. Dür and M. Elsig (eds.), *Trade Cooperation: The Purpose, Design and Effects of Preferential Trade Agreements*. Cambridge: Cambridge University Press.

Braithwaite, J., and P. Drahos. 2000. *Global Business Regulation*. Cambridge: Cambridge University Press.

Bulkeley, H. 2005. "Reconfiguring Environmental Governance: Towards a Politics of Scales and Networks." *Political Geography* 24/8: 875–902.

Bulkeley, H. 2015. *Accomplishing Climate Governance*. Cambridge: Cambridge University Press.

Busch, M.L., and E.R. Reinhardt. 2003. "Developing Countries and GATT/WTO Dispute Settlement." *Journal of World Trade* 37/4: 719–735.

Büthe, T. 2008. "The Globalization of Health and Safety Standards: Delegation of Regulatory Authority in the SPS-Agreement of 1994 Agreement Establishing the World Trade Organization." *Law and Contemporary Problems* 71/1: 219–255.

Büthe, T. 2009. "The Politics of Food Safety in the Age of Global Trade: The Codex Alimentarius Commission in the SPS-Agreement of the WTO," in C. Coglianese, A. Finkel, and D. Zaring (eds.), *Import Safety: Regulatory Governance in the Global Economy*. Philadelphia, PA: University of Pennsylvania Press.

Büthe, T. 2010a. "Engineering Uncontestedness? The Origins and Institutional Development of the International Electrotechnical Commission (IEC)." *Business and Politics* 12/3: 1–62.

Büthe, T. 2010b. "Global Private Politics: A Research Agenda." *Business and Politics* 12/3: 1–24.

Büthe, T. 2010c. "Private Regulation in the Global Economy: A (P)Review." *Business and Politics* 12/3: 1–38.

Büthe, T. 2014. "The Politics of Market Competition: Trade and Antitrust in a Global Economy," in L.L. Martin (ed.), *Oxford Handbook of the Politics of International Trade*. New York: Oxford University Press.

Büthe, T., and N. Harris. 2011. "The Codex Alimentarius Commission: A Hybrid Public-Private Regulator," in T. Hale and D. Held (eds.), *Handbook of Transnational Governance: Institutions and Innovations*. Oxford: Polity Press.

Büthe, T., and W. Mattli. 2011. *The New Global Rulers: The Privatization of Regulation in the World Economy*. Princeton, NJ: Princeton University Press.

Büthe, T., and H.V. Milner. 2008. "The Politics of Foreign Direct Investment into Developing Countries: Increasing FDI through International Trade Agreements?" *American Journal of Political Science* 52/4: 741–762.

Büthe, T., and S. Minhas. 2015. "The Global Diffusion of Competition Laws: A Spatial Analysis." Paper presented at the 6th Meeting of the UNCTAD Research Partnership Platform in the context of the 7th United Nations Conference to Review the Set of Multilaterally Agreed Equitable Principles and Rules for the Control of Restrictive Business Practices (Competition Policy), Geneva, July 10.

Cadbury, A. 1992. *The Financial Aspects of Corporate Governance (Cadbury Report)*. London: The Committee on the Financial Aspect of Corporate Governance (The Cadbury Committee) and Gee & Co.

Cafaggi, F., and K. Pistor. 2015. "Regulatory Capabilities: A Normative Framework for Assessing the Distributional Effects of Regulation." *Regulation and Governance* 9/2: 95–107.

Cafaggi, F. 2011. "New Foundations of Transnational Private Regulation." *Journal of Law and Society* 38/1: 20–49.

Canada Model Agreement for the Promotion and Protection of Investments [Canadian Model BIT]. 2004. Annex B. http://italaw.com/documents/Canadian2004-FIPA-model-en.pdf.

Caporaso, J.A. 1996. "The European Union and Forms of State: Westphalian, Regulatory or Post-Modern." *Journal of Common Market Studies* 34/1: 29–52.

Carpenter, S.R., H.A. Mooney, J. Agard, D. Capistrano, R.S. DeFries, S. Diaz, and H.M. Pereira. 2009. "Science for Managing Ecosystem Services: Beyond the Millennium Ecosystem Assessment." *Proceedings of the National Academy of Sciences* 106/5: 1305–1312.

Carruthers, B. 2016. "Credit Ratings and Global Economic Governance: Non-Price Valuation in Financial Markets," in G. Mallard and J. Sgard (eds.), *Contractual Knowledge: One Hundred Years of Legal Experimentation in Global Markets*. New York: Cambridge University Press.

Cashore, B. 2002. "Legitimacy and the Privatization of Environmental Governance: How Non-State Market-Driven (NSMD) Governance Systems Gain Rule-Making Authority." *Governance* 15/4: 503–529.

Cashore, B., G. Auld, and D. Newsom. 2004. *Governing Through Markets: Forest Certification and the Emergence of Non-State Authority*. New Haven, CT: Yale University Press.

Cerny, P.G. 1990. *The Changing Architecture of Politics: Structure, Agency, and the Future of the State*. London: Sage.

Cerny, P.G. 1994. "The Dynamics of Financial Globalization: Technology, Market Structure, and Policy Response." *Policy Sciences* 27/4: 319–342.

Charnovitz, S. 2007. "Trade and the Environment in the WTO." *Journal of International Economic Law* 10. GWU Legal Studies Research Paper No. 338; GWU Law School Public Law Research Paper No. 338. https://ssrn.com/abstract=1007028.

Cheit, R.E. 1990. *Setting Safety Standards: Regulation in the Public and Private Sectors*. Berkeley, CA: University of California Press.

Connor, J.M. 2015. "The Rise of ROW Anti-Cartel Enforcement." *Competition Policy International* (September 16).

Connor, J.M., and R.H. Lande. 2012. "Cartels as Rational Business Strategy: New Data Demonstrates the Crime Pays." Manuscript, American Antitrust Institute, March.

Cooley, A., and H. Spruyt. 2010. *Contracting States: Sovereign Transfers in International Relations*. Princeton, NJ: Princeton University Press.

Copelovitch, M.S., and J.C.W. Pevehouse. 2014. "Bridging the Silos: Trade and Exchange Rates in International Political Economy," in L.L. Martin (ed.), *Oxford Handbook of the Politics of International Trade*. New York: Oxford University Press.

Corbera, E., N. Kosoy, and M. Martínez Tuna. 2007. "Equity Implications of Marketing Ecosystem Services in Protected Areas and Rural Communities: Case Studies from Meso-America." *Global Environmental Change* 17/3–4: 365–380.

Corporate Europe Observatory and the Transnational Institute, Profiting from Injustice. 2012. http://corporateeurope.org/sites/default/files/publications/profiting-from-injustice.pdf

Cox, R.W. 1973. "Ilo: Limited Monarchy," in R.W. Cox and H.K. Jacobson (eds.), *The Anatomy of Influence*. New Haven, CT: Yale University Press.

Cox, R.W., H.K. Jacobson, and G. Curzon. 1973. *The Anatomy of Influence: Decision Making in International Organization*. Cambridge: Cambridge University Press.

Crockett, A., T. Harris, F.S. Mishkin, and E. White. 2003. "Conflicts of Interest in the Financial Services Industry: What Should We Do About Them?" *Geneva Reports on the World Economy* 5. Geneva: Center for Economic Policy Research.

Cutler, A.C., V. Haufler, and T. Porter (eds.). 1999. *Private Authority and International Affairs*. Albany, NY: State University of New York Press.

Dahan Dalmedico, A., and H. Guillemot. 2008. "Climate Change: Scientific Dynamics, Expertise and Geopolitical Challenges," in G. Mallard, C. Paradeise, and A. Peerbaye (eds.), *Global Science and National Sovereignty: Studies in Historical Sociology of Science*. New York: Routledge.

Dashwood, A. 1983. "Hastening Slowly: The Community's Path Toward Harmonization," in H. Wallace, W. Wallace, and C. Webb (eds.), *Policy-Making in the European Community*. London: John Wiley & Sons.

Davis, C.L., and S.B. Bermeo. 2009. "Who Files? Developing Country Participation in GATT/WTO Adjudication." *Journal of Politics* 7/3: 1033–1049.

Davis, K., A. Fisher, B. Kingsbury, and S.E. Merry (eds.). 2012. *Governance by Indicators: Global Power Through Classification and Rankings*. Oxford: Oxford University Press.

Deardorff, A.V., and R.M. Stern. 1985. *Methods of Measurement of Non-Tariff Barriers*. Geneva: UNCTAD.

Dempsey, J., and M.M. Robertson. 2012. "Ecosystem Services: Tensions, Impurities, and Points of Engagement within Neoliberalism." *Progress in Human Geography* 36/6: 758–799.

DeSombre, E.R., and J.S. Barkin. 2002. "Turtles and Trade: The WTO's Acceptance of Environmental Trade Restrictions." *Global Environmental Politics* 2/1: 12–18.

De Tocqueville, A. 1835. *De la démocratie en Amérique*. Paris: Flammarion.

Dezalay, Y., and B. Garth. 1996. *Dealing in Virtue: International Commercial Arbitration and the Construction of a Transnational Legal Order*. Chicago, IL: Chicago University Press.

Dezalay, Y., and B. Garth. 2002. *The Internationalization of Palace Wars: Lawyers, Economists, and the Contest to Transform Latin American States*. Chicago, IL: University of Chicago Press.

Di Chiro, G. 1996. "Nature as Community: The Convergence of Environment and Social Justice," in W. Cronon (ed.), *Uncommon Ground: Rethinking the Human Place in Nature*. New York: W.W. Norton & Company.

DiMaggio, P.J., and W.W. Powell. 1983. "The Iron Cage Revisited: Institutional Isomorphism and Collective Rationality in Organizational Fields." *American Sociological Review* 48/2: 147–160.

Dingwerth, K. 2008. "Private Transnational Governance and the Developing World: A Comparative Perspective." *International Studies Quarterly* 52/3: 607–634.

Djelic, M.-L., and K. Sahlin-Andersson (eds.). 2006. *Transnational Governance: Institutional Dynamics of Regulation*. New York: Cambridge University Press.

Douglas, Z. 2003. "The Hybrid Foundations of Investment Treaty Arbitration." *British Yearbook of International Law* 74/1: 151–289.

Drayton, R. 2000. *Nature's Government: Science, Imperial Britain, and the Improvement of the World*. New Haven, CT: Yale University Press.

Dresner, S. 2008. *The Principles of Sustainability*. 2nd ed. New York: Earthscan.

12

Drezner, D.W. 2007. *All Politics Is Global: Explaining International Regulatory Regimes*. Princeton, NJ: Princeton University Press.

Dryzek, J.S. 2013. *The Politics of the Earth: Environmental Discourses*. Oxford: Oxford University Press.

Eberlein, B., and A.L. Newman. 2008. "Escaping the International Governance Dilemma? Incorporated Transgovernmental Networks in the European Union." *Governance* 21/1: 25–52.

Ehrlich, S.D. 2007. "Access to Protection: Domestic Institutions and Trade Policy in Democracies." *International Organization* 61/3: 571–605.

Eichengreen, B.J. 1996. *Globalizing Capital: A History of the International Monetary System*. Princeton, NJ: Princeton University Press.

Ellerman, A.D. 2003. "Are Cap-and-Trade Programs More Environmentally Effective than Conventional Regulation?" Working paper, MIT Center for Energy and Environmental Policy Research. http://hdl.handle.net/1721.1/45008.

Elliott, K.A., and R.B. Freeman. 2003. *Can Labor Standards Improve under Globalization?* Washington, DC: Peterson Institute for International Economics.

Elyachar, J. 2005. *Markets of Dispossession: NGOs, Economic Development and the State in Cairo*. Durham, NC: Duke University Press.

Eriksen, S.H., A.J. Nightingale, and H. Eakin. 2015. "Reframing Adaptation: The Political nature of Climate Change Adaptation." *Global Environmental Change* 35: 523–533.

Esping-Andersen, G. 1996. "After the Golden Age? Welfare State Dilemmas in a Global Economy," in G. Esping-Andersen (ed.), *Welfare States in Transition: National Adaptations in Global Economies*. London: Sage.

Esserman, S., and R. Howse. 2003. "The WTO on Trial." *Foreign Affairs* 82: 288–298.

Esty, D.C., and D. Geradin. 1997. "Market Access, Competitiveness, and Harmonization: Environmental Protection in Regional Trade Agreements." *Harvard Environmental Law Review* 21: 265–283.

European Commission (TTIP). 2015. "Proposal for Investment Protection and Resolution of Investment Disputes: Transatlantic Trade and Investment Partnership, Chapter II – Investment." http://trade.ec.europa.eu/doclib/docs/2015/november/tradoc_153955.pdf.

Fairhead, J., M. Leach, and I. Scoones. 2012. "Green Grabbing: A New Appropriation of Nature?" *Journal of Peasant Studies* 39/2: 237–261.

Fayazmanesh, S. 2008. *The United States and Iran: Sanctions, Wars and the Policy of Dual Containment*. New York: Routledge.

Ferguson, J. 2005. "Seeing Like an Oil Company: Space, Security, and Global Capital in Neoliberal Africa." *American Anthropologist* 107/3: 377–382.

Ferguson, J., and A. Gupta. 2002. "Spatializing States: Toward an Ethnography of Neoliberal Governmentality." *American Ethnologist* 29/4: 981–1002.

Ferri, G., L.-G. Liu, and J.E. Stiglitz. 1999. "The Pro-Cyclical Role of Rating Agencies: Evidence from the East Asian Crisis." *Economic Notes* 28: 335–355.

Financial Action Task Force. 2008. "Typologies Report on Proliferation Financing." www.fatf-gafi.org/publications/methodsandtrends/documents/%20typologiesreportonproliferationfinancing.html

Flandreau, M. 2013. "Sovereign States, Bondholders Committees, and the London Stock Exchange in the Nineteenth Century (1827–68): New Facts and Old Fictions." *Oxford Review of Economic Policy* 29/4: 668–696.

Fligstein, N., and T. Shin. 2007. "Shareholder Value and the Transformation of the US Economy, 1984–2000." *Sociological Forum* 22: 399–424.

Flores-Zendejas, J. 2016. "Financial Markets, International Organizations and Conditional Lending: A Long-Term Perspective," in G. Mallard and J. Sgard (eds.), *Contractual Knowledge: One Hundred Years of Legal Experimentation in Global Markets*. New York: Cambridge University Press.

Follesdal, A., and S. Hix. 2006. "Why There Is a Democratic Deficit in the EU: A Response to Majone and Moravcsik." *Journal of Common Market Studies* 44/3: 533–562.

Forsyth, T. 2005. "Building Deliberative Public–Private Partnerships for Waste Management in Asia." *Geoforum* 36/4: 429–439.

Fortin, E. 2013. "Transnational Multi-Stakeholder Sustainability Standards and Biofuels: Understanding Standards Processes." *Journal of Peasant Studies* 40/3: 563–587.

Foucault, M. 1977. *Discipline and Punish: The Birth of the Prison*. London: Penguin Books.

Franck, S. 2005. "The Legitimacy Crisis in Investment Treaty Arbitration: Privatizing Public International Law Through Inconsistent Decisions." *Fordham Law Review* 73: 1521.

Frölich, M., D. Kaplan, C. Pagés, J. Rigolini, and D. Robalino (eds.). 2014. *Social Insurance, Informality, and Labor Markets*. New York: Oxford University Press.

Fukuyama, F. 2004. *State-Building: Governance and World Order in the 21st Century*. Ithaca, NY: Cornell University Press.

Gaughan, A. 2004. "Harvey Wiley, Theodore Roosevelt, and the Federal Regulation of Food and Drugs." Third Year Paper in Food and Drug Law, Harvard Law School, Legal Electronic Document Archive (LEDA). leda.law.harvard.edu/leda/data/654/Gaughan.pdf.

Gereffi, G., J. Humphrey, and T. Sturgeon. 2005. "The Governance of Global Value Chains." *Review of International Political Economy* 12/1: 78–104.

Giry-Deloison, Ph., and Ph. Masson. 1988. "Vers un marché financier mondial: les rouages de la globalisation." *Revue banque* 485: 725–729.

Goldin, I., and D. van der Mensbrugghe. 1997. "Assessing Agricultural Tariffication under the Uruguay Round," in W. Martin and L.A. Winters (eds.), *The Uruguay Round and the Developing Countries*. Cambridge: Cambridge University Press.

Goldstein, J., M. Kahler, R.O. Keohane, and A.M. Slaughter (eds.). 2001. *Legalization and World Politics*. Cambridge, MA: MIT Press.

Gordon, K., and J. Pohl. 2015. "Investment Treaties over Time: Treaty Practice and Interpretation in a Changing World." OECD Working Papers on International Investment 2015.

Goulder, L.H., and I.W.H. Parry. 2008. "Instrument Choice in Environmental Policy." *Review of Environmental Economics and Policy* 2/2: 152–174.

Gourevitch, P.A. 1999. "The Governance Problem in International Relations," in D.A. Lake and R. Powell (eds.), *Strategic Choice and International Relations*. Princeton, NJ: Princeton University Press.

Green, J.F. 2014. *Rethinking Private Authority: Agents and Entrepreneurs in Global Environmental Governance*. Princeton, NJ: Princeton University Press.

Grieco, J.M. 1990. *Cooperation Among Nations: Europe, America, and Non-Tariff Barriers to Trade*. Ithaca, NY: Cornell University Press.

Gulati, M., and R.E. Scott. 2013. *The Three and a Half Minute Transaction: Boilerplate and the Limits of Contract Design*. Chicago, IL: University of Chicago Press.

Guzman, A.T. 1998. "Why LDCs Sign Treaties That Hurt Them: Explaining the Popularity of Bilateral Investment Treaties." *Virginia Journal of International Law* 38: 639.

Haas, E.B. 1964. *Beyond the Nation-State: Functionalism and International Organization*. Stanford, CA: Stanford University Press.

Haggard, S., and L. Tiede. 2011. "The Rule of Law and Economic Growth: Where Are We?" *World Development* 39/5: 673–685.

Hall, R.B., and T.J. Biersteker (eds.). 2002. *The Emergence of Private Authority in Global Governance*. Cambridge: Cambridge University Press.

Halliday, T.C., and B.G. Carruthers. 2009. *Bankrupt: Global Lawmaking and Systemic Financial Crisis*. Stanford, CA: Stanford University Press.

Halliday, T.C., M. Levi, and P. Reuter. 2013. "IMF Assessments of Anti-Money Laundering and Combating the Financing of Terrorism in the Context of the Financial Action Task Force Standards, Methodology and Practices." Center on Law and Globalization, American Bar Foundation: Technical Paper to International Monetary Fund.

Halliday, T.C., and G. Shaffer. 2014. *Transnational Legal Orders*. New York: Cambridge University Press.

Hansen, T.B., and F. Stepputat. 2001. *States of Imagination: Ethnographic Explorations of the Postcolonial State*. Durham, NC and London: Duke University Press.

Haufler, V. 2001. *The Public Role of the Private Sector: Industry Self-Regulation in a Global Economy*. Washington, DC: Carnegie Endowment for International Peace.

Heckman, J.J., and C. Pagés. 2000. *The Cost of Job Security Regulation: Evidence from Latin American Labor Markets*. Cambridge, MA: NBER.

Helleiner, E. 1993. "When Finance was the Servant: International Capital Movements in the Bretton Woods Order," in Ph. Cerny and G. Aldershot (eds.), *Finance and World Politics: Markets, Regimes and States in the Post-Hegemonic Era (Studies in International Political Economy)*. Cheltenham: Edward Elgar.

Helleiner, E. 1996. *States and the Reemergence of Global Finance: From Bretton Woods to the 1990s*. Ithaca, NY: Cornell University Press.

Helleiner, E. 2008. "The Mystery of the Missing Sovereign Debt Restructuring Mechanism." *Contributions to Political Economy* 27/1: 91–113.

Hepple, B., and B. Veneziani (eds.). 2009. *The Transformation of Labour Law in Europe*. Oxford: Hart.

Héritier, A., and S. Eckert. 2008. "New Modes of Governance in the Shadow of Hierarchy: Self-Regulation by Industry in Europe." *Journal of Public Policy* 28/1: 113–138.

Hicks, A. 1988. "Social Democratic Corporatism and Economic Growth." *Journal of Politics* 50/3: 677–704. doi: 10.2307/2131463.

Ho, K. 1989. *Liquidated: An Ethnography of Wall Street*. Durham, NC and London: Duke University Press.

Hoekman, B., and C.A. Primo Braga. 1997. "Protection and Trade in Services: A Survey." *Open Economies Review* 8/3: 285–308.

Hooghe, L., and G. Marks. 2003. "Unraveling the Central State, But How? Types of Multi-Level Governance." *American Political Science Review* 97/2: 233–243.

Hough, J.F., and R. Grier. 2015. *The Long Process of Development: Building Markets and States in Pre-Industrial England, Spain, and Their Colonies*. New York: Cambridge University Press.

Hulme, M. 2010. "Problems with Making and Governing Global Kinds of Knowledge." *Global Environmental Change* 20/4: 558–564. doi:10.1016/j.gloenvcha.2010.07.005

Hulme, M. 2011. "Reducing the Future to Climate: A Story of Climate Determinism and Reductionism." *Osiris* 26/1: 245–266.

ILO. 1972 [1919]. *Consitution*. www.ilo.org/dyn/normlex/en/f?p=1000:62:0::NO:62:P62_LIST_ENTRIE_ID:2453907:NO.

ILO. 1999. *Decent Work: Report of the Director-General to the 87th Session of the International Labour Conference* Geneva: ILO.

ILO. 2008. *World of Work Report*. ILO: Geneva.

ILO. 2009. *World of Work Report*. ILO: Geneva.

ILO. 2015. *Global Wage Report 2014/15*. Geneva: ILO.

International Monetary Fund (IMF). 1997. *Good Governance: The IMF's Role*. Washington, DC: IMF.

IMF. 2003. *World Economic Outlook*. Washington DC: IMF.

Jayasuriya, K. 2002. "Governance, New Post-Washington Consensus, and the New Anti-Politics," in T. Lindsey and H.W. Dick (eds.), *Corruption in Asia: Rethinking the Governance Paradigm*. Leichhardt, NSW: Federation Press.

Jaysuriya, K. 2004. "The New Regulatory State and Relational Capacity." *Policy and Politics* 32/4: 487–501.

Jayasuriya, K. 2006. *Empire and Neoliberalism in East Asia* (ed. V.R. Hadiz). London: Routledge.

Jessop, B. 2007. *State Power: A Strategic-Relational Approach*. Cambridge: Polity Press

Joerges, Ch. 2004. "Transnational Governance and Its Legitimacy Problematics: The Example of Standardization and Food Safety." Paper presented at the seminar on Globalization and Its Discontents, NYU Law School, February 2. New York.

Johnson, S. 1995. *Starting Over in Eastern Europe: Entrepreneurship and Economic Renewal*. Cambridge, MA: Harvard Business Press.

Jolly, S.K. 2015. *The European Union and the Rise of Regionalist Parties*. Ann Arbor, MI: University of Michigan Press.

Jordan, A., and T. O'Riordan. 2004. "Institutions for Global Environmental Change." *Global Environmental Change* 14/4: 367.

Kahler, M., and D.A. Lake (eds.). 2003. *Governance in a Global Economy: Political Authority in Transition*. Princeton, NJ: Princeton University Press.

Kahler, M., and D.A. Lake. 2009. "Economic Integration and Global Governance: Why So Little Supranationalism?" in W. Mattli and N. Woods (eds.), *The Politics of Global Regulation*. Princeton, NJ: Princeton University Press.

Kaiser, K. 1969. "Das internationale System der Gegenwart als Faktor der Beeinträchtigung demokratischer Außenpolitik." *Politische Vierteljahresschrift* 10/1 (Sonderheft "Die anachronistische Souveränität," ed. E.-O. Czempiel).

Karabarbounis, L., and B. Neiman. 2014. "The Global Decline of the Labor Share." *Quarterly Journal of Economics* 129/1: 61–103. doi: 10.1093/qje/qjt032.

Kaufman, B.E. 2004. *The Global Evolution of Industrial Relations. Events, Ideas and the Ilra*. Geneva: ILO.

Kaufmann-Kohler, G. 2007. "Arbitral Precedent: Dream, Necessity or Excuse?." *Arbitration International* 23/3: 357.

Kaufmann-Kohler G., and M. Potestà. 2016. "Can the Mauritius Convention Serve as a Model for the Reform of Investor-State arbitration in Connection with the Introduction of a Permanent Investment Tribunal or an Appeal Mechanism? Analysis and Roadmap." CIDS Research Paper, June 3.

Kenworthy, L. 2002. "Corporatism and Unemployment in the 1980s and 1990s." *American Sociological Review* 67/3: 367–388.

Keohane, R.O. 2003. "Global Governance and Democratic Accountability," in D. Held and M. Koenig-Archibugi (eds.), *Taming Globalization: Frontiers of Governance*. Cambridge: Polity Press.

Keohane, R.O., and J.S. Nye (eds.). 1972. *Transnational Relations and World Politics*. Cambridge, MA: Harvard University Press.

Keohane, R.O., and J.S. Nye. 2001 [1977]. *Power and Interdependence*. 3rd ed. New York: Addison Wesley Longman.

Kim, M. 2008. "Costly Procedures: Divergent Effects of Legalization in the GATT/WTO Dispute Settlement Procedures." *International Studies Quarterly* 52/3: 657–686.

Kingsbury, B., N. Krisch, and R.B. Stewart. 2005. "The Emergence of Global Administrative Law." *Law and Contemporary Problems* 68/3/4: 15–61.

Klooster, D. 2005. "Environmental Certification of Forests: The Evolution of Environmental Governance in a Commodity Network." *Journal of Rural Studies* 21/4: 403–417.

Konadu-Agyemang, K. 2000. "The Best of Times and the Worst of Times: Structural Adjustment Programs and Uneven Development in Africa: The Case of Ghana." *Professional Geographer* 52/3: 469–483.

Kono, D.Y. 2006. "Optimal Obfuscation: Democracy and Trade Policy Transparency." *American Political Science Review* 100/3: 369–384.

Koremenos, B. 2007. "If Only Half of International Agreements Have Dispute Resolution Provisions, Which Half Needs Explaining?" *Journal of Legal Studies* 36/1: 189–212.

Krasner, S.D. 1991. "Global Communications and National Power: Life on the Pareto Frontier." *World Politics* 43/3: 336–366.

Krippner, G. 2005. "The Financialisation of the American Economy." *Socio-Economic Review* 3/2: 173–208.

Krisch, N. 2005. "International Law in Times of Hegemony: Unequal Power and the Shaping of the International Legal Order." *European Journal of International Law* 16/3: 369–408.

Kruck, A. 2011. *Private Ratings, Public Regulations: Credit Rating Agencies and Global Financial Governance*. London: Palgrave.

Krueger, A.O. 2002. *A New Approach to Sovereign Debt Restructuring*. Washington, DC: International Monetary Fund.

Kydland, F.E., and E.C. Prescott. 1977. "Rules Rather than Discretion: The Inconsistency of Optimal Plans." *Journal of Political Economy* 85/3: 473–491.

Langille, B.A. 2005. "Core Labour Rights – the True Story (Reply to Alston)." *European Journal of International Law* 16/3: 409–437. doi: 10.1093/ejil/chi124.

Langohr, H.M., and P.T. Langohr. 2008. *The Rating Agencies and Their Credit Ratings: What They Are, How They Work and Why They Are Relevant*. New York: Wiley.

Lascoumes, P., and P. Le Gales. 2007. "Introduction: Understanding Public Policy Through Its Instruments – From the Nature of Instruments to the Sociology of Public Policy Instrumentation." *Governance* 20/1: 1–21.

Layard, R., S. Nickell, and R. Jackman. 2005. *Unemployment: Macroeconomic Performance and the Labour Market*. Oxford and New York: Oxford University Press.

Leary, V.A. 1996. "Workers' Rights and International Trade: The Social Clause (GATT, ILO, NAFTA, US Laws)," in by J. Bhagwati and R. E. Hudec (eds.), *Free Trade and Harmonization: Prerequisites for Free Trade?* (Vol. 2.) Cambridge, MA: MIT University Press.

Lehmbruch, G., and P. Schmitter (eds.). 1982. *Patterns of Corporatist Policy-Making*. London: Sage.

Lemos, M.C., and A. Agrawal. (2006). "Environmental Governance." *Annual Review of Environment and Resources* 31/1: 297–325.

Levi, M. 1988. *Of Rule and Revenue*. Berkeley, CA: University of California Press.

Lindbeck, A., and D. Snower. 1988. *The Insider-Outsider Theory of Employment and Unemployment*. Cambridge, MA: MIT Press.

Liu, P. 2010. "Tracing and Periodizing China's Food Safety Regulation: A Study on China's Food Safety Regime Change." *Regulation and Governance* 4/2: 244–260.

Locke, R.M. 2013. *The Promise and Limits of Private Power: Promoting Labor Standards in the Global Economy*. Cambridge: Cambridge University Press.

Logie, D., and J. Woodroffe. 1993. "Structural Adjustment: The Wrong Prescription for Africa?" *BMJ: British Medical Journal* 307/6895: 41–44.

Lordon, F. 2010. *Capitalisme, désir et servitude: Marx et Spinoza*. Paris: La fabrique.

Loriaux, M. 1997. "The End of Credit Activism in Interventionist States," in M. Loriaux, M. Woo-Cumings, K. Calder, S. Maxfield, and S.A. Pérez (eds.), *Capital*

Ungoverned: Liberalizing Finance in Interventionist States. Ithaca, NY: Cornell University Press.

McLaughlin, P. 2011. "Climate Change, Adaptation, and Vulnerability Reconceptualizing Societal–Environment Interaction Within a Socially Constructed Adaptive Landscape." *Organization & Environment* 24/3: 269–291.

Mahony, M. 2014. "The Predictive State: Science, Territory and the Future of the Indian Climate." *Social Studies of Science* 44/1: 109–133. doi:10.1177/0306312713501407

Majone, G. 1994. "The Rise of the Regulatory State in Europe." *West European Politics* 17/3: 77–101.

Mallard, G. 2018. "Bombs, Banks and Sanctions: How Sanctions Against Nuclear Proliferators Changed the Making of Global Financial Regulations," in E. Brousseau, J.-M. Glachant, and J. Sgard (eds.), *Oxford Handbook on International Economic Governance.* Oxford: Oxford University Press.

Mallard, G., and J. Sgard. 2016. "Contractual Knowledge: One Hundred Years of Legal Experimentation in Global Markets," in G. Mallard and J. Sgard (eds.), *Contractual Knowledge: One Hundred Years of Legal Experimentation in Global Markets.* New York: Cambridge University Press.

Marceau, G., and J.P. Trachtman. 2002. "TBT, SPS, and GATT: A Map of the WTO Law of Domestic Regulation." *Journal of World Trade* 36/5 (October): 811–881.

Mattli, W. 2003. "Public and Private Governance in Setting International Standards," in M. Kahler and D.A. Lake (eds.), *Governance in a Global Economy: Political Authority in Transition.* Princeton, NJ: Princeton University Press.

Mattli, W., and T. Büthe. 2005. "Global Private Governance: Lessons From a National Model of Setting Standards in Accounting." *Law and Contemporary Problems* 68/3/4 (Summer/Autumn): 225–262.

Maupain, F. 2013. *The Future of the International Labour Organization in the Global Economy.* Oxford: Hart.

Maurer, B. 1999. "Forget Locke? From Proprietor to Risk-Bearer in New Logics of Finance." *Public Culture* 11/2: 47–67.

Mayer, F.W., and G. Gereffi. 2010. "Regulation and Economic Globalization: Prospects and Limits of Private Governance." *Business and Politics* 12/3 (October): 1–25.

Milner, H.V., and K. Kubota. 2005. "Why the Move to Free Trade? Democracy and Trade Policy in the Developing Countries." *International Organization* 59/1: 107–143.

Mirowski, P. 2013. *Never Let a Serious Crisis Go to Waste: How Neoliberalism Survived the Financial Meltdown.* New York: Verso.

Mishra, R. 1996. "The Welfare of Nations," in R. Boyer and D. Drache (eds.), *States Against Markets: The Limits of Globalization.* Abingdon: Routledge.

Moretti, F., and D. Pestre. 2015. "Bankspeak: The Language of World Bank Reports." *New Left Review* 92: 75–99.

Morrison, A., and K. Webb. 2004. "Bicycle Helmet Standards and Hockey Helmet Regulation: Two Approaches to Safety Protection," in K. Webb. (ed.), *Voluntary Codes: Private Governance, the Public Interest and Innovation.* Ottawa, ON: Carleton University Research Unit for Innovation, Science and Environment.

Mosley, L. 2011. *Labor Rights and Multinational Production.* New York: Cambridge University Press.

Murphy, C.N., and J.A. Yates. 2008. *The International Organization for Standardization (ISO): Global Governance through Voluntary Consensus.* London and New York: Routledge.

Nelson, S.C. 2014. "Playing Favorites: How Shared Beliefs Shape the IMF's Lending Decisions." *International Organization* 68/2: 297–328.

Neumann, R.P. 2004. "Moral and Discursive Geographies in the War for Biodiversity in Africa." *Political Geography* 23: 813–837.

Newell, P. 2012. *Globalization and the Environment: Capitalism, Ecology & Power.* Cambridge: Polity Press.

Nickell, S., L. Nunziata, and W. Ochel. 2005. "Unemployment in the OECD Since the 1960s. What Do We Know?" *The Economic Journal* 115/500: 1–27.

Noorbakhsh, F., and A. Paloni. 1999. "Structural Adjustment Programs and Industry in Sub-Saharan Africa: Restructuring or De-Industrialization." *Journal of Developing Areas* 33/4: 549–580.

Noorbakhsh, F., and A. Paloni. 2001. "Structural Adjustment and Growth in Sub-Saharan Africa: The Importance of Complying with Conditionality." *Economic Development and Cultural Change* 49/3: 479–509.

Ocasio, W., and J. Joseph. 2005. "Cultural Adaptation and Institutional Change: The Evolution of Vocabularies of Corporate Governance, 1972–2003." *Poetics* 33/3–4: 163–178.

OECD. 1994. *The OECD Jobs Study: Facts, Analysis, Strategies.* Paris: OECD.

OECD. 2008. *Growing Unequal? Income Distribution and Poverty in OECD Countries.* Paris: OECD.

Oka, C. 2015. "Improving Working Conditions in Garment Supply Chains: The Role of Unions in Cambodia." *British Journal of Industrial Relations* 54/3: 647–672. doi: 10.1111/bjir.12118.

Oreskes, N., and E. Conway. 2010. *Merchants of Doubt: How a Handful of Scientists Obscured the Truth on Issues from Tobacco Smoke to Global Warming.* New York: Bloomsberry Press.

Painter, J. 2012. "Regional Biopolitics." *Regional Studies* 47/8: 1–14.

Paparinskis, M. 2010. "Limits of Depoliticisation in Contemporary Investor-State Arbitration." *Select Proceedings of the European Society of International Law* 3: 271 (ed. J. Crawford).

Paparinskis, M. 2013. "Investment Treaty Arbitration and the (New) Law of State Responsibility." *European Journal of International Law* 24: 617.

Partnoy, F. 1999. "The Siskel and Ebert of financial markets: Two Thumbs Down for the Credit Rating Agencies." *Washington University Law Quarterly* 77: 619–712.

Partnoy, F. 2002. "The Paradox of Credit Ratings," in R.M. Levich, G. Majnoni, and C. Reinhart (eds.), *Ratings, Rating Agencies and the Global Financial System.* New York: Springer.

Peet, R., and M. Watts. 2004. *Liberation Ecologies: Environment, Development and Social Movements.* 2nd ed. London: Routledge.

Peluso, N. 1993. "Coercing Conservation?" *Global Environmental Change* June: 199–217.

Peluso, N.L., and P. Vandergeest. 2011. "Political Ecologies of War and Forests: Counterinsurgencies and the Making of National Natures." *Annals of the Association of American Geographers* 101/3: 587–608.

Pénet, P. 2015. "Rating Reports as Figuring Documents: How CRAs Build Scenarios of the Future," in M. Kornberger, L. Jusesen, J. Moursitsen, and A. Koed Madsen (eds.), *Making Things Valuable.* Oxford: Oxford University Press.

Pénet, P., and G. Mallard. 2014. "From Risk Models to Loan Contracts: Austerity as the Continuation of Calculation by Other Means." *Journal of Critical Globalization Studies* 7: 4–50.

Perkins, H.A. 2009. "Out from the (Green) Shadow? Neoliberal Hegemony Through the Market Logic of Shared Urban Environmental Governance." *Political Geography* 28/7: 395–405.

Pestre, D. 2008. "Challenges for the Democratic Management of Technoscience: Governance, Participation and the Political Today." *Science as Culture* 17/2: 101–119

Pestre, D. 2016. "La mise en économie de l'environnement comme règle. Entre théologie économique, pragmatisme et hégémonie politique," in D. Pestre et Soraya Boudia (ed.), *Ecologie et Politique* 52, Special issue *Les mises en économie de l'environnement* 19–44.

Peters, A., et al. 2009. *Non-State Actors as Standard Setters.* Cambridge: Cambridge University Press.

Petrie, M. 2015. "Jurisdictional Integration: A Framework for Measuring and Predicting the Depth of International Regulatory Cooperation in Competition Policy." *Regulation and Governance* 10/1: 1–111.

Piketty, T. 2014. *Capital in the Twentieth Century.* Cambridge, MA: Harvard University Press.

Polaski, S. 2006. "Combining Global and Local Forces: The Case of Labor Rights in Cambodia." *World Development* 34/5: 919–932.

Ponte, S. 2013. "'Roundtabling' Sustainability: Lessons from the Biofuel Industry." *Geoforum* 54: 261–271. doi: http://dx.doi.org/10.1016/j.geoforum.2013.07.008

Power, M. 1997. *The Audit Society: Rituals of Verification.* Oxford: Oxford University Press.

Purdon, M. 2003. "The Nature of Ecosystem Management: Postmodernism and Plurality in the Sustainable Management of the Boreal Forest." *Environmental Science & Policy* 6/4: 377–388.

Rajagopal, B. 2003. *International Law from Below: Development, Social Movements, and Third World Resistance.* New York: Cambridge University Press.

Rajan, R. 2010. *Fault Lines: How Hidden Fractures Still Threaten the World Economy.* Princeton, NJ: Princeton University Press.

Raustiala, K. 1997. "Domestic Institutions and International Regulatory Cooperation: Comparative Responses to the Convention on Biological Diversity." *World Politics* 49/4: 482–509.

Reed, D., P. Utting, and A. Mukherjee-Reed (eds.). 2012. *Business Regulation and Non-State Actors: Whose Standards? Whose Development?* London and New York: Routledge.

Reserve Bank of India. 1997. *Report of the Committee on Capital Account Convertibility*. Bombay: Reserve Bank of India.

Rickard, S.J. 2015. "PTAs and Public Procurement," in A. Dür and M. Elsig (eds.), *Trade Cooperation: The Purpose, Design and Effects of Preferential Trade Agreements*. Cambridge: Cambridge University Press.

Riles, A. 2011. *Collateral Knowledge: Legal Reasoning in the Global Financial Markets*. Chicago, IL: University of Chicago Press.

Risse-Kappen, T. (ed.). 1995. *Bringing Transnational Relations Back In: Non-State Actors, Domestic Structures and International Institutions*. New York: Cambridge University Press.

Rist, G. 2002. "Le prix des mots." *Les mots du pouvoir: Sens et non-sens de la rhétorique internationale, Cahiers de l'IUED* 13: 9–24.

Roberts, A. 2010. "Power and Persuasion in Investment Treaty Interpretation: The Dual Role of States." *American Journal of International Law* 104: 179.

Roberts, A. 2013. "Clash of Paradigms: Actors and Analogies Shaping the Investment Treaty System." *American Journal of International Law* 107: 45.

Roberts, A. 2014. "State-to-State Investment Treaty Arbitration: A Theory of Interdependent Rights and Shared Interpretive Authority." *Harvard International Law Journal* 55: 1.

Roberts, A. 2015. "Triangular Treaties: the Nature and Limits of Investment Treaty Rights." *Harvard International Law Journal* 56: 353.

Roberts, A., and R. Braddock. 2016. "Protecting Public Welfare Regulation Through Joint Treaty Party Control: A ChAFTA Innovation." *Columbia FDI Perspectives* 113. http://ccsi.columbia.edu/files/2013/10/No-176-Roberts-and-Braddock-FINAL.pdf.

Rona-Tas, A., and S. Hiss. 2011. "Forecast as Valuation: The Role of Ratings and Predictions in the Subprime Mortgage Crisis in the US," in J. Becker and P. Aspers (eds.), *Worth of Goods: Valuation and Pricing in the Economy*. Princeton, NJ: Princeton University Press.

Rose, N. 1999. *Powers of Freedom: Reframing Political Thought*. Cambridge: Cambridge University Press.

Rosenau, J.N., and E.-O. Czempiel (eds.). 1992. *Governance Without Government: Order and Change in World Politics*. Cambridge: Cambridge University Press.

Ruggie, J.G. 1983. "International Regimes, Transactions, and Change: Embedded Liberalism in the Postwar Economic Order," in S.D. Krasner (ed.), *International Regimes*. Ithaca, NY: Cornell University Press.

Ruggie, J.G. 2008. "Taking Embedded Liberalism Global: The Corporate Connection," in J.G. Ruggie (ed.), *Embedding Global Markets: An Enduring Challenge*. Burlington, VT: Ashgate.

Sabel, Ch., D. O'Rourke, and A. Fung. 2000. "Ratcheting Labor Standards: Regulation for Continuous Improvement in the Global Workplace." *KSG Working Paper* (00–010).

Saint-Paul, G. 2002. "The Political Economy of Employment Protection." *Journal of Political Economy* 110/3: 672–704.

Salacuse J.W., and N.P. Sullivan. 2005. "Do BITs Really Work? An Evaluation of Bilateral Investment Treaties and Their Grand Bargain." *Harvard International Law Journal* 46: 67.

Sammon, A. 2016. "A History of Native Americans Protesting the Dakota Access Pipeline." *Mother Jones*, September 9. www. motherjones. com/environment/2016/09/dakota-access-pipeline-protest-timeline-sioux-standing-rock-jill-stein.

Sassen, S. 1996. *Losing Control? Sovereignty in the Age of Globalization*. New York: Columbia University Press.

Scahill, J. 2011. *Blackwater: The Rise of the World's Most Powerful Mercenary Army*. London: Profile books.

Schill, S.W. 2009. *The Multilateralization of Investment Law*. Cambridge: Cambridge Unversity Press.

Scholte, J. Arte. 1997. "Global Capitalism and the State." *International Affairs* 73/3: 427–452.

Schreurs, M.A., and E. Economy (eds.). 1997. *The Internationalization of Environmental Protection*. New York: Cambridge University Press.

Scott, J.C. 1998. *Seeing Like a State How Certain Schemes to Improve the Human Condition Have Failed*. New Haven, CT: Yale University Press.

Seidman, G.W. 2007. *Beyond the Boycott: Labor Rights, Human Rights, and Transnational Activism*. New York: Russel Sage.

Sending, O.J., and I.B. Neumann. 2006. Governance to Governmentality: Analyzing NGOs, States, and Power. *International Studies Quarterly* 50/3: 651–672.

Shaffer, G.C. 2003. *Defending Interests: Public-Private Partnerships in WTO Litigation*. Washington, DC: Brookings.

Shaffer, G.C. 2010. "The World Trade Organization Under Challenge: Democracy and the Law and Politics of the WTO's Treatment of Trade and Environment Matters." *Harvard Environmental Law Review* 25: 1–93.

Shaffer, G.C., and M. Waibel. 2016. "The Rise and Fall of Trade and Monetary Legal Orders: From the Interwar Period to Today's Global Imbalances," in G. Mallard and J. Sgard (eds.), *Contractual Knowledge: One Hundred Years of Legal Experimentation in Global Markets*. New York: Cambridge University Press.

Shell, R.G. 1995. "Trade Legalism and International Relations Theory: An Analysis of the World Trade Organization." *Duke Law Journal* 44: 829–876.

Sherman, M. 2009. "A Short History of Financial Deregulation in the United States." *Center for Economic and Policy Research*. Washington, DC: Center for Economic and Policy Research.

Shihata, I. 1986. "Towards a Greater Depoliticization of Investment Disputes: The Role of ICSID and MIGA." *ICSID Rev. – Foreign Investment Law Journal* 1: 1.

Shingal, A. 2015. "Revisiting the Trade Effects of Services Agreements," in A. Dür and M. Elsig (eds.), *Trade Cooperation: The Purpose, Design and Effects of Preferential Trade Agreements*. Cambridge: Cambridge University Press.

Shove, E., and G. Walker. 2010. Governing Transitions in the Sustainability of Everyday Life. *Research Policy* 39/4: 471–476.

Silva, E. 1997. "Business Elites, the State and Economic Change in Chile," in S. Maxfield and B.R. Schneider (eds.), *Business and the State in Developing Countries*. Ithaca, NY: Cornell University Press.

Skocpol, T. 1992. *Protecting Soldiers and Mothers: The Political Origins of Social Policy in the United States*. Cambridge: Belknap Press of Harvard University Press.

Slaughter, A.-M. 2004. *A New World Order*. Princeton, NJ: Princeton University Press.

Spencer, D. 2010. "Governing Through Standards: Networks, Failure and Auditing." *Sociological Research Online* 15/4: 1–19.

Spruyt, H. 2001. "The Supply and Demand of Governance in Standard-Setting: Insights from the Past." *Journal of European Public Policy* 8/3: 371–391.

Standing, G. 2008. "The ILO: An Agency for Globalization?" *Development and Change* 39/3: 355–384.

Steffen, W., K. Richardson, J. Rockström, S.E. Cornell, I. Fetzer, E.M. Bennett, and S. Sörlin. 2015. "Planetary Boundaries: Guiding Human Development on a Changing Planet." *Science* 347: 6223. doi: 10.1126/science.1259855

Steinberg, R.H. 2002. "In the Shadow of Law or Power? Consensus-Based Bargaining and Outcomes in the GATT/WTO." *International Organization* 56/2: 339–374.

Stockhammer, E. 2013. "Why Have Wage Shares Fallen? An Analysis of the Determinants of Functional Income Distribution," in M. Lavoie and E. Stockhammer (eds.), *Wage-Led Growth*. London: Palgrave.

Stone, R.W. 2002. *Lending Credibility: The International Monetary Fund and the Post-Communist Transition*. Princeton, NJ: Princeton University Press.

Stone, R.W. 2004. "The Political Economy of IMF Lending in Africa." *American Political Science Review* 98/4: 577.

Stone, R.W. 2011. *Controlling Institutions: International Organiztions and the Global Economy*. New York: Cambridge University Press.

Strange, S. 1986. *Casino Capitalism*. Manchester: Manchester University Press.

Streeck, W. 2014. "The Politics of Public Debt: Neoliberalism, Capitalist Development and the Restructuring of the State." *German Economic Review* 15/1: 143–165.

Subrahmanyam, S. 2005. "On World Historians in the Sixteenth Century." *Representations* 91: 26–57.

Summers, H.L. 2014. "U.S. Economic Prospects: Secular Stagnation, Hysteresis, and the Zero Lower Bound." *Business Economics* 49/2: 65–73. doi: 10.1057/be.2014.13.

Supiot, A. 2015. *La Gouvernance par les nombres*, cours au Collège de France *(2012–2014)*. Paris: Fayard.

Swain, A. 1997. "Democratic Consolidation? Environmental Movements in India." *Asian Survey* 37/9: 818–832.

Swyngedouw, E. 2005. "Governance Innovation and the Citizen: The Janus Face oftGovernance-Beyond-The-State." *Urban Studies* 42/11: 1991–2006.

Teubner, G. 1996. "Global Bukowina: Legal Pluralism in the World-Society," in G. Teubner (ed)., *Global Law Without a State*. London: Dartsmouth.

Thomson, J.E., and S.D. Krasner. 1989. "Global Transactions and the Consolidation of Sovereignty," in E.O. Czempiel and J.N. Rosenau (eds.), *Global Changes and Theoretical Challenges*. Lexington, MA: Lexington Books.

Tsing, A. 2005. *Friction: An Ethnography of Global Connection*. Princeton, NJ: Princeton University Press.

UNCTAD. 2000. "Bilateral Investment Treaties, 1959–1999." www.ustr.gov/sites/default/files/BIT%20text%20for%20ACIEP%20Meeting.pdf

UNCTAD. 2011. "Interpretation of IIAs: What States Can Do." IIA Issues Note, No. 3. http://unctad.org/en/Docs/webdiaeia2011d10_en.pdf.

U.S. Model Bilateral Investment Treaty. 2012. www.ustr.gov/sites/default/files/BIT%20text%20for%20ACIEP%20Meeting.pdf

Vaccaro, I. 2007. "Sovereignty, Collective Ingenuity and Moral Economies: The Confluence of Transnational Trends, States and Local Strategies in the Pyrenees." *Environment and History* 13/1: 25–46.

Valdivia, G. 2008. "Governing Relations Between People and Things: Citizenship, Territory, and the Political Economy of Petroleum in Ecuador." *Political Geography* 27: 456–477.

Van Aaken, A. 2014. "Interpretational Methods as an Instrument of Control in International Investment Law." *ASIL Proceedings* 108.

Van Aaken, A., and T. Lehmann. 2013. "Sustainable Development and International Investment Law: An Harmonious View from Economics," in R. Echandi and P. Sauvé (eds.), *International Investment Law and Policy*. Cambridge: Cambridge University Press.

Vandevelde, K.J. 2010. *Bilateral Investment Treaties: History, Policy, and Interpretation*. Washington, DC: World Bank.

Veggeland, F., and S.O. Borgen. 2005. "Negotiating International Food Standards: The World Trade Organization's Impact on the Codex Alimentarius Commission." *Governance* 18/4: 675–708.

Vogel, D. 1995. *Trading Up: Consumer and Environmental Regulation in a Global Economy*. Cambridge, MA: Harvard University Press.

Vogel, D. 2005. *The Market for Virtue: The Potential and Limits of Corporate Social Responsibility*. Washington, DC: Brookings.

Vogel, S.K. 1996. *Freer Markets, More Rules: Regulatory Reform in Advanced Industrial Countries*. Ithaca, NY: Cornell University Press.

Wallerstein, M. 1999. "Wage-Setting Institutions and Pay Inequality in Advanced Industrial Societies." *American Journal of Political Science* 43/3: 649–680.

Waltz, K.N. 1999. "Globalization and Governance." *PS: Political Science and Politics* 32/4: 693–700.

Waverman, L., W.S. Comanor, and A. Goto (eds.). 1997. *Competition Policy in the Global Economy: Modalities for Cooperation*. London: Routledge.

Webb Yackee, J. 2010. "Do Bilateral Investment Treaties Promote Foreign Direct Investment? Some Hints from Alternative Evidence." *Virginia Journal of International Law* 51: 397.

Yarbrough, B.V., and R.M. Yarbrough. 1992. *Cooperation and Governance in International Trade: The Strategic Organizational Approach*. Princeton, NJ: Princeton University Press.

Zangl, B. 2008. "Judicialization Matters! A Comparison of Dispute Settlement Under GATT and the WTO." *International Studies Quarterly* 52/4: 825–854.

Zarate, J. 2013. *Treasury's Wars: The Unleashing of a New Era of Financial Warfare*. New York: Public Affairs.

Zeng, K., and J. Eastin. 2007. "International Economic Integration and Environmental Protection: The Case of China." *International Studies Quarterly* 51/4: 971–995.

Zürn, M. 2004. "Global Governance and Legitimacy Problems." *Government and Opposition* 39/2: 260–287.

13 Media and Communications*

Coordinating Lead Authors:[1]
Nick Couldry, Clemencia Rodriguez

Lead Authors:[2]
Göran Bolin, Julie Cohen, Gerard Goggin, Marwan Kraidy, Koichi Iwabuchi, Kwang-Suk Lee, Jack Qiu, Ingrid Volkmer, Herman Wasserman, Yuezhi Zhao

Contributing Authors:[3]
Olessia Koltsova, Inaya Rakhmani, Omar Rincón, Claudia Magallanes-Blanco, Pradip Thomas

---

*   The authors would like to thank the following: Miriam Rahali, doctoral researcher at the London School of Economics, for her huge support in managing the drafting process and bringing together the final version (with her skill and professionalism, the task would have been impossible!); Guy Berger of UNESCO and Anita Gurumurthy of ITforChange for their excellent comments on an earlier draft, as well as all those who contributed through IPSP's public comments process; and Emma Christina Montaña for her excellent work on the Spanish translation of the chapter.

[1]   Affiliations: NC: The London School of Economics and Political Science, UK; CR: Temple University, USA.

[2]   Affiliations: GB: Södertörn University, Sweden; JC: Georgetown University, USA; GC: University of Sydney, Australia; MK: University of Pennsylvania, USA; KI: Monash University, Australia; KSL: Seoul National University of Science and Technology, South Korea; JQ: The Chinese University, Hong Kong; IV: University of Melbourne, Australia; HW: University of Cape Town, South Africa; YZ: Simon Fraser University, Canada.

[3]   Affiliations: OK: National Research University, Russia; IR: University of Indonesia; OR: C3 – Fundación Friedrich Ebert, Colombia; CMB: Universidad Iberoamericana Puebla, Mexico; PT: University of Queensland, Australia.

Summary

Developments in digital technologies over the last 30 years have expanded massively human beings' capacity to communicate across time and space (Section 13.1). Media infrastructures have simultaneously acquired huge complexity. By "media" we mean technologies for the production, dissemination, and reception of communication, but also the contents distributed through those technologies and the institutions associated with their production, dissemination, and reception. The relations between media, communications, and social progress are complex. More people can now make meaning and be connected through media, providing an important resource for new movements for justice and social progress. Meanwhile the uneven distribution of opportunities to access and use media is itself a dimension of social justice.

Media infrastructures, and media access, have spread unevenly (Section 13.2), and media's consequences for social progress cannot be determined at a general level. Traditional and digital media have developed according to distinctive histories across the world (Section 13.2.1), with varying marketization and state control (case studies on China, Russia, Sweden, South Africa, Indonesia, and Mexico: Section 13.2.2). Inequalities of access to media infrastructures (Section 13.2.3) are stark, between and within regions and inside countries, with implications for the Sustainable Development Goals (SDGs). Cultural flows through media vary greatly within and between regions (Section 13.2.4).

Meanwhile (Section 13.2.5) people's increasing dependence on an online infrastructure that *mediates* daily life increases the importance of the corporations, which provide that infrastructure. This has transformed the governance of media infrastructures (Section 13.3), with a shift from formal to informal governance and the growing importance of transnational governance institutions and practices, whereby corporations, not states, exercise predominant influence (Section 13.3.2), including through the operations of algorithms, with ambiguous implications for corporate power and individual rights, for the public sphere and for social progress (Section 13.3.3).

Journalism has for centuries been a key institutional form for disseminating public knowledge, and so contributing to social progress (Section 13.4). While digital technologies have expanded who can do journalism (see Section 13.4.5 on citizens' media), other aspects of digitization have undermined the economics of public journalism (Section 13.4.3), with new threats to journalists from growing political instability (Section 13.4.4). Even so, there are new voices within global journalism (see Section 13.4.6 on TeleSUR and Al-Jazeera).

The increasing networking of communications changes citizenship too, as citizens find information, develop imaginative loyalties and make practical connections beyond national borders, not only within the Global North (Section 13.5) and with particular implications for global youth (Section 13.5.2). A more "connected" life is, however, not simply "better" (see Section 13.5.3's case study of life in a Chinese heritage village and Section 13.5.4 on the media-based oppression and resistance of precarious workers in East Asia).

Struggles for social justice through the democratization *of* media (Section 13.6) have acquired new prominence, echoing previous struggles (Section 13.6.1) and foregrounding the transparency and accountability of media infrastructures, and data flows in particular, (Section 13.6.2), with implications for the SDGs and Social Progress Index (SPI). Concerns include net neutrality, internet freedom, algorithms' discriminatory operations, and the automated surveillance on which most online businesses now rely. There are implications for state and corporate power (Section 13.6.5), which civil society has challenged (Section 13.6.4 on India and Facebook's Free Basics). A bold new model of internet governance has emerged in Brazil (Section 13.6.6 on *Marco Civil*).

Yet media remain the channel through which many struggles for social progress are pursued (Section 13.7). An important example of innovative media use for social progress was the Zapatistas in Mexico (Section 13.7.1), but social movements' uses of media technologies have taken many forms across the world, exposing important constraints (Section 13.7.2). Since old media generally do not disappear but are linked up in new ways through digital media, it is overall *ecologies* of media resource on which movements that struggle for social progress have drawn (Section 13.7.3), with struggles against the injustices faced by disabled people being an example of the creative use of media resources (Section 13.7.4).

Effective access to media is a necessary component of social justice (Section 13.8). But media's consequences for social progress are complicated by uneven media access, the plurality of spaces where people connect through media, and the multiple uses of communication resources (hate speech is enabled by the Internet too). The SPI should measure the distribution of opportunities for effective media access and use, and address communication rights. Media infrastructures are a common good whose governance should be open to democratic participation. Concerns about automated surveillance and the environmental costs of digital waste must also be addressed. Our action plan and toolkit list various measures to these ends.

13.1 Introduction: Media Infrastructures and Communication Flows

Media's role in social change, and potentially social progress, is often assumed, rather than fully investigated. "Media" are inherently complex, in themselves and in their consequences. By "media" we mean primarily *technologies for the production, dissemination, and reception of communications*, but (in accordance with the common usage of the word "media" and its equivalents in many languages) we include also *contents* distributed through those technologies and the *institutions* associated with their production, dissemination, and reception. By "social progress," we refer to the development of societies towards the progressive enablement of human beings to fulfil their needs and capabilities (Sen 1999; Stiglitz, Sen, and Fitoussi 2009; compare the Social Progress Index [Porter and Stern 2015], especially "Access to information and communication"). The consequences of media for social progress can be approached from many angles. Our main emphasis will be on media as providers of content and infrastructures of connection, since these are media's most important aspects for social progress.

13.1.1 Media as Infrastructures of Connection

Developments in media technologies over the past three decades have expanded massively the capacity of human beings and automated systems to create, use, disseminate, and store information and content of all types across time and space. This has happened through the emergence of the Internet, the digitization of previously analogue content, and the development of new platforms and devices. Changes have come so fast that it is easy to forget the much longer history of media's role in the formation of modern societies, polities, and economies. In this chapter we seek to recognize that longer history, while also reflecting upon the dramatic nature of media's transformations over the past three decades.

Media inherently involve the production, sharing, and interpretation of meanings, and so media processes are always contestable and open to further interpretation. Yet media remain at the same time infrastructure: networks of interdependencies that enable social, political, and economic action, but also encode both cultural and technological constraints. This double role of media, as both meaning and infrastructure (Boczkowski and Siles 2014; Sewell 2005), requires investigating both media cultures – what users and audiences do with the media, their "media-related practices" (Couldry 2012) – and media affordances: how media infrastructures shape the range of possible uses available to everyday users and audiences.

13.1.2 Media as Enablers of Increasing Cultural Complexity

Media infrastructures have acquired a particular complexity and reach in the past three decades due to the global but uneven spread of the Internet and social media platforms. Globalization has distributed flows of meaning more transnationally than before. Mundane exposure to media images and messages that flow from other parts of the world encourages people to become more reflexively open to the meanings

produced in other places. This has generated unprecedented cross-border connection, dialogue, and solidarity.

However, the basic patterns underlying contemporary media flows have much earlier origins. From the birth of the press through the development of postal, telephone, radio, and television networks, media flows and infrastructures have been crucial to successive modern forms of citizenship, providing information about governments and markets, connecting national populations and economies, providing forums for citizen practice and underpinning national identity (Anderson 1983). Media flows and infrastructures have also played central roles in projects of political and economic domination, providing the information necessary to govern empires, manage enterprises, and control populations. But media's spread across the world has been uneven, as Section 13.2 explains.

Despite increasing convergence of platforms for media delivery, proliferating media flows, and infrastructures have produced cultural complexity and increased the possibilities for cultural contestation, within and across national borders (Hannerz 1992; Iwabuchi 2002). Imagined communities, sustained by media, now proliferate involving, for example, marginalized people, diasporic communities, and political activists. Digital media have also enabled more people to become active producers and disseminators of images and meanings. This expanded productivity of meaning *through media* has itself become a practical precondition for new movements for social progress.

13.1.3 The Social Justice Issues Raised by Media and Communications

Through media, individuals and groups have more cultural resources with which to interpret and challenge cultural forms. Such access enriches the modalities of political action and protest, with consequences for social change and social progress (relevant SPI indicators are "Personal rights" and "Personal freedom and choice").[4] The political struggles against slavery in the nineteenth century and for the civil rights of all ethnic groups in the late twentieth century were also cultural struggles that drew on contemporary media resources. But because media impact is always contestable, the consequences of media practice and media innovations for social progress cannot be determined at a general level. Media globalization has both engendered indifference and disparity of attention and promoted dialogue and solidarity. Media and communications' contribution to social progress must always be considered at more specific levels.

Nonetheless, since connection is important to people's possibilities of action, *the uneven distribution of opportunities to access media and use them effectively is a dimension of social justice in its own right.* Improved "access to information and communications technology," including "universal affordable access to the Internet" by 2020, is rightly a Sustainable Development Goal (SDG 9.c),[5] but it raises fundamental social justice issues too. First, media are a key resource that enables the "reality" of particular social and political territories to be

---

4   The SPI report is found in Porter and Stern (2015).
5   The SDGs are found in United Nations (2015).

framed one way rather than another; as a result, media, through their operations, can perpetuate specific "injustices [in] framing" (Fraser 2005: 79) the social world. Second, because media have the symbolic power to construct general realities, media institutions comprise a resource whose long-term distribution can be unjust. Some battles for social progress contest particular media representations; others challenge media institutions' general control over symbolic power. In still other cases, media provide a forum for challenging injustices unconnected with media.

The relations between media, communications, and social progress are therefore inherently complex. Measures of social progress (such as the SPI) require considerable adjustment if they are to fully take account of media's contribution to social progress: measures of technological access alone are insufficient. Nor (see Section 13.2) is there a common pattern to how media institutions "work" in societies across the world. Even so, media and communications have important potential to contribute to particular struggles for social justice.

13.1.4　Media, Communications, and the Longer Global Struggle for Media Reform

Now is not the first time that the implications of media flows and infrastructures for social progress have been considered on a global scale. Such questions were central to the MacBride Report prepared for UNESCO in 1980 *(Many Voices, One World)*, which followed two decades of contested debate about "development." The report proposed a New World Information and Communication Order ("NWICO") and challenged the assumption that a global media infrastructure dominated by "the West" was good for democracy, social order and human rights. But the MacBride Report's proposals were not implemented, and a recent attempt to revive their broad agenda (the World Summit on the Information Society in 2003) has also achieved only limited success.[6] The history of "media reform" on a global scale is an interrupted one (MacBride and Roach 1989), which we discuss more fully in Section 13.6. Meanwhile, the relations between media and capitalist accumulation (Jin 2015; Schiller 1999) become ever more complex, and new market-based media infrastructures – for example, social media platforms and the vast infrastructures of data extraction on which they rely – pose increasingly urgent questions for social life and democratic practice.

13.2　Media Industries from Print to the Internet

This section introduces the *diversity* and *unevenness* of media infrastructures, media access, and media's cultural dynamics across the world. As such, it provides the reference point for later discussions of contemporary forms of communication inequality and opportunities for, or threats to, public knowledge (Sections 13.3 and 13.4) and the emergence of new spaces for citizenship (Section 13.5) and the long history of struggles for "democratization *of* media" and "democratization *through* media" (Zhao and Hackett 2005) (Sections 13.6 and 13.7).

6　For a reassessment, see WSIS Civil Society Plenary (2003).
7　Material on Russia in this case study written by Olessia Koltsova.

13.2.1　Traditional Media and the Internet as Infrastructures of Connection

Policy discourses about media have been dominated by the histories of how "modern" media (newspapers, radio, television, film) developed in Western Europe and North America. While scholarship on the complex regional flows of media has challenged the dominance of Western history (Boyd-Barrett 1977; Iwabuchi 2007; Schiller 1969; Sinclair and Jacka 1996), the same geographical skewing has been repeated in recent accounts of the rise of the Internet (Chan 2013). We will argue against this simplified view.

No universal history of media is possible on a global scale. Today's uneven global media landscape reflects many diverse histories: the contrasting reliance on public service versus commercial models of broadcasting in European and North American media systems; major linguistic and institutional diversity in Australasia and the Pacific; the contrasting roles played by state and market in India versus China; the super-fast growth of online connectivity in North-East Asian economies dominated by *Chaebols* (family-owned multinationals in South Korea); the contrasting legacies of colonialism in media development in Africa and Latin America; the distinctive role played by Gulf petro-monarchies in the Arab region's media. There are many possible relations between media, state, market, and society, each shaped differently by geopolitical forces, which rule out a universal narrative of "media and social progress." In what follows we present case studies from different regions to underscore not only media's diversity at a national level, but also how variously media and communication systems intersect to generate resources for social progress. Further case studies are added in later sections (Sections 13.4 and 13.6).

13.2.2　Case Studies

13.2.2.1　Country Case Study 1: China/Russia[7]

Today, Russia and China have large media systems that are highly distinctive in that, while incorporating various market features, they trace their historical origins to twentieth-century state-controlled non-commercial media systems, whose organization had intellectual roots in Marxist-Leninist critiques of capitalist and imperialist control of the media in the West. As such, both systems share the legacy of today's "social movement media," but are also internally complex and marked by nationalistic and sectorial struggles. Indeed, the Chinese system had distinctive differences from the Soviet model and by the early 1960s, the Soviet and Chinese media systems were in serious ideological conflict. By the late 1960s, the Chinese media system was destabilized in the onset of the Cultural Revolution. Nevertheless, what these historical systems had in common was their communist visions of achieving social progress through ideological mobilization and cultural enfranchisement. This vision provided many Third World postcolonial states with alternative models for media organization from those in the West while also providing inspiration for social struggles in the West, including US civil rights struggles (Dudziak 2000; Frazier 2015). However, bureaucratic ossification, and other forms of political, social, and cultural repression, as well as the influence of Western media, contributed to the transformations of China's and Russia's media systems from the early 1980s.

The collapse of the Soviet Union left Russia with a television-centered noncommercial media system. Liberalization, fractionalization of the postcommunist political elite, and economic difficulties led to privatization of state TV channels in the mid-1990s. Newly founded private television channels emerged as the economic situation improved, bringing more diversity into the media landscape. However, the early years of the twenty-first century have seen a gradual *renationalization* of most leading TV channels, outside the entertainment sector. The Russian government inherited from its Soviet predecessor direct control over transmission networks and appointment of the top television management. While the 1990s saw media wars between different television channels representing various political groups, the 2000s were marked by emergence of an identical pro-Kremlin picture on most TV channels. Social and media development is, however, very uneven across Russian provinces, varying from near subsistence farmers (with access to just 2–3 analogue TV channels and no Internet) to highly networked and cosmopolitan major cities. The government's television-based policy of media control is more effective in poorer, less connected regions. While the authorities have allowed a few oppositional media outlets (TV Dojd' [Rain] on the Internet; RBC [RosBusinessConsulting] on cable and satellite; Ekho Moskvy [Echo of Moscow] on the radio), they have very little influence on public opinion. On a global scale, given the denial for two decades to Russian television of broadcasting frequencies in most post-Soviet countries, the government launched Russia Today as a news provider, which is rapidly emerging as a major transnational satellite channel.

Against the trend of most other Russian industries, the Russian internet industry has been very successful. Russia is the only country where local internet businesses have beaten global giants without any protective barriers, with Yandex search engine more popular in Russia than Google, while Vkontakte and Odnoklassniki social networking sites are attracting much larger local audiences than Facebook. Nevertheless, the Russian government is facing a challenging choice with regard to internet management. It has been eager to make the Internet a "locomotive" for the rest of the Russian economy, but this risks disrupting the vision promoted by the government's continued control of Russian television, since government control of the Internet is weaker. Attempts to increase internet control through pro-government ownership of Russian social media sites such as LiveJournal and VKontakte might drive a key segment of the news reading internet audience to foreign competitors such as Facebook. The Russian government has developed three main tactics: gaining ownership over online media; producing its own "user-generated content"; and blocking websites. The result has been a dramatic polarization of Russian audiences between a loyal majority and a critical minority both online and offline. This policy coupled with state support of internet-based creativity, has encouraged the Russian IT sector to move away from politically sensitive issues.

China's post-1980 media system has developed very differently from the Russian system. China's media system retains its overall Leninist structure and core organizational principles, yet through post-Mao

China's economic growth and rapid industrial expansion, China's print and broadcasting media industries are both larger and more highly developed, *and* more tightly integrated and centrally controlled than Russia's. By mid-2015, China had over 2,000 newspaper titles, nearly 10,000 periodicals, more than 300 television stations with nearly 3,000 channels, with an audience reach of 1.35 billion. However, following nearly four decades of state-directed commercialization, market consolidation, global integration, and digital convergence, China's media also bear the hallmarks of market-driven systems familiar in other parts of the world.

At the core of China's media and communications infrastructure are state-controlled media and communications conglomerations organized at national and provincial levels, including Xinhua News Agency, People's Daily Group, CCTV, China National Radio and China Radio International, and state-owned telecommunication providers such as China Mobile, China Telecom, and China Unicom. Regional media conglomerates such as Shanghai Media and Entertainment Group, Guangdong Nanfang Media Group, and Hunan Satellite Television have also been highly influential in spearheading institutional reform, operational innovations, and content diversification. While state control, political direction, and censorship remain an enduring issue for China's media professional strata and citizens, particularly in relation to social media platforms, some outlets such as CCTV's well-known prime time investigative show *Focus Interviews* have played a significant role in spearheading social reforms.

Since the late 1990s, the Chinese state has systematically aimed to build the size and strength of its media and communication operations. Targeted national initiatives such as the "connecting every village" project have significantly improved access in China's remote areas, making China's media and communication infrastructure one of the most advanced in the Global South. At the same time, as part of the Chinese state's effort to address long-standing imbalances in global communication and promote its own vision of "globalization," it has systematically expanded the reach of its media and communication industries, with CCTV establishing branches in North America and Africa, and China Telecom and China Mobile expanding globally. The Chinese state's persistent effort to control the "commanding heights" of converging media and communication industries, regulate global media and communication flows, manage private and foreign capital investments, and pursue the latest technological innovations, has had a huge impact on the system's evolving structure and values (Hong 2017).

China's framework for developing its media and communications infrastructure does not therefore fit with the dominant Western liberal framework that treats press freedom (and "internet freedom"), defined always as freedom *from* government control, as the precondition of social progress. Each framework is explained by its distinctive historical and geopolitical context: accordingly, the more the Chinese media system evolves, the more the Communist Party of China seeks to emphasize its Leninist founding principles.

Since the early 1990s, the Chinese state has mounted an all-out effort for information technology development through various "golden projects" to integrate network applications with Chinese politics, economy, and society. In the aftermath of the 2008 global economic crisis, the Chinese state elevated the media, communication, internet, and cultural industries as a driver of economic restructuring (Hong 2017). In early 2015, Premier Li Keqiang unveiled the Chinese state's "Internet Plus Action Plan" to stimulate economic growth by integrating mobile internet, cloud computing, big data, and the "Internet of Things" with modern manufacturing. No other issue has received as much strategic emphasis by consecutive Chinese leaderships in the past three decades. By the time China-based internet firm Alibaba made a record-setting stock market debut in New York in 2014, China had established itself as the world's largest internet market in terms of the number of users, and in December 2015 China's internet population was 688 million – just over half of the national population (China Internet Network Information Center 2016). Yet in this project of making China into "a cyber power," the Chinese state treats citizen access and government control as not opposed, but indissolubly linked (Xinhua 2014). Meanwhile, various sectors of Chinese society have enthusiastically embraced the Internet (as less tightly controlled than the traditional media), turning it into a new terrain of discursive struggles over China's future.

These developments challenge any simplistic "state versus civil society" reading of how the Internet contributes to social progress: both the Chinese state *and* Chinese society have been empowered through the Internet (Zhang and Zheng 2012), with outcomes significantly different from the parallel history of media in Russia.

13.2.2.2   Country Case Study 2: Sweden

In contrast to government-controlled media regimes, Sweden's media is shaped by a welfare state system and characterized by a distinctive relation between media and state, market and civil society. Traditionally, Sweden has had high voter turnout, and high levels of media and information literacy, not least due to the national subsidy system for print newspapers, which have resulted in a plurality of local newspapers with high readership. Typically, the subsidy system provided for a plurality of political positions, with at least two local or regional newspapers representing two political viewpoints. Like other European countries, Sweden has had a strong public service broadcaster for radio and TV, which since the late 1980s has faced strong competition from commercial broadcasters. The communications infrastructure has been well developed, with high penetrations of landline phones, mobile phones, and computers.

The development of Sweden's news media has followed a similar pattern as other north European countries, with weakening public service media (due to audiences migrating to commercial channels), and a drift within the press from a focus on opinion formation to a closer tracking of market demand (Weibull 2016). Newspapers are today facing dramatic declines in readership, and advertising has migrated to the Internet. News consumption has also migrated from traditional press to social media such as Facebook and Twitter. This shift has challenged Sweden's distinctive relations between media and wider society.

Since the late 1990s Sweden has witnessed a tight horizontal integration of the media sector, with companies formerly working within one media developing tie-ins or purchasing companies in other markets: Sweden's largest media house Bonnier, a book publisher in the nineteenth century, moved early into publishing newspapers and weekly/monthly magazines, and today owns television, cinemas, advertising, and social marketing outlets. The development of "media houses," with particular regions' media being largely controlled by local or regional media houses, has also undermined the press subsidy system, undermining political variety in spite of continued state subsidy (Nygren and Zuiderveld 2011).

The digitization of media contents in particular has changed the power dynamics within the media industries, with the telecommunications industries acquiring increased importance because of their centrality to Wi-Fi and broadband networks. This infrastructural power was highlighted in 2016, when TeliaSonera closed an exclusive deal with Facebook for free surfing through their networks, perceived as unfair competition by Swedish news publishers in print and broadcasting and contrary to the EU regulation on net neutrality (compare Section 13.6.4 on Facebook India).[8]

Because of its well-developed infrastructure for high-speed internet, Sweden is also known as a safe haven for internet piracy, with The Pirate Bay party – its most prominent symbol (Andersson Schwarz 2013; Larsson 2013) – acting as a focus for debates on media governance issues.

13.2.2.3   Country Case Study 3: South Africa

South African media are arguably the most technologically advanced on the African continent, offering a wide range of content across print, broadcast, and digital platforms. Its media landscape involves a three-tiered model of public, commercial, and community media. South Africa became a democracy in 1994, with its early period post-independence from Britain (1961) better seen as the continuation of colonialism in internal form (the apartheid system) (Visser 1997). But in many ways the country's media show similarities with those elsewhere on the continent, where colonialism, the postcolonial transition, and globalization have shaped media systems.

The changes that South African public broadcasting has undergone illustrate some of these shifts. As in other African countries under military or one-party state rule, the South African Broadcasting Corporation (SABC) under apartheid acted as a state broadcaster. In 1991, the Windhoek Declaration, which was put together by independent African journalists and endorsed by UNESCO, initiated a move to greater freedom, pluralism, and independence as regards print media. This was followed 10 years later by the African Charter on Broadcasting, which created momentum for private, public, and community broadcasting. The Windhoek Declaration signaled a move towards greater independence of broadcasting continent-wide, even if in some countries like Zimbabwe there has been a deterioration in recent years (Kupe 2016). The Windhoek Declaration coincided with the period of negotiated

---

8   SVT Opinion, May 2, 2016. www.svt.se/opinion/telias-uppgorelse-med-facebook-ett-slag-mot-svenska-medieforetag.

transition in South Africa, which saw the SABC adopting a public service mandate and media freedom entrenched in the new Constitution. The SABC has, however, never been fully publicly funded, and is largely dependent on commercial funding (Kupe 2014: 29). As in other African countries, the SABC has recently seen a "push-back" from government (Kupe 2016): some argue its editorial independence has eroded under pressure from an ANC government increasingly intolerant of media criticism. Other negative signs have been the proposal of a statutory Media Appeals Tribunal that would impose harsher sanctions on offending journalists, and the Protection of State Information Bill that could criminalize whistleblowers, investigative journalists, and civil society activists who access information classified by government as secret (R2K 2015).

South Africa led the way in newspaper development in Anglophone Africa, with the publication of the Cape Town Gazette in 1800 (Karikari 2007:13), and a centuries-old private commercial press. Under apartheid, mainstream newspapers either supported the regime (the Afrikaans-language press) or provided a limited critique (the English press), while an alternative, underground press engaged in a more radical critique of apartheid and faced harassment, censure, and closures. Democratization largely eliminated the parallelism between language and political orientation, and most South African newspapers adopted a watchdog approach to the government and reflected a liberal, commercial consensus.

Meanwhile, South African media have been affected by global investment processes. The South African press was a major capitalist venture from its inception. For example, the South African media company Naspers has become a globalized conglomerate, while the Irish Independent group bought the largest English-language newspaper group in 1994, selling it in 2013 to the Sekunjalo consortium, in which Chinese business interests have a major stake. Widely seen as a vehicle for soft power in Africa, several state-owned Chinese media houses have offices on the continent (Kenya as well as South Africa), including the news agency Xinhua, the newspaper *China Daily*, China Central Television, and China Radio International. China has also funded Africa's media and communications infrastructure (Wu 2012). The influence of the Chinese media presence and investments in African media on journalistic norms and practices has been controversial, and challenges any simple regional or Western-dominated model of media diversity.

During the transition to democracy, a particular attempt was made to strengthen the community media sector through the establishment of the Media Development and Diversity Agency (MDDA) to fund media owned and controlled by the community they serve, especially to enable more Black ownership of media (Banda 2006). Another important development has been the rise of popular tabloid newspapers, which, although commercially owned, provide perspectives from the poor, mostly Black, working class rarely found in mainstream print media (Wasserman 2010). Some of the most interesting alternatives to the mainstream print media in South Africa have been online (the *Daily Maverick*, *The Con* and *Groundup)*. Such publications have provided critical analysis and investigative reporting often surpassing the mainstream press in South Africa in diversity and depth. Despite the obstacles in terms of access and reach, digital media platforms

are increasingly reshaping social relationships and public spheres in Africa (Mabweazara 2015: 2). Meanwhile, the mobile phone has had a massive impact as a platform for Internet access, for reconstituting traditional modes of sociality (Mabweazara 2015: 2–3), and, via social media platforms, providing spaces for citizens to engage in political debate and mobilize for social change.

13.2.2.4　Country Case Study 4: Indonesia[9]

An important case of a diverse media system is Indonesia, the largest economy in Southeast Asia with a population of 240 million, and the fourth largest democracy in the world. The establishment of Indonesia's modern media system owes greatly to the legacies of President Soeharto's five-year economic development plans, which centralized capital and inhabitants in Java. For decades the authoritarian state held strong control over media infrastructure and content, from the press, radio, film, satellite, to television. The media system was built to support state developmentalism, limiting civilians to accessing information provided by the state.

During the 1960s–1980s, Indonesia had a single, state broadcasting system, Television of the Republic of Indonesia. Although designed as a network system, television infrastructure and production relied heavily on central funding and programming (Sen and Hill 2000). The state-controlled television system shifted to an open, privatized, and more liberal system in the late 1980s as a consequence of the government's open market and open sky policy. These policies allowed foreign content via satellite television and cable networks (Hollander, d'Haenens, and Bardoel 2009), which catered to the needs of the expanding urban middle class. By the early 1990s, dozens of private television stations had been founded, owned by the President's close allies. This gave precedence to market demand over commercial news, and gradually weakened state control over information. Around the same time, the Internet came to Indonesia, providing an alternative source of information to a small elite in Java (Lim 2003; Sen and Hill 2000). Media liberalization and commercialization of information paved way for the growth of a civil society (Hill and Sen 2005; Hollander et al. 2009), which was the prelude to Indonesia's transition towards democracy.

The authoritarian regime finally broke under the weight of the Asian economic crisis of 1997, in the face of increasing public pressure and conflicting interests within the ruling elite, starting a social transformation among an expanding middle class amid conditions of unprecedented economic growth (Basri 2012). While market demand over commercial news had helped the push for democratic transition, since the early 2000s the development of the news media in Indonesia have relied more on market responses rather than having an independent democratic agenda (see Lim 2011). Television is Indonesia's most popular media with a penetration rate of 97 percent (Nielsen 2014), and it continues to attract the dominant share of advertising income.

Second to television, the Internet has the highest penetration rate of 34.9 percent in 2014 (APJII 2015) or 88 million users to 51.8 percent in 2016 (APJII 2016). Nielsen (2014) estimated that 48 percent of mobile

---

9　Case study written by Inaya Rakhmani.

phone owners use their phones to access the Internet. This has caused the closing of print versions of newspapers, while digital news has seen a steady rise. Over two decades, Indonesia's media have seen a convergence whereby established media companies, initially specialized in one form of media – print, television, or online – are expanding into other media, forming larger, multiplatform converged conglomerates (Tapsell 2015). Indonesia experienced the largest number of mergers and acquisitions in the history of its media system in 2011 (Nugroho, Putri, and Laksmi 2012), establishing four large media conglomerates, namely MNC Group, Jawa Pos Group, Kompas Gramedia Group, and Mahaka Group (Lim 2012). There has emerged a set of interconnected relationships between politicians and media proprietors, with various political leaders owning media companies. The CEO of MNC Group, Hary Tanoesoedibjo, founded and heads the political party Perindo, and ran for vice president of Indonesia in 2015. MNC Group owns three terrestrial television stations, one pay television station with 60 percent of market share, 14 local television stations, one newspaper, one online news portal, and several franchise magazines. This has allowed media conglomerates to republish the same news content on multiple platforms.

Significantly, the Internet infrastructure and service provision remain dominated by *state enterprises* Telkom and Indosat, which cater mostly to urban users in large cities. Media markets and conglomeration are concentrated in Jakarta and Java more broadly, monetizing the activities of internet users in large cities while excluding users in rural areas and small cities. Only 20 percent of women in Indonesia have internet access (World Wide Web Foundation 2016), which calls for new ways for inclusive approaches that are gender-informed (see Triastuti 2014). International forces are important too: in 2015, 70 percent of digital advertising revenue in Indonesia (USD 560 million) went directly to Google and Facebook, rather than national companies. Consequently, media systems in Indonesia today still reflect the centralization model that was established since the 1960s, while also registering the power of global digital platforms.

13.2.2.5   Country Case Study 5: Mexico[10]

The media system in Mexico is highly concentrated and deeply marketized. Its core is commercial broadcasting, owned by private corporations controlled by a handful of individuals. The power of those media corporations was built from alliances between powerful economic groups aligned with government interests that have benefited from discretionary grants, television and radio concessions, lucrative contracts for governmental advertising in print media, and ad hoc legislation (or lack of it) in favor of the sector's economic interests.

After the Mexican Revolution (1910–1920) the country adopted a capitalist economic model and initiated a corporatization of the Mexican State. From 1929 to 2000 all presidents were members of the *Partido Revolucionario Institucional* (PRI). Lack of regulation and communication policies led to a concentration of media in a few families. In the early twentieth century, well-established industrial families (railways, mining, and banking) invested in radio broadcasting. After the First

World War, US capital replaced European investments in Mexico, with large investments in the radio industry (radio stations, manufacture and sales of radio devices, records, phonographs). Today there are 1,600 radio stations, but 80 percent of them are owned by 13 commercial families.

In 1950 the Mexican television industry started, modeled on the US commercial system. The families who owned radio stations became, in turn, the owners of television stations, for example, the Azcárraga family, which, from its original concession of Channel 2, grew through mergers to create the now better known Televisa (Televisión Vía Satélite). From 1972 to 1993 Televisa was Mexico's only private television company, competing with three public television channels. From its origins, Televisa had a close link with the ruling party PRI. Televisa subsequently became the most influential global producer and distributer of Spanish-language audiovisual contents, and currently owns free-to-air television channels, restricted television systems (satellite and cable), a leading Spanish editorial house, radio stations, entertainment companies, soccer teams and stadiums, music recording companies, and cinema distribution companies. In the early 1990s the public television channels 7 and 13 were privatized. The Salinas Pliego family (owners of departmental stores and previously radio manufacturers) bought both channels and created Televisión Azteca offering contents similar to those of Televisa and aligning itself with the government.

The early 1990s also saw the privatization of telecommunications, generating another monopoly (Telmex-Telcel) in the hands of just one individual, Carlos Slim. Slim's monopoly started with landline telephone services (Telmex has 65 percent of the national market) and moved on to mobile telephony (Telcel has 65 percent of subscribers) and internet services (75 percent of subscribers). The government justified the sale of the nation's telephone company to a single owner by arguing that a monopoly would scale economies, lower costs, and increase the number of landlines. However, Mexico's mobile phone and internet service costs are actually in the middle of international rankings (International Telecommunications Union 2014), and, although, since the early 2000s, internet home users have grown from 5 percent to 61 percent of the population, the digital divide between urban and rural areas has widened.

Political reforms have continuously supported deregulation and privatization, and changes in legislation have meant more power and influence for media monopolies, generating a *mediacracy*, where members of senate and congress have direct links with the media industry. In 2012 the PRI party regained the presidency of Mexico, with Enrique Peña Nieto elected with the full support of the media industry, mainly Televisa. In 2013 Peña Nieto promoted a historic constitutional reform in telecommunications and broadcasting with the aim to increase competition in the sector. The new legislation enabled Televisa to enter the telecommunications market by offering *triple play services* (cable television, landline telephone services, and the Internet). Televisa now controls the market of restricted television (cable and satellite) with 60 percent of subscribers and in 2014 and 2015 purchased two new cable companies. The new legislation punishes Telmex by imposing strict restrictions on telephone carriers (cancellation of long distance fees; a prohibition on charging for interconnection services).

---

10   Case study written by Claudia Magallanes-Blanco.

There are also positive aspects to this new legislation. While public services are still offered by private entities through concessions regimes that distinguish between commercial, public, and social media (indigenous and cultural), with the latter not allowed to sell advertisements (previously community and indigenous media were not recognized, and so operated outside any legal framework), telecommunications and broadcasting have now been defined as fundamental human rights and public services (compare SDG 9.c). As for telecommunications, the new legislation reserves a portion of the spectrum for social concessions, reflecting the work done by the community cellular network in creating a network of mobile phone services for indigenous communities previously denied mobile phone services by the major telecommunication companies. Civil society activism in Mexico has begun slowly to correct for some of the excesses of previous marketization.

* * * * *

The section has introduced the diversity of the world's media systems and their organization: state, market, and civil society may work in isolation or together in multiple combinations, with varying consequences for how media and communications outputs provide a context for social progress and struggles for social justice.

13.2.3   Unevenness of Access

The stark differences in access to media between population sectors may have consequences for social progress. It is significant that basic levels of mobile phone subscriptions and internet access are included as items in the SPI, alongside concerns about state control of media registered in the press freedom index (compare SDG 9.c).

Effective media access depends on the interrelationship between media and other closely related factors: literacy, language, and education (SDG 4). This is the central lesson from the "digital divide" debate: *that simple availability of technology is not sufficient* for development or social progress. Empowerment of people through Media and Information Literacy is an important prerequisite for fostering equitable access to information and knowledge and promoting free, independent, and pluralistic media and information systems (UNESCO 2013). Adequate levels of media *use* require training and education, democratic participation, accessibility of formats and technology for people with disabilities and other distinctive needs, diverse content in appropriate languages, freedom of expression, and opportunities for community and citizen-produced media. The 2005 Tunis Agenda for The Information Society acknowledged these factors, and they have since been the focus of international efforts (WSIS 2005). The multifaceted nature of "access" is crucial to understanding media's integral role in achieving the Sustainable Development Goals, and broader social progress (International Telecommunications Union 2016) (SPI "Access to information and communications").

Globally, there has been progress on access to internet and mobile phones in the past 20 years (SPI "Access to information and communications"; "Mobile telephone subscriptions"). However, what such broad indicators of "access" mean on the ground is poorly understood: much depends on what kinds of media, internet, and mobile content people can affordably access. What media access do people need as the *minimum* for a "universal" service? Without closer attention to these questions, today's push to ever-greater digital connectivity only risks deepening digital exclusion.

There are *regions* with highly uneven media access. Asia, for instance, includes countries such as South Korea and Japan, both pioneers in digital media, as well as emerging powerhouses (India, China). India has gone from fewer than 1 percent of individuals using the Internet (in 2000–2001) to 18 percent in 2014; China has moved from 1.78 percent in 2000 to 49.3 percent in 2014. Yet other Asian countries have poor media infrastructure, including Bangladesh (9.6 percent internet users) and Laos (14.26 percent) (International Telecommunications Union 2015). In Latin America, the mobile phone landscape is not homogenous, but the rapid spread of mobile phones is in part explained by the previous lack of landlines. In a number of countries, total figures for mobile phone subscriptions are high – for instance, Chile, Argentina, and México (International Telecommunications Union 2016). However, on closer inspection, there is a significant proportion of the population in these and other countries without adequate access to mobile communication – either through not owning a phone or through restricted use of services due to affordability (Donner 2015).

Within *countries*, there are also striking disparities in access (SDG 9.c), especially in rural and remote areas, among different sociodemographics, cultural, ethnic, and racial groups, and groups with reduced or uncertain legal or citizenship status (for example migrants and internally displaced persons). Upon closer inspection, many cities with apparent "good infrastructure" display great differences between the media "have-less" and "have-mores." Yet other countries have seen extraordinary large-scale growth. Among China's 688 million internet users (2015), the vast majority (620 million) use social media applications such as Weibo and Tencent's Wechat; around 90 percent of China's internet-using population access the Internet through mobile phones, while internet use for online payments, access to online education and medical services, has become widespread among the middle classes.

We must, however, note the continuing lack of gender equity in access to and use of media. Significantly fewer women are connected to the Internet than men. In 24 of 29 European countries between 2008 and 2010, men outnumbered women users of the Internet. For the same time period in non-European countries, men outnumbered women users in 36 of 39 countries (comprising OECD and non-OECD countries). The "global internet user gender gap" widened from 11 percent in 2013 to 12 percent in 2016. In the poorest countries, the gap is large: 31 percent in the least developed countries. On a regional level, there is significant disparity in the gender gap: 23 percent in Africa compared to the Americas. In many countries, gender often intersects with other factors (e.g. location, age) to create even deeper inequalities. Only a few countries report higher internet use by women compared to men (International Telecommunications Union 2016).

Such figures give just a partial insight into a complex situation of inequality. Profound changes in media technologies are typically accompanied by promises to improve gender inequalities yet such technologies are often unaffordable for many groups of women, and gender is often neglected in design, education, and resource processes crucial to ensuring communication rights. The emergence of new technologies may generate new kinds of injustice and exclusion: misogyny and oppressive gender relations have taken disturbing forms on social media platforms. Such gendered aspects of media and ICTs significantly hinder social progress, as noted in the agenda laid out by UNESCO's Global Alliance on Gender and Media.

Media's contribution to social progress cannot therefore be understood without grasping both the *distribution* and *differentiation* of media access, and how they shape possibilities for political and social agency.

13.2.4   Cultural Flows of Media Within Regions

Putting the complexities of media infrastructure to one side, media's *cultural forms and consequences* also vary significantly from region to region. Western colonial powers such as the United Kingdom, France, and the United States dominated global information flows during and after the colonial period. Those media culture flows were unevenly shaped by the long-standing centrality of the United States, with which even the United Kingdom and France could not compete. Some Western countries (such as France) developed media regulation to contest US cultural dominance and foster "national culture."

In a globalized world, however, more complex flows of media culture have evolved. Cultural globalization does not simply homogenize the world, but instead reorganizes the production of cultural diversity (Hannerz 1996). By creatively localizing and indigenizing US cultural influences, some non-Western countries such as Brazil, Mexico, Nigeria, Japan, South Korea, and India have achieved high levels of media production capacity, especially in the last two decades. The media outputs of those countries circulate transnationally and are favorably received within and beyond their regions, generating important counterflows to US dominance.

In Latin America, the predominant mainstream cultural flow is *telenovelas*, or "soap opera" TV drama series, which have been exported globally. Export formats have evolved from selling program series to selling only the show's central idea or main character (Bitereyst and Meers 2000; La Pastina and Straubhaar 2005).[11] Mexican, Brazilian, and Colombian television content has shifted what Latin Americans watch on their screens. If 1970s and 1980s generations grew up watching mainly US-produced imports, today's Latin American audiences are exposed to the customs, lifestyles, and social fabric of Latin American communities themselves. And, although Latin American media content still privileges the visibility of upper class and predominantly White groups, some content does depict the experiences of working-class and non-White Latin Americans. Additionally, free trade agreements and the growing number of migrants from Latin American countries to North America have generated new North–South media content flows; since 1994, Spanish-language media has grown exponentially in the United States, and Univisión (owned by Hallmark) and Telemundo

(owned by Sony) are the two main Spanish-language cable television networks. Univisión benefits from an agreement with Mexico's Televisa, including a pipeline of Spanish-language content. Other lesser players in the global field of Spanish-language media include CNN, BBC, MTV, and Fox, with news and sports channels entirely in Spanish.[12] But overall the unevenness of mainstream audiences' daily media fare has not changed much since the mid-1990s: Latin American media include mostly Latin American and US content (music, films, TV), plus a trickle of Japanese anime and European media content (mainly BBC). Flows from other regions of the world (Africa, South and Southeast Asia) are still scarce.

The impact of globalization on African media has also shifted the flows and contraflows of media content and capital. After the long dominance of ex-colonial powers, many countries have recently developed media production capacities. A prominent example is the growth of the Nigerian film industry "Nollywood," which exports to a global audience (Krings and Onookome 2013; Larkin 2008). It has become the third largest global producer of feature films, next to Hollywood (United States) and Bollywood (India), relying increasingly on coproduction and distribution with the Ghanaian film industry. Also notable are the growing African and global footprint of the South African media giant Naspers, and significant foreign investment in African media firms, especially from China (Xinhua news agency, China Central Television: see Section 13.2.1).

In Asia, India, Hong Kong, and Japan have developed local film and TV industries and their outputs have circulated within the region for many years. However, circulation outside the region has jumped sharply in the last two decades. The global diffusion of Bollywood films has become much more prominent (Kavoori and Punathambekar 2008; Gopal and Moorti 2008). In East Asia, cultural products such as manga, animation, video games, and TV dramas produced in Japan have generated a regional and global media culture since the 1990s (Iwabuchi 2002). Even more notable is the so-called "Korean Wave" (or *Halryu*, a term first coined by Chinese reporters in 1999), whereby Korean cultural products such as films, television dramas, fashion, and popular music (K-pop) have penetrated other Asian markets (Chua and Iwabuchi 2008; Kim 2013), Europe, and Latin America. The Korean Wave offers an intriguing example of how national cultural policy can be used as a form of soft power, bolstering local production capacity and promoting the export of media culture by "creative industries." South Korea's interventionist cultural policies position the Korean cultural industry as a "sub-empire" of the Hollywood system in Asia. The "Korean Wave" thus signifies the Korean culture industry's ambiguous position *as both* a counterflow against the Hollywood system *and* a subflow co-opted by Hollywood.

This complexity characterizes counterflows in other regions too. The more counterflows to American media culture advance, the more market-driven governance encompasses them. Even though relatively independent from the cultural dominance of the "Hollywood empire," the rise of media culture flows in non-Western regions has given rise to new intraregional asymmetries. American media culture maintains

---

[11]   The best example is the Colombian *Ugly Betty*, which has a Mexican and a US adaptation, each completely different from the Colombian source, apart from the main character (Miller 2010).

[12]   http://palabraclave.unisabana.edu.co/index.php/palabraclave/article/viewFile/4669/pdf.

a pivotal presence, yet in a way that goes beyond a straightforward understanding of American cultural hegemony. Hollywood itself has striven to incorporate capital, talent, and narratives from many parts of the world and develop outsourcing of postproduction labor on a global scale (Miller et al. 2004). The rise of non-Western media cultures forms part of a market-driven *recentralization* in which diverse players across the world collaborate to penetrate transnational markets, engendering a new kind of governance via marketing, coproduction, distribution, and copyright monopoly. Section 13.3 will discuss the emergence of global governance infrastructures for the regulation of information and data.

This is not to underestimate the newly emerging landscape of media globalization. Together with the progress of digital communication technologies, the acceleration of human mobilities from and among non-Western regions (by migrants, expatriates, students) has complicated the cross-border circulation and consumption of media cultures. Meanwhile cultural *counter*flows between diverse regions and countries cultivate cross-border exchange and dialogue, with important implications for social progress. Regional circulation of diverse media cultures has enabled new kinds of cross-border connection, mutual understanding, and self-reflexivity by people about their own society and culture. The *mutual consumption* of media cultures, for example of entertainment genres popular with women audiences such as soap operas, has enabled mutual understanding of societies and cultures, for example in regions such as East Asia. However, as it is predominantly market-oriented forces that have advanced cross-border media circulation, it is the commercially and ideologically dominant elements of each country's media culture that tend to travel, under-representing marginalized voices (Iwabuchi 2002, 2015). Crucial questions thus remain: whose voices and concerns are excluded, what perceptions of self–other relationships are typically promoted, and which issues are under-represented, as the marketization of media culture flows advances? Section 13.5 considers the ambivalent consequences for practices of global citizenship that such media connections may foster.

13.2.5 Digital Disruptions and Transformations (Technological, Geo-Political)

Even before 2005, the global media landscape was highly uneven, and its implications for social progress correspondingly complex. Some key developments since the middle of the century's first decade (when Facebook, the world's current most successful social media platform, was launched) have increased this complexity considerably. Of course there is not today "one" Internet – much of the Internet is inaccessible in language to large sections of the world's population – but some key patterns are clear.

The key technological development has been the shift from so-called "web 1.0" – a system of media infrastructure based on discrete websites, connected by hypertext links, with access obtained from desktop or laptop computers – to "web 2.0" characterized by increasing use of *interactive* online platforms, in particular social media platforms. Today, both platforms and websites are increasingly accessed from phones and other mobile devices, and the applications (or "apps") embedded within them. This change from a "read only" to

a "read/write" interface has intensified internet use and its embedding in daily life, heightening institutional attention to how audiences can be reached online and stimulating the rise of a vast commercial infrastructure of online data collection and data processing. This shift in media as "infrastructure" has involved also a significant cultural shift, as patterns of use have changed (a shift in media as "meaning"). This double shift has multiple consequences.

First, the increasing dependence in daily life on a complex, distributed online infrastructure for *mediating* daily life changes the power dynamics within the media industries, leading to the increased importance of the telecommunications industries that provide infrastructures of connection (Wi-Fi and broadband networks). Market convergence means that telecommunications providers have the power of control "in the last instance" over the communication systems on which all content distribution depends (Bolin 2011). Consider the vast scale of some new media infrastructure companies: Google's annual revenue in 2015 was 74.5 billion USD, Facebook's 17.9 billion USD, and Amazon's 107 billion USD.[13]

But the global balance is no longer one of simple US dominance. By the end of 2014, of the top 10 internet companies in the world, 6 are US and 4 are Chinese. Indeed, the growing power of China's internet market, with its distinctive Chinese platforms (Sina's Weibo, Tencent's Wechat) is such that Shi (2015) has argued that cyberspace now has two camps, *GAFA* (Google, Amazon, Facebook, and Apple) and *BATJ* (Baidu, Alibaba, Tencent, Jingdong). As a result, "the material foundation for US–China co-governance of the Internet is in shape" (Shi 2015). This observation was made at the 2015 World Internet Conference Wuzhen Summit at which the Chinese state's effort promoted its goal of shaping the future of global internet governance, a strategy with profound implications not only for China, but also for global communication politics.

Second, such developing power concentrations have implications for evermore sectors of everyday life from government to health (SDG 3). Take also education (SDG 4): concerns are developing regarding school learning materials increasingly provided not by the state but by commercial media companies such as Apple and Google through initiatives such as Apple Education and Google for Education. Weaker welfare and public service systems are creating opportunities for market advances in areas such as education that were not previously much commercially exploited (Forsman 2014; Selwyn 2014).

Third, none of these developments would be possible without a huge double development in media's "infrastructures of connection": the vast infrastructure of data collection and processing that drives the activities of search engines and all sorts of digital platforms and, underpinning them, the default infrastructure of "cloud computing" (Mosco 2014) that provides the capacity necessary for such data collection and processing, and for the general expansion of computer-based information processing in everyday life (for example, the "Internet of Things"). Both developments expand what we mean by "media" and create new challenges for governance (see Section 13.3).

---

[13] www.statista.com/.

At the same time, deep *inequalities* of access remain, as noted in Section 13.2.2. The African continent, for example, remains characterized by widespread poverty, huge socioeconomic inequalities, and highly differentiated patterns of media access and use, with the central parts of the continent most deprived (Porter and Stern 2015: 17, 50). Such inequalities have important implications for citizens' ability to participate in any mediated public sphere (see Sections 13.4 and 13.5).

We cannot therefore say that the "whole world" is being transformed by media at the same time and in the same way. Yet the overall direction of these large-scale transformations is changing how we think about media's potential contribution to social progress.

13.3 The Governance of Media Infrastructures

As we showed in Section 13.2, the global media landscape is complex and uneven, reflecting many diverse histories. The often opaque structures of media governance that have emerged in the digital era are another factor that complicates media and communications' contribution to social progress.

13.3.1 The Evolving Relations Between Media Infrastructures and Government Regulation of Information Flows

Governments worldwide have expressed interests in regulating media infrastructures. In some cases, such interests take the form of laws directly prescribing the conditions of information access and exchange or the technical capabilities of media infrastructures. In others, legal incentives for the takedown of certain kinds of information produce regulatory effects.

Legal regimes in many countries protect freedom of expression, but all governments prohibit the publication and exchange of certain types of information. Additionally, "[m]any democracies now deploy national-level filtering systems through which all ISPs (or in some cases most major ones) are compelled to block designated lists of websites to address public concerns about … illegal activities conducted on the Internet" (MacKinnon 2012: 95). Typical subjects of legal prohibitions include child pornography, speech offering material assistance to terrorists, speech that infringes intellectual property rights, and speech ruled to be defamatory. Additionally, some countries prohibit the dissemination of hate speech, and many set limits on the collection, dissemination, and processing of personal information, although data protection regimes vary considerably from country to country. There are good reasons for all these prohibitions, but each involves governments in decisions about what is or is not prohibited, and therefore raises the possibility of overbroad interpretation leading to censorship of other, nominally protected expression. Such decisions necessarily have implications for the quality of social life and the possibilities for social progress.

In some situations, legal rules incentivize media infrastructure companies to create notice-and-takedown mechanisms for removal of prohibited information. To create an additional, more consistent set of incentives for removal, many countries have enacted legislation that provides safe harbor from copyright infringement liability if procedures are followed for removal of unauthorized copyright-protected materials from publicly available websites and/or exclusion of such materials from search results. The first copyright safe harbor legislation was enacted by the United States as part of the Digital Millennium Copyright Act of 1998.[14] Similar provisions have been enacted in many other countries, often following inclusion of such obligations in bilateral or multilateral free trade agreements negotiated by the United States (Fink and Reichenmiller 2006; see also Valdes and McCann 2014). More recently, European legal instruments regarding privacy and data protection have been interpreted to afford enforceable rights to deindexing and erasure of information made available online.[15] Those rulings have prompted some online information providers, including most notably Google, to develop notice-and-takedown mechanisms patterned after the copyright model (Powles and Chaparro 2015). Such legal structures play important roles in shaping the "rules of the game" regarding information flow in daily life.

Meanwhile, governments in some regions have invested heavily in the development of technologies for regulating citizens' informational activities more directly and on highly granular levels. South Korea, for example, for several years enforced a "real-name system" for internet access that prevented anonymous expression online. In 2012, the Constitutional Court of Korea struck down the real-name requirements, ruling that they violated internet users' freedom of speech.[16] Automated content filtering of information supplied via media infrastructures is pervasive. Such filtering is often justified by asserted needs that parallel the reasons offered for direct speech prohibitions (e.g. protection against pornography, copyright infringement, and/or defamation and harassment); in operation, however, it also seeks to police and deny access to content for political reasons (MacKinnon 2012).

On another level, not just governments but corporations (from Europe, North America, and Asia) are heavily involved in the *building* of media infrastructures, for example through the export of technologies to the Global South. Such infrastructures often include built-in capacities for censorship and surveillance. Chinese companies export technologies similar to those developed to Communist Party specifications for domestic use (MacKinnon 2012). When the Zimbabwean government jammed shortwave broadcasts in the run-up to the 2005 elections, it was believed to have done so by using jamming equipment provided by China (Wu 2012). But North American and European companies such as Cisco also export information technologies built to customer specification to enable informational control, and global platform companies have acceded to demands for censorship to gain access to local markets (Stirland 2008; Wu 2012).

---

14 Digital Millennium Copyright Act of 1998, Pub. L. No. 105–304, Title II: Online Liability Limitation, 112 Stat. 2860, codified as amended at 17 USC. § 512.

15 *Google Spain SL* v. *Agencia Española de Protección de Datos and Mario Costeja Gonzalez*, No. C-131/12, May 13, 2014.

16 Constitutional Court Decision 2010Hun-Ma47, August 23, 2012.

13.3.2 The Shift From Formal to Informal Governance and the Rise of New Global/Transnational Governance Institutions

Direct government mandates, prohibitions, and procurements are the most obvious mechanisms through which media infrastructures are governed, but other mechanisms are equally important. The emergence of a networked information economy and the globalization of mediated information flows have catalyzed two significant shifts in the nature and quality of governance. The first is a shift away from formal government regulation toward informal and often highly *corporatized* governance mechanisms. The second is a shift away from state-based governance (and global governance institutions organized around state membership) toward transnational governance institutions more directly responsive to the asserted needs of private entities, often also corporations, that are those institutions' "stakeholders." Both trends, if they continue unabated, may result in a serious imbalance inconsistent with SDG 16, which calls for the building of "effective, accountable and inclusive institutions at all levels."

Particularly in the Global North but also the Global South, the information networks and communication protocols that underlie media infrastructures are designed and operated by private, corporate entities. Direct technical authority over networks and protocols gives those entities an authority that is inherently regulatory. Global platform companies such as Google, Twitter, Facebook, Microsoft, and Apple, each of which occupies a dominant market position globally, enjoy correspondingly stronger and more pervasive regulatory power.

The regulatory effects of technology take a variety of forms and produce a variety of effects, some beneficial and others less so. For example, security measures designed to prevent unauthorized access to networks, servers, and accounts protect private, personal information, and important corporate and government information from prying eyes and malicious actors. Flawed or poorly implemented security measures can introduce vulnerabilities into the network, exposing individuals to identity theft, surveillance, censorship, and political persecution. Likewise, flawed or poorly implemented security measures can expose corporations, governments, and key power and communications infrastructures to espionage and cyberattack. But technical protections applied to media infrastructures and content flows can also have direct impacts on important aspects of social life: for example, affecting the information access necessary for education, self-development, cultural participation, informed voting, and open and democratic government (Citron 2008; Cohen 2012). Governance processes in relation to media infrastructures are therefore much more than a "technical" concern.

There are other examples of how media governance affects social life. Many platform companies (e.g. Google/YouTube, Facebook, Twitter) employ filtering algorithms to remove or de-list content that infringes copyright and related rights. Such automated mechanisms for content removal tend to be over-inclusive, removing both material that is clearly infringing and material that would be covered by the various limitations and exceptions to copyright (Quilter and Urban 2005; see also United Nations 2011).

In addition, many platform companies employ predictive algorithms to determine what information to display to their users. In networked digital media and particularly for mobile applications, access to information is comprehensively mediated by such algorithms, which process data collected from users, often in combination with data purchased from other information collectors and aggregators, and rely on what is known or inferred about users to generate correlations and predictions (Bolin 2011; Turow 2011). National security services engage in similar data collection and process, often sharing the results with one another and helping each other circumvent the restrictions that might apply to data collection and processing conducted within territorial boundaries (Privacy International 2013). Like the filtering algorithms used for content monitoring, the predictive algorithms used in commercial contexts are maintained as proprietary trade secrets, while their counterparts on the intelligence side are maintained as state secrets. In both cases, secrecy frustrates efforts to document and understand the effects of such filtering processes on the flow of daily life and on everyday freedoms (Cohen 2012; Pasquale 2015).

The relationships between governments and the corporate entities that exercise alternative forms of governance over media infrastructures are complex and often contested. For governments seeking greater regulatory authority over media infrastructures, the control exercised by corporate entities presents an obvious target for regulatory intervention (Birnhack and Elkin-Koren 2006; MacKinnon 2012; United Nations 2011). In China, for example, the coordination between state and private governance is relatively tight, fueled by close ties between the state/communist party and IT conglomerates.

In North America and Europe, by contrast, the interplay of state and private governance mechanisms is more complicated. There are powerful pressures to comply with government demands for access to information for law enforcement and national security purposes, as the Snowden revelations showed. In the wake of those revelations, however, some companies, including most notably Apple, have redesigned their products and services to offer users greater privacy for their communications with each other (though, as we discuss in Section 13.3.3, they have continued to collect other data streams for predictive targeting) and have more aggressively resisted government demands for access (Powles and Chaparro 2016; Yadron 2016).

Outside the law enforcement context, dynamics tend to be somewhat different, and reflect a greater perceived alignment of state and private interests. For example, US companies that engage in collection and processing of personal information often count government entities among their customers (Hoofnagle 2004), and have looked to the US government to protect their economic interests in relation to claims for stronger privacy and data protection regulation. European information companies, for their part, value cross-border trade but also look to the European Union for protection against US-based rivals. With regard to private economic rights in information, copyright safe harbour legislation effectively positions corporate information *businesses* as the regulators of first resort. So far, however, efforts to impose in law parallel takedown obligations on payment providers and domain name system registrars have not succeeded.

The second shift described in this section – from state-based to transnational governance – involves two types of transnational governance institutions: trade dispute resolution bodies and technical standards bodies, in both of which the relative regulatory influence of corporations is growing. The global trade system has become a key mechanism through which both nation-states and powerful corporate actors pursue their interests in regulating media infrastructures and controlling information flows. Many completed global, regional, and bilateral trade agreements – and many others currently under negotiation – contain key provisions dealing with recognition and enforcement of intellectual property rights and with flows of data and information services across borders (Calabrese and Briziarelli 2011; Freedman 2003). Although trade agreements typically contain provisions exempting protections for public health, environmental protection, and privacy rights from designation as nontariff barriers,[17] the extent of those exemptions is unclear and their scope contested (Public Citizen 2015a). Arbitral proceedings alleging violations of trade agreements therefore may work at cross purposes with efforts by domestic legislatures and courts and international human rights tribunals to set appropriate limits on right-holder control of information and on the collection, processing, and use of personal information to sort and categorize individuals and communities.

Meanwhile, technical standards bodies have attained increasing prominence and power. Networked digital communications operate via information transfer protocols. Such protocols determine the resources to which individuals and communities have access and, depending on their design, may enable particular types of surveillance or afford bottlenecks at which state or corporate regulatory authority can be brought to bear (DeNardis 2014; MacKinnon 2012). Those protocols are the responsibility of an interlocking network of global standards bodies, including the International Telecommunications Union (ITU), the Internet Corporation for Assigned Names and Numbers (ICANN), and the Internet Engineering Task Force (IETF). These bodies have different charges and varying degrees of connection to more traditional governance institutions.

For example, the ITU, which oversees standardization and implementation of a variety of protocols for telecommunication, broadcasting, and data transfer, is overseen by the United Nations and representation is state-based, whereas the ICANN, which oversees the Internet naming and addressing protocols and maintains a dispute resolution system for resolving trademark-related domain name disputes, is a standalone corporate body chartered under the laws of California, with policies set by an elected board of directors.

In these multiple ways, the ability of national governments, and indirectly national civil societies, to influence the workings of media in everyday life (through governance structures) has been challenged by the cross-cutting ability of corporate interests to impose governance through other means. In considering the potential implications of media for social progress we need therefore to take into account this underlying shift in regulatory power.

13.3.3 The Ambiguous Implications of Media-Based Governance for Social Progress

For citizens, networked digital media infrastructures may lower the costs of access to knowledge and enable new forms of participation in social, cultural, and economic life (see Section 13.5). At the same time, however, citizens' access to many important informational and cultural resources is subject to control by neo-authoritarian states and by information intermediaries of various sorts, including internet access providers, search engines, mobile applications developers, and designers of proprietary media ecosystems. Such control often materially affects the level and quality of access. The implications for social progress are clearest when particular materials are blocked or removed, but mediated access also produces a range of other effects, which may or may not be consistent with SDG 9 concerning the construction of "resilient infrastructures" and the promotion of "inclusive and sustainable industrialization."

The increasingly global regime for intellectual property protection both incentivizes worldwide distribution of informational and cultural resources and creates additional barriers for those seeking access to such resources. As already suggested in Section 13.2.5, licensing requirements for access to educational, professional, and technical materials can be onerous and the need to pay recurring fees for continued access to digitalized resources (rather than, for example, purchasing hard copies to which one may enjoy permanent access) disproportionately burdens public institutions and lower-resourced communities. In the Global South, the costs of access to copyrighted materials can render access infeasible even for educational institutions and libraries (Chon 2007; Okediji 2004, 2006). In addition, a 1967 Berne Convention protocol governing translation rights is not widely used because its protections are difficult for developing countries to invoke. Among other things, the protocol requires that a compulsory licensing system be fully implemented in domestic law and does not make adequate provision for minority languages.[18] The Global South has adopted a variety of ad hoc solutions, but the lack of a clear framework often stymies efforts to make informational and cultural works available to global audiences that are linguistically and culturally diverse (Cerda Silva 2012).

In many parts of the world and for large parts of the population, everyday life routinely involves online access to a wide variety of purveyors of news, information, and popular culture, as well as search engines, social networking platforms, and other content aggregators that seek to help users find, organize, and make sense of it all. Access to these resources may be offered at no financial cost to users on an advertiser-supported basis, but often such access has a price, in the form of the automated collection of information about personal reading, viewing, and listening habits (Hoofnagle and Whittington 2014). Such information can be used both to target advertising and to suggest content more likely to appeal to each user.

Such predictive targeting of information access has a number of troubling economic and political implications. Algorithms for predictive

---

targeting based on data about personal habits and preferences necessarily enable the identification of population segments sorted by, for example, race/nationality, cultural background, religious affiliation, socioeconomic status, and political preferences. Commercially, targeting based on such indicators raises the prospect of invidious *discrimination* in the distribution of goods and services, in decisions about employment and credit, and in myriad other ways (Barocas and Selbst 2016; Robinson and Yu 2014). The ability to conduct relatively granular price discrimination over those goods and services, in ways that deprive ordinary individuals of choice and corresponding marketplace leverage, sits in tension with free-market ideologies and raises profound distributive justice questions (Cohen 2015).

Turning to politics, micro-targeting of media content and political appeals that align with (inferences about) recipients' preexisting inclinations creates the prospect of an "echo chamber" or "filter bubble" effect, through which preexisting inclinations become reinforced and public opinion about political and cultural issues becomes correspondingly polarized (Pariser 2011; Sunstein 2009).[19] Individuals themselves can come to rely on filtering processes to simplify the information environment and reduce information overload (Andrejevic 2013). In an era in which descriptions of policy problems increasingly are subject to expert mediation – as with climate change or the global financial crisis – the filter bubble effect can work to entrench beliefs in ways that are highly resistant to scientific challenge or debunking (Andrejevic 2013: 12–18, 42–61, 113–132). This can undermine efforts to mobilize popular and political support for action toward social progress on various fronts (environmental sustainability, financial accountability, and so on).

A final set of ambiguities concerns the newly prominent transnational governance institutions described in Section 13.3.2. Governance of media infrastructures and information flows via trade and technical standards bodies provides harmonization that many argue is essential in an increasingly interconnected world. But the new transnational governance institutions are accountable neither to national governments nor to traditional international governance institutions, and many lack robust democratic traditions of their own. Participation in such institutions may be perceived as offering opportunities for powerful national and/or commercial interests to avoid roadblocks interposed by domestic regulation, by the international human rights framework, and by civil society groups (Benvenisti 2015). Within the global trade system, both negotiation and dispute resolution processes are highly responsive to corporate interests yet much less responsive to other interests. Trade dispute resolution panels convened by the World Trade Organization have, to date, ruled *against states* asserting protective regulation in all but one of the cases in which domestic protective regulations have been challenged (Public Citizen 2015a). In recent rounds of negotiation over high-profile multilateral agreements such as the Trans Pacific Partnership and the Transatlantic Trade and Investment Partnership, trade associations representing corporate interests have enjoyed privileged access to country-level negotiators and working drafts, while civil society groups and interested members of the public have been allowed only brief glimpses of later-stage

documents, and only on condition of confidentiality.[20] Technical standards bodies, meanwhile, are only gradually coming to terms with their own role as governance bodies (DeNardis 2009, 2014; MacKinnon 2012: 203–219).

The result is a landscape of everyday media consumption configured by forces that are increasingly *in tension* with shared flows of information and open, inclusive development. The multiple overlapping processes for governing media's underlying infrastructures are ever more secretive and resistant to civil society influence. This is the complex starting point for thinking about two important potential contributions of media and communications to social progress: the role of journalism in the production of public knowledge (Section 13.4) and the role of networked communications in enabling new forms of citizenship (Section 13.5).

13.4   Journalism and Public Knowledge

One key way in which media can contribute to social progress over the long term is through the provision of public knowledge (Sen 1999). The term "public knowledge" refers to the resources that citizens have for forming informed opinions about matters of public and general interest. Journalism has for centuries been a key institutional form for disseminating such knowledge.

13.4.1   Public Knowledge for Democracy and Social Progress

Digital media infrastructures create new opportunities for the dissemination of public knowledge. Although the decline in civic participation in established democratic societies has been widely lamented (Putnam 2000), other observers (Dahlgren 2009; Lewis, Inthorn, and Wahl-Jorgensen 2005) have pointed to the growth of new communities online and the growth in quantity and diversity in communication platforms outside of the traditional news media, where citizens can exchange information and participate in political debate. Additionally, whereas public knowledge traditionally was disseminated through news and information in the press, radio, and television, social networking platforms are becoming a major news source for citizens. A recent survey conducted in the United States found that 44 percent of respondents get their daily news from social media (IPSP 2017). The question of citizenship is complex, and cannot be dealt with at length here: we note, however, that large parts of the world's population live without citizenship, and citizenship in a nation-state does not protect citizens from rights-affecting actions controlled by institutions outside of the nation-state.

Early research on public knowledge overemphasized news distribution and correspondingly undervalued other sources of information, such as popular culture and entertainment (Corner 1991). Both sources of information can contribute to the formation of public knowledge and to social progress, as can be appreciated when we consider the political and cultural aspects of citizenship. Where *political citizenship* deals

---

[19]   In the United States, practices of political microtargeting are becoming widespread. See Beckett (2012).
[20]   See, for example, Inman (2016), Schneider (2014).

with issues related to the formal rights (and duties) of citizens, and is most often mediated by traditional categories of news about current affairs and politics, *cultural citizenship* deals with questions of recognition, identity, and the cultural rights (and duties) of citizens, and is mediated by various sorts of information that circulate in the cultural public sphere.

The distinction between political and cultural citizenship may become more blurred when the convergence of entertainment media and political citizenship is taken seriously (Hermes 2005; Van Zoonen 2005; Williams and Delli Carpini 2011). The rise of bots and algorithmic management of information introduces additional distortions of public deliberation (Tambini 2017). But none of this potential to create public knowledge matters if media content produced by an elite "professional" class of journalists does not resonate with audiences' everyday lived experience. Today various factors point in that direction, both in forms of propaganda and destabilizing communicative practices and in problems within systems of education, where much of the socializing of citizens take place (SPI "Access to basic knowledge").

In this section we outline, first, the special roles that journalism plays in public knowledge, and so why journalism is important for democracy and social progress. We will then give examples of the various "soft" and "hard" threats that we identify as detrimental to public knowledge, including both changes in business models, news reception, and new forms of "information management," and, more directly, various physical threats against news production, and journalists in conflict areas and unstable democracies. Third, we will point to areas where there are opportunities for countering this negative picture, for example the rise of citizen journalism and alternative media. We end this section with a double case study of organized attempts to construct alternative journalistic narratives in Latin America and the Middle East.

13.4.2   The Special Functions of Journalism and Journalistic Practice

Journalism is still associated, especially in the established democracies of the Global North, with the institutions and practices of democracy (Fenton 2010: 3). There are many examples, both historical and current, of how journalism has contributed to public knowledge for social progress (SDG 16). These include, for example, the antislavery campaigns that benefited from press assistance with the formation of abolitionist organizations (King and Haveman 2008), samizdat publications in the former Soviet Union (Feldbrugge 1975), information about environmental disasters such as the 2011 Fukushima nuclear accident that was spread not only by mainstream journalists but also by citizens on blogging and social media platforms (Friedman 2011), or the role of the underground press in the struggle against apartheid (Switzer and Adhikari 2000). For these reasons the contribution of journalism to public knowledge remains an important reference point in the broader context of global social progress.

The emergence of digital media infrastructures has had profound implications for traditional conceptions of news and journalism. These include a proliferation of the channels through which journalism is produced and consumed, and a blurring of the lines between news and entertainment through the rise of formats such as the "mockumentary," "docudrama," and satirical news. The participatory potential of digital technologies, aided by the widespread accessibility of technologies such as the mobile phone, has challenged previous claims by professional journalists to exclusivity in the purveying of news. Additionally, the business models for journalism have undergone a fundamental transformation in recent years, even as new opportunities have arisen for the creation of public knowledge and citizen participation in the construction of knowledge and public debate.

Against the background of rapid change, however, the expectation that news journalism will contribute to public knowledge, the monitoring of power, and the facilitation of public debate remains an ideal against which communication practices continue to be measured. The mere fact that information is publicly disseminated and available does not automatically result in an informed public. Additionally, in the context of changing frameworks of reception, citizens' ability to orientate themselves in today's increasingly complex media landscape, drawing perhaps on the skills provided by education, are ever more important.

13.4.3   Threats to Public Knowledge 1: System Pressures

The digitization and marketization of media (discussed in Section 13.2) have affected the institutional conditions for journalistic production. New economic conditions have led the news industries into a downward spiral where it has become ever more difficult to charge for content. In a recent survey conducted by the IPSP in the United States, 57 percent of respondents do not like to pay for news, and believe news should be freely accessible to all (IPSP 2017). Shrinking readership makes advertisers abandon print media to the benefit of online search and social networking.

The old business models of journalism are collapsing, and news producers have had to rethink their relation to audiences, leading in turn to changes in journalistic practice. New forms of "click-bait journalism," robot journalism, and algorithmically steered news production are increasingly common. These follow different logics from traditional journalism, and in their most extreme forms may produce echo chambers or filter bubbles (see Section 13.3) that in the long run fragment public debate and the public sphere more generally. The automated search for audiences through data processing also may further marginalize those audiences who are already on the margins of the public sphere. In countries where access to the digital public sphere mirrors huge social and economic equalities – for instance South Africa, India, China, and Brazil – these new practices could exacerbate such inequalities.

The reorganization of media production into large-scale media corporations with interests also in non-journalistic media production has meant that even financially successful journalistic and public knowledge operations cannot always reinvest their profits into news production, but instead have their profits reinvested in other activities. This lack of economic control makes it difficult to sustain long-term strategies of news production. While there has always been a tension between editorial and management teams within news organizations, large-scale media corporations shift economic decision-making farther away from news production environments, resulting in managerial decisions that direct journalistic practice from the outside.

There are also regulative threats to independent news media production, for example the noncommercial and license fee funded public service media. In Europe, the traditional freedom of public service broadcasters to choose their policy orientations has come under attack by newly powerful private broadcasters (SPI "Press freedom"). One result is the public value test instigated by the European Commission, which emerged from private broadcasters' intense lobbying efforts in relation to the European Commission (Donders and Moe 2011).

While online (including mobile) media have created new platforms for social agency and public participation, both in the creation of "user-generated content" (UGC) for mainstream media and in providing outlets for alternative news and views, the Internet has also become a space where reactionary views, racist representations, and hate speech can thrive. Social media like Facebook and Twitter contribute to the proliferation of this kind of communication. Misunderstandings of complex matters and online "lynch mobs" illustrate the *volatility* of networked digital media environments and offer testimony to the limits of social media for public debate. On a more fundamental level, well-meaning educational initiatives to foster "digital literacy" might produce relativistic approaches to scientific and social truths (Boyd 2017), and the journalistic ideals of balance of opinion might privilege a blurring of the distinction between facts and opinions, and where "truth" becomes more of an affective mood.

13.4.4   Threats to Public Knowledge 2: Coercive Force

Meanwhile, journalists can face harder forms of threat, whether through legal frameworks (press freedom or its opposite) or informal threats (through damage to journalists' physical and psychological security): these threats may exist separately or in combination.

In many parts of the world, growing *political* instability has affected journalism's ability to fulfil its broader public knowledge goals because of direct threats to press freedom (see SPI "Press Freedom"). For example, in some parts of Eastern Europe, political polarization has arisen as some post-Soviet states have sought closer ties with the EU. The Ukraine–Russia conflict is one, widely reported, outgrowth of this polarization, but the phenomenon is also visible in other post-Soviet countries (Richter 2015). Information warfare is on the rise, not only in the region itself, but also in international news media (for example, via TV channels such as Russia Today and Ukraine Today [Miazhevich 2014]). Initiatives for disinformation and propaganda/counterpropaganda, including so-called "troll-factories" maintained in Russia (and elsewhere),[21] make efforts to enhance public knowledge increasingly difficult. The sheer amount of seemingly contradictory information circulating puts high pressure on audiences' critical abilities (the much discussed phenomenon of "fake news"). A recent example of this

from the Ukraine–Russia conflict is the overload of contradictory information that surrounded the shooting down of Malaysian flight MH17 over eastern Ukraine in 2014, and the sharply divergent accounts that circulated on the Internet both before and after the Dutch Safety Board published their report of the crash.[22] Similar dynamics have emerged in the Middle East, leading to an increasingly polarized and propaganda-dominated public sphere (see Section 13.4.6).

In many African countries also, journalism for public knowledge remains an ideal rather than a practical reality. In the Windhoek Declaration on Promoting an Independent and Pluralistic African Press (UNESCO 1991), African journalists invoked the Universal Declaration of Human Rights as a motivation for the promotion of press freedom. At the same time, however, African resistance to colonialism and rejection of cultural imperialism engendered an insistence on "African values" in journalism, couched in the discourse of development but often implying uncritical and loyalist media support of postcolonial states. An example of an appeal to "African values" is Francis Kasoma's (1994, 1996) notion of "Afriethics," which rejects Western normative frameworks and counterposes an African value system that privileges communalism and an orientation towards the family and clan over individualism. Appeals to "African values" have often been criticized for their tendency to essentialize African culture and identity, without acknowledging the interpenetration of African and Western values in a globalized context (Banda 2009; Skjerdal 2012). Additionally, such appeals have served to justify repression of media freedom in many African countries (see Bourgault 1995; Karikari 2007).

Lastly, against the background of political instability, propaganda wars, and state repression, *violence* against journalists has also increased. Some examples include: Egypt clamping down on journalists, activists, and civil society; the consolidation of electoral autocracy and temporary closure of digital platforms in Turkey; and repressive measures from verbal threats to physical assaults and imprisonment in various African countries. In Poland, a new legal regime has circumscribed the freedom for journalists, making critical and investigative journalism more difficult and precarious.[23]

13.4.5   Opportunities for Public Knowledge: New Forms of Journalism and Citizens' Media

Meanwhile, digital media infrastructures have enabled the growth of new forms of citizen-created media for the production of public knowledge. In many African contexts where legacy media like newspapers and radio stations are owned and controlled by the state, digital media platforms have served as alternative outlets for the dissemination of news, political debate, and critique (Paterson 2013). In Zimbabwe, Facebook has provided users with more freedom to engage in political satire and offer alternative accounts of political developments (Mare 2014). The widespread penetration and use of mobile media in Africa have also provided users with a tool to engage more actively with mainstream news agendas. An example of this was the mobile

---

[21]   See www.theguardian.com/world/2015/aug/18/trolls-putin-russia-savchuk or www.theguardian.com/world/2015/apr/02/putin-kremlin-inside-russian-troll-house.

[22]   See www.onderzoeksraad.nl/.

[23]   See www.bbc.com/news/world-europe-35257105.

phone footage of police brutality against a Mozambican immigrant, Mido Macia, in Daveyton, South Africa. The footage of police dragging Macia, cuffed to a police vehicle, was captured by a bystander and sent to the tabloid the *Daily Sun*, who posted the video online and reported on it. The video went viral and made headlines internationally after Macia died in police custody, and led to the arrest and conviction of the police officers. This integration of citizen journalism, legacy media (especially tabloids), and online platforms such as Youtube or Facebook, has provided journalists and news consumers with new ways of creating public knowledge and serving the public interest.

In South Korea, citizen journalists have used digital networks for producing alternative civic discourses and for mobilizing enormous rallies of citizens to speak out on socially sensitive issues. More recently, social media have given rise to new alternative media such as *Newstapa* ("Rebuilding Investigative Journalism") launched in January 2012. Due to the government's control over public broadcasting, some former employees of the major TV networks and other small-sized production team members have come together to produce an investigative news program about social issues. *Newstapa* uses a variety of online outlets such as its own webpage views, YouTube clips, and podcast episodes, and the younger generations download and watch its weekly episodes using their smartphones. Social media also play a key role in spreading the news program's schedule and in enabling public fundraising to support production. *Newstapa* has gained a reputation as an influential news provider and as illustrating how, through regular practices of collaboration, citizens can build alternative *paradigms* of social justice against mainstream media and power elites.

Meanwhile, during the political turmoil and violence following the ousting of former President Yanukovich in Ukraine, faculty and students from the Mohyla School of Journalism in Kyiv created StopFake (stopfake.org), an organization aimed at debunking Russian propaganda and the distorted news produced by troll-factories. Another civic initiative formed during the political turmoil was The Ukraine Crisis Media Centre, which is a platform for information management that arranges press briefings with representatives of the Ukrainian military and government (Bolin, Jordan, and Ståhlberg 2016).

There are therefore many overlapping factors shaping media's possible contribution to public knowledge in different parts of the world today. In the next part of this section, we offer a double case study from Latin America and the Middle East that considers the possibilities of building new infrastructures for journalism that can offer alternative voices to counter perceived dominant narratives.

13.4.6   Double Case Study: TeleSUR and Al-Jazeera: Alternative Voices in Global News

The Venezuelan channel TeleSUR and the Qatari channel Al-Jazeera are often hailed as models of media with global reach that have challenged the North Atlantic domination of global news flows and reference points. These two channels have much in common: they were both made possible by the large political ambitions of their founders; both faced indifference or hostility in the world's power centers; and both evolved from single channels into multiplatform

networks. This section explores what can be learned from their contrasting achievements.

13.4.6.1   TeleSUR

Sponsored by the left-leaning government of Hugo Chávez in Venezuela (1999–2013), TeleSUR was formed in 2005 as a regional television network with the goal of broadcasting "from the South to the South" (Da Silva Mendes 2012). TeleSUR's achievements can only be understood against the history of media concentration and economic exploitation achieved by elites in Latin America since the eighteenth century. From the inception of electronic media, upper classes have controlled the media and used them to advance their own political and financial interests, at the exclusion of the interests of working-class majorities. Through control of commercial and public media, political and economic elites secured ideological control over, and the opportunity to profit from, mass audiences.

Former Venezuelan president Hugo Chávez created TeleSUR as a television network that would prioritize the information and communication needs of the oppressed majorities in the region and disseminate an autonomous Latin American perspective. Drawing explicitly from the language of the NWICO, TeleSUR defines itself as "a Latin American multimedia initiative dedicated to promoting unity among the peoples of the South; a space and a voice for the development of a new communication order" (www.teleSURtv.net). It defines "the South" as a "geopolitical concept that promotes the people's struggle for peace and self-determination and respect for human rights and social justice." TeleSUR has had two different goals: to offer an alternative to US and European news media, (e.g. BBC or CNN); and to shape a unified Latin American public sphere (Cañizalez and Lugo 2007). It is not a coincidence that TeleSUR emerged in 2005 at the same time that the region shifted to the left. Its slogan – "*Nuestro norte es el Sur*" (Our North is the South) – embodies this shift in perspective, and is evidenced by its coverage of key historical events such as the bombardment of Colombian FARC guerrilla camps by the military, or the demise of Gaddafi's government in Libya.

TeleSUR is cofinanced by various governments in Latin America (Da Silva Mendes 2012). Some Latin American analysts suggest that TeleSUR is more the loudspeaker of "Chavismo" (the political platform of late Venezuelan president Hugo Chávez) than a pan-Latin American voice (Moraes 2011), but TeleSUR makes an important contribution to public knowledge: information and news make up 80 percent of TeleSUR's programming and the rest centers on renowned Latin American personalities (Da Silva Mendes 2012; Rincón in press). In 2009 TeleSUR grew into a multimedia platform with a strong presence online and its own distribution system. TeleSUR currently has five satellites covering parts of Europe and the Americas, as well as the Middle East and North Africa.

13.4.6.2   Al-Jazeera

Al-Jazeera, the original Arabic-language channel, was formed in late 1996, following the break-up of BBC Arabic. It was founded by Hamad bin-Khalifa Al Thani to free Qatar from the influence of its larger neighbor, Saudi Arabia, and give the country a regional and global influence disproportionate to its small size.

Al-Jazeera's unbridled news coverage quickly offended Arab leaders accustomed to deference and Western powers unused to having their narratives of global affairs challenged. By early 2004, the government of Qatar had received more than 500 complaints from Arab governments focusing on Al-Jazeera (Lamloum 2004: 20). Originally hailed as a beacon of free speech by the West, Al-Jazeera became vilified as the loudspeaker of Al-Qaeda following the September 11, 2001 attacks. The channel became a global household name in the wake of the Anglo-American invasions of Afghanistan and Iraq in 2001 and 2003, when its deep coverage was reused by Western news organizations.

In the following years, Al-Jazeera grew from a single channel to a network of multiple channels, including Al-Jazeera *English*, a training center, and online platforms. The Arabic-language Al-Jazeera's editorial line was sympathetic to the centrist Islamism of the Muslim Brotherhood, to the Palestinian cause, and to the Global South. Some of these issues carried over into Al-Jazeera *English*, whose editorial line has significant overlap with TeleSUR's. Al-Jazeera *English* became a major global news player, with broadcast bureaus in Doha, London, New York, and Kuala Lumpur, and dozens of offices and correspondents worldwide. Al-Jazeera, however, faced problems from its inception regarding repeated political pressure to restrain its editorial line, internal frictions (Zahreddin 2011), and a conflict between two factions – one secular and Arab nationalist, the other Islamist and sympathetic to the Muslim Brotherhood (Kraidy and Khalil 2009; Talon 2011).

Al-Jazeera shifted its editorial line with the onset of the Arab uprisings in 2010. In Egypt, the channel supported the Muslim Brotherhood against Mubarak. In Syria, it also sided with the rebels against Assad. Although Al-Jazeera and Qatar gained some ground as a supporter of the Muslim Brotherhood, ensuing political shifts, driven by rapprochement between Qatar and Saudi Arabia, undermined Al-Jazeera's status as a news outlet that challenged dominant news agendas.

* * * * *

The contrasting cases of TeleSUR and Al-Jazeera illustrate both the opportunities for and the potential vulnerabilities of attempts to create public knowledge outlets from outside the Global North that have influence on a global scale. Such outlets can be established and have significant success, provided strong initial funding and support exists, but they remain vulnerable to the wider political influences that may lie behind their funding. That vulnerability, however, should not be seen in isolation from the vulnerabilities to political influence that commercially funded media outlets also face in many other parts of the world.

13.5   Networked Communications: Possibilities for Citizenship

We have argued in Section 13.4 that media's potential contribution to social progress through public knowledge faces significant threats

but, in a digital age characterized by an increasingly global media infrastructure, brings important opportunities too. In this section, we consider how *citizens* make use of the informational and imaginative materials that media provide to them.

13.5.1   Relations Between Media and Spaces of Citizenship

Today's new density of global communication not only enables continuous interaction across world regions, but also is beginning to shape new spheres of civic communication on every scale. Communication interfaces (from WhatsApp to WeChat) offer a new architecture of civic discourse that is no longer merely national or international: the resulting spaces where citizens interact are shaped not by the media spheres of particular territories but by individuals' choices of what to follow online. Furthermore, these networked spheres of civil communication are no longer accessible only in the Global North but engage citizens – with internet access – from all types of societies, including so-called failed states. Through this, media become involved in opening up new spaces of citizenship (SDG 16.7).

Although citizenship is national and the boundedness of state territory continues, communication is shaping a new form of civic identity, which is increasingly *embedded in* a globalized digital space. Rather than globalization operating outside and against the national, "the nation *is the site* of globalization" (Sassen 2007: 80, emphasis added). Today this merging of national and global takes different shapes in different societies. Even secluded states such as North Korea and failed states such as Syria, Somalia, and Afghanistan have their own modes of nation-based globalization. However, the point is particularly important in relation to public civic communication where national and global public spheres merge, and public deliberations, legitimacy, and accountability no longer develop solely through national debates. Rather, in contexts of climate change, governments are held accountable based on broader global discourses.

As with the history of media (Section 13.2), these developments are still mainly considered from the perspective of nations in the Global North, with narratives often not looking beyond Western communications theory and research (Farivar 2011). Similarly, accounts of diaspora's use of media often ignore political connectivity *between* expatriates of the Global South that link back to civic discourse in their countries of origin. The roles of nongovernmental actors in failed states and civic communications in post-conflict resolution constitute other examples of new forms of connection between citizens across borders. Citizens of the Global South such as forced migrants are communicating outside national media territories (Witteborn 2015). Networks of activism, deliberation, and mobilization, not possible in the past, are emerging whereby media provide new infrastructures of citizenship as part of what the MacBride report called the "many voices" of "one world."

Section 13.2 discussed the historical dominance of communication flows from the Global North, linked to colonial communication infrastructures and extended by satellite communication infrastructures emerging in the 1970s for the delivery of broadcasting content and, since the 1990s, for individual media reception. For most of the

13

twentieth century, the globalized "stretching" of human interactions through media – the "intensification of worldwide social relations which link distant localities in such a way that local happenings are shaped by events occurring many miles away and vice versa" (Giddens 1990: 64) – was, in its framing, dominated by news channels from the Global North, such as BBC, CNN, and Deutsche Welle, with few opportunities to contest it.

This situation has changed significantly since the second half of the 1990s due to three interrelated processes: the emergence of digital satellite platforms enabling the delivery of no longer just a few but hundreds of channels, the reduction of uplink costs for broadcasters, and the availability of cheap direct-to-home rooftop dishes. Furthermore, and most importantly, new regional media players have challenged the monopoly of political "breaking news" in times of world conflict. Such news is often delivered "live" worldwide and has influenced national foreign policy imperatives in various countries (Robinson 2005; Volkmer 1999), contesting the framing of world events by media corporations from the Global North (see also Section 13.4.6). Whereas CNN produced the only narrative of the first Gulf War (1990–1991) for a world audience, now there are hundreds of satellite news channels from the wider Arabic region, from Sudan, Pakistan, Tanzania, and at least 50 channels dedicated to news from India, South Korea, China, Mexico, and Brazil. In addition, some region-wide news channels, such as Channel News Asia and Africa 24, are available in several languages and target neighboring regions.

The resulting digital ecology for civic participation has two additional key characteristics. The first is the increasingly complex flow of media and information organized not just by media organizations, but by citizens' own efforts to upload or recirculate what interests them. It is a transnational public space, which enables a new density of communication between citizens. The results of such dense peer-to-peer civic communication may include attempts to influence individuals through hate speech (Phillips 2015), fake news and "bots" (see IPSP Chapter 10; IPSP Chapter 13 Toolkit "Knowledge as Commons" Column 2). At the same time, new forms of "reflective interdependence" (Volkmer 2014) may emerge whereby, through the sharing of reference points across borders, citizens acquire a new basis for shared political debate or activism on topics ranging from climate change, human rights violations, and crisis communication to political campaigns such as the "Occupy" movement. Under these new conditions, civic engagement no longer occurs in one "place," but across a network of places.

Although only a minority of the population is engaged in these new global networks, "their contribution to democracy cannot be underestimated" (Frere and Kiyindou 2009: 77, 79). In many countries, state monopolies on the inflow of foreign news are no longer possible. For example, it can be argued that African governments have "hardly any grip on the choices of the Internet user-consumer, who can freely choose the information that is interesting or useful and decide to join a particular 'virtual community'" (Frere and Kiyindou 2009: 78). This flexibility in the resources available through online media, including information and deliberation accessed across borders (Bohman 2007), potentially changes citizens' horizons of civic engagement.

13.5.2 New Forms of Communicative Citizenship: The Case of Global Youth

As an example of these emerging trends, young citizens in many countries are engaging with each other in unprecedented ways, in peer-to-peer interaction within and across borders. In order to assess the implications of these new digital ecologies for civic identity, we need to consider the interaction between local and global media practices and information flows.

The density of these interactions is revealed in an international comparative study on "Global Youth and Media, Notions of Cosmopolitanism in the Global Public Space" (discussed in Volkmer 2014). The study included more than 6,000 young people aged 14–17 in nine countries on five continents. The study asked how they use media, how they construct globalization, and perceive civic identity. The distinctive uses of local, national, and global media by particular generations have been little researched. While national television is the general population's preferred medium for political news, young people find news in parallel ways through Google news, MSN, and Yahoo. Across all society types, this younger generation mixes local and global information flows in a distinctive way that entitles them to the label of "in-betweeners." As a result, they consider themselves between skepticism and trust, between a realistic appreciation of global risks (indeed a strong sense of world insecurity) and the need for leadership. When asked if they feel that the world today has become more insecure since their parents were young, 80 percent agree. Yet more than half consider *international* political events more important than national and so seem to live out their citizenship on two connected scales, national and global. They distrust politicians and engage in global political spheres characterized by global themes such as "environment," "human rights," and "economy, wealth, and poverty."

A Mexican sociologist describes in the context of Central America the implications of such an engagement for local citizenship: "the protest movements with a global reach, and the presence of leadership of young people in them, bring to mind the emergence of a new political cosmopolitanism among youth. Its native land is the world, and its strength lies in its (seeming) absence of structure, its intermittence and the multiple nodes in which its utopia is anchored" (Reguillo 2009: 34). In this analysis Central America's young generation is both "disconnected and unequal" and "well situated, connected, and globalized" and increasingly engaged in national and transnational youth publics (Reguillo 2009: 23). Other regions provide further evidence of youth agency converging around local networks of publicity in Cairo (Arvizu 2009: 387), Tanzania (Tufte and Enghel 2009), and Chile (Munoz-Navarro 2009). In Kenya and other parts of the Global South, media provide platforms for youth to interact and participate in political debates worldwide, leading one analyst to comment that, for the Kenyan diaspora, social media is an "integral aspect [of] Kenya's social and political dynamics" (Mukhongo 2014: 325).

However, the implications of these emerging forms of public engagement in regional media cultures require more attention. For example, in Central Asia, urban youth are drawing increasingly on global sources of information and so "are increasingly judging the worldviews and behaviours of parents, teachers, political elites and other traditional authority figures against that global context … they are suddenly able to compare themselves with anyone, anywhere" (Ibold 2010: 532). As anticipated by Joshua Meyrowitz three decades ago (Meyrowitz 1985), but now on a global, not national, scale, media flows can work to challenge knowledge barriers and destabilize relations between generations, so forging new bases for civic identity and action.

13.5.3 Case Study: Connectivity and Social Progress in a Chinese Heritage Village

The world's rural population is at its largest ever today, even though the world's urban population is (slightly) larger. An understanding of *rural* connectivity and its relation to social progress is therefore indispensable. Located in the mountainous interior region of China's coastal Zhejiang Province, Heyang has a population of 3,670 and more than 1,100 years of history. It is a quintessential embodiment of China's agrarian civilization. Its well-preserved Ming-Qing era traditional architecture earned it a place in 2013 in the Chinese State Council's list of key sites of national cultural relics. However, this is also a modernized and globalized village: with part of its economy integrated into global circuits of production and more than half of its labor force now working outside the village (most of whom only return briefly to reunite with family during festival periods).

Village communications also cut across the traditional and the modern. The oral tradition remains strong: the village's Senior Center and popular street corners serve as sites of information and gossip exchange. Public announcements are posted at centrally located information boards and walls at different village corners. However, the village's lineage book, started more than 600 years ago by a Ming-Dynasty official from the village, issued its sixteenth edition in December 2016 with a grand ceremony. The book contains biographies of notable individuals and registers the names of all male descendants (female descendants were first recorded in its fifteenth edition, compiled in 1995).

Wired radio and communal film projection were the most popular forms of mediated communication and entertainment during the 1970s and early 1980s. Along with village assemblies, these low-tech forms of communication played pivotal roles in Mao-era political mobilization and cultural integration. Their embeddedness in communal life was instrumental to their success in linking villagers to the outside world and sustaining village cohesion. Starting, however, from the late 1980s, information reception and entertainment have become privatized and personalized. As villagers are exposed to wider and more diverse media flows, many feel more isolated from each other. Social stratification and income polarization, following the dismantling of the collective economy, have engendered a further sense of social dislocation and community disintegration.

The 1990s saw the village's further leap into the digital age: automated direct dial telephone started in 1990; cable television and analogue mobile telephony arrived in 1994 and by 1997, digital mobile telephony. Today, Heyang is among the 150,000 Chinese villages with broadband access (in 2015 China's State Council promised a 98 percent village broadband access rate by 2020). While desktop computers are rare, telephones, especially mobile phones, are widely used, but only the young and economically better-off have smartphones to connect themselves to the Internet.

In between lies a wide spectrum of communication patterns and circuits of connectivity that have made Heyang a small-scale model of China's highly stratified society. Square dancers in the village, for example, have used their smartphones to download videos of the latest dancing styles, in this way imagining themselves as part of a larger national dance community. A small minority, like their urban middle-class counterparts, engage in online stock trade. Wechat, the most popular Chinese social media platform, is popular among village elites, the young, and the economically well-off. One member of the Village Council has more than a dozen Wechat friend circles, with relatives, businessmen originally from the village, government officials, and students of Heyang's culture. However, with inclusion also comes exclusion: such Wechat friend circles are limited to this member's own professional and interpersonal networks, and so exclude the majority of villagers. Moreover, her Wechat communications are mostly externally directed, aiming at promoting Heyang as a tourist site, rather than at fellow villagers. Meanwhile, with the higher cost of a digital cable subscription, some poorer villagers have given up on cable television service altogether to opt for satellite television, which only requires the one-time purchasing cost of a satellite receiving dish. But such satellite television services do not include local municipal and county television channels. Consequently, these households end up with no access to local television news.

As a result, many local residents, especially those in the lower social strata, complain about their lack of communication with village leaders, lack of effective participation in village affairs, and a general sense of powerlessness in shaping the village's future. Caught in a complex web of local governance, land appropriation, village renovation, and tourist development, villagers resort to protests and blockages of village construction projects to communicate their demands and frustrations. In one case, in an attempt to make their voices heard, some residents refused to allow a CCTV crew to film their residential courtyard for the 2015 Spring Festival Gala; others have tried to derail the village's lineage book compilation project. A few villagers have also expressed a desire for the return of a village wired radio system and Mao-era face-to-face meetings of the village community as a whole.

But China's "great digital leap forward" has not created upwardly mobile opportunities for all. X. Zhu, a 24-year-old Heyang village youth, grew up in a well-off family with postsecondary education, but did not live to see a future in Heyang. He arranged his own suicide through the Internet in early 2010. Another 24-year-old netizen came all the way from Yunan Province in southwestern China to commit suicide together with Zhu. Theirs is one of the saddest stories of digital connectivity in the Network Age.

13.5.4 Networked Communications Among East Asian Precarious Workers

Networked communications offer opportunities in many countries for new forms of political and social connection, which may be especially important in spreading public knowledge where public broadcasting systems are under threat (see Section 13.4). But this opportunity may occur in the context of social conditions, particularly labor markets, where ICTs are intensifying the deterioration of working conditions and sustaining new structures of precarious labor (SDG 8.8). The resulting balance for social progress may therefore be highly ambiguous, and Northeast Asia offers an important example of these tensions.

The mobile phone has become deeply entangled with the precarious labor culture in Northeast Asia. Mobile communication technology has intersected with the emergence of increasingly insecure working conditions, particularly those of young Northeast Asian workers, who are situated within the "institutionalized precariousness" of a dual economy made up of a large reserve army "with no employment prospects, no future, [and] no plans" (Bourdieu 1998: 30f.), alongside a small privileged minority of secure workers with a regular wage. A "mobile precariat" (precarious workers who use mobile phones to sustain their living within an always-on-call working culture)[24] suffers from chronically insecure job positions as temporary staff or contract workers: they are trapped at the bottom of the pay scale, yet at the same time remain connected through media to the workplace (Qiu 2009). This mobile precariat is disadvantaged not only through the labor exploitation they endure, but also when it comes to seeking remedies for these injustices (see Seo and Kim 2009; Shaviro 2002 for important studies).

Employers' attitudes vary to mobile phone use among their precarious workers. Whereas in Japan and Taiwan, workers must leave their phones behind, beyond their reach, when they start work, in South Korea, where the conditions for workers are extremely insecure with the second longest working hours among OECD countries (2,124 hours/year as of 2014),[25] mobile phones are allowed at work. However, in all countries, possessing a mobile phone renders precarious workers vulnerable to a wider culture of surveillance. Many employers monitor their workers' lives outside of formal working hours by using mobile instant messaging services (KakaoTalk in Korea; WeChat in China; Line in Japan and Taiwan). Transgressing the normal boundaries of work, employers use phones to issue orders to their precarious workers on matters such as cleanliness, service management, and the employee code of conduct.

The outcomes are, however, unstable. In South Korea, young precarious workers have attempted to stir public opinion against unjust business practices, by posting images and chat messages on social media platforms. They, in turn, have been disciplined through remote monitoring on live surveillance mobile apps and mobile instant messaging. In Japan, there have been on- and offline protests against "black companies," notorious for exploiting precarious workers, with workers using the Internet and social media to disclose their unfair treatment in the workplace and share it with others. Given the collapse of the public broadcasting system in Japan, online citizen journalism and alternative journalism have also offered platforms for building alternative understandings of social justice in the workplace that go beyond the agendas of mainstream media.

In summary, Northeast Asia offers a clear example of how the mobile phone as an infrastructure of connection has become a new technique

for regulating labor in an always-on-call culture, yet continues to offer opportunities for movements for social justice and social progress.

13.6   Struggles for Social Justice Through the Democratization of Media

Having in Sections 13.4 and 13.5 considered how the outputs of media contribute variously to new forms of social connection and environments of public knowledge – two preconditions for action towards social progress – we turn in this section to the *new* social issues raised by the increasingly complex governance structures for media and communications outlined in Section 13.3. We first place those issues within the context of a longer-term struggle for media reform.

13.6.1   The Longer History of Democratizing Media

The expansion of media infrastructures into ever wider areas of life through digital platforms has generated new types of media activism (Milan 2016). Across the Global South and the Global North, today's media activists fight struggles on diverse fronts. However, popular attempts to shape media infrastructures into more democratic and inclusive social institutions did not begin with the media activists of the twenty-first century.

Just as media infrastructures have developed differently in each nation and region of the world (see Section 13.2), so efforts to reshape and reform the media are varied. Before the consolidation of the advertising-supported commercial press, radical working-class publications in the United Kingdom, United States, and Canada emerged to challenge the dominant press order (Hackett and Zhao 1998). With the rise of electronic communication, US media activists in the 1920s and 1930s demanded public ownership of the telegraph and noncommercial radio (McChesney 1993; Stein 2009). In Russia and China, communist and nationalist revolutionaries established alternative media systems as part of their attempts to seek social progress through anticapitalistic and nationalistic struggles; the resulting media structures, however, degenerated into ossified state-controlled systems. Nevertheless, anti-establishment communication forms (underground tabloids and samizdat in Russia; the big-character posters on China's Democracy Wall) testified to the radical democratic communication impulse of these post-revolutionary societies.

In the 1960s and 1970s, civil rights movements in the United States and Canada responded to poor media coverage of their struggles for social justice by demanding more access to the mainstream media, and developing their own media (Stein 2009). The battle around cable television regulation in these countries was one of the most salient victories of media reform movements, as cable companies are now mandated to establish community and educational channels free of charge (Halleck 2001) (SPI "Access to basic knowledge"). In Latin America, in response to the brutal dictatorships of the 1970s and 1980s, grassroots groups developed their own underground communication networks in a long

---

[24]   Also known as *Alba* [알바] in South Korea, [*xin gong ren* 新工人] in China, and Freeter [*furita* フリーター] in Japan.

[25]   OECD.StatExtract, 2016.

battle to pressure states to democratize the media (Rodríguez and Murphy 1997). Meanwhile, in several European countries, pirate radio was the precursor of later struggles for media regulation that guarantees space for public and community media (Jankowski, Prehn, and Stappers 1992).

In 1976, in one of the earliest *global* efforts to democratize the media, Amadou Mathar M'Bow, Director of UNESCO, appointed a commission of 16 experts to examine global communication problems. The commission's final report, known as the MacBride Report, described shocking information inequalities between First and Third World countries (UNESCO 1980). The report documented high levels of media concentration in a few transnational media corporations mostly located in rich, industrialized countries. Such concentration had many damaging consequences including highly unequal information flows between rich and poor countries; a lack of diversity among the voices and sources of information and communication; and a flow of media content from the North to the South that threatened the latter's local cultures. The MacBride Report argued that a New World Information and Communication Order was urgently necessary.

Efforts towards a NWICO, including recommendations for national communication policies, reduced media concentration, more South-to-South communication channels, and a mass media code of ethics, embroiled UNESCO in a high-profile dispute with the United States, who interpreted the report's recommendations as a threat to "freedom of the press," defined within the liberal framework as freedom from government control. In 2003, the Communication Rights for the Information Society Campaign (CRIS) emerged as a new moment of global media reform. The CRIS Campaign, which still continues, encompasses four pillars of *communication rights:* the right to participate in the public sphere; the right to knowledge; civil rights in communication; and cultural rights in communication (Siochrú 2005).

The first two decades of the twenty-first century have been marked by UNESCO's efforts to protect journalists and defend freedom of expression. The UN Human Rights Council's "Resolution on the Safety of Journalists" (2016) is welcome, but does not yet extend to Russia and China. In 2015, Member States endorsed the concept of "internet universality" which includes four principles for internet governance: human rights, openness, accessibility, and multistakeholder participation (UNESCO 2015).

Looking back over the past four decades, international governmental organizations and media activists have broadened their platforms and struggles to include communications as an important dimension of social progress. As Laura Stein notes: "communication policy activism spans the gamut from representational concerns with the end products of communication to the deep-seated political, economic, regulatory, and infrastructural issues that shape the larger cultural environment" (Stein 2009: 2–3). At stake in this continued battle is a foundational change in the governance of media and communications

infrastructures no less profound than that called for urban governance in Chapter 5. We turn for the rest of this section to specific struggles that target the underlying communications infrastructure of the digital age and its increasingly complex needs for governance.

13.6.2 Transparency and Accountability of Media Infrastructures and Mediated Data Flows

The last decade has seen the emergence of increasing global concern about the transparency and accountability of media infrastructures and the data flows that they carry (SDG 9; SPI "Access to information and communications"). In some cases, those concerns have prompted popular protests and engendered new forms and sites of resistance. One important category of concern about transparency and accountability relates to the conditions of access to information online. Populations worldwide have begun to pay attention to the effects of private agreements for preferential treatment that, behind the scenes, structure the universe of information they see (IPSP 2017).

Initially, struggles over preferential treatment took the form of efforts to secure formal enactment of the principle of "network neutrality." Proponents of network neutrality argued that internet access providers should treat all content, sites, and services equally without discriminating among different sources, services, or providers, while internet access providers sought greater leeway to experiment with differential quality of service. For the most part, countries around the world have resolved this debate in favor of network neutrality, although European regulations create a preferential exemption for certain specialized, high-bandwidth services.[26] Since there is no reason to believe that unregulated markets by themselves will preserve anything like network neutrality, this issue is likely to remain important for media's positive contribution to public knowledge.

Formal regulatory adoption of network neutrality mandates, however, has not resolved disputes about preferential access, but has simply shifted the terrain. Worldwide, regulatory implementation of network non-discrimination mandates has often been followed by so-called "zero-rating" initiatives. Zero-rating refers to an arrangement by which an internet access provider or mobile services provider agrees to exempt a particular content service from the data caps otherwise imposed on its users. Such agreements may be made in return for flat payments or in return for access to data about the behavior of users as they use the zero-rated service. Zero-rating agreements tend to drive traffic toward exempted data services, to the advantage of those providing them, so indirectly challenging the net neutrality principle.

A second important category of transparency and accountability issues relates to targeted removal of online information. Such removal may be mandated or initiated by an information intermediary (for example, a platform company). It may also involve the threatened (or feared) assertion of intellectual property rights, a request for removal, or

---

[26] For the US regulation, see "Protecting and Promoting the Open Internet," 80 Fed. Reg. 19,737 (April 13, 2015). For the European Union regulation, see Regulation 2015/2120 of the European Parliament and of the Council of 25 November 2015 laying down measures concerning open internet access and amending Directive 2002/22/EC on universal service and users' rights relating to electronic communications networks and services and Regulation (EU) No 531/2012 on roaming on public mobile communications networks within the Union, L 301/1.

de-indexing in connection with rights afforded under data protection regulation, enforcement of privately defined acceptable-content policies, or direct state censorship. Because the *failure* to remove some types of information can itself raise justice issues, targeted removal may sometimes be appropriate. Very often, however, such content filtering mechanisms remain secretive and unaccountable. Concerns about secret and unaccountable content filtering have sparked protests around the world, resulting in a new model of activism that takes digital media simultaneously as a site and *target* of protest activity. Such activity has achieved political gains, but arguably also accelerated the shift toward corporatized governance (described in Section 13.3.2).

In the United States, a protest movement that originated domestically and then spread globally defeated proposed legislation that tried to impose content filtering obligations on domain name registrars and payment providers (Herman 2013). Subsequently, however, major US payment providers have acceded to a set of voluntary "best practices" that involves them more actively in private intellectual property enforcement (Bridy 2015). In Australia, a popular protest movement opposed a government proposal that would have required internet service providers to perform mandatory content filtering; the government eventually withdrew the proposal after political opposition proved firm, and after the major Australian ISPs voluntarily agreed to block 1,400 sites previously identified as child pornography purveyors.[27] In China, where state involvement in filtering and suppression of dissident or otherwise disfavored expression is more direct, protest movements have taken correspondingly more indirect forms that involve the use of seemingly innocuous code words to discuss forbidden topics (Link and Xiao 2013).

Anticensorship and "internet freedom" activists have developed new, crowd-sourced methods of discovering and documenting content removal efforts and actions, producing websites such as chillingeffects. org, a US-based site that catalogues copyright takedown notices, and onlinecensorship.org, a project by the Electronic Frontier Foundation that catalogues content removals by social media sites. Some global platform companies, such as Twitter and Google, have begun to disseminate information about various types of targeted removals (e.g. Google's "transparency report"), although they have been much less forthcoming about their own acceptable-content protocols.

A final set of concerns about transparency and accountability relates to processes of automated, algorithmically processed mediation and filtering. Many dominant market providers – Google and Baidu in search, Facebook in social networking, Twitter in microblogging – use predictive algorithms to structure the universe of information that users see, and network neutrality mandates do not address those practices. Such algorithms operate invisibly to create displays to users that are tailored to what is known or inferred about that user. To individual users, however, the displays may appear universal and neutral. As we noted in Section 13.3, there are important, unresolved issues concerning the accountability of such automated filtering.

13.6.3 New Concentrations of Power Via Media Infrastructures and Mediated Data Flows

The new concentrations of power exerted via media infrastructures and mediated data flows have themselves generated rising levels of concern, prompting activism by civil society groups and sometimes more widespread protests and struggles (SDG 9).

One important cluster of issues involves proprietary claims to information networks and resources. Even as digital media activists and civil society groups have pushed for greater legal freedom to store, share, and modify content online, law enforcement authorities around the world have pushed to make outlaws of individuals and businesses who facilitate file-sharing. Enforcement has proceeded both via highly publicized litigation and by off-the-record efforts to seize or block access to internet domains (McCourt and Burkart 2003; Palmer and Warren 2013; see also Bridy 2015). In addition, as discussed in Section 13.3.2, both nation-states and powerful corporate actors have sought enhanced intellectual property protection through trade agreements. In Europe, popular opposition to the prospect of stepped-up intellectual property enforcement defeated ratification of the Anti-Counterfeiting Trade Agreement, which had been negotiated with the United States, Japan, and other countries. However, many provisions for enhanced enforcement have appeared in a different agreement, the Trans-Pacific Partnership (which was signed in 2016 but has not entered into force) (Public Citizen 2015b). Less is known about another agreement, the Trans-Atlantic Trade and Investment Partnership, now under negotiation between the United States and Europe.

Another set of issues relating to power exerted through today's fast-changing media infrastructures involves the surveillance conducted by powerful third parties, such as nation-states (IPSP 2017). In the wake of the revelations by Edward Snowden about the extent of the US National Security Administration's surveillance of global electronic communications, both ordinary citizens and governments worldwide protested NSA's lawless and seemingly unconstrained behavior. The Snowden revelations, however, also showed that national security services in multiple jurisdictions – including some of those now protesting most loudly – cooperated with the NSA and with each other, helping to form a network for evading existing domestic procedures for oversight (Privacy International 2013).[28]

Resistance to those efforts has taken varied forms. Some experts in computer security have formed ventures to develop and market secure "black phones" and online tools, while others have helped activists and civil society groups to explore, understand, and expose the full range of lawful and unlawful government surveillance activity.[29] As described in Section 13.3, some large information companies also have actively resisted the expansion of government surveillance. One country, Iceland, has resolved to develop comprehensive legislation establishing itself as a safe harbor for whistleblowers and investigative journalists.[30]

---

[27] See Ramadge (2008) and Charette (2012).

[28] See MacAskill and Ball (2013).

[29] See Laskow (2014), Rinehart (2015), Schneier, Seidel, and Vijayakumar (2016).

[30] International Modern Media Institute, "IMMI Resolution." https://en.immi.is/immi-resolution/.

Civil society organizations and, more recently, frustrated legislators, have put sustained pressure on trade negotiators to make treaty processes more transparent and democratically accountable.[31] New political movements and parties have formed around platforms for access to information and free culture (Beyer 2014), and the free/*libre*/open source software (FLOSS) movement has worked to foster the development and adoption of open systems that may be freely used and adapted (Coleman 2013; Gamalielsson and Lundell 2014).

A third cluster of struggles involves efforts by privacy activists and researchers to mobilize civil society groups and the public against commercial information power. This struggle needs to be understood within a wider diagnosis of contemporary media infrastructures' central role in the emergence of a new form of *surveillance capitalism*, whereby populations worldwide comprise a source of raw materials for new practices of surplus extraction (Cohen 2015; Zuboff 2015).

Disputes over these questions are as widely varied as the contexts and population groups involved. In the United States and Europe, commercial surveillance practices have engendered legal struggles over behavioral credit monitoring, drawing attention to the role of predictive profiling in the high-risk lending practices that contributed to the global financial crisis of 2008 (Pasquale 2015). Meanwhile, in an effort to enlist users themselves in both frustrating and exposing the practices of surveillance capitalism, teams of researchers have worked to design new privacy tools, such as ad blockers and tracker visualization tools (Eaglehardt and Narayanan 2016; Kennedy 2016).

In the Global South, struggles over the spread of surveillance capitalism have involved challenges to public–private partnerships for the delivery of services. In India, debates concerning the possible uses of a new national identification number have proved sharply divisive. In 2015, the Indian government launched the Digital India Initiative, which is based on the use of the Aadhar Unique Identity (UID) scheme for biometric authentication of recipients of government benefits and services. The Aadhar scheme, which is the world's largest biometrics-based database initiative, was developed by corporate technology partners, and critics charge that too little is known about its capabilities and potential future uses (see also the India case study in Section 13.6.4).[32] In sub-Saharan Africa, questions have been raised about the undisclosed uses of data collected via privately funded mobile telephony and banking initiatives (Hosein and Nyst 2013; Taylor 2016a; Taylor and Broeders 2015).

More generally, in the international development context, attention to data protection questions has highlighted how routine practices of data collection and sharing can put local populations at risk (Taylor 2016b) (SPI "Private rights"). There is a deep, if rarely noticed, continuity between these recent debates about control of networked information flows and the struggles of *indigenous peoples* against broadcasters for many decades. For example, Australia's Aboriginal communities have developed protocols that regulate how media makers – both individual media producers and media industries – can proceed on Aboriginal lands and among Aboriginal communities (Janke 1999; West 2014). Any individual producer or media industry intending to operate among Aboriginal communities must gain clearances from Aboriginal custodians before capturing, disseminating, reproducing, or archiving *data* about the land or the people. By defining a framework of respect, integrity, authenticity, and consultation with Aboriginal authorities and custodians, Aboriginal protocols have sought to ensure media accountability. Far from seeing such protocols as part of a "local culture" that unhelpfully resists "progress" (compare IPSP Chapter 15), we need to look to them as precursors of the fundamental changes needed in the governance of data flows. But no such protocols have yet been developed to govern data flows in the wider development context.

13.6.4 Case Study: Civil Society Activism in India: Facebook Free Basics[33]

Recent events in India offer an example of the ability of civil society activism to challenge the power of global digital platforms. We will focus here particularly on Facebook's proposed introduction of its "Free Basics" platform for internet access, but will situate the struggle over Free Basics in the broader context of other disputes over information rights in India in recent years.

Facebook's Free Basics platform is a joint private–public partnership ostensibly committed to expanding internet access for first-time users of the Internet in select countries in Asia, Latin America, and Africa. Facebook's CEO, Mark Zuckerberg, launched the initiative in 2013 (originally branded as Internet.org) in partnership with Samsung, Ericsson, MediaTek, Opera Software, Nokia, and Qualcomm. It was based on an "app" that enables smartphone users limited, free access to certain sites and services on the Internet, and that is designed to function on less robust 2G networks, potentially encouraging users to subscribe to mobile access packages (Hemple 2016).

From the Indian government's perspective, Free Basics represented an opportunity to expand its digital footprint into the daily lives of Indian citizens, by integrating Free Basics within its flagship Digital India initiative (discussed in Section 13.6.2). The Indian PM Narendra Modi's attempts to use social media including Twitter, Facebook, Youtube, Instagram, and other platforms for political purposes are well known (Pal, Chandra, and Vydiswaran 2016). In September 2015, he met Mark Zuckerberg in Silicon Valley, California (Mukherjee 2015). For Facebook, signing India to Free Basics would have given Facebook unrivalled access to the members of its second largest market (125 million users). The deal was celebrated on Facebook with both Modi's and Zuckerberg's profile pictures wrapped in the green, orange, and white of the Indian flag, leading millions of users to update their profiles with the tri-color.

Civil society activists, however, viewed Free Basics as an attempt by a commercial vendor to tether users to its product and monopolize the terms of access to the wider Internet, so compromising the tenets

---

[31] Perhaps as a result, some provisions of the Trans-Pacific Partnership's intellectual property chapter are less draconian than they had been in earlier, leaked versions of the proposed text. See Cox (2015).

[32] See Dreze (2015), Kakkar (2010), Masiero (2014), Punj (2012). See also Section 13.6.3.

[33] Case study written by Pradip Thomas.

of network neutrality (discussed in Section 13.6.2). While civil society groups in India had previously advocated specific reforms such as banning software patents and support for free and open source software (FOSS), a new "Save the Internet" campaign mobilized millions of users to petition the Telecom Regulatory Authority of India (TRAI) to uphold the broad principle of network neutrality. Facebook was completely caught off guard by the extent of the mobilization of Indian civil society in India against Free Basics.

In February 2016, the TRAI acted to uphold the principle of network neutrality. TRAI's regulation, titled "Prohibition of Discriminatory Tariffs for Data Services Regulation" provides that "no service provider shall offer or charge discriminatory tariffs for data services on the basis of content." TRAI's response was surprising given its previous support for industry interests over those of civil society (Abraham 2016). Additionally, while trade bodies such as the Cellular Operators Association of India (COAI) supported "differential pricing," others such as the National Association for Software and Services Companies (NASSCOM) opposed it.

This episode, which illustrates both the potential for cozy, mutually beneficial relationships between global platform companies and nation-state governments and the ability of civil society to challenge such relationships, needs to be put in the broader context of grassroots struggle for information rights in India in recent years (SPI "Access to information and communications"). Campaigns spearheaded by individuals such as Aruna Roy and Nikhil Dey and organizations such as the National Campaign for People's Right to Information led to the Indian government enacting the Right to Information Act in 2005. Such campaigns, along with a variety of social movements for information rights, created a broader recognition of the need for knowledge of entitlements and rights, facilitated access to information, and transparency and accountability in the disbursement of public funds.

This broad Right to Information movement laid the foundations for the subsequent struggles not only against Facebook's Free Basics initiative but also against the Aadhar Unique Identity (UID) scheme (discussed in Section 13.6.3). A number of the organizations that contested Free Basics also contest the Aadhar initiative. They have consistently highlighted shortfalls in the collection of biometric data, the security, and authentication issues that surround a centralized database on citizens, the potential for misuse of private information and for mass surveillance of citizens, and the absence of privacy laws. While the government has defended the scheme as a means to combat benefit fraud and protect national security, critics highlighted successfully the threat to basic freedoms from this expansion of the digital infrastructure.

13.6.5   Normative Implications of Media Infrastructures and Mediated Data Flows

The developments discussed in this section raise three broad sets of normative implications: for autonomy, economic justice, and political self-determination.

First and most basically, new and unaccountable concentrations of power exerted via media infrastructures and mediated data flows have implications for individual autonomy. As media infrastructures become more pervasive in everyday life, they increasingly mediate the human experience of the self, the other, and the world. As they connect individuals and communities, they also structure the universe of information and personalize informational exposure. The dynamics of continual, feedback-driven personalization invest information intermediaries with enormous power over processes of individual self-determination, which in a less intensively mediated world have been much more open textured and amenable to serendipity (Cohen 2012). Since individual autonomy is a necessary element of *any* form of social progress, it is essential to consider the implications of such large-scale media-based developments for the ongoing goal of social progress.

Second, as described in Section 13.3.3, the emergence of new economic models based on surveillance, social sorting, and predictive profiling has implications for economic justice (SDG 9). The necessary frameworks for protective regulation against such forms of data extraction are incompletely developed and unevenly implemented. Moreover, as privacy activists and civil society organizations worldwide have worked to raise public awareness of surveillance and its threats to privacy, they have struggled against an antiregulatory discourse that aims to defeat protective regulation by linking surveillance tightly with a generalized innovation imperative (Cohen 2016).

Finally, commercial and government practices of surveillance, social sorting, and predictive profiling have profound implications for political self-determination. The basic possibilities for political self-determination are important not just for political processes themselves, but also for wider processes of human development, richly understood (Sen 1999). Yet there is mounting evidence that predictive algorithms can be used to alter user behavior, in ways that implicate values of democratic self-governance and the rule of law. Facebook has publicly acknowledged conducting experiments on how personalization of the content in newsfeeds can affect users' moods and other experiments reminding users to go to the polls and vote (Grimmelmann 2015). There is no guarantee that future experiments would be disclosed, nor is Facebook subject to ethical guidelines similar to those that constrain human-subject experimentation in other contexts. Google's chief economist similarly has characterized Google's user base as subjects for experimentation (Varian 2014).

The prospect that large information intermediaries may enjoy wholly unaccountable power to manipulate the flows of social and public knowledge is alarming. More generally, the continuous, immanent, and highly granular regulatory processes by which such privately controlled intermediaries exert power via media infrastructures (and the new discourse of human development through the exploitation of "big data" that helps legitimate such power) exist in tension with broadly shared commitments to due process and the rule of law (Hildebrandt 2015).

We end this section with an important case where the broad social justice issues raised by the governance of media and communications infrastructures entered the political domain: the civil-society based NETmundial initiative that emerged in Brazil in the wake of the Snowden revelations.

13.6.6   Case Study: Brazil's *Marco Civil* on Internet Governance[34]

After the Snowden scandal of 2013 revealed mass electronic surveillance and espionage by US intelligence agencies, diverse global initiatives to defend the freedom of the Internet emerged from civil society. At the time of writing, the most progressive regulatory framework for the Internet is *Marco Civil da Internet* (Civil Rights Framework for the Internet), an initiative developed jointly by Brazil's civil society and the former government of Dilma Rousseff. Unlike authoritarian states who show greater concern over the implications of the Internet for regime stability than for freedom, and unlike liberal democracies in North America and Europe – who fear increased state control and often defer to private, corporatized governance of media infrastructures – Brazil supports universal free internet, while being also critical of the international governance structures that guide it (Trinkunas and Wallace 2015: 2). The *Marco Civil* is an exemplar of alternative ways of thinking about internet governance and its relation to wider social justice, without claiming that, by itself, a regulatory framework can create a different type of internet infrastructure, let alone address all the issues of power to which any communications infrastructure gives rise.

The *Marco Civil* sought to rethink what freedom and citizenship mean when it comes to the Internet. Adopted on April 23, 2014, the Civil Rights Framework is intended as a prototype for Internet regulation globally. The *Marco Civil* emerged from NETmundial, a conference convened by Brazil's national internet steering committee and organized as a multi-stakeholder dialogue between government, industry, and civil society. The framework that became the *Marco Civil* was developed through a series of online and offline deliberations that invited Brazilian citizens to shape a legal framework for internet regulation. It is significant not only as an initiative born from civil society in dialogue with government and private sectors, but also as a proposal emerging from the Global South, framed by social movements committed to the idea of communication rights. The *Marco Civil* has the *potential* to act as a balance to the global power of the United States on internet governance issues.

The Brazilian Civil Rights Framework for the Internet advances the commitment to respect for civil rights as an important component of internet regulation and governance. Recognizing the vulnerability of users, the *Marco Civil* emphasizes the Internet's social goals, protects the rights of internet users, and proposes the adoption of open source technologies that allow free access to information, knowledge, and culture. In the eyes of civil society activists (Gutiérrez 2014), the most important achievements of Brazil's *Marco Civil* include protection of freedom and privacy, open governance, universal inclusion, cultural diversity, and network neutrality.

The *Marco Civil* considers access to the Internet fundamental to democracy, as it is essential for participation in political life and cultural production, and part of the right to education and freedom of expression. It therefore advocates reducing inequalities in access to digital technologies and promotes the development of competencies to use digital platforms effectively. It proposes universal internet service with controlled rates and sufficient connection speed and also promotes education on the rights of consumers, ethical consumerism, and protection against misleading advertising and deceptive business methods (Compare SPI "Access to basic knowledge").

The *Marco Civil* stipulates that, while internet providers are free to compete, they are also responsible for guaranteeing freedom of speech, freedom of access to information, net neutrality, and protection of privacy. The *Marco Civil* forbids any type of discrimination based on disability, sexual orientation, or political or religious affiliations. It also provides for the protection of users' data and reputation and the right to the free development of personality,[35] and guarantees the right to access information and the right to rectification (SPI "Access to information and communications"). The *Marco Civil* states that citizens should be encouraged to move from being mere consumers of information, knowledge, and culture to becoming content creators. The framework calls for the development of appropriate digital tools to facilitate the creation of information, knowledge, and culture by citizens and states that the Internet should promote the production and circulation of such local content. Not surprisingly therefore movements that defend the freedom of knowledge strongly support this new code, to which Brazil's free software community was a principal contributor (Gutiérrez 2014). As initially proposed, the *Marco Civil* also mandated that all information and content about Brazil should be archived in Brazil, but that restriction was removed following lobbying by transnational internet corporations. Ultimately, the *Marco Civil* provided that all Brazilian internet content or content about Brazil is considered "Brazilian" and can be the object of observation. The *Marco Civil* eliminates criminal copyright penalties for content usage by citizens. However, it recognizes civil copyright laws that limit access to digital content and hinder collaborative creation, in tension with the goal of an entirely free digital culture.

The Brazilian Civil Rights Framework for the Internet mandates network neutrality (discussed in Section 13.6.2), and prohibits discriminatory action against any type of content or user, either by changing the speed of transmission or restricting content. Network neutrality ensures that all data travels at the same speed and without any restrictions based on the nature of the content or the nature of the user. Brazil's *Marco Civil* forbids blocking, monitoring, filtering, or analyzing content for commercial, political, moral, religious, or ideological reasons. The principle of network neutrality is here affirmed as essential to a collaborative and democratic digital culture.

The Brazilian Civil Rights Framework proposes a model of governance through multi-stakeholder, transparent, collaborative, and democratic mechanisms. The creators of the *Marco Civil* hoped to inspire activists and civil society organizations in other countries to demand similar laws (Gutierrez 2014), proposing "a global Internet that promotes freedom, inclusion, and diversity" (Trinkunas and Wallace 2015: 37). The code's provisions were in many cases opposed by global platform companies and sometimes defeated. It remains too early to determine the long-term influence of the model proposed, but its significance as an alternative to standard models of governance remains.

---

[34]   Case study written by Omar Rincón.

[35]   Compare the similar "right to free development of [the] personality" recognized in German law: Article 2 of the *Grundgesetz*.

13.7   Struggles for Social Justice Through Media

We come in this final main section of the chapter to consider the distinctive role that media and communications play in struggles for social justice and those struggles' overall contribution to social progress. The transformation of media infrastructures in the final decades of the twentieth century gave rise to new communication ecologies, which enabled divergent worldviews and political interests to draw on a multitude of media resources in their struggles for social justice.

13.7.1   Appropriating the Digital

Individuals and communities around the world have learned to appropriate media, especially digital communications infrastructures. The most notable late twentieth-century case of appropriating media for social justice was provided by the Zapatistas in Mexico.

In 1994, just as Mexico was preparing to sign the North American Free Trade Agreement (NAFTA) with the United States and Canada, the Ejército Zapatista de Liberación Nacional (EZLN) (Zapatista Army of National Liberation), an indigenous guerrilla organization, abruptly came to national attention by seizing towns in the region of Chiapas and demanding land, work, food, housing, education, independence, freedom, justice, and peace for Mexico's indigenous communities. The Mexican government attempted to annihilate the EZLN before news of the group reached the global public sphere but did not succeed. The EZLN's resistance has been analyzed from many perspectives, but in this chapter its importance lies not in its general repertoire of activism, but more as an exemplar of how, in the late twentieth century, media and culture came to be appropriated in new ways by social justice movements.

Using diverse media technologies and strategies, the Zapatistas activated a communication network that linked Mexican indigenous communities with social justice activists worldwide. In terms of media technology, Zapatista videos recorded on VHS tapes were carried out of the Lacandon jungle to the nearest urban centers and then on to Mexico City, where US activists picked them up and took them to Austin, Texas to be digitized and uploaded on computer listservs; meanwhile Zapatista audio recordings and texts were translated into multiple languages and disseminated via then-emerging digital platforms. In terms of cultural message, Subcomandante Marcos, the main spokesperson of the Zapatistas at the time, used these practical means to issue statements that framed the local struggles of marginalized Mexican indigenous communities as aligned with other social justice and identity struggles in the Global North and Global South (Rodríguez, Kidd, and Stein 2010), proposing himself as standing in for "every untolerated, oppressed, exploited minority that is … now beginning to speak" (Subcomandante Marcos 1994).

Through their distinctive use of communications (both technological and cultural) the Zapatistas served to link social justice collectives and individuals worldwide into a wave of international solidarity in the global public sphere, alerting the Mexican government and its army that the whole world was monitoring human rights abuses against indigenous communities in southern Mexico (Pianta and Marchetti 2007).

Social justice activists in many countries worldwide came to adopt Zapatista language, goals, and communication strategies. "Zapatismo" came for many to represent a new *type* of social justice activism, based less on formal institutional structures and more on "participation and deliberation, collective autonomy, and decentralized power structures" (Ferron 2012: 157). Marcos' specific manifesto for the "construction of a world where many worlds fit" (EZLN 1996) became exemplary for linking social justice to questions of culture (voice and diversity in public spheres) and questions of media (the need for inclusive media infrastructures).

The influence of this exemplar was shown in December 1999 by the actions of a wide coalition of protesters who met in Seattle to disrupt a World Trade Organization (WTO) summit. Because the Seattle protests originated a series of demonstrations against the dominant model of neoliberal globalization, the movement is sometimes labelled the "anti-globalization movement," but they refused that label, as they were not opposed to globalization, but to specific economic models that spread inequity worldwide. Learning from the EZLN, this movement insisted on producing their own media rather than allowing mainstream media to shape the narrative about their actions. The Seattle protest organizers set up the first Independent Media Center (Indymedia), and enabled protesters to produce and edit their own coverage of the protests by uploading to Indymedia's web page, which, in turn, incorporated Open Publishing software made available by media activist Matthew Arnison from Sydney's Community Activist Technology group (Arnison 2001; Kidd 2004). This model was replicated during the first decade of the twenty-first century in hundreds of cities worldwide under the motto "Don't hate the media, be the media."

Even in a world of corporate-owned digital platforms, these visions from the Lacandon jungle and Seattle still resonate through alternative models of how social justice activists can appropriate and redesign media technologies to meet their distinctive information and communication needs (Rodríguez 2001, in press).

13.7.2   Affordances and Constraints: From the Mobile Phone to Social Media and Beyond

If the circumstances of the Zapatistas' innovations were exceptional, broader changes in access to media technologies have been important too. With the introduction of prepaid accounts, low-cost handsets and relatively easy connectivity, mobile phone usage has spread across all social groups, including poor and marginalized populations. Despite stark inequalities in access, use, literacy, and resources (Donner 2015; Qiu 2014), much social innovation and activism with mobile phones has emerged, enabling collective action of all sorts, whether progressive or not. At the same time, the migration of activism to new digital platforms has encountered new constraints. We must always remember that the very same communication resources that benefit movements for social justice and social progress are also benefiting the movements that oppose them, including forces of right-wing extremism and authoritarian populism. Before discussing activism in more detail, it is important to note also that the affordances of mobile technologies and social networking platforms enable new kinds of everyday solidarity in contexts outside of politics. The use of mobile phones, the Internet, and social media has been important among migrants and their dispersed family, cultural, and political networks (Fortunati, Pertierra, and Vincent 2012). Filipino workers and other domestic workers (generally women) who spend years away from their families and communities use mobile phones and social media to maintain bonds and connection with friends and families (Madianou and Miller 2012). Chinese migrants who leave rural areas to find work in cities (Chu et al. 2012) also rely on mobile phones to create a new "modern" identity, spanning urban and rural settings (Wallis 2013). Outside the context of migration, diverse communities use mobile phones to redraw the boundaries between the private and personal and create "intimate publics" (Hjorth, King, and Kataoka 2014), for example to mourn or grieve (Cann 2014; Cuminsky and Hjorth 2016). In the wake of the earthquake and tsunami disaster of March 11, 2011 social media and mobile phones provided new channels for citizens to witness solidarity and contribute to disaster responses in Japan (Hjorth and Kim 2011).

One of the earliest places where uses of social media and mobile phones entered politics was Africa, where mobiles have been used for sharing information on health (SDG 3), "witnessing" human rights violations (through the incorporation of cameras into mobile phones), and citizen journalism, including election monitoring (Ekine 2010). An instructive case is Ushahidi (meaning "testimony" in Swahili), a mobile-based platform developed to share information and create maps to report on postelection violence in Kenya in 2008. In the South African elections of 2009, political groups and their supporters used different kinds of mobile software, combining instant messaging and chat functions to enhance communication (SDG 10). Labor struggles in Africa have also adopted the Internet and especially the mobile phone, alongside traditional media, for purposes of mobilization, coordination, and solidarity, for example the Marikana mine workers in South Africa (Walton 2014) and the El-Mahalla textile workers in Egypt. Section 13.5.4 discussed parallel developments in Northeast Asia.

Another important affordance of ICTs for social justice struggles is the ease with which they enable textual and multimedia commentary, protest, and dissent (SDG 16). Building on the early history of dial-up Bulletin Board Systems (BBS) from the late 1980s to late 1990s (Goggin and McLelland 2016), the growth of the World Wide Web in the 1990s saw the emergence of blogs as a flexible and powerful architecture of connection and commentary (Bruns and Jacobs 2006). In many countries, blogs enabled writers and activists, audiences and publics to engage and connect. Although this first attracted attention in the United States, it quickly became influential among social movements elsewhere, for example in the Middle East, especially Egypt (el-Nawaway and Khamis 2015) and Iran (Sreberny and Khiabany 2010). Blogs provide a way for religious, cultural, political, and linguistic communities to connect across territorial boundaries around religion (the various Muslim blogospheres: Russell and Echchaibi 2009), gender rights (Guta and Karolak 2015), health issues, and diasporic and sexual identities.

But the implications of information and communications technologies for achieving social justice and democracy are often ambiguous for several reasons. First, patterns of access and use remain very unequal. An example from the early 2000s comes from two post-Apartheid South

African social movements, the Treatment Action Campaign (TAC) and the Anti-Privatization Forum (APF): although they used websites and email to disseminate information, they needed to limit their mobile phone use to communications within their organizations. The use more recently of smartphones to communicate election messaging does not necessarily transform the public sphere overall or citizens' opportunities within it (Walton and Donner 2009). The use of different media for different functions may channel politics and related activity into particular elite domains (policy discussion by experts, for instance), rather than broadly based public spheres in which wider populations can participate (Wasserman 2007).

Second, debate continues about the role of social media platforms in creating new forms of solidarity and transnational mobilization. Facebook has been associated with various social and political movements, especially the "Arab Spring" uprisings of 2011, as well as the recent "Women's March" – a worldwide protest held in January 2017 to protect legislation and policies regarding human rights and environmental issues. Meanwhile, Twitter – relatively simple in its design, and without the cross-media integration of Facebook – has nonetheless helped incubate various initiatives based on "hashtag publics" (Weller et al. 2013), for example around Iran's 2009 election (Mottahedeh 2015), #BlackLivesMatter in the United States, and the #RhodesMustFall protests in South Africa.

At the same time, however, the infrastructure of social media and digital platforms remains tightly controlled by their corporate owners and managers (Andrejevic 2013), rather than by activists. Technological affordances that are key to solidarity – for example the hashtag function in Twitter – can be changed overnight by the parent corporation without consultation or participation of users. It remains very difficult for users or activists to have systematic input into the design and governance of commercial social media platforms (Mansell 2012). Social movements and social justice activists have learned that the potential of digital platforms to enhance their communication capabilities goes hand in hand with increased surveillance of their actions (Treré 2015). Finally, it is important to remember that the very same communication resources that benefit movements for social justice and social progress are also benefiting the movements that oppose them. We need therefore in reviewing the potential of new media technologies to acknowledge both affordances and constraints, and how they interact in specific contexts.

13.7.3   One Planet, Many Struggles, Many Media

Contemporary protest movements tend to draw on an "enlarged media ecology" (Qiu 2008) of old *and* new media, where traditional communication channels are mixed with new digital tools of activism. A variety of media ecologies have proved important in the context of different struggles for social justice across the world.

The interplay among traditional and digital media reached new heights as the Arab uprisings of 2010 and 2011 spawned a vibrant scene of dissident media and culture. The rise of political stand-up comedy was a hallmark of the uprising: in Bahrain, Syria, and Tunisia digital videos bore witness to atrocities, mocked dictators, and showcased a variety of animation, dance, theatre, and song. The media of artists and activists, often produced and disseminated under extremely risky conditions, is an important form of "creative insurgency" (Kraidy 2016). Meanwhile, media-based activism for gender equality and the empowerment of all women and girls is also growing worldwide. Through creative media strategies, advocacy groups have from the 1990s onwards made remarkable progress in the realm of gender equality from universal suffrage for women to rights for sexual minorities.

As another example, in the struggle against ISIS, activists have been running clandestine festivals of short films, shot on mobile phones, thereby defying local political censorship and moral prohibitions. The group "Raqqa Is Being Slaughtered Silently" has documented the atrocities of daily life under the Islamic State, propagating these on social media and connecting with mainstream journalists worldwide.

As these examples also illustrate, care is needed to contextualize the role of digital platforms in social movements. Digital technologies and social media platforms rarely drive political actions and protest in themselves. Social movements' communication strategies may involve not only digital technologies but also a wide range of non-digital media. In the 2013–2016 Gezi Square protests in Turkey, solidarity was built through a mix of media that combined photocopied zines and street performance with content shared via social media platforms (Saybaşılı 2014).

A significant new direction in media activism is as a space for political agency outside the sectarianism that dominates mainstream media and politics in polarized societies. In Lebanon, activists have mobilized around issues of environmental justice and the provision of utilities; the 2015 "You Stink" Movement, which used digital media to mobilize activism about inadequate removal services for municipal waste, was a key example of this trend.

Anticorruption campaigning has also harnessed diverse media capabilities. The most dramatic example of using the Internet as an infrastructure of connection to challenge not just corruption, but state and corporate power more generally, is the work of the activist group Anonymous with its "denial of service" and other attacks (Coleman 2014) and the whistleblower platform WikiLeaks (Brevini, Hintz, and McCurdy 2013). One of the largest civil society campaigns in recent years is the 2011 Indian anticorruption movement triggered by Anna Hazare's hunger strike in New Delhi.

In conclusion, all social justice and social progress initiatives depend on complex media ecologies that offer resources while simultaneously imposing risks and constraints. Activist individuals and communities, not technologies, drive social progress, by meeting the specific communication and information needs of each social justice context.

13.7.4   Creative Affordances: The Case of Disability Movements

An excellent case study of the role that the new affordances of digital media technology can play is disability. According to the landmark WHO 2011 *World Report on Disability*, more than 1 billion people in the world experience disability (15 percent of the world's population), of whom 110–190 million experience very significant disabilities (SDG 3).

Disability involves a wide range of impairment types from sensory disabilities to cognitive disabilities and psychosocial conditions. Prevalence of disability is growing due to population ageing and global increase in chronic health conditions. Disability is highly correlated with disadvantage but not "all people with disabilities are equally disadvantaged" (WHO 2011).

A roadmap for putting disability at the heart of the vision for social progress was proposed in 2006 by the UN Convention on Rights of Persons with Disabilities (CRPD). The CRPD has many provisions, which involve communication and technology rights, since media is pivotal for achieving human rights in relation to disability. People with disabilities generally experience inferior access to and affordability of media infrastructures, technologies, content, and participation, especially in the Global South. At the same time, disability becomes a paradigm case for rethinking both media and media's potential contribution to social progress. Disability is a key part of wider understandings of cultural and media diversity, but is of particular interest because of disability struggles' strong focus on digital technologies and their affordances.

Since the 1970s, the role of media in communicating negative attitudes, stereotypes, and myths about disability has been critiqued, commencing with the role of advertising in "charity" discourses of disability and a push towards affirmative images of disability. Although still very much in the minority, people with disabilities appear as characters of TV shows, increasingly reported in news, or, on occasion, as media workers, broadcasters, journalists, and celebrities themselves. However there remains a hierarchy of what is newsworthy, entertaining, and shareable, even in digital platforms. Mainstream media industries generally lag behind in offering work opportunities to people with disabilities (SDG 8). Disability still occupies a marginal place on media professionals' agendas.

However, in various countries, people with disabilities and their allies are using digital platforms in distinctive ways: for example, US Deaf protests in the Gaudallet "Deaf President" campaign; the use of video, photography, and social media by Bolivian disability activists in March 2016 to demand better social support (Goggin 2016); and British disability movement protests from 2012 against welfare cuts, using blogs, Facebook, and Twitter. Through social media, blogs, and websites a wide variety of disability publics have emerged. People with disabilities have also developed their own disability media: dedicated blogs (*Ouch!* established by BBC in the UK), disability comedy chatshow news genres (*The Last Leg*, Channel 4 in Britain), disability web-based programs (*Gimpgirl*), and crowd-funding platforms used to fund investigative journalism or entertainment.

Issues of accessibility to media infrastructures, as well as the potential affordances of these platforms, are particularly salient for people with disabilities, for example, captioning on TV and radio for the print handicapped. Despite their long histories, disability media such as Braille formats and sign language communication are still given little recognition in wider society, although there have been concerted international efforts on some aspects of digital technology (accessible computers and software, web accessibility, mobile phone accessibility, "apps" for people with disabilities).

Yet even in areas with the most concentrated effort, such as web accessibility, the situation remains inequitable: most government websites across the world have low levels of accessibility compliance, despite "digital first" government service, welfare, and e-government policies. The implementation of the CRPD requires widespread accessibility, especially across design of digital technologies, but national legislatures and media corporations have been slow to act.

The lack of social progress on disability and media is a central issue for wider social progress. It constrains the possibilities for social and cultural participation of people with disabilities (SPI "Health and wellness"). Yet disability has much to teach us about how communication occurs across the world's population: communication among, with, and by people with disabilities foregrounds issues of voice (Couldry 2010) and listening (MacNamara 2015): people with disabilities need access to public spheres where we can all listen not least governments, corporations, civil society, and a wide range of other organizations and agents (Goggin 2009). Without that the much-vaunted promises of new digital technologies are hollow.

13.8   Summary and Recommendations

This chapter has told two stories. On the one hand, the vast and varied media landscape we have depicted offers a complex set of resources for daily life and social movements. On the other, this landscape is marked by processes of power both old and radically new: new power processes include an emerging logic of *data extraction* tied to an imperative of data stimulation via increased message circulation (Sections 13.3 and 13.6). Through this transformation, unfamiliar forms of domination and exclusion are emerging, while public discourse and practices of government are subject to surprising new pressures. The long history of communications, and specifically media technologies, is now joining up with capitalism's development in striking new ways. The resulting global information environment requires urgent attention, if our understanding of social progress' dynamics is not to be dangerously oversimplified.

Media are an important resource for movements that promote social progress, and *effective* access to media is a necessary component of social justice (and a too-little recognized component of social progress itself). By "effective access" we mean that all individuals and communities should be able to use media infrastructures to produce content, access information and knowledge, and be active participants in the realms of politics, culture, and governance. Three major factors complicate the picture considerably.

First, the distribution of media resources (including traditional media and digital platforms) is skewed towards the rich and powerful, and away from the majority of the world's population, especially poor, marginalized, and excluded groups. This basic fact is ignored by the recurrent "social imaginary" (Taylor 2003) that sees media infrastructures as automatically progressive and socially transformative (for critique, see Herman, Hadlaw, and Swiss 2014; Mansell 2012; Mosco 2004). Although people rely on media platforms for connection and communication, they generally have very little influence over their design and pricing, or the conditions of access, use, or content production and distribution. Second, there is not *one* single space of connection enabled by media, but *many* such spaces, and the relations between them are highly uneven: questions of language and culture, unequal influence over Internet governance, software localization and technical design, all make the Internet, in particular, a highly uneven playing field for diverse groups, especially cultural and linguistic minorities. Third, even with access and more even distribution of opportunities for effective use, it may not be solidarity and dialogue that are facilitated when people come together via media (online abuse is also on the rise): the Internet's capacity, in principle, to enable multiple producers of content is not therefore sufficient. A central issue remains: how to design and sustain online spaces that encourage dialogue, free speech, respectful cultural exchange, and action for social progress? The governance of internet infrastructures is crucial in all of this, but itself highly contested and uneven.

In response to these challenges, we recommend that the key measure of "social progress" in the global policy community (the SPI) be adjusted to recognize effective media access as a new core component of social progress:

- While it is important that the SPI under "foundations of well-being" includes "access to information and communications" (defined in terms of numbers of internet users, mobile phone subscriptions, and a Press Freedom Index), this is insufficient: additional measures are needed for the distribution of opportunities for *effective* access *and use*. Such measures would concern not only access to the technological means to receive information and content, but also to appropriate pertinent and affordable technologies. The design of media infrastructures and digital platforms needs to be pertinent to diverse language communities, individuals with different ability levels, learning styles, and financial resources.
- While it is important that the SPI under "Opportunity" includes "personal rights" and "tolerance and exclusion," this is insufficient: *communication rights* must be added to the basket of *personal* rights, taking into account the direct relation between lack of participation and diversity *in the design and governance* of media infrastructures and lack of inclusion and tolerance *at a more general cultural level*.
- The *right to privacy* should also be added, including appropriate regulatory frameworks to protect against surveillance and data extraction.
- In addition, references to "tolerance" elsewhere in the SPI need to be interpreted to include tolerance in the media (that is, the absence of hate speech against the LGBTIQ community, women and girls, ethnic minorities, etc.)

In addition, we make the following broader recommendations:

- Media and communications infrastructures should be regarded as a common good, in the same way as other infrastructures (roads, railways, etc.). The recent wave of privatization and concentration in the media and information industries should be reviewed by regulators for its effects on the quality of media, its diversity, and its ability to meet people's needs. The encouragement of subsidy and spaces for nonprofit media should become an essential component of struggles for social progress and social justice. If progress is to be made towards these wider goals, major efforts are needed by civil society, governments, and international organizations to promote and sustain media that exist outside of market forces, and to secure noncommercial financial models for their existence (e.g. license fees).

- Internet *governance* should not be in the hands of organizations that make decisions, implement policy, and design online architectures behind closed doors. Popular participation and transparency should be the guiding principles that frame internet governance, policy, and regulatory frameworks.

- Equally, processes for the *design* of digital platforms and other means of accessing the Internet should recognize and effectively include representation from the full range of human communities.

- Media infrastructures need to work more effectively to facilitate the content creation by *diverse* communities. Access to media infrastructures as consumers, receivers, or audiences of content and information is not enough; individuals and communities need access as content creators; issues of language, affordability, user competencies, and technology design are fundamental.

- Core aspects of society such as *health care*, *social services*, and *financial services* will be increasingly provided over the Internet in the future, access to digital systems needs to be equally distributed among populations, and such access should come free of commercial tracking and surveillance.

- With increased state and corporate *surveillance*, *censorship*, and *data gathering* need to become the focus of extensive civic debate and regulatory attention.

- Sound, independent journalism, especially investigative journalism, is essential to democratic life. Citizens need curated, credible, verified, and contextualized information to be able to make reasonable decisions in political, cultural, and social arenas. Alternative forms of funding investigative journalism therefore need to compensate for the threat to the commercial newspaper business model.

- Serious attention is needed also on the impact on environmental sustainability of the waste generated by today's communication devices and the vast data-processing infrastructure that supports their use. This point has not emerged earlier in this chapter, but it is an unintended long-term side effect of intensified connection through media (Maxwell and Miller 2012).

In all these and many other respects media and communications flows and infrastructures are not mere background to social struggles, but themselves a *site of struggle*. We must acknowledge the overall lack of progress in media reform over the past 40 years. Since 1980 when the NWICO's MacBride Report was presented by UNESCO, numerous initiatives have attempted to reform media infrastructures, including the World Summit of the Information Society (WSIS), the Free Press movement in the United States, and the net neutrality and free software international movements. However, international organizations have not generally pursued such concerns. The international organizations responsible for proposing media policy (International Telecommunication Union (ITU); the Internet Corporation for Assigned Names and Numbers (ICANN)) have limited their scope to technical matters discussed with little input from civil society or social movements. A renewed and more inclusive debate on media reform must be launched.

Action plan

1. To add effective media access (as defined above) as a new core component of social progress in the SPI, to "ensure affordable, reliable, sustainable, and effective access to communication infrastructure," while acknowledging the long-term environmental waste from IT devices and data processing infrastructures.

2. To open a public discussion in which matters of inclusion, affordability, and diversity in media take center stage over markets and profit.

3. To position communication rights as central to official definitions of Social Progress. Communication rights include the right to be a content creator; the right to free expression; the right to knowledge and information; and the right to privacy.

4. To pressure international and national regulatory bodies and policy makers to design and implement processes for civil society participation in internet and media infrastructures' governance and policy. Media infrastructures should be governed by multi-stakeholder, transparent, and open bodies.

5. To pressure governments, the private sector, and universities to be accountable for designing media platforms that are accessible to input from diverse individuals and communities – especially marginalized communities such as communities of color, gender minorities, LGBTIQ communities, disabled communities, and communities in the Global South.

6. To push for media and internet regulation that protects users from state and/or corporate surveillance and data extraction for control or marketing purposes.

7. To promote media and internet regulatory regimes that forbid any type of censorship or discrimination based on disability, gender, sexual orientation, or political, religious, or ethnic affiliations.

8. To promote the notion that "access" also includes opportunities for content creation and not the mere technological access to platforms for media consumption. Media and information literacy, technical competencies, linguistic diversity, and capacity building are fundamental elements of access.

9. To re-establish independent, sound journalism as an essential element of democracy, and for this purpose to explore alternative funding models besides the commercial (innovative forms of public–private partnership, license fees, etc.).

10. To promote free access to software and free knowledge, as the commons of humankind.

Table 13.1 | Toolkit

Goals/values	Policy makers	International organizations	Corporate media and tech sector	NGOs	Citizens
Effective access to communication infrastructures	Develop regulatory regimes that guarantee affordability, cultural inclusion, and linguistic diversity of media and digital platforms Develop regulation that allocates a significant proportion of communication resources (frequencies, budgets, R&D) to citizens' media initiatives Develop regulatory systems to deal in an environmentally friendly way with waste from IT products and their use Promote net neutrality in national regulations	Promote the notion that "Effective access to media infrastructures" includes using technologies to create and disseminate content Monitor media and digital content for diversity, inclusivity, and access Sanction corporate media and technology corporations if they fail to comply	Produce tolerant, inclusive, and diverse media and digital content Design media and digital platforms that can be used by citizens to produce and disseminate their own content Adopt net neutrality	Promote and support citizens' media Promote media production and software design programs in schools Promote training in media and information literacy and writing code	Develop and support citizens' media (produced by local communities for local communities) Develop and support school media Implement citizen-run media and information literacy programs Demand tolerant, inclusive, and diverse media and digital content from the private and public media sectors Defend net neutrality
Transparency and accountability of media and digital platforms	Incorporate transparency and accountability in international and national legislation/regulation on media and the Internet	Organize multistakeholder international and regional forums to discuss the future of media and digital platforms	Help subsidize nonprofit media and digital platforms	Mobilize civil society to participate in global and local discussion about the future of media and digital platforms	Demand inclusion and voice in global and local discussions about the future of media and digital communication
Communication rights: • right to be a content creator • right to free expression • right to knowledge and information • right to privacy	Include communication rights as a fundamental human right in national legislations Develop the necessary regulatory frameworks for the implementation, regulation, and vigilance of communication rights	Include communication rights in SDGs, SPI, and any other similar global blueprint to assess progress, wellbeing, and sustainable development	Review and adjust business models for consistency with communications rights Advocate policies, regulations, and treaties that advance communication rights Produce and disseminate content that informs audiences about communication rights	Raise awareness around communication rights among social justice organizations and social movements	Demand communication rights from national governments, the private sector and international organizations
Participatory governance of media infrastructures and digital platforms	Design media and digital platforms regulatory regimes that include effective civil society participation, and in particular participation by representatives of indigenous people and people with disabilities	Establish a global international body responsible for monitoring and assessing access, inclusion, diversity, and communication rights in media infrastructures Promote the notion that civil society input is essential in the governance of media and digital platforms Implement educational programs for citizens about media and internet regulation and governance	Include civil society participation in all aspects of media and internet governance (e.g. ICANN, WAN-Ifra)	Promote the notion that civil society participation in media and internet governance is a right Implement media and internet regulation and governance	Demand the opportunity to participate in media and internet governance Implement citizen-run educational programs about media and internet regulation and governance

continued on next page →

Table 13.1 | (continued)

Goals/values	Policy makers	International organizations	Corporate media and tech sector	NGOs	Citizens
Participation of civil society in the **design** of media infrastructures and digital platforms	Budget public funds for inclusive citizen-led research and design of digital platforms and software, where "inclusive" means including, for example, women and girls, indigenous communities, disabled communities, and linguistic minorities	Monitor and assess the cultural appropriateness and inclusivity of media, digital platforms, and software for diverse communities Promote inclusive civil society participation and input in the research and design of communication technologies	Establish the necessary channels to incorporate inclusive citizen input into research and design of communication technologies, especially indigenous communities, disabled communities, and linguistic minorities	Promote research and design of communication technologies in schools Promote design of communication technologies and software driven by the needs of disadvantaged communities and specifically (a) women and girls, (b) indigenous peoples, and (c) disabled people Develop and fund initiatives for sharing knowledge, know-how, technical expertise, and content between disadvantaged communities	Implement inclusive citizen-run, local initiatives of communication technology research and design Demand participation in corporate and public communication technology research and design Promote the use of open access software
Protection from **surveillance** and data extraction	Design and implement regulation that protects citizens from surveillance and data extraction by media and internet corporations, governments, and security organizations Regulate the use of algorithms for marketing or surveillance purposes	Promote multistakeholder regional and international forums to address surveillance and data extraction Re-position civil society organizations as key participants in regulating the consequences of surveillance and data extraction Lead a public conversation about filtering and predictive algorithms	Review and adjust business models for consistency with rights of privacy and data protection Advocate policies, regulations, and treaties that advance rights of privacy and data protection Develop transparent and accessible conventions for disclosing sponsorship, and describing the use of predictive algorithms	Promote a public conversation on surveillance and data extraction as threats to privacy Expose unlawful government surveillance activities Support the design and distribution of ad blockers and tracker visualization tools	Demand the right to privacy and protection against data extraction by corporate or government entities Demand transparency and accountability of data collection, filtering and the use of predictive algorithms
Media infrastructures and digital platforms free from **censorship**	Develop regulatory regimes that demand transparency and accountability of content filtering mechanisms Develop legislation that protects whistleblowers and investigative journalists Include the social responsibility of media and digital platforms as a key element of international and national media and internet legislation	Monitor the transparency of content filtering mechanisms used by corporate and government media and digital platforms Promote the need for investigative journalism as an essential component of democratic life	Commit to supporting independent investigative journalism as the social responsibility of media and digital platforms	Fund civil society initiatives to monitor and catalogue content removal in digital platforms and social media Support independent investigative journalism initiatives (in universities, foundations, or government-sponsored organizations)	Demand access to knowledge and information Support investigative journalism as an essential element of democratic societies

Table 13.1 | (continued)

Goals/values	Policy makers	International organizations	Corporate media and tech sector	NGOs	Citizens
Media and information **literacy**	Promote the inclusion of media and information literacy as a core element in educational curricula	In collaboration with NGOs, civil society, and citizens' media, implement media and information literacy initiatives at the local level, especially targeting children and youth, disabled communities, ethnic minorities, and other vulnerable populations	Develop free and accessible media and information literacy initiatives in collaboration with NGOs and citizens	Fund/sponsor media and information literacy initiatives developed by international organizations, NGOs, civil society, and citizens' media Promote public conversation about the improvement of media and information literacy	Develop local initiatives of media and information literacy –linked e.g. to schools, universities, community organizations, and local citizens' media
Linguistic diversity	Implement policies that mandate subtitles and translation Design regulatory regimes that mandate the production of media content and software for linguistic minorities and disabled communities Include indigenous people and people with disabilities in the formulation of media and internet regulatory regimes	Coordinate and support local initiatives for linguistic diversity Enable global visibility of linguistic diversity	Produce content in various languages, including indigenous languages Design communication technologies and software appropriate and accessible to diverse linguistic communities and disabled communities	Promote alliances and collaboration between media and digital communication NGOs and indigenous NGOs and social movements Mobilize civil society and social movements to demand linguistic plurality in media infrastructures	Demand media content available in local languages Demand media content and digital platforms tailored to disabled communities
Human knowledge as **commons**, instead of commodities	Balance intellectual property rights with notions of information and knowledge as the commons of humankind, and the value of communication and dialogue	Pressure trade agreement negotiations to balance intellectual property protections with the rights to free knowledge and information Promote free culture and free/*libre*/open source software	Recognize the limits to proprietary claims over information, expression, and innovation Acknowledge the importance for social progress of the availability of nonproprietary information, expression, and innovation Advocate policies, regulations, and treaties that advance a global knowledge commons	Pressure schools to embrace free/*libre*/open source software in the classroom	Demand access to knowledge and information as a right, not a privilege

Note: we have allocated the tasks in the toolkit matrix to the actor who should have the *main* responsibility for each task, however, various tasks should be developed by multistakeholder bodies.

References

Abraham, S. 2016. "Facebook's Fall From Grace: Arab Spring to Indian Winter." *Tech 2*. http://tech.firstpost.com/news-analysis/facebooks-fall-from-grace-arab-spring-to-indian-winter-298412.html.

Anderson, B. 1983. *Imagined Communities*. London: Verso.

Andersson, S.J. 2013. *Online File Sharing*. New York: Routledge.

Andrejevic, M. 2013. *Infoglut*. New York: Routledge.

APJII. 2015. *Profil Pengguna Internet Indonesia (Profile of Indonesia Internet Users)*. Jakarta: Asosiasi Penyelenggara Jasa Internet Indonesia (The Indonesian Association for Internet Service Providers).

APJII. 2016. *Penetrasi dan Perilaku Pengguna Internet Indonesia (Penetration and Behaviour of Indonesian Internet Users)*. Jakarta: Asosiasi Penyelenggara Jasa Internet Indonesia (The Indonesian Association for Internet Service Providers).

Arnison, M. 2001. "Decisions and Diversity: Sydney Indymedia Volunteer." *Version 0.2*. http://purplebark.net/maffew/catk/decisions.html.

Arvizu, S. 2009. "Creating Alternative Visions of Arab Society: Emerging Youth Publics in Cairo." *Media, Culture and Society* 31/3: 385–407.

Banda, F. 2006. "Negotiating Distant Influences: Globalization and Broadcasting Policy Reforms in Zambia and South Africa." *Canadian Journal of Communication* 31/2: 459–467.

Banda, F. 2009. "Kasoma's Afriethics: A reappraisal." *International Communication Gazette* 71/4: 227–242.

Barocas, S., and A. Selbst. 2016. "Big Data's Disparate Impact." *California Law Review* 104: 1–62.

Basri, M.C. 2012. "Indonesia Role in the World Economy: Sitting on the Fence," in A. Reids (ed.), *Indonesia Rising*. Singapore: Institute for Southeast Asian Studies.

Beckett, L. 2012. "How Companies Have Assembled Political Profiles for Millions of Internet Users." ProPublica, October 22. www.propublica.org/article/how-companies-have-assembled-political-profiles-for-millions-of-Internet-us.

Benvenisti, E. 2015. "Democracy Captured: The Mega-Regional Agreements and the Future of Global Public Law." *GlobalTrust Working Paper Series*, August 2015. http://papers.ssrn.com/sol3/papers.cfm?abstract_id=2646882.

Beyer, J.L. 2014. "The Emergence of a Freedom of Information Movement: Anonymous, Wikileaks, the Pirate Party, and Iceland." *Journal of Computer-Mediated Communication* 19: 141–154.

Bilnack, M.D., and N. Elkin-Koren. 2006. "The Invisible Handshake: The Reemergence of the State in the Digital Environment." *Virginia Journal of Law and Technology* 8: 1–57.

Bilstereyst, D., and P. Meers. 2000. "The International Telenovela Debate and the Contra-Flow Argument: A Reappraisal." *Media Culture Society* 22/4: 393–413.

Birnhack, M.D., and N. Elkin-Koren. 2006. "The Invisible Handshake: The Reemergence of the State in the Digital Environment." *Virginia Journal of Law and Technology* 8: 1–57.

Boczkowski, P. J., and I. Siles. 2014. "Steps Toward Cosmopolitanism in the Study of Media Technologies: Integrating Scholarship on Production, Consumption, Materiality, and Content," in T. Gillespie, et al. (eds.), *Media Technologies*. Cambridge: MIT Press.

Bohman, J. 2007. *Democracy Across Borders*. Cambridge: MIT Press.

Bolin, G. 2011. *Value and the Media*. Farnham: Ashgate.

Bolin, G., P. Jordan, and P. Ståhlberg. 2016. "From Nation Branding to Information Warfare," in M. Pantti (ed.), *Media and the Ukraine Crisis*. New York: Peter Lang.

Bourdieu, P. 1998. *Acts of Resistance*. New York: The New Press.

Bourgault, L.M. 1995. *Mass Media in Sub-Saharan Africa*. Bloomington, IN: Indiana University Press.

Boyd, D. 2017. "Did Media Literacy Backfire?." *Points*, January 5. points.datasociety.net/did-media-literacy-backfire-7418c084d88d#.m76u6f177.

Boyd-Barrett, O. 1977. "Media Imperialism," in J. Curran et al. (eds.), *Mass Communications and Society*. London: Open University Press.

Brevini, B., A. Hintz, and P. McCurdy. 2013. *Beyond Wikileaks*. London: Palgrave Macmillan.

Bridy, A. 2015. "Internet Payment Blockades." *Florida Law Review* 67: 1523–1568.

Bruns, A., and J. Jacobs. 2006. *Uses of Blogs*. New York: Peter Lang.

Calabrese, A., and M. Briziarelli. 2011. "Policy Imperialism: Bilateral Trade Agreements as Instruments of Media Governance," in R. Mansell and M. Raboy (eds.), *The Handbook of Global Media and Communications Policy*. Oxford: Blackwell.

Cañizalez, A., and J. Lugo. 2007. "Telesur: Estrategia geopolítica con fines integracionistas." *Confines* 3/6: 53–64.

Cann, C.K. 2014. *Virtual Afterlives*. Lexington, KS: University of Kentucky Press.

Cerda Silva, A.J. 2012. "Beyond the Unrealistic Solution for Development Provided by the Appendix of the Berne Convention on Copyright." *Journal of the Copyright Society of the USA* 60: 581–633.

Chan, A. 2013. *Networking Peripheries*. Cambridge: MIT Press.

Charette, R.N. 2012. "Australian Government Gives Up on Filtering the Internet." IEEE Spectrum, November 12. http://spectrum.ieee.org/riskfactor/computing/it/australian-government-gives-up-on-filtering-the-Internet.

China Internet Network Information Center. 2016. "Zhongguo hulianwangluo fazhan zhuangkuang tongjibaogao." *China Internet Network Development State*. www.cnnic.net.cn/hlwfzyj/hlwxzbg/201601/P020160122469130059846.pdf.

Chon, M. 2007. "Intellectual Property 'From Below': Copyright and Capability for Education." *U.C. Davis Law Review* 40: 803–854.

Chu, R.W.-C., L. Fortunati, P.-L. Law, and S. Yang. 2012. *Mobile Communication and Greater China*. London: Routledge.

Chua, B.H., and K. Iwabuchi. 2008. *East Asian Pop Culture*. Hong Kong: Hong Kong University Press.

Citron, D.K. 2008. "Technological Due Process." *Washington University Law Review* 85: 1249–1313.

Cohen, J.E. 2012. *Configuring the Networked Self*. New Haven, CT: Yale University Press.

Cohen, J.E. 2015. "The Biopolitical Public Domain." http://papers.ssrn.com/sol3/papers.cfm?abstract_id=2666570.

Cohen, J.E. 2016. "The Surveillance-Innovation Complex: The Irony of the Participatory Turn," in D. Barney, et al. (eds.), *The Participatory Condition*. Minneapolis, MN: University of Minnesota Press.

Coleman, E.G. 2013. *Codin Freedom*. Princeton, NJ: Princeton University Press.

Coleman, G. 2014. *Hacker, Hoaxer, Whistleblower, Spy*. London: Verso.

Corner, J. 1991. "Meaning Genre and Context: The Problematics of 'Public Knowledge' in the New Audience Studies," in J. Curran and M. Gurevitch (eds.), *Mass Media and Society*. London: Edward Arnold.

Couldry, N. 2010. *Why Voice Matters*. London: Sage.

Couldry, N. 2012. *Media Society World*. Cambridge: Polity.

Cox, K. 2015. "Analysis of the Final TPP (Leaked) Text on Intellectual Property: Mixed Results." InfoJustice.org, October 15. http://infojustice.org/archives/35159.

Cuminskey, K., and L. Hjorth. 2016. *Haunting Hands*. Oxford: Oxford University Press.

Da Silva Mendes, G. 2012. "The (In)visibility of Telesur in Argentina Under the Communication Policies of Nestor Kirchner." *Comunicación y Sociedad* 21: 269–293.

Dahlgren, P. 2009. *Media and Political Engagement*. Cambridge: Polity.

DeNardis, L. 2009. *Protocol Politics*. Cambridge: MIT Press.

DeNardis, L. 2014. *The Global War for Internet Governance*. New Haven, CT: Yale University Press.

Donders, K., and H. Moe. 2011. *Exporting the Public Value Test*. Göteborg: Nordicom.

Donner, J. 2015. *After Access*. Cambridge: MIT Press.

Dreze, Jean. 2015. "Unique Identity Dilemma." *Indian Express*, March 19. http://indianexpress.com/article/opinion/columns/unique-identity-dilemma/.

Dudziak, M.L. 2000. *Cold War Civil Rights*. Princeton, NJ: Princeton University Press.

Eaglehardt, S., and A. Narayanan. 2016. "Online Tracking: A 1-Million Site Measurement and Analysis." http://randomwalker.info/publications/OpenWPM_1_million_site_tracking_measurement.pdf.

Ekine, S. 2010. *SMS Uprising*. Cape Town: Pambazuka Press.

El-Nawaway, M., and S. Khamis. 2015. *Egyptian Revolution 2.0*. Basingstoke: Palgrave.

EZLN (Ejército Zapatista de Liberación Nacional). 1996. *Crónicas Intergalácticas. Primer Encuentro Intercontinental por la Humanidad y Contra el Neoliberalismo*. Chiapas, Mexico: Planeta Tierra.

Farivar, C. 2011. *The Internet of Elsewhere*. New Brunswick, NJ: Rutgers University Press.

Feldbrugge, F.J-M. 1975. *Samizdat and Political Dissent in the Soviet Union*. Leyden: F.J.A. Sijthoff.

Fenton, N. 2010. "Drowning or Waving? New Media, Journalism and Democracy," in N. Fenton (ed.), *New Media, Old News*. London: Sage.

Ferron, B. 2012. "Les Répertoires Médiatiques del Mobilisations Altermondialistes. Contributions à une analyse de la Société Transnationale," unpublished doctoral thesis, Université de Rennes, France.

Fink, C., and P. Reichenmiller. 2006. "Tightening TRIPS," in R. Newfarmer (ed.), *Trade, Doha, and Development*. Washington, DC: World Bank.

http://documents.worldbank.org/curated/en/2006/01/7564325/trade-doha-development-window-issues.

Forsman, M. 2014. *Media and Information Literacy in Sweden*. Stockholm: Statens Medieråd.

Fortunati, L., R. Pertierra, and J. Vincent. 2012. *Migrations, Diaspora and Information Technology in Global Societies*. New York: Routledge.

Fraser, N. 2005. "Reframing Global Justice." *New Left Review* 36: 69–90.

Frazier, R.T. 2015. *The East Is Black*. Durham, NC: Duke University Press.

Freedman, D. 2003. "Cultural Policy-Making in the Free Trade Era: An Evaluation of the Impact of Current World Trade Organization Negotiations on Audio-Visual Industries." *International Journal of Cultural Policy* 9/3: 285–298.

Frere, M.-S., and A. Kiyindou. 2009. "Democractic Process, Civic Consciousness, and the Internet in Francophone Africa," in M. Fred, T. Wisdom, and B. Fackson (eds.), *African Media and the Digital Public Sphere*. New York: Palgrave Macmillan.

Friedman, S. 2011. "Three Mile Island, Chernobyl and Fukushima: An Analysis of Traditional and New Media Coverage of Nuclear Accidents and Radiation." *Bulletin of the Atomic Scientists* 67/5: 55–65.

Gamalielsson, J., and B. Lundell. 2014. "Sustainability of Open Source Software Communities Beyond a Fork: How and Why Has the LibreOffice Project Evolved?" *Journal of Systems and Software* 89: 128–145.

Giddens, A. 1990. *Modernity and Self-Identity in the Late Modern Age*. Cambridge: Polity.

Goggin, G. 2009. "Disability and the Ethics of Listening: New Models for Democracy and Media." *Continuum: Journal of Media and Cultural Studies* 23/4: 489–502.

Goggin, G. 2016. "Reimagining Digital Citizenship via Disability," in A. McCosker, S. Vivienne, and A. Johns (eds.), *Rethinking Digital Citizenship*. Lanham: Rowman & Littlefield.

Goggin, G., and M. McLelland. 2016. *Routledge Companion to Global Internet Histories*. New York: Routledge.

Gopal, S., and S. Moorti. 2008. *Global Bollywood*. Minneapolis, MN: University of Minnesota Press.

Grimmelmann, J. 2015. "The Law and Ethics of Experiments on Social Media Users," *Colorado Technology Law Journal* 13: 219–271.

Guta, H., and M. Karolak. 2015. "Veiling and Blogging: Social Media as Sites of Identity Negotiation and Expression Among Saudi Women." *Journal of International Women's Studies* 16/2: 115–127.

Gutiérrez, B. 2014. "Brasil aprueba el *Marco Civil* de Internet, modelo para la Carta Magna de la Red." *El Diario*. www.eldiario.es/turing/Brasil-marca-ritmo-neutralidad-Internet_0_243925947.html.

Hackett, R.A., and Y. Zhao. 1998. *Sustaining Democracy?* Toronto: Garamond Press.

Halleck, D.D. 2001. *Hand Held Visions*. New York: Fordham University Press.

Hannerz, U. 1992. *Cultural Complexity*. New York: Columbia University Press.

Hannerz, U. 1996. *Transnational Connections*. London: Routledge.

Hemple, J. 2016. "Inside Facebook's Ambitious Plan to Connect the Whole World." *Wired*. file:///Users/uqpthom4/Desktop/Inside%20Facebook's%20Ambitious%20Plan%20to%20Connect%20the%20Whole%20World%20%7C%20WIRED.webarchive.

Herman, A., J. Hadlaw, and T. Swiss. 2014. *Theories of the Mobile Internet*. London: Routledge.

Herman, B.D. 2013. *The Fight Over Digital Rights*. New York: Cambridge University Press.

Hermes, J. 2005. *Re-Reading Popular Culture*. Malden: Blackwell.

Hildebrandt, M. 2015. *Smart Technologies and the End(s) of Law*. Cheltenham: Edward Elgar.

Hill, D.T., and K. Sen. 2005. *The Internet in Indonesia's New Democracy*. London: Routledge.

Hjorth, L., and K.-H.Y Kim. 2011. "The Mourning After: A Case Study of Social Media in the 3.11 Earthquake Disaster in Japan." *Television and New Media* 12: 552–559.

Hjorth, L., N. King, and M. Kataoka. 2014. *Art in Asia-Pacific*. New York: Routledge.

Hollander, E., L. d'Haenens, and J. Bardoel. 2009. "Television Performance in Indonesia: Steering Between Civil Society, State and Market." *Asian Journal of Communication* 19/1: 39–58.

Hong, Y. 2017. *Networking China*. Urbana, IL: University of Illinois Press.

Hoofnagle, C.J. 2004. "Big Brother's Little Helpers: How ChoicePoint and Other Commercial Data Brokers Collect and Package Your Data for Law Enforcement." *North Carolina Journal of International Law and Commercial Regulation* 29: 595–637.

Hoofnagle, C.J., and J. Whittington. 2014. "Free: Accounting for the Costs of the Internet's Most Popular Price." *UCLA Law Review* 61: 606–670.

Hosein, G., and C. Nyst. 2013. "Aiding Surveillance: An Exploration of How Development and Humanitarian Aid Initiatives Are Enabling Surveillance in Developing Countries." www.privacyinternational.org/sites/default/files/Aiding%20Surveillance.pdf.

Ibold, H. 2010. "Disjuncture 2.0: Youth, Internet Use, and Cultural Identity in Bishkek." *Central Asian Survey* 29/4: 521–535.

Inman, P. 2016. "MPs Can View TTIP Files – But Take Only Pencil and Paper with Them." *Guardian*, February 18. www.theguardian.com/business/2016/feb/18/mps-can-view-ttip-files-but-take-only-pencil-and-paper-with-them.

International Panel on Social Progess (IPSP) 2017. Survey Done by Qualtrics for IPSP on a Representative Sample of 1,041 US Residents. March–April.

International Telecommunications Union. 2014. "Time Series by Country (until 2014) for: Percentage of Individuals Using the Internet and Mobile-Cellular Subscriptions." www.itu.int/en/ITU-D/Statistics/Pages/stat/default.aspx.

International Telecommunications Union. 2015. "ITU Releases 2015 ICT Figures. Statistics Confirm ICT Revolution of the Past 15 Years." www.itu.int/net/pressoffice/press_releases/2015/17.aspx.

International Telecommunications Union. 2016. "Report on the WSIS Stocktaking." www.itu.int/dms_pub/itu-s/opb/pol/S-POL-WSIS.REP-2016-PDF-E.pdf.

Iwabuchi, K. 2002. *Recentering Globalization*. Durham: Duke University Press.

Iwabuchi, K. 2007. "Contra-Flows or the Cultural Logic of Uneven Globalization? Japanese Media in the Global Agora," in D. Thussu (ed.), *Media on the Move*. London: Routledge.

Iwabuchi, K. 2015. *Resilient Borders and Cultural Diversity*. Lanham, MD: Lexington Books.

Janke, T. 1999. *Our Culture: Our Future – Report on Australian Indigenous Cultural and Intellectual Property Rights*. Sydney: Michael Frankel and Company.

Jankowski, N., O. Prehn, and J. Stappers. 1992. *The People's Voice*. London: John Libbey.

Jin, D.L. 2015. *Digital Platforms, Imperialism and Political Culture*. London: Routledge.

Kakkar, M. 2010. "Companies, Processes and Technology behind India's UID Project, Aadhaar." October 1. www.zdnet.com/article/companies-processes-and-technology-behind-indias-uid-project-aadhaar/

Karikari, K. 2007. "African Media Since Ghana's Independence," in E. Barratt and G. Berger (eds.), *50 Years of Journalism*. Johannesburg: The African Editors' Forum.

Kasoma, F.P. 1994. *Journalism Ethics in Africa*. Nairobi: ACCE.

Kasoma, F.P. 1996. "The Foundations of African Ethics (Afriethics) and the Professional Practice of Journalism: The Case for Society-Centred Media Morality." *Africa Media Review* 10/3: 93–116.

Kavoori, A.P., and A. Punathambekar. 2008. *Global Bollywood*. New York: NYU Press.

Kennedy, H. 2016. *Post, Mine, Repeat*. London: Palgrave Macmillan.

Kidd, D. 2004. "From Carnival to Commons: The Global IMC Network," in E. Yuen, D. Burton Rose, and G. Katsiaficas (eds.), *Confronting Capitalism*. New York: Softskull Press.

Kim, Y. 2013. *The Korean Wave*. London: Routledge.

King, M.D., and H.A. Haveman. 2008. "Antislavery in America: The Press, the Pulpit, and the Rise of Antislavery Societies." *Administrative Science Quarterly* 53/3: 492–528.

Kraidy, M.M. 2016. *The Naked Blogger of Cairo*. Cambridge: Harvard University Press.

Kraidy, M.M., and J.F. Khalil. 2009. *Arab Industries*. London: BFI/Macmillan.

Krings, M.M., and O. Onookome. 2013. *Global Nollywood*. Bloomington, IN: Indiana University Press.

Kupe, T. 2014. "Media Diversity," in U. Seery (ed.), *Media Landscape 2014: Celebrating 20 Years of South Africa's Media*. Pretoria: Department of Communications.

Kupe, T. 2016. "Media Freedom has Come a Long Way in Africa, But It's Still Precarious." *The Conversation*. https://theconversation.com/media-freedom-has-come-a-long-way-in-africa-but-its-still-precarious-58604.

Lamloum, O. 2004. *Al-Jazira, miroir rebellé et ambigu du monde arabe*. Paris: La Decouverte.

La Pastina, A.C., and J.D. Straubhaar. 2005. "Multiple Proximities Between Television Genres and Audiences: The Schism between Telenovelas' Global Distribution and Local Consumption." *International Communication Gazette* 67/3: 271–288.

Larkin, B. 2008. *Signal and Noise: Media, Infrastructure and Urban Culture in Nigeria*. Durham: Duke University Press.

Larsson, S. 2013. "Metaphors, Law and Digital Phenomena: The Swedish Pirate Bay Court Case." *International Journal of Law and Information Technology* 21/4: 354–379.

Laskow, S. 2014. "Is Communications Security for Reporters Improving?" *Columbia Journalism Review*, August 11. www.cjr.org/behind_the_news/is_communications_security_for.php.

Lewis, J., S. Inthorn, and K. Wahl-Jorgensen. 2005. *Citizens or Consumers?* Maidenhead: Open University Press.

Lim, M. 2003. "The Internet, Social Networks, and Reform in Indonesia," in N. Couldry and J. Curran (eds.), *Contesting Media Power*. Boulder, CO: Rowman & Littlefield.

Lim, M. 2011. *@Crossroads: Democratization and Corporatization of Media in Indonesia*. Jakarta and Tempe, AZ: Ford Foundation and Participatory Media Lab at Arizona State University.

Lim, M. 2012. *The League of Thirteen: Media Concentration in Indonesia*. Jakarta and Tempe, AZ: Ford Foundation and Participatory Media Lab at Arizona State University.

Link, P., and Q. Xiao. 2013. "From 'Fart People' to Citizens." *Journal of Democracy* 24/1: 79–85.

Mabweazara, H. 2015. "Mainstreaming African Digital Cultures, Practices and Emerging Forms of Citizen Engagement." *African Journalism Studies* 36/4: 1–11.

MacAskill E., and J. Ball. 2013. "Portrait of the NSA: No Detail Too Small in Quest for Total Surveillance." *Guardian*, November 2. www.theguardian.com/world/2013/nov/02/nsa-portrait-total-surveillance.

MacBride, S., and C. Roach. 1989. "The New International Information Order," in E. Barnouw (ed.), *International Encyclopedia of Communications*. Oxford: Oxford University Press.

McChesney, R.W. 1993. *Telecommunication, Mass Media and Democracy*. New York: Oxford University Press.

McCourt, T., and P. Burkart. 2003. "When Creators, Corporations and Consumers Collide: Napster and the Development of On-line Music Distribution." *Media, Culture and Society* 25/3: 333–350.

MacKinnon, R. 2012. *Consent of the Networked*. New York: Basic Books.

MacNamara, J. 2015. *Organizational Listening*. New York: Peter Lang.

Madianou, M., and D. Miller. 2012. *Migration and New Media*. London, UK: Routledge.

Mansell, R. 2012. *Imagining the Internet*. Oxford: Oxford University Press.

Mare, A. 2014. "Social Media: The New Protest Drums in Southern Africa?," in B. Patrut and M. Patrut (eds.), *Social Media in Politics*. Berlin: Springer.

Maxwell, R., and T. Miller. 2012. *Greening the Media*. New York: Oxford University Press.

Meyrowitz, J. 1985. *No Sense of Place*. New York: Oxford University Press.

Miazhevich, G. 2014. "Russia Today's Coverage of Euromaidan." *Russian Journal of Communication* 6/2: 186–191.

Milan, S. 2016. "Stealing the Fire: Lessons from the Margins of Cyberspace," in O. Hemer and T. Tufte (eds.), *Voice and Matter Communication, Development and the Cultural Return*. Sweden: NORDICOM, University of Göteborg.

Miller, J.L. 2010. "Ugly Betty Goes Global: Global Networks of Localized Content in the Telenovela Industry." *Global Media and Communication* 6/2: 198–217.

Miller, T., N., Govil, J., McMurria, R. Maxwell, and T. Wang. 2004. *Global Hollywood: No.2*. London: BFI.

Moraes, D. 2011. *Vozes abertas da América Latina*. Río de Janeiro: Mauad X/Faperj.

Mosco, V. 2004. *Digital Sublime*. Cambridge: MIT Press.

Mosco, V. 2014. *To the Cloud*. New York: Routledge.

Mottahedeh, N. 2015. *#iranelection: Hashtag Solidarity and the Transformation of Online Life*. Palo Alto, CA: Stanford University Press.

Mukherjee, A. 2015. "How to Win Friends FB Style." *Outlook*. www.outlookindia.com/magazine/story/how-to-win-friends-fb-style/295492.

Mukhongo, L.L. 2014. "Negotiating the New Media Platforms: Youth and Political Images in Kenya." *Triple C Journal for a Global Sustainable Information Society* 12/1: 328–341.

Munoz-Navarro, A. 2009. "Youth and Human Rights in Chile. Otherness, Political Identity and Social Change," in T. Tufte and F. Enghel (eds.), *Youth Engaging with the World*. Gothenburg, Sweden: Nordicom.

Nielsen. 2014. "Nielsen: Konsumsi Media Lebih Tinggi di Luar Jawa (Nielsen: Higher Media Consumption Outside of Java)." www.nielsen.com/id/en/press-room/2014/nielsen-konsumsi-media-lebih-tinggi-di-luar-jawa.html.

Nugroho, Y., D.A. Putri, and S. Laksmi. 2012. "Mapping the Landscape of the Media Industry in Contemporary Indonesia." Report Series. *Engaging Media, Empowering Society: Assessing Media Policy and Governance in Indonesia through the Lens of Citizens' Rights*. Jakarta: CIPG and HIVOS.

Nygren, G., and M. Zuiderveld. 2011. *En himla många kanaler*. Göteborg: Nordicom.

Okediji, R.L. 2004. "Africa and the Global Intellectual Property System: Beyond the Agency Model." *African Yearbook of International Law* 12: 207–251.

Okediji, R.L. 2006. *The International Copyright System: Limitations, Exceptions and Public Interest Considerations for Developing Countries*. UNCTAD-ICTSD Project on IPRs and Sustainable Development: Issue Paper No. 15. www.iprsonline.org/unctadictsd/docs/ruth%202405.pdf.

Pal, J., P. Chandra, and V.G.V. Vydiswaran. 2016. "Twitter and the Rebranding of Narendara Modi." *Economic and Political Weekly* 51/8: 52–60.

Palmer, D., and I.J. Warren. 2013. "Global Policing and the Case of Kim Dotcom." *International Journal for Crime, Justice and Social Democracy* 2/3: 105–119.

Pariser, E. 2011. *The Filter Bubble*. New York: Penguin Press.

Pasquale, F. 2015. *Black Box Society*. Cambridge: Harvard University Press.

Paterson, C. 2013. "Journalism and Social Media in the African Context." *Ecquid Novi: African Journalism Studies* (special issue) 34/1: 1–6.

Phillips, W. 2015. *This Is Why We Can't Have Nice Things*. Cambridge: MIT Press.

Pianta, M., and R. Marchetti. 2007. "The Global Justice Movements: The Transnational Dimension," in D. della Porta (ed.) *The Global Justice Movement*. Boulder, CO: Paradigm.

Porter, M.E., and S. Stern (with M. Green). 2015. *Social Progress Index 2015*. www.socialprogressimperative.org/wp-content/uploads/2016/05/2015-SOCIAL-PROGRESS-INDEX_FINAL.pdf.

Powles, J., and E. Chaparro. 2015. "How Google Determined Our Right to Be Forgotten." *Guardian*. www.theguardian.com/technology/2015/feb/18/the-right-be-forgotten-google-search.

Powles, J., and E. Chaparro. 2016. "In the Wake of Apple v FBI, We Need to Address Some Uncomfortable Truths." *Guardian*. www.theguardian.com/technology/2016/mar/29/apple-fbi-encryption-san-bernardino-uncomfortable-truths.

Privacy International. 2013. "Eyes Wide Open: Special Report, Version 1.0." www.privacyinternational.org/sites/default/files/Eyes%20Wide%20Open%20v1.pdf.

Public Citizen. 2015a. "Only One of 44 Attempts to Use the GATT Article XX/GATS Article XIV 'General Exception' Has Ever Succeeded: Replicating the WTO Exception Construct Will Not Provide for an Effective TPP General Exception." www.citizen.org/documents/general-exception.pdf.

Public Citizen. 2015b. "Secret TPP Text Unveiled: It's Worse Than We Thought." www.citizen.org/documents/analysis-tpp-text-november-2015.pdf.

Punj, S. 2012. "A Number of Changes." *Business Today*, March 4. http://businesstoday.intoday.in/story/uid-project-nandan-nilekani-future-unique-identification/1/22288.html.

Putnam, R. 2000. *Bowling Alone*. New York: Touchstone.

Qiu, J.L. 2008. "Mobile Civil Society in Asia: A Comparative Study of the People Power II and Nosamo Movement." *Javnost – The Public* 15/3: 39–58.

Qiu, J.L. 2009. *Working-Class Network Society*. Cambridge, MA: MIT Press.

Qiu, J.L. 2014. "'Power to the People!': Mobiles, Migrants, and Social Movements in Asia." *International Journal of Communication* 8: 376–391.

Quilter, L., and J. Urban. 2005. "Efficient Process or 'Chilling Effects'? Takedown Notices under Section 512 of the Digital Millennium Copyright Act." *Santa Clara Computer and High Technology Law Journal* 22: 621–693.

R2K (Right to Know Campaign). 2015. "R2K Condemns the Return of the Secrecy Bill!." www.r2k.org.za/2015/05/12/secrecy-bill-returns/.

Ramadge, A. 2008. "Get Up! Organizes Advertising Blitz to Protest Internet Filter." December 4. http://web.archive.org/web/20090215191458/www.news.com.au:80/story/0,24750766-2,00.html.

Reguillo, R. 2009. "The Warrior's Code? Youth, Communication and Social Change," in T. Tufte and F. Enghel (eds.), *Youth Engaging with the World*. Gothenburg, Sweden: Nordicom.

Richter, A.G. 2015. "Legal Response and Propaganda Broadcasts Related to Crises in and Around Ukraine 2014–2015." *International Journal of Communication* 9: 3125–3145.

Rincón, O. In press. *Hacia el periodismo-experiencia en las figuras del Dj y el militante.* Quito: Ciespal.

Rinehart, A. 2015. "Encryption Becomes a Part of Journalists' Toolkit." HuffPost Media, April 10. www.huffingtonpost.com/the-groundtruth-project/encryption-becomes-a-part_b_7041278.html.

Robinson, P. 2005. *The CNN Effect.* London: Routledge.

Robinson, P., and H. Yu. 2014. "Knowing the Score: New Data, Underwriting, and Marketing in the Consumer Credit Marketplace: A Guide for Financial Inclusion Stakeholders." www.teamupturn.com/static/files/Knowing_the_Score_Oct_2014_v1_1.pdf.

Rodríguez, C. 2001. *Fissures in the Mediascape: An International Study of Citizens' Media.* Cresskill: Hampton Press.

Rodríguez, C. In press. "Citizens' and Movements' Uses and Appropriations of Media Technologies," in V. Pickard and G. Yang (eds.), *Media Activism.* New York: Routledge.

Rodríguez, C., D. Kidd, and L. Stein. 2010. *Making our Media (Creating New Communication Spaces).* Cresskill: Hampton Press.

Rodríguez, C., and P. Murphy. 1997. "The Study of Communication and Culture in Latin America: From Laggards and the Oppressed to Resistance and Hybrid Cultures." *Journal of International Communication* 4/2: 24–45.

Russell, A., and N. Echchaibi. 2009. *International Blogging.* New York: Peter Lang.

Sassen, S. 2007. "The Places and Spaces of the Global: An Expanded Analytic Terrain," in D. Held and A. McGrew (eds.), *Globalization Theory.* Cambridge: Polity.

Saybaşılı, N. 2014. "The Magnetic Remanences: Voice and Sound in Digital Art and Media," in A. Downey (ed.), *Uncommon Grounds.* London: I.B. Tauris.

Schiller, D. 1999. *Digital Capitalism.* Cambridge: Cambridge University Press.

Schiller, H. 1969. *Mass Communications and American Empire.* Boulder, CO: Westview Press.

Schneier, B., K. Seidel, and S. Vijayakumar. 2016. "Worldwide Encryption Products Survey." Version 1.0, February 11. www.schneier.com/academic/paperfiles/worldwide-survey-of-encryption-products.pdf

Schneider, H. 2014. "Trade Deals a Closely Held Secret, Shared by More than 500 Advisers." *Washington Post*, February 28. www.washingtonpost.com/business/economy/trade-deals-a-closely-held-secret-shared-by-more-than-500-advisers/2014/02/28/7daa65ec-9d99-11e3-a050-dc3322a94fa7_story.html.

Selwyn, N. 2014. *Distrusting Educational Technology.* London: Routledge.

Sen, A. 1999. *Development as Freedom.* Oxford: Oxford University Press.

Sen, K., and D.T. Hill. 2000. *Media, Culture and Politics in Indonesia.* Melbourne: Oxford University Press.

Seo, E.-K., and J.-H. Kim. 2009. "Young South Koreans Become the '880,000 Won Generation.'" *Reuters.* www.taipeitimes.com/ News/bizfocus/archives/2009/04/12/2003440846.

Sewell, W. 2005. *Logics of History.* Chicago, IL: University of Chicago Press.

Shaviro, S. 2002. "Capitalist Monsters." *Historical Materialism* 10/4: 281–290.

Shi, A. 2015. "Approaching New Internet Information and Communication Order: The Role of Chinese Media." Speech at the World Internet Conference, *Wuzhen Summit.* Wuzhen, China, December 17.

Sinclair, J., and E. Jacka. 1996. *New Patterns in Global Television.* Oxford: Oxford University Press.

Siochrú, S. 2005. *CRIS Campaign: Assessing Communication Rights: A Handbook.*: http://cdn.agilitycms.com/centre-for-communication-rights/Images/Articles/pdf/cris-manual-en.pdf.

Skjerdal, T. 2012. "The Three Alternative Journalisms of Africa." *International Communication Gazette* 74/7: 636–654.

Sreberny, A., and G. Khiabany. 2010. *Blogostan.* London: I.B. Tauris.

Stein, L. 2009. "Introduction," in L. Stein, D. Kidd, and C. Rodríguez (eds.), *National and Global Movements for Democratic Communication: Volume II of "Making Our Media."* Euricom Monographs. Cresskill: Hampton Press.

Stiglitz, J., A. Sen, and J. Fitoussi. 2009. *Report of the Commission on the Measurement of Economic Performance and Social Progress.* http://library.bsl.org.au/jspui/bitstream/1/1267/1/Measurement_of_economic_performance_and_social_progress.pdf.

Stirland, S. 2008. "Cisco Leak: 'Great Firewall' of China was a Chance to Sell More Routers." *Wired.* www.wired.com/2008/05/leaked-cisco-do.

Subcomandante Marcos. 1994. *Comuniqué.* www.spunk.org/texts/places/mexico/sp000655.txt.

Sunstein, C.R. 2009. *Republic.com 2.0.* Princeton, NJ: Princeton University Press.

Switzer, L., and M. Adhikari. 2000. *South Africa's Resistance Press.* Athens, OH: Ohio University Center for International Studies.

Talon, C.-G. 2011. *Al-Jazeera: Liberté d'expression et petromonarchie.* Paris: Presses Universitaires de France.

Tambini, D. 2017. "Brexit: Triumph of Robopolitics? *Vanguardia Dossier* 63: 135–137.

Tapsell, R. 2015. "Platform Convergence in Indonesia Challenges and Opportunities for Media Freedom." *Convergence* 21/2: 182–197.

Taylor, C. 2003. *Modern Social Imaginaries.* Durham, NC: Duke University Press.

Taylor, L. 2016a. "Data Subjects or Data Citizens? Addressing the Global Regulatory Challenge of Big Data," in M. Hildebrandt and B. van den Burg (eds.), *Freedom and Property of Information.* New York: Routledge.

Taylor, L. 2016b. "Safety in Numbers? Group Privacy and Big Data Analytics in the Developing World," in L. Taylor, B. van der Sloot, and L. Floridi (eds.), *Group Privacy.* London: Springer.

Taylor, L., and D. Broeders. 2015. "In the Name of Development: Power, Profit and the Datafication of the Global South." *Geoforum* 64: 229–237.

Treré, E. 2015. "The Struggle Within," in L. Dencik and O. Leistert (eds.), *Critical Perspectives on Social Media and Protest.* Boulder, CO: Rowman & Littlefied.

Triastuti, E. 2014. "Indonesian Women's Blog Formats from Tanah Betawi to Serambi Mekah: Women Blogger's Choices of Technical Features." *International Communication Gazette* 76/4–5: 407–424.

Trinkunas, H., and I. Wallace. 2015. *Converging on the Future of Global Internet Governance: The United States and Brazil. Foreign Policy at Brookings.* The Brookings Institution. www.brookings.edu/~/media/research/files/reports/2015/07/InternetInternet-governance-brazil-us/usbrazil-global-InternetInternet-governance-web-final.pdf.

Tufte, T., and F. Enghel. 2009. "Youth Engaging with Media and Communication. Different, Unequal and Disconnected," in T. Tufte and F. Enghel (eds.), *Youth Engaging with the World.* Gothenburg: Nordicom.

Turow, J. 2011. *The Daily You.* New Haven, CT: Yale University Press.

UNESCO. 1980. *Many Voices, One World.* Paris: International Commission for the Study of Communication Problems.

UNESCO. 1991. *Declaration of Windhoek.* www.unesco.org/webworld/fed/temp/communication_democracy/windhoek.htm.

UNESCO. 2013. *Global Media and Information Literacy: Assessment Framework.* www.uis.unesco.org/Communication/Documents/media-and-information-literacy-assessment-framework.pdf.

UNESCO. 2015. *Internet Universality.* www.unesco.org/new/en/communication-and-information/crosscutting-priorities/unesco-internet-study/internet-universality/.

United Nations. 2011. *Report of the Special Rapporteur on the Promotion and Protection of the Right to Freedom of Opinion and Expression.* A/HRC/17/27. May 16.

United Nations. 2015. *Transforming Our World: The 2030 Agenda for Sustainable Development* (UNGA Resolution A/RES/70/1). https://sustainabledevelopment.un.org/content/documents/21252030%20Agenda%20for%20Sustainable%20Development%20web.pdf.

Valdes, R., and M. McCann 2014. "Intellectual Property Provisions in Regional Trade Agreements: Revision and Update." World Trade Organization Staff Working Paper. ERSD-2014-14. www.wto.org/english/res_e/reser_e/ersd201414_e.pdf.

Van Zoonen, L. 2005. *Entertaining the Citizen.* Lanham, MD: Rowman & Littlefield.

Varian, H.R. 2014. "Beyond Big Data." *Business Economics* 49: 27–31.

Visser, N. 1997. "Postcoloniality of a Special Type: Theory and its Appropriations in South Africa." *The Yearbook of English Studies* 27: 79–94.

Volkmer, I. 1999. *News in the Global Sphere.* Luton: University of Luton Press.

Volkmer, I. 2014. *The Global Public Sphere.* Cambridge: Polity.

Wallis, C. 2013. *Technomobility in China.* New York: New York University Press.

Walton, M. 2014. "Pavement Internet: Mobile Media Economies and Ecologies in South Africa," in G. Goggin and L. Hjorth (eds.), *The Routledge Companion to Mobile Media.* London: Routledge.

Walton, M., and J. Donner. 2009. "Read-Write-Erase: Mobile-Mediated Publics in South Africa's 2009 Elections," in J.E. Katz (ed.), *Mobile Communication: Dimensions of Social Policy.* New Brunswick, NJ: Transaction.

Wasserman, H. 2007. "Is a New Worldwide Web Possible? An Explorative Comparison of ICTs by Two South African Social Movements." *African Studies Review* 50/1: 109–131.

Wasserman, H. 2010. *Tabloid Journalism in South Africa.* Bloomington, IN: Indiana University Press.

Weibull, L. 2016. "Medieämnets etablering i Sverige," in M. Hyvönen, P. Snickars, and P. Westerlund (eds.), *Massmedieproblem*. Stockholm: Mediehistoriskt arkiv,.

Weller, K., A., Bruns, J., Burgess, M. Mahrt, and C. Puschmann. 2013. *Twitter and Society*. New York: Peter Lang.

West, D. 2014. "Participation in Digital Media Culture: Curating Community in Australia." Paper presented at 10th OURMedia Conference on Diverse Communities, *Diverse Media*. Goroka, Papua New Guinea.

Williams, B., and M. Delli Carpini. 2011. *After Broadcast News*. Cambridge: Cambridge University Press.

Witteborn, S. 2015. "Becoming (Im)Perceptible: Forced Migrants and Virtual Practice." *Journal of Refugee Studies* 28/3: 350–367.

World Health Organization. 2011. *World Report on Disability*. www.who.int/disabilities/world_report/2011/en/.

World Summit on the Information Society. 2005. *Tunis Agenda on the Information Society*. WSIS-05/TUNIS/DOC/6(Rev. 1)-E, November 18. www.itu.int/net/wsis/docs2/tunis/off/6rev1.html.

Word Wide Web Foundation. 2016. *Women's Rights Online Report Card Indonesia: Measuring Progress, Driving Action*.

WSIS Civil Society Plenary. 2003. *Shaping Information Societies for Human Needs. Civil Society Declaration to the World Summit on the Information Society*. Geneva, Switzerland. www.itu.int/net/wsis/docs/geneva/civil-society-declaration.pdf.

Wu, Y.-S. 2012. "The Rise of China's State-Led Media Dynasty in Africa." *SAIIA Occasional Paper* 117. Johannesburg: South African Institute of International Affairs.

Xinhua. 2014. "Xi Jinping Leads Internet Security Group." http://news.xinhuanet.com/english/china/2014-02/27/c_133148273.htm.

Yadron, D. 2016. "San Bernardino iPhone: US Ends Apple Case after Accessing Data without Assistance." *Guardian*. www.theguardian.com/technology/2016/mar/28/apple-fbi-case-dropped-san-bernardino-iphone.

Zahreddin, L. 2011. *Al-Jazeera … Is Not the End of the Journey*. Beirut: Bissan.

Zhang, X., and Y. Zheng. 2012. *China's Information and Communications Technology Revolution*. London: Routledge.

Zhao, Y., and R.A. Hackett. 2005. "Media Globalization, Media Democratization: Challenges, Issues and Paradoxes," in R.A. Hackett and Y. Zhao (eds.), *Democratizing Global Media*. Lanham: Rowman & Littlefield.

Zuboff, S. 2015. "Big Other: Surveillance Capitalism and the Prospects of an Information Civilization." *Journal of Information Technology* 30: 75–89.

14

Challenges of Inequality to Democracy

Coordinating Lead Authors:[1]
Richard Bellamy, Wolfgang Merkel

Lead Authors:[2]
Rajeev Bhargava, Juliana Bidadanure, Thomas Christiano, Ulrike Felt, Colin Hay, Lily Lamboy, Thamy Pogrebinschi, Graham Smith, Gayil Talshir, Nadia Urbinati, Mieke Verloo

[1]   Affiliations: RB: University College, London, UK and European University Institute, Italy; WM: WZB Berlin Social Science Center and Humboldt University, Germany.
[2]   Affiliations: RB: Center for the Study of Developing Societies, India; JB: Department of Philosophy, Stanford University, USA; TC: University of Arizona, USA; UF: Department of Science and Technology Studies, University of Vienna, Austria; CH: Centre d'études européennes, Sciences Po, France LL: Department of Political Science, Stanford University, USA; TP: WZB Berlin Social Science Center, Germany; GS: Centre for the Study of Democracy, University of Westminster, UK; GT: Hebrew University of Jerusalem, Israel; NU: Columbia University, USA; MV: Radboud University, Netherlands and IWM, Vienna, Austria.

Summary

Democracy, as we understand it, is a process of collective decision-making among persons, which issues in collectively binding norms for the society of those persons. It is a process of decision-making in which persons participate as equals in determining the legal and conventional norms that bind them and in which the group of persons, taken collectively, are sovereign. Democracy can be understood as a descriptive term, referring to political societies that actually exist, or as a normative ideal for the evaluation of political societies. Our focus in this chapter is primarily on the basic moral principles that can justify this egalitarian process of collective decision-making and on the challenges to understanding and realizing this ideal in the modern world. After an initial account of the basic principle and the social and institutional realization of this principle, we address the challenges to articulating and implementing this principle that arise due to the reality of economic inequality and the religious, ethnic, gender, and racial pluralism of modern societies, and to the fact that state-based democratic systems operate within a larger global society. We then discuss and evaluate the appropriateness of democratic institutions, procedures, and organizations to translate the moral principles into the structural grammar of present-day democracies and to what extent they can guarantee the fundamental principles and normative promises of democracy. As we will see, the ideas of equality and sovereignty at the base of democracy cannot be fully appreciated without a grasp of the pluralism, complexity, and global interconnectedness of modern societies.

14

14.1 Introduction: Democracy as Public Equality

Democracy, as we understand it, is a process of collective decision-making among persons, which issues in collectively binding norms for the society of those persons. It is a process of decision-making in which persons participate as equals in determining the legal and conventional norms that bind them and in which the group of persons, taken collectively, are sovereign. Democracy can be understood as a descriptive term, referring to political societies that actually exist, or as a normative ideal for the evaluation of political societies. Our focus in this chapter is primarily on the basic moral principles that can justify this egalitarian process of collective decision-making and on the challenges to understanding and realizing this ideal in the modern world. After an initial account of the basic principle and the social and institutional realization of this principle, we will address the challenges to articulating and implementing this principle that arise due to the reality of economic inequality and the religious, ethnic, gender, and racial pluralism of modern societies, and to the fact that state-based democratic systems operate within a larger global society. We then discuss and evaluate the appropriateness of democratic institutions, procedures, and organizations to translate the moral principles into the structural grammar of present-day democracies and to what extent they can guarantee the fundamental principles and normative promises of democracy. As we will see, the ideas of equality and sovereignty at the base of democracy cannot be fully appreciated without a grasp of the pluralism, complexity, and global interconnectedness of modern societies. The work of this chapter is a collaborative project.

14.1.1 The Basic Principle

We take public equality as the basic normative principle underwriting democracy and guiding our efforts to understand the challenges that democracy faces. The principle helps us think about democracy along two distinct dimensions: procedural and substantive. Democracy is grounded in the principle of equality in the sense that because persons have equal status and worth, the collective decision-making process is meant to realize the equal advancement of the interests of the members of the society. The ideal of democracy is a uniquely public realization of the equal status and worth of each citizen in the sense that all can see that they are treated as equals despite all the disagreements and conflicts of interest that arise in modern societies. Democracy achieves this by giving people an equal say in the making of collectively binding decisions and by protecting basic civil rights. This equal say involves equality in capacities to deliberate with fellow citizens and equal voting power and capacities to negotiate when disagreements persist. The challenge is to extend and deepen this idea in the context of highly pluralistic and globalizing societies.

Democracy addresses the question of who gets to decide on the collectively binding norms in circumstances of disagreement and conflicting interests. Under the assumption that persons and groups have only limited understandings of the perspectives and interests of other persons and groups, persons and groups are generally biased in favor of their own perspectives and interests even when they attempt to construct conceptions of the common good, it is important for all persons and groups to have a say in the collectively binding decisions

that constitute the social and political order of a society. Each person and group brings their limited and partial perspectives on how society ought to be organized and attempts by means of argument and negotiation to reconcile their limited points of view with those of others. Each thereby is able to stand up for his or her own perspectives and interests and is able to learn about those of others. In this way, the biases of each person are partly mitigated by a process of discussion and negotiation. They are unlikely to reach full agreement on how to live together. And thus each is unlikely to be fully satisfied that society is organized as it ought to be organized since the points of view and interests of many others will have to be accommodated. It is not just important that all have a say but that each has an equal say. Only in this way can the issue of who decides be settled in a way that recognizes and affirms the equal status and value of all persons (Christiano 2008).

The principle of public equality also grounds the fundamental civil rights of persons as well. There are certain basic civil and liberal rights whose respect and protection are as important to the public realization of the equal status and worth of persons as democracy itself is (Habermas 1992). And these rights must be respected and protected by democratic decision-making just as much as democracy itself if persons are to be treated publicly as equals. This substantive dimension of public equality is also a source of debate and contention (Bellamy 2007).

At the same time, the idea of equality at the heart of democracy is itself a contested notion. And the challenges addressed in the subsequent parts of this chapter bring out some of the main sources of contestation. And so the ideal of public equality itself must be subject to continual discussion and revision. In this sense, democracy is an ideal that is never fully realized among persons. So the ideal of public equality serves both as a standard for the evaluation of the procedural aspects of the democratic process as well as a principle for the assessment of the substantive outcomes of democracy. The most obvious way in which it does this is that democratic societies must decide how to reproduce democracy themselves in their constitutional forms as well as in the social bases of democratic participation. In this respect, the discussions of this chapter are designed to inform this continual process of reflection on and the reproduction of democracy.

14.1.2 Social and Institutional Realization of Democracy

The principle of public equality, according to which people are to be treated as equals in a way that they can see that they are treated as equals, is quite abstract and needs to be realized in social and political institutions. This chapter is in significant part about the challenges to this realization. In order to understand just how challenging this is it is important to lay out some elements of a conceptual framework. One distinction important for understanding how the collective decision-making of a society realizes public equality is between the deliberative and power dimensions of collective decision-making. The first looks at how societies enable people to participate as equals in the processes of deliberation and discussion that lead up to decision-making and that form the conceptions of the alternatives societies face and the considerations in favor of and against those alternatives. The second explores how institutions and societies distribute power to persons so that they can advance their views and interests. These are not exclusive categories. Many aspects of political decision-making involve both dimensions.

For the deliberative dimension, when a group of people make a decision that is binding on all of the members, they must engage in a process of discussion to learn about their interests and how those interests can be accommodated and advanced in a just and harmonious way. This discussion is necessary to constructing the decision and thinking about alternatives. This process of deliberation does not start merely when a decision has to be made, it is an ongoing process that occurs throughout the society over a long course of time. It requires processes of discussion within particular sectors of society in which interests and conceptions of the common good are formulated and debated. And it requires debate and discussion on a society-wide level. Of course in a highly pluralistic society the participants in this discussion have to listen to each other and try to understand each other even when their experiences and the problems they face are diverse and unfamiliar to each other. The democratic ideal is that they listen to each other as equals. This is an extraordinary challenge that many of the sections of this chapter are focused on. In particular, this refers to the challenge of including and listening to people from different ethnic, racial, and religious groups as well as different genders.

The dimension of power is involved when discussion and debate do not resolve all the issues and there is disagreement and conflict even though a decision has to be made. Then the distribution of power involved in voting, in organizing groups to vote and pressure representatives, in negotiating compromises with other groups in order to come to a unified standpoint despite disagreement, becomes essential to the democratic ideal of public equality. When discussion and debate fail to reach consensus, the distribution of power becomes essential.

To be sure, the dimensions of deliberation and power come together in a variety of ways. One especially prominent way is that some groups are not listened to because they are marginalized because of their ethnicity, race, gender, religion, or socioeconomic status. They are deprived of power because they cannot participate as equals in the process of deliberation (Young 2000). Another important way occurs when the inequality of wealth and income in the society play a large role in enabling some groups to get their views out and disabling others.

This suggests a second distinction between formal and informal mechanisms that is important to evaluating the democratic quality of a process of decision-making. There are formal mechanisms and rights for giving people power over the collective decision, such as the right to vote and the electoral system that aggregates these votes. And there are formal mechanisms that enable people to participate in deliberation such as the rights of each to express themselves and to associate with other likeminded or like interested people. There are also formal mechanisms of contestation such as the system of courts for contesting the legality of legislative or administrative action just to name a couple. These are formal because certain rights are assigned to people and the mechanism is designed so that the exercise of those rights has legal consequences for the society.

There is also the informal character of democracies that consists in the extent to which groups actually organize to advance certain interests or viewpoints. Are the conditions present so that all the diverse interests in society are enabled to advance their interests? There is also the previously mentioned question as to whether, when a group is formed to present its interests and viewpoints, the other members of the society listen to them and take them seriously. Modern democratic societies have done reasonably well in developing legal regimes that protect the basic political and civil rights of their citizens, though there are important issues to be dealt with here, as in the question about how future generations can be represented in collective decision-making. Great strides have been made in protecting the civil and political rights of minorities. But it remains the case that religious, racial, and ethnic minorities are often not accorded the respect owed to them as equal citizens in the societies. Some of the sections of our chapter are concerned with these fundamental inequalities in the deliberative and informal aspects of democratic equality.

Of course, the egalitarian dimensions of the informal aspects of political participation can be enhanced by legislative and constitutional action to some degree. For instance, one of the main ways in which interest groups find it difficult to organize and exert influence on the collective decision process is because the group is significantly poorer than the dominant majority. So they have less resources with which to participate in the deliberative and negotiating process. Furthermore, lower middle-class, working-class, and poorer citizens generally have distinctive interests in the society but find that they have significantly less resources with which to advance those interests. To some extent these inequalities can be mitigated by means of campaign finance reform. But the political platforms of major political parties and candidates seem to have less and less room for these interests in US and European societies. They seem to be less and less able to get people to listen to them (Bartels 2009). One consequence of this is that we see the rise of populist demagoguery in these societies as we discuss later in this chapter. We do not discuss the effects of socioeconomic inequality on political inequality in this chapter since it is well covered in Chapters 9 and 13. We will, however, suggest some recommendations for mitigating the effects of this inequality.

There is a further feature of democracy that is essential to a discussion of equality. This involves the ability of a democratic society to effectively govern itself. There are two major and connected challenges here. The first challenge involves the fact that democratic decision-making takes place in a context in which there are other powerful economic actors in a society that are able to impose costs on a democratic society when it makes certain decisions. Large economic firms can impose costs on a society when the society tries to regulate or tax their behavior and lessen their profitability as in the case of legislation to curb the production of pollution or increases in corporate taxes (Merkel 2014a). A firm can fulfill a threat to move to another jurisdiction if these measures are imposed and the legislature may forego important legislation in order to avoid the unemployment corporate moves would make. This is an exercise of power outside the normal democratic channels and so endows these entities with a kind of power in addition to their powers to participate in politics. The second challenge that arises here is that democratic societies must interact with other political societies to achieve certain aims in the international environment. They do this currently by means of treaties and agreements. But the processes of treaty-making and agreement-making can also be subjected to democratic norms of equality as we will discuss later. It should be noted that those two challenges are connected in that international cooperation among states can lessen the threats imposed by multinational firms by coordination on tax regimes or environmental regimes, to name just two examples.

14.1.3 Structure of the Chapter

We have structured the chapter along the fundamental challenges democracy is facing in the twenty-first century. The first part explores the challenges of socioeconomic inequality, gender inequality, religious inequality, racial inequality, generational inequality, and racial inequality. It then turns to globalization as an external threat to public equality, populism as an increasingly powerful internal threat within the OECD world, and the challenge science and technology pose to democracy. Though these single sections focus particularly on the challenges to democracy, they also provide some responses to them. The second part of the chapter changes the focus insofar as it deals mainly with responses, such as some proposals for reestablishing the demos and renationalizing democracy, democratic innovations in Europe and Latin America, and the democratic norms that should guide the procedures of supranational governance. We conclude with suggestions for limiting the effects of inequality of wealth on democratic decision-making and some different ways of organizing electoral systems for increasing minority participation.

14.2 Representation and (Social and Civic) Participation: Barriers to Public Equality

14.2.1 Socioeconomic Inequality

Democracy as public equality is constituted empirically within a political system possessing the following five components: (1) a democratic electoral regime; (2) political participation rights; (3) civil liberties; (4) the institutional safeguarding of mutual constraints and horizontal accountability; and (5) the de jure and de facto guarantees of the effective power to govern of democratically elected representatives. Socioeconomic inequality challenges each of these components.

14.2.1.1 The Electoral Regime

Voter turnout has declined moderately in Western Europe and drastically in Eastern Europe, while remaining at a problematically low level in the United States. Declining electoral participation is due to the political apathy of the lower social classes and not to their permissive abstention, as some conservative observers argue. While the gender gap has nearly closed, selectivity in terms of social class has significantly increased. The increasing socioeconomic inequality of the last three decades has translated into heightened inequalities in cognitive resources and political knowledge across social classes. The lower their political knowledge, the less the voters are able to translate their interests into corresponding voting preferences. The more unequal a society, the greater is the number of voters who are unwilling or unable to participate meaningfully in elections. The more unequal electoral

participation, in turn, the likelier it is that substantial representation on the parliamentary level becomes similarly distorted.

14.2.1.2 Political Rights and Opportunities

For almost three decades European party systems have been changing: the traditional "catch-all parties" are in decline, while more specialized or populist parties have emerged – from ecological parties and left-socialist parties to right-wing populist parties. While catch-all parties traditionally mobilized lower-class voters better than most other parties, the "new" parties rarely represent the interests of the lower classes. Attempts have been made to stop the trend toward political exclusion through democratic innovations such as referenda, deliberative assemblies, participatory budgeting, or citizen councils. However, given they are cognitively and politically more demanding than voting in general elections, they risk being even more socially exclusive. That said, this caveat may apply above all to advanced (post-)industrial societies and established democracies. Studies of Latin America show that in certain contexts, these new forms of political participation may intensify the involvement of citizens in political processes in their municipalities or even on the national level (Pogrebinschi 2012).

14.2.1.3 Civil Rights

Compared to the early 1960s, when women (Switzerland) or African-Americans (six US states) were not allowed to vote, when women did not enjoy the full range of economic and civil rights in many democracies, when homosexuals were criminalized, and discrimination against ethnic minorities was ubiquitous, the civil rights situation has improved considerably. Today's governments, parliaments, parties, and the political elites are under greater pressure to be more transparent. Contemporary civic associations are more numerous and more political, monitoring politics much more closely than some decades ago. John Keane (2011) has even spoken of an emerging "monitory democracy." Yet we are not living in a world where civil rights and the rule of law are unchallenged, as recent revelations of the surveillance practices of the American National Security Agency (NSA), the British Government Communications Headquarters (GCHQ), and secret services elsewhere in the world have shown. In the age of the Internet, private monopolies such as Google also pose a challenge to individual privacy rights. It is also true that democratic states must come up with more inclusive and lasting forms of selecting, accepting, and integrating immigrants into their societies and political systems. Indeed, hard-fought advances in equal rights for ethnic minorities have been recently challenged in Europe, the United States, Australia, and Asia. On the whole, however, there can be no doubt that the overall civil rights situation has improved within the OECD world in the past half-century.

14.2.1.4 Horizontal Accountability

The last decades have seen a weakening of national parliaments. Globalization and transnationalization have strengthened executives at the cost of parliaments. Governments, from Argentina to Greece to

14

Germany, are blackmailing their legislatures in the name of executive emergency rights and policy-making imperatives under the real or pretended pressures of crisis. The German chancellor Angela Merkel notoriously admonished the public and the parliament of the need for "market-conforming democracy," elevating the markets to the status of sovereign. Moreover, only governments are represented in supra- and international governance regimes such as the IMF, World Bank, WTO, and EU. Parliaments, the core bodies of representative democracies, have lost key legislative and monitoring powers vis-à-vis executives. Transparency and accountability have been among the first victims as a result.

14.2.1.5 Effective Power to Govern

What governments have gained in power vis-à-vis parliaments on the one side, they have lost to the markets on the other. Deregulation and globalization have empowered financial actors such as banks, hedge funds, investors, and global firms. "Markets" have become the principals, governments the agents. If these principals are hit by self-inflicted crises, as it has been the case with the financial crises after 2008, they can externalize their problems by forcing governments to bail them out.

14.2.1.6 Conclusion

In sum, four out of the five components of democracy have witnessed democratic erosions over the course of the last decades. Only the regime of civil rights has seen considerable improvements. The rights of women and minorities (ethnic, religious, sexual) have made impressive advances, de jure and de facto in most countries, although not completely up to the actual level of men and majorities. In times of globalization it seems easier for democratic governments to advance noneconomic identity rights than to halt the increasing socioeconomic inequalities (Merkel 2014a) in times of deregulated global markets and the dominant economic paradigm of austerity politics and policies.

We do not conclude that "democracy" (singular) is in crisis, since there is no theory that can tell us where the threshold between challenges to and crisis of the democratic system actually lies (Kneip and Merkel in press). It would be wrong to assume that the established democracies of the OECD world have already transformed into post-democracies, since there are, rather, asynchronous developments that have strengthened the proper working of democracies in certain ways and weakened it in others, as we have pointed out. We are also not facing the "end of representative politics" (Tormey 2015). But what will be discussed in the following sections is to what extent the multiple challenges of inequalities are undermining the very idea and practice of democracy and which democratic reforms and innovations can reduce the danger of shifting axes of democratic legitimacy in the twenty-first century.

14.2.2 Racial Inequality

For many, ethnic identity is a point of deep pride and personal connection. Ethnic groups create and transmit vital aspects of cultural knowledge and practice including philosophy, literature, music, art, food, and language. They also serve as powerful sites for social progress, facilitating bonds across individuals and allowing for mobilization. Yet ethnic and racial identities also pose deep challenges to democracy and the public equality that underlies it. This is in part because practices and beliefs differ across groups, and groups therefore struggle for power to determine the rules and practices of the society in which they live. But this is something of a red herring; most people, regardless of ethnicity, share a personal interest in safety, security, shelter, protection for civil liberties, and a society in which they are respected by their co-citizens. In this section, then, we focus on obstacles to public equality that stem not from ethno-racial *differences* but from ethno-racial *hierarchies* – structures that distribute power and advantage to members of some ethnic groups and not others.

Ethno-racial hierarchies are not natural, but instead are a product of historical and current structures established by groups seeking domination. These hierarchies are rooted in centuries-old patterns of colonialism, conquest, slavery, and/or forced migration. Groups identify common traits to bond them together and to justify practices that strip those outside the defined group of power. In the United States, this pattern began with European settler colonialism over Native Americans and chattel slavery of Africans. Although these practices came to a formal end, they leave an indelible mark on US society. In the nineteenth and twentieth centuries, for example, it became increasingly challenging for whites to use legal structures to oppress the Native American and Black populations. Scientists instead generated theories of "biological differences" between races, with whites being "naturally superior" and therefore fit to rule over non-white inhabitants. This justified stripping these inhabitants of rights and liberties, including claims to decent working and living conditions. While theories of biological racism have since been scientifically debunked, they still hold significant sway, showing up explicitly in white nationalist views and more subtly in the widely held belief that the United States is "post-racial" and that differences in outcomes between whites and nonwhites can be attributed to inherited differences in talent, motivation, and initiative rather than systemic barriers and institutionalized racism.

From here on out, references to "ethnicity" refer to both race and ethnicity. This is because ethnicity is an umbrella term that includes, but is not limited to, features associated with race such as skin color, hair type, and ancestry (Horowitz 1985). Membership in an ethnic group is based upon possessing traits "believed to be associated with descent" (Chandra 2006). By "believed to be associated with descent," we mean those traits "around which a credible myth of association with descent has been woven, whether or not such an association exists in fact" (Chandra 2006: 400). These traits are either genetically transmitted (skin color, hair type, physical features) or have to do with the language, religion, place of origin, tribe, caste, clan, nationality, or race of one's parents and ancestors (Chandra 2006). It is essential to recognize that racial and ethnic categories are not "fixed" but rather constructed. The salience of a cluster of "ethnic" features thus changes across time and space. Someone with the same phenotypically "black" features would encounter different obstacles and opportunities in Brazil than they would in France or Kenya. Indeed, each society has its own unique history of ethnic and racial hierarchy. Recognizing this, we nonetheless strive here to identity patterns, frameworks, and interventions that can help policy makers and activists worldwide understand the relationship between ethnic identity, public equality, and democracy.

Across the world, social and economic inequality tracks ethnic identity, threatening the underlying substantive equality essential for democratic practice. Residential segregation is one of the primary drivers of persistent group inequality. Segregation occurs due to housing discrimination, minority self-segregation, and patterns where families from the dominant ethnic group move away from neighborhoods when they become populated by ethnic minority groups (Anderson 2010). In Paris, for example, many low-income immigrants live in isolated suburban public housing communities. They have poor access to public transportation, quality food, good schools, and other public goods. They are also socially isolated, which means that they rarely interact with white French citizens, at least not on terms of respect. This threatens the deliberative component of the democratic ideal, decreasing understanding of and empathy for people outside one's ethnic group.

Limited interaction breeds stereotypical thinking: if you very rarely encounter someone from a minority ethnic group, then your opinions about a group are going to be limited to media exposure and a small number of personal interactions (Anderson 2010). Stereotyped thinking affects everyone in a society, from its lawmakers to its police officers. Biased laws, and the biased application of fair laws, significantly impedes public equality. Individuals acting on behalf of the state like judges, juries, and representatives frequently and unconsciously act in ways that deprive citizens of basic rights and liberties. Police officers and prosecutors perform one of the most essential tasks in a democracy: ensuring internal order. This job is challenging, requiring them to make frequent high-stakes decisions about who to pursue and how. Toward this end, officials worldwide use generalizations based on race, ethnicity, national origin, instead of evidence or individual behavior, as the basis for directing discretionary law enforcement actions" (OSJI 2009). This tactic, known as ethnic profiling, leads police officers to stop, question, arrest, and detain ethnic minorities at disproportionately high rates. In Spain, for example, Romany are 10 times more likely to be stopped on the street by police than "white" residents, Moroccans at 7.5 times the rate of whites, and Black Africans at 17 times the rate of whites (García Añón et al. 2013).

Despite its popularity, ethnic profiling is both ineffective and unjust. Because ethnic minorities are stopped at much higher rates, a disproportionate number of individuals killed during the pursuit of a suspected criminal are from minority groups. In cases where the suspect is not killed, the effects of ethnic profiling accumulate: disproportionate stops lead to disproportionate arrests, arrests lead to prosecutions, prosecutions lead to incarceration, and incarceration leads to difficulty finding employment and alienation from one's family and community. In all, the initial act of ethnic profiling in policing leads to much higher rates of prosecution and punishment for members of ethnic minority groups. This is compounded by the fact that juries and judges face severe obstacles to fair evaluation due to implicit bias. In some cases, police officers even kill people during stops. When this occurs, police officers are not typically held accountable, even when the victim was unarmed and not engaged in any criminal activity.

Given the clear problems associated with ethnic profiling, countries across the world are considering legislative and police reforms. First and foremost, it is essential that independent bodies are created to review officer-involved shootings. States must also build trust between police officers and the communities they serve by diversifying the population of police officers, conducting workshops on implicit bias, and explicitly teaching skills associated with conflict mediation and interethnic communication. Another promising reform involves officers wearing body cameras that record interactions with constituents. When an officer kills a constituent in the line of duty, stakeholders in the victim's community can see the footage and work with police to determine whether the officer was reacting appropriately given the level of danger at hand.

In addition to internal police reforms, there is need for legislation banning stops for "furtive" movements such as reaching for a waistband or acting nervous, stops for being in a high-crime area, and stops for matching a generalized description of a suspect. New York City requires officers to report the details of every stop that occurs including the location, race, and gender of the suspect, whether force was used, and whether a firearm was found. This has led to a sharp decrease in baseless stops. Finally, policy makers could decriminalize activities that do not threaten public security but give police officers easy justifications for stopping someone, including public alcohol consumption, marijuana possession, loitering, spitting, and jaywalking.

While these legislative and institutional reforms are essential to ending ethnic profiling, unfair policing is a symptom of larger societal problems that must be addressed, including the fact that public goods like education, safe roads, electricity, health care, and police protection are distributed unequally along ethnic lines. Unequal public goods provision is partially explained by opportunity and resource hoarding – a group with existing power and resources benefits from limiting access to these goods. Social scientists have found that cities with higher levels of ethnic diversity spend less overall on public goods (Alesina, Bagir, and Easterly 1999). This is because wealth levels map to an ethno-racial hierarchy, with certain ethnic groups possessing more wealth than others. In-group hoarding occurs when there are disparities in wealth along ethnic lines because well-resourced groups have more to lose, and poor individuals have more to gain from redistribution (Baldwin and Huber 2010). What's more, wealthy individuals are better able to substitute private goods for public goods (purchasing private education, private security, etc.), making them less sensitive to the levels of overall public goods provision. Consider the distribution of a public good – physical security – in Brazil. During the past decade, the murder rate for white citizens has decreased by 24 percent while the murder rate for Black and mixed-race citizens has increased by 40 percent. This is because white rich citizens are able to purchase private security, which both increases their safety and decreases their motivation to fund public security in the form of policing for others.

Political parties frequently mobilize voters along ethnic lines, explicitly promoting ideologies that play up "inherent" differences between ethnic groups. In the United States, for example, Black Americans are twice as likely to be unemployed and nearly three times as likely to live in poverty. Based on this, and drawing on centuries of bigoted stereotypes, white politicians often cast African-Americans as "lazy"

14

and "lacking work ethic." The reality is that African-Americans cannot access jobs due to poor access to education, employment discrimination, and other forms of oppression that result from the unequal distribution of public goods. To the extent that African-Americans are out of work, this is because whites "tend to limit access to stable jobs to fellow whites, relegating blacks to temporary, part-time, or marginal jobs in the secondary labor market" (Anderson 2010: 9). In short, political ideologies that play up "inherent" differences between ethnic groups "misrepresent the effect of group inequality as its cause" (Anderson 2010: 9).

Spatial segregation and unequal public goods provision undermine the substantive elements required for citizens to deliberate and determine the law as equals. Toward this end, spending on public schools ought to be equalized across ethnic groups, or in some cases even increased given the high need for supplemental "wrap-around" services like counseling, food, special education, and school supplies in high-poverty areas. Yet improving primary and secondary education is not a silver bullet; these efforts must be accompanied by steps to end residential segregation and increased spending on other public goods like childcare, paid family leave policies, health care, adult job training and employment, and access to nutritious food.

There is a tight relationship between the substantive and procedural conditions of public equality. Equal participation requires voter mobilization, campaigning, and lobbying financial capital, political knowledge, time, and access, which members of these groups frequently lack for the reasons described. As a result, they are less able to deliberate with fellow citizens on an equal footing. As was made clear earlier in this chapter, it is therefore urgent to put in place campaign finance laws distributing political resources across groups and limiting the influence of existing private wealth. Additionally, close attention must be paid to the interaction between existing ethnic hierarchy and democratic procedures. Direct democratic measures are on the rise in modern democracies. These practices that allow citizens to propose and vote directly on measures, are appealing to democratic theorists because they foster grassroots organizing, ensure numerical voting equality on issues, and allow those without powerful ties to politicians to have their voices heard. Yet careful attention to the empirical effects of these practices highlights how substantive inequalities and biases may infect democratic procedures. Voters bring in their own stereotyped beliefs and biases to the booth, which can result in a tyranny of the majority at the expense of minority groups.

In Switzerland, for example, foreign residents become naturalized in three stages: vetted first by the federal government, then the state, then at the municipal level. While some municipalities have their elected politicians vote on the applications, others allow voters to decide directly via secret ballot. A recent study found that, between 1970 and 2003, foreign residents were 50 percent more likely to get naturalized when elected politicians made the decision rather than voters (Hainmueller et al. 2016). The quality of the applicant pool was the same across districts, implying that voters discriminate against qualified applicants that would have been approved if accountable legislators had made the decision. In fact, the effect of switching from direct to representative democracy was notably stronger in areas where citizens were more xenophobic (Hainmueller et al. 2016). This

is because representatives, even if they hold the same prejudices as the voters, are publicly accountable for their choices and know their decisions are subject to evaluation in the courts. In short, under certain circumstances, direct democratic measures can be used to suppress the legitimate interests of ethnic minorities. Therefore, policy makers should be attentive to the circumstances under which ballot referenda are used, particularly when it comes to decisions concerning citizenship and the distribution of public goods.

Ethnic hierarchy poses a substantial threat public equality. One's membership in an ethnic group often determines whether one can access basic civil rights and liberties as well as the goods and resources essential for discourse on terms of mutual respect. This, in turn, poses clear challenges to democracy as a process of decision-making in which people have an equal ability to determine the laws and norms that bind them.

14.2.3 Religious Inequality

The defining feature of democracy, as already expressed in the introduction, is that all groups and persons be recognized as equally valued members of the society to which they belong. If this is so, and if, further, the collective decision-making process is the public realization of the equal worth of every citizen, then any practice that involves discrimination, exclusion, marginalization, or oppression of groups and persons violates the principle of democracy. For our purpose here, inequality may be viewed as a condition where such exclusionary and/or discriminatory practices thrive, where power is illegitimately deployed to thwart the basic interests and values of individuals and groups. A fully realized democracy then cannot coexist with inequality.

The focus of this section is on one such type of inequality, namely, religious inequality. Religious inequality can be of two kinds. In a society with multiple religions, members of one religious group may treat members of other religious groups as unequals, as when a government controlled by non-Muslims refuses permission to build a mosque with minarets, or when Hindus and Christians are debarred from standing for public office in an Islamic state. Let this be called interreligious inequality. A second kind of religious inequality also persists in many societies. Consider the persecution of Catholics by Protestants or the de-recognition of Ahmadiyas as Muslims. Here members of a broadly conceived religious group treat their own members as unequals. Let this be called intrareligious inequality. Another deeper form of intrareligious inequality also exists. For example, in India a whole group of people, formerly called "the untouchables" continue to find it difficult to enter many Hindu temples; in some places, women are still hounded because they are believed to be witches, women between the ages of 15 and 55 are not allowed entry into a temple because they are menstruating and therefore believed to be polluted.

The question before us is how should states deal with these different forms of religious inequalities. Are democratic states in a better position to address such inequalities than nondemocratic states? Furthermore, are some forms of democratic states better equipped to deal with religious inequalities than others? While the distinction between democratic and nondemocratic states is important, an even more important distinction for our purpose is between religion-centered and secular states. It is our view that all religion-centered states perpetuate religious inequalities and violate important principles of democracy. If the reduction of religious inequalities is our objective, then, it is argued here, religion-centered states must give way to secular states. Only a secular democratic state can undermine religious inequalities. But this simple answer does not suffice because all forms of secular-democratic states are not equally capable of addressing religious inequality. This begs the question: which form of secular-democratic state is best able to reduce both intra- and interreligious inequalities? To answer this question is the central objective of this section.

What are religion-centered and secular states? Religion-centered states grant privileged recognition to any one religion. They promote the values and interests of that religion and justify most of their laws and policies in terms of these values or interests. Sometimes, the entire apparatus of such states is run by religious personnel. The connection of states with religion is so strong and constitutive that their very identity is defined by religion. Such states then are Christian, Islamic, or Hindu.

Secular states are different. They withdraw privileges that any established religion had previously taken for granted. This they can do only when their primary ends or goals are defined independently of religion. Thus, a crucial requirement of a secular state is that it has no constitutive links with religion, that the ends of any religion not be installed as the ends of the state. For example, it cannot be the constitutive objective of the state to ensure salvation, nirvana, or moksha. No religious community in such a state can say that the state belongs exclusively to it. The identity of the state is defined independently of religion, and certainly independently of any one religion. Furthermore, laws and policies of such states cannot be justified solely in terms of reasons provided by any one religion.

Which of the two, religion-centered or secular states, can better undermine religious inequalities and build an inclusive society and polity on fair and equal terms? A cursory evaluation of these states shows that all religion-centered states are deeply troublesome. Take first historical instances of states that establish a single church, the unreformed established Protestant Churches of England, Scotland, and Germany, and the Catholic Churches in Italy and Spain. These states recognized a particular version enunciated by the church as the official religion, compelled individuals to congregate for only one church, punished them for failing to profess a particular set of religious beliefs, and levied taxes in support of one particular church (Levy 1994: 5). In such cases, not only was there inequality among religions (for example between Christians and Jews) but also among the churches of the same religion. Such multi-religious or multiple-denominational societies were frequently wrecked by interreligious or interdenominational wars and if not, their religious minorities faced persistent religious persecution (Jews in several European countries until the nineteenth century).

States with substantive establishments have not changed color with time. Wherever one religion is not only formally but substantively established, the persecution of minorities and internal dissenters continues today. One has only to cite the example of Saudi Arabia to prove this point (Ruthven 2002: 172–81). Or consider the situation in Pakistan where the virtual establishment of the dominant Sunni sect has proved to be disastrous to minorities, including to Muslim minorities. For example, Ahmedis have been deemed a non-Muslim minority, forbidden from using Islamic nomenclature in their religious and social lives (Bhargava 2010a: 63–108; 2010b: 81–102; Malik 2002: 10); and have been formally excluded by the state, both symbolically and materially, from its own religion. Moreover, by making adherence to Islam mandatory for anyone aspiring to the highest offices in the country, the Constitution ensures the exclusion of religious minorities from high politics (Malik 2002: 16). Likewise, many people in India believe that the establishment of a Hindu Rashtra would be disastrous, particularly for Muslim minorities, perhaps even for the Dalits (former untouchables). The Jewish state of Israel in effect fails to grant equal rights to its religious minorities.

So if religious inequalities are to be reduced, religion-centered states must be dismantled. However, while secular democratic states are committed to equality of citizenship, they also differ from one another in their respective understandings of how they must relate to religion. All agree that they must be separated or disconnected, but differ on how the metaphor of separation is to be unpacked. For one, separation is total disconnection or mutual exclusion. The state has neither a positive relationship with religion, for example there is no policy of granting aid to religious institutions nor a negative relationship with it; it is not within the scope of state activity to interfere in religious matters. The Constitutional state of the United States is frequently interpreted to instantiate this model, advocating mutual exclusion of state and religion (a wall) primarily for the sake of religious liberty and denominational pluralism. Thus by protecting religious freedom of all groups and ensuring interdenominational equality as also by ruling out discrimination in the official domain on grounds of religion, this model prevents certain forms of religious inequalities. However, it has two major limitations: (a) By its refusal to negatively intervene in religious practices, it may allow discriminatory, oppressive practices within a religion; (b) by eschewing any positive help to all religious groups, it may overlook that, to achieve equality, some vulnerable religious minorities require assistance from the state.

In another, second type, disconnection is partial and is conceived at the level of law and public policy in a wholly one-sided manner. Here to disconnect is to exclude religion from the affairs of the state but to allow virtually limitless intervention by the state in the affairs of religion to control, regulate, and even to destroy religion. Such secular states are decidedly antireligious. They often advocate one-sided exclusion primarily for the sake of a stringently guarded common public culture that gives a uniform and equal identity to citizens. In their authoritarian form this model is at least partly exemplified in Kemalist Turkey and Soviet Russia. Its democratic version is best enunciated in France.

These secular states (model 2) have one advantage over model 1. Since they are willing to intervene in religious affairs, they can undercut oppressive and exclusionary religious practices and achieve some forms of interreligious equality. However, by refusing to grant positive recognition or financial aid particularly to newly immigrated religious groups and by their obstinate refusal to acknowledge the entanglement of both official and public practices with a historically embedded

14

majority religion, they at least unwittingly perpetuate interreligious inequality.

Partial disconnection is also the form of state–religion relationship in the third (model 3) type of secular-democratic state. Disconnection is partial here because the state continues to partially support one religion, usually the dominant one, on the ground that it is part of the cultural inheritance and historical legacy of its citizens and therefore a significant public good. Such states are found in large parts of Western Europe. Such secular-democratic states, though not religion-centered, remain single-religion friendly. Why, if they provide to support to one religion, are such states secular?

There are several reasons for this: (a) because of a historical pattern of hostility to church and church-based religions on the ground that they were politically meddlesome and socially oppressive – a pattern explicit in the unchurching struggles in France but also found in most West European countries; and (b) because over time there has been a decline both in church belonging and in doctrinal adherence. Surely, if there is one place where secular humanism is perhaps naïvely taken for granted as the only ontological and epistemological game in town, it is Western Europe! Both (a) and (b) have had an impact on Europe's constitutional regimes. A fair degree of disconnection exists at the levels of ends, and so the same basket of formal rights (to different kinds of liberty, and forms of equality, etc.) are offered to all individuals regardless of their church affiliation and regardless of whether they are or are not religious. In the dominant political discourse, the self-definition of these states is that they are not religious (Christian) but (purely) liberal democratic.

However, it is equally true that some connection exists between state and religion. Several states continue to grant monopolistic privileges to one or the other branch of Christianity (The Presbyterian Church in Scotland, the Lutheran Church in most Nordic countries, the Orthodox Church in Greece, the Anglican Church in England). Moreover, at the level of law and public policy, state intervention exists in the form of support for the dominant church/churches. Thus though no longer religion-centered, they remain single-religion friendly states. State-religion connections combined with a significant degree of disconnection mean that these democratic states are at best modestly secular by the standards set by the idealized US model or the French model (Tariq Modood).

How do states of Western Europe fare when evaluated by norms of religious equality? Not all that well, it seems. Blind to the more complex dimension of interreligious inequalities, they do not even see that in this dimension they are not secular. Despite all changes, European states have continued to privilege Christianity in one form or another. The liberal democratization and the consequent secularization of many European states have helped citizens with non-Christian faiths to acquire most formal rights. But such a scheme of rights neither embodies a regime of interreligious equality nor effectively prevents religion-based discrimination and exclusion. Indeed, it masks majoritarian, ethno-religious biases. Thus, to go back to the example of schools run by religious communities, only two to five schools run by Muslims are provided state funding in England. In France there is at least one state-funded Muslim school

(in Réunion), and about four or five new private Muslim schools that are in the process of signing "contrats d'association" with the state. In Germany not a single school run by Muslims is funded by the state. Other examples exist in the failure of many Western European states to deal with the issue of headscarves (most notably France), in unheeded demands by Muslims to build mosques (Germany and Italy), in discrimination against ritual slaughter (Germany), and in unheeded demands by Muslims for proper burial grounds of their own (Denmark, among others).

So, do forms or conceptions of secular-democratic states that better address religious inequalities exist? One particular model outside the West (in the Indian subcontinent) that has tried, often unsuccessfully, to eliminate deep religious inequalities, and that currently lies in shambles everywhere, needs careful attention.

Several features of this fourth kind of secular-democratic state are worth mentioning. First, multiple religions exist in their background not as optional extras added on as an afterthought but as part of its foundation. These secular democratic states are inextricably tied to deep religious diversity. Second, they are committed to a deeply diverse set of values, not only liberty and equality but also fraternity (or sociability) – conceived not narrowly as pertaining only to individuals but interpreted broadly also to cover the relative autonomy of religious communities and, in limited and specific domains, their equality of status in society – as well as to foster a certain quality of relations among religious communities, perhaps even interreligious equality under conditions of deep religious diversity. They have a place not only for the right of individuals to profess their religious beliefs but also for the right of religious communities to, say, establish and maintain educational institutions crucial for the survival and sustenance of their distinctive religious traditions.

The acceptance of community-specific rights brings me to the third feature of this model. Because this form of secular democratic state was born in a deeply multi-religious society, it is concerned as much with interreligious inequality as it is with intrareligious inequality. Whereas other secular democratic states appear to provide benefits to minority religious groups only incidentally (e.g. Jews benefited in some European countries such as France not because their special needs and demands were met via public recognition but because of a more general restructuring of society guided by an individual-based emancipatory agenda), in these states some community-specific sociocultural rights are granted for their intrinsic value.

Fourth, such secular democratic states do not erect a wall of separation between religion and state. There are boundaries, of course, but they are porous. This situation allows the state to intervene in religions in order to help or hinder them without the impulse to control or destroy them. This intervention can include granting aid to educational institutions of religious communities on a non-preferential basis and interfering in socioreligious institutions that deny equal dignity and status to members of their own religion or to those of others; for example, the ban on untouchability and the obligation to allow everyone, irrespective of their caste, to enter Hindu temples, as well as, potentially, other actions to correct gender inequalities. In short, this form of secular democratic state interprets separation to mean not strict exclusion or strict neutrality, but what we call principled distance, poles apart from one-sided exclusion or mutual exclusion.

What does principled distance mean? First, religious groups have sought exemptions when states have intervened in religious practices by promulgating laws designed to apply neutrally across society. For example, Sikhs demand exemptions from mandatory helmet laws to accommodate religiously required turbans. Principled distance allows a practice that is banned or regulated in the majority culture to be permitted in the minority culture because of the distinctive status and meaning it has for the minority culture's members. Religious groups may demand that the state refrain from interference in their practices, but they may equally demand that the state interfere in such a way as to give them special assistance so that they are able to secure what other groups are routinely able to acquire by virtue of their social dominance in the political community. For example, subsidies are provided to schools run by all religious communities. Some holidays of all religious communities are granted national status.

Moreover, principled distance allows state intervention in some religions more than in others. Minority religions are granted a constitutional right to establish and maintain their educational institutions. Limited funding may be available to Muslims for Hajj. State engagement can also take a negative interventionist form. For the promotion of equality, special measures may be required in one religion. To undermine caste hierarchies, Hindu temples in India were thrown open to all, particularly to former untouchables should they choose to enter them. Likewise, constitutionally it is possible to undertake gender-based reforms in Hindu or personal Muslim personal law.

Fifth, such states are not compelled to choose between active hostility and passive indifference or between disrespectful hostility and respectful indifference toward religion. They combine the two, permitting necessary hostility as long as there is also active respect. This is a complex dialectical attitude to religion that Bhargava (2010) called critical respect. So, on the one hand, the state protects all religions, makes them feel equally at home, especially vulnerable religious communities, by granting them community-specific rights. But the state also hits hard at religion-based oppression, exclusion, and discrimination, in short all forms of religious inequalities.

This section has argued that secular-democratic states of the principled distance variety have a better chance of reducing religious inequalities. In sum, a society progresses the more it moves away from (a) a religion-centered to a secular-democratic state and (b) secular-democratic states hostile to or aloof from religions generally or friendly exclusively to one religion to those that keep a principled distance from all religions.

14.2.4 Gender Inequality

Gender equality is a Mission Impossible, now more than ever. First, there is an ongoing *perpetuum mobile* of gender inequality that is driven by structures and daily actions of human beings across all walks of life. Second, gender equality as an objective is deeply political

and inherently contested. Finally, while deep democracy is needed to mobilize and organize the inevitable ongoing feminist struggles against the tenacity and complexity of gender inequality, democracy currently seems to be shrinking rather than deepening and strengthening.

These triple troubles call for more attention to the linkages between the fates of democracy and of gender equality, and for more feminist engagement in struggles for deeper democracy. This means more attention for the pervasiveness and the tenacity of gender inequality in our societies, for the political nature of gender equality as a goal, and for a clearer perspective on democracy that shows the interrelation between gender equality and democracy. Given the current fate of democracy in Europe, this section will end with a call for action.

14.2.4.1 The Pervasiveness and the Tenacity of Gender Inequality in Our Societies

Even the briefest look at feminist history shows how significant victories in the past have never been enough to end gender inequality. Women's access to higher education, their legal personhood, women's suffrage, all these hard-won long battles by brave and engaged feminists have not brought an end to male domination. If anything, they have revealed the tenacity and complexity of gender inequality regimes. Gender inequality regimes have proven very flexible in readapting to changed contexts and structures. Laws and formal governmental regulations have not changed reality as intended. Progress is made, but mostly partial and never ensured. The impact of ongoing gender inequality on people's lives is huge, given that gender inequality restricts the lives of both women and men that do not fit well into conventional gender norms.

We now know something about the reasons why progress is so slow. The tenacity and complexity of gender inequality regimes is caused by the multilevel and multidimensional character of gender, its location in all social domains, and its deep connections to other inequalities. As the world is deeply social, none of this is fixed, and everything is in flux. The multilevel character of gender means that gender is part of societal structures and organizations, symbols and norms, identities and behavior. Identities, personalities, routinized behavior, symbols, norms, and structures are made and remade on a daily basis by the human beings on this planet. They make conscious decisions about this gendered world and their positioning in it, but also often just routinely follow the gendered scripts that history provides. It is hard to think of a domain where these gendered tracks or scripts would be absent. Gender inequality is both public and private, and is crucial to constructing what is seen as public and what is seen as private (similar to sexual inequality). Whether in economy, polity, violence, health, or knowledge, the gender unequal configurations of the past offer the material that people use to make their lives, provide the words and signs people use to be accepted and understood by others. In doing so, people reproduce and to some degree reorganize these gendered tracks, these gendered words, this gendered world across all domains. Whether people benefit or suffer from it depends on their gendered locations (men, women, or non-binary).

Feminist collective action – focused political pressure to change an element of these inequality regimes – such as quotas in politics, a more permissive abortion law, father's leave, or the opening of shelters for domestic violence victims, aims at change, and their hard-won victories matter. They are small steps with tremendous impact on the lives of some women (and men). Yet, there are intersectional caveats to most victories: not all women, not all men equally benefit from them. Quotas in politics might be opening space mostly for high-educated women, access to abortion might be almost impossible for rural women, gay fathers may not be eligible for paternity leave, minority women victims of domestic violence might have good reason not to engage with shelters organized by social workers for fear of being stigmatized in their communities or having custody of their children taken away from them.

It is clear then that it is very hard to fundamentally change the dynamics of gender inequality, or to abolish gender inequality. Collective action's role in inducing and supporting change is well demonstrated. But what are the conditions that foster such actions? What makes feminist collective action successful? How to ensure that these are victories for all women? To answer these questions, the quality of democracy is key. The quality of democracy matters for gender equality because the tenacity of gender inequality in our societies calls for better conditions for feminist collective action, and such action can only thrive in democracies. This is a matter of both theory and practice, of both a better understanding of the politics needed and more engagement to make such politics happen.

14.2.4.2   The Political Nature of Gender Equality as a Goal

If anyone should know what gender equality is, feminists should. And they do indeed, each and every one of them. Yet they give very different meanings to these goals, contradictory meanings even, including objections to the wording used here. Feminists fight fiercely about what the goal of feminism needs to be even if there are many examples of large-scale collective feminist actions for an agreed upon feminist cause. To make progress on how to deal with the challenge of the multitude of feminist goals – the challenge of the deep political nature of the feminist goal – two questions need to be addressed: What exactly are the bones of contention? Where do hegemonic understandings of gender equality come from? Intersectionality is key to address these questions because history shows, over and over again, that intersectional inequalities and the political choices that need to be made about them occupy center stage in internal feminist struggles and in the outcomes of these struggles. The intersection of class and gender was a bone of contention when feminists were fighting for the suffrage in Europe; the intersection of race and gender was at the heart of suffrage dynamics in the United States. In both Europe and the United States, sexual orientation deeply divided the feminist movement in the 1970s, and current conflicts over trans rights are equally divisive. At the level of feminist ideology and feminist theory, one of the strongest divides runs between liberal feminism – aiming for a gender-equal society within the settings of a capitalist world – and socialist feminism – aiming for a gender-equal society in which capitalist exploitation is

abolished or at least tamed. There is no way gender inequality can be understood or addressed separately from other major inequalities built around class, sexuality, and race.

This political nature of gender equality cannot be escaped, and the ongoing struggle of feminists and others about the meaning of gender equality is essential. Such "productive antagonism" (Butler 1993) or refusal of "ultimate truths" (J.W. Scott 1988) produces a dynamic understanding of feminism that can address the moving target of gender inequality by adapting to its changing forms, and that enables wider sets of coalitions to profit from emerging political opportunities. The format of ongoing struggle enables feminism to challenge domination as well as unstated "norms" of dominant groups within itself, to uncover and address processes of hegemonization within the feminist project (Hooks 1981). Open spaces and explicit rules are needed to include the perspectives of previously excluded subjects, ensuring that new inequalities are not made. For all the reasons stated, feminism as a political project needs democracy.

14.2.4.3   Democracy and Its Interrelation with Gender Equality

Gender inequality as a political problem and gender equality as a political goal are too dynamic to fit comfortably within classic formats of formal electoral representation. Formal representation and formal political actors, because of their acceptance of the boundaries of a certain nation or state, do not work well for giving voice to the non-represented, or for contributing to the articulation of political problems by those who are in one way or another not fully included in our societies. Social movements are the main actors that can introduce new actors to politics; that can develop and introduce new political problems to societies, and pursue political change to address these problems. For social movements to do this well, how citizenship is organized is key: who are included and excluded in societies, and who decides on this? Some degree of voice, of inclusive citizenship is needed for social movements to emerge and flourish. A first problem is that formal citizenship rights do not fully translate into actual access to participation in democratic institutions. The documented list of barriers for women in politics is long, ranging from non-inclusive language, to ridicule, absence of role models, biased electoral systems, problematic access to campaign funding, lack of compliance with formal rules, or outright harassment. Additionally, there are many individuals who are located at the intersection of gender and other inequalities and who lack basic rights in democracies as we know them. Consider the lack of bodily autonomy for women from states without abortion or contraception rights, the lack of resources for many women given the persisting wage gap, the lack of access to family rights for many lesbian and gay parents, the lack of freedom of movement for trans citizens from states without full trans rights, the lack of economic rights for asylum seekers in states that forbid them to be active on the labor market. Moreover, in order to really function as a democracy, a society needs to organize space not only for its subaltern groups, but also for disruptors of its way of functioning: for people who remind everyone that the political landscape does not cover all of society's problems, the political stage does not show all the actors actually involved in society, and change is needed to address newly politicized problems.

What kind of democracy does feminism – the political project that is home to feminist social movements – need? Authors such as Walby (2009) and Tilly (2007) show the need to expand on the classic procedural rules of electoral democracy with wider rules on citizenship and attention to the practices and outcomes those sets of rules produce in a society. The wider rules are non-exclusionary rules on citizenship that define how political arenas for debate and struggle are constructed (who is part of the demos), facilitate engagement of people in the societies relevant to them, and construct links between civil society and formal politics, thereby increasing the possibilities for democratic engagement toward gender equality. Following Tilly, state capacity is a crucial ingredient of democracy too, as it is essential to assure democratic practices. Including the practices and outcomes and not just the classic formal rules is also essential because of feedback effects between rules and outcomes.

14.2.4.4   Current Troubles with Democracy in Europe

Along with ongoing problems of democracy unrecognized by most political scientists, such as "democratic" states that are simultaneously monarchies or colonial powers, or have rules allowing parties to be ruled autocratically, there are substantial problems for democracy hindering further progress in abolishing gender inequality, as the following examples from the wider Europe illustrate. There is the *intrusion of the domain of the economy in the domain of the polity*, visible in the failure of democracies to constrain financial capitalism, the tendency to allow businesses to financially opt out of democratic decisions (TTIP), and the contagious spread of business reasoning in governance (as in NPM). All this weakens democracy, and expands the possibilities for gendered capitalist exploitation by either restricting welfare state arrangements or increasing the possibilities for precarious labor. Moreover, there is a renewed *strengthening of the political power of organized religion* as part of the polity, which is a major source of opposition to gender and sexual equality. While public attention centers mostly on Islamist states, the Vatican and Orthodox churches are much more important in the European context. There is also a *rise of authoritarianism* that is visible in the strengthening of the Radical Right and its connection to authoritarian-style geopolitics. There is a *rise in illiberalism and populism*, including criticism on independent thinking and on collective action. There are increasing calls for political restriction to academic autonomy (Turkey, Hungary), and laws that "gag" civil society in European Union member states (Spain, Hungary). Across European countries, there are *increasing (calls for) restrictions on citizenship based on racialized features* (religion, origin) across European countries. And there is an increase in sham democracies: mafia states adopting democratic masks to stage the theatre of their coercive power conquests. In sum, democratic structures supportive of women's rights – such as social democracy, welfare, civil society engagement, and academic freedom – are being eroded, with opposition to gender and sexual equality growing in frequency and strength (Verloo 2017).

14.2.4.5   Intersectional Challenges for Democratic Struggles About Gender Equality

Under conditions of endangered democracy, groups of women at the intersection of gender and sexuality, gender and class, and gender and race already encounter severe backlashes and further exclusion. Even for more privileged women, there is an urgent need for more wage equality and political representation, and less gender-based violence. But the challenges for various intersectional groups of women are far more substantial. The rise of authoritarianism and the extreme right in Europe increases the salience of certain inequality projects in politics and hinders working toward more gender, sexual, and racial inequality. Within conservative and extreme-right political ideologies, heteronormativity and traditional perspectives on gender prevail, with a centerpiece on fertility in the national interest. Sexual equality is almost always opposed and that impacts negatively on gender equality. The far-right's rise to power has set in motion backlashes against reproductive rights and has diminished hopes for such rights in countries lacking them. Racial inequality is at the heart of most far-right ideologies and proposed actions, constructing "racialized others" based on changing contextual configurations of skin color, religion (especially Judaism and Islam), origin (migration) or language. These variations in racialization complicate collective action against it. Class inequality is on the rise, linked to austerity measures leading to the weakening of welfare states in Europe. The weakening of social democratic parties, combined with their traditional blind spot for gendered class inequalities, seriously hinders action to reduce gendered class inequalities.

Strategically, the authoritarian preferences of far-right and populist parties strengthen the tendency to decrease the space given to civil society, further hindering collective action toward gender equality. The tendency for civil society restriction is exacerbated by the current terrorist attacks in Europe that trigger political responses that restrict civil liberties. In such contexts, it seems almost utopian to consider giving political space to the subaltern.

Summarizing, while a high need exists for more political engagement with gender equality, intersectional challenges to gender equality mean current developments all point to fewer opportunities to do so.

Gender equality and democracy are linked in an intricate and reinforcing feedback loop. The more democracy, the more chances for gender equality; the more gender equality there is, the more chances for democracy. Because of their interdependence, we need to be as clear and specific as possible about what kind of democratic principles and practices are needed to achieve real gender equality. As a set of principles, practices, and outcomes guiding, organizing, and producing the polity and civil society, democracy is utopian but the only hope for achieving real gender equality.

14.2.5   Generational Inequalities

There are at least three forms of generational inequalities that may constitute a challenge for the goal of democratic equality: (1)

inequalities between non-overlapping generations; (2) inequalities between coexisting birth cohorts; and (3) inequalities between age groups. These three forms of generational inequalities will be the focus of the sections that follow.

14.2.5.1   The Challenge of Justice Between Non-Overlapping Generations

Our unsustainable use of natural resources has created large problems that future generations will have to tackle. Deforestation, overfishing, and pollution have had a tremendous impact on biodiversity. The future is bleak with expected frequent natural catastrophes as a result of climate change. Some populations will be hit harder than others and, as entire territories will inevitably be replaced by water, millions will be forced to migrate. As a result, it is becoming more and more likely that future generations will have difficulties accessing the resources they need, including food, water, and clean air.

The environmental crisis and its myriads of consequences result in large part from the incapacity of present democratic institutions to reverse, stop, or at least stabilize climate change, global warming, and their various consequences. It epitomizes an endemic short-termism in democratic politics, and gives us the suspicion that our political institutions may not adequately promote long-term interests, in general, and the interests of future generations, in particular.

We face fundamental challenges such as global poverty that demand the urgent use of some non-renewable resources. But those important interests need to be balanced with those of future people. And yet, it is fair to worry that the fundamental inequality in power and representation of interests between current and future generations has translated into a radical form of political inequality. There are at least two ways in which this inequality is challenging from the point of view of democratic equality: one is procedural and the other is substantive.

First, in order for our decisions to have long-term procedural legitimacy, largely regardless of their actual content, adequate weight must be given to the interests of future generations. Even though in theory we can grant that their life and interests matter as much as ours do, it is not easy to ensure that they enjoy some presence in representative and deliberative bodies. It is even harder to make sure their interests are accounted for in voting procedures. But with the increasing realization that we are harming future generations, we ought to develop imaginative mechanisms that ensure they have some form of voice.

More controversially, the second challenge is substantive. It relates to the content of the policies that our democratic systems generate. Intergenerational justice requires at the very least that we make decisions that are sustainable. This goal of sustainability through time applies to other domains than the environment. It has implications for the levels of debt we are entitled to pass on to future generations, for the public infrastructure we invest in, for the budget we must devote to research, and for the extent to which we must protect heritage.

Sustainability is a substantive requirement of intergenerational justice, but also a demand of democratic equality. Indeed, the environmental

crisis threatens the basic subsistence and, in fact, the very existence of future generations. Future generations have a higher stake than current people in the long-term detrimental effects of current political decisions. If those interests are sidelined, then the basic foundations of the democratic ideal – that each person's interests matter equally, and that each person's basic liberties cannot be disregarded – are undermined. Therefore, the second challenge of intergenerational inequalities for democratic equality is substantive: to entrench the ideal of sustainability in democratic institutions.

We can distinguish at least four types of mechanisms that respond to the challenges that come from the structural invisibility of future generations. First, some institutions give a political voice to future generations. The introduction of parliamentary commissioners for future generations (as in Hungary) and the proposal for an International Ombudsperson for Future Generations are two such mechanisms. Another promising proposal is a committee for future generations in parliaments (as in Finland), whose role would be to scrutinize all policies from the perspective of future interests. Second, independent institutions that monitor progresses are proposed – for instance, an independent Council for the Future to complement parliamentary commissions. A third and fourth type of mechanisms consists in the constitutional entrenchment of intergenerational provisions and the implementation of institutions that directly promote a more sustainable future. The latter contributes to what we have identified as the substantive demand of democratic equality for future generations. From the proposal of a world climate bank, to the use of sovereign wealth funds with an individual dividend to give a stake to citizens in environmental management, those reforms can help bring about more sustainability in the management of non-renewable resources.

14.2.5.2   Inequalities Between Birth Cohorts

In addition to the general anxiety about the kind of future that we may leave to future generations, there is a growing concern for a lost generation – a large mass of young adults burdened with debts, structural unemployment, and precarious work. This concern has been particularly stark in European countries struggling with high rates of youth unemployment, as high as 50 percent in Greece and Spain, but often two to four times as high as for older age groups in other European countries. High rates of unemployment at a young age scar people in the long run and make them more likely to be unemployed or underpaid later in life compared to other cohorts at the same age; so young people are not likely to be compensated later in their life.

The emergence of a disadvantaged generation may be a challenge for our generational contract and for intergenerational justice, but not as such a challenge to the ideal of democratic equality the authors of this chapter subscribe to. Young cohorts may be worse off in terms of their job market-related opportunities or they may enjoy lower rates of benefits to contribution, but their basic civil rights and liberties may not be threatened in a fundamental manner. Nonetheless, as we will now show, there is ground to be concerned that such inequalities between birth cohorts might still pose a challenge to democracy.

Indeed, in addition to being massively at risk of social exclusion, young cohorts are at the margins of formal politics. They enjoy a low political power both through their low voting turnout and the ageing of the electorate. Voters' turnouts are strongly correlated with age. In the 2009 local elections in the UK, only 10 percent of 18- to 24-year-olds said that they had voted compared to 85 percent of people aged 65 years and over. The quantitative difference between potential voters, registered voters, and actual voters is directly correlated with age: the younger the voters, the higher the difference between potential and actual voting turnouts will be. This trend is widespread. One could go as far as arguing that there is an emerging "intergenerational democratic deficit" whereby young people are becoming marginalized within the democratic process (Berry 2012: 5).

Together, the socioeconomic concerns of current younger generations and their political disengagement from formal politics feed the suspicion that their interests may not be represented fairly by democratic institutions. The problem does not necessarily have to be that older generations are willingly trying to exclude or disadvantage younger generations. The concern is that they are more numerous, vote in higher proportions, and are overrepresented in parliamentary institutions. Older age groups may thus be in a privileged position to shape politics and parliaments with their values, attitudes, and interests. One recent example of this is the generational data of the Brexit referendum in the UK. Some studies show that up to 73 percent of the 18 to 24 age group have voted Remain when more than 60 percent of voters older than 65 years voted Leave.[3] Younger generations' views, values, and perceived interests may in fact get sidelined even when fundamental decisions that will affect them for longer than older age groups are taken.

There are a number of possible ways to improve youth involvement in formal politics. One set of solutions consists in re-enfranchising the young through lowering the voting age to 16. Youth participation can also be promoted through implementing easier voting systems and making registration simpler. Increasing funding for youth political initiatives, supporting the development of youth wings in political parties, and developing civic education in schools and universities are additional ways to work toward their reengagement.

14.2.5.3 Inequalities Between Age Groups

There is another form of generational inequality that is often hidden behind the aforementioned inequality between birth cohorts: inequalities between age groups. Age groups are groups of people of a given age at a given period of time. Individuals will only belong to one birth cohort in their life, but they will change age membership throughout their lives. Age-group and birth-cohort inequalities are distinct since inequalities between age groups do not necessarily translate into inequalities between birth cohorts. Age inequalities pose a separate challenge to democratic legitimacy, regardless of whether they translate into inequalities between successive birth cohorts. Let me focus on two examples.

First, age groups have access to unequal political rights. In most countries, young people below the age of 18 cannot vote or run for office.

For instance, while 16- and 17-year-olds were allowed to vote in the recent Scottish referendum, they were not allowed to vote in the Brexit referendum. One must also be of a certain age to be a member of the Senate (30 in the United States) or to run for president (35 in the United States). These age-based inequalities in basic rights are meant to capture unequal levels of competence, abilities, and sense of responsibility. But they are not unproblematic.

For a start, the young have a higher stake in the long-term consequences of decisions made today. There are very good reasons to keep children out of politics – which have to do with their autonomy and the fact that they could end up manipulated, for instance. But it is not clear that there are such reasons for older teenagers and young adults. Older teenagers are allowed to join the labor force, they can be imprisoned, and they can join the army in many countries. It seems consistent with this status that they should have the right to vote too.

A second example is the underrepresentation of young people between 18 and 35 years of age in parliaments. At the international level, fewer than 2 percent of representatives are younger than 30 years old in two-thirds of single and lower houses; and three-quarters of upper houses do not elect young parliamentarians at all (Inter-Parliamentary Union 2014). As many have pointed out, the underrepresentation of young adults in parliaments does not look as unfair as the exclusion of women or ethnic minority, since they are only unequally represented for a portion of their lives. Still, the underrepresentation of youth remains problematic since it reinforces the self-image of youth as apolitical and may have a negative impact on participation rates. Second, decision makers may be lacking experiential knowledge because of the lack of young representatives. As a result, they may often not give equal weight to the interests of old and young.

One radical policy to correct the underrepresentation of young people in parliaments is the introduction of youth quotas in the legislatures (Bidadanure 2017). Drawing on existing examples of youth quotas in the form of reserved seats for young people in parliament in Uganda, Kenya, and Morocco, the UNDP (2013) puts forward the introduction of youth quotas in electoral laws as a way to enhance youth representation and participation. The presence of young MPs can be expected to have at least two kinds of impacts on decision-making. The first is substantive. Regardless of their party membership, young MPs can be expected to contribute to expanding the available party policy packages through pushing for the better inclusion of youth concerns in political agendas. Quotas can prevent the important risk that policies and debates become driven by paternalism and condescendence, if conducted solely within some age groups and in exclusion of others.

The second potential impact of youth quotas relates to their symbolic role. If we consider that people's self-images are partly tied to their political images, then it seems that descriptive representation has meaning for whether given individuals are acknowledged as equals. Youth quotas would signal to society and young people that their contribution is valued and that they are considered with equal respect. The absence or underrepresentation of young people in parliament, on the contrary, signals the opposite and may contribute to an apolitical self-image of young adults.

---

[3]   http://lordashcroftpolls.com/2016/06/how-the-united-kingdom-voted-and-why/.

In summary, this section has considered three inequalities between generations that pose a challenge to democracy, and are yet often overlooked. We must devote more time and resources to understanding how each of those inequalities threatens democratic equality. The first challenge derives from the political invisibility of future generations and the endemic short-termism that comes with it. Mechanisms to give voice to future generations today (like parliamentary commissions) to legally entrench long-termist goals and to monitor progress and drawbacks must be considered. The "democratic deficit" between coexisting generations is the second intergenerational challenge that we considered: the risk is that small and/or disenfranchised cohorts may see their interests sidelined. Solutions there include simplifying registration and voting procedures, as well as investing in quality political education. The last challenge was identified as relating to age-group equality. Here we questioned the exclusion of some age groups (in particular teenagers and young adults) de jure or de facto from political institutions, including from electoral and parliamentary ones. We urged politicians to not take for granted those age-based differential treatments and to consider ways to make sure the interests of disenfranchised age groups are not sidelined. The potential benefits of the descriptive representation of young adults in parliaments for democratic equality were highlighted.

14.3 External and Internal Sources of Democratic Inequality

14.3.1 Globalization

Democracy has something of an ambivalent relationship to globalization. On the one hand, globalization is typically seen as a product of the highest stage of democratic development – a benign condition of healthy interdependence made possible by the attainment of a prior condition of democracy among its beneficiaries. Globalization is, in effect, the product of a democratic peace. On the other hand, the more detailed analysis of the consequences of globalization typically depicts globalization as a complex agent of de-democratization – something whose attainment makes the practice of democracy ever more difficult. Globalization produces, in other words, a democratic deficit.

The two perspectives are not strictly incompatible. But this kind of connection is rarely made, with the literature and wider public discourse of and about globalization typically resolving itself to a positive and benign view of globalization starkly counterposed to a negative view of globalization's corrosive effects.

The aim of this section is to bring these two opposed perspectives into greater dialogue. The argument is presented in two parts dealing, respectively, with the challenge posed by globalization and the responses to which it might give rise.

14.3.1.1   The Challenge of Globalization

14.3.1.1.1   Semantics

Globalization is in fact a generic term for a rather disparate array of things understood in a great variety of different ways. For the most part,

however, these understandings can be arrayed along a continuum. This ranges from the geographically least precise and unexacting to the geographically most restrictive and demanding. At the former end of the spectrum, to point to globalization means little more than to identify cross-border flows of goods and services, finance, migrants, pollutants, infectious agents, and so forth. By contrast, at the latter end of the spectrum, such flows need to be increasingly planetary in their scope to be regarded as evidence of globalization. Yet this is not the only definitional divide. It is important also to distinguish between contending understandings of globalization in terms of whether it is seen as a condition or property of the world system that has *already been achieved* or as a *still ongoing process* or tendency (which may be resisted) for the world system to become more global or global*ized* over time.

Such definitional choices have significant implications – both for whether we see evidence of globalization or not and, indeed, for the significance of any such observation for the viability of democratic systems of governance. Clearly, if to confirm the globalization thesis we need only show a proliferation of cross-border flows of goods, services, and so forth, then evidence of globalization abounds. But understood in this way globalization may be rather less significant a factor than we tend to assume. Conversely, if to confirm the globalization thesis we need to establish that such flows are in fact both increasingly *extensive* in their (planetary) scope and increasingly *intensive* in their magnitude, then evidence of globalization is going to be rather more difficult to find – but all the more significant if, as, and when we do find it.

There is clearly plenty of room for conceptual confusion here. Authors who may well agree on the facts themselves may nonetheless disagree over the extent of globalization simply because they impose upon the term different definitional standards. Indeed, on closer inspection what may seem at first like a dispute over the evidence itself often boils down to little more than a semantic difference of opinion.

The full implications of this become clear when we start to look in more detail at those theories that suggest that globalization and the respect for democratic choice are likely to be in significant tension with one another. For, as we shall see, what many of these share is a common analytical structure in which the effects for democracy of globalization (typically, a series of imperatives) are derived logically from stylized assumptions about both the behavior and motives of business and the degree of integration of world markets. It is to such theories directly that we now turn.

14.3.1.1.2   Globalization as a Source of Economic Imperatives

The idea that globalization is corrosive, if not of democracy itself, then of the effective space for democratic choice – since its effects serve to restrict the array of credible policy options – is not a new one. But in its contemporary form it is simply stated. In closed national economies, such as those that characterized the pre-globalization era, capital was essentially immobile and national in character; it had no "exit" option. In such an environment governments could impose punitive taxation regimes upon unwilling and relatively impotent national businesses with little cost to the domestic economy.

In a world of globalization, by contrast, open economy conditions pertain. Capital may now exit from national economies at minimal cost. Accordingly, by playing off the regulatory regimes of different economies against one another, capital can ensure for itself the highest rate of return on its investment. *Ceteris paribus*, capital will exit higher taxation jurisdictions for their lower taxation counterparts, comprehensive welfare states for residual states, highly regulated labor markets for flexible labor markets, and economies characterized by strict environmental regulations and high union density for those characterized by lapse environmental standards and low union density.

The process pits national economy against national economy in an increasingly intense competitive struggle. States must effectively clamber over one another in an ever more frenzied attempt to produce a more favorable investment environment for mobile ("footloose") foreign direct investors than their competitors. Yet this is not a one-shot game – and an early influx of foreign direct investment only increases the dependence of the state upon its continued "locational competitiveness." If investment is to be retained in such an environment, states must constantly strive to improve the investment opportunities they can offer relative to those of their competitors. Any failure to do so can only precipitate a hemorrhaging of invested funds, labor shedding and, eventually, economic crisis. Big government, and more importantly perhaps the democratic choice for big government, is rendered increasingly anachronistic – a guarantor not of the interests of citizens or even consumers, but a sure means to disinvestment and economic crisis.

If this is the general form of the argument, then there are two important extensions of it that are also important to consider. The first concerns financial markets – and the political imperatives arising from the financial market integration associated with globalization. The second is more specific to the period following the global financial crisis. It concerns public debt, the state's obligations to its creditors and the associated political imperatives arising from such financial dependence.

Globalization, of course, is not only associated with trade and foreign direct investment flows. Increasingly significant in accounts of globalization's political imperatives are financial flows, particularly short-term financial flows. Here the argument is again very simple. In a world of heightened financial interdependence, financial market actors can be seen, effectively, to "take positions" on the policy preferences exhibited by governments. In a sense they reward and penalize governments for their conduct of domestic economic governance. In so doing, they have the capacity to wreak almost instant domestic havoc through the positions they adopt in foreign exchange markets and/or by modifying the effective rate of interest on government debt. Understood in this way, governments have a need to appease financial market actors through their economic and social policy choices by, in effect, internalizing a series of external and non-negotiable financial imperatives (for fiscal prudence, deficit, and debt reduction through austerity and a hawkish commitment to price stability). Such imperatives, once again, circumscribe as they discipline democratic governance at the national level.

Finally, in a context of unprecedented levels of public (and, indeed, private) debt following the global financial crisis, such imperatives are typically seen to have been ratcheted up several notches. As Wolfgang Streeck (2014) puts it, today's nation-states are "consolidation states," simultaneously beholden to their citizens for democratic legitimacy and to global financial market institutions for the borrowing on which their spending relies. Here, as elsewhere, global economic interdependence makes democratic governance a more complex juggling of conflicting imperatives in which the capacity to respond directly to the demands of citizens is seemingly attenuated.

But is this credible? Insofar as we are right to accept the combined and mutually reinforcing logics of the argument democratic choice is, at the national level at least, profoundly threatened by economic globalization. The stakes could scarcely be higher. And for this reason, above all, we need to proceed with some caution.

While the logic is compelling and has proved exceptionally persuasive, not least among political elites, the evidence for the anticipated effects of such a logic is not nearly so strong. The problem here is the convenient simplicity of the analytical assumptions from which logics of this kind are derived that assumes, for instance, that all taxation is anathema to the interests of capital. It is but a short step to the imperative of fiscal and, hence, state retrenchment.

But this stands in marked contrast to the available empirical evidence. This shows, among other things, a strong, positive, and strengthening correlation between state expenditure and economic growth under conditions of globalization; a propensity for foreign direct investment to be attracted not by low but by high rates of corporate taxation, not by highly flexible but in fact tightly regulated labor markets and not by low but by high environmental standards; and a similar tendency for financial market actors to be comparatively lenient on budget deficits, accumulated debt, and even the inflationary preferences of governments (and central banks), at least in OECD countries.

The reason for all of this is relatively simple. State expenditure, and hence the taxation receipts out of which it is funded, is not nearly as damaging to competitiveness nor, relatedly, to the return on capital invested, than is typically assumed in such models. Foreign direct investors, it seems, seek not deregulated labor markets nor low corporate taxation so much as highly skilled and flexible labor, stable industrial relations regimes and privileged access to the kinds of affluent consumer economies typically characterized by the highest levels of social and other state expenditure. Similarly, in a context of incomplete and costly information, financial markets are less discriminating – and, crucially, less constraining – in their behavior than we tend to assume (Mosley 2003).

This suggests that the space for democratic deliberation and the national policy-making autonomy on which it relies is not as restricted as we might assume. But there is a catch. Insofar as our political elites are impressed by such logics they may well act as if such non-negotiable economic imperatives were real (Hay and Rosamond 2002). The effect is much the same, even if the mechanism by which it is achieved is very different.

14.3.1.2   The Prospects for Political Globalization

This is all very well – and for how we think about democratic governance at the national level, it is undoubtedly profoundly important. But it is to privilege the national level and, in a context of globalization, that is unquestionably problematic. Perhaps the simplest way to conceive of this is in terms of the uneven character of the process of, not economic, but *political* globalization. We might think of this in terms of the (uneven) globalization of political problems and the globalization of political solutions – the point, of course, being that there is a gross disparity between the former (evidence of which abounds) and the latter (where we are surely right to identify a governance deficit).

Both forms of political globalization pose problems for traditional forms of democratic governance, which tend to privilege the national level. Two examples serve particularly to reveal the extent of the difficulty. The first is the challenge of global climate change. Here, respect for the democratic preferences of citizens at the national level is likely to profoundly compromise the capacity and authority to impose solutions at a global level. And, while we still lack a vision of what a genuinely democratic, yet at the same time global, resolution of such a problem might entail, this disparity between national and global solutions is likely to manifest itself in terms of a political stalemate.

The second example, the problem of global financial market regulation, seems as yet no less intractable. Here again we witness the palpable disparity between the need for, and supply of, global governance. If, indeed, global financial market actors are as globally interconnected and interdependent as the global financial crisis reveals them to be, then regulation at a national level, however prudential, cannot guard against crisis through contagion. Clearly global governance is required. Yet in a context in which different states have, in effect, different exposures to and investments in the financial markets they ostensibly regulate there is a proliferation of potential veto players in the move from national to global regulation. The outcome is predictable. The transition from national to global governance, despite the inherent logic of such a move, has proved as yet impossible. Here the impediment is not so much the capacity to envision democratic global governance as to envisage genuinely global governance at all.

And herein lies the cusp of our contemporary dilemma. There is a demonstrable and palpable need for global governance and yet, at the same time, a clear and compelling argument that respect for the democratically expressed wishes of citizens at the national level is both anathema to, and will ultimately always thwart, the passing of political authority from the national to the transnational level. In the end there is only one solution to that problem – the envisioning of a form of global governance that is not only efficacious at a planetary level but also credibly democratic at the planetary level too. That is a tough ask – a challenge to political theorists as much as it is a challenge to proponents of democratic global governance.

Put bluntly, we have yet to make democracy and globalization compatible – and we have, for far too long, proceeded on the rather naively optimistic basis that, since globalization is a benign process, there is little or no risk to promoting its development in advance of any clear strategy for its democratization. We are rapidly reaching the point at which that comforting delusion no longer holds – and, in so doing, we reach a political watershed. The choice is ours.

14.3.2   Populism: The Danger to Be Avoided

After years of neglect, populism is now a central theme of political experience and research. Until recently, interest in the study of populism was traditionally strongest among scholars who saw it as a problem. Political scholars who have suggested that populism might have a positive role to play in contemporary democracy are thus rare. For this minority, however, populism's putative virtues include "folk politics" versus "institutionalized politics"; the concerns of large numbers over the interests of the few; the lived experience of local, the village, the neighborhood over an abstract, distant state; and finally the consistent actualization of popular sovereignty as the substance of the whole over and above constitutional rules (Canovan 1999; Mudde 2001). Populist scholars emphasize also the political directness, sincerity, and transparency of ordinary people versus the indirection and opacity of representative institutions; they oppose the "purity" of political purpose of the many to the bargaining games by the politicians, who are part of the few and the elite; they praise decisiveness (and also decisionism) over time-consuming parliamentary compromises, procedural formalism, and institutional obfuscation; they use the language of the organic unity of the populus rather than the artificial and abstract language of intellectuals and scholars; finally they stress the priority and homogeneity of the whole versus pluralism and the conflict of interests (Canovan 2002; Kazin 1995). They make the character of populism overlap with that of democracy and propose to see both of them as the best expressions of politics, the art of persuasion and decision by which means the people construct their community according to their will (Laclau 2005b).

Despite the power contrasts drawn by scholars sympathetic to populism, they have yet to converge on even a rough definition of it. Populism remains a deeply contested term, more useful polemically than analytically, often used merely to brand and accuse actual political movements or leaders; this explains the "repugnance with which words 'populism' and 'populist' are uttered," particularly among European scholars (D'Eramo 2013: 5). However, recent events in Europe and the United States and recent literature have helped shed light on populism and some agreement is possible upon basic definitions of it concerning its ideological character, its relation to democracy's promises of public equality, its sociocultural content, and its strategic mechanism.

14.3.2.1   Populism's Recognizable Characters

Although plural and diverse because it is socially and historically contextual, populism develops within representative democracies (not merely democracies) as a fight over the meaning and representation of the people, an extreme expression of intense majority politics and thus a straining of constitutional democracy to its extreme limits, beyond which a change of regime (tyranny or dictatorship) could occur. Recognizing populism's contextual specificity (thus its plural manifestations) is no impediment to using comparative analyses in view of understanding the reasons of its present success in democratic societies. All populist movements exhibit a strong reservation and even hostility to the mechanisms of representation, in the name of an almost unanimous collective affirmation of the will of the people under a leading figure and above party pluralism. Yet they do not renounce representation to institute direct democracy. Populism is "parasitical" not on democracy in general but rather on representative democracy in particular;[4] it is a distorted form developing from within it, rather than a regime of its own. The relationship of populism with democracy is an issue of contention rather than compatibility.

Populism is not external to representative democracy but competes with it about the meaning and use of representation as a strategy for claiming, affirming, and managing the will of the masses. Its representative claim is the source of its radical contestation of parliamentary democracy, its real target. Indeed, it treats pluralism (of interests and ideas, but also as manifested by parties) as litigious claims that fragment the body of popular sovereignty and thus must be simplified so as to create a polarized scenario that makes the people immediately know how to judge and with whom to side. *Simplification* and *polarization* are in the view of achieving a deeper unification of the masses against the existing elites and under an organic narrative that most of the time a leader embodies (Urbinati 2014). Benjamin Arditi has thus written (2008) that populism can be seen as representative democracy's "internal periphery" hardly conceivable without a politics of personality. Hence, we propose to identify populism with two intertwined political processes: one that goes toward polarization of the citizenry in two homogenous groups (the many and the few), and the other that goes toward a verticalization of the political system that minimizes the role of deliberation and mediation and exalts instead that of strong majorities and steadfast decisions. Polarization and Caesarism go hand in hand and both of them constitute a radical challenge to constitutional democracy. Populism can thus be rendered in the following way: it is a symptom of representative democracy's malaise as denunciation of the failure of constitutional democracy to be consistent with its promises of guaranteeing that all citizens enjoy an equal political power and that public equality is the norm leading institutions, politicians, and citizens.

14.3.2.2 The Promise of Democracy

Both in its classical and modern version, democracy promises to institute and guarantee legal, civil, and political equality. It promises isonomia or that all the members of the demos (the citizens) are equal as subjects to the law and are treated equally by the law. To make legal equality and civil equality certain and secure, modern constitutions incorporate a list of rights that limit the decision-making power of the government and watch over the equal treatment of all by the magistrates. Democracy promises also *isegoria* or that all adult citizens have the same identical political power when making decisions on public issues and the same chance to speak up frankly in public, to

associate for and promote their views. In representative government, this entails that as *electors* all are identical because their votes have equal weight (on this premise only majority rule achieves democratic legitimacy); and it entails that as *citizens* are all different in their social conditions and endowed with an equal right to give voice to their differences, to form and make public their opinions, to know what their government does, and finally to influence elected and electors as well.

Legal, civil, and political equality inspire both the mode and the substance of public behavior because identical as members of the demos and in their voting power, democratic citizens are not identical and not even equal when they give expression to their voice and cast their vote. In relation to its promises of equality, thus, democracy proposes things that at first glance seem contradictory: that political power should be distributed regardless of the social, cultural, and economic conditions of the citizens and that it should be used by the citizens to make sure that those conditions are not so unequal if the equal political power is to be effective. Democracy claims that procedures must ignore the social conditions of the citizens and yet that they will be used so that the citizens can make their social condition a close as possible to their political status. The tension between formal and substantial equality is in the very genes of democracy, not an accident or a defect because citizens' equality refers to both a way of making decisions (government form) and a way of participating in making them (political form). This makes a procedural conception of democracy simply an incomplete picture.

A purely procedural reading is too narrow to be explicative of the potentials and transformations that a democratic society is capable of. For sure it can hardly grasp populistic forms of representation but also ideological identifications among citizens and partisan aggregations animating the public forum. To complete our picture, we should consider that in nation-state based constitutional governments, the diarchic nature of democracy has been actualized through the construction of "the people" as the legal and legitimate sovereign of the law but also as the representative claimant that contests and proposes, that reclaims its visibility beyond its legal status. Like democracy, the people possess a double nature as is at once the norm or legal actor in whose name decisions are made and the concrete actor of the proposals and decisions.

De jure and de facto levels are intertwined and their tense combination makes a democratic society an amalgam in permanent and sometime turbulent motion, in which the promises of equality are at once working procedures and instigations to social criticism and innovation. This tension feeds populism, which represents an all-political transformation of the forum of opinions that becomes a force more authoritative than elections, often amplified by the media. Populism repudiates democracy's diarchy of opinion and decision in view of merging fully the way people think and the way people want. It is to representative democracy what demagoguery was to direct democracy.

---

[4] Following Arditi (2008) we take this definition of a parasite from Jacques Derrida (1988: 90): "The parasite then 'takes place.' And at the bottom, whatever violently 'takes place' or occupies a site is always something of a parasite. Never quite taking place is then part of its performance, or its success, as an event, or its 'taking place.'" Populism is a permanent possibility within representative democracy, and the "never taking place" refers to its being a permanent mobilizing possibility even when it is strong enough to manifest its power. If all the populist potentials were actualized it would replace representative democracy altogether but this would be a regime change (as, for example, what happened when fascism "took place").

According to Aristotle's pivotal analysis, demagoguery within democracy is: (a) a permanent possibility insofar as it relies upon the public use of speech and opinion like democracy; (b) a more intense use of the principle of the majority so as to make it almost absolute or a form of power more than a method for making decisions (populism is the rule of the majority rather than a politics that uses majority rule); and (c) a waiting room for a possible tyrannical regime. We may attribute the following four aspects to populism: it flourishes as a fellow traveler of democracy; is a radical form of democratic action as strong majoritarianism; develops in times of social distress and increasing inequality; and its outcome may be risky to constitutional democracy (Taggart 2000).

14.3.2.3   Populism's Contextual Specificity

A complex category hard to synthetize in a clear-cut definition, populism's factors and implications are deeply contextual and connected to the malaise of democratizing or democratic societies. In the United States, where the term was coined as a party name in the age of post-civil war industrial reconstruction and never brought upon a regime change, populism developed along with political democratization and was, and still is, predictably met positively by historians and political theorists because of its claim of inclusion of the many or not so well represented (Kazin 1995). Born when the country was ruled by an elected notabilate representing the interests of an oligarchy (before universal suffrage was implemented), the Declaration of Independence and the Bill of Rights became extant conditions for a more democratized polity, and populism a collective movement against the "domestic enemies of the people" (Frank 2010) in the name of an alleged purity of the origins of popular government and its adulteration by the artificial complexity of civilization and the institutional organization of the state (Lasch 1991). The bureaucratic and normative state apparatus, which started to be built in the mid-nineteenth century, made the work of the government more distant from the people and its operations more opaque and hard to understand for ordinary citizens.

On the other hand, in some Latin American countries, "the land of populism" in Carlos de la Torre's words (2016), populism has been met with mixed feelings in relation to its historical phases: thus whether it was evaluated at the beginning of its career or at the pick of its fulfillment as a regime; as an opposition party mobilizing against an existing government or as a regime itself; and then also, as a regime in its consolidation or facing a succession in power (Finchelstein 2014; Rovira Kaltwasser 2012). Like in the United States, populism in Latin America also emerged in the age of social modernization but much like fascism in Italy it governed the path toward modernity that used state power to protect and empower their popular classes, repress dissent, and meanwhile implement social-welfare policies (Germani 1978). Thus Ernesto Laclau (2005a) described populist (and Peronism in particular) as a strategy of hegemonic rebalancing within the "power blocs" through the incorporation of the popular-democratic ideology of the masses within the ruling majority. Finally, in Western Europe, populism made its appearance with democratization in the early twentieth century, along with colonial expansionism, militarization of society coinciding with the First World War, and the growth of ethnic

nationalism per effect of the distress that the war had caused. It helped justify xenophobic ideologies that aimed at homogenizing the nation and in fact promoted Fascist regimes based on mass propaganda, political simplification of friends/enemies divide, and Caesaristic leadership incorporating the people as one (Mueller 2011).

Populism is growing once again, not only in Latin America and in poor societies struggling to modernize and democratize. Populism is back in several European countries, within a supranational quasi-federative context and several decades of cosmopolitan culture of rights and toleration that lessened nationalistic politics. The European Union that developed as anti-totalitarian project after the Second World War, is a novel frontier of populism, which is emerging no longer and simplistically as a claim for going back to a pre-European Union order, but rather as a design for a new representation of the European peoples as ancestral totalities against external sources of contamination such as affluent cosmopolitan elites and migrants. Decline of socioeconomic well-being combines with an erosion of democratic legitimacy in relaunching populist leaders and movements in several European states and also the Unites States, which is experiencing resurgent nativism aimed against immigrants much like the old Europe and is no longer the exceptional and only place in which populism is the name of good democracy. To be sure, there are some left-wing forms of populism in both continents that claim to be inclusive of the new immigrants rather than exclusionary, yet they make their claim not in the name of the democratic promises but as a challenge to the constitutional fabric of representative democracy (Weyland 2013).

Renascent populism witnesses waning confidence in core representative democratic institutions such as parties, parliaments, and elections. As leading scholars have stressed, shrinking party membership and increasing estrangement between politicians and voters testify to disillusionment with representative democracy (Mair 2013; Manin 1997; Merkel 2014b; Rosanvallon 2015). Politicians are regularly accused of having lost touch with ordinary people's concerns and made politics into an insipid mainstreamism that chooses to neglect society's most grave needs and concerns in order not to compromise electoral consent. Yet antiparty sentiment is primed to damage constitutional democracy as citizens need to be offered recognizable political proposals in order to side with and against and choose and participate. Thus, in consolidated democracies populism seems to follow a cycle of electoral abstention and apathy, which is a side effect of mainstreamism and at the origin of citizens' mistrust in party politics, the growth of antiparty sentiments, and the attraction of the populist rebuff of "practical democracy" (Mair 2002). When elected politicians and citizens become two separate groups that make the opposition between "the many" and "the few" an easily grasped catchword, when ordinary citizens witness increase of social distress and gross violations of economic equality in the general indifference of their representatives and while the most powerful acquire more voice in politics, it may very well happen that people distrust "practical politics" (Mény and Surel 2002).

These are traditional factors that help explain the growth of populism in democratic societies: the quest for more intense power by the majority is primed to emerge from time to time like a symptom of mistrust in democracy's ability to fulfill its promise of equal political power. Yet some additional factors contribute today in reinvigorating the populist rhetoric, such as a globalized financial capitalism that weakens the decision-making power of sovereign states and a globalized market of labor force that narrows the possibility of striking a social-democratic compromise between capital and labor upon which democracy was rebuilt after the Second World War. The weakening of state sovereignty before global corporate business meets with the people's call for closed borders in several nation-states as if democratic citizens thought that the protection of their political power demands the containment of free movement of peoples and of free competition over salary and social benefits. Like in the past, populism associates politics of social redistribution with protectionist politics; in addition, the dramatic phenomenon of terrorism associated with Islamic extremism propels a politics of state security at the expense of civil rights and highlights the nationalistic character of democracy as a vital condition of cultural and religious homogeneity to be protected against external enemies. Hence, in several member-states of the European Union, anti-European sentiments, economic distress, and a cultural discourse dominated by cosmopolitan elites determine a representative deficit that can open a political space for those who have the perception of not having their voice represented: populist leaders are primed to find there an inviting milieu for their antiestablishment plans.

In a globalized world, populism comes to play two roles: that of denouncing social inequality and the privileges of the wealthy few and that of reclaiming the priority of the national unity of the people. Resuming the two ancient categories – *ethnos* and *demos* – whose mix steered the construction of post-eighteenth-century democratic "people," one might say that populism's renaissance in several democratic countries is both a symptom and a triggering force that can disrupt that mix. Indeed, on the one hand, the demos ("the people") tends to deflate its political meaning as the collective of equals in power (citizens/electors) and to translate it into a social unit identified with the majority and, on the other hand, the ethnos ("the nation"), which the political nation of the equal subjects to the law was meant to clear of all ancestral meanings, tends to be identified with pre-political characters not acquirable by simply being subjects to the law (Portinaro 2013). Briefly, populism combines two processes: of politicization of the ethnical aspect and of ethnicization of the political aspect that have made for "the popular sovereign" in modern democracy. It thus shows how weak and context-dependent the roots of representative democracy are.

14.3.2.4 Populism's Strategic Mechanisms

Based on these premises, a distinction has to be made between *populism as a popular movement* and *populism as a ruling power*, a prospective that allows us to face populism both in its rhetorical style, its propaganda tropes and ideology, and finally its aims and achievements. This double condition mirrors the diarchic character of democracy we have mentioned: power of decision and power of opinion qualify constitutional democracy as an order in which citizens have an equal right to make decisions by voting directly on issues (referenda) and for representatives and to construct the issues or claims that ask for decisions to be made, sustained, or revised.

Populism has to be evaluated and judged in relation to both authorities: as a movement of opinion and as a system of decision-making.

It is inaccurate to treat it as identical with "popular movements," movements of protest, or "the popular" as it can be much more than that. Hence there is populist rhetoric but not yet populist power when the polarizing and anti-representative discourse is made up of a social movement that wants to be a constituency independent of elected officials, wants to resist becoming an elected entity, does not have nor want representative leaders unifying its several claims, and wants to keep elected officials or the government under the scrutiny of the public. This was the case, for instance, in popular movements of contestation and protest like the Girotondi in Italy in 2002, Occupy Wall Street in the Unites States in 2011, and Indignados in Spain in 2011. Without an organizing narrative, the aspiration to win seats in the Parliament or the Congress and a leadership claiming its people to be the true expression of the people as a whole, a popular movement remains very much what it is: a sacrosanct democratic movement of opinion, protest, and contestation against a trend in society that betrays some basic principles of equality, which society itself has promised to respect and fulfill.

On the other hand, there is populist rhetoric and populist power when a movement does not want to be a constituency independent of the elected officials but wants instead to conquer the representative institutions and win a majority in order to model society on its own ideology of the people. This is, for instance, the case of Hungary's Fidesz party that in 2012 won a supermajority of the seats in Parliament and used it to scrap the old Constitution by amending it continuously, entrenching its own political vision at the expense of opposition parties and an independent judiciary. Similar events happened in Poland after the electoral victory of Kaczyński's PiS after 2014.

Populism, both as a movement and populism as an intrastate power, is parasitical on representative democracy either because it opposes representative democracy or wants to conquer it. But while a certain populist rhetoric is to be detected in almost all parties (particularly when they radicalize their claims close to elections), populism as a ruling power has some recognizable characteristics that can sharply contrast with "practical democracy" and the procedural structures of ordinary politics, like hostility toward party pluralism, the principles of constitutional democracy and the division of powers. Hence although ingrained in the ideology of the people and the language of democracy, populism as a ruling power tends to give life to governments that stretch the democratic rules toward an extreme majoritarianism, often discriminating against minorities. Populism in power is a *pars-pro-toto* project that may have devastating effects on constitutional democracy (Arato 2013). This makes me conclude that while a symptom of political and social malaise in democratic societies, populism can hardly be a cure. Factors driving populism can be found in the partial regimes of elections and political rights to participation within embedded democracies (see Section 14.1), where people at the lower end of the social strata feel systematically excluded and underrepresented or simply fear to be victims of threats they cannot face and control with ordinary legal and political means. In addition, a cause for populist discourse is also to be found in the partial regime of "power to govern" as national sovereignty is challenged by global markets and supranational governances such as the European Union. Yet regardless of its social specificity and the objective duress that fuels it, if populism comes to power it explicitly challenges the proper working of the "civil rights" regime and the regime of horizontal accountability granting too much power to the executive (decisionism and democracy of the leader) at the expenses of the legislature and the judiciary (deliberation and the rule of law). The problem is that although populist leaders seeking power promise to include the excluded and overturn an elected oligarchy, once in power they end up by attacking the institutions of liberal democracy, seizing central government, controlling and even repressing social movements and oppositions, limiting civil liberty, and contrasting media pluralism. For this reason, although a symptom of malaise of democratic societies, populism can hardly be a remedy.

14.3.3 Technology and Science

As contemporary societies increasingly build their governance structures and their imaginations about future developments around scientific knowledge, as they privilege specific kinds of expertise and embrace technological innovation as a sign of advancement, it is essential to carefully reflect how this politics of knowledge and technology is entangled with questions of inequality. When it comes to questions of democracy and inequality we often witness the coexistence of rather contradictory positions. Political leadership strongly tries to construct and keep alive an unquestioned ideal of scientific and technological rationality as a key governance principle, pretending that this would quasi-automatically improve democratic societies and render them more equal for its constituencies. However, simultaneously concerns are voiced that science and technology might contribute to reinforcing existing, or even creating new, inequalities. Indeed, access to the advancements in science and technology had become an important generator of power differentials both within and across societies.

The situation is complex. While both scientific knowledge and technologies have definitely created partial solutions to problems in the areas of health, food, energy, communication, or transport, inequalities persisted. Thinking democracy and inequality together, thus means to question the impact of the knowledge and technological infrastructures that form the basis of contemporary democracies, to be attentive to the many places and moments the performance of democracy is tied to questions of techno-scientific choices, and to unpack the new challenges citizens have to face in order to fully participate in contemporary societies.

(In)equality has to be understood as a situated outcome of specific forms of techno-scientific change that are always shifting. In analogy also "a democratic society cannot fully or at every moment be a democracy" and will "depend upon mutually reinforcing democratic ideas, political culture, political imaginaries, institutions, and practices" (Ezrahi 2012). Science and technology play an essential part in both, democracy and (in)equality. The aim is to think how we can bring them together reasonably well.

The attention therefore has to move from asking principled questions – is something democratic and do techno-scientific developments create conditions of equality – to the multiplicity of situations in which both democracy and equality are to be realized. This also means considering shifting socioeconomic conditions, the ways in which access to education and to different kinds of innovation is structured, the distribution of the

capacities to raise voice in relation to techno-scientific issues, and many more. And it becomes essential to investigate the structural conditions – that is, technological, educational, or market infrastructures – which might keep inequalities in place.

14.3.3.1 Values, Science, and Technology: Whose Values?

Scholarship in science and technology studies (STS) has shown how the knowledge and technologies we create and the dominant values and normative ideals we express in our societies have to be seen as deeply intertwined (Jasanoff 2004). As a consequence, we have to admit that the places where technologies are designed and knowledge is generated matter as well as the persons who hold the capacity to steer or at least to participate in these processes. Scientific knowledge and its technological realizations are thus imbued with values specific to the environment in which they were created; they have to be understood as (re)producing existing value orders. In terms of asking the democracy–equality question it is thus essential to pay attention to who gets imagined as potential user (groups) and who is forgotten; to who defines the problems to be solved and what counts as adequate solution; to the places where innovations are created; and, finally, how sets of values get imposed through the introduction of new technologies or the foregrounding of specific kinds of knowledge.

This calls us to pay attention to how specific technological arrangements are tacitly implemented for keeping certain social or political orders in place. In particular feminist scholars such as Judy Wajcman (2009) have pointed to the fact that the material forms in which technologies come, afford or inhibit certain gender power relations. If we consider the importance of broader economic and social circumstances of technological production, the exclusion of specific groups of people (women, members of lower socioeconomic classes, etc.) from technological domains points to a reinforcement of inequalities in a techno-scientific world. This then does not stay limited to questions of equal employment opportunities, but it is about how and for whom the world we live in gets shaped. The politics of knowledge and technology is thus integral to the renegotiation of power relations – with gender and other inequalities as the focus.

14.3.3.2 Ordering Societies Through Classification and Standardization: Whose Order?

A second site where questions of democracy and inequality are addressed are the classifications and standards that have become the basic infrastructures assuring that contemporary societies can work. Whether or not you are granted certain civil rights, have access to specific kinds of health care, or can chose your way of living, all this is related, in one way or another, to how well somebody is represented in such classifications and standardization processes. Thus, the very idea of equality and its realization in the political realm very much depend on the outcome of such orderings of society. Throughout the nineteenth and twentieth centuries we witness countless efforts of emerging nation-states to classify their constituency and thus make them calculable – efforts to design nation-states in line with what is believed to be scientific rationality (J.C. Scott 1999).

These processes of ordering society produced ever more extended collections of information on citizens, social relations, economic life, and many more, but also supported numerous planning efforts meant to realize desired futures. Such processes never simply describe the world as it is, but they make it through the description. The census, for example, contributed to the creation of communities that did not exist prior to the counting of and the accounting for them. In the end, it was a small elite who decided what should be counted and what order should prevail, thus allowing political power greater control over the lives of their subjects.

While classifications and standards are essential to extending our reach in space and time, we have to be aware that "each standard and each category valorizes some point of view and silences another" (Bowker and Star 1999). While we can argue that classifying is inescapable if we want to live in an ordered world, it is still related to value choices. Classifications and standards advantage some while pushing others to the margin, some areas get privileged while others suffer. The power of these classifications lies in the fact that over time they are regarded as "natural" and are taken for granted. They only become explicit when belonging to a specific category denies access or does not give the same rights as to others. In many ways ethnic and racial, but also gender and sexual categorizations, though used very differently in different national and supranational contexts, are excellent examples for the making of essential differences and thus defining relevant groups, to be cared for. Democratic societies therefore need to carefully reflect how these classifications are made, and how they are decided upon, giving voice to specific groups and individuals, while implicitly denying it to others.

Part of these questions of addressing differences have been more recently reformulated in an expanding diversity discourse, which tries to reevaluate what it means to attend to differences among human bodies and lives. Implementing the concept of diversity in health care, which is a key area where inequality matters, shows the difficulty of dealing with bringing together social justice concerns with evidence about the uneven distribution of health and disease across populations, with empowering and positive visions of differences and concerns of being able to uphold contemporary health care systems (Felt, Felder, and Penkler 2016). Access to health care is one such site where classifications potentially can both create better access and create (new) inequalities.

14.3.3.3   Living in an Experimental Society: Whose Benefit, Whose Voice?

More than two decades of scholarship have pointed at the experimental nature of contemporary societies, that is, at our limited capacity to anticipate the outcomes of techno-scientific change. The recent disaster in Fukushima has clearly pointed to the complexities and uncertainties of what it means to different groups of people to live with nuclear technologies. Or, when it comes to the impact of environmental damages, we clearly witness the unequal distribution of risks and benefits. Under the label of environmental justice STS scholars carefully investigated how the consequences of such real-world experiments often have to be carried in a disproportional manner by

marginalized groups, pointing to the importance of considering categories like race, gender, or class as they come to matter in important ways (e.g. Ottinger and Cohen 2011). Reflecting the nexus of democracy and inequality thus means asking: Who has the authority to design and do such experiments? Who is exposed to them? And, who might benefit from them? Answering these questions might lead us to understand how inequalities do both emerge and are kept in place.

These reflections have a quite immediate connection to two related debates: one on participatory justice in techno-scientific societies and the other on the role of information access in a world structured by new information and communication technologies (ICTs).

More than two decades ago, the question of an increased need for public participation started to be raised persistently with the crumbling of the strong belief that the spread of scientific knowledge and technologies across contemporary societies would lead to more democracy and equality. Concerns were voiced about the emergence of new hierarchies, allowing only a rather exclusive elite of knowledgeable subjects to direct societal choices. This has triggered a flurry of participatory exercises that were on a formal level deeply committed to openness, equality, representativeness, and transparency and in which citizens should be able to express their concerns regarding techno-scientific developments. However, science and technology studies scholars have pointed out the severe limitations such exercises meet in practice (Felt 2007). Not only are assumptions about who may legitimately speak in the name of society already built into participatory designs, in most exercises the questions were also pre-framed, severely limiting the potential outcomes. Furthermore, social orders are at work within the discussion settings, but a strong educational bias of those participating hinted at rather unequal conditions of participation (e.g. Chilvers and Kearnes 2016).

A number of case studies have successfully demonstrated the potential value of granting lay expertise space in shaping techno-scientific developments. Examples would be the AIDS movement in the 1970s that managed to change essential elements in treatment and prevention or, more recently, the citizen science groups forming around radiation measurements in the aftermath of the Fukushima disaster. In all these cases, we have seen how important it is to open up knowledge generation to different perspectives and how this allows important changes to be made to how democracy and equality can be connected in new ways.

This brings us to the question of ICTs, which feature prominently in debates concerning questions of science, technology, and inequality (Wyatt et al. 2001). When introduced, they were expected to free people from a number of limitations. Access to information from a broad variety of sources, participation in political processes from remote places as well as access to health expertise should become more equal. This should allow for a gain in overall justice and thus bring us closer to the ideal of democratic societies. This rather positive and inclusive view is, however, clearly opposed by analysts who argue that the "ICT revolution" might, quite to the contrary, be a source of new inequalities. Unequal access to the Internet between and within regions, but also the need to develop new skills in searching, sorting, and assessing information, creates advantages only for some while further disadvantaging others. Threats to exercise social control through different forms electronic surveillance would undermine the value of privacy held very high in liberal democracies and might affect vulnerable groups more than other parts of society. In the same move, we also witness new forms of segregation on the labor markets, given the information-intensive forms of work emerging. Finally, the spread of algorithms introduces unaccounted biases and calls for a broader public debate on these structures as one way to be able to reflect and navigate the information landscape in a self-defined manner.

To sum up, there is no doubt that science and technology have made essential contributions to the advancement of contemporary democracies. Yet, putting scientific and technological rationality at the core of governance has not necessarily led to creating more equality, both within nation-states as well as between regions of the world. It has in some areas even rendered societal inclusion more challenging than ever before. This means that we need to recognize that fostering science and technology alone will not suffice to create the desired outcome, but that new models assuring access to the benefits of techno-scientific advances for broader constituencies of societies and meaningful models of participation in the development of knowledge and innovations need to be developed. The challenge will remain, to achieve both building our democracies along techno-scientific rationalities and acknowledging that this is necessarily always also linked to ethical choices for which we need to take responsibility. Embracing science and technology can thus not be conceptualized as a moment of depoliticizing choices concerning the directions in which our societies develop, but much rather of acknowledging that this is politics by other means.

14.4   The Democratic Responses to These Challenges

14.4.1   Bringing the Demos Back In

"We the people" was a formative proposition, declaring many people a people and thereby constituting them as such. Moreover, it was a democratic people not only because the constitution organized fundamental democratic values – liberty, equality, well-being – into an institutional design, but also because the public debate between federalists and antifederalists created a democratic consciousness. A democratic people or demos is a body of political individuals that perceive themselves to be citizens within a state, one civic people, with conflicts and arguments, different representative institutions that nevertheless adhere to a set of rules, and feel part of a collective political identity. Democracy is government of the people, for the people and by the people: the people make the body politics of the sovereign state; the authors of its legitimacy. The demos rules by way of expressing the will of the people. This will is a shared will – to be part of the people, and to be involved in the decision-making and policy processes of the polity. Being a demos is a continuous prerequisite for democratic self-rule that embeds political equality: one person, one vote. Each citizen, being part of the body politic, has her own unique voice, cast as a vote. A vote for a candidate, party, worldview – that represents her through elections in the governing of the state. The will of the people is not one will of all the people, but an expression of the contingent will of the

majority, respecting the minorities, believing in continuous debate and the possibility of replacing the ruling power. Moreover, a citizen's political self-realization goes beyond just the vote, involving participation in political debate, the policy process, and the creation and recreation of the public will.

Much contemporary democratic practice and theory abandons the demos. However, while nationalism, populism, racism, and xenophobia are problems of and for contemporary democracy, democracy without a civic body within a sovereign state – that shares a political collective identity expressed through public media, public opinion, and public consciousness, and is based on shared values of freedom, self-realization, and crucially public equality – is a defective democracy.

14.4.1.1   Democracy and Inequality: The Structure of the Argument

Global inequality is becoming mixed up with social inequality. That is why the renationalization of democracy (through greater social cohesion and reappropriation of the political by citizens) is one way of combating both simultaneously. This struggle must therefore be a top priority for our time (Rosanvallon 2015: 299).

To suggest the renationalization of democracy in the post-national constellation of a globalized era sounds like a reactionary project. Yet renationalization – or, alternately, redemocratization of democracy by way of rethinking the demos as a core concept of democracy – is at the heart of democracy. Rosanvallon wants to renationalize democracy in order to combat economic inequality, analyzing capitalism as the driving force behind the crisis of democracy manifested in a crisis of equality. Yet the crisis of democracy is also a crisis of equality as a political concept. There are strong connections between economic inequalities and political disempowerment – but we consider democratic inequality on its own terms, as stemming from the disenchantment with the demos as the locus of the political collective identity. Re-instating the demos is thus a precondition for democratic equality.

This section addresses three basic challenges to the democratic state – cosmopolitanism, multiculturalism, and democratic governance – from the perspective of public equality. In contrast to some other contributions to this chapter, it argues that a demos is a fundamental part of democracy that embodies public equality and provides political dimension that the global or the local levels cannot replace.

14.4.1.2   Humanity as a Whole?

The argument for a cosmopolitan world community goes something like this: a state is an arbitrary, historically contingent invention; the ethical community that underlies all individuals is a cosmopolitan community, based on universal human rights, in a borderless world. Thus, since individuals possessing universal rights are all equal, the relevant moral community is the global one.

Is the idea of political community coextensive with a sovereign state redundant? From the ethical perspective, all humans possess human rights. But is the best way to protect human rights one unitary regime? Empirically, we live in a world of sovereign states with some international bodies that derive their legitimacy from agreements among the constituting states. There are no global political institutions whose legitimacy does not derive from states. Moreover, those international bodies enjoy declarative force but a minimal real ability to coerce or sanction against violations of human rights. Some members of the human rights council of the UN are far from protecting human rights in their own countries. Human rights may be universal in nature; yet, they are, today, best protected and practiced through being enshrined in the constitutions and public cultures and processes of democratic states. Thus, realizing human rights is not a given but a process. The idea of one ethical-political community actually undermines the legitimacy of sovereign states, thereby risking the only enclaves that actively protect human rights. But what about equality? Equality of the individuals is their equality as citizens within a state. There is a profound relation between their ability to experience self-autonomy and be active political citizens in a sovereign state. Being part of the policy process, of decision-making, of bringing about change – is crucial for the translation of autonomy into practice. It is hardly achievable in a global community.

Social policies, based on solidarity, are also under threat. It is one thing to pay taxes and gain national security, public health, and education, quite another to provide it to every traveler in a borderless society. Solidarity is an embodiment of the idea of public goods. The public good for humanity is almost an empty signifier. But the public goods that are being debated, decided upon, and acted on within a democracy are fundamental to democracy. In particular, the balance between economy and politics is a major function of states, which will be undermined by globalism. Neoliberalism – that seeks to weaken the state and let the market rule alone – would prevail. States are the only collective actors that act through fiscal and other means to change structures of inequality, to invest in the public domain, and to redistribute resources, as elected governments have the legitimacy to promote equality of opportunities. The poor would be poorer without states, and in a borderless world there would be no solidarity either with one's fellow citizens.

The third fundamental dimension of political equality that is being lost in a so-called global community is the demos as a discursive community. The "will of the people" is what emerges from political discussion, debates, conversations, contestations, and conflicts. Being part of the political discourse is what enables each citizen to be a political actor, who self-realizes herself in the public realm. The demos is not an ethnos, it is being part of a political community within a democratic state. Cosmopolitanism, for the sake of abstract universal rights, jeopardizes the protection of human rights via the rule of law and the fundamental role of the demos.

14.4.1.3   Multiculturalism: A Fragmented Political Arena?

The second challengers are voluntary associations – cultural, ethnic, religious, and local communities, usually situated in civil society. The argument is the following: the idea of shared values and active participation have a deeper political meaning in communities than in states,

where political behavior is reduced to voting and the national identity is loose. Local communities are more involving and relevant to the people than the abstract state. Politics as a way of life is best practiced in communities.

What happens to the concept of equality under a multicultural gaze? The liberal view assumes that community is the extension of the liberty of the individual; but what about equality? Free individuals are free to join different communities. But the main idea of equality is a second order one: equality of the groups to be different from one another. Equality of difference extended to communities. What happens to individuals under such a framework? Some might thrive; others might be sacrificing their human rights under the shared values of a particular community, women's rights in traditional communities notwithstanding. Still others may choose or find no significant community to be part of. The individual is no longer the building block of politics but of groups and hence is vulnerable. Who is to enshrine the individuals within those groups, and those without communities? The rule of law – the state.

What does multiculturalism mean for democracy? How do different communities collectively decide whether to go to war? Raise taxes? Decide what are the shared values or public goods? While communities act on their own interest, what authority do they have to act on behalf of individuals? Do African-Americans or Muslims or lesbians have shared ideas on fiscal policies, state/religion relations, or war and peace? Hardly. So communities perform a partial role and should not be viewed as alternatives to citizens acting together within states.

Finally, most communities are still based on a primordial association – one is born into an ethnos, religion, gender, or sex. A releasing power of democracy is that it treats individuals as equal. It provides a process of transformation of representation from identity into interests, ideology, and policy preferences. A citizen may choose whether she votes as a Catholic, worker, or feminist. It is not prescribed to her by a primordial identity. So communities may appear as much more engaging in nature but in fact fail to perform the roles of the democratic state in the various faces of equality. They may complement and revive the demos, not replace it.

14.4.1.4   Democratic Governance Beyond the Demos?

Contemporary theory argues that human societies are increasingly governed by a web of organizations that partake in the policy processes and provide global governance through deliberative democracy. Those voluntary associations – international NGOs, activists, social movements – are acting in the free market or civil society. This theory of governance connects the local with the global and gives only a partial role to states. But what is the account of public equality in a complex theory of governance?

14.4.1.4.1   Participation

Citizenship is a form of membership in the political game within democratic states. Active civil society extends participation far beyond voting. But moving participation from institutional democracy to global or local civil society entails moving from universal to voluntary participation; from individuals to organizations; from relatively compact participation – voting – into demanding engagement. The clear losers of such transformations are the disadvantaged groups. While voting is based on political equality, voluntary participation leaves those who lack time, resources, or education outside of the effective participation circle. True, in the minimal act of voting the dropping levels of participation is most dramatic for the poor. Yet, this would be even more the case in voluntary associations and deliberative processes in which the highly educated middle classes participate. Moreover, while within a democracy there is an institutionalized solidarity among the demos, enhancing public education and welfare, which facilitate participation, there is no such obligation in global civil society.

14.4.1.4.2   Political Representation

Voluntary associations, as the building blocks of new forms of representation, undermine the role of parties as the main representative actor in sovereign democracies. NGOs become the main actors. The move from the individual to the group is the first hindrance to equality. Politics of recognition – symbolic power and the right to be different communities – often works against economic equality. Also, in the party system the main ideological axis is the Left–Right axis: the major conflict in society is about redistribution of resources, life chances, and welfare. Identity politics moves the nexus of contestation from economics to culture and away from the state to global civil society, decreasing the centrality of economic and political equality on the political agenda.

14.4.1.4.3   Governing

As for governing, working through networks and deliberative governance means that the partners of policy-making are no longer elected representatives of the demos, but philanthropic or self-interested groups. Such groups have access to resources, decision makers, communication, media, and funding and thus discriminate against those who lack resources. There is no accountability. The main vow of democratic politics – self-rule of the people by the people for the people – is being severely damaged as the sovereign people has no priority in terms of decision-making, the public interest is not clear in a borderless world and it is not clear who governance networks work for – as they have no democratic legitimacy.

Crucially, networks of governance are almost always composed of those who have interests in the matter at hand. Instead of protecting the people from private and particular interest groups, which usually command the resources and the power, global governance adopts them as part of the web of decision makers. The silent majority is out of the web of stakeholders' deliberation. The self-selectivity of governance by networks, their lack of accountability and responsibility and the bias in their participation in the policy-making process, makes it highly problematic. Governing by networks actually undermines the legitimacy of sovereign states and democratic processes, as well as weakening the demos as the main unit of self-rule by incorporating those with clear interests into the policy-making process.

14.4.1.5   Reinstating the Demos Within Democracy

The crisis of democracy has led to advances that favor plurality and freedom over equality. Can the demos be reconstructed as a core concept of democracy in a post-national constellation? Democracy is an ongoing project. Citizenship is being extended from rich men to workers, to women, to immigrants. Politics is transformed and an active civil society enhances it. Yet at the core of the democratic project stands the individual, who becomes a political actor by way of belonging to a demos. Within this demos, a conversation and debates are going on about shared values, social policies, rights and wrongs. The basic value that holds this construction together is public equality between free individuals within a state, who form a political community. In our world, states can secure political rights. To go beyond the state should not mean to abandon the demos; multiethnic in its nature and hence remote from organic nationalism, and moving toward greater human rights on an international scale as a regulative norm, the evolving, equality-striving demos as a creation of democratic states is a guiding principle of humanism. It is therefore still a viable route to claim a civic demos at the heart of democratic polity as the main institutional design to embed public equality. Both universal rights as an ever-extending horizon for democracy and a rich active civil society within the public sphere, should enrich rather than undermine the ongoing discussion of the demos and provide new rather than fewer opportunities for equal citizens in sovereign states.

14.4.2   Democratic Innovations

New forms of participatory governance – often referred to as "democratic innovations" – are increasingly being enacted across the world in response to the failures of established institutions of representative government to promote and realize fully public equality. They are explicitly designed to increase and deepen participation by citizens in the political decision-making process. They are largely sponsored and organized by public authorities, although civil society organizations have also established democratic innovations independently or in collaboration with state actors. Such processes have engaged citizens in, for example, constitutional change, political reforms, formulation of public budgets, the implementation of social policies, and the monitoring of public services delivery. It is problematic, though, to generalize about their impact. Variations in design and implementation across the world mean that these institutions realize democratic goods in very different ways (Fung 2003; Smith 2009).

The spread of participatory practice does not entail that all democratic innovations respond effectively to political and social inequalities and exclusions and have meaningful impact. Many processes are poorly organized and can have detrimental effects, reinforcing inequalities and mistrust in public authorities and the democratic process.

But democratic innovations can be designed to overcome aspects of exclusion, giving voice to and increasing the well-being of politically and socially marginalized and disadvantaged social groups, increasing citizens' competence and political skills, and engaging citizens in the formulation and implementation of more just public and social policies. Citizens can exert meaningful influence, and in some cases control, over the decisions that affect their lives.

Given the complexity of practice, this section is necessarily selective and illustrative. We discuss briefly the practice of four democratic designs and the different ways in which they enhance public equality. Participatory budgeting, policy councils, and national public policy conferences originate from Latin America. This region has experienced an explosion of participatory governance following the period of redemocratization and decentralization that provided space for experimentation and institutionalization. The fourth innovation – randomly selected mini-publics – emerged in Europe and North America. Both participatory budgeting and mini-publics have experienced significant policy transfer.[5]

14.4.2.1 Participatory Budgeting

Participatory budgeting (PB) is arguably the best known democratic innovation and was designed with explicit recognition of the structural disadvantage suffered by poorer citizens. Typically operating at the municipal level, citizens participate in the definition, formulation, decision, and control of significant proportions of the municipal budget. PB was first established in Porto Alegre in 1989 and by the turn of the century around 16,600 citizens were participating annually in its popular assemblies, influencing the distribution of around $160 million in investments, Since then, PB has spread across Brazil and Latin America to more than 1,000 cities across Africa, Asia, Europe, North America, and Oceania. While there is evidence that PB can be transferred effectively, what has been implemented under the name of PB has not always reflected earlier Latin American experience. Much rests on the willingness of political authorities and pressure from civil society to embed more participatory and redistributive practices, in particular restructuring bureaucratic practices to build civic infrastructure in poorer neighborhoods and ensure swift implementation of decisions.

The attractiveness of PB, especially in Latin America, is tied to its capacity to ameliorate clientelism and corruption and generate a more equitable redistribution of public goods. Increased participation among disadvantaged, less educated, and lower-income groups reverses traditional patterns of influence on decision-making on budget distribution. There is evidence that PB improves social well-being, with increased spending in health care and decreases in infant mortality rates across Brazil's largest cities.

In its original form, PB was designed explicitly to separate demand-making and rule-making processes – both of which are controlled by citizens. In the demand phase, large numbers of citizens mobilize to propose and support local projects and hold the administration to account. In a separate rule-making phase, elected citizen representatives (with limited terms of office) from each district of the city establish and apply the rules to distribute the budget. As no district or partisan interest is able to dominate, the rules that guide the distribution of resources tend to reflect considerations of social justice, prioritizing the needs of the poor and infrastructure and services deficiencies (Smith 2009).

PB processes continue to innovate, developing digital and multichannel forms that broaden participation. For example, La Plata in Argentina combines offline, online, and remote (SMS) voting, which in its 2010 cycle directly engaged around 50,000 citizens: 10 percent of the local eligible population, many resident in remote and marginalized areas of the city. There has also been experimentation with specific policy areas, committees, and procedures (including quotas) dedicated to promoting the interests of women, young people, indigenous people, and other politically excluded groups.

14.4.2.2 Policy Councils

Policy councils bring together combinations of public officials, civil society organizations, ordinary citizens, private stakeholders, and service providers and users in areas such as development, infrastructure, and social policies. In some countries, such as Brazil and Paraguay, virtually all cities have a form of policy council and there are national level councils in several countries. In Mexico, for example, there are at least 163 councils at the federal level with an advisory role on various fields of public policy, including environment, rural and economic development, culture, education, health, and security. The design of policy councils has varied as their practice spread, as has their capacity to provide a space in which marginalized social groups are able to advance their interests.

The most common policy councils are advisory and restrict membership to state, civil society, and private sector leaders, although they can be more open and embedded in decision-making and administration at the local level. There is evidence that such structures can be used to promote inclusion, collaboration, transparency, and accountability.

A variation in design, management councils have a more explicit decision-making function, empowering citizens and civil society leaders in the formulation and implementation of policies in areas such as health, education, and housing. In Brazil, all 5,570 municipalities have a health council constituted by representatives of government institutions (25 percent), non-governmental organizations (25 percent), and citizens (50 percent), who meet at least once every month to formulate health policies and oversee their implementation. Explicit attention is given to participation of citizens from poorer and traditionally excluded social groups to improve the responsiveness of the national health system to their needs.

Where management councils are more concerned with redistributive policies and operate mostly at the local level, *representative councils* deal with recognition policies primarily at the national level. They are an explicit attempt to promote public equality and fight discrimination through the direct engagement of under-represented and minority groups in the policy process, particularly women, indigenous peoples, ethnic minorities, racial, and religious groups – and more recently youth and the elderly. Representative councils tend to have

---

[5] For further examples of democratic innovation, see Participedia http://participedia.net and LATINNO www.latinno.net/en/.

an agenda-setting and monitoring role. Both Ecuador and Brazil have national policy councils for women, the elderly, people with disabilities, and indigenous peoples. In Ecuador these and other councils were created in 2014 under the *Law of the National Councils for Equality* aimed at protecting minority rights. In Brazil, the national council for women's policy has been responsible for the drafting and enforcement of the first national policy plans exclusively addressed to their needs, improving women's representation and the realization of social rights (Pogrebinschi 2014).

14.4.2.3   National Public Policy Conferences

National public policy conferences (NPPCs) are designed to overcome challenges of scale associated with participation in national level policy-making. NPPCs connect citizens and civil society organizations through multiple and successive rounds of deliberation and representation at the local, regional, and federal levels. Brazil has a long tradition of experimenting with NPPCs in more than 50 policy areas including health, education, culture, cities, and racial equality. Again this democratic innovation has spread to other countries of Latin America with some interesting variation in format and scope (Pogrebinschi 2012).

While initiated by the federal government, the NPPC process begins at the municipal level, where the first round of deliberations is open to anyone to participate. Delegates are elected to represent the municipality in the state (regional) conferences where they deliberate with public officials on the policy proposals originated from the local stage. Proposals and delegates are then sent to the final, national, stage, which generates a set of policy recommendations. While these proposals are not binding, there is evidence that in Brazil the government has taken these inputs seriously in the formulation of federal policies and laws, including policy areas such as food security and nutrition. As NPPCs become institutionalized in some policy areas, they have begun playing an important role in policy evaluation and monitoring.

The NPPCs have been particularly important in increasing inclusion, with impressive numbers of citizens taking part (seven million people are reported to have participated in 82 NPPCs that took place between 2003 and 2011). Important social outcomes have been achieved, with NPPC proposals leading to progressive policy change in areas of gender, race, ethnicity, disabilities, and age. Many of these policies recognize new groups and enact rights – including constitutional rights – for groups previously excluded from the policy process (Pogrebinschi 2014).

14.4.2.4   Mini-Publics

Where the previous innovations have emerged from Latin America, mini-publics have been developed in North America and Europe, although their practice has spread to other continents. Mini-publics are defined by their use of random and stratified selection and facilitated deliberation among a diverse body of citizens who hear evidence from experts and witnesses and generate political recommendations. Mini-publics are typically used as consultative bodies by political decision makers. Examples include citizens' juries, consensus conferences, deliberative polls, citizens' assemblies, and G1000s. The number of citizens selected and length of time they are brought together varies between 12 to 1,000 citizens over one day to several weekends (Smith 2009).

Arguably the most impressive experimentation with mini-publics has been the citizens' assemblies in Canada, the Netherlands, and Ireland that have dealt with constitutional issues. Whereas other designs require citizens to participate for between one to five days, in Canada and the Netherlands citizens met over a series of weekends for a number of months, learning, deliberating, consulting, and deciding on a new electoral system. In British Columbia and Ontario the provincial governments committed to put recommendations to a province-wide referendum. The Irish Constitutional Convention took the unusual step of including one-third politicians as members alongside randomly selected citizens. There is evidence that its recommendations were critical in bringing forward legislation on same-sex marriage.

Mini-publics recruit a far more heterogeneous group of citizens than any legislature or other political institutions. Forms of random or stratified selection recall the fundamental democratic procedure of ancient Athenian democracy: no social group is systematically excluded; the equal status and value of all persons is recognized and affirmed. Inclusion in the deliberative process is promoted through active facilitation, ensuring that the process is not dominated by the politically confident.

Mini-publics are one of the most researched democratic innovations and there is evidence that structured deliberation among such a socially diverse group of participants increases sensitivity to the perspectives and arguments of others and defends against group polarization that is common among more homogenous groups. There is growing evidence that citizens are willing and able to come to sound judgments and recommendations on highly complex and technical issues, and that there are positive effects on participants' knowledge, interpersonal trust, and political efficacy, and that the broader public views the judgments of mini-publics as credible and trustworthy.

14.4.2.5   Institutionalizing Democratic Innovations

Democratic innovations can be designed to better realize public equality in very different ways – for example, through random selection, group representation, or rules that prioritize the interests of the politically marginalized. Institutional designs can empower minority groups, recognize new social and cultural identities, as well as incorporate historically marginalized groups in the public sphere. The practice of well-organized and politically salient innovations provides evidence that citizen participation can break political deadlocks, lead to decisions that redistribute state resources, refocus the delivery of public goods to those most in need, and provide access to public services for the poor.

The major challenge facing participatory governance is how democratic innovations can be embedded effectively within democratic systems. One aspect of this challenge is that the radical impulse and original designs of democratic innovations are often watered down as practice spreads. PB is a good example: many of the PBs across Latin America bear a strong family resemblance to early Brazilian practice. However, as it traveled to Europe and North America, many of the newer PBs were relatively poor imitations.

The second challenge is that democratic innovations are too often either not given decision-making power or are poorly coupled or integrated with existing decision-making processes. One lesson from Latin America is the importance of political, administrative, and fiscal autonomy for different levels of authority within a polity as a precondition for democratic experimentation and an opportunity to have a meaningful impact. But the decision to sponsor, organize, and respond to democratic innovations is often at the discretion of elected or appointed public officials. When innovations are not institutionalized through norms or law, they can lose their force and undermine citizen efficacy. The internationally renowned PB in Porto Alegre exemplifies this challenge: it was not codified and was weakened by the incoming mayor as soon as the Workers Party lost control of the city. In other parts of Latin America, such as Peru and the Dominican Republic, PB is mandatory under national law. However, legal or constitutional codification can be a break on creativity and further innovation.

An intriguing development is the emergence of autonomous public organizations charged with promoting public participation. The Quebec Environmental Public Hearings Board and the former Danish Board of Technology are rare examples of institutions that have been created by governments with the mandate to establish independent, high quality, and recurrent practices of participatory governance in specified areas of policy (Bherer, Gauthier, and Simard 2014).

Unsurprisingly, vested political and economic interests are suspicious of democratic innovations: when well designed, they open up the political process and promote public equality. But designing new and creative participatory institutions is not enough; it is crucial also to embed these practices within, alongside or, more radically, in place of representative institutions if democratic innovations are to contribute to overcoming political and social inequalities in contemporary democracies.

14.4.3 Democracy Below, Beyond, and Across the State? Equality Between Citizens or States?

We propose to give a unified account of the ideal of equality of voice across the domains of the domestic state and the international community. Some have thought that some variant of a democratic world state is the natural application of this idea. We argue that the ideal of political equality in the modern democratic state is a special case of a more general principle, which covers equality in collective decision-making traditionally conceived and a kind of equality in the conditions under which voluntary agreements are made among separate parties. We argue for a principle of proportionality, which asserts that persons ought to have a say in some issue area that is proportional to the stake they have in that area. Proportionality is particularly useful in the context of international decision-making where societies have very different stakes in the agreements they make. We define an ideal of fair negotiation among states that conforms to the broader ideal of

equality. This is an individualistic ideal in the sense that the ultimate entity that is to have a say is the individual. States act as representatives of individuals in the process of making voluntary agreements.

14.4.3.1 Globalization

The basic challenge of globalization to democracy is that the citizens of a democratic state are deeply affected by the policies and actions, or the lack thereof, of citizens in other states. Partly this is the consequence of the fact that certain goods, or bads such as pollution or the spread of disease, cannot be contained within the borders of states. Partly it is a consequence of decisions that states have made to increase openness to international trade and the movements of persons and capital. To the extent that the democratic principle implies that persons should have a voice in the basic conditions that affect their lives, there is a strong impulse to give citizenship a wider scope than it has had till now. Relatedly, the global community is currently facing some fundamental moral challenges, which can be recognized as such on virtually any scheme of morality. The aims include the preservation of international security and the protection of persons against serious and widespread violations of human rights. In addition, it must pursue the avoidance of global environmental catastrophe, the alleviation of severe global poverty, and the establishment of a decent system regulating international trade and the movements of people and capital. Meeting these challenges will require significant cooperation from many of the world's states. As a consequence, there are moral duties on the part of the people who are members of different states to attempt to achieve effective cooperation with other people in pursuing these mandatory aims.

All states have signed on to these aims (in the Millennium Development Goals, the United Nations Charter, the WTO, and various environmental agreements). They make sense from the standpoint of any moral theory that takes the promotion, protection, and respect for the fundamental interests of persons to be essential to a well-ordered political system. The morally mandatory aims specify certain very weighty aims that it makes sense to require the international community to pursue, given its current capacities and challenges.

14.4.3.2 Fairness

The question is, from the standpoint of democratic ideals, how are we to make decisions regarding how to pursue these aims? A natural thought here is that a fair process of decision-making among states would be a majoritarian one. But this majoritarian idea can take different forms. One can imagine a majoritarianism of states such as one state, one vote. There are two problems with this approach that arguably attend many of the majoritarian approaches to international rule-making. The first problem is that states are of very different size and so a majoritarian rule would not conform to the more fundamental principle that we want power apportioned to individuals in a way that treats individuals as equals.

The second problem is that a majoritarian rule of this sort violates in some way the political and legal integrity of political societies.

The political societies within what are initially arbitrary borders have developed highly integrated legal systems with integrated economic and social arrangements, as well as systems of accountability for transforming and adjusting these arrangements. States have arisen to establish justice and protect the basic needs of persons within limited areas. States have some interest in protecting the borders and the integrity of the systems operating within those borders in order to carry out their core responsibilities. From an international perspective, we have a kind of division of labor in which the world is divided into units that are capable of establishing justice in each unit (Goodin 1988).

Hence, it is through state consent that democratic ideals be realized. But the requirement of consent must be modified in three ways: first, unreasonable refusal of consent must be excluded; second, consent must be given under fair conditions; third, state consent must be broadly representative of the people of the state.

The justification for the state consent requirement is also grounded in the fact that there is a great deal of uncertainty as to how to pursue the morally mandatory aims. Though there is general agreement among scientists that the earth is warming up due to human activity, there is disagreement as to how much this is happening and how quickly or what a fair and efficient distribution of costs might be. The same uncertainties attend thinking about how to alleviate global poverty and how to protect persons from wide-spread human rights abuses. And there is significant disagreement about the limits of free trade and the methods for opening up trade as well as how to deal with the relationship between uneven development and trade. This kind of uncertainty, together with the centrality of states in making power accountable to persons, provides a reason for supporting a system of state consent with freedom to enter and exit arrangements because it supports a system that allows for a significant amount of experimentation in how to solve problems (Keohane and Victor 2011).

But the system of state consent must be heavily bounded given the morally mandatory need for cooperation. In the case of treaties that attempt to realize a system of cooperation that is necessary to the pursuit of morally mandatory aims, exit or the refusal to enter it must be accompanied by an acceptable explanation. States must lay out the reasons for thinking that the treaty would not contribute to solving the problem and that some alternative might be superior. The explanation must be in terms of the morally mandatory aims or in terms of a crushing or severely unfair cost of cooperation. The reasons given do not need to be the right reasons, but they must fall within the scope of what reasonable people can disagree on. For example, an explanation must not go against the vast majority of scientific opinion. A state must not free ride on others' contributions to morally mandatory aims, or refuse to shoulder the burden. The international community is permitted to pressure or coerce states that fail to provide adequate explanations for refusal to participate in cooperation for mandatory aims (Christiano 2015).

In this context we have to think about one of the major effects of globalization, which is the increase in the relative bargaining power of capital over labor as a consequence of the increasing mobility of capital. Democratic societies have had increasing difficulty in imposing constraints on capital because of the threat of flight. This imbalance can only be rectified by states cooperating in producing an international regime of taxation and regulation of capital.

How do we assess the fairness of state consent and the negotiations that lead up to this? A state's consent to a treaty must not be coerced by the other party and must not be the consequence of fraud by the other party. And states cannot validly create obligations that violate the *jus cogens* norms.

We can also see further norms through the lens of democratic theory. When a state engages in making agreements, contracts, and other arrangements with other states, it is in effect attempting to shape the social world surrounding it. It alters the rights, duties, and powers that other states have in relation to it. That world is the product of coordination and in part the product of conflict since states are able to shape this world more or less depending on how much social power they have.

Just as a citizen participates in shaping the overall character of the society she lives in by participating in collective decision-making about the overall collective features of the society, so a state shapes parts of the social world in which it exists by engaging in agreement making with others. The justification of these different powers of shaping the social world is grounded in the same common liberal concerns. Persons and the groups of which they are members have fundamental interests and concerns that often conflict and they disagree on how best to shape their common social worlds and so we give each person or group some power to pursue those interests.

We want to assert here as a general principle that persons ought to have a say in a collective decision in proportion to the legitimate stakes they have in the decision (Brighouse and Fleurbaey 2010). On the whole, persons ought to have an equal say in democratic decision-making within states because they have roughly equal stakes in the set of decisions overall. Where there are unequal stakes, we distribute power unequally, as in federalist arrangements.

Given the analogy of agreement-making to democratic participation, we can see that the principle of proportionality applies to agreement-making. In the case of voice, stakes are defined in terms of the whole range of plausible and legitimate alternatives in the different issue spaces. In the case of agreement-making, the fundamental determinant of stake is the outside option or what a person or group can expect if no agreement is made with the other party, in other words, the value of exit. We have a lot at stake in an agreement if we would be very badly off without it. You have a lot less at stake if you would not be so badly off without the agreement.

The fundamental argument for the principle of proportionality of power to stakes is that persons and groups of persons know their interests better than others do, normally. Thus in situations of conflict of interest, one should want the party with the most interest at stake to have more of a say if one is concerned with advancing the interests of persons.

There are four key differences directly relevant to fairness between states and persons that complicate the application of the ideas of fairness to interstate transactions. First, states come with different size populations; second, states have very different levels of wealth for which the present generation cannot be held responsible (usually); third, these conditions occur against a background in which there are no higher order political institutions with the capacity to rectify serious differences of opportunity and information; fourth, the negotiations that create international institutions are morally deeply fraught issues or at least more so than most ordinary negotiations. Two important structural differences also mark the transactions among states. Furthermore, there are a small number of states so the interactions among states never replicate the conditions of competitive markets, which sometimes play a large role in equalizing bargaining power among individual persons.

Population and wealth are two important determinants of stake for states. From the standpoint of democratic theory, the power of a particular state in negotiation ought to be proportioned to population so that each state has power apportioned to per capita stakes. The role of wealth is not so straightforward. Suppose one has two societies at very different levels of wealth entering a negotiation. When impoverished societies negotiate with wealthy societies, they have a lot less wealth at stake but they have more at stake in some fundamental sense since their abilities to finance basic goods for their populations are at stake.

One of the most fundamental puzzles in a system of free transactions among persons is that this principle of power proportionate to stakes can easily be violated. For example if you have two persons who depend on making an agreement to advance certain interests, the one who has the least stake will often have more power. This is because they can more easily afford no agreement. But this means that power is often inversely proportioned to stakes in a scheme of free transactions, while the normative principle tells us that power ought to be proportioned to stakes.

The problem of inequality of stakes in international politics is extremely hard to solve because there is no higher political entity capable of rectifying the imbalance of power. The poor and the vulnerable are frequently in very difficult bargaining positions relative to wealthy and powerful societies as we see in trade negotiations and in environmental negotiations. But it is not as if nothing can be done here. First of all, multilateral and inclusive conferences tend to be helpful to poorer societies. Here transparency can play a significant role in making negotiations fairer because though rich and powerful states are willing and able to engage in very hard bargaining with poorer states, they do not like to be seen to be doing so, either to their own citizens or to the global public. If hard bargaining becomes too open, it becomes damaging to the reputations of powerful states – reputations that are important assets in international politics. Two, coalition building among poorer countries can also offset the tremendous bargaining power that comes with wealth. This is because the great majority of the world's population is poor and the sheer size of this group can give it bargaining power (Narlikar 2012). This alteration of the bargaining situation is not unlike the change in bargaining between capital and labor that occurs when unions are allowed to form.

14.5   Conclusion: Meeting the Challenges

We have so far discussed the underlying principle of public equality and a number of important challenges to its realization. As we saw, three kinds of challenges stand out. First are the challenges that arise from socioeconomic inequality in society. Second are the challenges that arise from the marginalization of minorities, women, and the young. Third are the challenges stemming from globalization, which reinforce many of these others. All three kinds of challenges are manifested in the rise of populism. Our proposals here are essentially institutional proposals that supplement those offered in Sections 14.2 and 14.3 on age groups, future generations, enhancing participation through democratic innovations, and the prospects for global democracy.

The problems associated with the first challenge of socioeconomic inequality and its effect on the political system is discussed in much more detail in Chapters 9 and 13, but we will discuss here some institutional mechanisms by which the difficulties can be overcome. First let us get a quick characterization of the nature of the problem. The fundamental difficulty with the idea that economic inequality can issue in political inequality is that a society in which the affluent play the dominant role is one that violates the underlying principle of public equality. The idea is that the affluent have a much greater opportunity to influence the making of political decisions than do the less affluent. We hold to the fundamental democratic idea that persons' conceptions of the common good unwittingly reflect their interests and their distinctive experiences. So a society in which the affluent dominate the processes of persuasion and political choice is one in which their interests are likely to be much better served than those of the rest of the society. There are a number of mechanisms by which this can happen. One, if electoral campaigns are financed privately, then the affluent will play the role of selecting like-minded people to run for election. Campaign contributions in the United States tend to come almost entirely from the upper 10 percent of the income distribution. This implies that these people are playing a dominating role in the setting of the agenda in political decision-making. In this first mechanism, there need be no suggestion of corruption but it does imply that the interests of the affluent will be disproportionately advanced in these societies and the interests of others will be significantly ignored. But a second mechanism does suggest the possibility of corruption campaign finance contributions in return for promises to pass certain legislation favorable to the contributor. This is the main mechanism people think in terms of when they think of the influence of money on politics, but researchers have not found a great deal of evidence for this mechanism in the United States and Europe. A third mechanism relates in part to the process of globalization of markets. By virtue of its mobility, capital is able to secure good terms for itself from the political system simply by suggesting that it will move elsewhere or disinvest in some other way. It has a kind of independent political power in the political process. Charles Lindblom described this as the automatic punishment that business exercises over the political system. If stringent pollution controls are mandated by popular will, the business moves to an area where pollution controls are less, thus imposing a cost in the form of unemployment on the political system. Other theorists have described this as the structural dependence of the state on capital. A fourth mechanism influences the generation of political opinion in modern societies. Most people rely, as Anthony Downs argued, on heavily subsidized transmissions of opinions and arguments in modern societies. Inevitably the main source of the subsidization of opinion consists in the affluent. As a consequence there is likely to be a significant bias in the system of information and opinion generation toward the interests and concerns of the affluent.

All four of these mechanisms imply a great deal of inequality of opportunity to influence the democratic process and thus imply political inequality. Anthony Downs argued that inequality of political power is inevitable in modern societies. The question is: what kinds of institutions can mitigate these effects? Public financing of elections has been proposed as a partial solution to the first and second problems. A second kind of proposal is to have citizens assemblies of the sort analyzed in the democratic innovations (Section 14.4.2). They might deliberate about and propose potential pieces of legislation that would be subject to legislative votes or referenda. Here the idea is to insulate a significant part of the agenda-setting power in a legislature from the influence of money. Another proposal for mitigating the effects of the independent power of capital might consist in the restructuring of corporations so that their boards represent the workers in the corporations and perhaps other stakeholders. This would bring about decision-making that would be more reflective of the wider interests in society. It may also serve to mitigate some of the mechanism by which great inequality is created. A fourth proposal, suggested by Bruce Ackerman and Ian Ayres, would be to set up a voucher system for the support of interest groups and political parties, which might mitigate some of the domination of the affluent over the major media and interest groups. A fifth proposal is to attempt to revive and support organizations that advocate for the interests of working-class and poor people such as unions. This could create a kind of independent source of knowledge generation.

The second challenge is the subject of many of the sections on gender and minorities in this chapter. The problem is not primarily institutional though institutional reforms may help mitigate the problem. To put the point simply: for a democratic society to realize fully the equal citizenship of its members, people must see each other and treat each other as equals in the processes of democratic deliberation and communication generally. They must take each other seriously in the sense that they must listen to others and take their expressions of their conceptions of the common good and their own interests seriously. It is here that the marginalization of minorities and women can take an insidious and subtle form, but for all that a very powerful form. And of course, this marginalization can be compounded when persons are members of more than one marginalized group, as studies of intersectionality suggest. This constitutes a threat to the political equality of citizens to the extent that being able to communicate one's ideas and interests is essential to one's ability to influence the political process. If a majority of persons or even a significant minority cannot but think of one as not to be taken very seriously then one cannot communicate effectively and one's ability to influence the system is mitigated and one's interests are not likely to be advanced very well.

The marginalization of minorities and women in the democratic process can take two forms: as an overt denial of civil and political rights,

or it can involve a failure of processes to give voice to minority or marginalized voices. With regard to the former, common instances include voter suppression, enforced discrimination against minorities and women in the rules regulating economic and family life, and rules restricting the religious practices of minorities. There has been considerable progress over the last 50 years in many modern democracies toward the protection of the rights of minorities in terms of civil and political rights. There is some danger of backlash against these gains from the larger society, which has been discussed under the heading of populism. The latter forms of marginalization are more subtle and difficult to mitigate than those to the first. Probably the most prominent kinds of institutional fixes here are those having to do with representation. The idea is to give persons a stage on which they can express their views and which accords that expression legitimacy and authority. We have already looked at the role democratic innovations may play in this regard. Another, more mainstream, institution that may help with this is proportional representation. Thinking in terms of a kind of party-list proportional representation, such a system enables a greater plurality of voices to get a hearing in the society. Single-member district representation tends to displace the expression of the variety of interests and views in society to a less public place and takes it off the main legislative stage. Proportional representation tends to realize a more egalitarian representation of the plurality of views and interests in the society and it does so primarily by letting people choose for themselves what the important issues and identities are that they wish to associate themselves with. But to the extent that there are problems of marginalization that minorities wish to combat, it enables these minorities to form groups or play roles in shaping larger groups to be represented at the legislative level. So there may be better representation of interests and perspectives and there may also be better descriptive representation to the extent that minorities play the leading role in these parties. This can play a role in enhancing the legitimacy of minority voices and it may also put on display the diversity of voices within each minority. Proportional representation as an institution will not solve the problems entirely by any means. Other representation mechanisms may include quotas that ensure that a certain proportion of the representatives are women or are minorities.

References

Alesina, A., R. Bagir, and W. Easterly. 1999. "Public Goods and Ethnic Divisions." *Quarterly Journal of Economics* 114/4: 1243–1284.

Anderson, E. 2010. *The Imperative of Integration*. Princeton, NJ: Princeton University Press.

Arato, A. 2013. "Political Theology and Populism." *Social Research* 80/1: 143–172.

Arditi, B. 2008. *Politics on the Edge of Liberalism: Difference, Populism, Revolution, Agitation*. Edinburgh: Edinburgh University Press.

Baldwin, K., and J.D. Huber. 2010. "Economic Versus Cultural Differences: Forms of Ethnic Diversity and Public Goods Provision." *American Political Science Review* 104/4: 644–662.

Bartels, L. 2009. *Unequal Democracy*. Princeton, NJ: Princeton University Press.

Bellamy, R. 2007. *Political Constitutionalism*. Cambridge: Cambridge University Press.

Berry, C. 2012. *The Rise of Gerontocracy? Addressing the Intergenerational Democratic Deficit*. London: Intergenerational Foundation.

Bhargava, R. 2010a. *The Promise of India's Secular Democracy*. New Delhi: Oxford University Press.

Bhargava, R. 2010b. *What Is Political Theory and Why Do We Need It*. Oxford: Oxford University Press.

Bherer, L., M. Gauthier, and L. Simard. 2014. "Autonomy for What? Comparing the Role of Autonomous Public Organizations Dedicated to Public Participation." Paper presented at European Consortium for Political Research Joint Sessions, Salamanca, April 10–14.

Bidadanure, J. 2017. "Youth Quotas, Diversity and Long-Termism: Can Young People Act As Proxies for Future Generations?" in I. Gonzales-Ricoy and A. Gosseries (eds.), *Institutions for Future Generations*. Oxford: Oxford University Press.

Bowker, G., and S.L. Star. 1999. *Sorting Things Out: Classification and its Consequences*. London and Cambridge, MA: MIT Press.

Brighouse, H., and M. Fleurbaey. 2010. "Democracy and Proportionality." *Journal of Political Philosophy* 18/2: 137–155.

Butler, J. 1993. *Bodies that Matter: On the Discursive Limits of "Sex."* New York: Routledge.

Canovan, M. 1999. "Trust the People! Populism and the Two Faces of Democracy." *Political Studies* 47/1: 2–16.

Canovan, M. 2002. "Taking Politics to the People: Populism as the Ideology of Democracy," in Y. Mény and Y. Surel (eds.), *Democracies and the Populist Challenge*. Basingstoke: Palgrave.

Chandra, K. 2006. "What Is Ethnic Identity and Does It Matter?" *Annual Review of Political Science* 9: 397–424.

Chilvers, J., and M. Kearnes (eds.). 2016. *Remaking Participation: Science, Environment and Emergent Publics*. London: Routledge.

Christiano, T. 2008. *The Constitution of Equality*. Oxford: Oxford University Press.

Christiano, T. 2015. "Legitimacy and the International Trade Regime." *San Diego Law Review* 52: 981–1012.

D'Eramo, M. 2013. "Populism and the New Oligarchy" (trans. Gregory Elliott). *New Left Review* 82 (July–August): 5–28.

De La Torre, C. 2016. "Populism and the Politics of the Extraordinary in Latin America." *Journal of Political Ideologies* 21/2: 121–139. doi: 10.1080/13569317.2016.1150137.

Derrida, J. 1988. *Limited Inc*. Evanston, IL: Northwestern University Press.

Ezrahi, Y. 2012. *Imagined Democracies: Necessary Political Fictions*. Cambridge: Cambridge University Press.

Felt, U. 2007. *Taking European Knowledge Society Seriously. Report of the Expert Group on Science and Governance to the Science, Economy and Society Directorate, Directorate-General for Research, European Commission*. Luxembourg: Office for Official Publications of the European Communities.

Felt, U., K. Felder, and M. Penkler. 2016. "How Differences Matter: Tracing Diversity Practices in Obesity Treatment and Health Promotion." *Sociology of Health & Illness* 39/1: 127–142.

Finchelstein, F. 2014. *The Ideological Origins of the Dirty War: Fascism, Populism, and Dictatorship in Twentieth Century Argentina*. New York: Oxford University Press.

Frank, J. 2010. *Constituent Moments: Enacting the People in Postrevolutionary America*. Durham, NC: Duke University Press.

Fung, A. 2003. "Recipes for Public Spheres: Eight Institutional Design Choices and Their Consequences." *Journal of Political Philosophy* 11/3: 338–367.

García Añón, J., B. Bradford, J.A. García Sáez, A. Gascón Cuenca, and A. Llorente Ferreres. 2013. *Identificación Policial por Perfil Étnico en España: Informe Sobre Experiencias y Actitudes en Relación con las Actuaciones Policiales*. Valencia: Tirant Lo Branch.

Germani, G. 1978. *Authoritarianism, Fascism, and National Populism*. New Brunswick, NJ: Transaction Books.

Goodin, R. 1988. "What's So Special About My Fellow Countrymen?" *Ethics* 98: 663–686.

Habermas, J. 1992. *Faktizität und Geltung. Beiträge zur Diskurstheorie des Rechts und des demokratischen Rechtsstaats*. Frankfurt a. M.: Suhrkamp.

Hainmueller, J., D. Hangartner, and D. Lawrence. 2016. "When Lives Are Put on Hold: Lengthy Asylum Processes Decrease Employment Among Refugees." *Science Advances* 2/8 (August 3). http://advances.sciencemag.org/content/advances/2/8/e1600432.full.pdf.

Hay, C., and B. Rosamond. 2002. "Globalisation, European Integration and the Discursive Construction of Economic Imperatives." *Journal of European Public Policy* 9/2: 147–167.

Hooks, B. 1981. *Ain't We a Woman: Black Women and Feminism*. Boston, MA: South End Press.

Horowitz, D. 1985. *Ethnic Groups in Conflict*. Berkeley, CA: University of California Press.

Inter-Parliamentary Union. 2014. *Youth Participation in National Parliaments*. Geneva: Inter-Parliamentary Union.

Jasanoff, S. 2004. *States of Knowledge: The Co-Production of Science and Social Order*. London/New York: Routledge.

Kazin, M. 1995. *The Populist Passion: An American History*. New York: Basic Books.

Keane, J. 2011. "Monitory Democracy?" in S. Alonso, J. Keane, and W. Merkel (eds.), *The Future of Representative Democracy*. Cambridge: Cambridge University Press.

Keohane, R., and D. Victor. 2011. "The Regime Complex for Climate Change." *Perspectives on Politics* 9: 7–23.

Kneip, S., and W. Merkel (eds.). In press. *Democracy and Crisis: On the Difficult Relationship Between Theory and Empiricism*. Cham, Switzerland: Springer International.

Laclau, E. 2005a. *On Populist Reason*. London: Verso.

Laclau, E. 2005b. "Populism: What's in a Name?," in F. Panizza (ed.), *Populism and the Mirror of Democracy*. London: Verso.

Lasch, Ch. 1991. *The True and Only Heaven: Progress and Its Critics*. New York: Norton.

Levy, L.W. 1994. *The Establishment Clause: Religion and the First Amendment*. Chapel Hill, NC: University of North Carolina Press.

Mair, P. 2002. "Populist Democracy vs Party Democracy," in Y. Mény and Y. Surel (eds.), *Democracies and the Populist Challenge*. Oxford: Palgrave.

Mair, P. 2013. *Ruling the Void: The Hollowing of Western Democracy*. London: Verso.

Malik, I.H. 2002. *Religious Minorities in Pakistan*. London: Minority Rights Group International.

Manin, B. 1997. *The Principles of Representative Government*. Cambridge: Cambridge University Press.

Mény, Y., and Y. Surel. 2002. "The Constitutive Ambiguity of Populism," in Y. Mény and Y. Surel (eds.), *Democracies and the Populist Challenge*. Oxford: Palgrave.

Merkel, W. 2014a: "Is Capitalism Compatible with Democracy?" *Zeitschrift für Vergleichende Politikwissenschaft* 8/2: 109–128.

Merkel, W. 2014b. "Is There a Crisis of Democracy?" *Democratic Theory* 1/2: 11–25.

Mosley, L. 2003. *Global Capital and National Governments*. Cambridge: Cambridge University Press.

Mudde, C. 2001. "In the Name of the Peasantry, the Proletariat, and the People: Populisms in Eastern Europe." *East European Politics and Societies* 15/1: 33–53.

Mueller, J.-W. 2011. *Contesting Democracy: Political Ideas in Twentieth Century Europe*. New Haven, CT: Yale University Press.

Narlikar, A. 2012. "Collective Agency, Systemic Consequences: Bargaining Coalitions in the WTO," in A. Narlikar, M. Daunton, and R. M. Stern (eds.), *The Oxford Handbook on the World Trade Organization*. Oxford: Oxford University Press.

OSJI (Open Society Justice Initiative). 2009. *Ethnic Profiling in the European Union: Pervasive, Ineffective, and Discriminator*. New York: Open Society Foundations.

Ottinger, G., and B.R. Cohen (eds.). 2011. *Technoscience and Environmental Justice*. Cambridge, MA: The MIT Press.

Pogrebinschi, T. 2012. "Participation as Representation. Democratic Policymaking in Brazil," in M.A. Cameron, E. Hershberg, and K. Sharpe (eds.), *New Institutions for Participatory Democracy in Latin America. Voice and Consequence*. New York: Palgrave Macmillan.

Pogrebinschi, T. 2014. "Turning Participation into Representation: Innovative Policymaking for Minority Groups in Brazil," in C. Sirianni and J. Girouard (eds.), *Varieties of Civic Innovation: Deliberative, Collaborative, Network, and Narrative Approaches*. Vanderbilt Place, TN: Vanderbilt University Press.

Portinaro, P.P. 2013. "Ethnos e Demos. Per una genealogia del populismo." *Meridiana* 77: 47–66.

Rosanvallon, P. 2015. *Le bon gouvernement*. Paris: Seuil.

Rovira Kaltwasser, C. 2012. "The Ambivalence of Populism: Threat and Corrective for Democracy." *Democratization* 19/2: 184–208.

Ruthven, M. 2002. *A Futy for God: The Islamist Attack on America*. London: Granta Books.

Scott, J.W. 1988. "Deconstructing Equality-versus-Difference: or, the Uses of Poststructuralist Theory for Feminism." *Feminist Studies* 14/1: 33–50.

Scott, J.C. 1999. *Seeing Like a State: How Certain Schemes to Improve the Human Condition Have Failed*. New Haven, CT: Yale University Press.

Smith, G. 2009. *Democratic Innovations: Designing Institutions for Citizen Participation*. Cambridge: Cambridge University Press.

Streeck, W. 2014. *Buying Time*. London: Verso.

14

Taggart, P. 2000. *Populism*. Philadelphia, PA: Open University Press.

Tilly, C. 2007. *Democracy*. Cambridge: Cambridge University Press.

Tormey, S. 2015. *The End of Representative Politics*. Cambridge: Polity Press.

UNDP. 2013. *Enhancing Youth Political Participation Throughout the Electoral Cycle: A Good Practice Guide*. New York: UNDP.

Urbinati, N. 2014. *Democracy Disfigured: Opinion, Truth and the People*. Cambridge, MA: Harvard University Press.

Verloo, M. 2017. *Opposition to Gender Equality in Europe. Theory, Evidence and Practice*. London: Routledge.

Wajcman, J. 2009. "Feminist Theories of Technology." *Cambridge Journal of Economics* 34/1: 143–152.

Walby, S. 2009. *Globalization and Inequalities: Complexity and Contested Modernities*. Thousand Oaks, CA: Sage.

Weyland, K. 2013. "The Threat from the Populist Left." *Journal of Democracy* 24: 18–32.

Wyatt, S., F. Henwood, N. Miller, and P. Senker. 2001. *Technology and In/Equality. Questioning the Information Society*. London/New York: Routledge.

Young, I. 2000. *Democracy and Inclusion*. Oxford: Oxford University Press.

14

Authors

Introduction

Olivier Bouin, RFIEA
Marie-Laure Djelic, Sciences-Po
Marc Fleurbaey, Princeton University
Ravi Kanbur, Cornell University
Elisa Reis, Federal University of Rio de Janeiro

Chapter 9

Coordinating Lead Authors:
Donatella della Porta, Scuola Normale Superiore, Italy
Michael Keating, University of Aberdeen, UK

Lead Authors:
Gianpaolo Baiocchi, New York University, USA
Colin Crouch, University of Warwick, UK
Sheila Jasanoff, Harvard University, USA
Erika Kraemer-Mbula, University of Johannesburg, South Africa
Dina Kiwan, American University of Beirut
Abby Peterson, University of Gothenburg
Kenneth M. Roberts, Cornell University
Philippe C. Schmitter, European University Institute
Alberto Vannucci, University of Pisa
Antoine Vauchez, University of Paris
Asanga Welikala, University of Edinburgh

Chapter 10

Coordinating Lead Authors:
Peter Wallensteen, Uppsala University, Sweden and University of Notre Dame, USA
Michel Wieviorka, FMSH and EHESS, France

Lead Authors:
Itty Abraham, National University of Singapore, Singapore
Karin Aggestam, Lund University, Sweden
Alexander Bellamy, Queensland University, Australia
Lars-Erik Cederman, ETH Zentrum, Switzerland
Jerôme Ferret, EHESS-CNRS and University of Toulouse 1, France
Jean Baptiste Jeangène Vilmer, Collège d'études mondiales and Science Po, France
Wilhelm Heitmeyer, University of Bielefed, Germany
Angela Muvumba-Sellström, Uppsala University, Sweden
Laurie Nathan, University of Pretoria, South Africa
Hideaki Shinoda, Tokyo University, Japan
Ekaterina Stepanova, National Research Institute of World Economy and International Relations, Russia

Contributing Author:
Olga Odgers Ortiz, El Colegio de la Frontera Norte, Mexico

Chapter 11

Coordinating Lead Authors:
Hilary Charlesworth, University of Melbourne and the Australian National University, Australia
Sally Engle Merry, New York University, USA

Lead Authors:
B.S. Chimni, Jawaharlal Nehru University, India
Javier Couso, Universidad Diego Portales, Chile
Terence Halliday, American Bar Foundation, USA
Outi Korhonen, University of Turku, Finland
Vivian Lin, La Trobe University, Australia

Eden Medina, Indiana University, USA
Leslye Obiora, University of Arizona, USA
César Rodríguez-Garavito, Universidad de los Andes, Colombia
Gregory Shaffer, University of California, Irvine, USA
Rene Urueña, Universidad de los Andes, Colombia

Contributing Author:
Ruth Okediji, University of Minnesota Law School, USA

Chapter 12

Coordinating Lead Authors:
G. Balachandran, Graduate Institute of International and Development Studies, Switzerland
Grégoire Mallard, Graduate Institute of International and Development Studies, Switzerland

Lead Authors:
Olufunmilayo Arewa, University of California Irvine School of Law, USA
Lucio Baccaro, University of Geneva, Switzerland
Tim Büthe, Hochschule für Politik/Bavarian School of Public Policy at the Technical University of Munich (TUM), Germany and Duke University, USA
Andrea Nightingale, Swedish University of Agricultural Sciences, Sweden
Pierre Pénet, University of Geneva, Switzerland
Dominique Pestre, École des hautes études en sciences sociales, France
Anthea Roberts, School of Regulation and Global Governance (RegNet) at the Australian National University, Australia

Chapter 13

Coordinating Lead Authors:
Nick Couldry, The London School of Economics and Political Science, UK
Clemencia Rodriguez, Temple University, USA

Lead Authors:
Göran Bolin, Södertörn University, Sweden
Julie Cohen, Georgetown University, USA
Gerard Goggin, University of Sydney, Australia
Marwan Kraidy, University of Pennsylvania, USA
Koichi Iwabuchi, Monash University, Australia
Kwang-Suk Lee, Seoul National University of Science and Technology, South Korea
Jack Qiu, The Chinese University, Hong Kong
Ingrid Volkmer, University of Melbourne, Australia
Herman Wasserman, University of Cape Town, South Africa
Yuezhi Zhao, Simon Fraser University, Canada

Contributing Authors:
Olessia Koltsova, National Research University, Russia
Inaya Rakhmani, University of Indonesia
Omar Rincón, C3 – Fundación Friedrich Ebert, Colombia
Claudia Magallanes-Blanco, Universidad Iberoamericana Puebla, Mexico
Pradip Thomas, University of Queensland, Australia

Chapter 14

Coordinating Lead Authors:
Richard Bellamy, University College, London, UK and European University Institute, Italy
Wolfgang Merkel, WZB Berlin Social Science Center and Humboldt University, Germany

Lead Authors:
Rajeev Bhargava, Center for the Study of Developing Societies, India
Juliana Bidadanure, Department of Philosophy, Stanford University, USA

Thomas Christiano, University of Arizona, USA
Ulrike Felt, Department of Science and Technology Studies,
University of Vienna, Austria
Colin Hay, Centre d'études européennes, Sciences Po, France
Lily Lamboy, Department of Political Science, Stanford University, USA

Thamy Pogrebinschi, WZB Berlin Social Science Center, Germany
Graham Smith, Centre for the Study of Democracy, University of Westminster, UK
Gayil Talshir, Hebrew University of Jerusalem, Israel
Nadia Urbinati, Columbia University, USA
Mieke Verloo, Radboud University, Netherlands and IWM, Vienna, Austria

Index